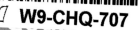

This coupon entitles you to special discounts when you book your trip through the

Hotels ♦ Airlines ♦ Car Rentals ♦ Cruises
All Your Travel Needs

Here's what you get: *

♦ A discount of $50 USD on a booking of $1,000** or more for two or more people!

♦ A discount of $25 USD on a booking of $500** or more for one person!

♦ Free membership for three years, and 1,000 free miles on enrollment in the unique Miles-to-Go™ frequent-traveler program. Earn one mile for every dollar spent through the program. Earn free hotel stays starting at 5,000 miles. Earn free roundtrip airline tickets starting at 25,000 miles.

♦ Personal help in planning your own, customized trip.

♦ Fast, confirmed reservations at any property recommended in this guide, subject to availability.***

♦ Special discounts on bookings in the U.S. and around the world.

♦ Low-cost visa and passport service.

♦ Reduced-rate cruise packages.

Visit our website at http://www.travnet.com/Frommer or call us globally at 201-567-8500, ext. 55. In the U.S., call toll-free at 1-888-940-5000, or fax 201-567-1838. In Canada, call toll-free at 1-800-883-9959, or fax 416-922-6053. In Asia, call 60-3-7191044, or fax 60-3-7185415.

---

* To qualify for these travel discounts, at least a portion of your trip must include destinations covered in this guide. No more than one coupon discount may be used in any 12-month period, for destinations covered in this guide. Cannot be combined with any other discount or program.

**These are U.S. dollars spent on commissionable bookings.

***A $10 USD fee, plus fax and/or phone charges, will be added to the cost of bookings at each hotel not linked to the reservation service. Customers must approve these fees in advance.

Valid until December 31, 1998. Terms and conditions of the Miles-to-Go™ program are available on request by calling 201-567-8500, ext 55.

NME123

Frommer's®

4th Edition

New Mexico

by Lisa Legarde & Don Laine

Macmillan • USA

ABOUT THE AUTHORS

Lisa Legarde was born in New Orleans and since early childhood has traveled extensively throughout Europe and North America. After receiving her degree in English from Wellesley College she worked as an assistant editor at Macmillan Travel, which sparked her career as a travel writer. Lisa is author or co-author of numerous Frommer's travel guides.

Don Laine has written about and traveled extensively throughout the Rocky Mountains and the Southwest. He and his wife, Barbara, have authored Frommer's guides to Colorado and are the regional editors of *Frommer's America on Wheels: Arizona and New Mexico*. The Laines, who reside in northern New Mexico, are currently at work on *Frommer's Utah*.

MACMILLAN TRAVEL

A Simon & Schuster Macmillan Company
1633 Broadway
New York, NY 10019

Find us online at **http://www.mgr.com/travel**
or on America Online at Keyword: **Frommer's**

ISBN 0-02-860907-7
ISSN 1053-2455

Editor: Suzanne Roe
Production Editor: Lori Cates
Design by Michele Laseau
Digital Cartography by Roberta Stockwell and Ortelius Design

SPECIAL SALES

Bulk purchases (10+ copies) of Frommer's and selected Macmillan travel guides are available to corporations, organizations, mail-order catalogs, institutions, and charities at special discounts, and can be customized to suit individual needs. For more information write to Special Sales, Macmillan General Reference, 1633 Broadway, New York, NY 10019.

Manufactured in the United States of America.

Contents

List of Maps

AN INVITATION TO THE READER

In researching this book, we discovered many wonderful places—hotels, inns, restaurants, shops, and more. We're sure you'll find others. Please tell us about them, so we can share the information with your fellow travelers in upcoming editions. If you were disappointed with a recommendation, we'd love to know that, too. Please write to:

Frommer's New Mexico, 4th Edition
Macmillan Travel
1633 Broadway
New York, NY 10019

AN ADDITIONAL NOTE

Please be advised that travel information is subject to change at any time—and this is especially true of prices. We therefore suggest that you write or call ahead for confirmation when making your travel plans. The authors, editors, and publisher cannot be held responsible for the experience of readers while traveling. Your safety is important to us, however, so we encourage you to stay alert and be aware of your surroundings. Keep a close eye on cameras, purses, and wallets, all favorite targets of thieves and pickpockets.

WHAT THE SYMBOLS MEAN

✪ Frommer's Favorites

Hotels, restaurants, attractions, and entertainment you should not miss.

⑤ Super-Special Values

Hotels and restaurants that offer great value for your money.

The following abbreviations are used for credit cards:

AE	American Express	EU	Eurocard
CB	Carte Blanche	JCB	Japan Credit Bank
DC	Diners Club	MC	MasterCard
DISC	Discover	V	Visa
ER	en Route		

The Best of New Mexico

There's so much to see and do in New Mexico that you might have a difficult time planning your trip or deciding which things are most important to you, so I've put together this chapter on the best of New Mexico to help make things a little easier for you. You shouldn't, however, limit yourself to the things I mention here—there are plenty of other interesting sights, activities, hotels, and restaurants that will become available to you during your travels. Take advantage of as many of them as possible and perhaps even set out to find some of your own favorite places.

1 The Best of Natural New Mexico

- **Capulin Volcano National Monument:** Last active 10,000 years ago, Capulin Volcano National Monument is located about 27 miles east of Raton. It offers opportunities for viewing gorgeous vistas of the surrounding area as well as a chance to hike into an ancient volcano vent. See chapter 9.
- **Blue Hole:** In Santa Rosa, "city of natural lakes," you'll find Blue Hole, a crystal clear 81-foot-deep artesian spring. It's a favorite spot for scuba divers. See chapter 9.
- **El Malpais National Monument:** An incredible volcanic landscape, El Malpais (The Badlands) features vast lava flows, lava tubes, ice caves, sandstone cliffs, and natural bridges. Located near Grants, El Malpais also features Anasazi ruins and ancient Native American trails. See chapter 10.
- **White Sands National Monument:** Located 15 miles southwest of Alamogordo, White Sands National Monument preserves the best part of the world's largest gypsum dune field. For a truly unforgettable experience, camp overnight so you can watch the sun rise on the smooth, endless dunes. See chapter 12.
- **Carlsbad Caverns National Park:** One of the world's largest and most complex cave systems is located in the extreme southeastern region of the state. The 80 known caves have spectacular stalagmite and stalactite formations. Explore the Big Room in a 1-mile self-guided tour, and then catch the massive bat flight from the cave entrance at sunset. See chapter 12.

2 The Most Interesting Native American Sights

- **Petroglyph National Monument:** This national monument outside Albuquerque preserves 10,500 petroglyphs that were etched into lava flows by prehistoric Native Americans. Plaques provide interpretations and there are four different hiking trails in differing levels of difficulty. See chapter 6.
- **Indian Pueblo Cultural Center:** Located in Albuquerque, the Indian Pueblo Cultural Center is a great way to learn more about Native American culture. There's a permanent exhibit that traces the development of represented pueblo communities. See chapter 6.
- **Coronado State Monument:** Excavated ruins reveal hundreds of rooms and unique murals, examples of which are displayed in the monument's small archeological museum. See chapter 6.
- **Pecos National Monument:** Ruins of a 14th-century pueblo and a 17th-century mission are what you'll find here. The pueblo, abandoned in 1838, had 660 rooms and several kivas. See chapter 7.
- **Puye Cliff Dwellings:** You'll have to hike 11 miles from Santa Clara Pueblo to get to Puye Cliff Dwellings, but once you're there you won't regret your effort. The dwellings were occupied by the Anasazi from 1250 to 1577. Visitors are permitted to explore the 740-room pueblo ruin where petroglyphs are still visible. See chapter 7.
- **Bandelier National Monument:** This was once an Anasazi cliff dwelling. It now features a visitors center and museum with self-guided or ranger-led tours. See chapter 7.
- **Taos Pueblo:** Perhaps the most photographed pueblo in the state, Taos Pueblo is still home to 1,500 Native Americans (Tiwas) as it has been for more than 900 years. The architecture is fascinating. See chapter 8.
- **Acoma Pueblo:** This spectacular walled adobe village is perched high atop a sheer rock mesa. Known as "sky city," it's worth the trip just for the view. See chapter 10.
- **Chaco Culture National Historical Park:** This not-to-be-missed park is comprised of the ruins of an ancient Anasazi Pueblo civilization. There is a self-guided trail as well as a campground for those who want to do more than a superficial exploration. See chapter 10.
- **Aztec Ruins National Monument:** These ruins of a 500-room Native American pueblo abandoned by the Anasazi more than 200 years ago include a kiva that is 50 feet in diameter. See chapter 10.

3 The Best Outdoor Activities

- **River Rafting:** Challenges await avid rafters in North Central New Mexico, the most daring of which is a trip through Taos Box. See individual chapters for information on outfitters.
- **Hiking:** From the alpine slopes of Taos and Santa Fe to the badlands of El Malpais there are literally thousands of great hiking trails in New Mexico.
- **Skiing:** New Mexico offers some fantastic skiing opportunities, especially in Santa Fe and Taos. And, if you're a little rusty and are in need of some pointers, the ski school at Taos Ski Valley is one of the best in the country.
- **Horseback Riding:** Dude ranches and adventures on horseback are both available in New Mexico. You can ride in groups or alone, depending on your skill level and needs, and you can choose a day trip or a week-long camping trip.

- **Ballooning:** One of New Mexico's most exciting and colorful activities, ballooning is most popular in the north central region of the state. On a clear day you can take a short balloon ride or opt for a longer one that involves brunch or lunch somewhere along the way.
- **Llama Trekking:** If you feel like hiking and camping but are tired of hauling your own gear and don't want to ride a horse, why not try llama trekking. It's one of New Mexico's newest and most unusual ways to "ride the range."
- **Golf:** New Mexico has a surprising number of excellent public golf courses in a wide variety of terrains. See city and regional chapters for more information.
- **Fishing:** For a state as dry as New Mexico, there's an incredible number of fishing holes around for the avid angler. Bass, trout, cutthroat, walleye, and perch are among the varieties of fish that are prevalent throughout the state.

4 The Best Scenic & Historic Drives

- **The Enchanted Circle:** If you're going to be spending some time in the Taos area, take the drive known as the Enchanted Circle. It's a 90-mile loop, listed as a National Forest Scenic Byway, that takes you through the towns of Questa, Red River, Eagle Nest, and Angel Fire. See chapter 8.
- **The Turquoise Trail:** The state-designated scenic and historic route known as the Turquoise Trail begins on NM 14 not far from Albuquerque and winds some 46 miles to Santa Fe along the eastern side of the Sandia Mountains. It will take you through the "ghost towns" of Madrid, Golden, and Cerrillos, where gold, silver, and turquoise were once mined in great quantities. See chapter 6.
- **The High Road to Taos:** Driving from Santa Fe to Taos, take your time and follow the "high road." It runs through tiny ridge-top villages overflowing with Hispanic tradition. See chapter 7.
- **The Jemez Mountain Trail:** From Albuquerque, take a slow-paced day trip on the Jemez Mountain Trail. Drive out of Albuquerque on Route 44 and then take Route 4. You can make stops at Jemez Pueblo and a variety of shops and galleries as you continue the drive along Route 4 to Bandelier National Monument and on up to Espanola. If you want to make a loop back to Albuquerque, veer off on Route 126 through Cuba and then back down on Route 44. See chapter 6.
- **The Camino Real:** If you want to trace a bit of New Mexico's trade history, drive the Camino Real, which once served as the major trade route between Mexico and New Mexico, stretching 1,800 miles from Santa Fe to Mexico City. It was originally known as the Camino Real de Tierra Adentro, or Royal Highway of the Interior Land, and can still be found paralleling major highways, including I-25 from Santa Fe to Las Cruces. For more information contact the Director, New Mexico State Monuments, Museum of New Mexico, P.O. Box 2087, Santa Fe, NM 87504.
- **The Santa Fe Trail:** Another important trade route, the Santa Fe Trail once served as a highway to businessmen from the eastern United States who were able to supply New Mexico with less expensive commercial goods than those that were imported from Mexico. The Santa Fe Trail became extremely important to New Mexico and great efforts were made to protect it after war was declared on Mexico in 1846. The war didn't eradicate the trail, but the Santa Fe Railway did take its place and effectively rendered it extinct until a few years ago when the Santa Fe Trail Association began to bring it back into the consciousness of the state. For more information on the Santa Fe Trail, contact the New Mexico Department of

Tourism, Room 751, Lamy Building, 491 Old Santa Fe Trail, Santa Fe, NM 87503. See chapter 9.

5 The Best Offbeat Travel Experiences

- **American International Rattlesnake Museum:** Located in Albuquerque, this museum, where you'll find living specimens as well as memorabilia dating from early American history, is completely unique and absolutely dedicated to this fearsome reptile. Kids love it. See chapter 6.
- **Bolack Trophy Museum:** If you're going to be in Bloomfield, don't forget to stop by the Bolack Trophy Museum, where you'll find former New Mexico governor Tom Bolack's collection of mounted animal trophies from around the world. See chapter 10.
- **Cumbres and Toltec Scenic Railroad:** The country's longest and highest narrow-gauge steam railroad, built in 1880, can be found at its depot in Chama (a town that's nothing more than a wide spot in the road) before it leaves on its 64-mile journey to Antonito, Colorado. See chapter 10.
- **Very Large Array (VLA):** This attraction is exactly what its strange name reveals—it's a very large array of dish-shaped antennae (each one is 82 feet in diameter) that forms a single gigantic radio telescope across the plains of San Agustin. VLA is located about an hour from Socorro. See chapter 11.
- **Rock Hound State Park:** If you're into rocks, maybe you won't find it odd that there's an entire park devoted to the pursuit of your hobby, but I'm certainly amazed by its existence. This is probably one of the only places in New Mexico where you're not only allowed, but encouraged, to take whatever you find. See chapter 11.
- **Dexter National Fish Hatchery:** It sounds like a strange place to visit on your vacation, but the Dexter National Fish Hatchery is actually quite fascinating. It is dedicated to the preservation, study, and raising of endangered fish species. Self-guided tours are available. See chapter 12.
- **Eagle Ranch Pistachio Groves:** Thought to be New Mexico's first and largest pistachio groves, Eagle Ranch offers tours on weekdays as well as a visitors center, art gallery, and gift shop. See chapter 12.

6 The Best Museums

- **Albuquerque Museum:** Dedicated to preserving the history of this historic city, the Albuquerque Museum features a permanent exhibit that chronicles the city's evolution from Coronado's 16th-century forays to its present-day status as a center of military research and high technology. See chapter 6.
- **Museum of Fine Arts:** Located in Santa Fe, the Museum of Fine Arts is a wonderful collection featuring the work of Georgia O'Keeffe, R. C. Gorman, and photographer Ansel Adams. Also represented are landscapes and portraits by all of the Taos masters. See chapter 7.
- **Museum of International Folk Art:** It's not as Southwestern as some of the other museums in Santa Fe, but it's well worth a visit. The collection includes art by craftspeople from around the world. See chapter 7.
- **Millicent Rogers Museum:** Located in Taos, this museum holds a wide variety of interesting Native American arts and crafts collected by its namesake, a wealthy Taos émigré, as well as more recent gifts and acquisitions. You'll find

everything from jewelry and pottery to rugs, kachina dolls, and basketry. See chapter 8.

- **Van Vechten Lineberry Taos Art Museum:** Recently opened, the Van Vechten Lineberry Taos Art Museum holds a fascinating (and excellent) collection of art created by the original Taos artists, as well as the work of the former wife of the museum's founder. See chapter 8.
- **Kit Carson Historic Museums:** Included in this group of museums is the Kit Carson Home and Museum of the West, a 12-room adobe home built in 1825; the Martinez Hacienda, a Spanish colonial hacienda that has been developed into a living museum featuring weavers, blacksmiths, and woodcarvers; and the Ernest L. Blumenschein Home and Museum, once home to one of the founders of the Taos Society of Artists. These historic homes are my favorite stops during a trip to Taos. See chapter 8.
- **Museum of the Horse:** I was a bit skeptical when I first heard of this place, located on racetrack grounds in Ruidoso, but I have to admit that I was very pleasantly surprised by what I found inside. It holds a collection of more than 10,000 horse-related items, including saddles, sleighs, a horse-drawn fire engine, a stagecoach, and paintings by artists such as Frederic Remington, Charles Russell, and Frank Tenney Johnson. See chapter 12.

7 The Most Interesting Historical Sites

- **Old Town:** Once the center of Albuquerque commerce, Old Town thrived until the early 1880s when businesses relocated nearer to the railroad tracks. It was rediscovered in the 1930s and from that time on has been a center of tourism. Today you can visit shops, galleries, and restaurants in Old Town, as well as the Church of San Felipe de Neri, the first structure built when colonists established Albuquerque in 1706. See chapter 6.
- **Palace of the Governors:** Now a state history museum, the Palace of the Governors, located in Santa Fe, was once the original capitol of New Mexico. Built in 1610 it has been in continuous public use longer than any other structure in the United States. See chapter 7.
- **Saint Francis Cathedral:** Located in Santa Fe, St. Francis Cathedral, built in the style of great European cathedrals for Archbishop Jean-Baptiste Lamy between 1869 and 1886, is an architectural anomaly in Santa Fe. However, it is beautiful and worth visiting. See chapter 7.
- **Loretto Chapel:** It seems that there are quite a few miraculous religious dedications in New Mexico. Loretto Chapel, with a spiral staircase that defies gravity, is another of them. See chapter 7.
- **Georgia O'Keeffe's Home:** Recently opened to the public, Georgia O'Keeffe's home in Abiquiu is a fascinating look into the life of the famous New Mexico artist. See chapters 7 and 10.
- **San Francisco de Asis Church:** Although it is often photographed, it's not the outside of this church that brings so many visitors to Ranchos de Taos—it's the painting inside. The Shadow of the Cross by Henri Ault (1896) seems to be somewhat magical. Go see for yourself. See chapter 8.
- **Fechin Institute:** A memorial to Russian artist Nicolai Fechin, the Fechin Institute was his home between 1927 and 1933. A true Renaissance man, Fechin was proficient at painting, drawing, sculpture, architecture, and woodworking, among other things. See chapter 8.

8   The Best Festivals & Events

- **Spanish Market:** People travel thousands of miles to attend Spanish Market in Santa Fe every year in July. More than 300 Hispanic artists from New Mexico and southern Colorado display and sell their work, which might include painted and carved saints (*santos*), textiles, tin work, furniture, and metal work. See "New Mexico Calendar of Events," in chapter 3.
- **Indian Market:** Also held in Santa Fe, and also extremely popular, Indian Market is the largest all–Native American market in the country. About 800 artisans display their baskets, blankets, pottery, wood carvings, rugs, paintings, and sculptures at rows and rows of booths. This is a huge event. See "New Mexico Calendar of Events," in chapter 3.
- **Intertribal Indian Ceremonial:** Fifty tribes from throughout the United States gather in Albuquerque for parades, rodeos, dances, athletic competitions, and an arts and crafts show during the second week of August. See "New Mexico Calendar of Events," in chapter 3.
- **New Mexico Arts and Crafts Fair:** Every year in June Albuquerque hosts the second-largest arts and crafts fair in the country. More than 300 New Mexico artisans are represented. See "New Mexico Calendar of Events," in chapter 3.
- **Kodak Albuquerque International Balloon Fiesta:** More than 800 colorful balloons come together in the world's largest balloon rally every October. There is a sunrise mass ascension and special events are scheduled throughout the week. See "New Mexico Calendar of Events," in chapter 3.
- **Chile Festival:** New Mexicans love their chiles, and every year they celebrate their favorite fiery food item with a festival in Hatch, New Mexico (chile capital of the world), on Labor Day weekend. See chapter 11.

9   The Best Family Experiences

- **Sandia Peak Tramway:** What kid wouldn't want to take a ride on the world's longest tramway? The scenery is fantastic, and once you reach the top, especially in the summer, you can let nature entertain the troops. See chapter 6.
- **Rio Grande Zoological State Park:** Soon to include an aquarium, Rio Grande Zoological State Park has always been a favorite place for kids to visit. They'll get to see a wide variety of animals at their own speed here. See chapter 6.
- **El Rancho de las Golondrinas:** A living museum, El Rancho de las Golondrinas re-creates an 18th- and 19th-century Spanish village. Kids like to visit the working molasses mill, the blacksmith shop, shearing and weaving rooms, and water mills. There are animals here as well. See chapter 7.
- **Santa Fe Children's Museum:** Interactive exhibits and hands-on displays keep everyone happy at the Santa Fe Children's Museum. In addition, there are regularly scheduled performances and family activities available. See chapter 7.
- **The New Mexico Museum of Mining:** Located in Grants, this place is wonderful for children. They'll get to go underground and touch actual mining tools and equipment, as well as ore cars and the like. Retired miners often lead the tours and kids love to hear their stories. See chapter 10.
- **White Sands National Monument:** If they've got some extra energy, take the kids to White Sands National Monument, where they'll be able to go dune surfing or just plain roll around in the sand. Bring extra clothing and lots of sunscreen (the reflection off the sand can cause some pretty nasty sunburns). See chapter 12.

- **Carlsbad Caverns National Park:** They won't like the fact that they can't go climbing on cave formations, but most kids are fascinated by these incredible caves nonetheless. See chapter 12.
- **Living Desert Zoo and Gardens State Park:** This zoo, located in Carlsbad contains more than 50 species of desert mammals, birds, and reptiles in native habitats. See chapter 12.

10 The Best Bed & Breakfast Inns

- **Hacienda Antigua** (Albuquerque; ☎ **800/201-2986**): Hacienda Antigua, not far from downtown Albuquerque, is quite a surprise. The grounds are absolutely gorgeous, and the rooms are beautifully decorated (and spotlessly clean). Claw-foot bathtubs are a real plus here. See chapter 6.
- **Spencer House** (Santa Fe; ☎ **800/647-0530**): Unique among Santa Fe bed-and-breakfast inns, Spencer House is surprisingly New England in decor. Romance oozes from every corner of the house, which won an award from the Santa Fe Historical Board for restoration. See chapter 7.
- **Adobe and Pines Inn** (Taos; ☎ **800/723-8267**): Absolutely my favorite B&B in New Mexico, the Adobe and Pines Inn in Taos is beautiful, charming, peaceful, and hosted by two of the most gracious individuals I've ever met. You absolutely will not be disappointed if you choose to stay here. See chapter 8.
- **Little Tree Bed and Breakfast** (Taos; ☎ **800/334-8467**): While there are lots of reasons to love this adorable, cozy B&B, it's tops on my list because it was built by the owners themselves with authentic adobe. You don't see many true adobes around anymore, and this one is a real treasure. See chapter 8.

11 The Best Historic Hotels

- **La Posada de Albuquerque** (☎ **800/777-5732**): Listed on the National Register of Historic Places, La Posada de Albuquerque was built in 1939 by famous hotelier Conrad Hilton as his very first inn. See chapter 6.
- **The W. E. Mauger Estate** (Albuquerque; ☎ **505/242-8755**): Listed on the National Register of Historic Places, this restored Queen Anne–style residence was constructed in 1897 for wool baron William Mauger. See chapter 6.
- **The Bishop's Lodge** (Santa Fe; ☎ **505/983-6377**): The original lodge was actually built for Bishop Jean-Baptiste Lamy, spiritual leader of northern New Mexico's Roman Catholic population, who used to retreat to the area when church politics became too taxing for him. The humble chapel he constructed is now listed on the National Register of Historic Places, and the lodge is a deluxe three-season resort. See chapter 7.
- **The Historic Taos Inn** (☎ **800/TAOS-INN**): Made up of a group of separate adobe buildings that date from the mid-1800s, The Historic Taos Inn was once home to Taos County's first physician, Dr. T. Paul Martin. It was also the first building in Taos to have indoor plumbing installed. See chapter 8.
- **St. James Hotel** (Cimarron; ☎ **800/748-2694**): Located in Cimarron, the St. James Hotel is famous for its former guests more than anything else. Annie Oakley's bed can be found within and so can a guest register with signatures of Buffalo Bill Cody and Jesse James. See chapter 9.
- **Casa de Patrón Bed and Breakfast** (Lincoln; ☎ **505/653-4676**): An adobe home built around 1860, Casa de Patron was once used as a hiding place by Billy the Kid during his time in Lincoln. See chapter 12.

12 The Best Restaurants

- **Le Marmiton** (Albuquerque; ☎ 505/821-6279): Le Marmiton is absolutely Albuquerque's best classical French restaurant. The atmosphere in the small restaurant (it seats only 40 at a time) is romantic and pleasant, and dishes like *caille* and *fantaisie aux fruits de mer* make for memorable dining. See chapter 6.
- **Prairie Star** (Bernalillo, outside Albuquerque; ☎ 505/867-3327): Located in Bernalillo, Prairie Star, which serves up contemporary American regional cuisine, has been a local favorite for years. The dining room is located in an adobe home built in the 1940s in Mission style. Recommended main courses include shrimp margarita, veal sweetbreads, and fresh pan-fried fish. See chapter 6.
- **Cafe Escalera** (Santa Fe; ☎ 505/989-8188): Modern in decor and cuisine, Cafe Escalera has been a local favorite since it opened several years back. Menu items include vegetarian black bean chile and a variation on salade Niçoise (grilled tuna with arugula, new potatoes, green beans, beets, and aioli). The menu also includes heartier selections as well as fantastic desserts. See chapter 7.
- **Coyote Cafe** (Santa Fe; ☎ 505/983-1615): If I mention the name Mark Miller I wonder how much more needs to be said about this great place that features contemporary Southwestern cuisine. Mark Miller, in case you've never heard of him, is a very talented chef who has authored several cookbooks as well as *The Great Chile Book* (something of a field guide to chiles). See chapter 7.
- **Double A** (Santa Fe; ☎ 505/982-8999): The Double A is one of the Santa Fe's newest hot spots for eating out. Contemporary American cuisine is the focus here, and you can get anything from the somewhat sophisticated cowboy coffee–rubbed quail served with toasted grits and summer squash casserole to the down-home Double A Burger with buttermilk onion rings. The desserts are wonderful. See chapter 7.
- **The Shed** (Santa Fe; ☎ 505/982-9030): A Santa Fe luncheon institution since 1954, The Shed occupies several rooms in part of a rambling hacienda that was built in 1692. The food is basic New Mexican, but the quality is unsurpassed and the festive atmosphere makes this a memorable dining experience for the whole family. See chapter 7.
- **Stakeout Grill and Bar** (Taos; ☎ 505/758-2042): For some reason Stakeout, located just outside of Taos, is very close to my heart. It could be their famous duck preparations or the views from the dining room at sunset. The reason is irrelevant, because I'm sure you'll enjoy dining here no matter what. See chapter 8.
- **Trading Post Café** (Taos; ☎ 505/758-5089): This is one of my favorite places in Taos. With its exhibition kitchen and devoted local following, the place is always packed—in fact, in the first couple of years after opening, the owners were forced to expand the dining room in order to accommodate the crowds. See chapter 8.
- **Valverde Steak House** (Socorro; ☎ 505/835-3380): Not spectacular by the highest of standards, Valverde Steak House is still quite good, especially for the Socorro area. See chapter 11.
- **Double Eagle** (Las Cruces; ☎ 505/523-6700): Continental cuisine is alive and well behind the walls of this historic hacienda (it's more than 150 years old) located in Las Cruces. The decor is lush and dramatic—chandeliers hung with Baccarat crystals—and the food is fantastic. See chapter 11.
- **Victoria's Romantic Hideaway** (Ruidoso; ☎ 800/959-1328): Dinner at Victoria's will be a romantic experience you'll never forget. Hidden away in

Victoria's Romantic Hideaway are plush, candlelit dining areas in which diners are absolutely spoiled during their three- to four-hour meals. The cuisine is Sicilian, and eight-course meals are not unusual. See chapter 12.

• **La Lorraine** (Ruidoso; ☎ **505/257-2954**): Not far from Victoria's Romantic Hideaway is a little piece of France known by locals as La Lorraine. Enter the adobe building and you're immediately transported to a small town in France, where specialties like pâté, duck a l'orange, and chateaubriand dominate the menu. See chapter 12.

2 Getting to Know New Mexico

Welcome to New Mexico. And prepare yourself for an assault on the senses.

The sights, sounds, smells, and tastes of this remarkable state have enraptured visitors for centuries. Probably no one who has ever trodden New Mexican soil can say he or she was unchanged.

What is it about the 47th state that is so special?

To some, it's the landscape. The state slopes gently upward from the Texas prairies and the Chihuahuan Desert to a wonderland of contorted canyons and high wilderness peaks, split by the life-sustaining river known as the Rio Grande. The mutable colors of the high plains, the sound of a coyote's howl, the smell of a storm-dampened creosote bush, the taste of a juicy prickly pear fruit—all these things are unforgettable.

Visitors also are entranced by New Mexico's unique blend of peoples and cultures. The most thoroughly tricultural of the contiguous 48 states, New Mexico is an overlay of Native Americans, Hispanics, and Anglos (non-Hispanic Caucasians). The groups live and work side by side, yet each preserves its distinct communities and cultural nuances.

Other visitors may point to its history for what makes New Mexico unique. Prehistoric culture reached its apex with the Anasazi (ca. A.D. 800–1300); when the Spanish first visited in the 16th century, they found a thriving post–Anasazi Pueblo culture. The newcomers built their capital at Santa Fe in 1610, spreading religion and politics across the region. In the 19th century, as the United States moved westward, New Mexico spawned legends like Billy the Kid and Geronimo, Kit Carson and the Cimarron Trail. Today, visitors can descend into the kivas of ancient Anasazi at Chaco Canyon and the Aztec Ruins; feel the damp earth at El Santuario de Chimayo, credited by pilgrims for two centuries of medical miracles; and relive the echoes of outlaws' gunfire in melodramatic re-creations at Fort Sumner and elsewhere.

There's something here for everyone. Hiking, skiing, and rafting for the outdoors lover; world-famous artists' and musicians' communities for the culture vulture; innovative and palate-pleasing cuisine for the gourmet; atomic and space museums for the amateur scientist. Excitement and relaxation for all.

1 The Natural Environment

It would be easy, and accurate, to call New Mexico "high and dry" and leave it at that. The lowest point in the state, in the southeastern corner, is still over 2,800 feet in elevation, higher than the highest point in at least a dozen other states. The southern Rocky Mountains, whose beginnings came during the Cenozoic era more than 70 million years ago, extend well into New Mexico, rising above 13,000 feet in the Sangre de Cristo range and sending a final afterthought above 10,000 feet, just east of Alamogordo. Volcanic activity created the mountain range and its aftereffects can be seen throughout the state—from Shiprock (the remaining core of a long-eroded volcano) to Capulin Volcano National Monument. Two fault lines, which created the Rio Grande Rift Valley, home to the Rio Grande, run through the center of the state and seismic activity continues to change the face of New Mexico even today.

While archeologists have discovered fossils indicating that most of New Mexico was once covered by ancient seas, the surface area of the state is now quite dry. The greater portion of New Mexico receives fewer than 20 inches of precipitation annually, the bulk of that coming either as summer afternoon thunderstorms or winter snowfall. In an area of 121,666 square miles—the fifth-largest American state—there are only 221 square miles of water. Rivers and lakes occupy less than 0.2% of the landscape. The most obvious and most important source of water is the Rio Grande, the "Big River" of Hispanic lore. It nourishes hundreds of small farms from the Pueblo country of the north to the bone-dry Chihuahuan Desert of the far south.

There is, however, more water than meets the eye in New Mexico. Systems circulating beneath the earth's surface have created all sorts of beautiful and fascinating geologic formations, including the natural wonder known as Carlsbad Caverns, one of the greatest cave systems in the world. Other caves have formed throughout the state, many of which have collapsed over the centuries creating large sinkholes. These sink holes have since filled with water and formed beautiful lakes. Bottomless Lakes State Park, located near the town of Roswell, is a good example of this type of geological activity.

Other natural wonders you'll encounter during a visit to New Mexico include red-, yellow-, and orange-hued high, flat mesas and the 275-square-mile White Sands National Monument that contains more than eight billion tons of pure white gypsum and is the largest field of sand dunes of this kind in the entire world. Here mountains meet desert and the sky is arguably bigger, bluer, and more fascinating than any other place in the country. Words can't do justice to the spectacular colors of the landscape: colors that have drawn contemporary artists from around the world for nearly a century, colors that have made Taos and Santa Fe synonymous with artists' communities. The blues, browns, greens, reds, oranges, and yellows in every imaginable variation make this land a living canvas. This is truly big sky country, where it seems you can see forever.

LIFE ZONES OF NEW MEXICO

Six of the earth's seven life zones are represented in New Mexico, from subtropical desert to alpine tundra. As a result, New Mexico is home to an unusually diverse variety of plant and animal life. You'll see sage-speckled plains and dense stands of pine trees, as well as cactus and tender perennials (typically found in much cooler climates). Living among the trees and out on the desert plains are deer, bear, scorpions, and rattlesnakes. The mélange of flora and fauna in New Mexico is simply overwhelming.

New Mexico

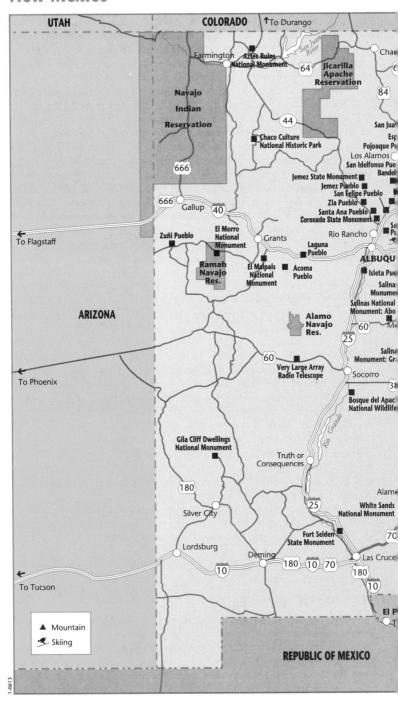

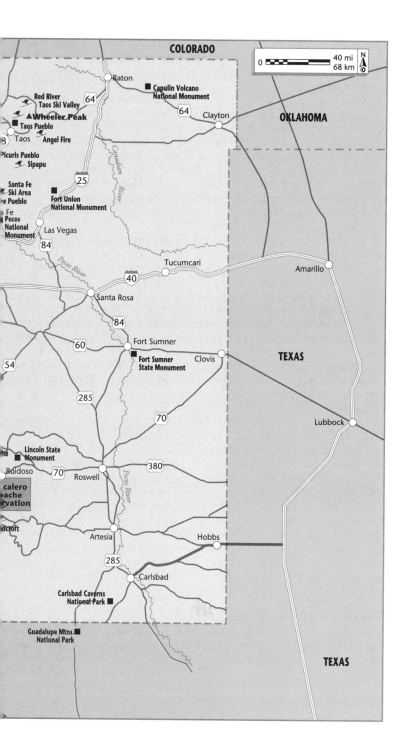

COLORADO

0 ━━━━━ 40 mi
68 km

N

Raton

Capulin Volcano
National Monument

Red River
Taos Ski Valley
64

▲Wheeler Peak

Taos Pueblo

Taos   Angel Fire

OKLAHOMA

64   Clayton

Picuris Pueblo
Sipapu

Santa Fe
Ski Area
Pueblo

25

Fort Union
National Monument

Fe
Pecos
National
Monument

Las Vegas

84

Canadian River

Pecos River

Tucumcari

40

Amarillo

Santa Rosa

84

60   Fort Sumner

Fort Sumner
State Monument

Clovis

TEXAS

54

285

70

Lubbock

Lincoln State
Monument

Ruidoso   70   Roswell

380

calero
ache
rvation

Pecos River

dcroft

Artesia

Hobbs

285

Carlsbad

Carlsbad Caverns
National Park

Guadalupe Mtns.
National Park

TEXAS

At the highest elevations (those above 12,000 feet) is the alpine zone, which offers very little in the way of a home for plants and animals. Areas in New Mexico that fall into the alpine zone include Wheeler Peak and several other mountains in the Enchanted Circle area near Taos. These peaks are above the timberline and conditions are harsh. Only a few animals, such as pikas and marmots, are able to survive at this elevation, and the only trees you'll see are bristlecone pines. In the "summer" only a few hardy wildflowers have the strength to bloom in the alpine zone.

Heading down the mountain to about 12,000 to 9,500 feet is the Hudsonian zone. At this altitude there is typically a great deal of snowfall in the late fall to late spring. There isn't much of a growing season in the Hudsonian zone, but there are more plants in this area than in the Alpine zone, creating more habitats for a greater number of animals. Rodents, birds, bighorn sheep, elk, mountain goats, and marmots live in New Mexico's Hudsonian zone among the bristlecone pine, blue spruce, and subalpine firs.

A very small percentage of New Mexico is in the Canadian zone, which includes certain areas of the White, Mogollons, Jemez, San Juan, and Sangre de Cristo Mountains. There you will find deer and elk (which migrate to warmer areas during the winter) as well as a variety of spruce, fir, and aspen trees.

With elevations between 8,500 and 6,500 feet, most of north-central New Mexico (primarily Santa Fe, Taos, and portions of Albuquerque) is well within the transition zone. This is where you'll find ponderosa pines standing alongside oak trees and juniper bushes. North-central New Mexico gets quite a bit more rain than other areas of the state and as a result you'll find a large number of wildflowers in bloom here in the spring and summer (columbine, pennyroyal, and New Mexico groundsel, to name a few), as well as a greater variety of wildlife. Keep your eyes open for black bears, mountain lions, deer, elk, quail, and wild turkey, especially if you're hiking in less-populated areas.

The northern portion of the state, from 6,500 to 4,500 feet, is in the upper Sonoran life zone. Here you'll find a combination of plants and animals found in the lower Sonoran life zone and the transition zone. Cacti are as prevalent as juniper, oak, and piñon; and rattlesnakes, scorpions, centipedes, and tarantulas make their homes here along with mountain lions, javelinas, and pronghorns.

The southern portion of the state, where the heat rises off dusty flatlands and the altitude is below 4,500 feet, falls within the lower Sonoran life zone. Traveling through Las Cruces, Alamogordo, and Carlsbad you'll see all sorts of cacti, including prickly pear and cholla. Don't expect, however, to see the giant saguaro cactus most commonly associated with the desert landscape. The arid environment in the lower Sonoran zone is home to animals that thrive in the heat and don't need as much water as those found at higher altitudes. It's the perfect climate for rattlesnakes, centipedes, tarantulas, and scorpions.

THE FLORA & FAUNA OF NEW MEXICO

As you can see, there are innumerable varieties and types of plants and animals in New Mexico, so it would be impossible to discuss all of them in this book. Below you'll find a list of the more unusual flora and fauna you're apt to encounter during your travels through the state.

FAUNA

Javelina   Also known as the collared peccary, the javelina is a small, wild pig with curved tusks. It is the only pig that is native to North and South America. The javelina can live in a variety of environments, but will most likely be found in the dry scrublands of New Mexico. Charcoal gray in color, the javelina has a white stripe around its neck and weighs up to 50 pounds. It travels in small groups feeding on insects, reptiles, worms, fruits, and roots.

Marmot A ground-living rodent with its roots in the squirrel family, the most common varieties of marmot are the chipmunk, prairie dog, and woodchuck. They live in burrows either in the plains or mountainous regions of North America and Eurasia and are active during daylight hours. Green plants are their food of choice. Their stout bodies are covered with brown, white-tipped fur. The yellow-bellied marmot makes its home in New Mexico.

Pika A relative of hare and rabbits, the pika is also known as the rock rabbit or mouse hare. They make their homes in rocky environments above the timberline in western North America and northern Asia, and they live in communities. Though they resemble the rabbit, they have shorter ears and their hind and forelegs are of equal length. Because they live in such cold environments their entire bodies, including the bottoms of their feet, are fur covered. Coloration varies from red to gray. Pika live on a diet of green plants, which are in short supply during the cold winter months. Pika circumvent this problem by cutting and drying vegetation in the sun for winter storage.

Pronghorn Very distantly related to the antelope of Asia and Africa, the pronghorn is sometimes called the American antelope, and is in fact native to the western United States—New Mexico, in particular. It is approximately three feet in height and has a light brown coat with distinctive white markings on its throat (two strips), rump, and underside. Both the male and female pronghorns have horns. These animals live on open plains and eat shrubs, such as sagebrush, and some grasses. Pronghorns are the fastest North American mammal. In spite of their speed, they are prey to wolves and coyotes. Unchecked hunting nearly caused the extinction of the pronghorn in the early part of this century; however, they are now a protected species and are making a strong comeback.

Roadrunner I would be remiss if I didn't mention the roadrunner, New Mexico's state bird. It is a member of the family of birds more commonly known as cuckoos. With its long tail, erect body, and heavy bill, the roadrunner is quite distinctive looking. Though it is a bird, it doesn't fly very well and prefers to run along the ground (hence its name) at high speeds. In fact, the roadrunner can run at a speed of up to 15 miles an hour. You'll see roadrunners all over the place during your travels around the state.

FLORA

Cholla The types of cholla, a variety of cactus, most commonly found in New Mexico are tree, plateau, cane, stanly club, and dagger club. Tree cholla, with tuberculate "branches," can grow up to 10 feet in height and has $3/4$- to $1^1/4$-inch-long spines. It grows primarily at elevations between 4,000 and 6,000 feet and produces magenta flowers. Plateau cholla is a short, shrublike plant that grows at elevations of 4,000 to 8,000 feet among other plants like piñon and juniper. If not surrounded by other bushes, grasses, and trees, plateau cholla can grow up to seven feet in height if the water supply is sufficient. In drier areas plateau cholla forms a short, wide mat along the ground. Spines are $3/4$ inch in length, and its flowers, which bloom in May, are pale to dark yellow. The fruit of this cactus is yellow when ripe. Cane cholla is similar to tree cholla in height and shape; however, it produces pink, purple, yellow, or white flowers. Stanly club and Dagger club cholla are short plants that form mats along the ground. Stanly club likes to grow on the mesas and plains of New Mexico, while Dagger club prefers rocky conditions. Both are extremely spiny and both produce small ($1^3/_4$- to 2-inch) yellow flowers.

Columbine Generally speaking, columbine is any perennial plant in the buttercup family. In New Mexico these delicate wildflowers can be seen growing at roadsides around Santa Fe and Taos. Hummingbirds love columbine, and Native Americans once used the seeds of this flower to cure headaches and fever.

Groundsel Groundsel is a name that encompasses any plant in the aster family. Groundsel might be found growing as a vine, shrub, or tree. However, the variety found in New Mexico simply resembles a small, yellow daisy. Native Americans have been known to use groundsel to heal open wounds as well as to stimulate menses.

Juniper An aromatic evergreen in the cypress family, juniper grows best in the temperate zone and is prevalent in New Mexico. Like other evergreens, juniper produces cones; however juniper cones look more like berries and are best known as juniper berries, which are used in cooking as well as in flavoring gin. Plains Indians used juniper as incense in religious gatherings.

Pennyroyal The American pennyroyal is an annual plant with small blue to purplish flowers. Admirers of the pennyroyal have discovered that the plant has more than aesthetic value. In fact, an oil found in pennyroyal is said to be excellent insect repellent, and a tea made from pennyroyal was once thought to be a cure for a variety of illnesses.

Prickly Pear Like the cholla cactus, there is also a wide variety of prickly pear cacti in New Mexico. There are simply too many to discuss here; however, most varieties can be identified by large, flat, spiny, teardrop-shaped branches and oblong purple or reddish fruit. Among the varieties seen in New Mexico are Fragile, Loose, Porcupine, Cliff, Starvation, Juniper, Red-Spined, Hair-Spined, Potts, Purple Fruited, Major, and Desert.

Yucca The state flower of New Mexico, yucca is a treelike succulent of the lily family. When they flower, yucca plants produce a long stalk of white or light purple flowers. It is interesting to note that the yucca plant is pollinated by the aptly named yucca moth, which depends on the plant as a "feeding ground" for its larvae. Without the yucca moth the yucca plant usually doesn't produce flowers or fruit.

2 The Regions in Brief

NORTH-CENTRAL NEW MEXICO The most highly populated and well traveled area of the state, north-central New Mexico roughly includes the cities of Albuquerque, Santa Fe, and Taos. It is also the economic center of New Mexico. In this portion of the state lush mountains, incredibly, seem to rise directly out of the parched plateaus that have made New Mexico's landscape famous. Temperatures are generally lower in this area than they are in the rest of the state, and skiing is one of the most popular winter activities in both Santa Fe and Taos.

NORTHEASTERN NEW MEXICO Covering the area north of Interstate 40 and east of the Sangre de Cristo Mountains, northeastern New Mexico is prairie land once inhabited and/or visited by some of the West's most legendary gunslingers. Towns to visit for a bit of Wild West history are Cimarron and Las Vegas. The northeastern portion of the state also includes attractions such as Fort Union National Monument, a portion of the Santa Fe Trail, Kiowa National Grasslands, and Capulin Volcano National Monument. Due to its abundance of state parks and wildlife reserves, as well as the fact that it borders the ski resort towns of Angel Fire, Taos, Red River, and Santa Fe, this region is an excellent area for sports enthusiasts.

NORTHWESTERN NEW MEXICO　　This region, which covers the upper left corner of the state, is the place to go if you're interested in Native American culture. Sandstone bluffs here mark the homes of Pueblo, Navajo, and Apache Indians in an area once inhabited by the Anasazi Indians of the past. My favorite places to visit in this section of the state are Acoma Pueblo, Chaco Culture National Historical Park, and Aztec Ruins National Monument. A major portion of the northwest region is part of a Navajo reservation, the largest in the country. This is also the gateway to the famous Four Corners region. The town of Grants, near Acoma, is a great spot for finding silver jewelry at reasonable prices. Railroad fanatics, hunters, and fishers should make the trip up to Chama, home of the Cumbres and Toltec Railroad and a popular starting point for hunting and fishing trips.

SOUTHWESTERN NEW MEXICO　　This region, like northeastern New Mexico, is another great place to visit if you're interested in the history of the Wild West and Native American culture, for it was once home to Billy the Kid and Geronimo. The Rio Grande, lifeline to this part of the state, acts as a border between the southwest and southeast portions of the state. Attractions west of the river include Gila National Forest, once home to the Mogollon Indians, whose past is preserved in the Gila Cliff Dwellings National Monument. The Chiricahua Apaches, a tribe once led by the famous Geronimo, also lived in this area. The town of Silver City, which survives today as an economic center of this area, was once a booming mine town. Surrounding ghost towns weren't as lucky. Las Cruces, located at the foot of the Organ Mountains, is the state's second largest city, and Truth or Consequences, named for a television and radio game show, is located north of Las Cruces off I-25. Socorro is a center of Hispanic culture, and Deming and Lordsburg are working ranch towns.

SOUTHEASTERN NEW MEXICO　　Bounded on the west by the Rio Grande River, to the north by Interstate 40, and to the east by Texas, southeastern New Mexico is home to two of the most interesting natural wonders in this part of the country: Carlsbad Caverns and White Sands National Monument. The underground caverns filled with stalactites and stalagmites are infinitely interesting and hauntingly beautiful. Snow-white dunes at White Sands National Monument, which rise out of the desert landscape, are an extraordinary sight as you make the drive to Alamogordo. White Sands is a great place to camp out and watch the sunrise. This portion of the state is yet another former home of Billy the Kid. It is also where he died. Southeastern New Mexico has something of a dubious past as well: The world's first atomic bomb was detonated here.

3　New Mexico Today

With a long history of uninterrupted habitation, Santa Fe was founded by Spanish colonists a full decade before the pilgrims set foot on Plymouth Rock. It is caught in a time warp between the 17th and 21st centuries, between traditional Native American and Hispanic cultures and a current-day onslaught of tourism.

A carefully considered plan to preserve and perpetuate pre–20th-century architecture has made downtown Santa Fe look like an adobe enclave. Much of the rest of this city has followed suit. For miles in all directions, flat-topped earth-colored homes, many of them valued in the millions of dollars, speckle the hills amid sparse piñon and mesquite forests. Most of the construction is actually stuccoed concrete. A standing joke in Santa Fe art circles is that the city sanctions the use of 42 shades of brown.

It's no laughing matter, however, that Santa Fe is fast becoming a victim of its own uniqueness. Known to residents and visitors as "The City Different," Santa Fe is rapidly attracting large numbers of new residents from around the country who want to escape the crime, pace, and closed-in spaces created by concrete skyscrapers. Unfortunately, they're bringing all of those things (except skyscrapers) with them. The real estate market was the first to fall victim to the onslaught of newcomers. At first, when the wealthy newcomers moved in, real estate prices went up. But then, as the area's less fortunate moved out because they could not afford these higher prices, home sales dropped. Over the past year, especially, real estate has taken a nosedive. The level of crime has increased: Muggings, almost unheard of in the past, are becoming commonplace; graffiti is showing up all over the city; homelessness is growing; and noise pollution is on the rise. (It should be noted, however, that comparatively speaking, Santa Fe is still one of this country's safest cities.) Due to these changes, tourism has declined and the city has begun to suffer economically. Some believe this is good news in its own way because hotel room rates have come down somewhat (though not significantly), and it's not as difficult as it once was to get a table at the more popular restaurants. Santa Fe remains a popular tourist destination; however, it is showing some wear and tear and has lost some of its original charm.

Taos, on the other hand, remains much the same as it was five years ago. Still a quaint small town, Taos seems to be attracting more visitors than it had in the past (perhaps due to Santa Fe's decline in popularity). The most significant event of late may have been the opening of a new museum, the Van Vechten Lineberry Taos Art Museum. It highlights the work of the 11 original Taos artists as well as Duane Van Vechten, the very talented wife of the museum's founder, Edwin C. Lineberry. This isn't to say that Taos has escaped the push for growth to which Santa Fe has fallen victim. There are plans to develop the land to the west of NM 68 (the road that leads into Taos town) just beyond Ranchos de Taos. Such plans will change not only the landscape, but the whole feeling of this charming little town. Fortunately, Taoseños have seen the negative consequences of changes in Santa Fe and are thus more aware of the problems that come with extensive development. It is my sincere hope that efforts will be made to keep Taos and its inhabitants from following in its neighbor's footsteps.

Albuquerque is completely different from Santa Fe and Taos in that it is truly a big city, skyscrapers and all. Most visitors to northern New Mexico fly into Albuquerque International Airport, rent a car, and head (literally) for the hills without stopping to take in the pleasures of the city. There are some wonderful museums, such as the New Mexico Museum of Natural History and Science, the Albuquerque Museum, and the Indian Pueblo Cultural Center, that should not be missed on a trip to New Mexico. They are constantly growing and changing. The latest addition to the scene is Albuquerque's new biological park (scheduled to open in the spring of 1997), which will include a zoo, an aquarium, and a plant conservatory. In addition, the nightlife offerings are expanding along Central Avenue in downtown Albuquerque. Furthermore, Albuquerque hosts the annual Kodak International Balloon Fiesta every October (it's the largest of its kind in the world) and is within a short driving distance of the spectacular Acoma Pueblo. For those who want to make an extended visit to Albuquerque but don't want to stay in a big downtown hotel, the good news is that many bed-and-breakfast inns are opening on the outskirts of the city in areas that are relatively free of the noise and traffic you'd experience downtown.

In the areas that surround and connect these three major tourist destinations, you will notice the development of many casinos and gaming palaces associated with the pueblos. These developments began in 1994 when a law was passed to permit gambling on Indian reservations. Not surprisingly, just about every pueblo, including Taos Pueblo, has taken advantage of this legislation. The casinos are a source of great debate among area residents and politicians and, no doubt, will continue to be in the years to come.

If you look at a map you'll no doubt come to realize that the outer regions of the state are primarily home to the national parks and monuments that make New Mexico unique. Capulin Volcano, White Sands National Monument, Carlsbad Caverns, and El Malpais National Monument continue to be major visitor attractions, but their faces remain relatively unchanged. Of course, there is greater interest in outdoor activities, making these areas more popular than before with tourists who, it is hoped, continue to respect these unique landscapes, leaving them as they found them. Surrounding towns maintain a slow pace, and major growth is unlikely.

So, as you can see, there's still something for everyone in New Mexico—the faster-paced area known as North Central New Mexico is great for those who love shopping and museums and good restaurants, while the outer areas are better for those who enjoy a more leisurely pace. This beautiful state is becoming more and more popular with visitors, but it still maintains much of the charm it held in earlier days.

4 A Look at the Past

CIVILIZATIONS   Archeologists say that humans first migrated to the Southwest, moving southward from the Bering Land Bridge, about 12,000 B.C. Sites such as Sandia Cave and Folsom—where weapon points were discovered that for the first time clearly established that our prehistoric ancestors hunted now-extinct mammals such as woolly mammoths—are internationally known. When these large animals died off during the late Ice Age (about 8,000 B.C.), people turned to hunting smaller game and gathering wild food.

Stable farming settlements, as evidenced by the remains of domestically grown maize, date from about 3,000 B.C. As the nomadic peoples became more sedentary, they built permanent residences—pit houses—and made pottery. Cultural differences began to emerge in their choice of architecture and decoration: The Mogollon people, in the southwestern part of modern New Mexico, created brown and red pottery and built large community lodges; the Anasazi, in the north, made gray pottery and smaller lodges for extended families.

The Mogollon, whose pottery dates from about 100 B.C., were the first of the sophisticated village cultures. They lived primarily in modern-day Catron and Grant counties. The most important Mogollon ruins extant today are in the Gila River Valley, including Gila Cliff Dwellings National Monument north of Silver City.

By about A.D. 700, and perhaps a couple of centuries earlier, the Anasazi of the northwest had absorbed village life and expanded through what is now known as the Four Corners Region (where

Dateline

- **3,000 B.C.** First evidence of stable farming settlements in region.
- **A.D. 700** Earliest evidence of Anasazi presence.
- **1540** Francisco Vásquez de Coronado marches to Cíbola in search of a Native American "city of gold."
- **1542** Coronado returns to New Spain, declaring his mission a failure.
- **1610** Immigration to New Mexico increases; Don Pedro de Peralta establishes Santa Fe as capital.
- **1680** Pueblo Indians revolt against Spanish.
- **1692** Spanish recapture Santa Fe.
- **1706** Albuquerque established.
- **1739** First French traders enter Santa Fe.
- **1779** Cuerno Verde, leader of rebellious Comanche tribes, falls to Spanish forces.
- **1786** Comanches and Utes sign treaty with Spanish.
- **1821** Mexico gains independence from Spain.
- **1828** Kit Carson, the legendary frontiersman, arrives in Taos.

continues

- 1846 Mexican War breaks out; Gen. Stephen Kearny takes possession of New Mexico for United States.
- 1847 Revolt in Taos against U.S. control; newly appointed governor Charles Bent killed.
- 1848 Under provisions of Treaty of Guadalupe Hidalgo, Mexico officially cedes New Mexico to United States.
- 1861 Victorious Confederate general proclaims all of New Mexico south of the 34th parallel the new, Confederate territory of Arizona.
- 1862 Confederates routed from New Mexico.
- 1864 Navajos relocated to Bosque Redondo Reservation.
- 1868 Navajos return to their homeland.
- 1879 Atchison, Topeka, and Santa Fe Railroad routes main line through Las Vegas, Albuquerque, El Paso, and Deming, where connection is made with California's Southern Pacific line.
- 1878–81 Lincoln County War erupts; comes to epitomize the lawlessness and violence of the Wild West.
- 1881 Legendary outlaw Billy the Kid killed by Pat Garrett.
- 1886 Apache chief Geronimo captured; signals end of New Mexico's Indian wars.
- 1898 Painters Ernest Blumenschein and Bert Phillips settle in Taos.
- 1912 New Mexico becomes the 47th state.
- 1914 Blumenschein and Phillips form Taos Society of Artists; Taos becomes a major center of influence in mid-century American art and letters.
- 1916 Construction of Elephant Butte Dam brings

continues

New Mexico, Arizona, Utah, and Colorado come together). Around A.D. 1000, their culture eclipsed that of the Mogollon. Chaco Canyon National Historic Park, Aztec Ruins National Monument, and Salmon Ruins all exhibit an architectural excellence and skill, and a scientific sensitivity to nature, that marks this as one of America's classic pre-Columbian civilizations.

Condominium-style communities of stone and mud adobe bricks, three and four stories high, were focused around central plazas. The villages incorporated circular spiritual chambers called *kivas*. The Anasazi also developed means to irrigate their fields of corn, beans, and squash by controlling the flow of water from the San Juan River and its tributaries. From Chaco Canyon, they built a complex system of well-engineered roads leading in four directions to other towns or ceremonial centers. Artifacts found during excavation, such as seashells and macaw feathers, indicate they had a far-reaching trade network. The incorporation of solar alignments into some of their architecture has caused modern archeoastronomers to speculate on the importance of the equinoxes to their religion.

The disappearance of the Anasazi culture, and the emergence of the Pueblo culture in its place, is something of a mystery today. Those who study such things are in disagreement as to why the Anasazi abandoned their villages around the 13th century. Some suggest drought or soil exhaustion; others, invasion, epidemic, or social unrest. But by the time the first Spanish arrived in the 1500s, the Anasazi were long gone and the Pueblo culture was well established throughout northern and western New Mexico, from Taos to Zuni, near Gallup. Most of the people lived on the east side of the Continental Divide, in the Rio Grande valley.

Certain elements of the Anasazi civilization had clearly been absorbed by the Pueblos, includ-ing the apartment-like adobe architecture, the creation of rather elaborate pottery, and the use of irrigation or flood farming in their fields. Agriculture, and especially corn, was the economic mainstay.

Each pueblo, as the scattered villages and surrounding farmlands were known, fiercely guarded its independence. When the Spanish arrived, there were no alliances between villages, even among those that shared a common language or dialect. No more than a few hundred people lived in any one pueblo, an indication that the natives had learned to keep their population (which totaled 40,000 to 50,000) down in order to preserve their soil and other natural resources. But not all was peaceful: They alternately fought and traded with each other, as well as with nomadic Apaches. Even before the Spanish arrived, a pattern had been established.

THE ARRIVAL OF THE SPANISH   The Spanish controlled New Mexico for 300 years, from the mid-16th to the mid-19th century. That's twice as long as the United States has. The Hispanic legacy in language and culture is stronger today in New Mexico than anywhere else in the Southwest, no doubt a result of the prominence of the Rio Grande valley as the oldest and most populous fringe province of the viceroyalty of New Spain.

The spark that sent the first European explorers into what is now New Mexico was a fabulous medieval myth that seven Spanish bishops had fled the Moorish invasion of the 8th century, sailed westward to the legendary isle of Antilia, and built themselves seven cities of gold. Hernán Cortés's 1519 discovery and conquest of the Aztecs' treasure-laden capital of Tenochtitlán, now Mexico City, fueled belief in the myth. When a Franciscan friar 20 years later claimed to have sighted, from a distance, "a very beautiful city" in a region known as Cíbola while on a reconnaissance mission for the viceroyalty, the gates were open.

Francisco Vásquez de Coronado, the ambitious young governor of New Spain's western province of Nueva Galicia, was commissioned to lead an expedition to the "seven cities." Several hundred soldiers, accompanied by servants and missionaries, marched overland to Cíbola with him in 1540, along with a support fleet of three ships in the Gulf of California. What they discovered, after six hard months on the trail, was a bitter disappointment: Instead of a city of gold, they found a rock-and-mud pueblo at Hawikuh, the westernmost of the Zuni towns. The expedition wintered at Tiguex, on the Rio Grande near modern Santa Fe, before proceeding to the Great Plains seeking more treasure at Quivira, in what is now Kansas. The grass houses of the Wichita Indians were all they found.

Coronado returned to New Spain in 1542, admitting failure. Historically, though, his expedition was a great success, contributing the first widespread knowledge of the Southwest and Great Plains, and discovering en route the Grand Canyon.

By the 1580s, after important silver discoveries in the mountains of Mexico, the Spanish began to wonder if the wealth of the Pueblo country might lie in its land

- irrigation to southern New Mexican farms.
- **1924** Native Americans granted full U.S. citizenship.
- **1943** Los Alamos National Laboratory built; "Manhattan Project" scientists spend two years in complete seclusion developing nuclear weapons.
- **1945** First atomic bomb exploded at Trinity Site.
- **1947** Reports of a flying saucer crash near Roswell make national headlines, despite U.S. Air Force's denials that it has occurred.
- **1972** Pioneer balloonist Sid Cutter establishes Albuquerque International Balloon Fiesta.
- **1981** The Very Large Array, the world's most powerful radio telescope, begins observations of distant galaxies from the desert west of Socorro.
- **1982** U.S. space shuttle *Columbia* lands at Holloman Air Force Base, near White Sands National Monument.
- **1984** New Mexico's last remaining section of famed Route 66, near San Jon, is abandoned.
- **1990** New Mexico's last uranium mine, near Grants, closes.
- **1992** The 70th anniversary of the Inter-Tribal Indian Ceremonial is held at Gallup.
- **1994** Under pressure from Congress, U.S. Air Force reopens investigation of the 1947 flying saucer crash reports, concluding that the debris found was likely from tests of a secret Cold War spy balloon; UFO believers allege a cover-up.

rather than its cities. They were convinced that they had been divinely appointed to convert the natives of the New World to Christianity. And so a northward migration began, orchestrated and directed by the royal government. It was a mere trickle in the late 16th century. Juan de Onate established a capital in 1598 at San Gabriel, near San Juan Pueblo, but a variety of factors led to its failure. Then in 1610, under Don Pedro de Peralta, the migration began in earnest.

It was not dissimilar to America's schoolbook stereotype. Bands of armored conquistadors did troop through the desert, humble robed friars striding by their sides. But most of the pioneers came up the valley of the Rio Grande with oxcarts and mule trains rather than armor, intent on transplanting their Hispanic traditions of government, religion, and material culture to this new world.

Peralta built his new capital at Santa Fe and named it La Villa Real de la Santa Fe de San Francisco de Asis, the Royal City of the Holy Faith of St. Francis of Assisi. His capitol building, the Palace of the Governors, has been continuously occupied as a public building ever since by Spanish, Mexicans, Americans, and for 12 years (1680–92) by the Pueblo Indians. Today it is a museum.

RELIGION & REVOLT   The 17th century in New Mexico was essentially a missionary era, as Franciscan priests attempted to turn the Indians into model Hispanic peasants. Their churches became the focal points of every pueblo, with Catholic schools a mandatory adjunct. By 1625 there were an estimated 50 churches in the Rio Grande valley. But the Native Americans weren't enthused about doing "God's work"—building new adobe missions, tilling fields for the Spanish, and weaving garments for export to Mexico—so soldiers backed the padres in extracting labor, a system known as *repartimiento*. Simultaneously, the *encomienda* system provided that a yearly tribute in corn and blankets be levied upon each Indian. The Pueblos were pleased to take part in Catholic religious ceremonies and proclaim themselves converts. To them, spiritual forces were actively involved in the material world. If establishing harmony with the cosmos meant absorbing Jesus Christ and various saints into their hierarchy of *kachinas* and other spiritual beings, so much the better. But the Spanish friars demanded they do away with their traditional singing and masked dancing, and with other "pagan practices." When the Pueblo religion was violently crushed and driven literally underground, resentment toward the Spanish grew and festered. Rebellions at Taos and Jemez in the 1630s left village priests dead, but the Pueblos were savagely repressed.

A power struggle between church and state in Nuevo Mexico weakened the hand of the Spanish colonists, and a long drought in the 1660s and 1670s gave the warlike Apaches reason to scourge the Spanish and Pueblo settlements for food. The Pueblos blamed the friars, and their ban on traditional rain dances, for the drought. The hanging of four medicine men as "sorcerers," and the imprisonment of 43 others, was the last straw for the Rio Grande natives. In 1680, the Pueblo Revolt erupted.

Impressions

For a greatness of beauty I have never experienced anything like New Mexico. . . . Just a day itself is tremendous there.
                              —D. H. Lawrence, "New Mexico," Survey Graphic, 1931

On the license plates in New Mexico it reads: "the Land of Enchantment." And that it is, by God! . . . Everything is hypnagogic, chthonian, and super-celestial. Here Nature has gone Gaga and Dada.
                              —Henry Miller, The Air-Conditioned Nightmare, 1945

Popé, a San Juan shaman, catalyzed the revolt. Assisted by other Pueblo leaders, he unified the far-flung Native Americans, who never before had confederated. They pillaged and burned the province's outlying settlements, then turned their attention upon Santa Fe, besieging the citizens who had fled to the Palace of the Governors. After nine days, having reconquered Spain's northernmost American province, they let the refugees retreat south to Mexico.

Popé ordered that the Pueblos should return to the lifestyle they had had before the arrival of the Spanish. All Hispanic items, from tools to livestock to fruit trees, were to be destroyed, and the blemish of baptism was to be washed away in the river. But the shaman misjudged the influence of the Spanish upon the Pueblo people. They were not the people they had been a century earlier, and they *liked* much of the material culture they had absorbed from the Europeans. What's more, they had no intention of remaining confederated; their independent streaks were too strong.

In 1692, led by newly appointed Governor Don Diego de Vargas, the Spanish recaptured Santa Fe without bloodshed. Popé had died, and without a leader to reunify them, the Pueblos were no match for the Spanish. Vargas pledged not to punish them, but to pardon and convert. Still, when he returned the following year with 70 families to recolonize the city, he had to use force. And for the next several years, bloody battles persisted throughout the Pueblo country.

By the turn of the 18th century, Nuevo Mexico was firmly in Spanish hands. This time, however, the colonists seemed to have learned from some of their past errors. They were more tolerant in their religion, less ruthless in their demands and punishments.

ARRIVAL OF THE ANGLOS   By the 1700s, there were signals that new interlopers were about to arrive in New Mexico. The French had laid plans to begin colonizing the Mississippi River, and hostile Native American tribes were on the warpath. The Spanish viceroyalty fortified its position in Santa Fe as a defensive bastion and established a new villa at Albuquerque in 1706.

In 1739, the first French trade mission entered Santa Fe, welcomed by the citizenry but not by the government. For 24 years, until 1763, a black-market trade thrived between Louisiana and New Mexico. It ended only when France lost its toehold on its North American claims during the French and Indian War against Great Britain.

The Native Americans were more fearsome foes. Apache, Comanche, Ute, and Navajo launched repeated raids against each other and the Rio Grande settlements for most of the 18th century, which led the Spanish and Pueblos to pull closer together for mutual protection. Pueblo and Hispanic militias fought side by side in campaigns against the invaders. But by the 1770s, the attacks had become so savage and destructive that the viceroy in Mexico City created a military jurisdiction in the province, and Governor Juan Bautista de Anza led a force north to Colorado to defeat the most feared of the Comanche chiefs, Cuerno Verde ("Green Horn"), in 1779. Seven years later, the Comanches and Utes signed a lasting treaty with the Spanish and thereafter helped keep the Apaches in check.

France sold the Louisiana Territory to the young United States in 1803, and the Spanish suddenly had a new intruder to fear. The Lewis and Clark expedition of 1803 went unchallenged, much as the Spanish would have liked to challenge it; but in 1807, when Lt. Zebulon Pike built a stockade on a Rio Grande tributary in Colorado, he and his troops were taken prisoner by troops from Santa Fe. Pike was taken to the New Mexican capital, where he was interrogated extensively, and then to Chihuahua, Mexico. The report he wrote upon his return to the United States was Atlantic America's first inside look at Spain's frontier province.

At first, pioneering American merchants—excited by Pike's observations of New Mexico's economy—were summarily expelled from Santa Fe or jailed, their goods confiscated. But after Mexico gained independence from Spain in 1821, traders were welcomed. The wagon ruts of the Santa Fe Trail soon extended from Missouri to New Mexico, and from there to Chihuahua. (Later, it became the primary southern highway to California.)

As the merchants hied to Santa Fe, Anglo American and French Canadian fur trappers headed into the wilderness. Their commercial hub became Taos, a tiny village near a large pueblo a few days' ride north of Santa Fe. Many married into native or Hispanic families. Perhaps the best known was Kit Carson, a sometime federal agent, sometime Indian scout, whose legend is inextricably interwoven with that of early Taos. He spent 40 years in Taos, until his death in 1868.

In 1846, the Mexican War broke out and New Mexico became a territory of the United States. There were several causes of the war—the U.S. annexation of Texas in 1845, disagreement over the international boundary, unpaid claims owed to American citizens by the Mexican government—but foremost was the prevailing U.S. sentiment of "manifest destiny," the belief that the Union should extend "from sea to shining sea." Gen. Stephen Kearny marched south from Colorado; in the Las Vegas plaza, he announced that he had come to take possession of New Mexico for the United States. His arrival in Santa Fe on August 18, 1846, went unopposed.

An 1847 revolt in Taos resulted in the slaying of the new governor of New Mexico, Charles Bent, but U.S. troops defeated the rebels and executed their leaders. That was the last threat to American sovereignty in the territory. In 1848, the Treaty of Guadalupe Hidalgo officially transferred title of New Mexico, along with Texas, Arizona, and California, to the United States.

Kearny promised New Mexicans that the United States would respect their religion and property rights and would safeguard their homes and possessions from hostile Indians. His troops behaved with a rigid decorum. The United States upheld Spanish policy toward the Pueblos, assuring the survival of their ancestral lands, their traditional culture, and their old religion—which even three centuries of Hispanic Catholicism could not do away with.

THE CIVIL WAR   As conflict between the North and South flared east of the Mississippi, New Mexico found itself caught in the debate over slavery. Southerners wanted to expand slavery to the western territories, but abolitionists fought a bitter campaign to prevent that from happening. New Mexicans themselves voted against slavery twice, while their delegate to Congress engineered the adoption of a slavery code. In 1861, the Confederacy, after its secession from the Union, laid plans to make New Mexico theirs as a first step toward capturing the West.

In fact, southern New Mexicans, including those in Tucson (Arizona was then a part of the New Mexico Territory), were disenchanted with the attention paid them by Santa Fe and already were threatening to form their own state. So when Confederate Lt. Col. John Baylor captured Fort Fillmore, near Mesilla, and on August 1, 1861, proclaimed all of New Mexico south of the 34th parallel to be the new territory of Arizona, there were few complaints.

The following year, Confederate Gen. Henry Sibley assembled three regiments of 2,600 Texans and moved up the Rio Grande. They defeated Union loyalists in a bloody battle at Valverde, near Socorro; easily took Albuquerque and Santa Fe, which were protected only by small garrisons; and proceeded toward the federal arsenal at Fort Union, 90 miles east of Santa Fe. Sibley planned to replenish his supplies there before continuing north to Colorado, then west to California.

On March 27–28, 1862, the Confederates were met head-on in Glorieta Pass, about 16 miles outside of Santa Fe, by regular troops from Fort Union supported by a regiment of Colorado Volunteers. By the second day, the rebels were in control, until a detachment of Coloradans circled behind the Confederate troops and destroyed their poorly defended supply train. Sibley was forced into a rapid retreat back down the Rio Grande. A few months later, Mesilla was reclaimed for the Union, and the Confederate presence in New Mexico was ended.

THE LAND WARS   The various tribes had not missed the fact that whites were fighting among themselves, and they took advantage of this weakness to step up their raids upon border settlements. In 1864, the Navajos, in what is known in tribal history as "The Long Walk," were relocated to the new Bosque Redondo Reservation on the Pecos River at Fort Sumner, in east central New Mexico. Militia Col. Kit Carson led New Mexico troops in this venture, a position to which he acceded as a moderating influence between the Navajos and those who called for their unconditional surrender or extermination.

It was an ill-advised decision: The land could not support 9,000 people; the government failed to supply adequate provisions; and the Navajo were unable to live peacefully with the Mescalero. By late 1868, the tribes retraced their routes to their homelands, where the Navajos gave up their warlike past. The Mescalero's raids were squashed in the 1870s and they were confined to their own reservation in the Sacramento Mountains of southern New Mexico.

Corraling the rogue Apaches of southwestern New Mexico presented the territory with its biggest challenge. Led by chiefs Victorio, Nana, and Geronimo, these bands wreaked havoc upon the mining region around Silver City. Eventually, however, they succumbed, and the capture of Geronimo in 1886 was the final chapter in New Mexico's long history of Indian wars.

As the Native American threat decreased, more and more livestock and sheep ranchers established themselves on the vast plains east of the Rio Grande, in the San Juan basin of the northwest, and in other equally inviting parts of the territory. Cattle drives up the Pecos Valley, on the Goodnight-Loving Trail, are the stuff of legend; so, too, was Roswell cattle baron John Chisum, whose 80,000 head of beef probably represented the largest herd in America in the late 1870s.

Mining grew as well. Albuquerque blossomed in the wake of a series of major gold strikes in the Madrid Valley, close to ancient turquoise mines; other gold and silver discoveries through the 1870s gave birth to boomtowns—now mostly ghost towns—like Hillsboro, Chloride, Mogollon, Pinos Altos, and White Oak. The copper mines of Santa Rita del Cobre, near Silver City, are still thriving.

In 1879, the Atchison, Topeka, and Santa Fe Railroad sent its main line through Las Vegas, Albuquerque, El Paso, and Deming, where it joined with the Southern Pacific line coming eastward from California. (The Santa Fe station was, and is, at Lamy, 17 miles southeast of the capital.) Now linked by rail to the great markets of America, New Mexico's economic boom period was assured.

But ranching invites cattle rustling and range wars, mining beckons feuds and land fraud, and the construction of railroads has often been tied to political corruption and swindles. New Mexico had all of them, especially during the latter part of the 19th century. Best known of a great many conflicts was the Lincoln County War (1878–81), which began as a feud between rival factions of ranchers and merchants. It led to such utter lawlessness that Pres. Rutherford B. Hayes ordered a federal investigation of the territorial government and the installation as governor of Gen. Lew Wallace (whose novel *Ben-Hur* was published in 1880).

One of the central figures of the Lincoln County conflict was William "Billy the Kid" Bonney, a headstrong youth (b. 1858) who became probably the best-known outlaw of the American West. He blazed a trail of bloodshed from Silver City to Mesilla, Santa Fe to Lincoln, and Artesia to Fort Sumner, where he was finally killed by Sheriff Pat Garrett in July 1881.

By the turn of the century, most of the violence had been checked. The mineral lodes were drying up, and ranching was taking on increased importance. Economic and social stability were coming to New Mexico.

STATEHOOD, ART & ATOMS Early in the 20th century, its Hispanic citizens having proved their loyalty to the United States by serving gallantly with Theodore Roosevelt's Rough Riders during the Spanish-American War, New Mexico's long-awaited dream of becoming an integral part of the Union was finally recognized. On January 6, 1912, Pres. William Howard Taft signed a bill making New Mexico the 47th state.

Within a few years, Taos began gaining fame as an artists' community. Two painters from the East Coast, Ernest Blumenschein and Bert Phillips, settled in Taos in 1898, lured others to join them, and in 1914 formed the Taos Society of Artists, one of the most influential schools of art in America. Writers and other intellectuals soon followed, including Mabel Dodge Luhan, novelists D. H. Lawrence and Willa Cather, and poet-activist John Collier. Other artists settled in Santa Fe and elsewhere in northern New Mexico; the best known was Georgia O'Keeffe, who lived miles from anywhere in tiny Abiquiu. Today, Santa Fe and Taos are world renowned for their contributions to art and culture.

The construction in 1916 of the Elephant Butte Dam near Hot Springs (now Truth or Consequences) brought irrigated farming back to a drought-ravaged southern New Mexico. Potash mining boomed in the southeast in the 1930s. Native Americans fared well, gaining full citizenship in 1924, two years after the All Pueblo Council was formed to fight passage in Congress of a bill that would have given white squatters rights to Indian lands. And in 1934, with ex-Taos intellectual John Collier as commissioner of Indian Affairs, tribes were accorded partial self-government. The Hispanics, meanwhile, became the most powerful force in state politics, and remain so today.

But the most dramatic development in 20th-century New Mexico was induced by the Second World War. In 1943, the U.S. government sealed off a tract of land on the Pajarito Plateau, west of Santa Fe, that previously had been an exclusive boys' school. On the site, in utter secrecy, it built the Los Alamos National Laboratory, otherwise known as Project Y of the Manhattan Engineer District—the "Manhattan Project." Its goal: to split the atom and develop the world's first nuclear weapons.

Under the direction of J. Robert Oppenheimer, later succeeded by Norris E. Bradbury, a team of 30 to 100 scientists lived and worked in almost complete seclusion for two years. Their work resulted in the atomic bomb, tested for the first time at the Trinity Site, north of White Sands, on July 16, 1945. The bombings of Hiroshima and Nagasaki, Japan, three weeks later, signaled to the world that the nuclear age had arrived.

Even before that time, New Mexico was climbing the ladder of stature in America's scientific community. Robert H. Goddard, considered the founder of modern rocketry, conducted many of his experiments near Roswell in the 1930s, during which time he became the first person to shoot a liquid-fuel rocket faster than the speed of sound. Clyde Tombaugh, the discoverer of the planet Pluto in 1930, helped establish the department of astronomy at New Mexico State University in Las Cruces.

And former Sen. Harrison (Jack) Schmitt, an exogeologist and the first civilian to walk on the moon in 1972, is a native of the Silver City area.

Today the White Sands Missile Range is one of America's most important astrophysics sites, and the International Space Hall of Fame in nearby Alamogordo honors men and women from around the world who have devoted their lives to space exploration. Aerospace research and defense contracts are economic mainstays in Albuquerque, and Kirtland Air Force Base is the home of the Air Force Special Weapons Center. Los Alamos, of course, continues to be a national leader in nuclear technology.

Despite the rapid approach of the 21st century in many parts of the state, there are other areas still struggling to be a part of the 20th. Many Native Americans, be they Pueblo, Navajo, or Apache, and Hispanic farmers, who till small plots in isolated rural regions, hearken to a time when life was slower paced. But life in New Mexico was never simple, for anyone.

5 Art, Architecture & Literature

ART   Since prehistoric times, New Mexico has been a cradle of artistic genius for its native peoples. Prehistoric Mogollon, Mimbres, and Anasazi pottery is unique in its design and color. Today's Pueblo Indians are noted not only for their pottery—each pueblo being distinctive in its touches from the next—but also for their textile crafts. Navajos are renowned for their silver jewelry, often with turquoise, and for their weaving and sand painting; Apaches are master basket makers.

Hispanic art was by nature either religious, rustic, or both. Cut off for centuries from most of the rest of the world, save through the rarely traveled colonial lifeline to Mexico, artisans handcrafted their own ornate furnishings. Paintings (*retablos*) and carved icons (*santos*) underscored the creators' devotion to their Roman Catholic faith. Traditional decorative tinwork and furniture are popular today, along with weaving and silversmithing.

New Mexico wasn't discovered by Anglo-American artists until the end of the 19th century. Two East Coast painters, Ernest Blumenschein and Bert Phillips, happened upon Taos in 1898 and were hypnotized by the dramatic light. They returned to make the valley their home, and in 1914 founded the Taos Society of Artists. The society disbanded in 1927, a victim of its own success—it so widely marketed the works of the town's isolated masters that other artists thronged to Taos. Today, the art community is prolific, indeed: By some estimates, more than 10% of the permanent population of Taos are painters, sculptors, writers, musicians, or others who earn income from artistic pursuits.

Santa Fe grew as an art community on the heels of Taos. By 1921, Los Cinco Pintores, a group of five avant-garde painters, were establishing names for themselves. The quintet included Jozef Bakos, Fremont Ellis, Walter Mruk, Willard Nash, and Will Shuster. The number of full-time professional artists in Santa Fe today exceeds 700, and that doesn't include writers or musicians. Thousands more dabble in the creative professions.

Santa Fe is home to the School of Indian Art, where many of today's leading Native American artists studied, including Apache sculptor Allan Houser. It's also the site of the Institute of American Indian Arts. The best-known Native American painter today is R. C. Gorman, an Arizona Navajo who has made his home in Taos since the 1960s. Now in his early 50s, Gorman is internationally acclaimed for his bright, somewhat surrealistic depictions of Navajo women.

ARCHITECTURE In a land as dry and treeless as most of New Mexico, it's not surprising that adobe has long been the principal construction material. Clay, mixed with grasses for strength, is placed in a mold and dried in the sun. The bricks are then stacked to create the building and reinforced with more wet clay. Almost every structure in New Mexico prior to 1879, when the railroad arrived, was built in this style by Pueblo Indians, Hispanics, and Anglos.

Architectural elements in adobe buildings usually include a network of *vigas,* long beams supporting the roof, their ends protruding through the facade; *latillas,* smaller stripped crossbeams layered between the vigas; corbels, carved wooden supports for the vertical posts and the vigas; a portal, usually shading a brick floor set into the ground; and a plastered adobe-brick *banco,* or fireplace, set into an outside wall.

The Territorial style of architecture became popular in the late 19th century, when railroads could carry in bricks, large logs, and other building materials. Today, adobe is again in vogue—for aesthetics, for price (it's cheap, and there's no shortage of mud!), and for its ability to retain heat for extended periods.

Modern architectural styles prevalent throughout the Western world are of course seen in New Mexico, especially in innovative downtown Albuquerque. But it's tradition that visitors find stunning. Santa Fe is the center of attention, as strict building codes have maintained the traditional architectural integrity of the city's core since the 1950s.

LITERATURE Many noted writers have made their homes in New Mexico in the 20th century. In the 1920s, the most noted were D. H. Lawrence and Willa Cather, both short-term Taos residents. Lawrence, the romantic and controversial English novelist, was here for parts of 1922–25 and reflected on that period in *Mornings in Mexico and Etruscan Places.* Though he died in Europe years later, a family shrine north of Taos is a popular place of pilgrimage for Lawrence devotees. Lawrence's Taos period is described in *Lorenzo in Taos,* written by his patron, Mabel Dodge Luhan. Cather, a Pulitzer Prize winner famous for her depictions of the pioneer spirit, penned *Death Comes for the Archbishop,* a fictionalization of the career of 19th-century Santa Fe bishop Jean-Baptiste Lamy, as a result of her stay.

Many well-known contemporary authors live in and write about New Mexico. John Nichols of Taos, whose *The Milagro Beanfield War* was turned into a popular movie in 1987, writes with insight about the problems of poor Hispanic farming communities. Tony Hillerman of Albuquerque is renowned for two decades of weaving mysteries around Navajo tribal police in such books as *Listening Woman* and *Thief of Time.* Hispanic novelist Rudolfo Anaya's *Bless Me, Ultima* and Pueblo writer Leslie Marmon Silko's *Ceremony* capture the lifestyles of their respective peoples. Of desert environment and politics, no one wrote better than the late Edward Abbey; *Fire on the Mountain,* set in New Mexico, was one of his most powerful works.

6 Religion & Ritual

Religion has always been at the heart of Indian life. Throughout the Southwest, the cosmos is viewed as a single whole. Within that whole, all living creatures are seen as mutually dependent, and every relationship, whether with another person, an animal, or even a plant, carries spiritual meaning. A hunter will pray before killing a deer, for instance, to ask the creature to give itself to the tribe. The slain deer is then treated as a guest of honor before the hunter ritually sends its soul back to its comrades to be reborn. Even the harvesting of a plant requires prayer, thanks, and ritual.

Pueblo Indians believe their ancestors originally lived underground, the source of life (and the place from which plants spring). Encouraged by burrowing animals, they

entered the world of humans—the "fifth" world—through a hole, a *sipapu,* by clinging to a web woven for them by Spider Woman.

The Pueblo peoples honor Mother Earth and Father Sun. In this dry land, the sun
can mean life and death. The tribes watch the skies closely, tracking solstices and planetary movements, to determine the optimum timing for crop planting cycles.

Dances are ritual occasions. Usually held in conjunction with the feast days of
Catholic saints (including Christmas Eve for Jesus Christ), the ceremonies demonstrate how the Pueblos absorbed certain aspects of Christianity from the Spanish without surrendering their traditional beliefs.

There are medicine dances, fertility rites, prayers for rain and for good harvests.
The spring and summer corn or *tablita* dances are among the most impressive. Ceremonies begin with an early morning mass and procession to the plaza honoring an
image of the saint. The rest of the day is devoted to song, dance, and feasting, with
performers masked and clad as deer, buffalo, eagles, and other creatures.

The all-night Shalako festival at Zuni Pueblo in late November or early December is the most spectacular of the Pueblo ceremonies. Colorfully costumed *kachinas,*
or spirit dancers, act out the Zuni story of creation and evolution. Everyone awaits
the arrival of the *shalakos,* 12-foot-tall kachinas who bless new and renovated homes
in the village.

Visitors are normally welcome to attend Pueblo dances but should respect the
Native Americans' requests that they not be photographed or tape-recorded.

Navajos believe in a hierarchy of supernatural beings, the Holy Ones, who can
travel on a sunbeam, a thunderbolt, or the wind. At their head is Changing Woman,
the earth mother, who vigilantly assures humans' well-being by teaching them to live
in harmony with nature. Her children, the Hero Twins, ward off our enemies—all
but Old Age and Death. Religious symbolism, which pervades art and music, under-
scores the Navajo belief that their homeland was created by the Holy Ones for them
to live in. Typical of Navajo dancing are the *yeibichai* rituals, curative ceremonies
marked by circular social dances with long song cycles.

The Apaches have a similar creation belief. They were created by Father Sun and
Mother Earth ("the White Painted Lady") to live in the Southwest region, and the
Holy Ones' twin sons helped them ward off wicked creatures by teaching them how
to ride horses and use a bow and arrow. The most important ceremony among the
Apaches today, including the Mescaleros, is the four-day puberty ritual for young
girls. The colorful masked *gahans,* or mountain spirits, perform to celebrate the
subject's womanhood, when the White Painted Lady resides within her body.

Outside the pueblos and reservations, the most visible places of worship are those
of the Roman Catholics. Santa Fe's Cathedral of St. Francis is the state's best-known
church, but a close second is El Santuario de Chimayo, an hour north of the state
capital. Constructed in 1816, it has long been a site of pilgrimage for Catholics who
attribute miraculous powers of healing to the earth in the chapel's anteroom. Most
Hispanic Catholics believe strongly in miracles.

7 New Mexican Cuisine

New Mexican cuisine isn't the same as Mexican cooking, or even those American
concoctions sometimes called "Tex-Mex" or "Cal-Mex." It's a consequence of
Southwestern history, a unique blend of Hispanic and Pueblo recipes. As the Native
Americans taught the Spanish conquerors about their corn—how to roast it, how to
make corn pudding, stewed corn, cornbread, cornmeal, and *posole* (hominy)—the
Spanish introduced their beloved chiles, adding spice to the cuisine.

You Say Chili, They Say Chile

It's never "chili" in New Mexico. New Mexicans are adamant that *chile,* the Spanish spelling of the word, is the only way to spell it—no matter what your dictionary might say.

Go ahead, look up *chile.* It's not in there. I guarantee it. Well, maybe it is, but only as a secondary spelling for the word *chili.* Personally, I think that's only been put there to appease the population of New Mexico.

The peppers that New Mexicans will identify only as chiles are grown throughout the state. The climate is perfect for cultivating and drying the small but powerful red and green New Mexican varieties. The state's residents have such a personal attachment to their most famous agricultural product that in 1983 they directed their senior U.S. senator, Pete Domenici, to enter New Mexico's official stand on the spelling of *chile* into the Congressional Record.

The town of Hatch, New Mexico, bills itself as the chile capital of the world. But wherever you travel, chiles make an appearance on every menu in the state. Just about everything you'll order during your stay in New Mexico will be covered with a sauce made from chiles. As a general rule, green chile sauce is hotter than the red chile sauce, but be sure to ask. No matter which you order, your eyes will start watering, your sinuses will drain, and your palate will be on fire after one heaping forkful. Be warned: No amount of water or beer will take the sting away. (Drink milk. A sopaipilla drizzled with honey also might help, too.)

Don't let my words of caution scare you away from genuine New Mexico chiles. The pleasure of eating them outweighs the pain. Start slow, with salsas and chile sauces first, maybe *rellenos* (stuffed peppers) next, then *rajas* (roasted peeled chiles cut into strips). Before you know it, you'll be buying *chile ristras* (dried chiles strung together for cooking as well as decorative use). You might even buy bags of chile powder and maybe a chile plant to bring home. By then you will have realized that you've never had a chili that tasted quite like this—and you'll know why it's a chile.

Lovers of tacos, burritos, and enchiladas will find them here, although they may not be quite as you've had them before. Tacos, for instance, are more often served in soft rolled tortillas than in crispy shells. Tamales are made from cornmeal mush, wrapped in husks and steamed. Chile rellenos are stuffed with cheese, deep-fried, then covered with green chile.

Many dishes include unusual local ingredients, such as piñon nuts, jicama, and prickly pear cactus. Here's a sampling of some of the more regional dishes that might be hard to find outside the Southwest:

Blue corn   Pueblo vegetable that produces a crumbly flour widely used in tortilla shells, especially for enchiladas.

Carne adovada   Tender pork marinated in red chile, herbs, and spices, then baked.

Chorizo burrito   (also called a breakfast burrito) Mexican sausage, scrambled eggs, potatoes, and scallions wrapped in a flour tortilla with red or green chile and melted Jack cheese.

Empanada   A fried pie with nuts and currants.

Fajitas   Strips of beef or chicken sautéed with onions, green peppers, and other vegetables, and served on a sizzling platter.

Green chile stew   Locally grown chiles cooked in a stew with chunks of meat, beans, and potatoes.

Huevos rancheros   Fried eggs on corn tortillas, topped with cheese and red or green chile, served with pinto beans.

Pan dulce   Indian sweet bread.

Posole   A corn soup or stew (called hominy in other parts of the South), sometimes with pork and chiles.

Sopaipillas   A lightly fried puff pastry served with honey or stuffed with meat and vegetables.

8 Recommended Books

For additional reading on the general history of New Mexico, there are quite a few excellent sources of information. Look for Robert L. Casey's *Journey to the High Southwest: A Traveler's Guide* (Pacific Search Press, 1985); Lance and Katherine Chilton's *New Mexico: A New Guide to the Colorful State* (University of New Mexico Press, 1984); Myra Ellen Jenkins and Albert H. Schroeder's *A Brief History of New Mexico* (University of New Mexico Press, 1974); and Marc Simmons's *New Mexico: An Interpretive History* (University of New Mexico Press, 1988).

A trip to New Mexico will likely intensify your interest in Native American and Hispanic culture, and while I've tried to cover both in this book there will undoubtedly be something you'd like to learn more about. If your interest lies in Hispanic arts and crafts, E. Boyd's *Popular Arts of Spanish New Mexico* (Museum of New Mexico Press, 1974) is an excellent source. Edward P. Dozier's *The Pueblo Indians of North America* (Holt, Rinehart and Winston, 1970) is a comprehensive look at the Pueblo Indians not only of New Mexico, but of other parts of the continent as well. Leslie Marmon Silko's *Ceremony* (Viking, 1977) and Ray A. Williamson's *Living the Sky: The Cosmos of the American Indian* (University of Oklahoma Press, 1987) are excellent sources of information on Native American religious ceremony and ritual.

Novels set in New Mexico include Willa Cather's *Death Comes for the Archbishop* (Random House, 1971); Tony Hillerman's *Thief of Time* (Harper and Row, 1988), as well as anything else by Tony Hillerman; and John Nichols's *The Milagro Beanfield War* (Ballantine, 1988). In addition, look for the writings of D. H. Lawrence (*Mornings in Mexico and Etruscan Places;* Penguin, 1967); Mabel Dodge Luhan (*Lorenzo in Taos;* Knopf, 1932); and Georgia O'Keeffe (*O'Keeffe;* Viking, 1976).

Planning a Trip to New Mexico

As with any trip, a little preparation is essential before you start your journey to New Mexico. This chapter will provide you with a variety of planning tools, including information on when to go, how to get there, how to get around once you're there, and some suggested itineraries.

1 Visitor Information

The best place to obtain detailed information is the **New Mexico Department of Tourism** in the Lamy Building, 491 Old Santa Fe Trail, Santa Fe, NM 87503 (P.O. Box 20002, Santa Fe, NM 87504-2004, ☎ **800/545-2040**). You can also visit the New Mexico Department of Tourism Internet site at http://www.newmexico.org.

The various cities and regions of the state are represented by convention and visitors bureaus and/or chambers of commerce. Their addresses and telephone numbers (and in some cases, their Internet addresses) are listed in the appropriate chapters in this book.

2 When to Go

THE CLIMATE Summers are hot throughout most of the state, though distinctly cooler at higher elevations. Winters are relatively mild in the south, harsher in the north and in the mountains. Spring and fall are pleasant all over. Rainfall is sparse except in the higher mountains; summer afternoon thunderstorms and winter snows account for most precipitation.

Santa Fe and Taos, at 7,000 feet, have midsummer highs in the 80s, overnight midwinter lows in the teens. Temperatures in Albuquerque, at 5,000 feet, often run about 10° warmer. Snowfall is common from November through March, and sometimes as late as May, though it seldom lasts long. Santa Fe averages 32 inches total annual snowfall. At the high-mountain ski resorts, as much as 300 inches (25 feet) may fall in a season—and stay. The plains and deserts of the southeast and south commonly have summer temperatures in excess of 100°.

New Mexico Temperatures & Precipitation

	Jan High–Low	Apr High–Low	July High–Low	Oct High–Low	Annual Precip. (inches)
Alamogordo	57–28	78–40	95–65	79–42	7.5
Albuquerque	47–28	70–41	91–66	72–45	8.9
Carlsbad	60–28	81–46	96–67	79–47	13.5
Chama	33–3	54–22	73–37	52–18	9.3
Cloudcroft	41–19	56–33	73–48	59–36	25.8
Farmington	44–16	70–36	92–58	70–37	7.5
Las Cruces	56–26	79–45	95–66	82–47	8.6
Roswell	56–24	78–42	91–65	75–45	12.7
Ruidoso	50–17	65–28	82–48	67–31	21.4
Santa Fe	40–18	59–35	80–57	62–38	14.0
Taos	40–10	62–30	87–50	64–32	12.1
Truth or Conseq.	54–27	75–44	92–66	75–47	8.5

NEW MEXICO CALENDAR OF EVENTS

January

- **New Year's Celebrations.** Several pueblos have public celebrations for the New Year. Among them are Cochiti (☎ **505/465-2244**), Jemez (☎ **505/834-7235**), and Santa Ana (☎ **505/867-3301**) pueblos. January 1.
- **Three Kings' Day.** Most pueblos honor their new tribal officers with ceremonies. Traditional dancing is held at Cochiti, Jemez, Laguna, Nambe, Picuris, Sandia, San Felipe, San Ildefonso, San Juan, Santa Ana, Santa Clara, Santo Domingo, Taos, Tesuque, and Zia pueblos. January 6.
- **Winter Wine Festival.** A variety of food and wine offerings and tastings prepared by local chefs takes place mid-January in the Taos Ski Valley. Call **505/776-2291** for more information.

February

- **Candelaria Day Celebration,** San Felipe Pueblo (☎ **505/843-7270**). Traditional dances. February 2.
- ✪ **Winter Fiesta.** Santa Fe's annual retreat from the midwinter doldrums appeals to skiers and nonskiers alike. Highlights include the Great Santa Fe Chili Cook-off; ski races, both serious and frivolous; snow-sculpture contests; snowshoe races; and hot-air balloon rides.

  Where: Santa Fe Ski Area. **When:** The last weekend in February. **How:** Call **505/982-4429** for details.
- **Mount Taylor Winter Quadrathlon.** Bicycling, running, cross-country skiing, and snowshoeing. Near Grants. Third weekend in February.

March

- **Fiery Food Show.** Annual trade show featuring chiles and chile products. Albuquerque. Call **505/873-9103** for more information. Early March.
- **Rio Grande Arts and Crafts Festival,** a juried show featuring 200 artists and craftspeople from around the country takes place at the State Fairgrounds in Albuquerque during the second week of March. Call **505/292-7457** for details.
- **Easter Celebrations.** At Cochiti, Nambe, Picuris, San Felipe, San Ildefonso, Santa Ana, Santo Domingo, and Zia pueblos, with masses, parades, and dances,

including the corn dance. There's a street party in the historic district of Silver City, and a balloon rally at Truth or Consequences. Late March or early April.

April

- **Albuquerque Founders' Day.** Parade, auction, and street entertainment in Old Town. Albuquerque. Call **505/768-3561** for more information. Third weekend in April.
- **Gathering of Nations Powwow.** Miss Indian World contest, dance competitions, arts and crafts exhibitions, fitness runs and walks. University of New Mexico arena. Albuquerque. Call **505/842-9918.** Mid- to late April.
- **American Indian Week,** Indian Pueblo Cultural Center, Albuquerque. A celebration of Native American traditions and culture. Call **505/843-7270** for details. Mid- to late April.

May

- **Cinco de Mayo Fiestas.** The restoration of the Mexican republic (from French occupation 1863–67) is celebrated at Hobbs, Las Cruces (Old Mesilla Plaza), Silver City, and Truth or Consequences. First weekend in May.
- **¡Magnifico! Albuquerque Festival of the Arts,** a 17-day celebration featuring more than 200 special events, attractions, and exhibits. The visual, performing, literary, and culinary arts are honored throughout the city. Call **505/842-9918** for more information. Early to mid-May.
- **Taos Spring Arts Celebration.** Three-week survey of visual, performing, and literary arts. Taos. Late April to mid-May. Call **505/758-3873** for details.

June

- **Rails and Trails Days.** Rodeo, train rides, fiddlers contest, quilt and art shows. Las Vegas. Call **800/832-5947** for more information. First weekend in June.
- ✪ **New Mexico Arts and Crafts Fair.** The second-largest event of its type in the United States presents more than 200 New Mexico artisans demonstrating and selling their crafts, plus nonstop entertainment for the whole family.

  Where: State Fairgrounds, Albuquerque. **When:** The last weekend in June. **How:** Admission varies. For information, call **505/884-9043.**
- **Santa Fe Opera.** World-class Santa Fe Opera season runs from the end of June to the end of August. Call **505/986-5900** for more information.

July

- **Fourth of July Celebrations.** Parades, fireworks, and various other events at Albuquerque, Capitan, Carlsbad, Clayton, Farmington, Gallup, Grants, Las Vegas, Lordsburg, Moriarty, Red River, Roswell, and Socorro. July 4.
- **Apache Maidens' Puberty Rites.** Rodeo and ceremonial Dance of the Mountain Spirits, Mescalero. Call **800/223-6424** for more information. July 4.
- **Nambé Waterfall Ceremonial.** Several rarely seen traditional dances are presented at Nambé Falls, Nambé Pueblo. For more information, call **505/455-2036.** July 4.
- **Rodeo de Santa Fe.** Parade, dance, and four rodeo performances. Santa Fe. Call **505/471-8643** for details. Weekend after July 4.
- **Taos Pueblo Powwow.** Intertribal competitions in traditional and contemporary dances, Taos Pueblo. For more information, call **505/758-1028.** Second weekend in July.
- **Billy the Kid–Pat Garrett Historical Days.** Lectures, tours, stew cook-off, Western music and dance, at Cedar Creek Park, Ruidoso. Call **505/355-2555** or 505/355-9935 for details. Third weekend in July.

- **Eight Northern Pueblos Artist and Craftsman Show.** More than 600 Indian artists exhibit their work. Traditional dances, food booths, and more at San Juan Pueblo. Call **505/852-4265** for more information. Third weekend in July.
- **Spanish Market.** Santa Fe Plaza. More than 300 Hispanic artists from New Mexico and southern Colorado exhibit and sell their work. Event also features special demonstrations and Hispanic music, food, and pageantry. For more information, call **505/983-4038.** Last weekend in July.

August

- **Bat Flight Breakfast.** Carlsbad Caverns National Park. An early morning buffet breakfast is served while participants watch the bats return to the cave. Call **505/785-2232** for details and exact date. Early August.
- **Old Lincoln Days and Billy the Kid Pageant,** Lincoln. Call **505/653-4025** for more information. First weekend in August.
- **Intertribal Indian Ceremonial.** Fifty tribes from the United States and Mexico participate in rodeos, parades, dances, athletic competitions, and an arts and crafts show, at Red Rock State Park, east of Gallup. For more information, call **505/863-6604.** Second week in August.
- **Connie Mack World Series Baseball Tournament.** Teams of teenagers from throughout the United States and Puerto Rico compete in a seven-day, 17-game series. Ricketts Park, Farmington. Call **505/327-9673** for details. Second week in August.
- **Annual Indian Market.** Juried Native American art competition, musical entertainment, dances, food booths. Santa Fe Plaza. For more information, call **505/983-5520.** Third weekend in August.
- **Great American Duck Race.** Parade, ballooning, tortilla toss, dances, and, of course, the duck race. Southwestern New Mexico State Fairgrounds, Deming. Call **800/848-4955** for details. Fourth weekend in August.

September

- **New Mexico State Fair.** Third-largest state fair in the United States. Seventeen days of Spanish and Indian villages, midway, livestock exhibits, arts and crafts, country-and-western entertainment, and rodeo. Albuquerque State Fairgrounds. Call **505/265-1791** for more information. Begins Friday after Labor Day.
- **Fiesta de Santa Fe.** Santa Fe Plaza. The oldest community celebration in the United States. Events include masses, parades, mariachi concerts, and dances. Call **505/988-7575** for more information. Second weekend in September.
- **Stone Lake Fiesta.** Apache festival with rodeo, ceremonial dances, and footrace. Jicarilla Reservation. Dulce. Call **505/759-3242,** ext. 275, for more information. September 14 to 15.
- **Mexican Independence Day.** Parade and dances in Carlsbad (San Jose Plaza) and Las Cruces (Old Mesilla Plaza), with a rodeo in Carlsbad. September 16.
- **Old Taos Trade Fair.** Reenactment of Spanish colonial living in the 1820s, with craft demonstrations, food, and entertainment. Martinez Hacienda, Taos. For more information, call **505/758-0505.** Third weekend in September.
- **Taos Fall Arts Festival.** Gallery openings, concerts, crafts fair. Taos. Call **800/732-8267** for more information. Third weekend in September to first weekend of October.
- **Shiprock Navajo Fair.** Rodeo, traditional dancing and singing, parade, arts and crafts exhibits. Shiprock. Call **800/448-1240** for details. Late September or early October.

October
- **Rio Grande Arts and Crafts Festival.** Features artists and craftspeople from around the country. Albuquerque. For more information, call **505/292-7457.** First and second weekend in October.
- **Kodak Albuquerque International Balloon Fiesta.** World's largest balloon rally, with races, contests, and special events, including weekend mass ascensions. Albuquerque. For more information, call **800/733-9918.** First to second weekend in October.

November
- **Southwest Arts Festival.** New Mexico's only juried national art event, held at the fairgrounds in Albuquerque. Call **505/262-2448** for details. Early November.
- **Festival of the Cranes.** Bosque del Apache National Wildlife Refuge. Socorro. For more information, call **505/835-0424.** Mid-November.
- **Indian National Finals Rodeo.** Indian rodeo riders from throughout the United States and Canada compete. Powwow, ceremonial dancing, Miss Indian Rodeo pageant, arts and crafts. Albuquerque State Fairgrounds. Third weekend in November.

December
- **Yuletide in Taos.** *Farolito* tours, candlelight dinners, dance performances, art events, ski-area activities. Taos. For more information, call **800/732-8267.** First to third weekends in December.
- **Our Lady of Guadalupe Fiesta.** Pilgrimage to Tortugas Mountain and torchlight descent, followed by mass and traditional Hispanic dances. Tortugas, near Las Cruces. Call **505/526-8171** for more information. December 10 to 12.
- **Sundown Torchlight Procession of the Virgin.** Vespers and Matachines dance at San Ildefonso, Santa Clara, Taos, and Tesuque pueblos. December 24.
- **Luminaria Tours.** Albuquerque (☎ **800/733-9918**) and Canyon Road in Santa Fe (☎ **505/988-7575**). Christmas Eve.

3 Health & Insurance

STAYING HEALTHY   One thing that sets New Mexico apart from most other states is its altitude. Most of the state is above 4,000 feet in elevation, and many heavily touristed areas, including Santa Fe, are at 7,000 feet or above. Getting plenty of rest, avoiding large meals, and drinking lots of nonalcoholic fluids (especially water) can help make the adjustment easier for flatlanders.

The reduced oxygen and humidity can bring on some unique problems, not the least of which is acute **mountain sickness.** Characterized in its early stages by headaches, shortness of breath, appetite loss and/or nausea, tingling in the fingers or toes, and lethargy and insomnia, it ordinarily can be treated with aspirin and a slower pace. If it persists or worsens, you must descend to a lower altitude.

Sunburn and hypothermia are other dangers of higher elevations, and should not be lightly regarded. To avoid dehydration, drink water as often as possible.

Other things to be wary of are **arroyos,** or flash floods, which can occur without warning in the desert. If water is flowing across a road, DO NOT try to drive through it because chances are the water is deeper and is flowing faster than you think. Just wait it out. Arroyos don't last long.

Finally, if you're an outdoorsperson, be on the lookout for **snakes**—particularly rattlers. Avoid them. Don't even get close enough to take a picture (unless you have a very good zoom lens).

INSURANCE   Before setting out on your trip, check your medical insurance policy to be sure it covers you away from home. If it doesn't, it's wise to purchase a traveler's policy, widely available at banks, travel agencies, and automobile clubs. Coverage offered by numerous companies is relatively inexpensive. In addition to medical assistance, including hospitalization and surgery, it should include the cost of an accident, death, or repatriation; loss or theft of baggage; costs of trip cancellation; and guaranteed bail in the event of a suit or other legal difficulties.

4   Tips for Travelers with Special Needs

FOR TRAVELERS WITH DISABILITIES   Throughout New Mexico, steps have been taken to provide access for people with disabilities. Most hotels and even some bed-and-breakfasts have wheelchair-accessible rooms. If you call the Developmental Disabilities Planning Council (☎ **800/552-8195**), they will provide you with free information about traveling with disabilities in New Mexico. The brochure *Art of Accessibility* lists hotels, restaurants, and attractions in Albuquerque that are accessible to travelers with disabilities. *The Directory of Recreational Activities for Children with Disabilities* is a list of accessible camps, national forest campgrounds, amusement parks, and individual city services throughout New Mexico. *Access Santa Fe* lists accessible hotels, attractions, and restaurants in the state capital. No matter what, it is advisable to call hotels, restaurants, and attractions in advance to be sure that they are fully accessible.

FOR SENIORS   Travelers over the age of 65—in many cases 60, sometimes even 55— may qualify for special discounts. Some hotels offer seniors rates 10% to 20% lower than the published rates. Many attractions give seniors discounts of up to half off the regular adult admission price. Get in the habit of asking about discounts. Seniors who plan to visit national parks and monuments in New Mexico should consider getting a Golden Age Passport, which gives anyone over 62 lifetime access to any national park, monument, historic site, recreational area, or wildlife refuge that charges an entrance fee. Golden Age Passports can be obtained at any National Park Office in the country. There is a one-time $10 processing fee. In New Mexico, contact the National Park Service Office of Communications at **505/988-6012** for more information.

If you're retired and are not already a member of the American Association of Retired Persons (AARP), consider joining. The AARP card is valuable throughout North America in your search for travel bargains.

In addition, there are 24 active Elderhostel locations throughout the state. For information, call New Mexico Elderhostel at **505/473-6267.**

A note about health: Senior travelers are more often susceptible to changes in altitude and may experience heart or respiratory problems. Speak with your physician before your trip.

FOR FAMILIES   Children are often given discounts that adults, even seniors, never dream of. For instance, many hotels allow children to stay free with their parents in the same room. The upper age limit varies from 12 to 18.

Youngsters are almost always entitled to discounts on public transportation and admission to attractions. Though every entrance requirement is different, you'll often find that admission for kids five and under is free and for elementary school–age children it's half price; older students (through high school) may also be offered significant discounts.

FOR STUDENTS Always carry your student identification with you. Tourist attractions, transportation systems, and other services may offer discounts if you have appropriate proof of your student status. Don't be afraid to ask. A high-school or college ID card or an International Student Card will suffice.

Student-oriented activities abound on and around college campuses, especially the University of New Mexico in Albuquerque. In Santa Fe, there are two small four-year colleges: the College of Santa Fe and St. John's College.

5 Getting There

BY PLANE The recently expanded and renovated **Albuquerque International Airport** (☎ 505/842-4366 for the administrative offices; call the individual airlines for flight information) is the hub for travel to most parts of New Mexico. A secondary hub for southern New Mexico is El Paso, Texas. Both airports are served by **American** (☎ 800/433-7300), **America West** (☎ 800/235-9292), **Continental** (☎ 800/525-0280), **Delta** (☎ 800/221-1212), **Southwest** (☎ 800/435-9792), and **USAir** (☎ 800/882-4358).

BY CAR Three interstate highways cross New Mexico. The north-south I-25 bisects the state, passing through Albuquerque and Las Cruces. The east-west I-40 follows the path of the old Route 66 through Gallup, Albuquerque, and Tucumcari in the north; while I-10 from San Diego crosses southwestern New Mexico until intersecting I-25 at Las Cruces.

Here are the approximate mileages to Albuquerque from various cities around the United States:

Distances to Albuquerque (in miles)

From	Distance	From	Distance
Atlanta	1,404	New Orleans	1,157
Boston	2,220	New York	1,997
Chicago	1,312	Oklahoma City	542
Dallas	644	Phoenix	458
Denver	437	St. Louis	1,042
Houston	853	Salt Lake City	604
Los Angeles	811	San Francisco	1,109
Miami	1,970	Seattle	1,453
Minneapolis	1,219	Washington, D.C.	1,883

BY TRAIN **Amtrak** has two routes through the state. The *Southwest Chief,* which runs between Chicago and Los Angeles, passes through New Mexico once daily in each direction, with stops in Gallup, Grants, Albuquerque, Lamy (for Santa Fe), Las Vegas, and Raton. A second train, the *Sunset Unlimited,* skims through the southwest corner of the state three times weekly in each direction—between Los Angeles and New Orleans—with stops in Lordsburg, Deming, and El Paso, Texas. Greyhound/Trailways bus lines provide through-ticketing for Amtrak between Albuquerque and El Paso.

You can get a copy of Amtrak's National Timetable from any Amtrak station, from travel agents, or by contacting Amtrak, 400 N. Capitol St. NW, Washington, DC 20001 (☎ 800/USA-RAIL).

New Mexico Driving Times & Distances

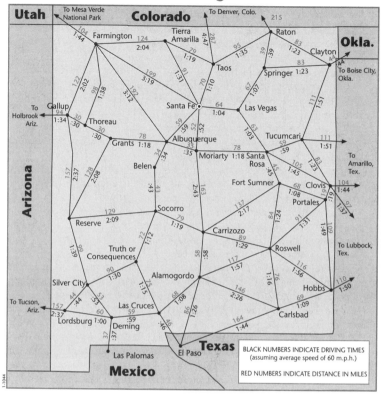

BLACK NUMBERS INDICATE DRIVING TIMES
(assuming average speed of 60 m.p.h.)

RED NUMBERS INDICATE DISTANCE IN MILES

BY BUS   **Greyhound Lines** and **TNM&O Coaches** (Texas, New Mexico, and Oklahoma) have extensive networks that penetrate every corner of the state, with daily connections virtually everywhere. Call **505/243-4435** for information on schedules and rates.

PACKAGE TOURS   Of course, you don't really need to take a package tour when traveling to New Mexico, but they are available and may be less expensive than if you booked the trip yourself because group tour operators often secure better rates than individual travelers. Tours within the state of New Mexico are offered by the following inbound operators:

   Jack Allan Tours, P.O. Box 11940, Albuquerque, NM 87192 (☎ **505/266-9688**).

   Destination Southwest, 121 Tijeras NE, Suite 1100, Albuquerque, NM 87102. (☎ **800/999-3109** or 505/766-9068).

   Gray Line of Albuquerque, 800 Rio Grande NW, Suite 22, Albuquerque, NM 87104 (☎ **800/256-8991** or 505/242-3880).

   Rojo Tours and Services, P.O. Box 15744, Santa Fe, NM 87501 (☎ **505/474-8333**).

   Sun Tours, 4300 San Mateo Blvd. NE, Suite B-155, Albuquerque, NM 87110 (☎ **505/889-8888**).

   Travel New Mexico, 6101 Candelaria NE, Albuquerque, NM 87110 (☎ **800/333-7159** or 505/883-9718).

6 Getting Around

BY CAR   Visitors who plan to drive their own car to and around New Mexico should give their vehicle a thorough road check before starting out. There are lots of wide-open desert and wilderness spaces in New Mexico, and it is not fun to be stranded in the heat or cold with a vehicle that doesn't run. Check your lights, windshield wipers, horn, tires, battery, drive belts, fluid levels, alignment, and other possible trouble spots. Make sure your driver's license, vehicle registration, safety-inspection sticker, and auto-club membership (if you have one) are valid. Check with your auto insurance company to make sure you're covered when out of state, and/or when driving a rental car.

Unless otherwise posted, the speed limit on open roads is 65 MPH (105 km/h). Minimum age for drivers is 16. Safety belts are required for drivers and all passengers age five and over; children under five must use approved child seats.

Indian reservations are considered sovereign nations, and they enforce their own laws. For instance, on the Navajo reservation (New Mexico's largest), it is prohibited to transport alcoholic beverages, to leave established roadways, or to travel without a seat belt. Motorcyclists must wear helmets.

Gas is readily available at service stations throughout the state. Prices are cheapest in Albuquerque and 10% to 15% more expensive in more isolated communities. All prices are subject to the same fluctuations as elsewhere in the United States.

An excellent state highway map can be obtained from the New Mexico Department of Tourism, Lamy Building, 491 Old Santa Fe Trail, Santa Fe, NM 87503 (☎ 800/545-2040). More specific county and city maps are available from the State Highway and Transportation Department, 1120 Cerrillos Rd., Santa Fe, NM 87501 (☎ 505/827-5100).

The State Highway and Transportation Department has a toll-free hot line (☎ 800/432-4269) providing up-to-the-hour information on road closures and conditions.

In case of an accident or road emergency, contact the New Mexico State Police. District offices are in Alamogordo (☎ 505/437-1313), Albuquerque (☎ 505/841-9256), Clovis (☎ 505/763-3426), Espanola (☎ 505/753-2277), Farmington (☎ 505/325-7547), Gallup (☎ 505/287-4141), Hobbs (☎ 505/392-5588), Las Cruces (☎ 505/524-6111), Las Vegas (☎ 505/425-6771), Raton (☎ 505/445-5571), Roswell (☎ 505/622-7200), Santa Fe (☎ 505/827-9300), Socorro (☎ 505/835-0741), and Taos (☎ 505/758-8878).

Members of the American Automobile Association can get free emergency road service wherever they are, 24 hours, by calling AAA's emergency number (☎ 800/336-4357).

Car rentals are available in every sizable town and city in the state, always at the local airport, and usually also downtown. Widely represented agencies include: **Alamo** (☎ 800/327-9633), **Avis** (☎ 800/331-1212), **Budget** (☎ 800/527-0700), **Dollar** (☎ 800/369-4226), **Hertz** (☎ 800/654-3131), and **Thrifty** (☎ 800/367-2277). Drivers who need wheelchair-accessible transportation should call **Wheelchair Getaways of New Mexico,** 1015 Tramway Lane NE, Albuquerque (☎ 800/408-2626 or 505/247-2626); they rent vans by the day, week, or month.

A word of warning: US 666 between Gallup and Shiprock has been labeled America's "most dangerous highway" by *USA Today.* New Mexico has the highest per capita rate of traffic deaths of any American state. Drive carefully!

BY PLANE   **Mesa Airlines** (☎ **800/MESA-AIR**) flies from Albuquerque to Alamogordo, Carlsbad, Clovis, Farmington, Gallup, Hobbs, Las Cruces, Roswell, Santa Fe, Silver City, and Taos.

BY TRAIN   **Amtrak's** northern New Mexico line, the *Southwest Chief,* runs west-east and east-west once daily, with stops in Gallup, Grants, Albuquerque, Lamy (for Santa Fe), Las Vegas, and Raton. The *Sunset Unlimited* connects Lordsburg and Deming with El Paso, Texas, three times weekly each direction. Greyhound/Trailways bus lines provide through-ticketing for Amtrak passengers between Albuquerque and El Paso. For information, call **800/USA-RAIL**.

BY BUS   Bus service links every sizable city in the state: Alamogordo, Albuquerque, Artesia, Belen, Carlsbad, Clayton, Clovis, Costilla, Cuba, Deming, Espanola, Farmington, Gallup, Grants, Hatch, Hobbs, Jal, Las Cruces, Las Vegas, Lordsburg, Portales, Raton, Roswell, Ruidoso, Santa Fe, Santa Rosa, Shiprock, Silver City, Socorro, Springer, Taos, Truth or Consequences, Tucumcari, and other communities en route.

Service is provided by **Greyhound/Trailways** (Albuquerque ☎ **505/243-4435**) and **TNM&O** (Texas, New Mexico, and Oklahoma; ☎ **505/243-4435** in Albuquerque). Many of the two coach companies' routes are now combined.

SUGGESTED ITINERARIES

If You Have 1 Week

Days 1–2   Spend your first two nights in Albuquerque. Wander around Old Town, visit the Albuquerque Museum and Indian Pueblo Cultural Center, and take the tramway up Sandia Peak. Then drive to Santa Fe, not much more than an hour north.

Days 3–5   Stay three nights in Santa Fe, and be sure to include a day trip to Los Alamos and Bandelier National Monument.

Days 6–7   Drive to Taos in the morning, taking the "High Road" through Chimayo. Stay overnight in Taos to see the pueblo, the art galleries, and the historic properties.

Day 7   In the afternoon, return to Albuquerque for the flight home.

If You Have 2 Weeks

Spend Days 1 to 6 as described above.

Day 7   In the afternoon drive west from Taos on US 64 to Chama to spend the night.

Day 8   Spend the day in Chama on the famous Cumbres and Toltec narrow-gauge steam railroad. After the train trip, continue west on US 64 to Farmington to spend two nights.

Day 9   Take an easy day trip from Farmington to Aztec Ruins National Monument, the Salmon Ruins, or Shiprock, on the Navajo Reservation.

Day 10   Start out early to spend most of the day at fascinating Chaco Culture National Historic Park. Then drive to Gallup for two nights.

Day 11   Explore the pawn shops of Gallup, and visit Zuni Pueblo, perhaps the most culturally unique pueblo in New Mexico.

Day 12   Drive to Grants for lunch, stopping at El Morro National Monument on the way. In the afternoon visit historic Acoma Pueblo as you head back to Albuquerque.

Day 13   Do a loop tour of the pueblos north of the city, or to drive to the three divisions of Salinas National Monument southeast of Albuquerque.

Day 14   Day 14 is your departure date from Albuquerque airport.

If You Have 3 Weeks

Spend the first two weeks as described above.

Day 15   Drive south from Albuquerque on I-25, stopping en route to explore Socorro and the Bosque del Apache National Wildlife Refuge. Stay the night in Truth or Consequences.

Day 16   Get an early start and visit Gila Cliff Dwellings National Monument. Spend the night in Silver City.

Day 17   Drive to Las Cruces, southern New Mexico's largest city, and its historic suburb of La Mesilla via City of Rocks State Park and Deming.

Day 18   Drive over the Organ Mountains to Alamogordo, being sure not to miss White Sands National Monument or the International Space Hall of Fame.

Day 19   If you get an early start, you can lunch in Carlsbad, check into your hotel, then spend the entire afternoon at Carlsbad Caverns.

Day 20   Take a trip to Ruidoso, a picturesque mountain resort town, via Roswell and the Old West village of Lincoln.

Day 21   Head back to Albuquerque for your departure.

FAST FACTS: New Mexico

American Express   Atlas American Express, 1301 Wyoming Blvd. NE, Albuquerque (☎ **505/291-6575**). To report a lost card, call **800/528-4800.** To report lost traveler's checks, call **800/221-7282.**

Banks and ATMs   Major statewide banks are the Bank of New Mexico, First Interstate Bank, First National Bank in Albuquerque, SunWest Bank, United New Mexico Bank, and Western Bank. They're typically open Monday to Thursday 10am to 3pm and Friday 10am to 6pm. Drive-up windows may be open later. Some may also open Saturday morning. Most branches have cash machines available 24 hours.

Business Hours   In general, business hours are Monday to Friday 9am to 5pm, with many stores also open Friday night and Saturday. Some cities may have different hours; in Las Cruces, for instance, many merchants close their doors on Monday but are open all day Saturday.

Car Rentals   See "Getting Around," earlier in this chapter.

Climate   See "When to Go," earlier in this chapter.

Consulates and Embassies   See Chapter 4, "For Foreign Visitors."

Driving Rules   See "Getting Around," earlier in this chapter.

Drugstores   Twenty-four-hour prescription services are available at selected Walgreens Drug Stores around the state. Prices at Thrifty and Wal-Mart outlets might be somewhat less. If you're having trouble getting a prescription filled, call the nearest hospital pharmacy.

Emergencies   For emergency medical help or information, call the New Mexico Medical Crisis Center at **800/432-6866.** The center is open 24 hours a day. In most cities, for police, sheriff, fire department, or ambulance, dial **911** at any time; otherwise, dial **0** and ask the operator to connect you.

Hitchhiking   Hitching a ride is legal in New Mexico, and in summer you may find backpack-laden vagabonds at interstate highway entrances, at road junctions, in the Navajo Indian Reservation, and on secondary roads.

Information   See "Visitor Information," earlier in this chapter.

Language   English is the common language, but Spanish is almost as frequently spoken. You'll also hear Native American languages—Navajo (the most widely spoken surviving North American Indian dialect), Apache, Zuni, Tanoan, and Keresan.

Liquor Laws   Drinking age is 21. Bars close at 2am; on Sunday they are open noon to midnight. Wine, beer, and spirits are sold at licensed supermarkets and liquor stores. A special allowance must be granted for liquor to be dispensed in proximity to any church. It is illegal to transport liquor through most Indian reservations.

Maps   The official state highway map is published by the State Tourism and Travel Division; county and city maps can be obtained from the State Highway and Transportation Department. Many local visitors bureaus or chambers of commerce publish their own city or regional maps. The American Automobile Association (AAA) supplies detailed state and city maps free to members.

Newspapers and Magazines   Larger cities and regional hubs have daily newspapers, and many smaller towns publish weeklies. The *Albuquerque Tribune,* published mornings, and the *Albuquerque Journal,* published evenings, are widely available around the state. The *El Paso Times* is favored in southern New Mexico. National newspapers like *USA Today* and the *Wall Street Journal* can be purchased in cities and major hotels. The state's favorite magazine is *New Mexico,* a high-quality monthly published by the State Tourism and Travel Division since 1923.

Pets   Dogs, cats, and other small pets are accepted at motels in most parts of the state, though not as universally in Albuquerque and Santa Fe as elsewhere. Some properties require owners to pay a damage deposit in advance. If you bring your pet, keep it well dusted with flea powder: Plague bacilli, a disease borne by fleas, is endemic to New Mexico.

Police   In the event of any emergency, contact the New Mexico State Police. Call **911** or **0** for an operator. Regional telephone numbers are listed in "Getting Around," earlier in this chapter.

Taxes   The 6.875% state tax on gross receipts includes hotel bills. Local governments tack their own lodging tax on top of that, which ranges from 2.75% to 5.812% depending upon the city.

Telephone and Fax   The area code for the entire state of New Mexico is **505.** No matter where you are in the state, if you're placing a call outside city limits you must use the **505** area code.

Time   New Mexico is on mountain standard time, one hour ahead of the West Coast and two hours behind the East Coast. Daylight saving time is in effect from April to October.

Tipping   A tip of $1 per bag is appropriate for hotel valets and airport porters. If you're staying longer than a night or two in a hotel or motel, tip about $1 per night for chamber service. Restaurant servers should get 15% to 20% of your bill for service.

4 For Foreign Visitors

Although American fads and fashions have spread across Europe and other parts of the world so much that the United States may seem like familiar territory before your arrival, there are still many peculiarities and uniquely American situations that any foreign visitor will encounter.

The **Santa Fe Council on International Relations,** P.O. Box 1223, Santa Fe, NM 87501 (☎ **505/982-4931;** fax 505/982-3953), assists foreign visitors by providing community information. An office in Room 281 of La Fonda Hotel on the Plaza is open Monday through Friday from 9:30am to 12:30pm.

1 Preparing for Your Trip

ENTRY REQUIREMENTS

Immigration laws are a hot political issue in the United States these days, and the following requirements may have changed by the time you plan your trip. Check at any U.S. embassy or consulate for current information and requirements.

DOCUMENT REQUIREMENTS

Canadian citizens may enter the United States without passports or visas; they need only proof of residence.

The U.S. State Department has a **Visa Waiver Pilot Program** allowing citizens of certain countries to enter the United States without a visa for stays of up to 90 days. At press time these included Andorra, Austria, Belgium, Brunei, Denmark, Finland, France, Germany, Iceland, Ireland, Italy, Japan, Liechtenstein, Luxembourg, Monaco, the Netherlands, New Zealand, Norway, San Marino, Spain, Sweden, Switzerland, and the United Kingdom. Citizens of these countries need only a valid passport and a round-trip air or cruise ticket in their possession upon arrival.

Note that citizens of these visa-exempt countries who first enter the United States may then visit Mexico, Canada, Bermuda, and/or the Caribbean islands and then reenter the United States, by any mode of transportation, without needing a visa. Further information is available from any U.S. embassy or consulate.

Citizens of all other countries, including Australia, must have two documents:

- a valid **passport** with an expiration date at least six months later than the scheduled end of their visit to the United States; and
- a **tourist visa,** available without charge from the nearest U.S. consulate. To obtain a visa, the traveler must submit a completed application form (either in person or by mail) with a 1¹/₂-inch-square photo and must demonstrate binding ties to a residence abroad.

Usually you can obtain a visa at once or within 24 hours, but it may take longer during the summer rush from June to August. If you cannot go in person, contact the nearest U.S. embassy or consulate for directions on applying by mail. Your travel agent or airline office may also be able to provide you with visa applications and instructions. The U.S. embassy or consulate that issues your visa will determine whether you will be given a multiple- or single-entry visa and any restrictions regarding the length of your stay.

MEDICAL REQUIREMENTS

No inoculations are needed to enter the United States unless you're coming from, or have stopped over in, areas known to be suffering from epidemics, particularly cholera or yellow fever.

If you have a disease requiring treatment with medications containing narcotics or drugs requiring a syringe, carry a valid signed prescription from your physician to allay any suspicions that you are smuggling drugs.

CUSTOMS REQUIREMENTS

Every adult visitor may bring in free of duty: 1 liter of wine or hard liquor; 200 cigarettes or 100 cigars (but no cigars from Cuba) or 3 pounds of smoking tobacco; and $100 worth of gifts. These exemptions are offered to travelers who spend at least 72 hours in the United States and who have not claimed them within the preceding six months. It's altogether forbidden to bring into the country foodstuffs (particularly cheese, fruit, cooked meats, and canned goods) and plants (vegetables, seeds, tropical plants, and so on). Foreign tourists may bring in or take out up to $10,000 in U.S. or foreign currency with no formalities; larger sums must be declared to Customs on entering or leaving the country. For more information, you can contact the **U.S. Customs Service Albuquerque Field Office** (☎ **505/766-2621**).

INSURANCE

Unlike Canada and Europe, there is no national health-care system in the United States, and the cost of medical care is extremely high. For this reason, we strongly advise every traveler to secure health insurance coverage before setting out. You may want to take out a comprehensive travel policy that covers sickness or injury costs (medical, surgical, and hospital); loss or theft of your baggage; trip-cancellation costs; guarantee of bail in case you are arrested; and costs of accidents, repatriation, or death.

Packages such as "Europe Assistance Worldwide Services" in Europe are sold by automobile clubs and travel agencies at attractive rates. **Travel Assistance International (TAI)** (☎ **800/821-2828** or 203/347-2025) is the agent for Europe Assistance Worldwide Services, so holders of this company's policies can contact TAI for assistance while in the United States.

Canadians should check with their provincial health scheme offices or call **HealthCanada** (☎ **613/957-3025**) to find out the extent of their coverage and what documentation and receipts they must take home in case they are treated in the United States.

MONEY

The foreign-exchange bureaus so common in Europe are rare even at airports in the United States and nonexistent outside major cities. Try to avoid having to change foreign money (or traveler's checks denominated in a currency other than U.S. dollars) at a small-town bank or even a branch bank in a big city. In fact, leave any currency other than U.S. dollars at home—it may prove a greater nuisance to you than it's worth. For Albuquerque, Santa Fe, and Taos banks that handle foreign-currency exchange, see the "Fast Facts" sections in chapters 6, 7, and 8, respectively.

CURRENCY

The U.S. monetary system has a decimal base: one American **dollar ($1) = 100 cents (100¢)**.

Dollar bills commonly come in $1 ("a buck"), $5, $10, $20, $50, and $100 denominations (the last two are not welcome when paying for small purchases and are not accepted in taxis). There are also $2 bills (seldom encountered).

There are six denominations of coins: 1¢ (one cent or "penny"), 5¢ (five cents or "nickel"), 10¢ (ten cents or "dime"), 25¢ (twenty-five cents or "quarter"), 50¢ (fifty cents or "half dollar"), and the rare $1 piece.

TRAVELER'S CHECKS

Traveler's checks *denominated in U.S. dollars* are readily accepted at most hotels, motels, restaurants, and large stores. But the best place to change traveler's checks is at a bank. Do not bring traveler's checks denominated in other currencies.

CREDIT CARDS

The method of payment most widely used is the credit card. Cards commonly used in the United States include Visa (BarclayCard in Britain), MasterCard (EuroCard in Europe, Access in Britain, Chargex in Canada), American Express, Diners Club, Discover, and Carte Blanche. You can save yourself trouble by using "plastic money" rather than cash or traveler's checks in most hotels, motels, restaurants, and retail stores (a growing number of food and liquor stores now accept credit cards). You must have a credit card to rent a car. It can also be used as proof of identity (often carrying more weight than a passport) or as a "cash card," enabling you to draw money from banks and automated-teller machines (ATMs) that accept it.

SAFETY
GENERAL

While tourist areas are generally safe, crime is on the increase everywhere, and U.S. urban areas tend to be less safe than those in Europe or Japan. Visitors should always stay alert. This is particularly true of large U.S. cities. Ask the tourist office if you are in doubt about which neighborhoods are safe. Avoid deserted areas, especially at night.

Remember that hotels are open to the public, and in a large hotel, security may not be able to screen everyone entering. Always lock your room door; don't assume that once inside your hotel you are automatically safe and need no longer be aware of your surroundings.

DRIVING

Safety while driving is important. Question your rental agency about personal safety, or ask for a brochure of traveler safety tips when you pick up your car. Obtain written directions, or a map with the route clearly marked, from the agency showing how to get to your destination. And, if possible, arrive and depart during daylight hours.

Recently, more and more crime has involved cars and drivers. If you drive off a highway into a doubtful neighborhood, leave the area as quickly as possible. If you have an accident, even on the highway, stay in your car with the doors locked until you assess the situation or until the police arrive. If you are bumped from behind on the street or are involved in a minor accident with no injuries and the situation appears to be suspicious, motion to the other driver to follow you to the nearest police precinct, well-lighted service station, or all-night store. *Never* get out of your car in such situations.

If you see someone on the road who indicates a need for help, do *not* stop. Take note of the location, drive on to a well-lighted area, and telephone the police by dialing **911.**

Park in well-lighted, well-traveled areas if possible. Always keep your car doors locked, whether the car is attended or unattended. Look around you before you get out of your car, and never leave any packages or valuables in sight. If someone attempts to rob you or steal your car, do *not* try to resist the thief/carjacker—report the incident to the police department immediately.

Also, make sure that you have enough gasoline in your tank to reach your intended destination, so that you're not forced to look for a service station in an unfamiliar and possibly unsafe neighborhood, especially at night.

You may want to contact the local tourist information bureau in New Mexico before you arrive. They can provide you with a safety brochure. (See "Visitor Information," in specific city or regional chapters.)

2 Getting to & Around the U.S.

GETTING THERE

Travelers from overseas can take advantage of the **APEX (Advance-Purchase Excursion) fares** offered by all the major international carriers. Albuquerque is the hub for air travel to New Mexico.

British travelers should check out **British Airways** (☎ **081/897-4000** in the United Kingdom, 800/247-9297 in the U.S.), which offers direct flights from London to Houston and Dallas with connections to Albuquerque. **Continental** (☎ **4412/9377-6464** in or outside the United Kingdom) also has direct service from London to Houston with connections to Albuquerque, while **American Airlines** (☎ **0180/572-555** in or outside the United Kingdom) has service from London to Dallas with connections to Albuquerque.

For Canadian travelers, both **American** and **Canadian Airlines** (☎ **800/ 665-9933** in Canada, 800/426-7000 in the United States) have service from Toronto and Montreal to Chicago with connections to Albuquerque. **Delta** has service from Montreal to Albuquerque via Cincinnati.

From Australia, **American Airlines, Quantas** (☎ **1800/062 123** in Australia, 800/227-4500 in the United States and Canada), and **United** all offer nonstop service from Sydney to Los Angeles. **Air New Zealand** (☎ **0800/737-000** in Auckland, or 64-3/379-5200 in Christchurch) also flies to Los Angeles.

Some large American airlines (for example, American Airlines, Delta, Northwest, TWA, and United) offer travelers on their transatlantic or transpacific flights special discount tickets under the name **Visit USA,** allowing travel between any U.S. destinations at minimum rates. These tickets are not sold in the United States, and must, therefore, be purchased before you leave your foreign point of departure. This system is the best, easiest, and fastest way to see the United States at low cost. You should obtain information well in advance from your travel agent or the office of the airline concerned, since the conditions attached to these discount tickets can be changed without advance notice.

The visitor arriving by air, no matter what the point of entry, should cultivate patience and resignation before setting foot on U.S. soil. Getting through Immigration control may take as long as two hours on some days, especially summer weekends. Add the time it takes to clear Customs and you'll see that you should make very generous allowances for delays when coordinating connections between international and domestic flights—an average of two to three hours at least.

In contrast, travelers arriving by car or by rail from Canada will find that the border-crossing formalities have been streamlined practically to the vanishing point. And air travelers from Canada, Bermuda, and some places in the Caribbean can sometimes go through Customs and Immigration at the point of departure, which is much quicker and less painful.

For further information about transportation to New Mexico, see chapter 3, "Planning a Trip to New Mexico."

GETTING AROUND THE U.S.

BY CAR Car culture reigns supreme in America, and driving will give you the freedom to make, and alter, your own itinerary. And it offers the possibility of visiting some of the off-the-beaten-path locations, places than cannot be reached easily by public transportation. For information on renting cars in the United States, see "Getting Around" in chapter 3, and "Automobile Organizations" and "Automobile Rentals" in "Fast Facts: For the Foreign Traveler," below.

Please note that in the United States we drive on the **right side of the road** as in Europe, not on the left side as in the United Kingdom, Australia, and New Zealand.

BY TRAIN Long-distance trains in the United States are operated by **Amtrak** (☎ 800/872-7245), the national rail passenger corporation. International visitors can buy a **USA Railpass,** good for 15 or 30 days of unlimited travel on Amtrak. The pass is available through many foreign travel agents. (With a foreign passport, you can also buy passes at some Amtrak offices in the United States, including locations in Boston, Chicago, Los Angeles, Miami, New York, San Francisco, and Washington, D.C.) In 1996 a 15-day pass cost $245 off-peak, $355 peak; a 30-day pass cost $350 off-peak, $440 peak. The peak seasons are from mid-June to mid-August and around major holidays such as Thanksgiving and Christmas. Reservations are generally required and should be made for each part of your trip as early as possible. Even cheaper than the above are **regional USA Railpasses,** allowing unlimited travel through a specific section of the United States.

With a few notable exceptions (for instance, the Northeast Corridor line between Boston and Washington, D.C.), train service is rarely up to European standards: Delays are common, routes are limited and often infrequently served, and fares are rarely much lower than discount airfares. Thus, cross-country train travel should be approached with caution.

BY BUS Although ticket prices for short bus trips between cities are often the most economical form of public transit, at this writing, bus passes are priced slightly higher than similar train passes. **Greyhound** (☎ 800/231-2222), the sole nationwide bus line, offers a **New Ameripass** for unlimited travel anywhere on its system. In 1996, prices for a 7-day pass started at $179; 15 days at $289; 30 days at $399; and 60 days at $599. Senior citizen discounts are available. Bus travel in the United States can be both slow and uncomfortable, so this option is not for everyone.

FAST FACTS: For the Foreign Traveler

Automobile Organizations   Auto clubs will supply maps, suggested routes, guidebooks, accident and bail-bond insurance, and emergency road service. The major auto club in the United States, with 955 offices nationwide, is the **American Automobile Association (AAA).** Members of some foreign auto clubs have reciprocal arrangements with the AAA and enjoy its services at no charge. If you belong to an auto club in your home country, inquire about AAA reciprocity before you leave. You may be able to join the AAA even if you're not a member of a reciprocal club; to inquire, call the AAA at **800/222-4357.** The AAA can provide you with an **International Driving Permit,** validating your foreign license. In addition, some automobile-rental agencies now provide many of these same services. Inquire about their availability when you rent your car.

Automobile Rentals   To rent a car you will need a major credit or charge card and a valid driver's license. In addition, you usually need to be at least 25 years old (some companies do rent to younger people but add a daily surcharge). Be sure to return your car with the same amount of gas you started out with; rental companies charge excessive prices for gasoline. See "Getting Around by Car," in individual city and regional chapters.

Business Hours   See "Fast Facts: New Mexico," in chapter 3.

Climate   See "When to Go," in chapter 3.

Currency   See "Preparing for Your Trip," earlier in this chapter.

Currency Exchange   See "Preparing for Your Trip," earlier in this chapter.

Drinking Laws   You must be 21 to purchase alcoholic beverages in New Mexico.

Electricity   The United States uses 110–120 volts A, 60 cycles, compared with 220–240 volts A, 50 cycles, as in most of Europe. In addition to a 100-volt transformer, small appliances of non-American manufacture, such as hair dryers or shavers, will require a plug adapter, with two flat, parallel pins.

Embassies and Consulates   There is one consulate in New Mexico, the Mexican Consulate, Western Bank Bldg., 401 5th St. NW, Albuquerque, NM 87102 (☎ **505/247-2147** or 505/247-2139). All embassies are located in the national capital, Washington, D.C.; some consulates are located in major U.S. cities, and most countries maintain a mission to the United Nations in New York City. The embassies and consulates of the major English-speaking countries—Australia, Canada, the Republic of Ireland, New Zealand, and the United Kingdom—are listed below. If you are from another country, you can get the telephone number of your embassy by calling "Information" in Washington, D.C. (☎ **202/555-1212**).

The embassy of **Australia** is at 1601 Massachusetts Ave. NW, Washington, DC 20036 (☎ **202/797-3000**). There is an Australian consulate at Century Plaza Towers, 19th Floor, 2049 Century Park East, Los Angeles, CA 90007 (☎ **310/229-4800**). The consulate in New York is located at the International Building, 630 Fifth Ave., Suite 420, New York, NY 10111 (☎ **212/408-8400**).

The embassy of **Canada** is at 501 Pennsylvania Ave. NW, Washington, DC 20001 (☎ **202/682-1740**). There's a Canadian consulate in Los Angeles at 550 S. Hope St., 9th floor, Los Angeles, CA 90071 (☎ **213/346-2700**). The one in

New York is located at 1251 Avenue of the Americas, New York, NY 10020 (☎ **212/596-1600**).

The embassy of the **Republic of Ireland** is at 2234 Massachusetts Ave. NW, Washington, DC 20008 (☎ **202/462-3939**). The consulate in New York is located at 345 Park Ave., 17th floor, New York, NY 10022 (☎ **212/319-2555**). The consulate in San Francisco is at 655 Montgomery St., Suite 930, San Francisco, CA 94111 (☎ **415/392-4214**).

The embassy of **New Zealand** is at 37 Observatory Circle NW, Washington, DC 20008 (☎ **202/328-4800**). The consulate in New York is located at 780 3rd Ave., Suite 1904, New York, NY 10017-2024 (☎ **212/832-4038**). The consulate in Los Angeles is located at 12400 Wilshire Blvd., Suite 1150, Los Angeles, CA 90025 (☎ **310/207-1605**).

The embassy of the **United Kingdom** is at 3100 Massachusetts Ave. NW, Washington, DC 20008 (☎ **202/462-1340**). The consulate in New York is located at 845 Third Ave., New York, NY 10022 (☎ **212/745-0200**). The consulate in Los Angeles is located at 11766 Wilshire Blvd., Suite 400, Los Angeles, CA 90025 (☎ **310/477-3322**).

Emergencies   Call **911** to report a fire, call the police, or get an ambulance. This is a toll-free call (no coins are required at a public telephone). Another useful way of reporting an emergency is to call the telephone company operator by dialing **0.**

If you encounter traveler's problems, check the local telephone directory to find an office of the **Traveler's Aid Society,** a nationwide, nonprofit, social-service organization geared to helping travelers in difficult straits. Their services might include reuniting families separated while traveling, providing food and/or shelter to people stranded without cash, or even offering emotional counseling. If you're in trouble, seek them out.

Gasoline (Petrol)   One U.S. gallon equals 3.8 liters or .83 Imperial gallon. There are usually several grades (and price levels) of gasoline available at most gas stations, and their names change from company to company. Unleaded gas with the highest octane ratings are the most expensive; however, most rental cars take the least expensive "regular" unleaded gas. Additionally, the price is often lower if you pay in cash instead of by credit or charge card. Finally, many gas stations now offer lower-priced self-service gas pumps—in fact, some gas stations, particularly at night, are all self-service.

Holidays   On the following legal national holidays, banks, government offices, post offices, and many stores, restaurants, and museums are closed: January 1 (New Year's Day), the third Monday in January (Martin Luther King Day), the third Monday in February (Presidents' Day, Washington's Birthday), the last Monday in May (Memorial Day), July 4 (Independence Day), the first Monday in September (Labor Day), the second Monday in October (Columbus Day), November 11 (Veterans' Day/Armistice Day), fourth Thursday in November (Thanksgiving Day), and December 25 (Christmas). Also, the Tuesday following the first Monday in November is Election Day and is a legal holiday in presidential-election years (next in 2000).

Legal Aid   The well-meaning foreign visitor will probably never become involved with the American legal system. However, there are a few things you should know just in case. If you are stopped for a minor infraction (for example, of the highway code, such as speeding), never attempt to pay the fine directly to a police officer; you may wind up arrested on the much more serious charge of attempted bribery. Pay fines by mail or directly to the clerk of the court. If you're accused of a more serious offense, it's wise to say and do nothing before consulting a lawyer. Under U.S. law, an arrested person is allowed one telephone call to a party of his or her choice. Call your embassy or consulate.

Mail   If you want your mail to follow you on your vacation and you aren't sure of your address, your mail can be sent to you, in your name, **c/o General Delivery** (Poste Restante) at the main post office of the city or region where you expect to be. (For the addresses and telephone numbers in Albuquerque, Santa Fe, and Taos, see the "Fast Facts" sections in chapters 6, 7, and 8, respectively.) The addressee must pick it up in person and must produce proof of identity (driver's license, credit or charge card, passport, etc.).

Domestic **postage rates** are 20¢ for a postcard and 32¢ for a letter. Check with any local post office for current international postage rates to your home country.

Generally found at intersections, **mailboxes** are blue with a red-and-white stripe and carry the designation U.S. MAIL. If your mail is addressed to a U.S. destination, don't forget to add the five-digit **postal code,** or ZIP (zone improvement plan) code, after the two-letter abbreviation of the state to which the mail is addressed (CA for California, NM for New Mexico, NY for New York, and so on).

Medical Emergencies   For emergency medical help or information, call the New Mexico Medical Crisis Center at **800/432-6866.** The center is open 24 hours a day.

Newspapers and Magazines   With a few exceptions, such as *The New York Times, USA Today,* and the *Wall Street Journal,* daily newspapers in the United States are local, not national. National news weeklies include *Newsweek, Time,* and *U.S. News and World Report.* For information on local publications, see the "Fast Facts" sections in chapters 6, 7, and 8.

The airmail editions of foreign newspapers and magazines are on sale only belatedly, and only at airports and international bookstores in the largest cities.

Post   See "Mail" above.

Radio and Television   Audiovisual media, with four coast-to-coast networks— ABC, CBS, NBC, and Fox—plus the Public Broadcasting System (PBS) and the cable news network CNN, play a major part in American life. In big cities, televiewers have a choice of several dozen channels (including basic cable), most of them transmitting 24 hours a day, not counting the pay-TV channels that show recent movies or sports events. All options are usually indicated on your hotel TV set. You'll also find a wide choice of local radio stations, both AM and FM, each broadcasting particular kinds of talk shows and/or music—classical, country, jazz, pop, gospel—punctuated by news broadcasts and frequent commercials.

Safety   See "Safety" in "Preparing for Your Trip," earlier in this chapter.

Taxes   In the United States there is no VAT (value-added tax) or other indirect tax at a national level. Every state, and each county and city in it, has the right to levy its own local tax on purchases, including hotel and restaurant checks, airline tickets, and so on. Taxes are already included in the price of certain services, such as public transportation, cab fares, telephone calls, and gasoline. The 6.875% New

Mexico state tax on gross receipts includes hotel bills. Local governments tack their own lodging tax on top of that, which ranges from 2.75% to 5.812% depending upon the city.

Telephone and Fax   The telephone system in the United States is run by private corporations, so rates, especially for long-distance service and operator-assisted calls, can vary widely—even on calls made from public telephones. Local calls in the United States usually cost 25¢ (they're 25¢ throughout New Mexico).

Generally, hotel surcharges on long-distance and local calls are astronomical. It's generally cheaper to call collect, use a telephone charge card, or use a **public pay telephone,** which you'll find clearly marked in most public buildings and private establishments as well as on the street. Outside metropolitan areas, public telephones are more difficult to find. Stores and gas stations are your best bet.

Most **long-distance and international calls** can be dialed directly from any phone (stock up on quarters if you're calling from a pay phone or use a telephone charge card). For calls to Canada and other parts of the United States, dial **1** followed by the three-digit area code and the seven-digit number. For international calls, dial **011** followed by the country code (Australia, 61; Republic of Ireland, 353; New Zealand, 64; United Kingdom, 44), then the city code (for example, 171 or 181 for London, 121 for Birmingham) and the telephone number of the person you wish to call.

For reverse-charge or collect calls, and for person-to-person calls, dial 0 (zero, *not* the letter "O") followed by the area code and number you want; an operator will then come on the line, and you should specify that you are calling collect, or person-to-person, or both. If your operator-assisted call is international, ask for the overseas operator.

For local **directory assistance** ("information"), dial **411;** for long-distance information, dial **1,** then the appropriate area code and **555-1212.**

Most hotels have **fax** machines available for guest use (be sure to ask about the charge to use it), and many hotel rooms are even wired for guests' fax machines. You'll probably also see signs for public faxes in the windows of local shops.

Telephone Directory   There are two kinds of telephone directories available to you. The general directory is the so-called **White Pages,** in which private and business subscribers are listed in alphabetical order. The inside front cover lists the emergency number for police, fire, and ambulance, and other vital numbers (like the poison-control center, crime-victims hotline, and so on). The first few pages are devoted to community-service numbers, including a guide to long-distance and international calling, complete with country codes and area codes.

The second directory, printed on yellow paper (hence its name, **Yellow Pages**), lists all local services, businesses, and industries by type of activity, with an index at the back. The listings cover not only such obvious items as automobile repairs by make of car or drugstores (pharmacies), often by geographical location, but also restaurants by type of cuisine and geographical location, bookstores by special subject and/or language, places of worship by religious denomination, and other information that the tourist might otherwise not readily find. The Yellow Pages also often include city plans or detailed area maps, often showing ZIP codes and public transportation routes.

Time   The United States is divided into six **time zones:** From east to west, eastern standard time (EST), central standard time (CST), mountain standard time (MST), Pacific standard time (PST), Alaska standard time (AST), and Hawaii standard time (HST). Always keep the changing time zones in mind if you are traveling (or even telephoning) long distances in the United States. For example, noon in New York City (EST) is 11am in Chicago (CST), 10am in Santa Fe (MST), 9am in Los Angeles (PST), 8am in Anchorage (AST), and 7am in Honolulu (HST).

New Mexico is on mountain standard time (MST), seven hours behind Greenwich mean time. **Daylight saving time** is in effect from the first Sunday in April through the last Saturday in October (actually, the change is made at 2am on Sunday), except in Arizona, Hawaii, part of Indiana, and Puerto Rico. Daylight saving time moves the clock one hour ahead of standard time. (Americans use the adage "spring ahead, fall back" to remember which way to change their clocks and watches.)

Tipping This is part of the American way of life, based on the principle that one should pay for any special service received. (Often service personnel receive little direct salary and must depend on tips for their income.) Here are some rules of thumb:

Bartenders: 10–15%

Bellhops: at least 50¢ per piece; $2–$3 for a lot of baggage

Cab drivers: 15% of the fare

Cafeterias, fast-food restaurants: no tip

Chambermaids: $1 a day

Checkroom attendants (restaurants, theaters): $1 per garment

Cinemas, movies, theaters: no tip

Doormen (hotels or restaurants): not obligatory

Gas-station attendants: no tip

Hairdressers: 15–20%

Redcaps (airport and railroad stations): at least 50¢ per piece, $2–$3 for a lot of baggage

Restaurants, nightclubs: 15–20% of the check

Sleeping-car porters: $2–$3 per night to your attendant

Valet parking attendants: $1

Toilets Foreign visitors often complain that public toilets are hard to find in most U.S. cities. True, there are none on the streets, but the visitor can usually find one in a bar, restaurant, hotel, museum, department store, service station, or train station. Some public places are equipped with pay toilets, which require you to insert one or more coins into a slot on the door before it will open.

5 The Active Vacation Planner

If outdoor activities are what you're looking for, I can't think of a better place to visit than New Mexico. From the dry flatlands of the southern regions of the state to the mountains and forests of north central New Mexico, there is something available for everyone in every corner of the state. Whether you're interested in a short day hike or overnight horse trips, groomed ski trails or backcountry adventures, you won't be disappointed. In addition there's plenty of fishing, hunting, and white-water rafting available. Golf is also becoming more and more popular in New Mexico, in spite of the dry, arid conditions.

This chapter discusses New Mexico's most popular active vacation choices with information on where to go to pursue the activity of your choice, as well as where to get more information, supplies and equipment if necessary.

For more in-depth coverage of the activities that follow, contact some of the local outfitters or organizations covered in the separate regional chapters that appear under "Outdoor Activities" and "Getting Outside" later in this book.

1 Skiing/Snowboarding

Most people, particularly those who don't ski very often, have no idea that skiing is possible in New Mexico. The fact is that it's not only possible, but it's where you'll find some of the best skiing in this country. With most downhill ski areas above 10,000 feet and many above 12,000 feet, there are several ski areas with vertical drops over 2,000 feet. Average annual snowfall at the 10 major areas is anywhere from 100 to 300 inches each winter. Many areas, aided by vigorous snow-making efforts, are able to open around Thanksgiving, and most open by mid-December, making New Mexico a popular vacation spot around the holidays. As a result, you'll see a definite rise in hotel room rates in or around ski areas during the holiday season. Ski season runs through March and often into the first week in April.

In Taos and at the surrounding resort towns of Angel Fire and Red River is where you'll find some of the best skiing in the state (see chapter 8). Additionally, Taos Ski Valley is home to one of the best ski schools in the country. All ski areas in New Mexico offer runs for a variety of skill levels (20% to 35% beginner, 35% to 50% intermediate, and 10% to 50% expert), and lift tickets range in price from $25 to $45 for an adult all-day ticket.

Snowboarding is permitted at all New Mexico ski areas with the exception of Taos Ski Valley, and some of the best **cross-country skiing** in the region can be found at the Enchanted Forest near Taos Ski Valley.

Equipment for downhill and cross-country skiing, as well as for snowboarding, can be rented at ski areas and nearby towns. Lessons are widely available.

For more information about individual ski areas, see regional and city chapters later in this book.

2 Hiking

Everywhere you go in New Mexico there are opportunities for hiking adventures. The terrain and climate are as varied as you might find during a trip to three or four different states. There's the heat and flatness of the desert plains and the cold, forested alpine areas of the northern region of the state. You can visit both (going from 3,000 to 13,000 feet in elevation) and anything in between in the same day without much trouble. As you read in chapter 2, the plant and animal life you'll see along the way is as varied and interesting as the terrain. You can go hiking virtually anywhere you please (except on private land or Native American land without permission); however, most maintained and developed trails can be found in the northern region of the state. You can hike on your own or with a guide, or even with a llama to carry your gear for you.

In this chapter I list some of the best hiking trails in each region of the state. See later chapters for details about outfitters, guides, llama trekking services, and who to contact for maps and other information. For general information, contact the **U.S. Forest Service,** 517 Gold Ave. SW, Albuquerque, NM 87102 (☎ **505/842-3292**); or specific forests: **Carson National Forest,** P.O. Box 558, Taos, NM 87571 (☎**505/758-6201**); **Cíbola National Forest,** 10308 Candelaria Blvd. NE, Albuquerque, NM 87112 (☎ **505/761-4650**); **Gila National Forest,** 2610 N. Silver St., Silver City, NM 88061 (☎ **505/388-8201**); **Lincoln National Forest,** 11th and New York streets, Alamogordo, NM 88310 (☎**505/434-7200**); or **Santa Fe National Forest,** 1220 St. Francis Dr., Santa Fe, NM 87504 (☎ **505/988-6940**).

An excellent book for avid hikers is *The Hiker's Guide to New Mexico* by Laurence Parent (Falcon Press Publishing Co., 1995). It includes a large number of hikes for a wide range of ability levels.

BEST HIKES   If you're around **Santa Fe,** I'd recommend hiking Santa Fe Baldy. It's a hike you can do in a day if you start out early, or if you'd like a less strenuous walk, plan to spend one night camping. This is a good first hike for those who came from lower altitudes but who are in good shape. Once you get to the top you'll have great views of the Sangre de Cristo and Jemez mountains, as well as the Rio Grande Valley. See chapter 7 for details.

If you're looking for something more challenging in the **North Central region** of the state, head up to Taos and give Wheeler Peak your best shot. The hike up New Mexico's highest peak is about 15 miles round-trip. If you're incredibly well conditioned you might be able to do the hike in a day. Others should plan on hiking and camping for several days. The pain of getting to the top is well worth it—at the top you'll find some of New Mexico's most spectacular views. See chapter 8 for details.

If you want a much less difficult hike in the Taos area, try hiking down into Rio Grande Gorge. It's beautiful and can be hiked year-round. See chapter 8 for details.

In the **Northeastern region** of New Mexico I'd recommend taking the 2-mile loop around Capulin Volcano. From the volcano's crater rim you'll get great views and you'll be able to look down into the crater. It's a nice, easy walk for those who'd rather not overexert themselves. The best time to hike Capulin Volcano is during the spring and fall. See chapter 9 for details.

If you're heading to the **Northwestern region** of the state, try hiking the Bisti Badlands, just south of Farmington. Some of the attractions on this 4-mile round trip are pinnacles and hoodoos. Out of hard-packed clay beds rise great sandstone monoliths and very little vegetation. The elevation changes by less than 100 feet on this hike, making it one of the easiest ones listed here. See chapter 10 for details.

This region is also home to El Malpais National Monument, where you can hike into great lava tubes. The hiking is easy, but it's also easy to get lost in this area, so be sure to carry a compass and a topographical map. Also in El Malpais National Monument is the Zuni-Acoma Trail, which used to connect the pueblo villages of Zuni and Acoma. It is a trail thought to be close to 1,000 years old. If you're up for this moderate to difficult 14-mile (round-trip) hike, you'll be hiking across three lava flows and you won't have to fight for trail space with other hikers. This hike is a good one to take any time of the year. See chapter 10 for details.

In the **Southeastern region,** you'll find one of my favorite places in all of New Mexico: White Sands National Monument. Hiking the white sand dunes is easy, but the magnificence of the view is unsurpassed. Be sure to take a compass and plenty of water on this hike; it's difficult to tell one dune from another here.

Of course, there are hundreds of other hikes from which to choose. Your best bet is to purchase a hiking book or to contact the national forests directly.

3 Mountain Biking

Just like the rest of the country, New Mexico has seen a huge jump in the number of mountain bikers seeking to conquer its desert plains and mountain forests in the last few years. Just about the entire state is conducive to the sport, making it the most popular place in the United States for avid mountain bikers.

You might be surprised to learn that there are trails around Albuquerque, and some of them make good day rides; however, because many of them are overused there tends to be trail damage, mud, and overcrowding. A far more interesting area from the mountain biker's point of view is located only about an hour from Albuquerque near Grants and El Morro and El Malpais National Monuments. It's one of the best riding areas, in terms of scenic variety, in the state. See Chapter 10 for details.

For more information on mountain biking in New Mexico, contact the **New Mexico Touring Society,** 4115 12th St. NW, Albuquerque, NM 87107 (☎ **505/ 344-1038**). Two books to check out are *Mountain Biking in Northern New Mexico* (University of New Mexico, 1994), which lists the 25 best rides in the area, and Sarah Bennett's *Mountain Biker's Guide to New Mexico* (Falcon Press, 1994). If you don't want to strike out on your own, **New Mexico Mountain Bike Adventures,** 6 Grasshopper Rd., Madrid, NM 87010 (☎ **505/474-0074;** fax 505/473-1374) sponsors day and half-day trips as well as 3- to 6-day camping trips for all levels of ability. Multiday trips include the Jemez Mountains, a Continental Divide ride, and the Apache and Gila National Forests.

4 Fishing & Hunting

There are scores of **fishing** opportunities in New Mexico. Warm-water lakes and streams are home to large- and small-mouth bass, walleye, stripers, catfish, crappie, and bluegill. In cold water lakes and streams, look for the state fish, the Rio Grande cutthroat, as well as rainbow, brown, lake, and brook trout, and kokanee salmon.

Two of the best places for fishing are the San Juan River near Farmington, and Elephant Butte Lake, not far from Truth or Consequences. The San Juan River offers excellent trout fishing and is extremely popular with fly fishers. Elephant Butte is great for bass fishing; in fact, it is considered one of the top 10 bass fishing locations in the United States. Of course, there are all sorts of other possibilities, such as the Rio Grande River, the Chama, Jemez, and Gila watershed areas, and the Pecos River. It would be impossible to describe them all in any detail here, so I recommend you buy Ti Piper's *Fishing in New Mexico* (University of New Mexico Press, 1994). It's an excellent and wonderfully comprehensive book that describes absolutely every waterway in New Mexico in great detail. It even includes information about regulations and descriptions of the types and varieties of fish you're likely to catch in New Mexico.

Fishing licenses, required of anyone 12 or older, cost $41. A one-day license costs $9, and a five-day license is $16. A Wildlife Habitat Improvement stamp ($6) must also be purchased for fishing in national forests or Bureau of Land Management–controlled waters.

Hunting opportunities also abound in New Mexico. Big game include deer, elk, and antelope. Turkey, grouse, quail, and ducks are also found throughout the state. Hunters must also be licensed.

For a fishing map and hunting and fishing regulations, you should contact the **New Mexico Department of Game and Fish** at **505/827-7911.** For recorded information regarding licensing and everything else you might need to know, call **800/ASK-FISH.**

It's important to note that while it is not necessary to have a fishing license in order to fish on Indian reservation land, you must still receive written permission and an official tribal document before setting out on any fishing trips. Phone numbers for individual tribes and pueblos are listed separately in the regional and city chapters later in this book.

5 Water Sports

Water sports in New Mexico? Absolutely! Here you'll find a variety of water sports activities, ranging from pleasure boating to white-water rafting and windsurfing.

There are fantastic opportunities in New Mexico for **white-water rafting** and **kayaking.** The water on the Chama River and the Rio Grande is generally at its best during the spring and summer (late May to late July); however, some areas of the Rio Grande are negotiable year-round, especially those that fall at lower elevations where temperatures are warmer. If you opt not to schlep your own rafting gear with you to New Mexico, there are many companies that will supply you with everything you need. I'd recommend contacting some of the outfitters listed in later chapters no matter what you've brought with you or what your level of experience is because white-water rafting and kayaking in certain areas of New Mexico (like Taos Box) can be quite dangerous. You should get tips from the professionals before you set out on your own. In addition to calling outfitters, you can also contact the **Bureau of Land Management,** 224 Cruz Alta Rd., Taos, NM 87571 (☎ **505/758-8851**) for information.

Opportunities for **pleasure boating** are available on many of New Mexico's lakes and reservoirs. There are boat ramps at more than 45 state parks, dams, and lakes. Elephant Butte Lake is one of the best and most beautiful spots for boating (see chapter 11). Unfortunately, the rules and regulations vary greatly from one body of water to another, so you'll have to contact the governing agencies for each place in which you intend to go boating.

The **U.S. Army Corps of Engineers** (P.O. Box 1580, Albuquerque, NM 87103; ☎ 505/766-2681) oversees the following lakes: Abiquiu, Cochiti, Conchas, Jemez, John Martin, Santa Rosa, and Trinidad. Most other boating areas are regulated by the **State Park and Recreation Division** (408 Galisteo, Santa Fe, NM 87504; ☎ 505/827-7465) or by the **New Mexico Department of Game and Fish** (P.O. Box 25112, Santa Fe, NM 87504; ☎ **505/827-7911** or 505/827-7880). Some are, of course, overseen by tribes and pueblos, and in those cases you'll have to contact them directly.

Another incredibly popular pastime, particularly at Cochiti and Storrie Lakes, is **windsurfing.** Elephant Butte is good all year.

6 Bird-Watching

Bird-watchers know that New Mexico is located directly on the Central Flyway, which makes it a great spot for this activity all year long. Each different region of the state offers refuge to a wide variety of birds, including everything from doves, finches, bluebirds, and roadrunners (the state bird) to the rare and wonderful whooping crane. The bald eagle is also frequently spotted during winter and spring migrations. There are several wildlife refuge centers in New Mexico, including the **Bosque del Apache National Wildlife Refuge** (93 miles south of Albuquerque, ☎ 505/835-1828), the **Rio Grande Nature Center** (Albuquerque, ☎ 505/344-7240), the **Las Vegas National Wildlife Refuge** (☎ 505/425-3581), and **Bitter Lake National Wildlife Refuge** (the Salt Creek Wilderness area of Bitter Lake is open to the public, ☎ 505/622-6755). Some common sightings at these areas might include sandhill cranes, snow geese, a wide variety of ducks, and falcons. New Mexico is also home to an amazing variety of hummingbirds. In fact, in early 1996, New Mexico was able to add the Cinnamon Hummingbird to its list of birds. Its sighting in Santa Teresa marked the occasion of only its second sighting in the United States. Four other birds were also added to New Mexico's list in 1996—the Acadian Flycatcher, the Berylline Hummingbird, the Black Skimmer, and the Ruff. This is simply astonishing, considering the fact that most states are removing species from their lists. The number of verified species in New Mexico is now 481. New Mexico ranks fourth (behind Texas, California, and Arizona) in the number of birds that live in or have passed through the state.

If you're interested in bird-watching during your trip to New Mexico, contact the state office of the **National Audubon Society** (P.O. Box 9314, Santa Fe, NM 87504; ☎ **505/983-4609**). They'll be able to tell you who to contact in individual towns and cities for more information.

7 Rockhounding

There are those people, like me, who pick up rocks by streams, in fields, or on mountain trails purely for their aesthetic value without the slightest idea of what they're looking for or at. Then, there are also those who know exactly what they're looking for—those who spend a great deal of time hunting for just the right rock, mineral, or gem. No matter which category you fall into, you'll enjoy New Mexico's rockhounding opportunities. Of course, you can't just go around picking up and taking rocks whenever it strikes your fancy to do so—in many places it's illegal to take rocks; however, there are a few places that not only allow rockhounding, they encourage it. **Rock Hound State Park** (☎ 505/546-6182), located not far from Deming, is one such place (see chapter 11 for more information). Rock hounds from all over the country descend on this part of the state specifically for the purpose of finding great rocks like agate, jasper, turquoise, and opal. At Rock Hound State Park you're allowed to camp and load up on as many rocks as your heart desires. For information on other popular rockhounding sites, contact the **New Mexico Bureau of Mines and Mineral Resources** (☎ **505/835-5410**).

8 Aerial Sports

You can't hear about New Mexico without hearing about **hot-air ballooning**—the two seem to go hand in hand. In fact, one of the state's greatest attractions is the annual Kodak Albuquerque International Balloon Fiesta in early October. Thousands of people travel from all over to see hundreds of huge, colorful balloons take flight simultaneously, and every year, hundreds more take the opportunity to experience a flight on their own. It is possible to charter hot-air balloon rides in all regions of the state. Most companies offer a variety of packages from the standard flight to a more elaborate all-day affair that includes meals. For more information you should contact individual chambers of commerce.

    Hang gliding and **soaring** have reached new levels of popularity in New Mexico in the past few years. Favorite spots for hang gliding (basically, an activity that requires one or two human beings and a giant kite with a harness) include the Sandia Mountains near Albuquerque and the area around Hobbs. Soaring, or gliding, is popular in Santa Fe, Taos, and Albuquerque. It's a wonderful experience—you'll feel like you're just floating in midair surrounded by absolute silence. See individual city or regional chapters for more information, or contact local chambers of commerce.

9 Other Activities

In addition to the activities listed above, there are many other recreational opportunities available in New Mexico. **Hot springs,** for example, are quite popular with both locals and visitors alike. They take many different forms and offer a wide variety of facilities and amenities (some, which aren't owned and operated by anyone but Mother Nature, offer no amenities). You'll find hot springs in the North Central and Southwestern regions of New Mexico. Many of them are listed later in this book. You might also try calling local chambers of commerce to see if they have any information on area hot springs.

    Tennis and **golf** remain popular pastimes, as do **swimming, horse racing, horseback riding,** and **rodeos** (see individual city and regional chapters for more information).

10 Tips for Staying Healthy

New Mexico is unique for many reasons, not the least of which is the altitude. Visitors should be aware of New Mexico's high elevation for two reasons. The first is clothing: Don't come at any time of year, even in the middle of summer, without at least a warm sweater and rain gear. The second is health: Don't push yourself too hard during your first few days here. The air is thinner, the sun more direct. If you haven't engaged in physical activity on a regular basis, see your doctor before your trip just to be sure you're in good condition. Under the best of circumstances at these altitudes, you should expect to sunburn more easily and stop to catch your breath more frequently.

Hantavirus Pulmonary Syndrome: What You Should Know

Recent news reports regarding the rare but often fatal respiratory disease known as Hantavirus have frightened some potential visitors to New Mexico. First recognized in 1993, the disease has afflicted just over 100 people, and half of those cases were reported in the Four Corners states of Utah, Colorado, New Mexico, and Arizona. It is believed that the disease is spread through urine and droppings of deer mice and other rodents, so outdoor enthusiasts are in one of the highest categories of risk. While there is some cause for alarm, there are ways of protecting yourself (recommended by the Centers for Disease Control) and your family against Hantavirus:

- Avoid camping or sleeping in areas with signs of rodent droppings.
- Before using cabins that have been closed up for the winter or for an extended period of time, open them up and air them out for a while before spending any length of time inside. Check for rodent infestation as well.
- If you see a rodent burrow or den, do not disturb it or try to chase the animals out of the area—just set up camp somewhere else.
- Don't sleep on the bare ground. Use a mat or an elevated cot if possible.
- Don't set up camp near a woodpile.
- Keep foods in airtight, rodent-proof containers, and dispose of garbage promptly and efficiently.

If you have some exposure to rodents and begin to exhibit symptoms of the disease (difficulty breathing, headache, flulike fever, abdominal, joint, and lower back pain, and sometimes nausea), see a doctor immediately, and be sure to tell them where and when you were in contact with rodents. The sooner you seek medical attention the better your chances for survival.

New Mexico also has the dubious distinction of having the highest per capita lightning deaths in the country. If you get caught in a fast-developing thunderstorm, seek lower ground immediately. Rain in New Mexico can also cause serious problems. If it begins to rain while you're out hiking, stay out of ditches and narrow canyons; flash floods are not uncommon at certain times of the year and they're very dangerous. If out driving and you suddenly find that water is covering part of the roadway, don't try to drive across. It's best to wait it out. The rain will stop and the water will recede—more quickly than you might imagine.

It is unfortunate that I have to warn you about drinking stream water while partaking in outdoor activities, but I'd be remiss if I didn't. There are still places where it's safe to drink water directly from its source; however, it's easier and more prudent to simply filter all water before you drink it if you're out hiking. You can buy mechanical filtration units at outdoors shops, or you can use chemical treatment such as chlorination. If you're going to drink from natural sources, try to get your water from springs located upstream from campgrounds. If you're only going hiking or biking for the day or have a place in mind to stop for the night where you can pick up provisions, it's much better to carry your own drinking water.

The only other thing you might be concerned about during outdoor activities is wildlife. Basically, you should keep your eyes and ears open, but most wildlife will be more afraid of you than you are of it. You should, however, watch out for snakes, especially rattlers, and avoid them when you see them.

Albuquerque 6

With a population of about half a million, Albuquerque is New Mexico's largest city. But it holds onto the bustling spirit of Western towns of half a century ago when *progress* was a fashionable word and growing bigger was unquestionably synonymous with getting better.

The historic center of Albuquerque is Old Town, where it was founded in 1706. The city jumped away from its origins when the railroad came through in 1880 and caused a new Albuquerque to be planted around the passenger and freight depots. This *Saturday Evening Post*–style center, so reminiscent of hundreds of small plains cities of the thirties and forties, still exists along Central Avenue between Second and Sixth streets. But a new downtown, with an impressive new convention center, luxury hotels, financial district of glass skyscrapers, and underground shopping mall, is emerging just a few steps north. And vast commercial and shopping complexes are part of the urban expanse east of downtown, within quick reach by car via the long, wide, straight, flat streets and avenues of the sprawling grid that reach nearly to the foot of the Sandia Mountains 20 miles east of the old center.

In spite of the leveling, gentrifying effect of the spread of chain restaurants, interchangeable condos, and placeless superhighways, Albuquerque retains strong elements of its original Western spirit. It feels somehow closer to the plains to the east, the directness of the Texan, than to the thin, chic optimism and faddishness of California. It is a young city: The people are young in years and in energy. The University of New Mexico plays a central role in life here, both by its geography just east of downtown and for the part it takes in the life of its city through its outstanding museums and cultural programs.

The city does have its unsightly commercial strips along the main east-west highway. The notorious old Route 66, where mid–20th-century pioneers heading west used to "get their kicks," still goes straight through town, though most of its traffic has been diverted to I-40. But it was not all that long ago that Albuquerque had for a main drag a movie-set–like row of false-front hotels, bars, and stores lined in front with hitching posts and wooden sidewalks along a muddy, rutted roadway crowded with wagons and buggies and figures on horseback.

That shot-in-the-arm railroad connection a little over a century ago gave Albuquerque the impetus to grow, to build, to move out in every direction without a thought for the future—without any plan at all. The city grew so big and so much, before there was any thought of saving any of its land for public use, that it wasn't until 1975 that any serious attempt at growth control took place. That action has provided citizens (and visitors) with some green spaces, and there are more to come. First-time visitors, viewing the city from a car speeding in over the interstate, which makes a huge cross in the middle of town with its east-west and north-south trajectories meeting and corkscrewing in and around one another, might suppose themselves lost in a Los Angeles–style wasteland of urban sprawl. But parts of Albuquerque are very special indeed—you just have to make sure to find them.

One of these is the plaza of Old Town, which rivals the plazas of Santa Fe and Taos for historical interest, architectural beauty, and lively shopping and dining scenes. Another is the innovative complex of glass-and-steel bank buildings clustered around a tiled open space, containing a pool and a fountain, terraces and tables with parasols, the whole of which conceals First Plaza—a brightly lighted futuristic warren of underground shops, bars, and eating places that could make you imagine you've come to Montreal on the Rio Grande. That good old Western-style downtown is just outside in case you feel a dire need for a touch of reality.

The city was long a supply center for the region. Today it has added to its original mercantile base by developing supply depots for military bases and building experimental scientific laboratories in a wide variety of specialized fields. Its warm, sunny climate and healthful altitude—varying from 4,200 to 6,000 feet—also bring in many vacationers and retirement residents.

The fairgrounds is the site for the annual state fair and for a colorful and locally renowned annual arts-and-crafts show. Indian pueblos in the area welcome tourists, and along with other pueblos throughout New Mexico have worked together to create the Pueblo Cultural Center, a showplace of Indian crafts of both past and present. The country's longest aerial tramway takes visitors to the top of Sandia Peak, which protects the city's eastern flank.

1 Orientation

ARRIVING

BY PLANE   **Albuquerque International Airport** is in the south-central part of the city, between I-25 on the west and Kirtland Air Force Base on the east, just south of Gibson Boulevard. A major renovation and expansion, completed in early 1990, gave the city a sleek and efficient air terminal.

The airport is served by eight national airlines: **America West** (☎ 800/235-9292), **American** (☎ 800/433-7300), **Continental** (☎ 800/525-0280), **Delta** (800/221-1212), **Southwest** (☎ 800/435-9792), **TWA** (☎ 800/325-4933), and **USAir** (☎ 800/428-4322).

Most hotels have courtesy vans to take new arrivals to their accommodations. **Shuttlejack** (☎ **800/452-2665** outside New Mexico, or **505/243-3244**) and **Checker Airport Express** (☎ **505/765-1234**) also offer service to city hotels and on to Santa Fe. **Sun Tran** (☎ **505/843-9200**), Albuquerque's public bus system, also makes airport stops. There's efficient taxi service to and from the airport, and numerous car-rental agencies.

BY CAR   If you're driving, you'll probably arrive in the city either via the east-west Interstate 40 or the north-south Interstate 25. Exits are well marked. For

Greater Albuquerque

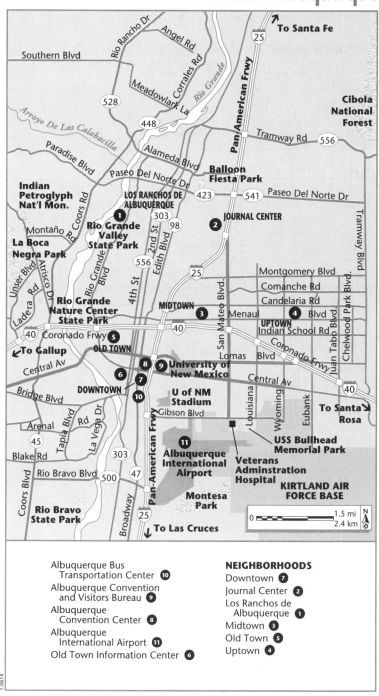

information and advice on driving in New Mexico, see the "Getting Around" section in chapter 3.

BY TRAIN   Amtrak's *Southwest Chief* arrives and departs daily from and to Los Angeles and Chicago. The station is at 214 First St. SW, two blocks south of Central Avenue (☎ **800/USA-RAIL** or 505/842-9650). Note: A new train station is currently in the planning stages, so call ahead to make sure the address listed here is still current.

BY BUS   Greyhound/Trailways (☎ **505/231-2222** for schedules and information) and **TNM&O Coaches** (☎ **505/243-4435**) arrive and depart from the Albuquerque Bus Transportation Center near the train station at 300 Second St. SW.

VISITOR INFORMATION

The main office of the **Albuquerque Convention and Visitors Bureau** is at 20 First Plaza NW (☎ **800/284-2282** or 505/243-3696). It's open Monday to Friday from 8am to 5pm. In addition, the bureau operates information centers at the airport, bottom of the escalator in the lower level, open from 9:30am to 8pm daily; and in Old Town at 303 Romero St. NW, Suite 107, open daily from 9am to 5pm. Tape recorded information about current local events is available from the bureau after 5pm weekdays and all day Saturday and Sunday. Call **800/284-2282.** The bureau also publishes a wide variety of visitor information, including the city's official annual visitors guide, brochures about local and regional attractions and accommodations, and quarterly calendars of events. If you have access to the Internet and the World Wide Web, the address for the Albuquerque Convention and Visitors Bureau is http://www.abqcvb.org.

CITY LAYOUT

Lay a map of Albuquerque before you and notice how the crossroads of I-40 and I-25 divide the city into four neat quadrants. The southwest quadrant is the location of Downtown and Old Town. Central Avenue (the old "Route 66") and Lomas Boulevard flank downtown on the south and north, respectively; they come together 2 miles west of downtown near the Old Town Plaza. The Rio Grande greenbelt lies about a half mile southwest of Old Town.

Lomas and Central continue east across I-25, staying about a half mile apart as they pass by first the University of New Mexico, then the New Mexico State Fairgrounds. The airport is due south of the UNM campus, about 3 miles via Yale Boulevard. Kirtland Air Force Base—site of Sandia National Laboratories and the National Atomic Museum—is an equal distance south of the fairgrounds on Louisiana Boulevard.

Roughly paralleling I-40 to the north is Menaul Boulevard, focus of the Midtown and Uptown shopping and hotel districts. (Think of Midtown as extending from I-25 to San Mateo Boulevard, about $2^1/2$ miles, and Uptown from there to Eubank Boulevard, another 3 miles.) As Albuquerque expands northward, the Journal Center business park area, about $4^1/2$ miles north of the freeway interchange, is getting more attention. Broad San Mateo Boulevard links Journal Center with Midtown and Uptown. East of Eubank are the Sandia Foothills, where the alluvial plain slants a bit more steeply toward the mountain.

For address purposes, Central Avenue divides the city into north and south, and the railroad tracks—which run just east of First Street, downtown—split it into east and west. Street names are followed by a directional: NE, NW, SE, or SW.

The most comprehensive Albuquerque street map is the one published by Sun West Bank and distributed by the Convention and Visitors Bureau. Gousha's laminated FastMap is also quite helpful.

2 Getting Around

A city of half a million people might seem intimidating to maneuver, but actually Albuquerque is easy to get around, thanks to its wide thoroughfares and grid layout combined with its efficient transportation systems.

BY CAR   The yellow pages list more than 30 **car-rental** agencies in Albuquerque. Among the well-known national firms are **Alamo,** 2601 Yale Blvd., SE (☎ **800/ 327-9633** or 505/842-4057), **Avis,** airport (☎ **800/331-1212** or 505/842-4080), **Budget,** airport (☎ **800/527-0700** or 505/768-5900), **Dollar,** airport (☎ **800/ 800-4000** or 505/842-4304), **Hertz,** airport (☎ **800/654-3131** or 505/842-4235). **Rent-a-Wreck,** 501 Yale Blvd. SE (☎ **800/535-1391** or 505/242-9556), and **Thrifty,** 2039 Yale Blvd. SE (☎ **800/367-2277** or 505/842-8733). Those not in the airport itself are nearby, and provide rapid airport pickup and delivery service.

When you return your vehicle to the rental agency, it's a good idea to fill the tank before you get back to the airport. Service stations near the airport often jack up their prices for gasoline 33% higher than stations a mile or two away.

Parking is generally not difficult in Albuquerque—nor, for that matter, is rush hour a serious problem (yet). Meters operate from 8am to 6pm weekdays and are not monitored at other times. Most hotels do not charge for parking, with the exception of the large downtown properties.

BY TAXI   **Yellow-Checker Cab** (☎ **505/765-1234**) serves the city and surrounding area 24 hours a day.

BY BUS   **Sun Tran of Albuquerque** (☎ **505/843-9200**) cloaks the arterials with its city bus network. Call for information on routes and fares.

FAST FACTS: Albuquerque

Airport   See "Arriving," earlier in this chapter.

American Express   The American Express office is at 6600 Indian School Rd. (☎ **800/219-1023** or 505/883-3677; fax 505/884-0008). To report lost credit cards, call **800/528-4800.**

Car Rentals   See "Getting Around," earlier in this chapter.

Climate   See "When to Go," in chapter 3.

Currency Exchange   Foreign currency can be exchanged at any of the branches of Sun West Bank (its main branch is at 303 Roma St. NE, ☎ **505/765-2211**); or at any of the branches of First Security Bank (its main office is at Twenty-First Plaza, ☎ **505/765-4000**).

Dentists   Call the Albuquerque District Dental Society at **505/260-7333** for emergency service.

Doctors   Call the University of New Mexico Medical Center Physician Referral Service at **505/843-0124** for a recommendation.

Embassies/Consulates   See "Fast Facts: For the Foreign Traveler," in chapter 4.

Emergencies For police, fire, or ambulance, dial **911.**

Hospitals The major facilities are **Presbyterian Hospital,** 1100 Central Ave. SE (☎ **505/841-1234,** or 505/841-1111 for emergency services); and **University of New Mexico Hospital,** 2211 Lomas Blvd. NE (☎ **505/843-2411** for emergency services).

Information See "Visitor Information," earlier in this chapter.

Libraries The main branch of the **Albuquerque/Bernalillo County Public Library** is downtown at 501 Copper Ave. NW (☎ **505/768-5140**). There are 13 other branches, including the notable **Ernie Pyle Branch** at 900 Girard Ave. SE (☎ **505/256-2065**). The **University of New Mexico Libraries** are headquartered on campus near Central Avenue and University Boulevard (☎ **505/277-5761**).

Maps See "City Layout," earlier in this chapter.

Newspapers/Magazines The two daily newspapers are the *Albuquerque Tribune,* published mornings, and the *Albuquerque Journal,* published evenings. *Albuquerque Monthly* magazine, which covers many aspects of city life, is widely available.

Police For emergencies, call **911.** For other business, contact the Albuquerque City Police (☎ **505/768-1986**) or the New Mexico State Police (☎ **505/841-9256**).

Post Offices The Main Post Office, 1135 Broadway NE (☎ **505/245-9561**) is open daily from 7:30am to 6pm. There are 18 branch offices, with another 13 in surrounding communities.

Radio/TV Albuquerque has some 30 local radio stations catering to all musical tastes. Albuquerque television stations include KOB, Channel 4 (NBC affiliate); KOAT, Channel 7 (ABC affiliate); KGGM, Channel 13 (CBS affiliate); KNME, Channel 5 (PBS affiliate); and KGSW, Channel 14 (Fox and independent). There are, of course, numerous local cable channels as well.

Taxes In Albuquerque, the hotel tax is 10.81%; it will be added to your bill.

Taxis See "Getting Around," earlier in this chapter.

Time Zone Albuquerque is on mountain time, one hour ahead of the West Coast and two hours behind the East Coast.

Transit Info **Sun Tran of Albuquerque** is the public bus system. Call **505/843-9200** for schedules and information.

Useful Telephone Numbers For time and temperature call **505/247-1611;** road information **800/432-4269;** emergency road service (AAA) **505/291-6600.**

3 Accommodations

New Mexico's largest city has some 9,000 hotel rooms. Although Albuquerque is growing as a convention destination, a high percentage of the rooms remain vacant during much of the year. That means visitors can frequently request, and obtain, a room rate lower than the one posted. The exceptions would be during peak periods— the New Mexico Arts and Crafts Fair in late June, the New Mexico State Fair in September, and the Kodak Albuquerque International Balloon Fiesta in early October—when hoteliers may raise their rates as much as 50% and still fill every room.

Central Albuquerque Accommodations

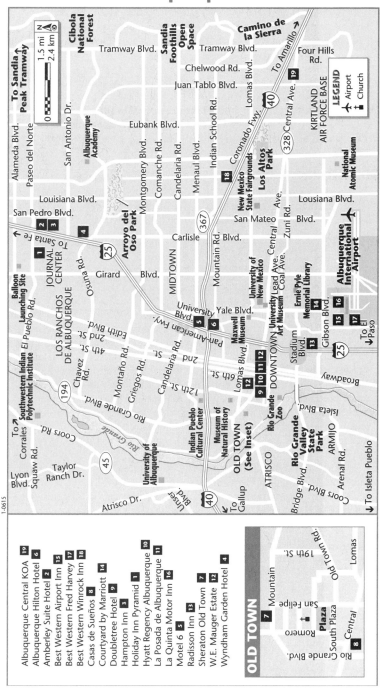

In the listings below, the following categories define price ranges: **expensive,** $90 and up per night double; **moderate,** $60 to $90; and **inexpensive,** $30 to $60. An additional tax is imposed on every hotel bill. Parking at most hotels is free (unless otherwise indicated).

Most hotels reviewed offer rooms for nonsmokers and for people with disabilities. In addition to the accommodations listed below, Albuquerque also has its share of budget hotel chains, including **Motel 6,** which has three locations in the city: 1701 University Blvd. NE at I-40, Albuquerque, NM 87102 (☎ **505/843-9228** or 505/891-6161); 13141 Central Ave. NE, I-40 at Tramway Boulevard Exit 67 (☎ **505/294-4600**); and at 6015 Iliff Rd. NW, I-40 at Coors Road Exit 155 (☎ **505/831-3400**).

DOWNTOWN/OLD TOWN

This area is the best location to stay if you want to be close to many of the major sights and attractions. All of the following accommodations are between I-25 and the Rio Grande, and between I-40 and Route 66 (Central Avenue).

EXPENSIVE

Casas de Sueños. 310 Rio Grande Blvd. SW, Albuquerque, NM 87104. ☎ **800/242-8987** or 505/247-4560. 19 rms. TV TEL. $85–$250 single or double. AE, CB, DC, DISC, MC, V.

You'll know Casas de Sueños by the bright sign and the snail-shaped front of the main building. The buildings that comprise Casas de Sueños were once private homes—a compound that was once an artists' colony. Most of them face a garden courtyard that was a gathering place for artists and their admirers. In the spring and summer, the gardens, filled with roses and seasonal displays, are maintained by a resident gardener, making the place an oasis right in the middle of Albuquerque.

Each of the rooms has an individual theme. For instance, the Rio Grande Suite is done in black, white, and pink and has a claw-foot bathtub—a nice romantic getaway. The Kachina room has many little *kachinas* (storyteller dolls) scattered about. Some of the rooms have kitchens, and La Miradora has two bedrooms (with king- and queen-size beds), a living room with a fireplace, a full bath with a two-person Jacuzzi, and a back porch with a swing overlooking a golf course. All the rooms have private entrances.

Kurt and Cathy Kubitz, the managers, serve a delicious full breakfast in the main building every morning. Works by local artists are displayed in the breakfast room (once an artist's studio and gallery). Guests have sports club privileges, and there is a massage therapist on the premises. No smoking is permitted indoors. Pets are not accepted, but children 12 and older are welcome.

Doubletree Hotel. 201 Marquette St. NW, Albuquerque, NM 87102. ☎ **800/528-0444** or 505/247-3344. Fax 505/247-7025. 294 rms, 10 suites. A/C TV TEL. $84–$134 double; $270–$375 suite. Rates include breakfast. AE, CB, DC, DISC, ER, MC, V.

A pillared lobby with a marble floor—as well as a plateful of chocolate chip cookies—greets arrivals to this elegant property. But perhaps the most remarkable feature of the Doubletree, which adjoins the Albuquerque Convention Center, is the two-story waterfall that cascades from the lobby to the restaurant and lounge below. An underground passageway links the hotel to the convention center and a shopping mall.

All rooms in the 15-story hotel are decorated in pastel shades and Southwestern designs, including custom-made furnishings. Each has a cable TV (with in-house movies) hidden in an armoire and a good-sized desk for business travelers.

Dining/Entertainment: La Cascada Restaurant, an airy coffee shop, serves a variety of food, from sandwiches and pastas to New Mexican specialties and meat, fish, and chicken main courses. Drinks are served in the Bistro Bar, adjacent to the waterfall; the Lobby Lounge has live music daily during happy hour.

Services: Room service from 6am to midnight, valet laundry.

Facilities: Swimming pool, weight room, gift/sundry shop, American Airlines ticket counter.

Hyatt Regency Albuquerque. 330 Tijeras Ave. NW, Albuquerque, NM 87102. ☎ **800/ 233-1234** or 505/842-1234. Fax 505/842-1184. 395 rms, 14 suites. A/C TV TEL. $144–$164 double; $310–$725 suite. Weekends $89 single or double. AE, CB, DC, DISC, MC, V. $8 self-parking; $11 valet.

This 20-story, $60 million property became a city landmark the day it opened in August 1990. Marble pillars, Irish carpets, and an extensive use of mahogany contribute to the feeling of opulence. A pyramid skylight nourishes palms surrounding a fountain in the lobby. The hotel boasts a $500,000 collection of public art, including an original sculpture by Frederic Remington.

The spacious rooms feature such touches as remote-control television, clock radios, full-length mirrors, mahogany desks, even data-port jacks for business travelers. In Southwestern fashion, each boasts a potted cactus.

Dining/Entertainment: McGrath's offers a gourmet grill menu in a rich atmosphere of black cherry and mahogany. A casual lounge adjoins the restaurant. A lobby bar has whimsical oil paintings on its walls, depicting saloons where the deer and the antelope play.

Services: Limited room service, concierge, valet laundry, courtesy van.

Facilities: Heated outdoor swimming pool, health club with massage service and large weight and exercise room, gift shop, several upscale art galleries, Delta Airlines desk, Budget car-rental desk, hair salon, florist, optician, travel agency.

✪ **La Posada de Albuquerque.** 125 2nd St. NW (at Copper St.), Albuquerque, NM 87102. ☎ **800/777-5732** or 505/242-9090. Fax 505/242-8664. 114 rms, 5 suites. A/C TV TEL. $98– $110 double; $180–$275 suite. AE, CB, DC, DISC, MC, V. Complimentary valet parking.

Built in 1939 by Conrad Hilton as the famed hotelier's first inn in his home state of New Mexico, this hotel is listed on the National Register of Historic Places. The atmosphere is of a 19th-century hacienda courtyard in old Mexico. In the center of the tile floor is an elaborate Moorish brass-and-mosaic tile fountain, and beyond it, a piano bar surrounded by plush leather-upholstered seating. Tin chandeliers hang from the two-story-high ceiling.

The guest rooms, which were becoming outdated, have just undergone a major facelift (completed in the fall of 1996). As in the lobby, all furniture is handcrafted, but here it's covered with cushions of stereotypically Southwestern design. There are limited-edition lithographs on the white walls and an ample desk opposite the wood-shuttered windows.

Dining/Entertainment: Conrad's Downtown (see "Where to Dine," below) is the hotel restaurant. In the evening, the Lobby Bar is a nice spot for a cocktail or after-dinner drink. On weekdays a pianist entertains during happy hour, and on Friday and Saturday you can enjoy the sounds of a jazz combo.

Services: Room service, valet laundry.

Facilities: Gift shop.

Sheraton Old Town. 800 Rio Grande Blvd. NW, Albuquerque, NM 87104. ☎ **800/ 237-2133,** 800/325-3535, or 505/843-6300. Fax 505/842-9863. 190 rms, 20 suites. A/C MINIBAR TV TEL. $110–$120 double; $140 suite. Children free with adult. AE, CB, DC, V.

Within five minutes' walk of the Old Town Plaza and overlooking two of Albuquerque's major museums, the Sheraton is an ideal spot for visitors without their own vehicles who don't want to be at the mercy of taxis or rental cars.

Each guest room is characterized by a Pueblo Indian craft on the wall over the beds. All furniture, including dressers, desks, and chairs, is handmade. South-side rooms, facing Old Town, have private balconies.

Dining/Entertainment: The Customs House Restaurant, which specializes in seafood and regional cuisine, is open for lunch during the week, dinner daily, and brunch on Sunday. There's also a coffee shop and a bar.

Services: Room service, concierge, valet laundry, secretarial, baby-sitting.

Facilities: Outdoor swimming pool and Jacuzzi, exercise room. Sheraton owns and operates Old Town Place, a shopping center to which it is directly connected. Shops include art dealers, bookstore, beauty salon, and manicurist.

MIDTOWN/UPTOWN

This area, which extends from I-25 to Eubank Boulevard, and between Central Avenue and Montgomery Boulevard, is a popular resting place for business travelers, shoppers, and other visitors seeking a central location. It includes Freeway Loop, which surrounds the interchange of I-25 and I-40; several major hotels are on Menaul and University boulevards nearby.

EXPENSIVE

Albuquerque Hilton Hotel. 1901 University Blvd. NE, Albuquerque, NM 87102. ☎ **800/27-HOTEL** or 505/884-2500. Fax 505/889-9118. 264 rms, 7 suites. A/C TV TEL. $95–$135 double; $375–$475 suite. Weekend discounts available. AE, CB, DC, DISC, MC, V. Free parking.

White stuccoed corridors with petroglyph-style paintings are a trademark of this hotel. Many of the rooms are in a high-rise tower that offers panoramic views of the Sandia Mountains or of the downtown area and western mesa. Two floors comprise a VIP level for business travelers; cabana rooms with 15-foot cathedral ceilings surround the outdoor pool.

Dining/Entertainment: The Ranchers Club, built like a British hunting lodge transported to the high plains, is one of Albuquerque's finest restaurants. Casa Chaco is open daily for three meals. The Cantina, with its fajitas grill and piano bar, serves as the hotel lounge.

Services: Room service (during restaurant hours), valet laundry, shoeshine stand, Avis car-rental desk.

Facilities: Indoor and outdoor swimming pools, whirlpool, saunas, tennis courts, fitness center, gift shop, and business center.

MODERATE

Best Western Winrock Inn. 18 Winrock Center NE, Albuquerque, NM 87110. ☎ **800/866-5252** or 505/883-5252. Fax 505/889-3206. 173 rms, 2 suites. A/C TV TEL. $55–$125 single or double; $59–$135 suite. Rates include full breakfast buffet. AE, CB, DC, DISC, MC, V.

Located just off I-40 at the Louisiana Boulevard interchange, the Winrock is attached to Albuquerque's second-largest shopping center, Winrock Center. Its buildings are wrapped around a private lagoon and garden featuring Mandarin ducks, giant koi (carp), and an impressive waterfall.

The comfortable rooms, many of which have private patios overlooking the lagoon, feature a pastel Southwestern-motif decor. The Club Room offers a breakfast buffet each morning. The hotel offers valet laundry, a heated outdoor swimming pool, and guest Laundromat.

AIRPORT

This district lies south of Central Avenue (Route 66) and primarily east of I-25, and includes Kirtland Air Force Base and Albuquerque International Airport. Most accommodations here are along Yale or Gibson boulevards near the airport entrance.

MODERATE

Best Western Fred Harvey. 2910 Yale Blvd. SE, Albuquerque, NM 87106. ☎ **800/ 227-1117** or 505/843-7000. Fax 505/843-6307. 266 rms. A/C TV TEL. $93–$103 double. AE, CB, DC, DISC, MC, V. Free parking.

No accommodation is closer to the airport than the Best Western Fred Harvey, which is literally a stone's throw north of the main terminal. It caters to air travelers with a 24-hour desk, shuttle service, and overnight valet laundry. The rooms are furnished with king-size or double beds, four-drawer dressers, leather easy chairs with ottomans, cable TV/radios, and phones. There are two restaurants on the premises. Room service, courtesy van, valet laundry, and complimentary shoeshine are available. Facilities include an outdoor swimming pool, self-service laundry, coed sauna, two all-weather tennis courts, and a gift shop.

✪ **Courtyard by Marriott.** 1920 Yale Blvd. SE, Albuquerque, NM 87106. ☎ **800/321-2211** or 505/843-6600. Fax 505/843-8740. 150 rms, 12 suites. A/C TV TEL. $89 double; $84–$103 suite. Weekend packages available. AE, CB, DC, DISC, MC, V.

Opened in 1990, this four-story member of the Marriott family is built around an attractively landscaped courtyard reminiscent of a village green, complete with shake-roofed bandstand. The white-marbled lobby floor is also filled with greenery. Families appreciate the security system: Access is only by key card between 11pm and 6am. The rooms feature walnut furniture and decor in pastel tones. Among the nicer touches are coffee and tea service from a 190° faucet, full-length mirrors, full-size writing desks, voice mail, clock radios, and massage showerheads. Refrigerators are available by request at no charge.

The coffee shop is open daily for breakfast and dinner. There is an adjacent lounge. The hotel provides valet laundry, courtesy van, and rooms for nonsmokers. Guest facilities include an indoor swimming pool, whirlpool, exercise room, and Laundromat.

Ⓢ **Radisson Inn.** 1901 University Blvd. SE, Albuquerque, NM 87106. ☎ **800/333-3333** or 505/247-0512. Fax 505/843-7148. 148 rms. A/C TV TEL. $75–$85 double. AE, CB, DC, DISC, MC, V. Free parking.

The Spanish Colonial–style Radisson (which is scheduled for renovation in 1997) is a mile from the airport. It's nice to be away from the hubbub, especially when you can lounge on the spacious deck of the swimming pool on the landscaped grounds. The rooms are furnished with king- or queen-size beds, two-drawer credenzas, tables and chairs, and Spectravision movie channels. In addition, each room is equipped with a hair dryer and every guest room features voice-mail phone systems with data ports.

Diamondback's Restaurant specializes in Southwestern and American cuisine. Coyote's Cantina is a popular watering hole. The hotel offers limited room service, valet laundry, 24-hour courtesy van, year-round outdoor swimming pool and whirlpool, and guest use of a nearby health club.

INEXPENSIVE

Best Western Airport Inn. 2400 Yale Blvd. SE, Albuquerque, NM 87106. ☎ **800/528-1234** or 505/242-7022. Fax 505/243-0620. 120 rms. A/C TV TEL. $62–$69 double. Rates include breakfast. AE, CB, DC, DISC, MC, V.

A landscaped garden courtyard behind the hotel is a lovely place to relax on cloudless days. The rooms, not the most attractive in town, contain standard furnishings and cable TV; local phone calls are free. Deluxe units have refrigerators. Breakfast is served free in rooms, or guests can get a coupon good for $3 off their morning meal at the adjacent Village Inn. The hotel has a courtesy van on call from 6am to midnight and offers valet laundry. Guests may use the outdoor swimming pool and Jacuzzi.

La Quinta Motor Inn. 2116 Yale Blvd. SE, Albuquerque, NM 87106. ☎ **800/531-5900** or 505/243-5500. Fax 505/247-8288. 105 rms. A/C TV TEL. $68 double. AE, CB, DC, DISC, ER, JCB, MC, V.

Rooms at La Quinta are appointed in pleasant, modern tones. Each has one king-size or two extralong double beds, a credenza, a table and chairs, a satellite TV/radio with pay in-house movies, and individually controlled heating and air-conditioning. Local phone calls are free. There's also an outdoor swimming pool. Coffee is on 24 hours in the lobby, and Goody's restaurant is adjacent to the motel.

Other La Quinta Motor Inns in Albuquerque are located at 5241 San Antonio Dr. NE, off I-25 at Journal Center (☎ **505/821-9000,** fax 505/821-2399; 130 rooms); and at I-40 and San Mateo Boulevard (☎ **505/884-3591;** 106 rooms). All have the same rates and facilities, including adjacent restaurants.

JOURNAL CENTER/NORTH CITY

North of Montgomery Boulevard, the focal point is the I-25 interchange with Osuna Road and San Mateo Boulevard. On the west side of the freeway, the Journal Center business park is dominated by the giant pyramid of the Holiday Inn. East of the freeway, at San Mateo and Academy boulevards, numerous hotels, restaurants, and shopping complexes dominate.

EXPENSIVE

Amberley Suite Hotel. 7620 Pan American Fwy. NE, Albuquerque, NM 87109. ☎ **800/333-9806** or 505/823-1300. Fax 505/823-2896. 170 rms, all suites. A/C FRIDGE TV TEL. $94–$104 single or double, $20 higher during balloon fiesta. Discounts for longer stays, weekend arrivals, or corporate or government travelers. Extra person $10. AE, CB, DC, DISC, MC, V.

Every room in the recently renovated Amberley Suite Hotel is a one- or two-room suite. They're fully carpeted units, most with a living room/kitchenette and separate bedroom; the deluxe king is an efficiency studio with a kitchen area. Kitchen facilities include a refrigerator filled with complimentary beverages, microwave oven, coffeemaker, pots, pans, and utensils. Each living room has a swivel rocker with an ottoman and cable television. Every bathroom is provided with a built-in hair dryer. Watson's Cafe and Deli serves an all-you-can-eat breakfast buffet and a summer patio barbecue Tuesday through Thursday. The hotel manager hosts a happy-hour reception Wednesday at 5:30pm with cocktails, hors d'oeuvres, live music, and trivia games. The hotel also provides a 24-hour courtesy car (within 2-mile radius), free airport shuttle, and valet laundry. Guest facilities include an outdoor swimming pool, sauna, hot tub, weight/exercise room, and Laundromat.

✪ **Holiday Inn Pyramid.** 5151 San Francisco Rd. NE, Albuquerque, NM 87109. ☎ **800/544-0623**, 800/HOLIDAY, or 505/821-3333. Fax 505/828-0230. 311 rms, 55 suites. A/C TV TEL. $110–$140 double; $115–$300 suite. AE, CB, DC, DISC, JCB, MC, V.

Driving north from Albuquerque toward Santa Fe, you can't help being startled by the spectacular stepped Aztec pyramid that seems to rise from nowhere on the west side of the I-25 freeway. It's meant to catch your attention: This is a major hotel and convention complex. Reached via the Paseo del Norte Exit 232 from I-25, it's a monument to the possibilities of modern-day hotel architecture. The 10 guest floors focus around a "hollow" skylit core. Vines drape from planter boxes on the balconies, and a fountain falls five stories between the two glass elevators to a pool below. The Aztec theme is perpetuated in the sand-and-cream–colored decor and the figures etched into the glass facing the fountain, opposite the entrance. The color scheme extends to the spacious rooms. Rooms with kitchenettes are available.

Dining/Entertainment: The Terrace Restaurant is open daily for breakfast, lunch, and dinner. The Palm Court, located adjacent to the Terrace, has a baby grand piano bar which opens daily at 11am. The Pyramid Club, a high-energy dance club, is open Wednesday through Saturday and features some of the Southwest's best DJs.

Services: Room service, full-service concierge, 24-hour courtesy airport shuttle, valet laundry.

Facilities: Indoor/outdoor swimming pool, sauna, two whirlpools, health club with weights and exercise room. Jogging trails wind through the 313-acre Journal Center business park.

MODERATE

ⓢ **Wyndham Garden Hotel.** 6000 Pan American Fwy. NE (I-25 at San Mateo Blvd.), Albuquerque, NM 87109. ☎ **800/996-3426** or 505/821-9451. Fax 505/858-0239. 151 rms. A/C TV TEL. $94 double. AE, CB, DC, DISC, MC, V.

The Wyndham doesn't try to be as grand as the Pyramid (see above), but it does have a five-story lobby atrium with fountains of its own. All rooms have private balconies (patios on the ground floor), as well as standard, comfortable furnishings, coffeemakers, in-room safes, and computer data ports. *USA Today* is delivered to guest rooms Monday through Friday.

The Garden Cafe is open daily for the breakfast buffet, lunch, and dinner. The Atrium Lounge is a quiet, comfortable place to enjoy cocktails or after-dinner drinks. Services and facilities include complimentary airport shuttle (from 7am to 11pm), guest laundry, fax and copy service, and an indoor/outdoor heated swimming pool.

INEXPENSIVE

Hampton Inn. 5101 Ellison NE, Albuquerque, NM 87109. ☎ **800/HAMPTON** or 505/344-1555. Fax 505/345-2216. 125 rms. A/C TV TEL. $65 double. Children under 18 stay free in parents' room. Rates include continental breakfast. AE, CB, DC, DISC, MC, V.

These sound-insulated rooms offer cost-conscious travelers standard furnishings, remote-control cable TV, and free local phone calls. The inn has an outdoor swimming pool, and guests have privileges at a health club located one mile away. This hotel is a particularly good choice for those attending the annual balloon fiesta in October, or for people who are planning trips to Santa Fe. The coffeepot is on in the lobby 24 hours.

BED-&-BREAKFASTS
DOWNTOWN/OLD TOWN

The W. E. Mauger Estate. 701 Roma Ave. NW, Albuquerque, NM 87102. ☎ **505/242-8755.** Fax 505/842-8835. 8 rms, 1 suite. $79–$115 double. Rates include full breakfast. AE, DC, MC, V.

A restored Queen Anne–style home constructed in 1897, this former residence of wool baron William Mauger is listed on the National Register of Historic Places. Today it is a wonderfully atmospheric Old West/Victorian–style bed-and-breakfast, with high ceilings and rich brass appointments. It's located close to downtown and Old Town, just five blocks from the convention center and only 5 miles from the airport. All rooms feature period furnishings, private baths with showers, and one has a balcony. A full breakfast is served each morning, in indoor and outdoor dining rooms.

ON THE OUTSKIRTS

✪ **Casa del Granjero.** 414 C de Baca Lane NW, Albuquerque, NM 87114. ☎ **800/701-4144** or 505/897-4144. Fax 505/897-4144. 7 rms. $79–$149 double. Extra person $20. Rates include breakfast. MC, V.

From the pygmy goats to the old restored wagon out front, Casa del Granjero ("The Farmer's House") is true to its name. The Great Room has an enormous sculptured adobe fireplace, comfortable bancos (benches) for lounging, a library, and scores of Old West and Native American artifacts. The guest rooms are beautifully furnished and decorated. Most have fireplaces. In the morning, breakfast is served at the spectacular dining room table or on the portal. Catered lunches and dinners are also available by arrangement. There's an outdoor hot tub available for guest use. Smoking is permitted outdoors only, and pets are not permitted.

Hacienda Antigua. 6708 Tierra Dr., NW, Albuquerque, NM 87107. ☎ **800/201-2986** or 505/345-5399. 5 rms (all with bath). A/C. $85–$125 double. Extra person $25. Rates include breakfast. AE, CB, DISC, MC, V.

Located on the north side of Albuquerque (20 minutes from the airport), just off Osuna Road, this 200-year-old adobe home was once the first stagecoach stop out of Old Town in Albuquerque. Owned for two centuries by the Yrissaris family, the hacienda retained its old world charm; when Ann Dunlap and Melinda Moffit bought it, they were careful to preserve the building's historic aspects while transforming it into a beautiful bed-and-breakfast.

A traditional "ducking door" in the Don Pablo Suite allows guests access to the beautifully landscaped courtyard. La Capilla, the home's former chapel, is furnished with a queen-size bed, a fireplace, and a beautiful carving of San Ysidro (the patron saint of farmers). The Emilia Room features a private courtyard entrance, a massive adobe fireplace, and an oversize clawfoot bathtub that dates from 1897. All rooms have unstocked minirefrigerators. A gourmet breakfast is served in the garden during warm weather and by the fire in winter. Guests also have use of the pool and hot tub.

La Hacienda Grande. 21 Baros Lane, Bernalillo, NM 87004. ☎ **505/867-1887.** Fax 505/867-4621. 6 rms (all with bath). A/C. $89–$115 double. Extra person $10. Rates include breakfast. AE, DISC, MC, V. Free parking.

This completely restored adobe home, with two-foot-thick walls, is more than 250 years old. It was one of two original stagecoach stops and is reported to have had the very first adobe stables and an adobe corral, built to prevent horse theft. It sits on four acres of land that were once part of the original 100-square-mile Spanish land grant; the kitchen was once used as a chapel for this area. The courtyard, surrounded by high adobe walls, has a vortex, which had special significance to the local native tribespeople who often came here to pray and hold ceremonies. Not long after they purchased the property, the owners learned that during the Civil War gold and silver were often stored here because the walled courtyard was a perfect fortress (its roofline was easily patrolled).

The guest rooms, all featuring custom-crafted furniture, are comfortable and inviting. All rooms have small sitting areas, and five have wood-burning kiva fireplaces (one is a lovely freestanding clay fireplace). Brick or tile floors are covered with throw rugs. There are phone jacks in each room, and phones are available at the front desk.

In addition, televisions and VCRs are available upon request. Early each morning, thermoses of coffee are left outside each guest room, and later breakfast is served in the dining room. Smoking is prohibited except on the patio.

Hacienda Vargas. El Camino Real (P.O. Box 307), Algodones, NM 87001. ☎ **800/261-0006** or 505/867-9115. 7 rms (all with bath). $79–$149 double. Extra person $15. MC, V.

Unassuming in its elegance, Hacienda Vargas is located right on old Route 66. Owned and operated by the DeVargas family, the inn is situated in the small town of Algodones, about 20 miles from Albuquerque. It's a good place to stay if you're planning on spending time in both Santa Fe and Albuquerque. The walls in the entry hallway are hung with the works of local artists (for sale), and each of the guest rooms has a private entrance. All rooms are furnished with New Mexican antiques; each is individually decorated, and all have handmade kiva fireplaces. A full breakfast is served every morning in the dining room. The only drawback here is that train tracks run directly parallel to the back of the house—during my stay the last train went by at around midnight. At all other times, the inn is very quiet and restful.

The Sandhill Crane Bed-and-Breakfast. 389 Camino Hermosa, Corrales, NM 87048 ☎ **800/375-2445** or 505/898-2445. Fax 505/898-2445. 3 rms. A/C TV TEL. $75–$145 double. Rates include breakfast. AE, MC, V. Free parking.

This lovely bed-and-breakfast is located about 20 minutes from Albuquerque in the sleepy little town of Corrales. It's a great place to stay if you want to explore the city but don't want to stay right downtown. Wisteria-draped walls surround the renovated adobe hacienda, and each room is uniquely decorated in a Southwestern style. For families or friends traveling together, the Outlaw Wing (two rooms with connecting bath, small kitchen, and private entrance) is a great choice. All rooms have cable TV and phone jacks for those who want a TV or telephone. Breakfast, which is served on the patio in warmer weather, includes fruit drinks, bagels, muffins, or homemade bread, as well as a special hot entrée on weekends.

Sarabande. 5637 Rio Grande Blvd. NW, Albuquerque, NM 87107. ☎ **800/506-4923** or 505/345-4923. Fax 505/345-9130. 3 rms (all with bath or shower). A/C TV. $85–$125 double. Rates include breakfast. MC, V. Free parking.

"Absolutely charming" is the best way I can describe this bed-and-breakfast. Once you pass through the front gate and into the beautifully tended, fountained courtyard gardens, you'll forget that you're staying on the fringes of a big city. The rooms are modern and bright. The Rose Room has a wonderful Japanese soaking tub and kiva fireplace. The Iris Room, with its stained-glass window depicting irises, has a king-size bed. Both rooms open out onto a wisteria-shaded patio. Out back are a 50-foot heated lap pool and a hot tub (it can be used through the winter). On the other side of the lap pool is the Garden Room, which is my favorite. The light is spectacular, and one of the focal points of the room is an enormous old-time refrigerator (now used for storage). The Garden Room has a shower only. There is a library stocked with magazines, books by local authors, and books about New Mexico (including local sports and recreation). The owners are avid hikers and will be happy to recommend hiking options for you. All-terrain bikes are available for guest use free of charge. Breakfast may be served in the courtyard or the dining room.

CAMPING

Albuquerque Central Koa. 12400 Skyline Rd. NE, Albuquerque, NM 87123. ☎ **505/296-2729.**

Facilities include 200 sites, bathhouse, guest laundry, outdoor swimming pool (open summers only), convenience store. Cabins available.

Albuquerque North Koa. 555 Hill Rd., Bernalillo, NM 87004. ☎ **800/624-9767** or 505/867-5227.

Facilities include 101 sites, laundry, outdoor swimming pool (open May to October), playground, convenience store, cafe, free outdoor movies. Free pancake breakfast daily. Reservations recommended.

Albuquerque West RV Park and Campground. 5739 Ouray NW, Albuquerque, NM 87120. ☎ **505/831-1912.**

103 sites, restrooms, shower, laundry, phones, limited groceries/RV supplies. There is a pool.

American RV Park of Albuquerque. 13500 Coronado Fwy. SW, Albuquerque, NM 87121. ☎ **800/282-8885** or 505/831-3545.

Facilities include 186 sites, picnic area, bathhouse, guest laundry, heated swimming pool, playground, outdoor games area, movies, convenience store.

4 Dining

DOWNTOWN/OLD TOWN
EXPENSIVE

Antiquity. 112 Romero NW (in Old Town). ☎ **505/247-3545.** Reservations recommended. Main courses $16.95–$24.95. AE, DC, DISC, MC, V. Daily 5–9pm. FRENCH/CONTINENTAL.

Antiquity is something of a surprise in this Old Town neighborhood, which is filled with snack shops and Mexican restaurants that have been around for decades, but it's a nice surprise. Antiquity has been around long enough now (10 years) to have earned a good reputation. Small dining rooms, punctuated by an enormous open grill, are subtly decorated in Southwest style with Mexican touches, making this an intimate spot for a romantic dinner. Classical music adds a finishing touch. Appetizers include standard, well-prepared dishes, such as escargots and French onion soup. The house special is a dish known as Henry the Fourth (fillet of beef served with an artichoke heart and béarnaise), and it is excellent. The salmon en papillote, my favorite, is perfectly done, tender and flaky. Desserts like chocolate mousse and crepes are normally quite rich but well worth the workout you'll have to do the next morning.

Conrad's Downtown. 2nd at Copper NW (in La Posada de Albuquerque). ☎ **505/242-9090.** Reservations recommended. Main courses $12.50–$18.75; lunch $5.95–$7.25. AE, CB, DC, DISC, MC, V. Daily 6:30–2pm and 5:30–10pm. Tapas bar daily 11am–10pm. SPANISH/MEXICAN.

Conrad's, one of Albuquerque's best restaurants, is located on the first floor of the historic La Posada hotel built by Conrad Hilton, just off the lobby. A large, classic bar is the focal point around which diners enjoy Spanish and Mexican specialties such as tapas and a delicious *huachinango con tequila toronja vinagre* (sautéed red snapper topped with tequila vinaigrette and grapefruit) at lunch. Dinner entrées include a delicious *cordoorniz negrado con chipotle y mantequilla con tequila* (blackened quail with a mixture of lime and tequila, chipotle, and cilantro in a creamy butter sauce) and an interestingly textured *trucha con maiz azul y tequila mantequilla* (red trout breaded in a spicy blue-corn meal with a lime and tequila butter). A few beef and pork dishes are offered as well. All entrées are served with polenta, black beans, and Spanish rice or pesto poblano. The paellas (for one or two) are quite good here as well, though

Central Albuquerque Dining

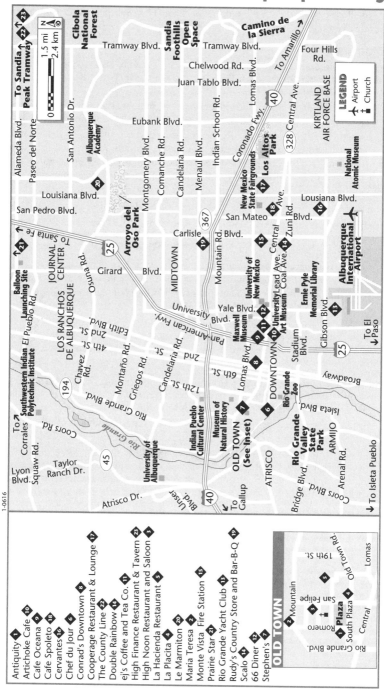

you'll have to wait 20 to 30 minutes for them. The atmosphere is casual. Conrad's offers complimentary valet parking.

MODERATE

⊕ **Artichoke Cafe.** 424 Central Ave. SE. ☎ **505/243-0200.** Reservations recommended. Main courses $8.95–$19.95. AE, CB, DC, DISC, MC, V. Mon–Fri 11am–2:30pm; Mon–Sat 5:30–10pm. CONTINENTAL.

The no-frills decor here is clean and tasteful, with modern art prints on azure walls, white linens on tables shaded by standing plants, and classical music playing in the background. Start your meal with an artichoke appetizer, then go on to a main dish such as baked chicken stuffed with goat cheese, spinach, and roasted red peppers (wonderful!), or baby clams in a sauce of white wine, garlic, leeks, and cream. Crepes, pastas, salads, sandwiches, and the like are popular at lunch. The cafe has an excellent list of Californian and French wines. Over the years, the Artichoke Cafe has, in my opinion, consistently been one of the area's best restaurants.

High Noon Restaurant and Saloon. 425 San Felipe St. NW. ☎ **505/765-1455.** Reservations recommended. Main courses $8.75–$19.25. AE, CB, DC, DISC, MC, V. Mon–Sat 11am–3pm and 5–10pm, Sun noon–9pm. STEAKS/SEAFOOD/NEW MEXICAN.

One of Albuquerque's oldest buildings, this restaurant (now in business for more than 20 years) boasts a 19th-century saloon atmosphere with stuccoed walls, high and low ceiling beams, and historical photos on the walls. One photo depicts the original 1785 structure, which now comprises the building's foyer and santo room. The dinner menu offers a choice of beef dishes, such as the house-specialty pepper steak sautéed with brandy; fish dishes, including red trout amandine; game dishes, including buffalo, venison, and caribou; and regional favorites, such as burritos, enchiladas, and fajitas.

La Hacienda Restaurant. 302 San Felipe St. NW (at North Plaza). ☎ **505/242-3131.** Reservations recommended for large parties. Main courses $7.25–$14.95; lunch $4.50–$8.95. AE, CB, DC, MC, V. Daily 11am–9:30pm. NEW MEXICAN/AMERICAN.

A mural girding La Hacienda's outer wall depicts the establishment of Albuquerque and the construction of this Villa de Albuquerque at the turn of the 18th century. Diners enter this cozy restaurant through a large gift shop. The interior, with an intimate, laid-back atmosphere, is adorned with hanging plants and chile *ristras* (dried chiles strung together for cooking as well as decorative use). The menu is predominantly regional, with such house specialties as beef or chicken fajitas, *carne adovada* (sautéed dried pork smothered in red chile), *tostadas compuestas* (a corn tortilla cup topped with beef, beans, melted cheese, and red or green chile), and tortilla-chile soup. Steaks, shrimp, and other American meals are also offered. Desserts include the traditional flan and fried ice cream.

⊕ **Maria Teresa.** 618 Rio Grande Blvd. NW. ☎ **505/242-3900.** Reservations recommended. Main courses $13–$26. AE, MC, V. Daily 11am–2:30pm, 5–9pm. NEW MEXICAN/CONTINENTAL.

The city's most beautiful and classically elegant restaurant, Maria Teresa is located in the 1840s Salvador Armijo House, a National Historic property furnished with Victorian antiques and paintings. Built with 32-inch-thick adobe walls, the house exemplifies 19th-century New Mexican architecture, when building materials were few and defense a prime consideration. The house had 12 rooms, 7 of which (along with a large patio) are now reserved for diners. Another room is home to the 1840 bar and lounge.

The menu features salads, pastas, sandwiches, seafood, and New Mexican specialties for lunch; and a wide choice of traditionally continental gourmet dinners, from seared filet mignon with béarnaise sauce or seared New York cut venison with sun-dried tomatoes and olives to poached salmon with Dijon basil hollandaise.

✪ **Stephens.** 1311 Tijeras Ave. NW (at 14th St. and Central Ave.). ☎ **505/842-1773.** Reservations recommended. Main courses $7.25–$24.95. AE, DC, MC, V. Mon–Fri 11am–2pm; Sun–Thurs 5:30–9:30pm, Fri–Sat 5:30–10:30pm. CONTEMPORARY AMERICAN.

This modern, open, and airy restaurant was inspired by Mexico City's Hacienda Angel and features interior decor by the noted designer Richard Worthen. French windows provide a view of the European-style garden and elegant fountain. Start with a fine baked Brie with almonds, apples, and honey in puff pastry or the black bean pasta ravioli stuffed with Montrachet and Fontina cheeses served with a roasted red pepper sauce. If you're dining on a Friday or Saturday night, I would recommend the chicken Anasazi (chicken breast stuffed with spinach, sun-dried tomatoes, and pistachio pesto served on spinach fettucine); otherwise, the shrimp and scallop pastry box (with fresh mushrooms in a light champagne sauce) is a good choice. Other dishes on the menu include filet mignon, loin lamb chops, New York strip steak, and several pasta creations. There is a spa menu as well as daily dessert specials, and the award-winning wine list features more than 300 choices.

INEXPENSIVE

Chef du Jour. 119 San Pasquale SW. ☎ **505/247-8998.** Menu items $2.50–$6.75. No credit cards. Mon–Fri 11am–2pm. ECLECTIC.

The decor certainly isn't much to talk about at Chef du Jour, but that's not why people are flocking to this popular lunch spot located just a block from Old Town. Once you get a taste of what's on the menu (which changes every week), you'll be coming back for more. Recent menu offerings included spicy garlic soup, a great garden burger, green-corn tamales (served with Southwest mango salsa), and marinated grilled chicken breast (on whole wheat fruit and nut bread with Jamaican banana ketchup). There are also sandwiches and a salad du jour. Chef du Jour has both indoor and some outdoor tables; if you call in advance, the restaurant will fax you a copy of its current menu.

⑤ **La Placita.** 208 San Felipe St. NW (Old Town Plaza). ☎ **505/247-2204.** Reservations recommended for large parties. Lunch $4.25–$7.25; dinner $6.25–$14.50. AE, DISC, MC, V. Daily 11am–9pm. NEW MEXICAN/AMERICAN.

Native American artisans spread their wares on the sidewalk outside the old Casa de Armijo, built by a wealthy Hispanic family in the early 18th century. The 283-year-old adobe hacienda, which faces the Old Town Plaza, features hand-carved wooden doorways, deep-sunk windows, and an ancient patio. Fine regional art and furnishings decorate the five dining rooms and an upstairs gallery. The house favorite is a full Mexican dinner, which includes an enchilada colorado de queso, chile rellenos, taco de carne, frijoles con queso, arroz español, ensalada, and two sopaipillas. There is also a variety of beef, chicken, and fish selections.

MIDTOWN/UPTOWN
MODERATE

Cafe Oceana. 1414 Central Ave. SE. ☎ **505/247-2233.** Reservations recommended. Main courses $11.95–$13.95. AE, DC, DISC, MC, V. Mon–Thurs 11am–11pm, Fri 11am–11:30pm, Sat 5–11:30pm. Oyster hour Mon–Thurs 3–6:30pm and 10–11pm, Fri 3–6:30pm and 10:30–11:30pm, Sat 5–7pm and 10:30–11:30pm. SEAFOOD.

The Cafe Oceana is and has long been Albuquerque's favorite oyster bar and fresh seafood cafe. In a New Orleans–style dining room with high ceilings and hardwood floors, you can enjoy fresh oysters, fresh fish daily, scallops, crab rellenos (for the New Mexican touch), and the house special: beer-batter-fried shrimp Oceana. The daily oyster hour features two-for-one oysters and boiled shrimp. If you're really in the mood for New Orleans cuisine, you can also order red beans and rice here.

Cooperage Restaurant and Lounge. 7220 Lomas Blvd. NE. ☎ **505/255-1657.** Reservations recommended. Main courses $9–$22; lunch $4–$8. AE, CB, DC, DISC, MC, V. Mon–Fri 11am–2:30pm, Sat noon–2:30pm; Mon–Thurs 5–10pm, Fri–Sat 5–11pm, Sun noon–9pm. STEAKS & SEAFOOD.

The Cooperage is shaped to make you feel as if you're in a gigantic beer barrel. Circular and wood paneled, its walls are decorated with reproductions of 19th-century paintings and depictions of coopers at work making barrels.

The dinner menu features a variety of seafood and beef dishes, including lobster and prime rib. The restaurant also has a great 40-item salad bar, and is fully licensed. There's live music for dancing Wednesday through Saturday nights.

Cooperage West is at 10200 Corrales Rd. NW, in Corrales (☎ **505/898-5555**).

✪ **Monte Vista Fire Station.** 3201 Central Ave. NE, Nob Hill. ☎ **505/255-2424.** Reservations recommended. Main courses $12.95–$17.95. AE, MC, V. Mon–Fri 11am–2:30pm; Sun–Thurs 5–10:30pm, Fri–Sat 5–11pm. Bar open to 2am Mon–Sat, to midnight Sun. CONTEMPORARY AMERICAN.

The Fire Station has been a city landmark since it was built in pure Pueblo Revival style in 1936. Its occupants no longer make fire calls, however—they concentrate instead on serving a unique menu in an art deco setting. Luncheon diners can start with crab cakes served with goat cheese on assorted baby greens with ancho chile aioli, then go on to seared tenderloin tips surrounding a currant almond couscous timbal with a Cajun cream sauce. Popular dinner appetizers are citrus marinated ostrich fajitas with onions, peppers, roasted poblano chiles and pineapple salsa; and grilled pheasant and chicken sausage with mixed peppers served on greens with caramelized apples and currants and wild mushroom potato cakes. Main courses include blue corn dusted poblano rellenos and wild mushroom tamales served with ancho chile sauce, as well as chile-honey glazed grilled salmon served with gourmet greens, ginger red onion relish, and sweet potato puree. Try the tiramisu for dessert.

✪ **Scalo.** 3500 Central Ave. SE (Nob Hill). ☎ **505/255-8782.** Reservations recommended. Main courses $7.95–$16.95; lunch $5.75–$9. AE, CB, DC, DISC, MC, V. Mon–Sat 11:30am–2:30pm and 5:30–11:30pm, Sun 5–9pm. Bar, Mon–Sat 11am–1am. NORTHERN ITALIAN.

Scalo has a simple bistro-style elegance, with white linen-clothed tables indoors, and outdoor tables in a covered, temperature-controlled patio. The kitchen, which makes its own pasta and breads, specializes in contemporary adaptations of classical northern Italian cuisine.

Seasonal menus focus on New Mexico–grown produce. Featured appetizers include *calamaretti fritti* (fried baby squid served with a spicy marinara and lemon aioli) and *caprini con pumante* (local goat cheese with fresh foccacia, capers, tapenade, and a roasted garlic spread). There's a selection of pastas for lunch and dinner, as well as meat, chicken, and fish dishes. The *filetto con salsa balsamica* (grilled fillet of beef with rosemary, green peppercorns, garlic, and a balsamic demi-glacé sauce) is one of my favorites, and the *Battuta di Vitello Mandorlata* (veal scaloppini prepared with toasted almonds, sun-dried cranberries, and Pinot Grigio) is also quite good.

INEXPENSIVE

Double Rainbow. 3416 Central Ave. SE. ☎ **505/255-6633.** Reservations not accepted. All menu items under $8. AE, DISC, MC, V. Daily 6:30–midnight. CAFE/BAKERY.

If you're a people-watcher worth your salt, you shouldn't miss the Double Rainbow, located in Albuquerque's historic Nob Hill district. Of course, people-watching is only one reason to stop by—Double Rainbow has great sandwiches, ice cream, breads, pastries, cakes, and coffee. All baking is done on the premises daily. One of the best things about this place is its enormous selection of magazines—more than 700 titles, ranging from comic books to film and fashion magazines to a travel magazine for gays and lesbians. Double Rainbow has another branch at 4501 Juan Tabo NE (☎ **505/275-8311**), which features a large outdoor patio, a slightly more extensive menu, and live music on Thursday nights as well as Saturday and Sunday mornings.

☉ ej's Coffee and Tea Co. 2201 Silver Ave. SE. ☎ **505/268-CAFE.** Breakfast $2.50–$5.95; lunch $3.95–$7.50; dinner $5.25–$8.75. MC, V. Mon–Thurs 7am–11pm, Fri 7am–midnight, Sat 8am–midnight, Sun 8am–9pm. NATURAL FOODS.

A popular coffeehouse just a couple of blocks from the UNM campus, ej's caters to natural-foods lovers. Breakfasts include granola and croissants from ej's own bakery. Lunch features homemade vegetarian soups, tempeh burgers, organic turkey sandwiches, and cheese enchiladas. The gourmet dinner menu lists shrimp linguine, spinach fettuccine Alfredo, Monterey chicken, and a vegetarian stir-fry.

Rudy's Country Store and Bar-B-Q. 2321 Carlisle NE (at I-40). ☎ **505/884-4000.** Main courses $3.75–$10.95. AE, DISC, MC, V. Daily 10am–10pm. BARBECUE.

Don't be put off by the picnic tables in this otherwise nondescript barbecue spot. This is the place for delectable barbecue brisket, spare ribs, short ribs, chicken, and turkey, among other things. The sauce, which is quite thin and spicy with lots of vinegar, is up to you (bottles are on each table).

⑤ 66 Diner. 1405 Central Ave. NE. ☎ **505/247-1421.** $2.95–$6.95. AE, DISC, MC, V. Mon–Thurs 11am–11pm, Fri 11am–midnight, Sat 8am–midnight, Sun 8am–10pm. AMERICAN.

Like a trip back in time to the days when Martin Milner and George Maharis got "their kicks on Route 66," this thoroughly 1950s-style diner comes complete with Seeburg jukebox and full-service soda fountain. The white caps make great hamburgers, along with meat loaf sandwiches, grilled liver and onions, and chicken-fried steaks. Ham-and-egg and pancake breakfasts are served Saturday and Sunday mornings. For those of you who may have visited 66 Diner in the past you'll notice some changes, and that's because the original restaurant suffered a devastating fire a couple of years back. Thanks to tremendous community spirit and a great deal of hard work, 66 Diner is once again up and running. Beer and wine are available.

AIRPORT
MODERATE

Rio Grande Yacht Club. 2500 Yale Blvd. SE. ☎ **505/243-6111.** Reservations suggested at dinner. Main courses $9.95–$17.95; lunch $4.50–$7.95. AE, CB, DC, MC, V. Mon–Fri 11am–2pm; daily 5:30–10:30pm. SEAFOOD.

Red, white, and blue sails are draped beneath the skylight of this large room, which is dominated by a tropical garden. Jimmy Buffett himself, the contemporary sailor's chanteur, couldn't have created a better milieu for the Caribbean yachtsman-wannabe. Fresh fish, of course, is the order of the day. Catfish, whitefish, bluefish, salmon, grouper, sole, mahimahi, and other denizens of the deep are prepared in a variety of ways. Diners can also opt for shrimp, certified Angus beef steaks and ribs, chicken, and seafood-and-steak or prime rib combinations. Sandwiches and salads are served at lunch. The cozy lounge has a full bar and an outdoor courtyard.

INEXPENSIVE

Cervantes. 5801 Gibson Blvd. at San Pedro Blvd. ☎ **505/262-2253.** Reservations suggested at dinner. Lunch $3.50–$6.25; dinner $5.75–$12.95. AE, CB, DC, MC, V. Daily 11am–10pm. Closed major holidays. NEW MEXICAN.

An impressive classical Spanish decor hides behind Cervantes's rather unimpressive exterior, near Kirtland Air Force Base. New Mexican dinners with all the trimmings are extremely reasonably priced: A taco, tamale, enchilada, and carne adovada combo plate, for instance, is just $5.75, including beans, rice, chile, and sopaipillas.

There's another Cervantes, this one with a piano bar, at 10030 Central Ave. NE, near Manzano Mesa (☎ **505/275-3266**).

JOURNAL CENTER/NORTH CITY

EXPENSIVE

High Finance Restaurant and Tavern. 40 Tramway Rd., atop Sandia Peak. ☎ **505/243-9742.** Reservations requested. Main courses $13.95–$35. Tramway $10 with dinner reservations ($13 without). AE, DC, DISC, MC, V. Daily 11am–4pm and 5–9:30pm. CONTINENTAL.

Perched atop Sandia Peak, 2 miles above Albuquerque and the Rio Grande valley, diners at High Finance have a breathtaking panorama of New Mexico's largest city. The atmosphere inside is elegant yet casual. The menu focuses on prime rib, steaks, and fresh seafood. Diners can also choose pasta or Mexican main courses. Many tram riders just drop in for the view and a drink at the casual full-service bar. Smoking is permitted only in the bar.

✪ **Le Marmiton.** 5415 Academy Blvd. NE. ☎ **505/821-6279.** Reservations recommended. Dinner $13.95–$18.95. AE, DC, MC, V. Mon–Thurs 5–9pm, Fri–Sat 5:30–9:30pm, Sun 5:30–9pm. FRENCH.

The name means "the apprentice," but there's nothing novice about the food or presentation here. The 15 tables seat 40 people in a romantic French provincial atmosphere, with lace curtains and antique plates on shelves.

Recommended main courses include *fantaisie aux fruits de mer,* a mixture of shrimp, scallops, and crab in a mushroom-cream sauce on pastry, and *cailles,* two whole quail finished with a shallot sherry-cream sauce. If you arrive early for dinner (between 5 and 6pm) Monday through Thursday, you can take advantage of the fixed-price light dinners, which include soup or salad, a choice of main course, and coffee or tea for $7.95. There's a long wine list and great cinnamon-apple crepes for dessert.

MODERATE

Cafe Spoleto. 2813 San Mateo NE. ☎ **505/880-0897.** Reservations recommended, especially on weekends. Main courses $10–$16.25. Tues–Sun 6–9:30pm. DISC, MC, V. MEDITERRANEAN.

If you've grown a bit weary of New Mexican cuisine (if that's possible) and are looking for a nice, unpretentious Mediterranean restaurant with a casual atmosphere, try Cafe Spoleto. Salads include a grilled raddichio wrapped in pancetta with melon, which is quite nice. My pasta choice was the farfalle with sugar snap peas, mushrooms, applewood smoked bacon, and shaved Spanish manchego cheese. The natural chicken under a brick with grilled portobello mushrooms and sherry is also very tasty, and the grilled homemade sausages are definitely worth trying. There's also always a fish selection (like sautéed halibut with a spicy sweet pepper sauce with Pernod). You won't be disappointed here.

The County Line. 9600 Tramway Blvd. NE. ☎ **505/856-7477.** Reservations not accepted. Main courses $8.95–$14.95. AE, CB, DC, DISC, MC, V. Mon–Thurs 5–9pm, Fri–Sat 5–10pm, Sun 4–9pm. BARBECUE.

Although this extremely popular spot doesn't take reservations, if you call before you leave your hotel, they'll put your name on the waiting list, and by the time you get there you'll probably be next in line. If not, you can always wait at the ever-crowded bar. The restaurant is loud and always busy, but it has a spectacular view of the city lights and great food.

When you finally get a table, you'll be given a Big Chief Writing Tablet menu offering great Southwestern barbecue at very reasonable prices. You might opt for barbecued chicken or a steak grilled to perfection, along with a baked potato (with your choice of toppings), beans, and coleslaw. If you're not very hungry you should probably consider going somewhere else.

OUT OF TOWN

Some of Albuquerque's finest restaurants are outside the city. Prairie Star is about 20 miles north, via I-25 and NM 44, near Bernalillo; the Luna Mansion is about 24 miles south, also via I-25.

EXPENSIVE

✪ **Prairie Star.** 1000 Jemez Canyon Dam Rd., Bernalillo. ☎ **505/867-3327.** Reservations recommended. Main courses $15–$24. AE, DISC, MC, V. Daily 5–10pm (lounge opens at 4pm); brunch Sun 11am–2:30pm. CONTEMPORARY REGIONAL.

A sprawling adobe home, with a marvelous view across the high plains and a golf course adjacent to Sandia Peak, is host to this intimate dining experience. The 6,000-square-foot house, on a rural site leased from Santa Ana Pueblo, was built in the 1940s in Mission architectural style. Exposed vigas and full latilla ceilings, as well as hand-carved fireplaces and bancos, complement the thick adobe walls in the dining room. The art displayed on the walls is for sale. There is a lounge at the top of the circular stairway.

Diners can start with smoked quail or baked cheese in puff pastry (a blend of mascarpone and Gruyère cheese scented with toasted hazelnuts and fresh tarragon). Main courses include shrimp margarita (shrimp sautéed and flambéed with tequila, fresh tomatoes, and roasted poblano chiles, and finished with lime juice and butter), veal sweetbreads (served in puff pastry with a tarragon and wild-mushroom cream sauce), lamb loin (stuffed with roast garlic, pine nuts, basil, and goat cheese), and pan-fried Truchas trout with piñon nuts. There are daily specials.

MODERATE

The Luna Mansion. Hwys. 6 and 314, Los Lunas. ☎ **505/865-7333.** Reservations recommended. Main courses $7.95 –$19.95. AE, MC, V. Brunch Sun 11am–2pm; daily 5–9pm. AMERICAN.

This national historic landmark, 1 1/2 miles east of I-25, was built in 1881 by the Santa Fe Railroad as compensation to the Don Antonio Jose Luna family when the railroad built a track through their existing hacienda. While the two-story mansion is Southern Colonial in style, its basic construction material is adobe. A solarium, a front portico, and impressive ironwork were added in the 1920s.

The menu offers such gourmet dishes as piñon-crusted pork loin medallions with a red chile cream sauce, and chicken breast stuffed with cilantro pesto and Monterey Jack cheese. New Mexican food is also featured, and the new "Homestyle" menu ($7.95 to $9.95), which includes dessert and beverage, offers a variety of complete dinners such as sliced roast sirloin and green chile chicken pot pie. There is a full bar.

5 What to See & Do

Albuquerque's original town site, today known as Old Town, is the central point of interest for visitors to the city today. Here, centered around the plaza, are the venerable Church of San Felipe de Neri and numerous restaurants, art galleries, and crafts shops. Several important museums stand nearby.

But don't get stuck in Old Town. Elsewhere in the city are the Sandia Peak Tramway, Kirtland Air Force Base and the National Atomic Museum, the University of New Mexico with its museums, and a number of natural attractions. Within day-trip range are several Native American pueblos and a trio of national monuments.

EXPLORING OLD TOWN

A maze of cobbled courtyard walkways lead to hidden patios and gardens where many of Old Town's 150 galleries and shops are located. Adobe buildings, many refurbished in Pueblo Revival style in the 1950s, focus around the tree-shaded **Old Town Plaza,** created in 1780. Pueblo and Navajo Indian artisans often display their pottery, blankets, and silver jewelry on the sidewalks lining the plaza.

The buildings of Old Town once served as mercantile shops, grocery stores, and government offices. But the importance of Old Town as Albuquerque's commercial center declined after 1880, when the railroad came through 1.2 miles east of the plaza and businesses relocated nearer the tracks. Old Town clung to its historical and sentimental roots, but the quarter was disintegrating until it was rediscovered in the 1930s and 1940s by artisans and other shop owners and tourism took off.

The first structure built when colonists established Albuquerque in 1706 was the **Church of San Felipe de Neri,** facing the plaza on its north side. The house of worship has been in almost continuous use for 285 years. When the original building collapsed about 1790, it was reconstructed and subsequently expanded several times, all the while remaining the spiritual heart of the city. The windows are some 20 feet from the ground and its walls are four feet thick—structural details needed to make the church also serviceable as a fortress against Indian attack. A spiral stairway leading to the choir loft is built around the trunk of an ancient spruce. Confessionals, altars, and images are hand carved; Gothic spires, added in the late 19th century, give the church a European air from the outside. The church's annual parish fiesta, held the first weekend in June, brings food and traditional dancing to the plaza.

Next door to the church is the **Rectory,** built about 1793. Also on the north plaza is **Loyola Hall,** the Sister Blandina Convent, built originally of adobe in 1881 as a residence for Sisters of Charity teachers who worked in the region. When the Jesuit fathers built **Our Lady of the Angels School,** 320 Romero St., in 1877, it was the only public school in Albuquerque.

The **Antonio Vigil House,** 413 Romero St., is an adobe-style residence with traditional *viga* ends sticking out over the entrance door. The **Florencio Zamora Store,** 301 Romero St., was built in the 1890s of "pugmill" adobe for a butcher and grocer. The **Jesus Romero House,** 205 Romero St., was constructed by another

Central Albuquerque Attractions

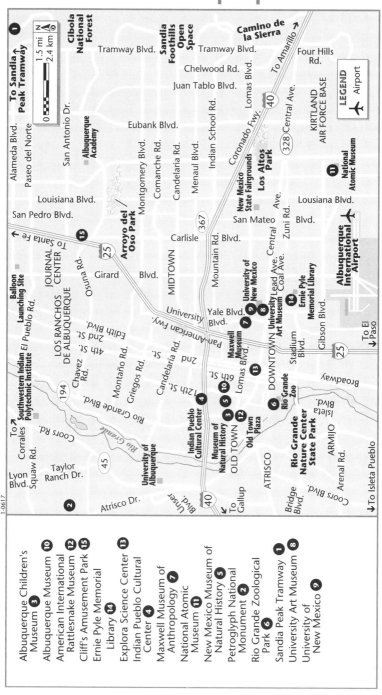

To Sandia Peak Tramway ↑

N

1.5 mi
2.4 km
0

Cibola National Forest

Sandia Foothills Open Space

Camino de la Sierra ↗

Tramway Blvd.

Tramway Blvd.

Chelwood Rd.

Juan Tablo Blvd.

To Amarillo →

Four Hills Rd.

LEGEND

✈ Airport

Alameda Blvd.

Paseo del Norte

San Antonio Dr.

Albuquerque Academy

Eubank Blvd.

Montgomery Blvd.

Comanche Rd.

Candelaria Rd.

Menaul Blvd.

Indian School Rd.

Coronado Fwy.

Lomas Blvd.

40

328 Central Ave.

KIRTLAND AIR FORCE BASE

National Atomic Museum

⓫

Louisiana Blvd.

San Pedro Blvd.

Louisiana Blvd.

Arroyo del Oso Park

New Mexico State Fairgrounds

Los Altos Park

San Mateo

Central Ave.

Zuni Rd.

Lousiana Blvd.

Blvd.

Albuquerque International Airport

✈

← To Santa Fe

JOURNAL CENTER

25

⓯

367

Carlisle

Mountain Rd. Blvd.

Balloon Launching Site

Osuna Rd.

Girard

Blvd.

MIDTOWN

University of New Mexico

University Art Museum

Lead Ave.

Coal Ave.

Ernie Pyle Memorial Library

⓮

LOS RANCHOS DE ALBUQUERQUE

El Pueblo Rd.

Edith Blvd.

2nd St.

University Blvd.

⑦ ⑨ ⑧

Yale Blvd.

Stadium Blvd.

Gibson Blvd.

To El Paso →

To Corrales

Southwestern Indian Polytechnic Institute

194

Chavez Rd.

Montaño Rd.

Griegos Rd.

4th St.

Candelaria Rd.

2nd St.

12th St.

6th St.

Maxwell Museum

⓭

Pan-American Fwy.

DOWNTOWN

Rio Grande Zoo

25

To El Paso →

Coors Rd.

Rio Grande Blvd.

Rio Grande

University of Albuquerque

⑫

Indian Pueblo Cultural Center

Museum of Natural History

OLD TOWN

③ ⑤ ⑩

④

Old Town Plaza

⑥

Rio Grande Nature Center State Park

ATRISCO

Isleta Blvd.

ARMIJO

Broadway

Lyon Blvd.

Taylor Ranch Dr.

Squaw Rd.

45

Unser Blvd.

Rio Grande

Atrisco Dr.

②

40

To Gallup →

Bridge Blvd.

Coors Blvd.

Arenal Rd.

→ To Isleta Pueblo

1-0617

Albuquerque Children's Museum ③

Albuquerque Museum ⑩

American International Rattlesnake Museum ⑫

Cliff's Amusement Park ⓯

Ernie Pyle Memorial Library ⓮

Explora Science Center ⓭

Indian Pueblo Cultural Center ④

Maxwell Museum of Anthropology ⑦

National Atomic Museum ⓫

New Mexico Museum of Natural History ⑤

Petroglyph National Monument ②

Rio Grande Zoological Park ⑥

Sandia Peak Tramway ①

University Art Museum ⑧

University of New Mexico ⑨

grocer in 1915 in "Prairie-Mediterranean" style. Just down the street, the **Jesus Romero Store,** built in 1893, has Territorial and Queen Anne structural features. On the south plaza, the **Manuel Springer House** had a hipped roof and bay windows, still visible under its commercial facade of today. The adjacent **Cristobal Armijo House,** a banker's two-story adobe, was completed in 1886 in combined Italianate and Queen Anne architectural styles.

Casa Armijo, in the 200 block of San Felipe Street, dates from before 1840; it was a headquarters for both Union and Confederate troops during the Civil War days. The nearby **Ambrosio Armijo House and Store,** also on San Felipe, an 1882 adobe structure, once had the high false front of wooden boards so typical of Old West towns in movies. The **Herman Blueher House,** at 302 San Felipe St., built by a businessman in 1898, is a three-story Italianate mansion with fancy porches on two levels, now obscured by storefronts.

The Albuquerque Museum conducts guided **walking tours** of Old Town's historic buildings during the summer at 11am Tuesday through Friday and 1pm Saturday and Sunday. The $2-per-person price includes museum admission. For visitors who don't find those times convenient, the museum publishes a brochure for a self-guided walking tour of Old Town.

The Old Town Easter Parade, held annually on the Saturday preceding Easter, brings the Easter Bunny to the streets of the quarter, along with a variety of floats and marching bands. On Christmas Eve, thousands of *luminarias* or *farolitos*—brown paper bags filled with sand and lighted candles—line the narrow streets and flat-roofed buildings surrounding the plaza.

OTHER TOP ATTRACTIONS

✪ **Sandia Peak Tramway.** 10 Tramway Loop NE. ☎ **505/856-7325** or 505/856-6419. Admission $13 adults, $10 seniors and children 5–12. Memorial Day to Labor Day daily 9am–10pm; spring and fall Thurs–Tues 9am–8pm, Wed 5–9pm; ski season Mon–Tues and Thurs–Fri 9am–8pm, Wed noon–8pm, Sat–Sun 8:30am–8pm.

The world's longest tramway extends 2.7 miles from Albuquerque's northeastern city limits to the summit of 10,378-foot Sandia Peak. A 15-minute ride up the tram is a memorable experience, rising from urban desert at its base to lush mountain foliage in the Cíbola National Forest at its peak—and dropping about 20° in temperature in the process. Animals viewed on the wild slopes from the tram occasionally include bears, bighorn sheep, deer, eagles, hawks, and a rare mountain lion. The view from the observation deck encompasses more than 11,000 square miles, well beyond Santa Fe and Los Alamos to the north.

Winter skiers often take the tram to the **Sandia Peak Ski Area,** where visitors can couple their trip with a ride on the resort's 7,500-foot double-chair lift through the spruce and ponderosa pine forests on the mountain's eastern slope. (A single ride costs $4; the chair operates from 10am to 3pm in summer, 9am to 4pm in winter.)

The Sandia Peak tram is a "jigback"; in other words, as one car approaches the top, the other nears the bottom. The two pass halfway through the trip, in the midst of a 1 1/2-mile "clear span" of unsupported cable between the second tower and the upper terminal.

There is a popular and high-priced restaurant at the tramway's summit, **High Finance** (☎ **505/243-9742;** see "Dining," above). Special tram rates apply with dinner reservations.

To reach the base of the tram, take I-25 north to the Tramway Road Exit 234 then proceed east about 5 miles on Tramway Road (NM 556); from I-40 take Exit 167 (Tramway Boulevard) and go north for approximately 9 miles.

✪ Indian Pueblo Cultural Center. 2401 12th St. NW. ☎ **800/766-4405** or 505/843-7270. Admission $3 adults, $2 seniors, $1 students; free for children 4 and under. Daily 9am–5:50pm; restaurant 7:30am–4pm. Closed New Year's Day, Thanksgiving Day, and Christmas.

Owned and operated as a nonprofit organization by the 19 pueblos of New Mexico, this is a fine place to begin an exploration of Native American culture. Located about a mile northeast of Old Town, this museum—modeled after Pueblo Bonito, a spectacular 9th-century ruin in Chaco Culture National Historic Park—consists of several parts.

In the basement, a permanent exhibit depicts the evolution from prehistory to present of the various pueblos, including displays of the distinctive handcrafts of each community. Note especially how pottery differs in concept and design from pueblo to pueblo. The displays include a series of remarkable photographs of Pueblo people taken between 1880 and 1910, a gift of the Smithsonian Institution. The Pueblo House Children's Museum, also located on the premises, is a hands-on museum that gives children the opportunity to learn about and understand the evolution of Pueblo culture.

Upstairs is an enormous (10,000-square-foot) gift shop featuring fine pottery, rugs, sandpaintings, kachinas, drums, and jewelry, among other things. Southwestern clothing and souvenirs are also available.

Every weekend throughout the year, Native American dancers perform and artisans demonstrate their crafts expertise in an outdoor arena surrounded by original murals. An annual craft fair is held on the July 4 holiday weekend, the first weekend in October, and Thanksgiving weekend.

A restaurant, open from 7:30am to 4pm, offers traditional Native American foods.

✪ Albuquerque Museum. 2000 Mountain Rd. NW. ☎ **505/243-7255.** Free admission, but donations are appreciated. Tues–Sun 9am–5pm. Closed major holidays.

The largest U.S. collection of Spanish colonial artifacts is housed here. Included are arms and armor used during the Hispanic conquest, medieval religious artifacts and weavings, maps from the 16th to 18th centuries, and coins and domestic goods traded during that era. A multimedia audiovisual presentation, *Four Centuries: A History of Albuquerque,* depicts the history of the mid–Rio Grande region from the Spanish conquest to the present. "History Hopscotch" is a hands-on history exhibit designed specifically for children. There's also a gallery of early and modern New Mexico art, with permanent and changing exhibits; a major photo archive; and a sculpture garden. Some of the exhibits scheduled for 1997 are: *Rodin: Sculpture from the B. Gerald Cantor Collection; Larry Bell Retrospective; Inventing the Southwest: Fred Harvey Company and Southwest Native Art;* and *The Art of Tibet.* From time to time children's exhibits and classes are offered. A gift shop offers a variety of souvenirs and other wares.

MORE ATTRACTIONS
University of New Mexico. Yale Blvd. NE north of Central Ave. ☎ **505/277-0111.**

The state's largest institution of higher learning stretches across an attractive 700-acre campus about 2 miles east of downtown Albuquerque, north of Central Avenue and east of University Boulevard. The six campus museums, none of which charge admission, are constructed (like other UNM buildings) in a modified Pueblo style. Popejoy Hall, in the south-central part of campus opposite Yale Park, hosts many performing arts presentations, including those of the New Mexico Symphony Orchestra; other public events are held in nearby Keller Hall and Woodward Hall.

The **Maxwell Museum of Anthropology** (☎ 505/277-4405), an internationally acclaimed repository of Southwestern anthropological finds, is situated on the west side of campus on Redondo Drive at Ash Street NE. Permanent galleries include *Ancestors,* describing four million years of human evolution, and *Peoples of the Southwest,* a 10,000-year summary. Mimbres and Pueblo pottery, Hopi kachina dolls, Navajo weavings, and a variety of regional jewelry, basketry, and textiles are on display. The collections support education and research in anthropology, archeology, and ethnology. Native American art and books about the state's cultural heritage are on sale in the museum's gift shop. It's open Monday through Friday from 9am to 4pm, Saturday from 10am to 4pm, and Sunday from noon to 4pm. Closed holidays.

The **University Art Museum** (☎ 505/277-4001), in the Fine Arts Center adjoining Popejoy Hall on Cornell Street, just north of Central Avenue, is a multilevel museum focusing on 19th- and 20th-century American and European artists. The prides of its permanent collection are an exhibit of early modernist work and exhibitions covering the history of photography and prints. It's open from September through May, Tuesday from 9am to 4pm and 5 to 9pm, Wednesday through Friday from 9am to 4pm, and Sunday from 1 to 4pm; closed holidays. A gift shop offers many art books and periodicals, as well as some prints of the works displayed.

The intimate **Jonson Gallery** (☎ 505/277-4967), at 1909 Las Lomas Blvd. NE on the north side of the central campus, features more than 2,000 works by the late Raymond Jonson, a leading modernist painter in early 20th-century New Mexico, as well as works by contemporary artists. The gallery is open Tuesday 9am to 4pm and 5 to 8pm, Wednesday to Friday 9am to 4pm.

Located in Northrop Hall (☎ 505/277-4204), about halfway between the Maxwell Museum and Popejoy Hall in the southern part of campus, the adjacent **Geology Museum** and **Meteoritic Museum** (☎ 505/277-2747) cover the gamut of recorded time from dinosaur bones to meteorites. The 3,000 meteorite specimens held here comprise the sixth-largest collection in the United States. The Geology Museum is open Monday through Friday from 8am to 5pm; the Meteoritic Museum, Monday through Friday from 9am to noon and 1 to 4pm.

Finally, the **Museum of Southwestern Biology** (☎ 505/277-5340) in the basement of Castetter Hall (the biology building next to Northrop Hall) has few displays, but has an extensive research collection of global flora and fauna. The holdings especially represent Southwestern North America, Central America, South America, East Asia, and parts of Europe. Visitors must call ahead for an appointment.

✪ **National Atomic Museum.** Wyoming Blvd. and K St. (P.O. Box 5800), Kirtland Air Force Base. ☎ **505/284-3243.** Free admission. Visitors must obtain passes (and a map) at the Wyoming or Gibson Gate of the base. Children under 12 not admitted without parent or adult guardian. Daily 9am–5pm.

This museum is the next-best introduction to the nuclear age after the Bradbury Science Museum in Los Alamos. It traces the history of nuclear weapons development beginning with the top-secret Manhattan Project of the 1940s, including a copy of the letter Albert Einstein wrote to Pres. Franklin D. Roosevelt suggesting the possible development of an atomic bomb. A 51-minute film, *Ten Seconds That Shook the World,* is shown every hour.

There are full-scale models of the "Fat Man" and "Little Boy" bombs, displays and films on the peaceful application of nuclear technology and other alternative energy sources. Fusion is explained in a manner that a layperson might understand; other exhibits deal with the problem of nuclear waste. Outdoor exhibits include a B-52 "Stratofortress," an F-1015D "Thunderchief," and a 280mm atomic cannon. An hour-long tour takes visitors through the development of the first nuclear weapons to today's technology. You'll also see a solar-powered TV and be able to test your budgeting skills as you use the Energy-Environment Simulator to manipulate energy allocations to make the planet's supplies last longer. The museum is directly across the street from the International Nuclear Weapons School, adjacent to Sandia National Laboratory.

Ernie Pyle Memorial Library. 900 Girard Blvd. NE. ☎ **505/256-2065.** Free admission. Tues and Thurs 12:30–9pm; Wed and Fri–Sat 9am–5:30pm.

The 1940 home of America's favorite war correspondent is now a library. Memorabilia and poignant exhibits recalling the Pulitzer Prize–winning journalist, killed in action during World War II, stand in display shelves between the book stacks.

GETTING CLOSE TO NATURE

Petroglyph National Monument. 4735 Unser Blvd. NW, west of Coors Rd. ☎ **505/839-4429.** Admission $1 per vehicle ($2 on weekends). Summer daily 9am–6pm; winter 8am–5pm. Closed state holidays.

Albuquerque's western city limits are marked by five extinct volcanoes. The ancient lava flows here were a hunting ground for prehistoric Native Americans, who camped among the rocks and left a cryptic chronicle of their lifestyle etched and chipped in the dark basalt. Over 15,000 of these petroglyphs have been found in several concentrated groups at this archeological preserve. Self-guiding brochures interpret the rock drawings—animal, human, and ceremonial forms—for visitors, who may take four hiking trails, ranging from easy to moderately difficult, winding through the lava. The 45-minute Mesa Point trail is the most strenuous, but also the most rewarding.

Camping is not permitted in the park; it is strictly for day use; picnic areas, drinking water, and rest rooms are available.

Rio Grande Nature Center State Park. 2901 Candelaria Rd. NW. ☎ **505/344-7240.** Admission $1 adults, 50¢ children 6 and older, free for children under 6. Daily 10am–5pm.

Located on the Rio Grande Flyway, an important migratory route for many birds, this wildlife refuge extends for nearly a mile along the east bank of the Rio Grande. Numerous nature trails wind through the cottonwood *bosque*, where a great variety of native and migratory species can be seen at any time of year. The center publishes a checklist to help visitors identify them, as well as several self-guiding trail brochures. Housed in a unique building constructed half above ground and half below, the visitor's center contains classrooms, laboratory space, a library, and exhibits describing the history, geology, and ecology of the Rio Grande valley. Interpreted hikes and bird walks are scheduled every weekend.

Rio Grande Zoological Park. 903 10th St. SW. ☎ **505/764-6200.** $4.25 adults, $2.25 children and seniors. Children under 12 must be accompanied by an adult. Mon–Fri 9am–4:30, Sat–Sun 9am–5:30pm.

Open-moat exhibits with animals in naturalized habitats are a treat for zoo-goers. Major exhibits include the giraffes, sea lions (with underwater viewing), the cat walk, the bird show, and ape country with its gorilla and orangutans. More than 1,200 animals of 300 species live on 60 acres of riverside bosque among ancient cottonwoods. The zoo has an especially fine collection of elephants, mountain lions, koalas, reptiles, and native Southwestern species. A children's petting zoo is open during the summer, and in the fall of 1996 an aquarium and botanical garden were opened. There are numerous snack bars on the zoo grounds, and La Ventana Gift Shop carries film and souvenirs.

ORGANIZED TOURS

Albuquerque is very spread out and doesn't lend itself to **walking tours,** except in Old Town. Old Town Walking Tours, Plaza Don Luis, 303 Romero NW no. S 202, (☎ **505/246-9424**) offers daily walking tours of Old Town and the surrounding neighborhood from March to November. Reservations aren't necessary. Tours depart at 9:30am and 1:30pm.

Consult any of the following **tour operators** for city and regional tours: **Jack Allen Tours,** P.O. Box 11940, Albuquerque, NM 87192 (☎ **505/266-9688**), and **Destination Southwest,** 121 Tijeras NE, Ste. 1100, Albuquerque, NM 87102 (☎ **800/ 999-3109** or 505/766-9068). For other, more specific activity tours, see Outdoor Activities, below.

A good way to explore the Albuquerque arts scene is to take advantage of one of the monthly **ArtsCrawls.** During the free ArtsCrawl, usually the third Friday of the month, galleries in a convenient geographic area stay open late and free art exhibits, receptions, and demonstrations are featured. For walking or driving maps, contact the Albuquerque Convention and Visitors Bureau (☎ **800/284-2282** or 505/ 243-3696).

6 Especially for Kids

If you're traveling with children, you'll be happy to know that there are a number of Albuquerque attractions that are guaranteed to keep the kids interested. One of the city's best child-oriented activities takes place on Sundays year-round on Romero Street in the Old Town, where costumed actors re-create **Wild West shoot-outs.** You'll know they're about to begin when you hear the warning shots five minutes before show time. Call **505/266-9011** for more information. On weekends, there are also regular puppet plays at the **Old Town Puppet Theatre** (☎ **505/243-0208**).

✪ **New Mexico Museum of Natural History and Science.** 1801 Mountain Rd. NW. ☎ **505/841-2800.** Admission to Museum only, $4 adults, $3 seniors, $2 children 3–11. Museum and Dynamax, $7 adults, $5 seniors, $3 children 3–11. Children under 12 must be accompanied by an adult. Daily 9am–5pm. Closed Mon in Jan and Sept.

Two life-size bronze dinosaurs stand outside the entrance to this modern museum, located opposite the Albuquerque Museum. The pentaceratops and albertosaur greeting them are only the first of the museum's displays that kids will love.

When the museum opened in 1986, on money drawn mostly from taxes on oil, gas, and coal produced in the state, it began nearly from scratch, without any major collections of artifacts or other materials. Today it contains permanent and changing exhibits on regional zoology, botany, geology, and paleontology.

Innovative video displays, polarizing lenses, and black lighting enable visitors to stroll through geologic time. You can walk a rocky path through the Hall of Giants, as dinosaurs fight and winged reptiles swoop overhead; step into a seemingly live volcano, complete with simulated magma flow; or share an Ice Age cave, festooned with stalagmites, with saber-toothed tigers and woolly mammoths. Hands-on exhibits in the Naturalist Center permit visitors to use a video microscope, view an active beehive, and participate in a variety of other activities. Don't miss the new, public-view Fossil Works lab where volunteers are removing the bones of Seismosaurus, the longest dinosaur that ever lived (a native of New Mexico). The giant-screen Dynamax Theater features large-format films on natural history topics. Shows are every hour on the hour from 10am to 5pm.

There's a gift shop on the ground floor, and a Subway sandwich shop is on the mezzanine.

Albuquerque Children's Museum. 800 Rio Grande Blvd. NW. ☎ **505/842-1537.** Admission $3 children 2–12, $1 13 and up, under 2 free. Tues–Sat 10am–5pm, Sun noon–5pm.

The Albuquerque Children's Museum has something for everyone: bubbles, whisper disks, a computer lab, a giant loom, a dress-up area, zoetropes, a capture-your-shadow wall, art activities, and special changing exhibits in a variety of changing subjects. The museum also sponsors wonderful educational workshops. *The Me I Don't Always See* was a health exhibit designed to teach children about the mysteries of the human body, and recently, the museum sponsored a "Great Artists" series that featured live performances depicting artists' lives and work followed by an art activity. Special family performances are offered on weekends. Call ahead for a current schedule of events.

American International Rattlesnake Museum. 202 San Felipe St. NW. ☎ **505/242-6569.** Admission $2 adults, $1 children. Daily 10am–6:30pm.

This unique museum has living specimens, in naturally landscaped habitats, of common, not so common, and rare rattlesnakes of North, Central, and South America. More than 20 species can be seen, including such oddities as albinos and patternless rattlesnakes. Especially popular with the kids are the baby rattlesnakes. A seven-minute film explains the rattlesnake's contribution to the ecological balance of our hemisphere. Throughout the museum are rattlesnake artifacts from early American history, Native American culture, medicine, the arts, and advertising. A gift shop sells Southwestern jewelry, T-shirts, and other mementos, with an emphasis on rattlesnakes, of course.

Explora Science Center. 40 1st Plaza/Galleria no. 68 (at Second and Tijeras NW). ☎ **505/842-6188.** $2 adults, $1 children 5–17 and seniors 62 and older, free for children 4 and under. Wed–Sat 10am–5pm, Sun noon–5pm.

Children and adults alike will enjoy a trip to the Explora Science Center, a hands-on science and technology museum. Kids will learn about air pressure by firing an air cannon, flying a model plane, and floating a ball on a stream of air. The light and electricity exhibits allow museum-goers to create their own laser shows and freeze their shadows. There are also motion, health and body, fluid, and sound exhibits—all hands on.

Cliff's Amusement Park. 4800 Osuna Rd. NE. ☎ **505/881-9373.** General admission $2.50; ride pass $11.95. May Sat noon–midnight, Sun 1–7pm; Memorial Day to Labor Day Sat noon–10pm, Sun 1–9pm, Tues–Fri 6–10pm (1–7pm Mon holidays); Sept Sat noon–9pm, Sun 1–7pm.

This is New Mexico's largest amusement park. Children of all ages love the 23 rides, video arcades, picnic ground, and live entertainment.

7 Outdoor Activities

BALLOONING   Visitors not content to watch the colorful crafts rise into the clear-blue skies have a choice of several hot-air balloon operators; rates start at about $100 per person: **Braden's Balloons Aloft,** 3212 Stanford NE (☎ **505/281-2714**); **Rainbow Ryders,** 10305 Nita Pl. NE (☎ **505/293-0000**); and **World Balloon Corporation,** 4800 Eubank Blvd. NE (☎ **505/293-6800**).

The annual **Kodak Albuquerque International Balloon Fiesta** is held the first through second weekends of October (see "New Mexico Calendar of Events," in chapter 3, for details).

BIKING   Albuquerque is a major bicycling hub in the summer, both for road racers and mountain bikers. Bikes can be rented from **Big River Bike** (1613 Virginia NE; ☎ **505/294-6800**), **REI** (1905 Mountain Rd., NW; ☎ **505/247-1191**), and **Rio**

Mountain Sport (1210 Rio Grande NW; ☎ **505/766-9970**). Big River Bike and REI supply bikers with helmets, maps, and locks.

A great place to mountain bike is Sandia Peak Ski Area in Cíbola National Forest. You can't take your bike on the tram; instead you'll have to drive to the ski area. To reach the ski area, take 1-40 east to Exit 175 (Cedar Crest); then take NM 14 north and veer off onto NM 536, following the signs to the Sandia Peak Ski Area. Once at the ski area, however, Chairlift no. 1 is available for up- or downhill transportation with a bike. If you'd rather not rent a bike from one of the above-mentioned sports stores, bike rentals are available at the top and bottom of the chairlift. The lift ride one-way with a bike is $6, all day with a bike will cost you $10. Helmets are mandatory. Bike maps are available; the clearly marked trails range from easy to very difficult. Mountain Bike Challenge Events are held on Sandia Peak in May, July, and August. For more information on biking on Sandia Peak, call **505/242-9133.** For information about other mountain bike areas, contact the Albuquerque Convention and Visitors Bureau or ask for bike maps at the bike-rental outlets listed above.

BIRD-WATCHING One of the best spots for bird-watching in the entire state is the Bosque del Apache National Wildlife Refuge, located about 90 miles south of Albuquerque on I-25. For more on the refuge, which was established in 1939 as a breeding ground for migratory birds and other wildlife, see chapter 11, "Southwestern New Mexico." Wildlife at the refuge includes snow geese, sandhill cranes, whooping cranes, and bald eagles.

FISHING There are no real fishing opportunities in Albuquerque as such, but there is a nearby fishing area known as **Shady Lakes.** Nestled among cottonwood trees, it's located near I-25 on Albuquerque's north side. The most common catches are rainbow trout, black bass, bluegill, and channel catfish. To get there take I-25 north to the Tramway Exit. Follow Tramway Road west for a mile and then go right on NM 313 for a half mile. Call **505/898-2568** for information. **Sandia Lakes Recreational Area** (☎ **505/897-3971**), also located on NM 313, is another popular fishing spot. There is a bait and tackle shop there.

GOLF There are quite a few public courses in the Albuquerque area. The **Championship Golf Course** at the University of New Mexico (3601 University Blvd., SE ☎ **505/277-4546**) is one of the best courses in the Southwest and was rated one of the country's top 25 public links by *Golf Digest.* **Paradise Hills Golf Course** (10035 Country Club Lane, NW; ☎ **505/898-7001** for tee times and information) is a popular 18-hole golf course that has recently been completely renovated.

Other Albuquerque courses are **Ladera,** located at 3401 Ladera Dr., NW (☎ **505/836-4449**); **Los Altos** at 9717 Copper NE (☎ **505/298-1897**); **Puerto del Sol,** 1800 Girard SE (☎ **505/265-5636**); and **Arroyo del Oso,** 7001 Osuna NE (☎ **505/888-8115**).

If you're willing to take a short drive just outside Albuquerque, you can play at the **Santa Ana Golf Club at Santa Ana Pueblo** (288 Prairie Star Rd. [P.O. Box 1736], Bernalillo, NM 87004; ☎ **505/867-9464**), which was rated by *The New York Times* as one of the best public golf courses in the country. Rentals are available (call for information), and greens fees range from $20 to $50 depending on where you want to play.

In addition, **Isleta Pueblo** is currently in the process of building an 18-hole golf course. It is expected to open for play in the summer of 1996.

HIKING The 1.6-million-acre **Cíbola National Forest** offers ample opportunities. In the Sandia Ranger District alone are 16 recreation sites, though only two allow overnight camping. For details, contact Sandia Ranger Station, NM 337 south toward Tijeras (☎ **505/381-3304**).

Elena Gallegos/Albert G. Simms Park, near the base of the Sandia Peak Tramway at 1700 Tramway Blvd. NE (☎ **505/291-6224** or 505/768-3550), is a 640-acre mountain picnic area with hiking-trail access to the Sandia Mountain Wilderness.

For a guided tour, contact **South Mountain Wilderness Tours,** P.O. Box 638, Edgewood, NM 87015 ☎ **505/ 281-9638.** You'll do the hiking and mules will carry the load. Women-only hiking trips are available.

HORSEBACK RIDING There are a couple of places in Albuquerque that offer guided or unguided horseback rides. At **Sandia Trails Horse Rentals** (10601 N. 4th St.; ☎ 505/898-6970), you'll have the opportunity to ride on Sandia Indian Reser-vation land along the Rio Grande. The horses are friendly and are accustomed to children. In addition, **Turkey Track Stables** (1306 US 66 East Tijeras; ☎ **505/ 281-1772**), located about 15 miles east of Albuquerque, offers rides on trails in the Manzano foothills. Riding lessons are available.

RIVER RAFTING This sport generally takes place farther north, in the area surrounding Santa Fe and Taos.

In mid-May each year, the **Great Race** takes place on a 14-mile stretch of the Rio Grande through Albuquerque. Eleven categories of craft, including rafts, kayaks, and canoes, race down the river. Call **505/768-3490** for details.

SKIING The **Sandia Peak Ski Area** has twin base-to-summit chairlifts to its upper slopes at 10,360 feet, and a 1,700-foot vertical drop. There are 25 runs (35% beginner, 55% intermediate, 10% advanced) above the day lodge and ski-rental shop. Four chairs and two pomas accommodate 3,400 skiers an hour. All-day lift tickets are $30 for adults, $21 for children; rental packages are $14 for adults, $11 for kids. The season runs from mid-December to mid-March. Contact 10 Tramway Loop NE (☎ **505/242-9133**) for more information, or call the hotline for ski conditions (☎ **505/242-9052**). To reach the ski area, take I-40 east to the Cedar Crest Exit 175, then take NM 14 north and veer off to NM 536; from there just follow the signs.

Cross-country skiers can enjoy the trails of the Sandia Wilderness from the ski area, or they can go an hour north to the remote Jemez Wilderness and its hot springs.

TENNIS There are 29 public parks in Albuquerque with tennis courts. Because of the city's size, your best bet is to call the Albuquerque Convention and Visitors Bureau to find out which park is closest to your hotel.

8 Spectator Sports

BASEBALL The Albuquerque Dukes, 1994 champions of the Class AAA Pacific Coast League, are a farm team of the Los Angeles Dodgers. They play 72 home games from mid-April to early September in the city-owned 10,500-seat Albuquerque Sports Stadium, 1601 Stadium Blvd. SE (at University Boulevard) ☎ **505/243-1791.**

BASKETBALL The University of New Mexico team, nicknamed "The Lobos," plays an average of 16 home games from late November to early March. Capacity crowds cheer the team at the 17,121-seat University Arena (fondly called "The Pit") at University and Stadium Boulevards. The arena was the site of the National Collegiate Athletic Association championship tournament in 1983.

FOOTBALL The UNM Lobos football team plays a September to November season, usually with five home games, at the 30,000-seat University of New Mexico Stadium, opposite both Albuquerque Sports Stadium and University Arena at University and Stadium boulevards.

HORSE RACING   **The Downs at Albuquerque,** New Mexico State Fairgrounds (☎ **505/266-5555** for post times), is near Lomas and Louisiana boulevards NE. Racing and betting—on thoroughbreds and quarter horses—take place on Wednesday, Friday, and Saturday from late January to June and during the state fair in September. The Downs has a glass-enclosed grandstand, exclusive club seating, valet parking, and complimentary racing programs and tip sheets. General admission is free; reserved second floor seating is $2.

9 Shopping

Nowhere in the state could one get a better shopping "fix" than in Albuquerque. In addition to having the two largest malls in the state, Coronado Center and Winrock Center (both on Louisiana Boulevard just north of I-40), there's Old Town, which features more than 100 shops and galleries.

Other areas of the city also feature art galleries; however, they're not as concentrated as they are in Santa Fe and Taos, so you'll have to do some driving to find them. In addition, the Sandia Pueblos run their own crafts market on their reservation land off I-25 at Tramway Road, just beyond Albuquerque's northern city limits.

Business hours vary from store to store and from shopping center to shopping center. In general, it's safe to say that shops will be open Monday through Saturday from 10am to 6pm, but many have extended hours; some have reduced hours; and a few, especially in shopping malls or during the high tourist season, are open Sunday.

BEST BUYS

Look for Southwestern regional items in Albuquerque. These include arts and crafts of all kinds, from traditional Native American and Hispanic to contemporary works. In Native American art, look for silver and turquoise jewelry, pottery, weavings, baskets, sand paintings, santos, and Hopi kachina dolls. Hispanic folk art, including handcrafted furniture, tinwork, and *retablos* (religious paintings), is worth seeking out. Contemporary art focuses primarily on painting, sculpture, jewelry-making, ceramics, and fiber art, including weaving. By far the greatest concentration of galleries is in Old Town; others are spread around the city, with smaller groupings in the university district and the northeast heights. Consult the brochure published by the Albuquerque Gallery Association, *A Select Guide to Albuquerque Galleries,* or Wingspread Communications's annual *The Collector's Guide to Albuquerque,* widely distributed at shops.

You should note that every month **ArtsCrawl** organizes art exhibits, artist receptions, and demonstrations in a convenient geographic area. Galleries in that area stay open late during the ArtsCrawl, and all events are free. You can get walking and driving maps from the Albuquerque Convention and Visitors Bureau (☎ **800/284-2282** or 505/243-3696).

Other things to keep your eyes open for are fashions in Southwestern print designs; gourmet items, including blue-corn flour and chile ristras; and other souvenirs unique to the region, especially Native American and Hispanic creations.

A SHOPPER'S GUIDE TO OLD TOWN

Adobe Gallery. 413 Romero St. NW, Old Town. ☎ **800/821-5221** or 505/243-8485.

Art of Southwestern Native Americans is featured here. The gallery also carries numerous contemporary and antique Indian items, including pottery, weavings, pawn jewelry, baskets, paintings, and kachina dolls. There is a large selection of books on

How to Buy a Navajo Rug

After you arrive in New Mexico, you'll begin noticing beautiful hand-loomed Navajo rugs in shops, hotels, and museums. The colors and designs are so striking, chances are you'll quickly begin looking for one to take home.

There are several things to keep in mind when shopping for a Navajo rug. First of all, be sure the shop where you're browsing has a good reputation (ask for recommendations at your hotel). Although all Navajo rugs are authentic, they may not all be good quality (none is completely perfect, however). Of course, you want to buy a rug that pleases you aesthetically, but it is not wise to buy on impulse because you will be spending quite a lot of money. Take your time looking. Spread the rugs out completely to make sure there are no obvious flaws (holes or fraying wool). Then check to make sure the design and color are uniform throughout. The weave lines should be straight, without any visible loose ends. The rug should be of equal thickness throughout. If the rug you like meets all of the above criteria and the price is right, buy it—you'll have regrets later if you don't.

Southwest Native American and Hispanic culture, and the gallery also features a small selection of American arts and crafts and Mission Oak antique furniture.

Amapola Gallery. 2045 S. Plaza St. ☎ **505/242-4311.**

Cooperative gallery featuring the work of more than 50 local artists and craftspeople.

Andrews Pueblo Pottery and Art Gallery. 303 Romero St. NW, Plaza Don Luis, Old Town. ☎ **505/243-0414.**

Probably no place in New Mexico has a wider selection of contemporary and pre-Columbian Pueblo pottery. The gallery also carries baskets, serigraphs, fetishes, and kachina dolls.

The Candy Lady. 524 Romero St. NW, Old Town. ☎ **505/243-6239.**

What a fun place to visit, even if you're not a chocoholic! Chocolate candies and cakes of all kinds are made on the premises, and there's a side room "for over 18 only" with more ribald chocolate delights. Opposite the intersection of Mountain Road and Rio Grande Boulevard NW.

Casa de Avila. 324 San Felipe St. NW, Old Town. ☎ **505/242-3753.**

Southwest contemporary gifts, jewelry, Zapotec rugs, and home designs are retailed here.

Chili Pepper Emporium. 328 San Felipe St. NW, Old Town. ☎ **505/242-7538.**

Old Town's "hot spot" carries everything to do with chili and chiles, from ground powders to the hottest chili pods in the world. You'll find all sorts of salsas and jams, as well as chile ceramics, jewelry, T-shirts, aprons, and oven mitts. They'll ship it home for you, too. Other locations in Albuquerque are 89 Winrock Center (☎ **505/881-9225**) and C-198 Cottonwood Mall (☎ **505/897-2883**).

El Condor West. 400 San Felipe, NW Ste. 7, Old Town. ☎ **505/243-4363.**

This shop features crafts and wearable items from North and South America, as well as beautiful Oaxacan wood carvings, Zapotec weavings, and jewelry.

Estevan's Custom Jewelry. 2 Patio Market NW, Old Town. ☎ **505/247-4615.**

Master goldsmith Estevan B. Garcia designs and handcrafts his own contemporary Southwestern pieces.

Gus's Trading Company. 2026 Central Ave. SW, Old Town. ☎ **505/843-6381.**

Gus sells and repairs Hopi, Navajo, Zuni, and Santo Domingo Indian jewelry. He also carries kachina dolls, pottery, and original Native American paintings.

Hernandez Fine Art. 323 Romero St. NW no. 4. ☎ **505/242-9557.**

Hand-pulled serigraphs by internationally known artist Fermin Hernandez.

La Piñata. 2 Patio Market NW, Old Town. ☎ **505/242-2400.**

Piñatas and paper flowers are the specialty here; they can be custom ordered and shipped.

Mariposa Gallery. 113 Romero St. NW, Old Town. ☎ **505/842-9097.**

The collection at Mariposa Gallery (open since 1974) includes fine jewelry, clay of many kinds, tapestries, wood, glass, and mixed media works, and a variety of delightful contemporary folk art. Mariposa hosts an annual invitational theme show in addition to shows for individual artists several times a year.

Michael C. McCullough Fine Arts. 323 Romero St. NW, Old Town. ☎ **505/242-8667.**

Fine quality Southwestern artwork, including works by local artists are offered, as well as bronze sculptures by Ken Payne and originals by Amado Pena.

New Mexico Bead and Fetish. 323 Romero St. NW, Old Town. ☎ **505/243-6200.**

If you've fallen in love with Native American beadwork, this is the place to stop during your visit to Old Town. Here you'll find a great selection of beads and beading supplies.

Nizhoni Moses Ltd. 326 San Felipe St. NW, Old Town. ☎ **505/842-1808.**

Fine Native American art is featured here, including Pueblo pottery, Navajo weavings and mud toys, and a variety of contemporary and antique jewelry.

R. C. Gorman Navajo Gallery Old Town. 323 Romero St. NW, Old Town. ☎ **505/843-7666.**

The painting and sculpture of famed Navajo artist Gorman, a resident of Taos, are shown here daily from 11am to 5pm. Most works are available in limited-edition lithographs. Another artist represented is Ken Nunez, a kachina carver.

Schelu Gallery. 306 San Felipe St. NW, Old Town. ☎ **505/765-5869.**

A collection of handcrafts for the home by talented Southwestern artisans featuring stoneware, furniture, raku, pottery, pillows, candles, florals, and many other unique items.

Tanner Chaney Gallery. 410 Romero St. NW, Old Town. ☎ **505/247-2242.**

Contemporary and traditional Native American art, jewelry, weavings, sculpture, pottery, and baskets are displayed in this gallery, one of New Mexico's oldest. Lodged in a Civil War–era adobe hacienda, it also has notable historic collections.

Tecolote Tiles and Gallery. 303 N. Romero St. NW, Ste. 207N, Old Town. ☎ **505/243-3403.**

Handmade art tile and furniture, as well as pottery by Lawrence Vargas, collectibles, and Native American art are featured.

Treasure House. 2012 S. Plaza NW, Old Town. ☎ **505/242-7204.**

Decorative tiles, ironwood carvings, Navajo sand paintings, Native American and gemstone jewelry, and other interesting items are available. The shop has been open since the 1940s.

OTHER SHOPPING RESOURCES

ANTIQUES

Brandywine Galleries. 120 Morningside Dr. SE. ☎ **505/255-0266.**

In an elegant setting of period furniture, porcelain, and silver are displayed some of the outstanding representational works of art of 19th- and 20th-century New Mexico, including pieces by the original Taos and Santa Fe schools. The gallery specializes in art and antique appraisals and restorations.

Classic Century Square. 4616 Central Ave. SE. ☎ **505/265-3161.**

More than 100 individual dealers in antiques, collectibles, and arts and crafts exhibit here, between the University of New Mexico and the State Fairgrounds. Jewelry, china, crystal, silver, books, dolls, home accessories, and other items are available.

ART

Absolutely Neon. 3903 Central NE. ☎ **505/265-6366.**

Southwestern, one-of-a-kind neon art pieces.

Coleman Gallery. 311 South Broadway. ☎ **505/842-6712.**

Contemporary abstract and figurative two- and three-dimensional works by local and nationally known artists are offered here.

Dartmouth Street Gallery. 3011 Monte Vista NE. ☎ **505/266-7751.**

This gallery features vapor mirage works of Larry Bell, paintings by Angus Macpherson, tapestries, sculpture, and works on paper by contemporary New Mexico artists.

Frank's Fly Fishing Art Gallery. 5852 Osuna NE. ☎ **505/881-0755.**

Fly-fishing enthusiasts should take note of this unique gallery. It's devoted to fly-fishing art and features aromatic cedar fly-tying benches as well as some beautiful display cases.

New Mexico Art League. 3407 Juan Tabo NE. ☎ **505/293-5034.**

Established almost 60 years ago, the New Mexico Art League is a nonprofit organization that features the work of successful and emerging New Mexico artists. The gallery holds a great mix of styles and media.

Weyrich Gallery (Rare Vision Art Galerie). 2935-D Louisiana Blvd. at Candelaria Rd. ☎ **505/883-7410.**

Contemporary paintings, sculpture, textiles, jewelry, and ceramics by regional and nonregional artists are exhibited at this spacious midtown gallery.

BOOKS

Bookworks. 4022 Rio Grande Blvd. NW. ☎ **505/344-8139.**

This store, selling both new and used books, has one of the most complete Southwestern nonfiction and fiction sections. Recently enlarged, Bookworks carries major offerings in children's books, gift books, travel, art, literature, gardening, cooking, and architecture.

Corner Bookstore. 3500 Central Ave. SE. ☎ **505/266-2044.**

Located in the nostalgic Nob Hill section, Corner Bookstore has an especially fine collection of nonfiction and fine arts books. A superb source for a wide collection of travel, language, and Southwest books.

✪ **Page One.** 11018 Montgomery Blvd. NE. ☎ **505/294-2026.**

New Mexico's largest bookstore has more than 135,000 titles in stock, close to 5,000 foreign and domestic magazines, and more than 150 out-of-state and foreign newspapers. It also carries road maps, computer books and software, and compact discs.

COOKING SCHOOLS

Jane Butel's Cooking School. 800 Rio Grande NW, no. 14. ☎ **800/472-8229.** Fax 505/243-8297.

If you've fallen in love with New Mexican and Southwestern cooking during your stay in New Mexico (or even before you've arrived), you might like to sign up for cooking classes with Jane Butel, a leading Southwestern cooking authority and author of 14 cookbooks. You'll learn the history and techniques of Southwester cuisine, and you'll develop cooking techniques through hands-on preparation. If you opt for the weeklong session, you'll start by learning about chiles. The second and third days you'll try your hand at native breads and dishes; the fourth day focuses on more innovative dishes, and the final day centers on appetizers, beverages, and desserts. There are also weekend sessions available. Call, write, or fax for current schedules and fees.

CRAFTS

Bien Mur Indian Market Center. I-25 at Tramway Rd. NE. ☎ **505/821-5400.**

The Sandia Pueblo's crafts market is on its reservation, just beyond Albuquerque's northern city limits. The market sells turquoise and silver jewelry, pottery, baskets, kachina dolls, handwoven rugs, sand paintings, and other arts and crafts. The market is open Monday through Saturday from 9am to 5:30pm and Sunday from 11am to 5pm.

Gallery One. In the Nob Hill Shopping Center, 3500 Central SE. ☎ **505/268-7449.**

This gallery features folk art, jewelry, contemporary crafts, cards and paper, and natural fiber clothing.

The Pueblo Loft. In the Nob Hill Shopping Center, 3500 Central SE. ☎ **505/268-8764.**

Owner Kitty Trask takes pride in the fact that all items featured at The Pueblo Loft are crafted by Native Americans. For nine years, her slogan has been, "Every purchase is an American Indian work of art."

✪ **Wright's Collection of Indian Art.** Park Square, 6600 Indian School Rd. NE. ☎ **505/883-6122.**

This gallery, first opened in 1907, features a free private museum and carries fine handmade Native American arts and crafts, both contemporary and traditional.

FASHIONS

Fashion Square. San Mateo and Lomas blvds. NE.

Upscale boutique lovers congregate at this award-winning midtown shopping area. The various shops feature retail fashions, jewelry, gift items, home furnishings, and luggage. There's also a florist, a beauty salon, and restaurants. Most shops are open Monday through Saturday from 10am to 6pm; some remain open Monday and Friday until 8pm and Sunday from noon to 5pm. Extended holiday hours are in effect Thanksgiving through Christmas.

Western Warehouse. 6210 San Mateo Blvd. NE. ☎ **505/883-7161.**

Family Western wear, including an enormous collection of boots, is retailed here.

FOOD

La Mexicana. 1523 4th St. SW. ☎ **505/243-0391.**

This is a great place to go shopping if you're a diehard fan of Mexican food. Many items at La Mexicana are imported directly from Mexico, and others, like tortillas, tamales, and Mexican pastries, are made fresh daily.

My Santa Fe Connection. 517½ Central Ave. NW. ☎ **505/842-9564.**

This mail-order company specializes in native New Mexican food and gift items, including decorated chile ristras, and ships them anywhere.

Rocky Mountain Chocolate Factory. 380 Coronado Center. ☎ **505/888-3399.**

Old-fashioned candy made right before your eyes. All chocolates are hand made.

FURNITURE

Ernest Thompson Furniture. 4531 Osuna NE. ☎ **800/568-2344** or 505/344-1994.

Original design, handcrafted furniture is exhibited in the factory showroom. Thompson is a fifth-generation furniture maker who still uses traditional production techniques.

Strictly Southwestern. 1321 Eubank Blvd. NE. ☎ **505/292-7337.**

Solid oak Southwestern-style furniture is manufactured and sold directly to the buyer. Lighting, art, pottery, and other interior items are also available.

GIFTS/SOUVENIRS

New Mexico's Own Bernalillo Store. 925 Camino del Pueblo, Bernalillo. ☎ **505/867-3004.**

Just north of Albuquerque in the town of Bernalillo is this wonderful store, which showcases a large selection of cottage-industry products, all of which were made in New Mexico. Inside you'll find gourmet food products, furniture, handmade clothing, cosmetics, and artwork.

JEWELRY

✪ **Ortega's Indian Arts and Crafts.** 726 Coronado Center NE. ☎ **505/881-1231.**

An institution in Gallup, adjacent to the Navajo Reservation, Ortega's now has this Albuquerque store. They do sales, repairs, engravings, and appraisals of silver and turquoise jewelry.

✪ **The Silver Bird.** 3821 Menaul Blvd. NE, at Carlisle Blvd. ☎ **505/881-2780.**

Visitors can make appointments to view the factory workshop, where Native Americans make jewelry and concho belts. Pottery, ceramics, paintings, mandalas, storytellers, sand paintings, and other crafts are also sold here. A second location is at 2436 Menaul Blvd. NE.

Skip Maisel's Wholesale Indian Jewelry and Crafts. 510 Central Ave. SW, downtown. ☎ **505/242-6526.**

The largest selection of Native American jewelry, along with other arts and crafts, can be found at this downtown outlet. Zuni, Hopi, Navajo, and Santo Domingo Pueblo jewelry is featured.

MARKETS

Flea Market. New Mexico State Fairgrounds.

Every Saturday and Sunday, year-round, the fairgrounds hosts this market from 8am to 5pm. There's no admission; just come and look around.

WINERIES

In addition to everything else New Mexico has to offer, wineries seem to be springing up all over the state. Wineries in Albuquerque or within short driving distance of the city include **Anderson Valley Vineyards** at 4920 Rio Grande Blvd. NW, Albuquerque, NM 87107 (☎ **505/344-7266**); **Sandia Shadows Vineyard and Winery,** 11704 Coronado NE, Albuquerque, NM 87122 (☎ **505/856-1006**); **Las Nutrias Vineyard and Winery,** 4627 Corrales Rd., Corrales, NM 87048 (☎ **505/897-7863**); and **Gruet Winery,** 8400 Pan-American Fwy. NE, Albuquerque, NM 87113 (☎ **505/821-0055**).

10   Albuquerque After Dark

Albuquerque has an active performing arts and nightlife scene, as befits a city of half a million people. The performing arts are naturally multicultural, with Hispanic and (to a lesser extent) Native American productions sharing time with Anglo works; they include theater, opera, symphony, and dance. In addition, many national touring companies appear in the city. Country music predominates in nightclubs, though aficionados of rock, jazz, and other forms of music can find them here as well.

Full information on all major cultural events can be obtained from the Albuquerque Convention and Visitors Bureau (☎ **800/284-2282** or 505/243-3696), with a tape recording of local events after business hours. Current listings can be found in the two daily newspapers: Detailed weekend arts calendars can be found in the Thursday evening *Tribune* and the Friday morning *Journal.* The weekly *Albuquerque Voice,* launched in 1990, and the monthly *On the Scene* also carry entertainment listings.

Tickets for nearly all major entertainment and sporting events can be obtained from **Ticketmaster,** 4004 Carlisle Blvd. NE (☎ **505/884-0999** for information, or **505/842-5387** to place credit-card orders on American Express, MasterCard, or Visa). This computerized ticket service is located in Smith's Food and Drug Stores, with 10 outlets in the greater Albuquerque area, and at the box offices of the New Mexico Symphony Orchestra, the Albuquerque Civic Light Opera Association, and Popejoy Hall on the University of New Mexico campus. You can also get tickets through **PROTIX** (☎ **800/905-3315** or 505/851-5050).

Discount tickets are often available for midweek and matinee performances. Check with specific theaters or concert halls.

Don't miss the free entertainment from May to August on Civic Plaza, at Third and Marquette streets NW. Musicians serenade outdoor diners during the Friday noon hour, while ethnic performers take to the plaza every Saturday evening, from 5 to 10pm, as part of Summerfest.

THE PERFORMING ARTS

CLASSICAL MUSIC & OPERA

In addition to the listings below, the **June Music Festival** (9910 Indian School Rd. NE, Ste. 102, Albuquerque, NM 87112; ☎ **505/295-2468**) is worth your consideration if you're in town on one of the concert dates. June Music Festival is a series of five concerts, featuring nationally and internationally known string quartets with guest artists from leading symphony orchestras. It takes place during the first two weeks following Memorial Day. It also presents the Albuquerque Chamber Soloists Series throughout the year. The festival celebrated its 50th anniversary year in 1991.

Season subscription tickets are $65 to $80; single tickets, $16 to $20 for adults, $10 for students.

Chamber Orchestra of Albuquerque. 2730 San Pedro Dr. NE, Suite H-23. ☎ **505/ 881-0844.** Tickets $12–$25.

This 31-member professional orchestra, conducted by music director David Oberg, performs from September to June, primarily at St. John's United Methodist Church, 2626 Arizona St. NE. There is a subscription series of six classical concerts (in October, November, January, March, May, and June), an all-baroque concert in February, concerts for children in February and April, and a joint concert with the University of New Mexico Chorus. The orchestra regularly features guest artists of national and international renown.

New Mexico Symphony Orchestra. 3301 Menaul Blvd. NE, Suite 4. ☎ **800/251-6676** for tickets and information, or 505/881-9590. Ticket prices vary with concert; call for details.

NMSO musicians may be the busiest performing artists in New Mexico. During its 1996–97 season, the orchestra will perform about 30 classical, pops, baroque, and family concerts from September to May, plus ensemble programs in all Albuquerque elementary schools and tours to a dozen communities throughout the state. Concert venues range from Popejoy Hall on the University of New Mexico campus to the 2,500-seat Hoffmantown Baptist Church to the outdoor bandshell at the Rio Grande Zoo.

Albuquerque Civic Light Opera Association. 4201 Ellison Rd. NE. ☎ **505/345-6577.** Tickets $10–$18.50 adults, $8–$16.50 students and seniors.

Five major Broadway musicals are presented each year at Popejoy Hall during a March-to-December season. Each production is staged for three consecutive weekends, including two Sunday matinees.

DANCE

New Mexico Ballet Company. 3620 Wyoming Blvd. NE (P.O. Box 21518). ☎ **505/ 292-4245.** Tickets $10–$16 adults, $5–$8 students.

Founded in 1972, the state's oldest ballet company performs an October-to-April season at Popejoy Hall. Typically there is a fall production, such as *The Legend of Sleepy Hollow,* a December performance of *The Nutcracker* or *A Christmas Carol,* and a contemporary spring production.

THEATER

La Compañía de Teatro de Albuquerque. 518 First St. NW. ☎ **505/242-7929.** Tickets $9 adults Thurs and Sun, $10 Fri–Sat; $8 students, seniors, and children Thurs and Sun, $9 Fri–Sat.

One of the few major professional Hispanic companies in the United States and Puerto Rico, La Compañía stages a series of productions every year between October and June. Comedies, dramas, and musicals are offered, along with one Spanish-language play a year.

Albuquerque Little Theatre. 224 San Pasquale Ave. SW. ☎ **505/242-4750.**

The Albuquerque Little Theatre has been offering a variety of productions ranging from comedies to dramas to musicals since 1930. Six plays are presented here annually during a September-to-May season. Located across from Old Town, Albuquerque Little Theatre offers plenty of free parking. The 1996–97 schedule includes *The Cemetery Club, Sleuth, The Secret Garden, A Comedy of Errors, A Few Good Men,* and *The Good Doctor.*

Rodey Theatre and Experimental Theatre. Fine Arts Center, University of New Mexico. ☎ **505/277-4332.** Tickets $10 adults, $6 faculty, $3.50 students and children.

Major student dramatic productions and dance recitals, from classical ballet to modern jazz dance, hold forth at the 440-seat Rodey Theatre. The adjacent Experimental Theatre, which seats 75 to 150 (depending upon configuration), hosts a variety of unique productions, from one-acts to dance recitals.

Vortex Theatre. Buena Vista (just South of Central Ave.). ☎ **505/247-8600.** Tickets $8 adults, $7 students and seniors, $6 children 13 and under; $6 for everyone Sun.

An 18-year-old community theater known for its innovative productions, the Vortex is Albuquerque's "Off-Broadway" theater, presenting a range of plays from classic to original. The company mounts 10 shows a year, including (in 1996) *Six Degrees of Separation.* Performances take place on Friday and Saturday at 8pm and on Sunday at 6pm. The black-box theater seats 90.

Albuquerque Children's Theatre. 4139 Prospect Ave. NE. ☎ **505/888-3644.** Tickets $4 for public (senior) shows.

Playwright Bill Hayden established this troupe at his ballet school in the late 1950s, and it has grown to become one of the country's most unique children's theaters. Hayden's philosophy was to produce shows for children, by children, and to give the participating kids a nonstressful introduction to theater: just 90 minutes of rehearsal each week. When he died in 1989, after three decades of instruction, he left a legacy of original plays and adaptations of such classics as *Cinderella, Snow White,* and *Puss in Boots.* There are three companies: seniors (ages 12 to 16) do January and July shows at Popejoy Hall or Rodey Theatre at UNM. Juniors (ages 8 to 11) and play actors (ages 4 to 7) also do two shows a year, but theirs are at the Hayden School of Ballet.

THE MAJOR CONCERT HALLS & ALL-PURPOSE AUDITORIUMS

✪ **KiMo Theatre.** 423 Central Ave. NW. ☎ **505/848-1370** for information, or 505/764-1700 for tickets (Mon–Fri 11am–5pm). Tickets $5–$30. Series tickets are available at a discount, and there are discounts for children.

Albuquerque's historic showcase of the performing arts is a tribute to the region's Native American cultures. Opened in 1927, the KiMo's architecture is a colorful adaptation of an adobe pueblo, and its interior decor emphasizes Native American motifs. Handmade tiles adorn the lobby; wall paintings simulate Navajo sand paintings; murals of the legendary "Seven Cities of Cíbola" stand outside the balcony seating area; even the design of the box office is based on a kiva. And then there's the remarkable lighting: White plaster buffalo heads with lights in their eye sockets adorn the mezzanine columns and outline the ceiling of the theater itself.

The 750-seat theater, owned by the city of Albuquerque, is the home of Opera Southwest and La Compañia de Teatro de Albuquerque. In addition, it hosts numerous dance, music, and theater groups. The KiMo and the city also sponsor a series of touring shows of national and international importance.

Popejoy Hall. Cornell St. at Redondo Dr., University of New Mexico. ☎ **505/277-3121.** Tickets, Broadway series, $20–$38 general admission (depending upon production), with discounts for students, faculty, staff, and seniors. For prices of other events, see descriptions of specific companies.

A multipurpose performing arts facility, Popejoy Hall is Albuquerque's leading venue for major musical entertainment. Seating 2,094, it is the home of the New Mexico Symphony Orchestra, the Albuquerque Civic Light Opera Association, the New Mexico Ballet Company, and UNM's highly popular September to April "Broadway" series, featuring major New York productions. For information on each of the local companies, see the descriptions above and below.

South Broadway Cultural Center. 1025 Broadway Blvd. SE. ☎ **505/848-1320.** Tickets $6 adults, $2 children 12 and under for touring shows.

Funded by the city of Albuquerque, SBCC presents a diversity of multicultural programming in the performing arts—from blues singers to avant-garde comedy, Mexican dance theater to medieval troubadour melodies. The center, which seats 315, includes a 3,000-square-foot gallery space and a 2,000-square-foot multipurpose room. There is also a large, well-stocked branch library. Open Monday through Saturday from 9am to 5:30pm. It's located on the northwest corner of Broadway and Garfield SE, three blocks north of Stadium Boulevard.

THE CLUB & MUSIC SCENE
COMEDY CLUBS/DINNER THEATER

Laffs Comedy Caffè. 3100-D Juan Tabo Blvd. (at Candelaria Rd. NE). ☎ **505/296-JOKE.**

Top acts from each coast, including comedians who have appeared on the *Late Show with David Letterman* and HBO, are booked at Albuquerque's top comedy club. Show times are Tuesday through Sunday at 8pm, with second shows on Friday and Saturday at 10:30pm. Tuesday is "Best of Albuquerque Night." Wednesday is smoke-free night; Thursday and Sunday are Laff's T-shirt nights. The cafe serves dinner nightly from 6pm.

Mystery Cafe. 125 Second NW. (in La Posada de Albuquerque). ☎ **505/237-1385.**

If you're in the mood for a little dinner theater, the Mystery Cafe might be just the ticket. You'll help the characters in this ever-popular, delightfully funny show solve the mystery as they serve you a four-course meal. Reservations are a must. Call for show times and prices.

COUNTRY MUSIC

Caravan East. 7605 Central Ave. NE. ☎ **505/265-7877.** Cover Fri–Sat $3; free other nights.

"Always a dance partner," boasts this large country-and-western club, located east of the State Fairgrounds. Two bands share stage time Monday through Saturday from 5pm to 2am and Sunday from 4:30pm to midnight; there are occasional national acts. Tuesday is ladies' night. Happy hour is from 4:30 to 7:30pm, and there's a free dinner buffet from 5 to 7pm.

Midnight Rodeo. 4901 McLeod Rd. NE (near San Mateo Blvd.). ☎ **505/888-0100.** Cover Fri–Sat $3.

The Southwest's largest nightclub of any kind, Midnight Rodeo not only has bars in all corners of its enormous domicile, it even has its own shopping arcade, including a boutique and gift shop. A DJ spins records daily until closing; the 5,000-square-foot hardwood dance floor is so big it resembles an indoor horse track. Free dance lessons are offered Sunday, Tuesday, and Thursday. A busy kitchen serves simple but hearty meals to dancers who work up appetites, and there's a $3 happy hour buffet from Monday to Friday.

ROCK/JAZZ

Beyond Ordinary. 211 Gold SW. ☎ **505/764-8858.** Cover $4.

Albuquerque's alternative rock hangout has live music, including reggae, and a DJ spinning progressive disks Friday and Saturday from 7pm to 1:30am and Sunday from 7pm to midnight. An art gallery exhibits equally alternative paintings. Happy hour is Wednesday through Friday from 4 to 8pm.

Brewsters Pub. 312 Central SW. ☎ **505/247-2533.** Cover varies.

Wednesday through Saturday nights, Brewsters Pub offers live entertainment in a sports-bar setting. There are 24 beers on tap, as well as a wide variety of bottled beer. Sports fans can enjoy the day's game on a big-screen TV. Barbecue is served at lunch and dinner.

The Cooperage. 7220 Lomas Blvd. NE. ☎ **505/255-1657.** Cover $3–$5.

Jazz, rhythm-and-blues, rock, and salsa keep dancers hopping Friday and Saturday nights inside this gigantic wooden barrel (see "Dining," above).

Dingo Bar. 313 Gold SW. ☎ **505/243-0663.** Cover varies according to performers.

The Dingo Bar is one of Albuquerque's premier rock clubs. The nightly live entertainment runs from punk to classic rock to jazz.

The Zone Niteclub. 120 Central SW. ☎ **505/343-7933.** Cover varies.

The Zone, with four bars on four separate levels and three different music venues, can entertain up to 1,000 people at once. It's almost overwhelmingly huge, but if you're looking for rock and popular music in a big-city club atmosphere, this is the place.

MORE ENTERTAINMENT

The best place to catch foreign films, art films, and limited-release productions is the **Guild Cinema,** 3405 Central Ave. NE (☎ **505/255-1848**). For film classics, check out the **UNM SUB Theater,** on the UNM campus, with double features Wednesday through Sunday, changing nightly.

If you're feeling lucky some night, you might also want to check out the **Isleta Gaming Palace,** 11000 Broadway Blvd. SE (☎ **505/869-2614**), a luxurious, air-conditioned casino that also offers music for special events and occasional closed-circuit televised sporting events. There are more than 400 slot machines, blackjack, craps, live keno, roulette, Caribbean stud, poker, and bingo. Call **505/869-5920** for information about daily poker tournaments. The casino is open 24 hours, seven days a week. There is a full service restaurant. A brand new golf course is scheduled to open directly across the street from the casino as this book goes to press.

ONLY IN ALBUQUERQUE

Albuquerque's best nighttime attraction is the **Sandia Peak Tramway** (see "Attractions," above), and its two restaurants, **High Finance** at the summit and the **Firehouse** at the base (see "Dining," above). Both offer a view nonpareil of the Rio Grande valley and the city lights.

11 Touring the Pueblos Around Albuquerque

Ten Native American pueblos are located within an hour's drive of central Albuquerque. Two of them, Acoma and Laguna, are discussed in chapter 10, "Northwestern New Mexico." The others, from south to north, are discussed here along with Coronado and Jemez state monuments, which preserve ancient pueblo ruins.

When visiting pueblos, it is important to observe certain **rules of etiquette:** Remember to respect them as people's homes. Don't peek into doors and windows, and don't climb on top of buildings. Stay out of cemeteries and ceremonial rooms, such as kivas, as these are sacred grounds. Do not speak during dances or ceremonies, nor applaud after their conclusions: Silence is mandatory. Most pueblos require a permit to carry a camera or to sketch or paint on location. Many pueblos prohibit picture taking at any time.

Pueblo Etiquette: Do's & Don'ts

Those who are not Native American are welcome to visit Indian pueblos and reservations; however, there are some guidelines you should follow as a guest on tribal land. The first thing you should know is that Native American reservations and pueblos have their own systems of government and, therefore, their own laws and regulations. If you don't follow their laws you will be subject to punishment as outlined by the Indian government. The best thing that could happen is that you'd simply be asked to leave (which I've seen on a number of occasions because visitors were not behaving in a respectful manner). Remember, these are not museums or tourist attractions in their own right; they are people's homes.

If you want to take pictures, make video, or sketch anything on pueblo or reservation land, find out about fees in advance. Do not wander around on your own if the Indians have asked that you visit the pueblo only by guided tour. If, on a guided tour, you are asked not to take pictures of something, or are asked to stay out of a certain area, please follow the guidelines. If you don't have to visit by guided tour, don't go into private buildings without being escorted by someone who lives there or who has the authority to take you inside. Be respectful of ceremonial dances and don't applaud at the end of the dance—they aren't dancing for your amusement, they are dancing as part of their ceremony.

In short, be respectful and courteous and don't do anything you wouldn't do in your own mother's house.

AREA PUEBLOS
ISLETA PUEBLO

Located just 14 miles south of Albuquerque, off I-25 or US 85, Isleta Pueblo (P.O. Box 1270, Isleta, NM 87022; ☎ **505/869-3111**) is the largest of the Tiwa-speaking pueblos, comprising several settlements on the west side of the Rio Grande. The largest village, Shiaw-iba, contains the Mission of San Agustin de Isleta, one of the few mission churches not destroyed in the 17th-century Pueblo rebellion. Grasslands and wooded bosques along the river are gradually becoming part of Albuquerque's growing urban sprawl; already, some governmental agencies and commercial interests are leasing property from the Isleta. Most of the pueblo's 3,000 residents work in Albuquerque; others are employed in farming and ranching or private business.

Isleta women potters make red wares distinctive for their red-and-black designs on white backgrounds. The tribe operates a casino (see "Albuquerque After Dark," above) and fishing and camping areas at Isleta Lakes. Permits ($2 to $7 daily) can be purchased at the recreation area.

The Isleta hold an evergreen dance in late February, and stage a Spanish fiesta with a carnival, food stands, and religious events on August 28. The big day of the year is the feast day honoring St. Augustine, September 4, when a midmorning mass and procession are followed by an afternoon harvest dance.

The pueblo is open to visitors during daylight hours, seven days a week. Admission is free. Photography is limited to the church.

SANDIA PUEBLO

Established about 1300, Sandia Pueblo (P.O. Box 6008, Bernalillo, NM 87004; ☎ **505/867-3317**) was one of the few pueblos visited by Coronado's contingent in 1540. Remains of that village, known as Nafiat, or "sandy," are still visible near the present church. The Sandia people temporarily fled to Hopi country after the Pueblo rebellion of 1680, but returned to the Rio Grande in 1742. Many of today's 300 Tiwa- (Tanoan) speaking inhabitants work in Albuquerque or at Pueblo Enterprises. They also run the Bien Mur Indian Market Center on Tramway Road (☎ 800/365-5400 or 505/821-5400). It's about 14 miles north of Albuquerque off I-25.

The pueblo celebrates its St. Anthony feast day on June 13 with a midmorning mass, procession, and afternoon corn dance. Another dance honors newly elected governors in January.

The pueblo is open to visitors during daylight hours, and admission is free. No photographing, recording, or sketching are allowed.

SANTA ANA PUEBLO

Though partially abandoned and closed to visitors except for ceremonial events, the Santa Ana Pueblo (Star Route, Box 37, Bernalillo, NM 87004; ☎ **505/867-3301**) on the lower Jemez River claims a population of about 550. Many "residents" who maintain family homes at the pueblo actually live nearer the stream's confluence with the Rio Grande, in a settlement known as Ranchos de Santa Ana near Bernalillo, where farming is more productive.

Pottery, wood carvings, ceremonial bands, red cloth belts, and unique wooden crosses with straw inlay are produced in the old village by a handful of craftspeople. Marketing is handled by the Ta-Ma-Myia Cooperative Association.

Guests are normally welcomed only on ceremonial days. Pueblo members perform the turtle and corn dances on New Year's Day; the eagle, elk, buffalo, and deer dances on January 6, Three Kings Day; the spring corn basket dance at Easter; various dances for St. Anthony's Day on June 29 and St. Anne's Day on July 26; and several days of dances at Christmastime.

The pueblo is about 30 miles north of Albuquerque, reached via I-25 to Bernalillo, then 8 miles northwest on NM 44. Admission is free; photography is prohibited.

ZIA PUEBLO

Zia pueblo (San Ysidro, NM 87053; ☎ **505/867-3304**) of 720 inhabitants blends in so perfectly with the soft tans of the stone and sand of the desertlike land around it that it's very hard to see—it's like a chameleon on a tree trunk. The pueblo is best known for its famous sun symbol—now the official symbol of the state of New Mexico—adapted from a pottery design showing three rays going in each of the four directions from a sun, or circle. It is hailed in the pledge to the state flag as "a symbol of perfect friendship among united cultures."

Zia has a reputation for excellence in pottery making. Zia pottery is identified by its unglazed terra-cotta coloring and traditional geometric designs and plant and animal motifs painted on a white slip. Paintings, weaving, and sculptures are also prized products of the artists of the Zia community; their work can be viewed and purchased at the Zia Cultural Center located at the pueblo. Our Lady of the Assumption, the patron saint, is given a celebratory corn dance on her day, August 15.

The pueblo is about 8 miles northwest of the Santa Ana Pueblo, just off NM 44. It's open to visitors during daylight hours, and admission is free. Photography is not permitted.

JEMEZ PUEBLO

The 2,400 Jemez natives—including descendants of the Pecos Pueblo, east of Santa Fe, abandoned in 1838—are the only remaining people to speak the Towa dialect of the Tanoan group. The Jemez are famous for their excellent dancing and

Side Trips from Albuquerque

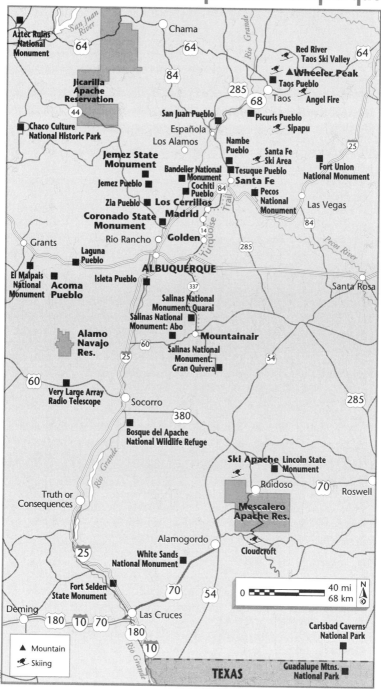

Aztec Ruins National Monument
64
San Juan River
Chama
64
84
285
Red River
Taos Ski Valley
64
Wheeler Peak
Taos Pueblo
68
Taos
Angel Fire
Jicarilla Apache Reservation
44
San Juan Pueblo
Picuris Pueblo
Sipapu
Española
Chaco Culture National Historic Park
Los Alamos
Nambe Pueblo
Santa Fe Ski Area
25
Jemez State Monument
Bandelier National Monument
Tesuque Pueblo
Fort Union National Monument
Jemez Pueblo
Cochiti Pueblo
Santa Fe
84
Pecos National Monument
Las Vegas
Zia Pueblo
Los Cerrillos
Madrid
Coronado State Monument
84
Turquoise Trail
Pecos River
Grants
Rio Rancho
14
Golden
Laguna Pueblo
285
El Malpais National Monument
Acoma Pueblo
ALBUQUERQUE
Isleta Pueblo
337
Santa Rosa
Alamo Navajo Res.
Salinas National Monument: Quarai
Salinas National Monument: Abo
Mountainair
25
60
Salinas National Monument: Gran Quivera
54
60
Very Large Array Radio Telescope
Socorro
380
285
Bosque del Apache National Wildlife Refuge
Rio Grande
Ski Apache
Lincoln State Monument
Ruidoso
70
Roswell
Truth or Consequences
Mescalero Apache Res.
Alamogordo
70
Cloudcroft
25
White Sands National Monument
40 mi
N
0
68 km
Fort Selden State Monument
Deming
180
10
70
Las Cruces
70
54
180
10
Rio Grande
Carlsbad Caverns National Park
▲ Mountain
Skiing
Guadalupe Mtns. National Park
TEXAS

I-0331

feast-making; their feast days attract residents from other pueblos, turning the celebrations into multitribal fairs. Two rectangular kivas are central points for groups of dancers. Try to attend the Feast of Our Lady of Angels on August 12; the Feast of San Diego on November 12, when the Pecos bull dance is performed; or the Feast of Our Lady of Guadalupe on December 12 for the Matachines dance, based on a Spanish morality play.

Woven belts, plaited yucca-fiber baskets, and cloth for garments are the primary crafts. A famous native potter who lives at Jemez Pueblo is Estella Loretto (☎ **505/834-7444**), who has studied ceramics from Italy to Japan, the South Pacific to the Himalayas.

There is fishing and picnicking along the Jemez River on government forest lands, and camping at the Dragonfly Recreation Area. Pueblo stores sell fishing permits at $2 to $5 daily, and permits for game hunting may be bought from the pueblo governor's office.

The pueblo (P.O. Box 78, Jemez, NM 87024; ☎ **505/834-7235**) is 42 miles northwest of Albuquerque via I-25 to Bernalillo, NM 44 to San Ysidro, and NM 4 for 43 final miles. The pueblo is open to visitors daylight hours daily, although it may be closed certain ceremonial days. Admission is free; no photography is permitted.

SAN FELIPE PUEBLO

This conservative pueblo of 2,400 people, located on a mesa on the west bank of the Rio Grande, is known for its beautiful ritual ceremonies. The plaza has been worn into the shape of a bowl by the feet of San Felipe's dancers over the centuries. In the grandest of these dances, hundreds of men, women, and children move through their rhythmic steps all day long in the spring corn dance on May 1, performed in honor of the pueblo's patron, St. Philip (San Felipe). The dancing is done to a great chorus of male singers intoning music that reaches back into prehistory and evokes strong emotions in participants and in visitors, too. Other ceremonial events here are a January 6 corn dance, a February 2 buffalo dance for Candelaria Day, and many dances over several days around Christmastime.

San Felipe (P.O. Box A, San Felipe, NM 87001; ☎ **505/867-3381**) is 30 miles northeast of Albuquerque via I-25 and an access road. Admission is free. Photography is not permitted. The pueblo is open to visitors during daylight hours.

SANTO DOMINGO PUEBLO

One of New Mexico's largest pueblos, with 3,450 residents, this farming community on the east bank of the Rio Grande is also one of the state's most traditional. Craftspeople are known for their beautiful silver jewelry, unique necklaces of *heishi* (shell fragments), innovative pottery, and fine weaving. They are renowned as astute traders and often will swap with visitors for the value of their crafts rather than sell them for cash.

At the dramatic Santo Domingo Pueblo feast day, August 4, the corn dance is performed as it is done nowhere else. It is a lavish production involving clowns, scores of singers and drummers, and 500 tireless and skilled dancers in imaginative traditional costumes. Other festive occasions during the year include Three Kings Day, January 6, with elk, eagle, buffalo, and deer dances; Candelaria Day, February 2, with the buffalo dance; the Easter spring corn dance and basket dance; the San Pedro's Day corn dance, June 29; and many traditional dances in the Christmas season.

Santo Domingo (P.O. Box 99, Santo Domingo, NM 87052; ☎ **505/465-2214**) is 50 miles northeast of Albuquerque via I-25 north to NM 22. The pueblo is open to visitors during daylight hours. Admission is free, but no photography or sketching is permitted.

COCHITI PUEBLO

Occupied continuously since the 14th century, Cochiti Pueblo (P.O. Box 70, Cochiti Pueblo, NM 87041; ☎ **505/465-2244**), the northernmost of the Keresan-speaking pueblos stretches along the Rio Grande. Its Church of San Buenaventura, though rebuilt and remodeled since, still contains sections of its original 1628 structure.

Cochiti (pop. 920) is well known for its pottery, especially the famous "storyteller" figures created by Helen Cordero. Beadwork and soft leather moccasins are other craft specialties. The pueblo's double-headed dance drums, made from hollowed-out cottonwood logs and covered with leather, are used in ceremonies throughout the Rio Grande area.

San Buenaventura Feast Day is July 14, when the corn and rain dances are performed. Other events include a New Year's Day turtle dance and corn dance; eagle, elk, buffalo, and deer dances on January 6, Three Kings Day; the spring corn dance and basket dance for Easter; more such dances on May 3, Santa Cruz Day; and ceremonies for several days around Christmas.

The pueblo is about 40 miles north of Albuquerque, via US 85, then north on NM 22 and NM 16. It is open to visitors daily during daylight hours; admission is free. No photography or sketching is permitted. Fishing and bird hunting on pueblo grounds requires purchase of a permit from the pueblo governor for $2 to $7. Cochiti Lake is popular for water sports among Albuquerque citizens.

TWO STATE MONUMENTS IN THE AREA

Coronado State Monument. NM 44 (P.O. Box 95), Bernalillo, NM 87004. ☎ **505/867-5351.** Admission $2 adults, children 16 and under free. May 1–Sept 15 9:30am–5:30pm; Sept 16–Apr 30 8:30am–4:30pm; closed major holidays. To get to the site (20 miles north of Albuquerque), take I-25 to Bernalillo and NM 44 west.

When the Spanish explorer Coronado traveled through this region in 1540–41 while searching for the Seven Cities of Cíbola, he wintered at a village on the west bank of the Rio Grande—probably one located on the ruins of the ancient Anasazi pueblo known as Kuaua. Those excavated ruins have been preserved in this state monument. Hundreds of rooms can be seen, and a kiva has been restored so that visitors may descend a ladder into the enclosed space, once the site of sacred rites. Unique multicolored murals, depicting human and animal forms, were found on successive layers of wall plaster in this and other kivas here; some examples are displayed in the monument's small archeological museum.

An adjacent state park has sheltered campsites, hot showers, and RV hookups.

Jemez State Monument. NM 4 (P.O. Box 143), Jemez Springs, NM 87025. ☎ **505/829-3530.** Admission $2.50 per person; 16 and under free. May 1–Sept 15 9:30am–5:30pm, Sept 16–Apr 30 8:30am–4:30pm. From Albuquerque, take NM 44 to NM 4, and then continue on NM 4 for about 18 miles.

All that's left of the Mission of San Jose de los Jemez, founded by Franciscan missionaries in 1621, is preserved at this site. Visitors find the mission's massive walls standing alone, its sparse, small door and window openings underscoring the need for security and permanence in those times. The mission was excavated between 1921 and 1937, along with portions of a prehistoric Jemez pueblo. The pueblo, near the Jemez Hot Springs, was called Giusewa—"place of the boiling waters."

A small museum at the site exhibits artifacts found during the excavation, describes traditional crafts and foods, and weaves a thread of history from Anasazi to the 21st century in a series of displays. An interpretive trail winds through the ruins.

12 Also Worth a Look: Salinas Pueblo Missions National Monument

The Spanish conquistadors' Salinas Jurisdiction, on the east side of the Manzano Mountains (southeast of Albuquerque), was an important 17th-century trade center because of the salt extracted by the Native Americans from the salt lakes. Franciscan priests, using Native American labor, constructed missions of adobe, sandstone, and limestone for their converts. The ruins of some of the most durable—along with evidence of preexisting Anasazi and Mogollon cultures—are highlights of a visit to Salinas Pueblo Missions National Monument. The monument consists of three separate units: the ruins of Abo, Quarai, and Gran Quivira. They are centered around the quiet town of Mountainair, 75 miles southeast of Albuquerque at the junction of US 60 and NM 55.

Abo (☎ 505/847-2400) boasts the 40-foot-high ruins of the Mission San Gregorio de Abo, a rare example of medieval architecture in the United States. Quarai (☎ 505/847-2290) preserves the largely intact remains of the Mission of La Purisima Concepción de Cuarac (1630). Its vast size—100 feet long and 40 feet high—contrasts with the modest size of the pueblo mounds. A small museum in the visitor center has a scale model of the original church, with a selection of artifacts found at the site. Gran Quivira (☎ 505/847-2770) once had a population of 1,500. Las Humanes has 300 rooms and seven kivas. Rooms dating from 1300 can be seen. There are indications that an older village, dating from 800, may have previously stood here. Ruins of two churches (one almost 140 feet long) and a convent have been preserved. At the visitor center, you'll be able to view many artifacts from the site, a 40-minute movie showing the excavation of some 200 rooms, and a short history video of Las Humanes.

All three pueblos and the churches that rose above them are believed to have been abandoned in the 1670s. Self-guided tour pamphlets can be obtained at the units' respective visitor centers and at the Salinas Pueblo Missions National Monument Visitor Center in Mountainair, one block west of the intersection of US 60 and NM 55 on US 60. This main visitor center offers an audiovisual presentation on the region's history, a bookstore, and an art exhibit.

JUST THE FACTS Abo is 9 miles west of Mountainair on US 60. Quarai is 9 miles north of Mountainair on NM 55. Gran Quivira is 25 miles south of Mountainair on NM 55. All roads are paved. The monument sites are open daily from 9am to 5pm, and admission is free. A visitor center in Mountainair is open daily from 8am to 5pm. The monument is closed Christmas and New Year's Day. For more information, write P.O. Box 496, Mountainair, NM 87036, or call **505/847-2585.**

13 En Route to Santa Fe Along the Turquoise Trail

New Mexico Highway 14 begins 16 miles east of downtown Albuquerque, at I-40's Cedar Crest exit, and winds 46 miles to Santa Fe along the east side of the Sandia Mountains. Best known as the Turquoise Trail, this state-designated scenic and historic route traverses the revived "ghost towns" of Golden, Madrid, and Cerrillos, where gold, silver, coal, and turquoise were once mined in great quantities.

Modern-day settlers, mostly artists and craftspeople, have brought a renewed frontier spirit to these old mining towns.

Before reaching the first of these towns, however, travelers can make a turn at **Sandia Park,** 6 miles north of the I-40 junction, to begin climbing 10,678-foot **Sandia Crest** on NM 536. The road is paved, well maintained, and wide enough to accommodate tour buses, with no severe hairpin turns; there is parking at the summit overlook. Sandia Crest is the high point of the Sandia Mountains and, like Sandia Peak, offers a spectacular panoramic view in all directions. Many miles of **Cíbola National Forest** trails, including the popular north-south Sandia Crest Trail, run through here; box lunches can be provided for day hikers by the **Sandia Crest House Restaurant and Gift Shop** (☎ **505/243-0605**). The restaurant is open daily May to October from 10am to 9pm, 10am to one hour after sunset the rest of the year.

En route to the summit, on NM 536 in Sandia Park, is the **Tinkertown Museum** (☎ **505/281-5233**), a miniature wood-carved western village with more than 10,000 objects on display, including 500 animations—among them a turn-of-the-century circus. There are also antique dolls and old-time music machines. In 1994 a 45-foot antique wooden sailing ship (built in England in 1936) was added to the museum collection. Tinkertown is open April 1 to October 31 daily from 9am to 6pm. Admission is $3 for adults, $2.50 for seniors, and $1 for children under 16.

If you turn north off NM 536 onto the unpaved NM 165 and proceed about 5 tortuous miles on the rough, narrow byway, you'll come to **Sandia Cave,** a short walk from the road. Artifacts identified as those of "Sandia Man," dating from 23,000 B.C, were found in this cave. They are some of the oldest evidence of humankind ever discovered in the United States.

Golden is 10 miles north of the Sandia Park junction on NM 14. Its sagging houses, with their missing boards and the wind whistling through their broken eaves, make it a purist's ghost town. There is a general store open, though, as well as a bottle seller's "glass garden." Nearby are ruins of an Indian pueblo called Paako, abandoned around 1670. Such communities of mud huts were all the Spaniards ever found on their avid quests for the gold of Cíbola.

Madrid (pronounced with the accent on the first syllable) is 12 miles north of Golden. Madrid and neighboring Cerrillos were in a fabled turquoise-mining area dating back into prehistory. This semiprecious stone, known in the Old World since 4000 B.C, got its name from the French for "Turkish." In Mexico it was sacred to the Aztec royal house and was forbidden to commoners; it was believed to have an affinity to its owner, to grow pale in prophecy of a coming misfortune, or to glow richly with its wearer's good health. A visitor might still find a bit of raw turquoise in the tailings of an ancient pit mine. The Spanish worked these mines, using local Native American slave labor, until 1680, when a rockfall killed 30 of the miners. Their lack of concern was one of the final sparks contributing to the Pueblo revolt of that year.

Gold and silver mines followed, and when they faltered, there was still coal. The Turquoise Trail towns supplied fuel to locomotives of the Santa Fe Railroad until the 1950s, when the railroad converted to diesel fuel. Madrid used to produce 100,000 tons of coal a year.

In 1919, an idealistic mine owner named Huber transformed a gloomy scene into a showcase village with a new recreation center, hotel, hospital, school, church, post office, department store, drugstore, auto showroom, beauty shop, fire station, dental office, tennis and basketball courts, golf course, shooting range, a brass band, and a Christmas light show; early transcontinental planes used to detour over the town for a look. But the town emptied when the mine closed in 1956.

Twenty years later, the owner's son sold everything at auction: tipple, breaker, tavern, church, store, houses, roads—the lot. A handful of diehards, many of them artists and craftspeople, bought property and stayed on. Today the village seems stuck in the 1960s: Its funky, ramshackle houses have many counterculture residents, the "hippies" of yore, who operate several crafts stores and import shops.

Madrid's **Old Coal Mine Museum** (☎ **505/473-0743**) is an on-site museum that features mining and railroad relics, including antique cars, tools, workshops, and a fully restored 1900 Baldwin Steam Locomotive—you can even climb aboard and ring the bell! The museum is open daily, weather permitting, and the admission price is $3.50 for adults, $2.50 seniors, $1.50 children under 12.

Next door, the **Mine Shaft Tavern** continues its lively career with buffalo steaks on the menu and live music daily, attracting folks from Santa Fe and Albuquerque. It's adjacent to the **Madrid Opera House,** claimed to be the only such establishment on earth with a built-in steam locomotive on its stage. (The structure was an engine repair shed; the balcony is made of railroad track.)

Cerrillos, 3 miles north of Madrid, is a village of dirt roads that sprawls along Galisteo Creek. It appears to have changed very little since it was founded during a lead strike in 1879; the old hotel, the saloon, even the sheriff's office have a flavor very much like an Old West movie set.

Cerrillos once had eight daily newspapers, several hotels, and two dozen saloons, serving miners from 30 mines. Today only the Palace Hotel stands, in ruins, used as a stable for llamas that go on backcountry pack trips. The general store sells flea-market items, antiques, and some old turquoise. The Cerrillos Bar—part of the original Tiffany Saloon, founded by the New York jewelry family—has billiard tables in an ornate Victorian setting. And an old adobe house called Casa Grande shelters an unusual trading post.

It's another 15 miles to Santa Fe and I-25.

Santa Fe

The New Mexico state capital is caught in a time warp between the 17th and 21st centuries, between traditional Native American and Hispanic cultures and the modern onslaught of tourism. The longest continuously occupied capital city in the United States, it has been under the rule of five governments: Spain (1610–80 and 1692–1821), the Pueblos (1680–92), Mexico (1821–46), the United States (since 1846), and the Confederacy (for a short time in 1862).

Nestled at 7,000 feet in the pastel foothills of the Sangre de Cristo Mountains is this community of 60,000 people. Residents call it "The City Different."

Santa Fe is nothing if not aesthetically pleasing and artistically involved. It has a famous art colony, larger (though not as historically rich, perhaps) than that of Taos; the world-renowned Santa Fe Opera and other acclaimed performing-arts companies; a highbrow literary segment; an active festival life; and more than its fair share of energetic, creative citizens in all pursuits.

Santa Fe has always been close to the earth. For its first two centuries and longer, it was a town of one- and two-story adobes. When the United States took over the territory from Mexico in 1846 and trade began flowing from the eastern states, new tools and materials began to change the face of the city. The old adobe took on brick facades and roof decoration in what became known as the Territorial style. But the flat roofs were retained so that the city never lost its unique, low profile, creating a sense of serenity to be found in no other American city, and only in a few of the smaller towns of the Southwest, such as Taos.

Bishop Jean-Baptiste Lamy, the inspiration for the character of Bishop Latour in Willa Cather's *Death Comes for the Archbishop,* built the French Romanesque St. Francis Cathedral shortly after he was appointed to head the diocese in 1851. Other structures still standing include what is claimed to be the oldest house in the United States, built of adobe by Native Americans an alleged 800 years ago. The San Miguel Mission is the oldest mission church in the country, while the state capital, built in the circular form of a ceremonial Indian *kiva,* is among the newest in the United States.

The city was originally named La Villa Real de la Santa Fe de San Francisco de Asis (The Royal City of the Holy Faith of St. Francis of Assisi) by Spanish governor Don Pedro de Peralta, who founded it. Peralta built the Palace of the Governors as his capitol on the north side of the central Plaza, where it stands today as an excellent museum of the city's four centuries of history. It is one of the major attractions in the Southwest, and under its portico, Pueblos sit cross-legged, hawking their crafts to eager tourists, as they have done for decades.

The Plaza is the focus of Santa Fe's mid-September fiesta, celebrated annually since 1770 to commemorate the reconquest of the city by Spanish governor Don Diego de Vargas in 1692, following the years of the Pueblo revolt. It was also the terminus of the Santa Fe Trail from Missouri, and of the earlier Camino Real (Royal Road) up from Mexico, when the city thrived on the wool and fur of the Chihuahua trade.

1 Orientation

Part of the charm of Santa Fe is that it's so easy to get around. Like most cities of Hispanic origin, it was built around a parklike central plaza, with its centuries-old adobe buildings and churches lining the narrow streets. Many of them now house shops, restaurants, art galleries, and museums.

Santa Fe sits high and dry at the foot of the Sangre de Cristo Range. Santa Fe Baldy rises to more than 12,600 feet a mere 12 miles northeast of the Plaza. The city's downtown straddles the Santa Fe River, a tiny tributary of the Rio Grande that is little more than a trickle for much of the year. North is the Española Valley (a beautiful view of which is afforded from the Santa Fe Opera grounds) and beyond that, the village of Taos, 66 miles distant. South are ancient Indian turquoise mines in the Cerrillos Hills; southwest is metropolitan Albuquerque, 58 miles away. To the west, across the Caja del Rio Plateau, is the Rio Grande, and beyond that, the 11,000-foot Jemez Mountains and Valle Grande, an ancient and massive volcanic caldera. Native American pueblos dot the entire Rio Grande valley an hour's drive in any direction.

ARRIVING
By Plane

The **Santa Fe Municipal Airport** (☎ 505/473-7243), just outside the southwest city limits on Airport Road off Cerrillos Road, is primarily used by private planes. In conjunction with United Airlines, commuter flights are offered by United Express, which is operated by **Mountain West Airlines** (☎ 800/241-6522). There are four daily departures from Denver during the week, and three on weekends. When departing from Santa Fe, passengers can connect to other United Airlines flights in Denver. Call for schedules and fares. For charter services call **Santa Fe Aviation** (☎ 505/471-6533).

GETTING TO AND FROM THE AIRPORT   Typically, air travelers to Santa Fe arrive in Albuquerque and either rent a car there or take the **Shuttlejack** bus (☎ 505/982-4311 in Santa Fe, 505/243-3244 in Albuquerque). This express service travels direct from the Albuquerque airport to central Santa Fe hotels and back. The fare is $20, payable to the driver, and there's service every 2¹/₂ hours or so between 5am and 10:15pm. **Greyhound Lines** (☎ 505/471-0008) also runs three round-trips daily between the Albuquerque airport and the Santa Fe bus station at 858 St. Michael's Drive. Fare to or from Albuquerque runs around $14; however, because the bus station is several miles south of the city center, travelers often need a taxi to get to their hotels. It may be more convenient to pay a few extra dollars for an airport-to-hotel shuttle. **Faust's Transportation** (☎ 505/758-3410) shuttles between Albuquerque and Taos with a stop in Santa Fe each direction.

BY CAR

Santa Fe is only about 58 miles northeast of Albuquerque via I-40. I-25 skims past Santa Fe's southern city limits, connecting it north and south with points from Billings, Montana, to El Paso, Texas. I-40, the state's major east-west thoroughfare that bisects Albuquerque, affords coast-to-coast access to "The City Different." (From the west, motorists leave I-40 in Albuquerque and take I-25 north; from the east, travelers exit I-40 at Clines Corners, an hour's drive east of Albuquerque, and continue 52 miles to Santa Fe via US 285.) For travelers coming from the northwest, the most direct route is via Durango, Colorado, entering Santa Fe on US 84.

BY TRAIN

Amtrak (☎ **800/872-7245** or 505/842-9650) runs the *Southwest Chief* between Los Angeles and Chicago, making a stop at the frontier village of Lamy, 14 miles southeast of Santa Fe.

BY BUS

Greyhound Lines and **TNM&O Coaches** (☎ **505/471-0008**) offer regular daily service between Santa Fe and Albuquerque, Taos, Denver, Phoenix, Dallas, and points around the state and the country. The Santa Fe bus station is at 858 St. Michael's Dr. For more information on bus service from Albuquerque to Santa Fe, see "Getting to and from the airport," above.

VISITOR INFORMATION

The **Santa Fe Convention and Visitors Bureau** is located at 201 W. Marcy St., in Sweeney Center at the corner of Grant Street downtown (P.O. Box 909), Santa Fe, NM 87504-0909 (☎ **800/777-CITY** or 505/984-6760). The **New Mexico Department of Tourism** is in the Lamy Building, 491 Old Santa Fe Trail (☎ **800/ 545-2040**). If you would like information before you leave home but don't want to wait for it to arrive by mail, try this Internet address: http://www.santafe.org. It will take you directly to the Santa Fe Convention and Visitors Bureau's home page.

CITY LAYOUT

MAIN ARTERIES AND STREETS   The limits of downtown Santa Fe are demarcated on three sides by the horseshoe-shaped **Paseo de Peralta,** and on the west by **St. Francis Drive,** otherwise known as US 84/285. **Alameda Street** follows the north shore of the Santa Fe River through downtown, with the State Capitol and other federal buildings on the south side of the stream, and most buildings of historic and tourist interest on the north, east of Guadalupe Street.

The **Plaza** is Santa Fe's universally accepted point of orientation. Its four diagonal walkways meet at a central fountain, around which a strange and wonderful assortment of people of all ages, nationalities, and lifestyles can be found at nearly any hour of the day or night.

If you stand in the center of the Plaza looking north, you're gazing directly at the Palace of the Governors. In front of you is Palace Avenue; behind you, San Francisco Street. To your left is Lincoln Avenue and to your right **Washington Avenue,** which divides downtown avenues into "East" and "West." St. Francis Cathedral is the massive Romanesque structure a block east, down San Francisco Street. Alameda Street is two blocks behind you.

Streaking diagonally to the southwest from the downtown area, beginning opposite the state office buildings on Galisteo Avenue, is **Cerrillos Road.** Once the main north-south highway connecting New Mexico's state capital with its largest city, it is now a 6-mile-long motel and fast-food "strip." St. Francis Drive, which crosses Cerrillos Road three blocks south of Guadalupe Street, is a far less pretentious byway, linking Santa Fe with I-25 4 miles southeast of downtown. The **Old Pecos Trail,** on the east side of the city, also joins downtown and the freeway. **St. Michael's Drive** interconnects the three arterials.

FINDING AN ADDRESS   Because of the way the city is laid out, it's often difficult to know exactly where to look for a particular street address. It's best to call ahead for directions.

MAPS   Free city and state maps can be obtained at tourist information offices. An excellent state highway map is published by the New Mexico Department of Tourism, 491 Old Santa Fe Trail, Santa Fe, NM 87504 (P.O. Box 20002, Santa Fe, NM 87504, ☎ **800/733-6396** or 505/827-7336). There's also a Santa Fe Visitors Center in the same building. More specific county and city maps are available from the State Highway and Transportation Department, 1120 Cerrillos Rd., Santa Fe, NM 87501 (☎ **505/827-5100**). Members of the American Automobile Association, 1644 St. Michael's Dr. (☎ **505/471-6620**), can get maps at no cost from the AAA office. Other good regional maps can be purchased at area bookstores. Gousha publishes a laminated "FastMap" of Santa Fe and Taos that has proved indispensable during my travels.

2 Getting Around

BY CAR   Cars can be rented from any of the following firms in Santa Fe: **Avis,** Garrett's Desert Inn, 311 Old Santa Fe Trail (☎ **505/982-4361**); **Budget,** 1946 Cerrillos Rd. (☎ **505/984-8028**); **Enterprise,** 1911 Fifth St., Suite 102 (☎ **505/ 473-3600**); and **Hertz,** Santa Fe Hilton, 100 Sandoval St. (☎ **505/982-1844**). For toll-free numbers, see "Car Rentals" in the appendix.

If Santa Fe is merely your base for an extended self-driving exploration of New Mexico, be sure to give the vehicle a thorough road check before starting out. There are a lot of wide-open desert and wilderness spaces in New Mexico, and if your car were to break down you could be stranded for hours in extreme heat or cold before someone might pass by.

Street **parking** is difficult to find during the summer months. There's a parking lot near the federal courthouse, two blocks north of the Plaza; another one behind Santa Fe Village, a block south of the Plaza; and a third at Water and Sandoval Streets. If you stop by the Santa Fe Convention and Visitors Bureau, at the corner of Grant and Marcy streets, you can pick up a wallet-size guide to Santa Fe parking areas. The map shows both street and lot parking.

BY BUS   In 1993, Santa Fe opened **Santa Fe Trails** (☎ **505/984-6730**), its first public bus system. There are six routes, and visitors may pick up a map from the convention and visitors bureau. Buses operate from 6am to 9pm Monday through Friday and from 8am to 8pm on Saturdays. There is no service on Sundays or holidays. Call for current schedule and fare information.

BY TAXI   It's best to telephone for a cab, for they are difficult to flag from the street. Taxis have no meters; fares are set for given distances. Expect to pay an average of about $2.50 per mile. **Capital City Cab** (☎ **505/438-0000**) is the main company in Santa Fe.

BY BICYCLE/ON FOOT   A bicycle is an excellent way to get around town. Check with **Palace Bike Rentals,** 409 E. Palace Ave. (☎ **505/984-2151**), for rentals.

The best way to see downtown Santa Fe is on foot. Free walking-tour maps are available at the tourist information center in Sweeney Center, 201 W. Marcy St. (☎ **800/777-CITY** or 505/984-6760).

FAST FACTS: Santa Fe

American Express   There is no office in Santa Fe; the nearest one is in Albuquerque (see "Fast Facts: Albuquerque," in chapter 6).

Airport   See "Arriving," above.

Baby-Sitters   Most hotels can arrange for sitters on request. Alternatively, call the Santa Fe Kid Connection (☎ **505/471-3100**).

Business Hours   **Offices and stores** are generally open Monday through Friday from 9am to 5pm, with many stores also open Friday nights, Saturday, and Sunday in the summer season. Most **banks** are open Monday through Thursday from 10am to 3pm and on Friday from 10am to 6pm; drive-up windows may be open later. Some may also be open Saturday mornings. Most branches have cash machines available 24 hours. See also "Liquor Laws," below.

Car Rentals   See "Getting Around," above.

Climate   Santa Fe is consistently 10°F cooler than the nearby desert but has the same sunny skies, averaging more than 300 days of sunshine out of 365. Midsummer (July and August) days are dry and sunny (around 80°F), often with brief afternoon thunderstorms; evenings are typically in the upper 50s. Winters are mild and fair, with occasional and short-lived snow (average annual snowfall is 32 inches, although the ski basin gets an average of 225 inches). The average annual rainfall is 14 inches, most of it in summer; the relative humidity is 45%. (See also "When to Go," in chapter 3.)

Currency Exchange   You can exchange foreign currency at two banks in Santa Fe: Sun West Bank, 1234 St. Michael's Dr. (☎ **505/471-1234**) and First Security Bank, 121 Sandoval St. (☎ **505/983-4312**).

Dentists   Located in the geographic center of the city is Dr. Leslie E. La Kind, at 400 Botulph Lane (☎ **505/988-3500**). Dr. La Kind offers emergency service. You might also call the Dental Referral Services (☎ **800/917-6453**) for help in finding a dentist.

Doctors   The Lovelace Alameda Clinic, 901 W. Alameda St. (☎ **505/995-2900**), is in the Solano Center near St. Francis Drive. It's open daily from 8am to 8pm for urgent care, with no appointments required. For Physicians and Surgeons Referral and Information Services, call the American Board of Medical Specialties (☎ **800/776-2378**).

Embassies/Consulates   See chapter 4, "For Foreign Visitors."

Emergencies   For police, fire, or ambulance emergency, dial **911.**

Eyeglass Repair   The Quintana Optical Dispensary, 109 E. Marcy St. (☎ **505/988-4234**), provides one-hour prescription service Monday through Friday from 9am to 5pm and on Saturday from 9am to noon. They will also repair your current glasses.

Hospitals   St. Vincent Hospital, 455 St. Michael's Dr. (☎ **505/983-3361**), is a 268-bed regional health center. Patient services include urgent and emergency-room care and ambulatory surgery. Other health services include the AIDS Wellness

Program (☎ **505/983-1822**) and Women's Health Services Family Care and Counseling Center (☎ **505/988-8869**). Lovelace Health Systems has a walk-in office at 901 W. Alameda St. (☎ **505/995-2900**).

Hotlines   The following hotlines are available in Santa Fe: battered families (☎ **505/473-5200**), poison control (☎ **800/432-6866**), psychiatric emergencies (☎ **505/983-3361**), and sexual assault (☎ **505/473-7818**).

Information   See "Visitor Information," above.

Libraries   The Santa Fe Public Library is half a block from the Plaza at 145 Washington Ave. (☎ **505/984-6780**). There are branch libraries at Villa Linda Mall and at 1713 Llano St., just off St. Michael's Drive. The New Mexico State Library is at 325 Don Gaspar Ave. (☎ **505/827-3800**). Specialty libraries include the Archives of New Mexico, 404 Montezuma St., and the New Mexico History Library, 110 Washington Ave.

Liquor Laws   The legal drinking age is 21 throughout New Mexico. Bars may remain open until 2am Monday through Saturday and until midnight on Sunday. Wine, beer, and spirits are sold at licensed supermarkets and liquor stores. There are no package sales on Sunday and no sales of any alcohol on election days. It is illegal to transport liquor through most Indian reservations.

Lost Property   Contact the **city police** at ☎ **505/473-5000.**

Newspapers and Magazines   The *New Mexican,* Santa Fe's daily paper, is the oldest newspaper in the West. Its offices are at 202 E. Marcy St. (☎ **505/983-3303**). The weekly *Santa Fe Reporter,* published on Wednesday, is often more willing to be controversial; its entertainment listings are excellent. Regional magazines published locally are *New Mexico Magazine* (monthly, statewide interest), the *Santa Fean Magazine* (monthly, local interest), *Santa Fe Lifestyle* (quarterly, local interest), and *Southwest Profile* (eight times a year, regional art).

Pharmacies   The **R&R Professional Pharmacy,** at 1691 Galisteo St. (☎ **505/988-9797**), is open Monday through Friday from 9am to 6pm and on Saturday from 9am to noon. Emergency and delivery service is available.

Photographic Needs   Everything from film purchases to camera repairs to one-hour processing can be handled by the Camera Shop, 109 E. San Francisco St. (☎ **505/983-6591**). Twenty-four–hour processing is available at Camera and Darkroom, 216 Galisteo St. (☎ **505/983-2948**).

Police   In case of emergency, dial **911.**

Post Offices   The Main Post Office is at 120 S. Federal Place (☎ **505/988-6351**), two blocks north and a block west of the Plaza. The Coronado Station branch is at 541 W. Cordova Rd. (☎ **505/438-8452**). Both are open Monday through Friday from 8am to 4pm and on Saturday from 9am to 1pm. Most of the major hotels have stamp machines and mailboxes with twice-daily pickup. The ZIP code for central Santa Fe is 87501.

Radio   Santa Fe's radio stations include KMIK-AM 810 (all-news CBS affiliate), KTRC-AM 1400 (nostalgia music and early radio dramas), KSFR-FM 90.7 (classical), KNYN-FM 95.5 (country), KBAC-FM 98.1 (adult contemporary), KLSK-FM 104.1 (adult alternative), KBOM-FM 106.7 (Spanish), and KVSF-AM 1260 (news and talk). Albuquerque stations are easily received in Santa Fe.

Safety   Generally speaking, Santa Fe is an extremely safe city; however, as changes take place, Santa Fe is becoming more and more like any large U.S. city.

Indeed, there have been increased reports of crime in recent years. It's easy to get a false sense of security in a city as attractive and friendly as Santa Fe, but I would advise visitors today to be as aware of their surroundings as they would be in any other major city in this country.

Taxes   A city bed tax of 3.875% and the state gross-receipts tax of 6.875% are added to all lodging bills.

Taxis   See "Getting Around," above.

Television   Two local independent television stations are KKTO-TV (Channel 2) and KCHF-TV (Channel 11); the latter offers Christian programming. The three Albuquerque network affiliates—KOB-TV (Channel 4, NBC), KOAT-TV (Channel 7, ABC), and KQRE-TV (Channel 13, CBS) all have offices at the State Capitol.

Time Zone   New Mexico is on mountain standard time, one hour ahead of the West Coast and two hours behind the East Coast. When it's 10am in Santa Fe, it's noon in New York, 11am in Chicago, and 9am in San Francisco. Daylight saving time is in effect from early April to late October.

Useful Telephone Numbers   Information on road conditions in the Santa Fe area can be obtained from the state police (☎ **505/827-9300**). For time and tempera-ture, call ☎ **505/473-2211**.

Weather   For weather forecasts, call ☎ **505/988-5151.**

3 Accommodations

Although Santa Fe has more than 60 hotels, motels, bed-and-breakfast establish-ments, and other accommodations, rooms can still be hard to come by at the peak of the tourist season. Year-round assistance is available from **Santa Fe Central Res-ervations,** 320 Artist Rd., Suite 10 (☎ **800/776-7669** or 505/983-8200; fax 505/984-8682). This service will also book tickets for the Santa Fe Opera, Chamber Music Festival, Maria Benitez Teatro Flamenco, and the Desert Chorale, as well as Jeep trips into the High Country, white-water rafting, horseback riding, mountain bike tours, and golf packages. **Emergency Lodging Assistance,** especially helpful around Fiesta time in September, is available free after 4pm daily (☎ **505/986-0043**).

Accommodations are often booked solid through the summer months, and most establishments raise their prices accordingly. Rates are usually increased further for Indian Market, the third weekend of August. But there's little agreement on the dates marking the beginning and end of the tourist season; whereas one hotel may not raise its rates until July 1 and may drop them again in mid-September, another may have higher rates from May to November. Some hotels recognize a shoulder season or in-crease rates again over the Christmas holidays. It pays to shop around during these "in-between" seasons of May through June and September through October.

In any season, senior, group, corporate, and other special rates are often available. If you have any questions about your eligibility for these rates, be sure to ask.

In these listings, the following categories define midsummer price ranges: **very expensive** rooms average $200 and over per night double; **expensive** rooms average $150 to $200; **moderate** rooms average $75 to $150; **inexpensive** rooms average up to $75 per night double. Remember that an additional 10.125% tax is imposed on every hotel bill. Parking is usually free, unless otherwise indicated. Most accommo-dations have rooms for nonsmokers and people with disabilities.

DOWNTOWN

Everything within the horseshoe-shaped Paseo de Peralta, and east a few blocks on either side of the Santa Fe River, is considered downtown Santa Fe. None of these accommodations is beyond walking distance from the Plaza.

VERY EXPENSIVE

Eldorado Hotel. 309 W. San Francisco St., Santa Fe, NM 87501. ☎ **800/955-4455** or 505/988-4455. Fax 505/995-4544. 219 rms, 18 suites, 8 condo suites. A/C MINIBAR TV TEL. Jan 1–Feb 1, $129–$239 double; Feb 2–May 2 and Oct 27–Dec 19, $159–$269 double; May 3–June 26 and Aug 25–Oct 26, $199–$309 double; June 27–Aug 24, $229–$339 double; Dec 20–Dec 31, $179–$299 double. Year-round $249–$950 suites. Ski and other package rates are available. AE, DC, DISC, MC, V. 24-hour valet parking.

A five-story pueblo-style structure built around a lovely courtyard one block west of the Plaza, the Eldorado boasts a Southwestern interior with an art collection appraised at more than $1 million, including antique furniture, Native American pottery, carved animals, and other works mainly by local artists. The guest rooms continue the regional theme. Many of them feature traditional kiva fireplaces, handmade furniture, and decks or terraces. The upper rooms in particular afford outstanding views of the surrounding mountains. Just down the street from the main hotel is Zona Rosa, which houses two-, three-, and four-bedroom condo suites with full kitchens.

Dining/Entertainment: The innovative and elegant **Old House** restaurant was built on the preserved foundation of an early 1800s Santa Fe house. It features a creative Southwestern cuisine. More casual meals are served in the spacious **Eldorado Court.** The lobby lounge offers low-key entertainment.

Services: Room service, concierge, butlers, laundry, twice-daily maid service, nightly turndown, safe-deposit boxes.

Facilities: Heated rooftop swimming pool and Jacuzzi, exercise room, saunas, professional masseuse, beauty salon, shopping arcade, and business center.

✪ **Inn of the Anasazi.** 113 Washington Ave., Santa Fe, NM 87501. ☎ **800/688-8100** or 505/988-3030. Fax 505/988-3277. 59 rms. A/C MINIBAR TV TEL. Nov–Mar, $199–$345 double; Apr–Oct, $235–$395 double. Holiday and festival rates may be higher. AE, CB, DC, DISC, MC, V. Valet parking $10 per night.

Located near the Palace of the Governors, the Inn of the Anasazi is definitely a luxury hostelry. It's named for the "enduring and creative spirit" of the Native American people known as the Anasazi. Opened in 1991, it is a collaborative project of the Washington Avenue Limited Partnership, a group that wanted to blend cultural, community, and environmental concerns to create a unique Santa Fe hotel and restaurant. Every piece of paper used at the inn is recycled; the guest room fireplaces burn gas rather than wood; the linens, soaps, and shampoos are all natural; and the food served in the restaurant is organic and free of chemicals.

This is not to say that the hotel skimps on amenities—there are VCRs in all rooms, as well as minibars, private safes, coffeemakers, bathroom telephones, and walk-in closets. Original artwork is featured throughout the hotel, and there's a living room with a fireplace, as well as a library where you can sit and relax before dinner.

Dining/Entertainment: The **Inn of the Anasazi Restaurant** serves breakfast, lunch, and dinner daily, and features Native American and northern New Mexican food. (See below for a full description.)

Services: Room service, concierge, twice-daily maid service, complimentary newspaper, tours of galleries and museums, massage and aromatherapy treatments, stationary bicycles available for use in guest rooms; use of spas and fitness centers can easily be arranged.

Downtown Santa Fe Accommodations

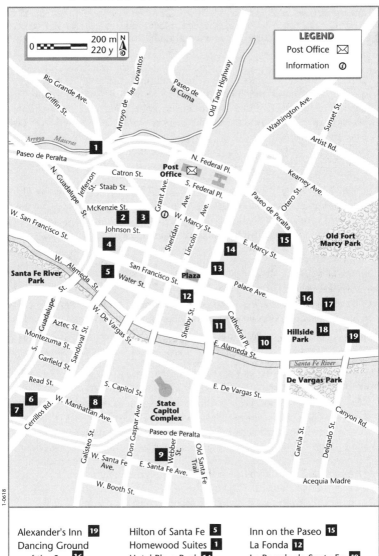

Alexander's Inn **19**

Dancing Ground
  of the Sun **16**

Eldorado Hotel **4**

El Farolito **8**

Four Kachinas Inn **9**

Grant Corner Inn **3**

Hilton of Santa Fe **5**

Homewood Suites **1**

Hotel Plaza Real **14**

Hotel Santa Fe **7**

The Inn at Loretto **11**

Inn of the Anasazi **13**

Inn on the Alameda **10**

Inn on the Paseo **15**

La Fonda **12**

La Posada de Santa Fe **18**

The Preston House **17**

Santa Fe Motel **6**

Spencer House
  Bed & Breakfast **2**

✪ **The Inn at Loretto.** 211 Old Santa Fe Trail (P.O. Box 1417), Santa Fe, NM 87501. ☎ **800/ 528-1234** or 505/988-5531. Fax 505/984-7988. 143 rms, 3 suites. A/C FRIDGE TV TEL. $175– $215 double; $300–$700 suite. Extra person $15. Children 12 and under free with parent. AE, CB, DC, DISC, MC, V.

This handsome, Pueblo Revival–style building was constructed on the site of the Loretto Academy, a Catholic girls' school built in the late 19th century under the direction of Bishop Lamy. Bits and pieces of the original academy remain, including the famous chapel of Our Lady of Light with its mysterious spiral staircase (see "Attractions," below). Another unique element of the Inn at Loretto is the use of hand-painted Mimbres designs. There are about 1,000 of these colorful motifs, all different, on lobby, corridor, guest room, meeting room, and restaurant walls throughout the building. Artist Ross Martinez re-created work found on pottery of the 11th- and 12th-century Mimbres people of southwestern New Mexico.

The hotel, a little over one block from the southeast corner of the Plaza, is horseshoe-shaped, with room balconies or patios surrounding a landscaped outdoor courtyard with a pool. Southwest decor dominates. All rooms have either a sofa or an easy chair or an activity table with two chairs.

Dining/Entertainment: Cafe Loretto, styled after the rambling haciendas of northern New Mexico, is open daily. On warm summer days, service is extended to the patio. Cocktails are available in the lobby bar.

Services: Room service, concierge, valet laundry.

Facilities: Outdoor swimming pool. Shopping arcade with an art gallery, four boutiques, a gold designer, a bookstore, gift shops, a sundries shop, and a hair salon.

✪ **Inn on the Alameda.** 303 E. Alameda St., Santa Fe, NM 87501. ☎ **800/289-2122** or 505/984-2121. Fax 505/986-8325. 67 rms, 9 suites. A/C TV TEL. Nov–Feb, $150–$200 single or double; $210–$320 suite. Mar–June, $165–$220 single or double; $235–$345 suite. June– Oct, $180–$235 single or double; $250–$360 suite. Holiday and special event rates may be higher. Rates include breakfast. AE, CB, DC, DISC, MC, V. Free parking.

This might be just the ticket for visitors who prefer more intimacy than large hotels can offer. Located opposite the Santa Fe River at the corner of Paseo de Peralta, the Inn on the Alameda preserves the spirit of old Santa Fe behind an exterior of adobe and adz-hewn wood pillars. You'll feel it as soon as you enter the lobby, with its traditional viga-latilla ceiling construction. Just past the unobtrusive reception desk is a sitting room/library with handcrafted furnishings, soft pillows, and a rocking chair grouped around an inviting kiva fireplace.

The theme continues in the guest rooms, which are decorated in warm pastel shades of contemporary Southwestern decor. Fresh-cut flowers brighten each room, charming prints hang on the walls, and wood-slat blinds add warmth and privacy. Some rooms feature outdoor patios or private balconies, refrigerators, and kiva fireplaces.

A new wing provides 19 more rooms, guest laundry, fitness facility, and massage room. Eight individually designed suites provide such luxuries as enclosed courtyards and portals, traditional kiva fireplaces, TVs in both living room and bedroom, and minirefrigerators. These suites are set away from the main building and have their own parking areas.

Dining/Entertainment: An elaborate continental "Breakfast of Enchantment" is served each morning in the Agoyo Room, outdoor courtyard, or your own room. A full-service bar is open nightly.

Services: Limited room service, concierge, valet laundry, complimentary morning newspaper; child care can be arranged. The hotel offers a pet program that features pet amenities and pet-walking map.

Facilities: Two open-air Jacuzzi spas, fitness facility, massage room, and guest laundry.

EXPENSIVE

Hilton of Santa Fe. 100 Sandoval St. (P.O. Box 25104), Santa Fe, NM 87504-2387. ☎ **800/ 336-3676,** 800/HILTONS, or 505/988-2811. Fax 505/986-6439. 158 rms, 6 suites. A/C MINIBAR TV TEL. Jan 1–May 1 and Oct 29–Dec 21, $89–$219 double; May 2–June 29 and Sept 4–Oct 28, $119–$239 double; June 30–Sept 3, $139–$260 double; Dec 22–Dec 31, $160– $260 double. Year-round, $380–$520 suites. Extra person $20. AE, CB, DC, DISC, MC, V. Free parking.

With its city-landmark bell tower, the Hilton encompasses a full city block (between Sandoval, San Francisco, Guadalupe, and Alameda streets) and incorporates most of the historic landholdings of the 350-year-old Ortiz family estate. It's built around a central pool and patio area and is an excellent blend of ancient and modern styles.

The guest rooms are well appointed and spacious. In June 1994 the Hilton opened Casa Ortiz de Santa Fe, a small building adjacent to the main hotel, which houses three exclusive casitas. Each has a living room with kiva fireplace, fully stocked kitchenette, and bathroom with whirlpool tub. One of the one-bedroom units offers a fireplace in the bedroom.

Dining/Entertainment: The **Piñon Grill** offers intimate candlelight dinner (as well as daily lunch) service. The **Chamisa Courtyard,** which serves breakfast, features casual garden-style tables amid lush greenery under a large skylight; it's built on the home's enclosed patio. Breakfast, lunch, and dinner are also served at **El Cañon** wine and coffee bar.

Services: Room service, concierge, courtesy car, valet laundry.

Facilities: Outdoor swimming pool, Jacuzzi, gift shop, car-rental agency, travel agency.

Homewood Suites. 400 Griffin St., Santa Fe, NM 87501. ☎ **800/225-5466** or 505/ 988-3000. Fax 505/988-4700. 105 suites. A/C TV TEL. Jan–April 30 and Oct 16–Dec 15, $99– $119 one-bedroom suite; $225 two-bedroom suite. May 1–Oct 15 and Dec 16–31, $150–$170 one-bedroom suite; $310 two-bedroom suite. Rates include continental breakfast. AE, DC, DISC, MC, V. Free parking.

Homewood Suites is Santa Fe's only downtown all-suite hotel. The apartment-style units are perfect for families or single travelers who like to cook for themselves while on vacation. Each suite has a living room, bedroom, kitchen, and bathroom with separate dressing area. Many of the suites have fireplaces, and all offer ironing boards and irons, as well as recliner chairs and VCRs. Both living rooms and bedrooms are furnished with TVs, and the living room couches convert into full-size beds (perfect for kids). Business travelers can enjoy free use of a computer, copier, and typewriter at the hotel's business center.

Services: Complimentary shopping service and complimentary local shuttle service.

Facilities: Outdoor pool and hot tubs, exercise center (with bikes, weights, a step machine, and a rower), activity court, guest laundry, business center, "Suite Shop" (for sundries, food, and video rentals).

Hotel Plaza Real. 125 Washington Ave., Santa Fe, NM 87501. ☎ **800/279-7325** or 505/ 988-4900. Fax 505/983-9322. 56 rms, 44 suites. A/C TV TEL. Nov–Apr, $130–$209 double; May–June, $139–$219 double; July–Oct, $159–$249 double. Year-round, $295–$475 suite. Extra person $15; children under 12 stay free in parents' room. Rates include breakfast. AE, CB, DC, DISC, MC, V. Parking $6 per day.

This three-story hotel, opened in 1990, is located half a block north of the Plaza. It's built in traditional Territorial style, with red-brick coping along the roof lines and white-trimmed windows. Native American designs and wood beams complement the Santa Fe–style furnishings in the rooms, most of which offer fireplaces and outdoor patios. Rooms overlook a peaceful inner courtyard, away from the bustle of the Plaza. Breakfast (plus the daily paper) is served in the Santa Clara Room and Patio or delivered to your room. **La Piazza** is the hotel's sidewalk cafe where guests can enjoy pastries, cappuccino, sandwiches, and cocktails. An intimate lounge also serves cocktails in the evening. Services include concierge, complimentary walking tour, 24-hour desk, and valet laundry.

Hotel Santa Fe. 1501 Paseo de Peralta, Santa Fe, NM 87505. ☎ **800/825-9876** or 505/982-1200. Fax 505/984-2211. 131 rms, 91 suites. A/C MINIBAR TV TEL. Jan 1–Apr 10, $89–$109 double; from $119 suite. Apr 11–June 19 and Sept 2–Oct 19, $139–$159 double; from $169 suite. June–Sept 1 and Dec 20–Dec 30, $159–$179 double; from $199 suite. Extra person $10; children 17 and under stay free in parents' room. AE, CB, DC, DISC, MC, V. Free parking.

This is the first-ever partnership in New Mexico between a Native American tribe—in this case, Picuris Pueblo—and a private business located off reservation trust land. The three-story Pueblo-style building, cruciform in shape and featuring Picuris tribal motifs throughout, is about five blocks south of the Plaza.

Most of the rooms have California king-size beds, and all have Taos-style furnishings, remote-control TVs, and fully stocked minibars. Each suite has a separate living room and bedroom, with a TV and phone in each room, a safe-deposit box, and microwave oven.

Dining/Entertainment: The hotel offers an extended continental breakfast menu and the Corn Dance Cantina offers Native American cuisine. The Lobby Lounge serves complimentary hors d'oeuvres daily from 5 to 7pm.

Services: Valet laundry, 24-hour security, safe-deposit boxes, courtesy shuttle to the Plaza and Canyon Road, in-room massage, limited room service, twice-daily maid service, baby-sitting services, secretarial services, concierge.

Facilities: Massage room, guest laundry, Picuris Pueblo gift shop, pool, whirlpool; use of the Club International fitness center can be arranged.

✪ **La Fonda.** 100 E. San Francisco St. (P.O. Box 1209), Santa Fe, NM 87501. ☎ **800/523-5002** or 505/982-5511. Fax 505/988-2952. 153 rms, 21 suites. A/C TV TEL. $174 standard double, $189 deluxe double; $200–$500 suite. Extra person $15; children under 12 stay free in parents' room. AE, CB, DC, MC, V. Parking $4 per day in three-story garage.

"The Inn at the End of the Trail" occupies a full block between the southeast corner of the Plaza, where a marker denotes the terminus of the Santa Fe Trail, and Bishop Lamy's St. Francis Cathedral. When the first Americans who pioneered the trail arrived in Santa Fe in 1821, they found an inn—a *fonda*—on this site. As trappers, traders, and merchants began flocking to Santa Fe, a saloon and casino were added. Among the inn's 19th-century patrons were President Rutherford B. Hayes, General Ulysses S. Grant, and General William Tecumseh Sherman. The original inn was dying of old age in 1920 when it was razed and replaced by the current La Fonda. Its architecture is Pueblo Revival, imitation adobe with wooden balconies and beam ends protruding over the tops of windows.

Every room is distinct. Each piece of hand-carved Spanish-style furniture is individually painted with a Hispanic folk motif and is color-coordinated with other pieces in the room. Suites and deluxe rooms have minirefrigerators, tiled baths, and sophisticated artwork. Full suites feature fireplaces, private balconies, antique furniture, Oriental carpets, and lots of closet and shelf space. Two-bedroom suites have kitchenettes.

Dining/Entertainment: La Plazuela Restaurant, a tiled skylit garden patio, is open for three meals daily. Cuisine is regional with a contemporary flair. The adjacent **La Fiesta Lounge** offers nightly entertainment. The **Bell Tower Bar,** at the southwest corner of the hotel, is the highest point in downtown Santa Fe, a great place for a cocktail and a view of the city.

Services: Room service, concierge, tour desk, laundry.

Facilities: Outdoor swimming pool, two indoor Jacuzzis, cold plunge, massage room, ballroom, and shopping arcade.

✪ **La Posada de Santa Fe.** 330 E. Palace Ave., Santa Fe, NM 87501. ☎ **800/727-5276** or 505/986-0000. Fax 505/982-6850. 119 rms, 40 suites. A/C TV TEL. May–Oct plus the Thanksgiving and Christmas seasons, $110–$297 single or double; $189–$397 suite. Nov–Apr (except holidays), $77–$215 single or double; $125–$285 suite. Various packages available. AE, CB, DC, DISC, MC, V. Free parking.

This lovely hotel has 119 adobe-style buildings spread across six acres of thoughtfully landscaped grounds. It's constructed around the Staab House, a historic mansion built two blocks east of the Plaza in 1882 by Abraham Staab, a German immigrant, for his bride, Julia. Today, several rooms have been fully restored in classical fashion as a Victorian lounge, with period furnishings and museum-quality 19th-century art. Julia Staab, who died in 1896, continues to haunt half a dozen upstairs bedrooms. Mischievous but good-natured, she is Santa Fe's best-known and most frequently witnessed ghost.

Each of the hotel's charming rooms is unique, with variations in size, shape, layout, and detail. But the *casitas* ("little houses") share many common traits: outside entrances with carved wood portals, handcrafted furniture, wood floors with throw rugs, and painted tiles built into walls. Eighty-six rooms are equipped with fireplaces or woodstoves; piñon firewood is provided daily. Some larger units have refrigerators, walk-in closets, and dressing tables.

Dining/Entertainment: New Mexican cuisine is a house specialty at the **Staab House Restaurant,** open for three meals daily. From spring to early fall, food is also served outside on a big patio. The lounge has seasonal happy-hour entertainment (usually local musicians).

Services: Room service, concierge, valet laundry.

Facilities: Outdoor swimming pool, guest use of local health club, boutique, beauty salon.

INEXPENSIVE

Santa Fe Motel. 510 Cerrillos Rd., Santa Fe, NM 87501. ☎ **800/999-1039** or 505/982-1039. Fax 505/986-1275. 21 rms, 1 house. A/C TV TEL. May–Oct, $85–$95 double; $180 Thomas House. Nov–Apr, $70–$80 double; $150 Thomas House. Continental breakfast included May–Sept. AE, MC, V. Free parking.

One of the bonuses of staying at this adobe-style motel south of the Santa Fe River is that most rooms have kitchenettes. Southwestern motifs predominate in the rooms, spread across four turn-of-the-century buildings. Fresh-brewed coffee is served each morning in the office, where a bulletin board lists Santa Fe activities. The nearby Thomas House, on West Manhattan Drive, is a fully equipped rental home with living and dining rooms and off-street parking. A recent renovation at the Santa Fe

Family-Friendly Hotels

The Bishop's Lodge *(see p. 126)*   A children's pony ring, riding lessons, tennis courts with instruction, a pool with lifeguard, stocked trout pond just for kids, a summer daytime program, horseback trail trips, and more make this a veritable day camp for all ages.

El Rey Inn *(see p. 127)*   Kids will enjoy the play area, table games, and pool; parents will appreciate the kitchenettes and laundry facilities.

Motel brought a new level of charm to eight of the hotel's rooms. One now has a fireplace, another features skylights, viga ceilings were added in some cases, and several have their own private patio entrances.

NORTHSIDE

This area, within easy reach of the Plaza, includes accommodations that lie beyond the loop of the Paseo de Peralta to the north.

VERY EXPENSIVE

✪ **The Bishop's Lodge.** Bishop's Lodge Rd. (P.O. Box 2367), Santa Fe, NM 87504. ☎ **505/ 983-6377.** Fax 505/989-8739. 68 rms, 20 suites. A/C TV TEL. European plan (meals not included), Mar 25–May 26 and Sept 6–Dec, $140 standard double, $215 deluxe double, $245 superdeluxe double; $170 standard suite, $285 deluxe suite. May 27–June, $160 standard double, $245 deluxe double, $275 superdeluxe double; $210 standard suite, $315 deluxe suite. July–Sept 5, $195 standard double, $295 deluxe double, $325 superdeluxe double; $245 standard suite, $355 deluxe suite. Modified American plan (available May 27 to Labor Day), $236–$271 standard double, $321–$371 deluxe double, $351–$401 superdeluxe double; $286–$321 standard suite, $391–$431 deluxe suite. Jan–Mar 24, $95 standard double, $175 deluxe double, $210 superdeluxe double, $125 standard suite, $249 deluxe suite. AE, DISC, MC, V. Free parking.

More than a century ago, when Bishop Jean-Baptiste Lamy was the spiritual leader of northern New Mexico's Roman Catholic population, he often escaped clerical politics by hiking 3¹/₂ miles north over a ridge into the Little Tesuque Valley. There he built a retreat he named Villa Pintoresca (Picturesque Villa) for its lovely vistas, and a humble chapel (now on the National Register of Historic Places) with high-vaulted ceilings and a hand-built altar. Today Lamy's 1,000-acre getaway has become the Bishop's Lodge. Purchased in 1918 from the Pulitzer family (of publishing fame) by Denver mining executive James R. Thorpe, it has remained in his family's hands to this day.

The guest rooms, spread through 10 buildings, all feature handcrafted cottonwood furniture and regional artwork. Guests receive a complimentary fruit basket upon arrival. Standard rooms provide balconies and either king-size beds or two twin beds. Deluxe rooms feature traditional kiva fireplaces, private decks or patios, and walk-in closets; some older units have flagstone floors and viga ceilings. Super-deluxe rooms offer a combination bedroom/sitting room. The deluxe suites are extremely spacious, with living rooms, separate bedrooms, private patios and decks, and artwork of near-museum quality. All "deluxe" units come with fireplaces, refrigerators, and in-room safes. The Lodge is an active resort three seasons of the year; in the winter, it takes on the character of a romantic country retreat. Furthermore, the tax rate here is slightly lower than that of rooms in downtown Santa Fe. The Bishop's Lodge is exceptionally well tended—in fact, each year approximately 10 rooms are renovated.

Dining/Entertainment: Three large adjoining rooms with wrought-iron chandeliers and wall-size Native American–theme oil paintings comprise the Bishop's Lodge dining room. Santa Feans flock here for breakfast, lunch, Sunday brunch, and dinner (featuring creative regional cuisine with continental flair). Attire is casual at breakfast and lunch but more formal at dinner (men generally wear a sport coat, though they aren't required). There's a full vintage wine list, and El Rincon Bar serves before- and after-dinner drinks.

Services: Room service, seasonal cookouts, valet laundry.

Facilities: Daily guided horseback rides, introductory riding lessons, children's pony ring; hiking and self-guided nature walk (the Lodge is a member of the Audubon Cooperative Sanctuary System); four surfaced tennis courts, pro shop and instruction; supervised skeet and trap shooting; outdoor pool with lifeguard, saunas, and whirlpool; aerobics classes; stocked trout pond for children; Ping-Pong; summer daytime program with counselors for children.

EXPENSIVE

Radisson Hotel Santa Fe. 750 N. St. Francis Dr., Santa Fe, NM 87501. ☎ **800/333-3333** or 505/982-5591. Fax 505/988-2821. 116 rms, 12 suites, and 32 condominium units. A/C TV TEL. Jan–Apr, $98–$199 double; May–Dec, $128–$199. Children 12 and under free with parent. AE, DC, MC, V.

If you're in town for the Santa Fe Opera, you'll have a hard time finding an accommodation closer than this one. The amphitheater is only 3 miles north up US 84/285; the Radisson provides free drop-off and pickup. In fact, there's complimentary shuttle service to Santa Fe Plaza, 1 mile southeast, from 7am to 10pm daily. Once you're in this landscaped garden-style hotel, though, you may find it hard to leave. You can have free run of facilities at the adjacent Santa Fe Spa, the city's top health club. Standard rooms have typical hotel furnishings, whereas the more spacious premium rooms feature Santa Fe–style furnishings and private balconies. Parlor suites have a traditional kiva fireplace in the living room, a big dining area, a wet bar and refrigerator, and a jetted bathtub. Cielo Grande condo units have fully equipped kitchens, fireplaces, and private decks.

Dining/Entertainment: The Santa Fe Salsa Company Restaurant and Bar serves three meals a day. A jazz combo plays Friday through Sunday in the bar, and the nightclub features the Spanish quicksteps of New Mexico's best-known flamenco dancer and her Estampa Flamenco troupe.

Services: Room service, complimentary shuttle, valet laundry, complimentary *USA Today.* Child care can be arranged.

Facilities: Outdoor swimming pool, hot tub, Santa Fe Spa (indoor pool, weights, massage, steamrooms, aerobics, dance, yoga, and karate classes), coin-op guest Laundromat.

SOUTHSIDE/CERRILLOS ROAD

Santa Fe's major commercial strip, Cerrillos Road, is US 85, the main route to and from Albuquerque and the I-25 freeway. It's about 5¼ miles from the Plaza to the Villa Linda Mall, which marks the southern extent of the city limits. Most motels are on this strip, although one—the Residence Inn—is a couple of miles east, closer to St. Francis Drive (US 84).

MODERATE

✪ **El Rey Inn.** 1862 Cerrillos Rd. (P.O. Box 4759), Santa Fe, NM 87502-4759. ☎ **800/521-1349** or 505/982-1931. Fax 505/989-9249. 95 rms, 8 suites. A/C TV TEL. $56–$115, single or double; $95–$155 suite. Rates include continental breakfast. AE, CB, DC, MC, V.

"The King" is notable for its carefully tended, shaded grounds and thoughtfully maintained recently renovated units. The white-stucco buildings are adorned with bright trim around the doors and hand-painted Mexican tiles in the walls. No two rooms are alike. Most have viga ceilings and Santa Fe–style wood furnishings, a walk-in closet, and a handsome tiled bathroom. Some have kitchenettes, others refrigerators and/or fireplaces. Ten new rooms that surround a Spanish Colonial courtyard are individually decorated with the work of regional artists. Eight poolside terrace units feature private outdoor patio areas. Facilities include a Territorial-style sitting room with library and game tables; a swimming pool; an in-ground, tiered hot tub; picnic area; children's play area; and coin-op laundry.

INEXPENSIVE

Cactus Lodge. 2864 Cerrillos Rd., Santa Fe, NM 87501. ☎ **505/471-7699.** 25 rms, 4 suites. A/C TV TEL. Mar 15–Oct 31, $48–$68 double with one bed, $68–$75 double with two beds; Nov 1–Mar 14, $32–$48 double with one bed, $38–$58 double with two beds. Extra person $4. AE, DISC, MC, V.

Typical of many small, privately owned motels on the Cerrillos Road strip, the Cactus Lodge includes four two-bedroom suites that can sleep up to seven people. Each room is furnished with a queen-size or double beds, a desk or three-drawer dresser, a table and chairs, and has cable TV. Some rooms have microwaves and refrigerators.

Super 8 Motel. 3358 Cerillos Rd., Santa Fe, NM 87501. ☎ **800/800-8000** or 505/471-8811. Fax 505/471-3239. 96 rms. A/C TV TEL. May–Sept, $49.88 double; Oct–Apr, $44.88 double. AE, CB, DC, DISC, MC, V. Free parking.

It's nothing flashy, but this boxlike motel attracts a regular following who know precisely what to expect: a clean, comfortable room with standard furnishings, double beds, working desk, TV, and phone that allows free local calls. The motel has a 24-hour desk.

BED-&-BREAKFASTS

Alexander's Inn. 529 E. Palace Ave., Santa Fe, NM 87501. ☎ **505/986-1431.** 8 rms (6 with bath). A/C. $75–$150 double. MC, V.

Located not too far from the center of downtown Santa Fe in a quiet residential area, Alexander's Inn is unlike most of the other places in town because it isn't done in Southwestern decor. Instead, the 10-year-old inn (actually constructed in 1903) is done in a Victorian/New England style with stenciling on the walls, Oriental and hook rugs, muted apricot and lilac tones, and white-iron or four-poster queen-size beds. You might begin to think you're in a country inn in Vermont. One of the rooms has a private deck. There's also a new cottage, complete with kitchen, living room (with a kiva fireplace), Jacuzzi tub, and a porch. All guests can enjoy privileges at El Gancho Tennis Club. Mountain bikes are available for guest use. A gourmet continental breakfast of homemade baked goods is served every morning, and every afternoon tea and cookies are available to guests.

✪ **Dancing Ground of the Sun.** 711 Paseo de Peralta, Santa Fe, NM 87501. ☎ **800/645-5673** or 505/986-9797. 8 rooms. TV TEL. Nov–Apr, $75–$210 double; May–Oct and all holidays, $95–$245 double. Rates include breakfast. MC, V. Free parking.

The owners of Dancing Ground of the Sun put a great deal of thought and energy into decorating their units, and it shows. Each of the eight rooms, the majority of which are casitas, has been outfitted with handcrafted Santa Fe–style furnishings made by local artisans, and the decor of each room focuses on a mythological Native American figure, whose likeness has been hand-painted on the walls of that unit. Four of the casitas feature fireplaces, and all have fully equipped kitchens; the

Buffalo and Rainbow casitas are equipped with washers and dryers. Spirit Dancer and Deer Dancer, completed in 1996, are the inn's newest rooms. Each morning breakfast is delivered (along with the paper) to your front door in a basket for you to enjoy at your leisure. Smoking and pets are not permitted.

El Farolito. 514 Galisteo St., Santa Fe, NM 87501. ☎ **505/988-1631.** 7 casitas. TV TEL. Nov–Mar, $75–$90 double; Apr–Jun, $85–$100 double; July–Oct, $110–$125 double. Additional person $15 extra. MC, V.

El Farolito is just a five-minute walk from downtown Santa Fe, but it's far enough away from the center of town to offer guests a quiet refuge after a long day of shopping and sightseeing. All seven of the casitas here have kiva fireplaces, and all are decorated in true Santa Fe style. The floors in each room are either brick or tile and are covered with Mexican rugs; walls are adobe colored, and bedspreads are Southwestern in style. All rooms have private patios and some have wet bars. A continental breakfast is served each morning in the breakfast room (which also has a fireplace).

Four Kachinas Inn. 512 Webber St., Santa Fe, NM 87501. ☎ **800/397-2564** or 505/982-2550. 4 rms (all with bath). TV TEL. $88–$120 double. MC, V.

Located on a quiet residential street, but still well within walking distance of downtown Santa Fe, the Four Kachinas Inn is a wonderful little bed-and-breakfast. The rooms are decorated with Southwestern artwork, including beautiful antique Navajo rugs, kachinas, and handmade furniture (in fact, some of the furniture was made from the wood salvaged from the old barn that was once on the property here). Three of the rooms are on the ground floor. The upstairs room has a beautiful view of the Sangre de Cristo Mountains. In a separate building, which is constructed of adobe bricks that were made on the property, there is a guest lounge where guests can gather at any time during the day to enjoy complimentary beverages and snacks. The snacks, whatever they are that day, will be a treat—one of the owners won "Best Baker of Santa Fe" at the country fair a couple of years ago. Also in the guest lounge are pieces of art for sale, and a library of art and travel books. One of the rooms here is completely accessible for people with disabilities.

✪ **Grant Corner Inn.** 122 Grant Ave., Santa Fe, NM 87501. ☎ **505/983-6678** for reservations, or 505/984-9001 for guest rooms. 11 rms. A/C TV TEL. June–Oct and major holidays, $95–$130 standard double, $150–$155 deluxe double; Nov–May except holidays, $65–$85 standard double, $135–$140 deluxe double. Rates include breakfast. No children 8 or under. MC, V.

This early 20th-century manor at the corner of Johnson Street is just three blocks west of the Plaza. Each room is furnished with antiques, from brass or four-poster beds to armoires and quilts. Most rooms also have ceiling fans and small refrigerators, and five have private baths. But each room also has its own character. No. 3, for instance, has a hand-painted German wardrobe closet dating from 1772 and a washbasin with brass fittings in the shape of a fish. No. 8 has an exclusive outdoor deck which catches the morning sun. No. 11 has an antique collection of dolls and stuffed animals. The inn's office doubles as a library and gift shop and has hot coffee and tea available at all hours.

Breakfast is served each morning in front of the living-room fireplace, or on the front veranda during the warm months of summer. The meals are so good that an enthusiastic public pays $10.50 a head ($7 for young children) to brunch here Saturday from 8 to 11am and Sunday from 8am to 1pm. (It's included in the room price for Grant Corner Inn guests, of course.) The menu changes daily, but always includes a fruit frappé, a choice of two gourmet main courses, homemade pastries, and coffee and tea.

Inn on the Paseo. 630 Paseo de Peralta, Santa Fe, NM 87501. ☎ **800/457-9045** or 505/984-8200. Fax 505/989-3979. 18 rms, 2 suites. A/C. $75–$165 double. MC, V.

Located just a few blocks from the Plaza, the Inn on the Paseo is a good choice for travelers who want to be able to walk to the shops, galleries, and restaurants, but would rather not stay in one of the larger hotels. When you enter the inn, you'll be welcomed by the warmth of the large fireplace in the foyer. Southwestern furnishings dot the spacious public areas, and the work of local artists adorns the walls. The guest rooms are large, meticulously clean, and very comfortable. Many of the rooms have fireplaces. The owner is a third-generation quilter; she made all of the quilts you'll see hanging throughout the inn. A breakfast buffet is served out on the sun deck in warmer weather, indoors by the fire on cooler days. Complimentary refreshments are served every afternoon.

🅢 **The Preston House.** 106 Faithway St., Santa Fe, NM 87501. ☎ **505/982-3465.** 15 rms. A/C TV TEL. High season, $75–$85 double with shared bath, $106–$118 with private bath; $150 cottage or adobe suite. Low season, $48–$58 double with shared bath, $78–$98 with private bath; $115 cottage or adobe suite. Extra person $20. Children over 10 only. MC, V.

This is a different sort of building for the City Different—a century-old Queen Anne home. That style of architecture is rarely seen in New Mexico, especially painted sky blue with white trim. The house's owner, noted silk-screen artist and muralist Signe Bergman, adores its original stained glass.

Located three blocks east of the Plaza, off Palace Avenue near La Posada hotel, the Preston House has several types of rooms. Six in the main house have period antiques and exquisitely feminine decor, with floral wallpaper and lace drapes. Many have brass beds covered with quilts; some have decks, several have fireplaces, and only two must share a bath. Seven more rooms with private baths and TVs are in an adobe building catercorner from the house. Two private cottages in the rear of the Preston House and an adobe home across the street have more deluxe facilities. All rooms are stocked with sherry and terry-cloth robes. A continental buffet breakfast is served daily from 8 to 10am, and full tea and dessert are served every afternoon.

✪ **Spencer House Bed and Breakfast Inn.** 222 McKenzie St., Santa Fe, NM 87501. ☎ **800/647-0530** (7am–7pm) or 505/988-3024. 4 rms, 1 cottage. A/C $85–$115 double. Rates include breakfast. MC, V. Free parking.

The Spencer House is unique among Santa Fe bed-and-breakfasts. Instead of Southwestern-style furnishings, you'll find beautiful antiques from England, Ireland, and colonial America. One guest room features an antique brass bed, another a pencil-post bed, yet another an English panel bed. Each bed is also outfitted with a fluffy down comforter. All bathrooms are completely new, modern, and very spacious. In summer a full breakfast is served on the outdoor patio. In winter guests dine indoors by the wood-burning stove. A full afternoon tea is served in the breakfast room. Keith and Michael, who live next door, received an award from the Santa Fe Historical Board for the restoration of Spencer House.

RV PARKS & CAMPGROUNDS
RV PARKS

At least four private camping areas, mainly for recreational vehicles, are located within a few minutes' drive of downtown Santa Fe. Typical rates are $20 for full RV hookups, $15 for tents. Be sure to book ahead at busy times.

Babbitt's Los Campos RV Park. 3574 Cerrillos Rd., Santa Fe, NM 87501. ☎ **505/473-1949.** Fax 505/471-9220.

The resort has 95 spaces with full hookups, picnic tables, showers, restrooms, laundry, and grocery store. It's just 5 miles south of the Plaza.

Rancheros de Santa Fe Campground. Exit 290 off I-25 (Rte. 3, Box 94, Santa Fe, NM 87505). ☎ **505/466-3482.**

Tents, motor homes, and trailers requiring full hookups are welcome here. The park's 130 sites are situated on 22 acres of piñon and juniper forest. Facilities include tables, grills and fireplaces, hot showers, rest rooms, laundry, grocery store, swimming pool, playground, games room, free nightly movies, public telephones, and propane. Cabins are also available. It's located about 6 miles southeast of Santa Fe and is open from March 15 to October 31.

Santa Fe KOA. Exit 290 or 294 off I-25 (Rte. 3, Box 95A, Santa Fe, NM 87501). ☎ **505/466-1419,** or 505/KOA-1514 for reservations.

This campground offers full hookups, pull-through sites, tent sites, picnic tables, showers, restrooms, laundry, store, Santa Fe–style gift shop, playground, recreation room, propane, and dumping station. It's located about 11 miles northeast of Santa Fe.

Tesuque Pueblo RV Campground. US 84/285 (Rte. 5, Box 360H, Santa Fe, NM 87501). ☎ **800/TRY-RV-PARK** or 505/455-2661.

This campground has full hookups, pull-through sites, tent sites, showers, restrooms, laundry, seasonal swimming pool and hot tub, and a store that sells Native American jewelry and fishing gear. It's approximately 10 miles north of Santa Fe.

CAMPGROUNDS

There are three forest sites along NM 475 going toward the Santa Fe Ski Basin. All are open from May to October. Overnight rates start at about $6, depending on the particular site.

Hyde Memorial State Park. NM 475 (P.O. Box 1147, Santa Fe, NM 87503). ☎ **505/983-7175.**

This park is about 8 miles from the city. Its campground includes shelters, water, tables, fireplaces, and pit toilets. Maps of Santa Fe showing where firewood can be found are supplied. Seven RV pads with electrical pedestals and an RV dump station are available. The park also features a small ice-skating pond and nature trails.

Santa Fe National Forest. NM 475 (P.O. Box 1689, Santa Fe, NM 87504). ☎ **505/988-6940.**

Black Canyon campground, with 44 sites, is located just before you reach Hyde State Park; it has potable water and sites for trailers up to 32 feet long. Big Tesuque campground, with 10 newly rehabilitated sites, is about 12 miles from town. Both Black Canyon and Big Tesuque campgrounds, located along the Santa Fe Scenic Byway, NM 475, are equipped with vault toilets.

4 Dining

There are literally hundreds of restaurants in Santa Fe, from luxury establishments with strict dress codes right down to corner hamburger stands. This is a sophisticated city, and there is a great variety of cuisines here. Some chefs create new recipes by incorporating traditional Southwestern foods with other kinds of ingredients; their restaurants are referred to in this listing as "creative Southwestern."

DOWNTOWN
EXPENSIVE

Cafe Escalera. 130 Lincoln Ave., 2nd floor. ☎ **505/989-8188.** Reservations recommended. Main courses $14.50–$24.50; lunch $8.50–$14.50. AE, MC, V. Mon–Fri 11:30am–2:30pm, Mon–Wed 5:30–9pm, Thurs–Sat 5:30–9:30pm. CREATIVE CONTINENTAL/MEDITERRANEAN.

Cafe Escalera has, over the past six years, become one of Santa Fe's best and most popular restaurants. The spacious, open, warehouselike space is bright, airy, and filled with energy. The decor is understated in a modern way—the focus here is on the food. At lunch I like to start with an order of Mediterranean olives and perhaps roasted almonds. If you're in the mood for a more substantial appetizer, try the roasted peppers and goat cheese or the vegetarian black-bean chili. On my last visit to Cafe Escalera for lunch, I enjoyed the mussels in a spicy broth. Dinner appetizers are usually the same as at lunch, but the main courses differ greatly. The risotto timbale with summer squash, spinach, and basil pesto is a good choice, and so is the grilled king salmon with a tomato-basil vinaigrette. Those with a heartier appetite may like the Niman-Schell Ranch fillet steak with garlic mashed potatoes. The menu changes daily. For dessert you really can't go wrong if you order the Blanco y Negro or the Creme Brolles or pots de cremes. The waitstaff here is among the best in Santa Fe.

Coyote Cafe. 132 W. Water St. ☎ **505/983-1615.** Reservations recommended. Main courses $6.50–$15.95 (Rooftop Cantina); fixed-price dinner $39.50 (Coyote Cafe). AE, DC, DISC, MC, V. Oct–Apr daily 11:30am–2pm and 6–9pm; Apr–Oct Sat–Sun 11:30am–2pm, daily 6–9pm; Rooftop Cantina open daily 11am–9pm. MODERN SOUTHWESTERN.

This is still the number-one "trendy" place to dine in Santa Fe. Owner Mark Miller has talked extensively about his restaurant and cuisine on national television, which has invariably identified him with "Santa Fe cuisine." Tourists throng here: In fact, during the summer, reservations are recommended days in advance. The cafe overlooks Water Street from tall windows on the second floor of a downtown building. Beneath the skylight, set in a cathedral ceiling, is a veritable zoo of animal sculptures in modern folk-art forms. Smoking is not allowed here.

The cuisine, prepared on a pecan-wood grill in an open kitchen, is Southwestern with a modern twist. The menu changes seasonally, but diners might start with roasted red pepper soup with grilled Yucatán chicken sausage and fennel confit or grilled buttermilk corn cakes with chipotle shrimp and salsa fresca. Main courses might include pecan-grilled fillet of beef served with red chile, huitlacoche taquitos, and a chanterelle-grilled yellow tomato salsa; or grilled ahi with a spicy tomatillo avocado sauce and tortilla salad. A vegetarian special is offered daily. Andrew Maclauchlan, the new pastry chef, has added a wonderfully creative variety of treats to the menu, including peach star anise upside-down cake with iced gingered peach sauce and vanilla bean ice cream and apricot and black mission fig linzer tart with brown sugar cream and blueberry ice cream.

The Coyote Cafe has two adjunct establishments. The **Rooftop Cantina** serves light Mexican fare and cocktails. On the ground floor is the Coyote Cafe General Store, a retail gourmet Southwestern food market, featuring the Coyote Cafe's own food line (called Coyote Cocina), as well as hot sauces and salsas from all over the world.

Double A. 331 Sandoval. ☎ **505/982-8999.** Reservations recommended. Main courses $14–$26; lunch $7–$9. AE, MC, V. Mon–Fri 11:30am–2pm and 5:30–10pm; Sat–Sun 5:30–10pm. The bar is open until 2am Mon–Sat and until 11pm on Sun. AMERICAN.

Downtown Santa Fe Dining

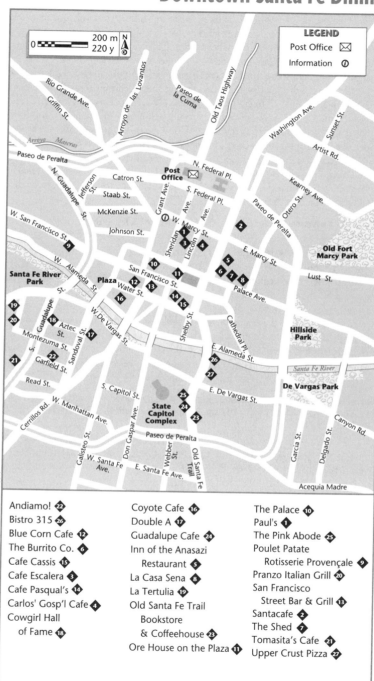

Andiamo! **22**
Bistro 315 **26**
Blue Corn Cafe **12**
The Burrito Co. **6**
Cafe Cassis **15**
Cafe Escalera **3**
Cafe Pasqual's **14**
Carlos' Gosp'l Cafe **4**
Cowgirl Hall
   of Fame **18**

Coyote Cafe **16**
Double A **17**
Guadalupe Cafe **24**
Inn of the Anasazi
   Restaurant **5**
La Casa Sena **8**
La Tertulia **19**
Old Santa Fe Trail
   Bookstore
   & Coffeehouse **23**
Ore House on the Plaza **11**

The Palace **10**
Paul's **1**
The Pink Abode **25**
Poulet Patate
   Rotisserie Provençale **9**
Pranzo Italian Grill **20**
San Francisco
   Street Bar & Grill **13**
Santacafe **2**
The Shed **7**
Tomasita's Cafe **21**
Upper Crust Pizza **27**

1-0619

133

Every year a number of new restaurants open in Santa Fe, but only one or two keep the locals coming back for more. The Double A, which opened in June 1995, is destined to be one of those places. Chef Marion Gillchrist (previously chef at Santacafe) and sous chef Tom Atkins (previously a banquet chef at the Inn of the Anasazi) make a great team and, so far, turn out consistently good American fare night after night. I really enjoyed the penne with buffalo sausage in roasted tomato-garlic sauce, as well as the quail served with toasted grits and summer squash casserole. Other menu items include the Double A Burger with buttermilk onion rings or spaghettini with roasted corn, arugula, and shaved Parmesan. For an additional sum you can have a side order of toasted grits, oven-roasted potatoes, horseradish mashed potatoes, or matchstick potatoes. Desserts include sweet potato shortcake with brandied peaches and buttermilk-pecan cream and warm fudge cake served with peanut butter crunch ice cream, toasted bananas, and a warm chocolate sauce. The wine list is well chosen, but only a few bottles are priced at less than $25.

✪ **Encore Provence.** 548 Agua Fria St. ☎ **505/983-7470.** Reservations recommended. Main courses $14–$18.50. AE, MC, V. Sun–Thurs 6–9pm, Fri–Sat 6–9:30pm. FRENCH.

Encore Provence, a delightful little restaurant decorated in French country style, is one of Santa Fe's lesser-known jewels. The menu features dishes reminiscent of the heart of the French countryside. Begin with a lovely serving of mussels provençal (served off the shell in garlic and parsley butter) or the brandade (puree of salt cod, potatoes, garlic, and extra-virgin olive oil served with sweet bell peppers and olive tapenade). My choice for a main course would be the seven-hour leg of lamb served with mashed potatoes or the scallops wrapped in bacon and served with a cream of French lentils and spinach. For dessert, the crème brûlée, as might be expected, is quite good, as is the *schuss* (light raspberry and kirsch fromage blanc cheesecake with a raspberry coulis). The wine list here is superb.

Geronimo. 724 Canyon Rd. ☎ **505/982-1500.** Reservations recommended. Main courses $16.50–$21. AE, MC, V. Daily 11:30am–2:15pm; Sun–Thurs 6–10pm, Fri–Sat 6–10:30pm. CREATIVE CONTINENTAL.

When Geronimo opened in 1991, no one was sure if it would succeed because so many previous restaurants at this site had failed miserably. But Geronimo has done more than just survive—it has flourished. Occupying an old adobe structure known as the Borrego House, built by Geronimo Lopez in 1756, the restaurant has been completely restored. Numerous small dining rooms help it retain the comfortable feel of an old Santa Fe home. On a recent visit, I enjoyed cornmeal-dusted, pan-seared, free-range chicken served with baby spinach and roasted new potatoes. Additional offerings included mesquite-grilled Black Angus ribeye burger with grilled Anaheim chile-pineapple salsa and Gruyère cheese served with chile-dusted shoestring potatoes, and Chicken Mole Relleno served with jalapeño peach salsa and crème fraîche. For dessert try the mocha pot de crème—you won't be disappointed, especially if you're a chocoholic. The menu changes seasonally, and there is an excellent wine list. Outdoor dining is available in warm weather.

Inn of the Anasazi Restaurant. 113 Washington St. ☎ **505/988-3236.** Reservations recommended. Main courses $17.50–$29; lunch $8–$11.75; breakfast $5.25–$9.50. AE, DC, DISC, MC, V. Daily 7–10:30am, 11:30am–2:30pm, and 5:30–10pm. NORTHERN NEW MEXICAN/ NATIVE AMERICAN.

In keeping with the principles of the Inn of the Anasazi (see above), everything served at this restaurant is all natural. The meats are chemical-free and the fruits and vegetables are organic whenever possible. They serve water only upon request "in the interest of conservation." The setting is comfortable, with an exposed-beam ceiling, exposed adobe walls, and traditional Southwestern decor.

For breakfast you can have anything from fruit to scrambled egg quesadillas with apple smoked bacon, tomatoes, and guacamole. At lunch, you might try the Anasazi flatbread with fire-roasted sweet peppers and tomato-olive salsa to start, followed by coconut tempura prawns with jicama-poblano slaw and chile passion fruit coulis. For dinner, try tortilla soup with ginger pork potstickers, then perhaps follow with cinnamon- and chile-rubbed tenderloin of beef with chipotle and white cheddar mashed potatoes and mango salsa. Or maybe you'd rather have plantain-crusted halibut served with a peach-citrus coulis, green chile risotto, and tropical fruit salsa.

There are daily specials, as well as a nice list of wines by the glass and special wines of the day.

✪ **La Casa Sena.** 125 E. Palace Ave. ☎ **505/988-9232.** Reservations recommended. Fixed-price dinner $29; lunch $7.75–$10. La Cantina, main courses $8.50–$17. AE, CB, DC, DISC, MC, V. Mon–Sat 11:30am–3pm; daily 5:30–10pm. Brunch Sun 11am–3pm. CREATIVE SOUTH-WESTERN.

Opposite St. Francis Cathedral, two restaurants face a spacious garden patio. The elegant main dining room occupies a Territorial-style adobe house built in 1867 by Civil War hero Major José Sena for his wife and 23 children. Today it's a veritable art gallery with museum-quality landscapes on the walls and Taos-style handcrafted furniture. In the adjacent **La Cantina,** waiters and waitresses sing numbers from Broadway shows as they carry platters from kitchen to table.

The cuisine in the main dining room might be described as northern New Mexican with a continental flair. Lunches include chicken enchiladas on blue-corn tortillas and almond-encrusted salmon with gazpacho salsa. In the evening, diners might start with a salad of mixed organic greens, goat cheese, and a fresh herb vinaigrette, then move to American corn-fed lamb chops with habañero-papaya sauce, tropical fruit ensalada, and crispy root vegetables.

The more moderately priced **Cantina** menu offers the likes of country fried ribeye and carne adovada burrito (prime pork roasted with red-chile sauce, served with Hatch green chile and cheeses). Both restaurants have exquisite desserts. The award-winning wine list features more than 850 wines.

The Pink Adobe. 406 Old Santa Fe Trail. ☎ **505/983-7712.** Reservations recommended. Main courses $10.75–$23.25; lunch $4.75–$8.75. AE, CB, DC, DISC, MC, V. Mon–Fri 11:30am–2:30pm; daily 5:30–9:30pm. CONTINENTAL/SOUTHWESTERN.

San Pasqual, patron saint of the kitchen, keeps a close eye on this popular restaurant in the center of the 17th-century Barrio de Analco and across the street from the San Miguel mission. A Santa Fe institution since 1946, it occupies an adobe home believed to be at least 350 years old. Guests enter through a narrow side door into a series of quaint, informal dining rooms with tile or hardwood floors. Stuccoed walls display original modern art or Priscilla Hoback pottery on built-in shelves.

At the dinner hour the Pink Adobe offers the likes of escargots and shrimp rémoulade as appetizers. Main courses include shrimp rémoulade, poulet Marengo, steak Dunnigan (a house specialty), lamb curry, and porc Napoléone. Lunch has more New Mexican and Cajun dishes, including a house enchilada topped with an egg, turkey-seafood gumbo, and gypsy stew (chicken, green chile, tomatoes, and onions in sherry broth). The food here isn't the greatest, to be sure, but people don't flock here for the cuisine; they come for the atmosphere.

Smoking is allowed only in the **Dragon Room,** the lounge across the alleyway from the restaurant. Under the same ownership, the charming Dragon Room (which is much more popular with locals than the Pink Adobe's main dining room) has its own menu offering traditional Mexican food. The full bar is open daily from 11:30am to 2am, until midnight on Sunday, and there's live entertainment Sunday through Thursday.

Poulet Patate Rotisserie Provencale. 446 W. San Francisco St. ☎ **505/820-2929.** Reservations recommended. Main courses $14.25–$24; lunch $9–$18. AE, DISC, MC, V. Daily 11am–2:30pm and 6–10pm. CONTINENTAL.

Featuring a six-by-six-foot wood-burning rotisserie oven, Poulet Patate is best known for its spit- or fire-roasted rotisserie chickens. The food is authentically French—the house specialty is an excellently prepared Herbes de Provence Chicken. Another good choice is the rotisserie duck stuffed with oranges and rosemary and glazed with honey and lavender. The leg of lamb offered here is traditionally French in its preparation. Everybody's favorite dessert here is Berries on a Cloud. In addition to dining room service, Poulet Patate also offers a takeout menu.

✪ **Santacafe.** 231 Washington Ave. ☎ **505/984-1788.** Reservations recommended. Main courses, $18–$24; lunch, $8–$12. AE, MC, V. Mon–Sat 11:30am–2pm; daily 6–10pm (5:30–10:30pm in summer). CONTEMPORARY AMERICAN.

A casually formal restaurant in the 18th-century Padre Gallegos House, 2^{1}/$_{2}$ blocks north of the Plaza, the service and presentation here are impeccable. Noted for its minimalist decor, art-free soft white adobe interior, and "Zen-inspired" courtyard, Santacafe has been a favorite of tourists and locals alike since 1983. Each room has a fireplace, and the courtyard is available for summer dining. Santacafe's unique modern American cuisine also reveals Southwestern and Asian influences. Menus change seasonally, but recent offerings included Dungeness crab cakes with cucumber and carrot salad and house-smoked chicken spring rolls with a three-chile dipping sauce as appetizers. Main courses included red chile ravioli filled with goat and feta cheeses, fresh oregano, sun-dried tomato, and a basil green chile sauce, and Atlantic salmon with roasted new potatoes. All breads and desserts are homemade, and the full bar offers wines by the glass.

MODERATE

Andiamo! 322 Garfield St. ☎ **505/995-9595.** Reservations recommended. Main courses $12–$18. AE, DISC, MC, V. Wed–Mon 5:30–10pm. ITALIAN.

Quite a few new restaurants have sprung up in Santa Fe over the last year, several of which are the creations of former staff members at some of the city's most popular eateries—Andiamo! is one of those that's making a successful go of it. Chris Galvin, once the sous chef at Cafe Escalera, has joined forces with business partner Joan Gillcrist at this fine restaurant to create an authentically Tuscan atmosphere in which a daily changing menu features antipasto, pasta, and excellent desserts. I particularly enjoyed the Caesar salad and the crispy polenta with rosemary and Gorgonzola as well

---

🔵 Family-Friendly Restaurants

Bobcat Bite *(see p. 142)*   The name and the ranch-style atmosphere will appeal to families looking for great steaks and huge hamburgers at low prices.

Cowgirl Hall of Fame *(see p. 137)*   Kids love the Kid's Corral where, among other things, they can play a game of horseshoes.

Upper Crust Pizza *(see p. 141)*   Many people consider this the best pizza in town, and they'll deliver to tired tots and their families at downtown hotels.

as the cannelloni (stuffed with spinach). For dessert I'd recommend the polenta pound cake with lemon crème anglaise. Beer and wine are served, and the dining room is smoke-free.

Bistro 315. 315 Old Santa Fe Trail. ☎ **505/986-9190.** Reservations recommended. Main courses $16–$24 at dinner. AE, DISC, MC, V. Daily 11:30am–2pm and 6–9pm. CONTINENTAL.

Bistro 315 has enjoyed instant success since its opening in 1995, and it's no wonder with two powerhouses like Matt Yohalem, a graduate of Johnson and Wales and Chef Poissonier at Le Cirque under Chef Daniel Boulud, and Jack Shaab, who formerly worked with both Larry Forgione and Mark Miller (Coyote Cafe). The restaurant is tiny (only 27 tables), but always packed, and with good reason. The food is excellent. The menu changes seasonally; on my last visit there I started with croquettes with goat cheese and bell pepper coulis and moved on to piñon-crusted halibut served with spinach and scallion beignets (Yohalem's experience working at Commander's Palace in New Orleans shows in dishes like this one). The grilled tomato soup is also excellent, and I've been fortunate to be here on a night when the grilled smoked chicken was offered. My favorite dessert is the warm *tarte tatin* served with crème fraîche. Because the restaurant is so small and so popular, reservations are an absolute must.

Cafe Cassis. 103 E. Water St. ☎ **505/989-1717.** Main courses $6.50–$15.75. AE, MC, V. Mon–Fri 11am–9pm, Sat–Sun 9am–3pm and 4–9pm. CONTEMPORARY AMERICAN.

Twenty-foot ceilings make the dining room at this small, contemporary restaurant seem much bigger and entertainment is provided by cooks who throw pizza dough into the air as though they've been doing it all their life. The specialty here is oak-fired pizzas with perfectly crisp crusts and creative toppings (like mushrooms and spinach pesto). One of Chef Ivan Walz's specialties is piñon-breaded pan fried chicken that is sauced with a chipotle and lingonberry combination. This is the place for good food at reasonable prices. There is a bar.

ⓢ Cafe Pasqual's. 121 Don Gaspar Ave. ☎ **505/983-9340.** Reservations highly recommended for dinner. Main courses $15.95–$24; lunch $6.25–$8.95; breakfast $4.75–$7.75. AE, MC, V. Mon–Sat 7am–3pm; Sun 8am–2pm; Sun–Thurs 6–10pm; Fri–Sat 6–10:30pm. NEW MEXICAN/AMERICAN.

This classic New Mexican–style establishment one block southwest of the Plaza is a big favorite of locals and travelers alike. Omelets, pancakes, cereals, and huevos motulenos—like rancheros but with fried bananas—are among the breakfast options. Soups, salads, sandwiches, and Mexican dishes are popular at lunch; there's a delectable grilled salmon burrito with black beans, herbed goat cheese, and cucumber salsa. There are also daily specials.

The frequently changing dinner menu offers grilled meats and seafoods, plus vegetarian specials. Oaxacan mango with citrus salsa, warm French brie with whole roasted garlic, and corn cakes are frequently offered appetizers. Main courses might include charcoal-grilled Yucatán-spiced breast of free-range chicken with saffron rice and fire-roasted poblano, red peppers, and zucchini; Thai shrimp sautéed in a lemongrass-coconut sauce with flash-fried ginger and steamed baby bok choy; and grilled rack of New Mexico lamb with mint-tomato salsa, white rose potatoes, and sugar snap peas.

Cowgirl Hall of Fame. 319 S. Guadalupe St. ☎ **505/982-2565.** Reservations recommended. Main courses $4.25–$12.95; lunch $2.95–$7.50. AE, DISC, MC, V. Mon–Thurs 11am–10:30pm; Fri–Sat 11am–11:30pm; Sun 10am–10pm. The bar is open every night until 2am (Sun until midnight). REGIONAL AMERICAN/BARBECUE.

Mention the Cowgirl Hall of Fame to any Santa Fean and you'll hear one word: *fun*. Everything at this restaurant has been done with a playful spirit, from the cowgirl paraphernalia decorating the walls to menu items such as "chicken wing dings" (eight chicken wings in a "dandy" citrus-Tabasco marinade served with a special dressing) and chuck wagon chili. The bunkhouse smoked brisket with potato salad, barbecue beans, and coleslaw is excellent, as is the cracker-fried catfish with jalapeño-tartar sauce. Recent specialties of the house included butternut squash casserole and grilled salmon soft tacos. There's even a special "kid's corral" with horseshoes, a ridin' rockin' horse, a horse-shaped rubber tire swing, hay bales, and a bean-bag toss to keep children entertained during dinner. The dessert specialty of the house is the original ice cream baked potato (ice cream molded into a potato shape, rolled in spices, and topped with green pecans and whipped cream). Happy hour is from 4 to 6pm. There is live music or comedy performances almost every night.

⑤ La Tertulia. 416 Agua Fria St. ☎ **505/988-2769.** Reservations recommended. Main courses $7.75–$18.50; lunch $4.95–$7.25. AE, MC, V. Tues–Sun 11:30am–2pm and 5–9pm. NEW MEXICAN.

Housed in a former 18th-century convent, La Tertulia's thick adobe walls separate six dining rooms, among them the old chapel and a *sala* (living room) containing a valuable Spanish colonial art collection. There's also an outside garden patio for summer dining. Dim lighting and viga-beamed ceilings, shuttered windows and wrought-iron chandeliers, lace tablecloths and hand-carved *santos* in wall niches lend a feeling of historic authenticity. La Tertulia means "The Gathering Place."

Gourmet regional dishes include filet y rellenos, carne adovada, pollo adovo, and *camarones con pimientas y tomates* (shrimp with peppers and tomatoes). If you feel like dessert, try *natillas* (custard). Many diners order a pitcher of the homemade sangría from the bar.

Ore House on the Plaza. 50 Lincoln Ave. ☎ **505/983-8687.** Reservations recommended. Main courses $12.95–$22.95. AE, MC, V. Daily 10:30am–2:30pm and 5:30–10pm. STEAKS/SEAFOOD.

The Ore House's second-story balcony, at the southwest corner of the Plaza, is an ideal spot from which to watch the passing parade while enjoying lunch or cocktails. When the weather gets chilly, radiant heaters keep the balcony warm, and there's a big fireplace indoors. The decor is Southwestern, with plants and lanterns hanging from white walls and over booths.

The menu is heavy on fresh seafood and steaks. Daily fresh fish specials include salmon and swordfish (poached, blackened, teriyaki, or lemon), rainbow trout, lobster, and shellfish. Steak Ore House, wrapped in bacon and topped with crabmeat and béarnaise sauce, and chicken Ore House, a grilled breast stuffed with ham, Swiss cheese, green chile, and béarnaise, are local favorites. Vegetable platters are also available. Luncheon diners often opt for the spinach salad or the prime rib sandwich.

The bar, with weekend entertainment, is proud of its 100 "custom margaritas." It also has an excellent wine list (a *Wine Spectator* award winner three years running). An appetizer menu is served from 2:30 to 10pm daily, and the bar stays open until midnight or later (only until midnight on Sunday).

The Palace. 142 W. Palace Ave. ☎ **505/982-9891.** Reservations recommended. Main courses $9.50–$18.95; lunch $5–$10.50. AE, MC, V. Mon–Sat 11:30am–4pm; daily 5:45–10pm. NORTHERN ITALIAN/CONTINENTAL.

When the Burro Alley site of Doña Tules's 19th-century gambling hall was excavated in 1959, an unusual artifact was discovered: a brass door-knocker, half shaped like a horseshoe, and the other half like a saloon girl's stockinged leg. That knocker has become the logo of the Palace, which maintains the Victorian flavor but none of the negative associations of its predecessor.

The brothers Lino, Pietro, and Bruno Pertusini have brought a long family tradition into the restaurant business: Their father was chef at the Villa d'Este on Lake Como, Italy. The Pertusinis' menu is northern Italian with a few French and continental dishes. Lunch features Caesar salad and roasted "7 Aromas" chicken salad, bruschetta caprini, ruby trout, housemade pasta, and breads. Dinner includes crab-stuffed shrimp, *scaloppine di vitello Ortolana* (veal, eggplant, and zucchini in a Pinot Grigio parsley sauce), New Mexican lamb, and a variety of vegetarian dishes. There are fresh pastas daily; the wine list is long and well considered. Outdoor dining is available, and the bar is open Monday through Saturday from 11:30am to 2am and Sunday from 5:45pm to midnight with nightly entertainment.

✪ **Paul's.** 72 W. Marcy St. ☎ **505/982-8738.** Reservations recommended for dinner. Main courses $12.95–$18.95; lunch $4.95–$7.50. AE, DISC, MC, V. Mon–Sat 11:30am–2:15pm; Sun–Thurs 5:30–9pm; Fri–Sat 6–10pm. INTERNATIONAL.

Once just a home-style deli, then a little gourmet restaurant called Santa Fe Gourmet, Paul's (which opened in 1990) is a wonderful place for lunch or dinner. The lunch menu has a nice selection of main courses, such as salad Niçoise, dill salmon cakes, and an incredible pumpkin bread stuffed with pine nuts, corn, green chile, red chile sauce, queso blanco, and caramelized apples. Sandwiches are also available at lunch. At dinner, the lights are dimmed and the bright Santa Fe interior (with folk art on the walls and colorfully painted screens dividing the restaurant into smaller, more intimate areas) becomes a great place for a romantic dinner. The menu might include red chile duck wontons in a soy ginger cream to start, and pecan-herb–crusted baked salmon with sorrel sauce as an entrée. The grilled ahi with roasted pepper, artichoke heart, and green olive salsa is excellent. Every dish is artistically exquisite in its presentation. Paul's won the "Taste of Santa Fe" award for the best main course in 1992 and the best dessert in 1994. His chocolate ganache is exquisite. A wine list is available. Smoking is not permitted anywhere in the restaurant.

✪ **Pranzo Italian Grill.** 540 Montezuma St., Sanbusco Center. ☎ **505/984-2645.** Reservations recommended. Main courses $5.95–$18.50; lunch $5.95–$9.95. AE, DC, DISC, MC, V. Mon–Sat 11:30am–3pm; Sun–Thurs 5–10pm, Fri–Sat 5–11pm. REGIONAL ITALIAN.

Housed in a renovated warehouse, and freshly redecorated in warm Tuscan colors, this sister of Albuquerque's redoubtable Scalo restaurant caters to local Santa Feans with a contemporary atmosphere of modern abstract art and food prepared on an open grill. Homemade soups, salads, creative pizzas, and fresh pastas are among the less expensive menu items. *Bianchi e nere al capesante* (black-and-white linguine with bay scallops in a light seafood sauce) and *pizza pollo affumicato* (with smoked chicken, pesto, and roasted peppers) are consistent favorites. Steak, chicken, veal, and fresh seafood grills—heavy on the garlic—dominate the dinner menu. The bar offers the Southwest's largest collection of grappas, as well as a wide selection of wines and champagnes by the glass. The upstairs rooftop terrace is lovely for seasonal moon-watching over a glass of wine. **Portare Via Cafe,** adjacent to the restaurant, is a great place for a light breakfast or lunch. The cinnamon rolls and scones are particularly good, and cappuccino and pastries are served throughout the day. Sandwiches are available at lunch.

INEXPENSIVE

Blue Corn Cafe. 133 W. Water. ☎ **505/984-1800.** Reservations accepted for parties of 8 or more. Main courses $4.95–$8.25. AE, DC, DISC, MC, V. Daily 11am–11pm. The bar stays open until 2am. NEW MEXICAN.

This lively, attractively decorated Southwestern-style restaurant opened in 1992 and is just what southside Santa Fe needed: great food at low prices. The interior is notable for its blue, green, red, and yellow painted patch floor. While you peruse the menu your waiter will bring freshly made tortilla chips to your table. The Blue Corn Cafe is known for its chile rellenos, and I have enjoyed the achiote grilled half chicken with epazote cream sauce as well as the carne adovada quesadilla (red chile marinated pork, wrapped in a flour tortilla with green chile and jack and cheddar cheese served with guacamole and sour cream). The tortilla burger (beef patty covered with cheeses and red or green chile, wrapped in a flour tortilla and served with chile fries) is another good bet. And for those who can't decide, the combination plates offer a nice variety. For dessert, try the Mexican brownies, the homemade caramel flan, or the fried ice cream. The bar features 34 varieties of tequila and an interesting list of specialty margaritas. Live bands play on Friday and Saturday nights.

The Burrito Co. 111 Washington Ave. ☎ **505/982-4453.** $1.85–$4.75. MC, V. Mon–Sat 7:30am–11pm. NEW MEXICAN.

This is probably downtown Santa Fe's best fast-food establishment. You can people-watch as you dine on the outdoor patio, or enjoy the garden-style poster gallery indoors. Order and pick up at the counter. Breakfast burritos are popular in the morning; after 11am you can get traditional Mexican meals with lots of chiles.

Ⓢ **Carlos' Gosp'l Cafe.** 125 Lincoln Ave. ☎ **505/983-1841.** Menu items $2.65–$6.65. No credit cards. Mon–Sat 11am–4pm. DELI.

You'll want to sing the praises of the "Say Amen" desserts at this cafe, located in the inner courtyard of the First Interstate Bank Building. First, though, try the tortilla or hangover (potato-corn) soup, or the deli sandwiches. Carlos' has outdoor tables, but many diners prefer to sit indoors, reading newspapers or sharing conversation at the large common table. Gospel and soul music play continuously; oil paintings of churches and of many performers cover the walls.

Ⓢ **Guadalupe Cafe.** 422 Old Santa Fe Trail. ☎ **505/982-9762.** Main courses $6.95–$15.95; lunch $6–$12; breakfast $4.50–$8.75. DISC, MC, V. Tues–Fri 7am–2pm; Tues–Sat 5:30–10pm; Sat–Sun 8am–2pm. NEW MEXICAN.

Santa Feans line up at all hours to dine in this casually elegant cafe, which was recently featured in *Bon Appetit* magazine. Breakfasts include spinach-mushroom burritos and huevos rancheros, while the lunch menu features chalupas, stuffed sopaipillas, burritos, chimichangas, and burrito plates, as well as a wide variety of salads and burgers. Dinner specialties include the excellent breast of chicken relleno (boneless breast of chicken filled with jack and cheddar cheese, breaded in corn meal, deep fried, and finished in the oven with green chile and cheese). For those who don't enjoy Mexican food there are hamburgers and a selection of traditional favorites like chicken fried steak, turkey piñon meat loaf, and chicken salad. Daily specials are available; don't miss the famous chocolate-amaretto adobe pie for dessert. Beer, wine, and margaritas are served.

La Choza. 905 Alarid St. ☎ **505/982-0909.** Reservations not accepted. Lunch $4.50–$5.50; dinner $5.50–$6.50. MC, V. Mon–Sat 11am–9pm. NEW MEXICAN.

The sister restaurant of the Shed (see below) is located near the intersection of Cerrillos Road and St. Francis Drive. A casual eatery with round tables beneath a viga ceiling, it's especially popular on cold days when diners gather around the wood-burning stove and fireplace. The menu offers traditional enchiladas, tacos, and burritos on blue-corn tortillas, as well as green-chile stew, chili con carne, and carne adovada. Vegetarians and children have their own menus. Beer and wine are available.

Old Santa Fe Trail Bookstore and Coffeehouse. 613 Old Santa Fe Trail. ☎ **505/988-8878.** Reservations not accepted. Main courses $5–$10.50. AE, DISC, MC, V. Sun–Thurs 8am–10pm; Fri–Sat 8am–11pm. CAFE.

If you're one of the literati (or just enjoy being around the literati), the Old Santa Fe Trail Bookstore and Coffeehouse has become the place to see and be seen. Sandwiches, coffees, and pastries dominate the menu here, so you can grab a bite to eat while listening to the latest reading or attending the latest book signing. Local talent is featured, and chocolate decadence dessert and cappuccino are the perfect way to enjoy the atmosphere.

⑤ **San Francisco Street Bar and Grill.** 114 W. San Francisco St. ☎ **505/982-2044.** Reservations not accepted. Lunch $5.25–$6.75; dinner $5.25–$12.50. AE, DISC, MC, V. Daily 11am–11pm. AMERICAN.

This easy-going eatery offers casual dining amid simple decor in three seating areas: the main restaurant, an indoor courtyard beneath the three-story Plaza Mercado atrium, and an outdoor patio with its own summer grill. Although the restaurant may be best known for its hamburgers, it does offer a variety of daily specials. The lunch menu consists mainly of soups, sandwiches, and salads; dinner dishes include a tasty chicken breast with roasted red pepper aioli, grilled pork tenderloin with apple and green chile salsa, and New York strip steak. There are also nightly pasta specials like spinach linguini al Greque (housemade spinach linguini with sun-dried tomatoes, kalamata olives, feta cheese, olive oil, and garlic). The full bar service includes draft beers and daily wine specials.

⑤ **The Shed.** 113¹/₂ E. Palace Ave. ☎ **505/982-9030.** Reservations accepted at dinner. Main courses $6.75–$13.95; lunch $4.75–$7. DISC, MC, V. Mon–Sat 11am–2:30pm; Thurs–Sat 5:30–9pm. NEW MEXICAN.

Lines often form outside The Shed, located half a block east of the Palace of the Governors. A luncheon institution since 1953, it occupies several rooms and the patio of a rambling hacienda that was built in 1692. Festive folk art adorns the doorways and walls. The food is basic but delicious, a compliment to traditional Hispanic Pueblo cooking. Enchiladas, tacos, and burritos, all served on blue-corn tortillas with pinto beans and posole, are menu staples. The green-chile soup is a local favorite. The Shed recently hired a new chef, Joshua Carswell, who has added vegetarian and low-fat Mexican foods to the menu as well as a wider variety of soups and salads. There are dessert specials, and beer and wine are available. The Shed is once again open for dinner (this meal had not been available for some 30 years).

⑤ **Tomasita's Cafe.** 500 S. Guadalupe St. ☎ **505/983-5721.** Main courses $4.75–$9.75; lunch $4.25–$9.25. MC, V. Mon–Sat 11am–10pm. NEW MEXICAN.

This may be the restaurant most consistently recommended by local Santa Feans. Why? Some point to the atmosphere; others cite the food and prices. Hanging plants and wood decor accent this spacious brick building adjacent to the old Santa Fe railroad station. Traditional New Mexican main courses like chile rellenos and enchiladas (house specialties), as well as stuffed sopaipillas, chalupas, and tacos are served. Offerings also include vegetarian dishes and daily specials, and there's full bar service.

Upper Crust Pizza. 329 Old Santa Fe Trail. ☎ **505/983-4140.** Reservations not accepted. Main courses $3.95–$12.95. No credit cards. Winter Mon–Sat 11am–10pm, Sun noon–10pm; Summer Mon–Sat 11am–11pm, Sun noon–11pm. PIZZA.

Santa Fe's best pizzas may be found here, in an adobe house where the front gate adjoins the old San Miguel mission. Meals-in-a-dish include the Grecian gourmet pizza (feta and olives) and the whole wheat vegetarian pizza (topped with sesame seeds). You can either eat here or request free delivery (it takes about 30 minutes) to your downtown hotel. Beer and wine are available, as are salads, calzones, and stromboli.

SOUTHSIDE/CERRILLOS ROAD
MODERATE

✪ **Old Mexico Grill.** 2434 Cerrillos Rd., College Plaza South. ☎ **505/473-0338.** Reservations requested at dinner for parties of 6 or more. Main courses $8.75–$16.95. DISC, MC, V. Mon–Fri 11:30am–2:30pm; Sun–Thurs 5:30–9pm; Fri–Sat 5:30–9:30pm. Extended hours in summer. MEXICAN.

Here's something unique in Santa Fe: a restaurant that specializes not in northern New Mexico food, but in authentic regional Mexican cuisine. Waitpersons offer attentive service; the centerpiece is an exhibition cooking area with an open mesquite grill and French rotisserie, behind bright blue tiles and beneath a raft of hanging copper ware.

A tempting array of fajitas, tacos al carbón, and other specialties are prepared on the grill. Popular dishes include turkey mole poblano and *costillas de puerca en barbacoa de Oaxaca* (hickory-smoked baby back ribs baked in a chipotle and mulato chile, honey, mustard barbecue sauce). There's a good choice of soups and salads at lunch, and a selection of homemade desserts. A full bar serves Mexican beers and margaritas.

✪ **Steaksmith at El Gancho.** Old Las Vegas Hwy. ☎ **505/988-3333.** Reservations recommended. Main courses $8.95–$23.95. AE, MC, V. Daily 5:30–10pm. STEAKS/SEAFOOD.

Santa Fe's most highly regarded steak house is a 15-minute drive up the Old Pecos Trail toward Las Vegas. Guests enjoy attentive service in a pioneer setting with adobe walls and viga ceilings. New York sirloin, filet mignon, and other complete steak dinners are served, along with barbecued ribs and such nightly fresh seafood specials as oysters, trout, and salmon. A creative appetizer menu ranges from ceviche Acapulco to grilled pasilla peppers and beef chupadero.

Szechwan Chinese Cuisine. 1965 Cerrillos Rd. ☎ **505/983-1558.** Reservations recommended. Main courses $5.95–$11.95; lunch $5–$7. DISC, MC, V. Daily 11am–9:30pm. NORTHERN CHINESE.

The spicy northern Chinese cuisine served here pleases the Southwestern palate. The seafood platter of shrimp, scallops, crab, fish, and vegetables stir-fried in a wine sauce is excellent. Other specialties include Lake Tung Ting shrimp, sesame beef, and General Chung's chicken. Wine and Tsingtao beer from China are served.

INEXPENSIVE

⑤ **Bobcat Bite.** Old Las Vegas Hwy. ☎ **505/983-5319.** Reservations not accepted. Main courses $3.50–$11.95. No credit cards. Tues–Sat 11am–7:50pm. STEAKS/BURGERS.

This local classic (in operation for over forty years), located about 5 miles southeast of Santa Fe, is famed for its high-quality steaks—such as the 13-ounce ribeye—and huge hamburgers, including a remarkable green-chile cheeseburger. The ranch-style atmosphere appeals to families.

⑤ **Maria's New Mexican Kitchen.** 555 W. Cordova Rd. near St. Francis Drive. ☎ **505/983-7929.** Reservations accepted but not essential. Main courses $5.75–$15.95; lunch $5.25–$8.95. MC, V. Mon–Fri 11am–10pm, Sat–Sun noon–10pm. NEW MEXICAN.

Built in 1949 by Maria Lopez and her politician husband, Gilbert (current owners are Laurie and Al Lucero), this restaurant is a prime example of what charm can come from scavenging: Its bricks came from the old New Mexico State Penitentiary, and most of its furniture was once used in La Fonda Hotel. The five wall frescoes in the cantina were painted by master muralist Alfred Morang (1901–58) in exchange for food.

Maria's boasts an open tortilla grill, where cooks can be seen making flour tortillas by hand. Generous portions are on every plate, from the award-winning beef, chicken, and vegetarian fajitas to blue-corn enchiladas, chile rellenos, green chile and posole stews, and huge steaks. If you're a margarita fan, this is the place to taste a variety of them—Maria's features more than 40 "Real Margaritas" ranging in price from $3.75 to $20. Children's plates are available. Strolling mariachi troubadours perform nightly. The restaurant offers patio dining in the summer, and two fireplaces warm the dining room in winter.

✪ **Natural Cafe.** 1494 Cerrillos Rd. ☎ **505/983-1411.** Reservations recommended at dinner. Lunch $5–$8; dinner $8.50–$17. Tues–Fri 11:30am–2:30pm; Tues–Sun 5–9:30pm. CREATIVE INTERNATIONAL.

An international menu of tasty and healthful dishes is served in an artsy garden atmosphere by a competent cosmopolitan staff. No fewer than five national cuisines—Mexican (black-bean enchiladas), Chinese (Szechuan chicken), Indonesian (tempeh burger), Thai (vegetable gai tua), and American—are represented on the everyday menu. Several seafood and chicken specials are offered daily, including salmon with lemon caper sauce and chicken romesco (charcoal-grilled free-range chicken served with red pepper and hazelnut sauce). A children's menu is available. Homemade desserts are sweetened with maple syrup, raw sugar, or honey. Wine and beer are served.

❸ **Tecolote Cafe.** 1203 Cerrillos Rd. ☎ **505/988-1362.** Main dishes $2.95–$9.25. AE, CB, DC, DISC, MC, V. Tues–Sun 7am–2pm. NEW MEXICAN/AMERICAN.

This is a breakfast-lover's favorite. The decor is simple, but the food is elaborate: eggs any style, omelets, huevos rancheros—all served with fresh-baked muffins or biscuits and maple syrup. Give the atole piñon hotcakes (made with blue cornmeal) a try. Luncheon specials include carne adovada burritos and green-chile stew, served with beer or wine.

5 What to See & Do

Nearly all of Santa Fe's top attractions are directly on or adjacent to the city's bustling central plaza. **The Plaza** has been the heart and soul of Santa Fe since it was established with the city in 1610. Originally designed as a meeting place, it has been the location of innumerable festivals as well as other historical, cultural, and social events; for many years, it was a dusty hive of activity as the staging ground and terminus of the Santa Fe Trail. Today, those who sit around the Plaza's central fountain are afforded the best people-watching in New Mexico.

For information on what the Plaza has to offer in addition to the points of interest discussed below, visit the historic Tully House, located directly on the Plaza at 136 Grant Ave. and home to the Historic Santa Fe Foundation. There, you can pick up the foundation's publication, *Old Santa Fe Today,* which provides detailed descriptions, accompanied by a map and photos, of 50 sites within walking distance of the Plaza.

THE TOP ATTRACTIONS

✪ **Palace of the Governors.** North Plaza. ☎ **505/827-6483.** Admission $5 adults, free for children under 17. Four-day passes good at all four branches of the Museum of New Mexico cost $8 for adults. Jan–Feb, Tues–Sun 10am–5pm; Mar–Dec, daily 10am–5pm. Closed Mon in Feb.

Greater Santa Fe

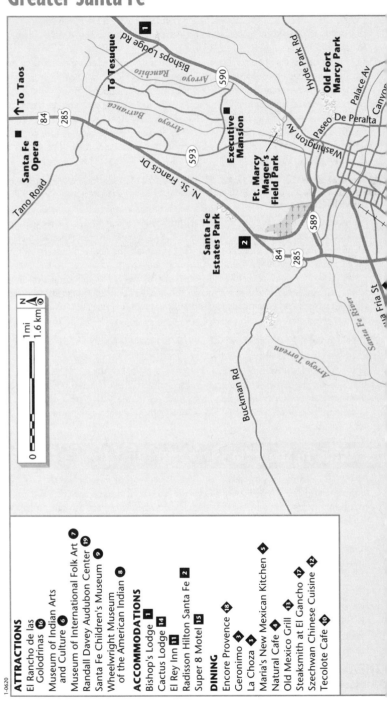

ATTRACTIONS
El Rancho de las
  Golodrinas 16
Museum of Indian Arts
  and Culture 6
Museum of International Folk Art 7
Randall Davey Audubon Center 19
Santa Fe Children's Museum 9
Wheelwright Museum
  of the American Indian 8

ACCOMMODATIONS
Bishop's Lodge 1
Cactus Lodge 14
El Rey Inn 11
Radisson Hilton Santa Fe 2
Super 8 Motel 15

DINING
Encore Provence 18
Geronimo 3
La Choza 3
Maria's New Mexican Kitchen 5
Natural Cafe 4
Old Mexico Grill 13
Steaksmith at El Gancho 17
Szechwan Chinese Cuisine 12
Tecolote Cafe 10

1-0620

144

6
7
8

del
Jo
e Trail

To Roswell
& Las Vegas

285
25
84
25

Las Vegas Hwy

Old Pecos Trail

9

Don Ca

E San Mateo Rd

Lupita Rd

Botulph Rd

Rodeo Road

300

Pe rez Park

5

St Michael's Dr

Calisteo St

S St Francis Drive S

84
285

W San Mateo Rd

St Mateo Rd

Zia Rd

25 466

The Institute
of American
Indian Arts

Ashbaugh
Park

10

11

12 13

College of
Santa Fe

Siringo Rd

Arroyo de los Chamisos

Ragle
Park

25

To Albuquerque

Agua Fri

Santa Fe River

588

14

Gen Franklin
E Miles Park

Cerrillos Rd

85

15

Rodeo Road

300

16

Villa Linda
Mall

Built in 1610 as the original capitol of New Mexico, the Palace has been in continuous public use longer than any other structure in the United States. Designated the Museum of New Mexico in 1909, it has become the state history museum, with an adjoining library and photo archives. Some cutaways of doors and windows reveal the early architecture.

A series of exhibits chronicles four centuries of New Mexico's Hispanic and American history, from the 16th-century Spanish explorations through the frontier era to modern times. Among the Hispanic artifacts, there are maps dating from the early 1700s. There's even an entire mid–19th-century chapel, with a simple, bright-colored altarpiece made in 1830 for a Taos church by folk artist José Rafael Aragón.

Governors' offices from the Mexican and 19th-century U.S. eras have been restored and preserved. Displayed artifacts from early New Mexican life include a stagecoach, an early working printing press, and a collection of *mestizajes,* portraits of early Spanish colonists depicting typical costumes of the time. Also on display are pieces from the silver service used aboard the battleship USS *New Mexico* from 1918 to 1939 and a tiny New Mexico state flag (three by four inches) that went to the moon on one of the *Apollo* missions.

Most Native American artifacts (previously housed here) have been moved to the Museum of Indian Arts and Culture. Among those that remain are some pieces of ancient pottery from the Puye Plateau culture and photographs depicting a museum-sponsored study of Mayan sites in Mexico's Yucatán.

There are two shops of particular interest. One is the bookstore, which has one of the finest selections of art, history, and anthropology books in the Southwest. The other is the print shop and bindery, where limited-edition works are produced on hand-operated presses.

One of the most lasting impressions of Santa Fe that visitors are likely to take home is not of the museum itself, but of the Native American artisans sitting shoulder-to-shoulder beneath the long covered portal facing the Plaza. Here on the shaded sidewalk, several dozen colorfully dressed members of local Pueblo tribes, plus an occasional Navajo, Apache, or Hopi, spread out their handcrafts: mainly jewelry and pottery, but also woven carpets, beadwork, and paintings.

The Palace is the flagship of the Museum of New Mexico system; the main office is at 113 Lincoln Ave. (☎ **505/982-6366,** or 505/827-6463 for recorded information). The system comprises five state monuments and four Santa Fe museums: the Palace of the Governors, the Museum of Fine Arts, the Museum of International Folk Art, and the Museum of Indian Arts and Culture.

✪ **Museum of Fine Arts.** Palace and Lincoln aves. ☎ **505/827-4455.** Admission $5 adults, free for youth under 17 (4-day passes are available). Tues–Sun 10am–5pm. Closed Mon.

Located catercorner from the Plaza and immediately opposite the Palace of the Governors, this was the first Pueblo Revival–style building constructed in Santa Fe, in 1917. As such, it was a major stimulus in Santa Fe's development as an art colony earlier in this century.

The museum's permanent collection of more than 8,000 works emphasizes regional art and includes landscapes and portraits by all the Taos masters as well as Georgia O'Keeffe, and more recent works by such contemporary greats as R.C. Gorman and Amado Pena Jr.

The museum also has a collection of Ansel Adams photography. Modern artists, many of them far from the mainstream of traditional Southwestern art, are featured in temporary exhibits throughout the year. Two sculpture gardens present a range of three-dimensional art from the traditional to the abstract.

Beautiful St. Francis Auditorium, patterned after the interiors of traditional Hispanic mission churches, adjoins the Museum of Fine Arts. (See "Santa Fe After Dark," below.) A museum shop sells books on Southwestern art, plus prints and postcards of the collection.

✪ **St. Francis Cathedral.** Cathedral Place at San Francisco St. (P.O. Box 2127). ☎ **505/982-5619.** Donations appreciated. Open daily. Visitors may attend mass Mon–Sat at 6 and 7am and 5:15pm and Sun at 6, 8, and 10am, noon, and 7pm.

Santa Fe's grandest religious structure, named after Santa Fe's patron saint, is just a block east of the Plaza. An architectural anomaly in Santa Fe, it was built between 1869 and 1886 by Archbishop Jean-Baptiste Lamy to resemble the great cathedrals of Europe. French architects designed the Romanesque building and Italian masons assisted with its construction.

The small adobe Our Lady of the Rosary Chapel on the northeast side of the cathedral reflects a Spanish style. Built in 1807, it is the only parcel remaining from Our Lady of the Assumption Church, founded with Santa Fe in 1610. The new cathedral was built over and around the old church.

A wooden icon set in a niche in the wall of the north chapel, *La Conquistadora,* "Our Lady of Conquering Love," is the oldest representation of the Madonna in the United States. Rescued from the old church during the 1680 Pueblo rebellion, it was carried back by Don Diego de Vargas on his peaceful reconquest 12 years later, thus the name. Today *La Conquistadora* plays an important part in the annual Feast of Corpus Christi in June and July.

In 1986 a $600,000 renovation project relocated an early 18th-century wooden statue of St. Francis of Assisi to the center of the altar screen. Around the cathedral's exterior are front doors featuring 16 bronze door panels of historic note, and a plaque memorializing the 38 Franciscan friars who were martyred in New Mexico's early years. There's also a large bronze statue of Bishop Lamy himself; his grave is under the main altar of the cathedral.

MORE ATTRACTIONS
MUSEUMS

Catholic Museum & the Archbishop Lamy Commemorative Garden. 223 Cathedral Place. ☎ **505/983-3811.** Donations appreciated. Mon–Fri 8:30am–4:30pm; Sat hours vary (call ahead).

Housed in a complex of buildings that date from 1832, the Catholic Museum is one of New Mexico's newest. Visitors here have the opportunity to learn about the development and significance of Catholicism in New Mexico. Opened in 1994 by the Archdiocese of Santa Fe, the museum houses a collection of religious relics, including a book printed by Padre Antonio José Martinez of Taos, the Lamy chalice that was given to Archbishop Lamy by Pope Pius IX in 1854, and the document that formally reestablished royal possession of the Villa and Capital of Santa Fe and was signed by Diego de Vargas in 1692. There are also photographs on display, documenting events pertaining to the 11 archbishops of Santa Fe. The museum shop is stocked with books on New Mexico's history and religious items.

Institute of American Indian Arts Museum. 108 Cathedral Place. ☎ **505/988-6211.** Admission (2-day pass) $4 adults, $2 seniors and students, free for children 16 and under. Tues–Sat 10am–5pm, Sun noon–5pm.

The Institute of American Indian Arts (IAIA) is the nation's only congressionally chartered institute of higher education devoted solely to the study and practice of the artistic and cultural traditions of all American Indian and Alaska native peoples. Many

New Mexico & Georgia O'Keeffe: The Transformation of a Great American Artist

In June 1917, during a short tour of the Southwest, painter Georgia O'Keeffe (b. 1887) visited New Mexico for the first time. She was immediately enchanted by the place—her mind wandered frequently to the arid land and undulating mesas even after she returned to the vibrant sights and sounds of New York. It wasn't until she was coaxed back by arts patron and "collector of people" Mabel Dodge Luhan 12 years later, however, that O'Keeffe returned to the multihued desert of her daydreams.

When she arrived in Santa Fe in April 1929, O'Keeffe was reportedly ill, both physically and emotionally. New Mexico seemed to soothe her spirit and heal her physical ailments almost immediately. Only two days after Georgia's arrival, Mabel Dodge convinced the artist to move to her home in Taos. There, she could be free to paint and socialize as she liked.

In Taos, O'Keeffe began painting some of her best-known canvasses—close-ups of desert flowers and objects such as cow and horse skulls. "The color up there is different . . . the blue green of the sage and the mountains, the wildflowers in bloom," O'Keeffe once said of Taos. "It's a different kind of color from any I've ever seen— there's nothing like that in north Texas or even in Colorado." Her personality, as well as her art, was transformed by Taos's influence. She bought a car and learned to drive (in that order). Sometimes, on warm days, she ran stark naked through the sage fields. That August, a new, rejuvenated O'Keeffe rejoined her husband, photographer Alfred Stieglitz, in New York.

The artist returned to New Mexico year after year, spending time with Mabel Dodge as well as staying at the isolated Ghost Ranch. She drove through the countryside in her snappy Ford, stopping to paint in her favorite spots. But, until 1949, O'Keeffe always returned to New York in the fall. Three years after Stieglitz's death, though, she relocated permanently to New Mexico, spending her winters and springs in Abiquiu, summers and falls at Ghost Ranch. Georgia O'Keeffe died in Santa Fe in 1986.

of the best Native American artists of the last three decades have passed through the IAIA. Their works can often be seen in one or another of the many exhibitions offered at the museum throughout the year. The museum's National Collection of Contemporary Indian Art comprises painting, sculpture, ceramics, textiles, jewelry, beadwork, basketry, and graphic arts. The institute's museum is the official repository of the most comprehensive collection of contemporary Native American art in the world and has loaned items from its collection to museums all over the world. The museum presents the artistic achievements of IAIA alumni, current students, and other nationally recognized Native American and Alaskan artists.

✪ **Museum of Indian Arts and Culture.** 710 Camino Lejo. ☎ **505/827-6344.** Admission $5 adults, children under 17 free. Tues–Sun 10am–5pm.

Next door to the Museum of International Folk Art, this museum opened in 1987 as the showcase for the adjoining Laboratory of Anthropology. Interpretive displays detail tribal history and contemporary lifestyles of New Mexico's Pueblo, Navajo, and Apache cultures. More than 50,000 pieces of basketry, pottery, clothing, carpets, and jewelry, much of it quite ancient, are on continual rotating display.

Downtown Santa Fe Attractions

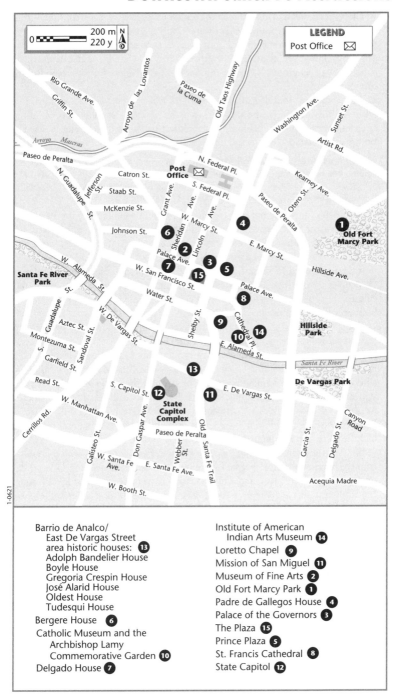

Barrio de Analco/
  East De Vargas Street
  area historic houses: **13**
    Adolph Bandelier House
    Boyle House
    Gregoria Crespin House
    José Alarid House
    Oldest House
    Tudesqui House
Bergere House **6**
Catholic Museum and the
  Archbishop Lamy
  Commemorative Garden **10**
Delgado House **7**

Institute of American
  Indian Arts Museum **14**
Loretto Chapel **9**
Mission of San Miguel **11**
Museum of Fine Arts **2**
Old Fort Marcy Park **1**
Padre de Gallegos House **4**
Palace of the Governors **3**
The Plaza **15**
Prince Plaza **5**
St. Francis Cathedral **8**
State Capitol **12**

There are frequent demonstrations of traditional skills by tribal artisans and regular programs in a 70-seat multimedia theater. Native American educators run a year-round workshop that encourages visitors to try such activities as weaving and corn grinding. There are also regular performances of Native American music and dancing by tribal groups. Concession booths purvey Native American foods during summer months.

The laboratory, founded in 1931 by John D. Rockefeller Jr., is a point of interest in itself. Designed by the well-known Santa Fe architect John Gaw Meem, it is an exquisite example of Pueblo Revival architecture. Since the museum opened, the lab has expanded its research and library facilities into its former display wing.

✪ **Museum of International Folk Art.** 706 Camino Lejo. ☎ **505/827-6350.** Admission $5 adults, free for children under 17. Tues–Sun 10am–5pm. The museum is located about 2 miles south of the Plaza, in the Sangre de Cristo foothills. Drive southeast on Old Santa Fe Trail, which becomes Old Pecos Trail, and look for signs pointing left onto Camino Lejo.

This branch of the Museum of New Mexico may not seem quite as typically Southwestern as other Santa Fe museums, but it's the largest of its kind in the world. With a collection of around 130,000 objects from more than 100 countries, it is my personal favorite of the city museums.

It was founded in 1953 by the Chicago collector Florence Dibell Bartlett, who said: "If peoples of different countries could have the opportunity to study each others' cultures, it would be one avenue for a closer understanding between men." That's the basis on which the museum operates today.

The special collections include Spanish Colonial silver, traditional and contemporary New Mexican religious art, Mexican tribal costumes, Mexican majolica ceramics, Brazilian folk art, European glass, African sculptures, East Indian textiles, and the marvelous Morris Miniature Circus. Particularly delightful are numerous dioramas, all done with colorful miniatures, of people around the world at work and play in typical town, village, and home settings. Recent acquisitions include American weathervanes and quilts, Palestinian costume jewelry and amulets, and Bhutanese and Indonesian textiles. Children love to look at the hundreds of toys on display. About half the pieces were given in 1982 by Alexander and Susan Girard.

In 1989 the museum opened a new Hispanic Heritage Wing, which houses the country's finest collection of Spanish Colonial and Hispanic folk art. Folk-art demonstrations, performances, and workshops are often presented. The 80,000-square-foot museum also has a lecture room, a research library, and a gift shop where a variety of folk art is available for purchase.

Wheelwright Museum of the American Indian. 704 Camino Lejo. ☎ **505/982-4636.** Donations appreciated. Mon–Sat 10am–5pm, Sun 1–5pm.

Though not a member of the state museum system, the Wheelwright is often included when people plan a trip to the folk-art and Native American arts museums because of its proximity: It's next door. Once known as the Museum of Navajo Ceremonial Art, the Wheelwright was founded in 1937 by Boston scholar Mary Cabot Wheelwright in collaboration with a Navajo medicine man, Hastiin Klah, to preserve and document Navajo ritual beliefs and practices. Klah took the designs of sand paintings used in healing ceremonies and adapted them into the woven pictographs that are a major part of the museum's treasure.

In 1976 the museum's focus was changed to include the living arts of all Native American cultures. Built in the shape of a Navajo hogan, with its doorway facing east (toward the rising sun) and its ceiling formed in the interlocking "whirling log" style, it offers rotating shows of silverwork, jewelry, tapestry, pottery, basketry, and paintings. There's a permanent collection (although it is not always on display) plus an outdoor sculpture garden with works by Allan Houser and other noted artisans.

In the basement is the Case Trading Post, an arts-and-crafts shop built to resemble the typical turn-of-the-century trading post found on Navajo reservations. Storyteller Joe Hayes captivates the attention of his listeners outside a tepee at dusk on certain days in July and August.

✪ **El Rancho de Las Golondrinas.** 334 Los Pinos Rd. ☎ **505/471-2261.** Admission $3.50 adults, $2.50 seniors 62 and over and teens, $1.50 children 5–12. Rates are slightly higher on festival weekends. June–Sept Wed–Sun 10am–4pm. Guided tours Apr–Oct by advance arrangement.

This 200-acre ranch, 15 miles south of the Santa Fe Plaza via I-25, was once the last stopping place on the 1,000-mile El Camino Real from Mexico City to Santa Fe. Today, it is a living 18th- and 19th-century Spanish village, comprising a hacienda, village store, schoolhouse, and several chapels and kitchens. There's also a working molasses mill, wheelwright and blacksmith shops, shearing and weaving rooms, a threshing ground, a winery and vineyards, and four water mills, as well as dozens of farm animals. A walk around the entire property is 1³/₄ miles in length.

Annual highlights at Las Golondrinas (The Swallows) are the Spring Festival (the first weekend of June) and the Harvest Festival (the first weekend of October). On these festival Sundays, the museum opens with a procession and mass dedicated to San Ysidro, patron saint of farmers. Other festivals and theme weekends are held throughout the summer. Authentically costumed volunteers demonstrate shearing, spinning, weaving, embroidery, wood carving, grain milling, blacksmithing, tinsmithing, soap making, and other activities. There's an exciting atmosphere of Spanish folk dancing, music, and theater, and traditional oven-cooked food.

CHURCHES

✪ **Loretto Chapel.** The Inn at Loretto, 211 Old Santa Fe Trail at Water St. ☎ **505/984-7971.** Admission $1 adult, children 6 and under free. Daily 9am–5pm. Entry is through the Inn at Loretto.

Though no longer consecrated for worship, the Loretto Chapel is an important site in Santa Fe. Patterned after the famous Sainte-Chapelle church in Paris, it was constructed in 1873—by the same French architects and Italian masons who were building Archbishop Lamy's cathedral—as a chapel for the Sisters of Loretto, who had established a school for young ladies in Santa Fe in 1852.

The chapel is especially notable for its remarkable spiral staircase: It makes two complete 360° turns, with no central or other visible support! (A railing was added later.) Legend has it that the building was nearly finished in 1878 when workers realized the stairs to the choir loft wouldn't fit. Hoping for a solution more attractive than a ladder, the sisters made a novena to St. Joseph—and were rewarded when a mysterious carpenter appeared astride a donkey and offered to build a staircase. Armed with only a saw, a hammer, and a T-square, the master constructed this work of genius by soaking slats of wood in tubs of water to curve them, and holding them together with wooden pegs. Then he disappeared without waiting to collect his fee.

Mission of San Miguel. Old Santa Fe Trail at E. De Vargas St. ☎ **505/983-3974.** Free admission; donations welcomed. Mon–Sat 11:30am–4pm, Sun 1–4:30pm. Summer hours start earlier. Mass 5pm daily.

This is one of the oldest churches in America, having been erected within a couple of years of the 1610 founding of Santa Fe. Tlaxcala Indians, servants of early Spanish soldiers and missionaries, may have used fragments of a 12th-century pueblo found on this site in its construction. Severely damaged in the 1680 Pueblo revolt, it was almost completely rebuilt in 1710, and has been altered numerous times since.

Because of its design, with high windows and thick walls, the structure was occasionally used as a temporary fortress during times of raiding Native Americans. One painting in the sanctuary has holes that, according to legend, were made by arrows.

The mission and a nearby house—today a gift shop billed as "The Oldest House," though there's no way of knowing for sure—were bought by the Christian Brothers from Archbishop Lamy for $3,000 in 1881; the order still operates both structures. Among the treasures in the mission are the San Jose Bell, reputedly cast in Spain in 1356 and brought to Santa Fe via Mexico several centuries later, and a series of buffalo hides and deerskins decorated with Bible stories.

Santuario de Nuestra Señora de Guadalupe. 100 Guadalupe St. at Agua Fria St. ☎ **505/ 988-2027.** Donations accepted. Mon–Sat 9am–4pm. Closed weekends Nov–Apr.

Built between 1776 and 1795 at the end of El Camino Real by Franciscan missionaries, this is believed to be the oldest shrine in the United States honoring the Virgin of Guadalupe, patron of Mexico. The sanctuary's adobe walls are almost three feet thick, and the deep-red plaster wall behind the altar was dyed with oxblood in traditional fashion when the church was restored earlier this century.

On one wall is a famous oil painting, *Our Lady of Guadalupe,* created in 1783 by renowned Mexican artist Jose de Alzibar. Painted expressly for the church, it was brought from Mexico City by mule caravan.

Today administered as a museum by the nonprofit Guadalupe Historic Foundation, the sanctuary is frequently used for chamber music concerts, flamenco dance programs, dramas, lectures, and religious art shows.

GETTING CLOSE TO NATURE

Old Fort Marcy Park. Artist Rd.

Marking the 1846 site of the first U.S. military reservation in the Southwest, this park overlooks the northeast corner of downtown. Only a few mounds remain from the fort, but the Cross of the Martyrs, at the top of a winding brick walkway from Paseo de Peralta near Otero Street, is a popular spot for bird's-eye photographs. The cross was erected in 1920 by the Knights of Columbus and the Historical Society of New Mexico to commemorate Franciscans killed in the Pueblo Revolt of 1680. It has since played a role in numerous religious processions.

Randall Davey Audubon Center. Upper Canyon Rd. ☎ **505/983-4609.** $1 donation requested. Daily 9am–5pm. House tours conducted sporadically during the summer; call for hours.

Named for the late Santa Fe artist who willed his home to the National Audubon Society, this wildlife refuge occupies 135 acres at the mouth of Santa Fe Canyon. More than 100 species of birds and 120 types of plants live here, and a variety of mammals have been spotted, including black bears, mule deer, mountain lions, bobcats, raccoons, and coyotes. Trails winding through more than 100 acres of the nature sanctuary are open to day hikers.

ESPECIALLY FOR KIDS

In addition to the listing below, don't miss taking the kids to the Museum of International Folk Art, where they'll love the international dioramas and the toys, and to El Rancho de las Golondrinas, a living Spanish colonial village.

Santa Fe Children's Museum. 1050 Old Pecos Trail. ☎ **505/989-8359.** Admission $2.50 adults, $1.50 children under 12. Wed, Thurs, Sat 10am–5pm, Fri 9am–5pm, Sun noon–5pm. The museum is open the first Friday of every month until 8pm.

Designed for whole families to experience, this museum offers interactive exhibits and hands-on activities in the arts, humanities, science, and technology. Special performances and hands-on sessions with artists and scientists are regularly scheduled.

6 Organized Tours

WALKING TOURS

Afoot in Santa Fe. At the Inn at Loretto, 211 Old Santa Fe Trail. ☎ **505/983-3701.**

Personalized 2^1/$_2$-hour tours are offered twice daily from the Inn at Loretto. Reservations are not required.

The Walking Tour of Santa Fe. 107 Washington Ave. ☎ **800/338-6877** or 505/983-6565.

One of Santa Fe's best walking tours begins at the northwest corner of the Plaza (at 9:30am and 1:30pm) and lasts about 2^1/$_2$ hours. The tour costs $10 for adults. Children are free.

BUS, CAR & TRAM TOURS

Gray Line Tours. 1330 Hickox St. ☎ **505/983-9491.**

The trolleylike Roadrunner departs several times daily in summer (less often in winter) from the Plaza, beginning at 9am, for 2^1/$_2$-hour city tours. Buy tickets as you board. Daily tours to Taos, Chimayo, and Bandelier National Monument are also offered.

LorettoLine. At the Inn at Loretto, 211 Old Santa Fe Trail. ☎ **505/983-3701.**

For an open-air tour of the city, contact LorettoLine. Tours last 1^1/$_2$ hours and are offered seven days a week from May to October. Tour times are at 10am, noon, and 2pm. Tickets are $9 for adults, $4 for children.

Rocky Mountain Tours. 217 W. Manhattan St. ☎ **505/984-1684.**

With this service, you can arrange a custom tour with a private guide (in your car or a four-wheel-drive vehicle) to Chaco Canyon (usually requires an overnight stay), the Four Corners region (usually requires two nights on the road), and other areas. River-rafting trips, hot-air balloon flights, airplane sightseeing rides over Santa Fe, and horseback riding trips are also offered.

MISCELLANEOUS TOURS

Pathways Customized Tours. 161-F Calle Ojo Feliz. ☎ **505/982-5382.**

Don Dietz offers several planned tours, including a downtown Santa Fe walking tour, a full city tour, a trip to the cliff dwellings and native pueblos, a "Taos adventure," and a trip to Georgia O'Keeffe country; he will try to accommodate any special requests you might have. These tours last anywhere from 1^1/$_2$ to 9 hours, depending on the one you choose. Don has extensive knowledge of the area's culture, history, geology, and flora and fauna and will help you make the most of your precious vacation time.

Rain Parrish. 535 Cordova Rd., Suite 250. ☎ **505/984-8236.**

A Navajo anthropologist, artist, and freelance curator offers custom guide services focusing on cultural anthropology, Native American arts, and the history of the Native Americans of the Southwest. Ms. Parrish includes visits to local pueblo villages.

Recursos de Santa Fe. 826 Camino de Monte Rey. ☎ **505/982-9301.**

This organization is a full-service destination management company, emphasizing custom-designed itineraries to meet the interests of any group. They specialize in the archeology, art, literature, spirituality, architecture, environment, food, or history of the Southwest.

Rojo Tours and Services. P.O. Box 15744. ☎ **505/474-8333;** fax 505/474-2992.

Customized private tours are arranged to pueblos, cliff dwellings, and ruins, as well as adventure travel such as river rafting and horseback riding.

Santa Fe Detours. 107 Washington Ave. ☎ **800/DETOURS** or 505/983-6565.

Santa Fe's most extensive tour-booking agency accommodates almost all travelers' tastes, from bus and rail tours to river rafting, backpacking, and cross-country skiing.

Southwest Safaris. P.O. Box 945, Santa Fe, NM 87504. ☎ **800/842-4246** or 505/988-4246.

One-day combination air/land natural history tours are offered from Santa Fe to Monument Valley, Grand Canyon, Canyon de Chelly, Mesa Verde, and Arches/Canyonlands.

7 Outdoor Activities

Note: In addition to all the activities and recreation centers listed below, there will be a new full-service family recreation center in Santa Fe by early to mid-1998. The complex will include a 25-meter pool, leisure and therapy pools, an ice-skating rink, three gyms, a workout room, racquetball courts, and an indoor running track. Contact the Santa Fe Convention and Visitors Bureau for more information.

BALLOONING   New Mexico is known for its spectacular Balloon Fiesta, which takes place annually in Albuquerque. If you've always wanted to take a ride, this is the place to do it. **Rocky Mountain Tours,** at 217 W. Manhattan St. (☎ **800/231-7238** outside New Mexico, or 505/984-1684), offers year-round hot-air-balloon flights daily on a reservations-only basis. Flights take place at dawn. The flight includes continental breakfast or snacks and champagne after the flight. Rates begin at around $135 a flight. If you've got your heart set on a balloon flight, I would suggest that you make your reservations early in your trip because flights are often canceled due to weather. This way, if you have to reschedule, you'll have time to do so.

BIKING   You can cycle along main roadways and paved country roads year-round in Santa Fe, but be aware that traffic is particularly heavy around the Plaza and you need to be especially alert. Mountain biking is popular in the spring, summer, and fall. The Santa Fe Convention and Visitors Bureau can supply you with bike maps. *The New Mexican Mountain Bike Guide* (Big Ring Press) by Brant Hayeng and Chris Shaw is an excellent guide to trails in Santa Fe, Taos, and Albuquerque. The book outlines tours for beginner, intermediate, and advanced riders. **Palace Bike Rentals,** 409 E. Palace Ave. (☎ **505/984-0455**), rents mountain bikes and caters to tourists. Half-day, full-day, and weekly rentals can be arranged. Accessories, maps, and trail information are also supplied.

In June cyclists participate in seven days of bicycle races known as the **Pedal the Peaks Bicycle Tour** (☎ **800/795-0898** for more information). Courses traverse areas around Santa Fe, Taos, and Albuquerque as well as Los Alamos and Las Vegas.

FISHING   In the lakes and waterways around Santa Fe, anglers typically catch trout (there are five varieties in the area). Other local fish include bass, perch, and Kokanee salmon. The most popular fishing holes are Cochiti and Abiquiu Lakes as well as the Rio Chama and Pecos streams. Fly-fishing is popular in the Rio Grande. Check with the **New Mexico Game and Fish Department** (☎ **505/827-7911**) for information and licenses. **High Desert Angler,** 435 S. Guadalupe St. (☎ **505/988-7688**), specializes in fly-fishing gear and guide service.

GOLF   There are two public courses in the Santa Fe area: the 18-hole **Santa Fe Country Club,** on Airport Road (☎ **505/471-2626**); and the oft-praised, 18-hole **Cochiti Lake Golf Course,** 5200 Cochiti Hwy., Cochiti Lake, about 35 miles southwest of Santa Fe via I-25 and NM 16 and 22. The **Santa Fe Golf and Driving Range,** 4680 Wagon Rd. (☎ **505/474-4680**) is also open to the public throughout the year. It has 42 practice tees, golf merchandise, and rental clubs and will provide instruction.

HIKING   It's hard to decide which of the 1,000 miles of nearby national forest trails to challenge. Four wilderness areas are especially attractive: **Pecos Wilderness,** with 223,000 acres east of Santa Fe; **Chama River Canyon Wilderness,** 50,300 acres situated west of Ghost Ranch Museum; **Dome Wilderness,** 5,200 acres of rugged canyonland adjacent to Bandelier National Monument; and **San Pedro Parks Wilderness,** 41,000 acres located west of Los Alamos. Also, visit the 58,000-acre Jemez Mountain National Recreation Area. Information on these and other wilderness areas is available from the **Santa Fe National Forest,** 1220 St. Francis Dr. (P.O. Box 1689), Santa Fe, NM 87504 (☎ **505/988-6940**). If you're looking for company on your trek, contact the Santa Fe branch of the **Sierra Club** (☎ **505/983-2703**) or **Tracks,** 417 San Pasqual, Santa Fe, NM 87501 (☎ **505/982-2586**). You might also consider purchasing *The Hiker's Guide to New Mexico* (Falcon Press Publishing Co.) by Laurence Parent; it outlines 70 hikes throughout the state.

One of the most popular hikes in Santa Fe National Forest is the 7-mile hike to Santa Fe Baldy. To reach the trailhead, take Hyde Park Road/NM 475 15 miles northeast of Santa Fe to the parking area for the Santa Fe Ski Area (☎ **505/983-9155**). From there, the hike ascends to 12,622 feet along an easy-to-follow trail to the top of one of the highest peaks in the region. I also enjoy taking a chairlift ride to the summit of the ski area and hiking around up there in the spring and summer months.

HORSEBACK RIDING   Trips ranging in length from a few hours to overnight can be arranged by **Santa Fe Detours,** 107 Washington Ave. (☎ **800/338-6877** or 505/983-6565). You'll ride with "experienced wranglers," and can even arrange a trip that includes a cookout or brunch. Rides are also major activities at a local guest ranch: **The Bishop's Lodge** (see "Accommodations," above). In addition, **Rocky Mountain Tours,** 217 W. Manhattan St., Santa Fe, NM 87501 (☎ **505/984-1684**) arranges escorted rides for individuals of all ability levels as well as families. Trips can run from 90 minutes to a full day. Special packages like "Raft and Ride" and "Design Your Own Ride" are also available.

HUNTING   Mule deer and elk are taken by hunters in the Pecos Wilderness and Jemez Mountains, as well as occasional black bears and bighorn sheep. Wild turkeys and grouse are frequently bagged in the uplands, geese and ducks at lower elevations. Check with the **New Mexico Game and Fish Department** (☎ **505/827-7911**) for information and licenses.

RIVER RAFTING   Although Taos is the real rafting center of New Mexico, several companies serve Santa Fe during the April to October white-water season. They include the **Southwest Wilderness Adventures,** P.O. Box 9380, Santa Fe, NM 87501 (☎ **800/869-7238** or 505/983-7262); **New Wave Rafting,** 107 Washington Ave. (☎ **505/984-1444**); and the **Santa Fe Rafting Co.,** 80 E. San Francisco St. (☎ **505/988-4914**).

HANG GLIDING/SOARING   Soaring is available for those who don't believe the sky is the limit. For information and rates, call **Santa Fe Soaring** (☎ **505/ 470-4571**).

SKIING   There's something available for every ability level at the **Santa Fe Ski Area,** about 16 miles northeast of Santa Fe via Hyde Park (Ski Basin) Road. Built on the upper reaches of 12,000-foot Tesuque Peak, the area has an average annual snowfall of 225 inches and a vertical drop of 1,650 feet. Seven lifts, including a 5,000-foot triple chair and a new quad chair, serve 39 runs and 590 acres of terrain, with a total capacity of 7,300 an hour. Base facilities, at 10,350 feet, center around La Casa Mall, with a cafeteria, lounge, ski shop, and boutique. Another restaurant, Totemoff's, has a midmountain patio.

The ski area is open daily from 9am to 4pm; the season often runs from Thanksgiving to April 6, depending on snow conditions. Rates for all lifts are $37 for adults, $23 for children and seniors, free for kids less than 46 inches tall (in their ski boots), and free for seniors 73 and older. For more information, contact the **Santa Fe Ski Area,** 1210 Luisa St., Suite 5, Santa Fe, NM 87505 (☎ **505/982-4429**). For 24-hour taped reports on snow conditions, call **505/983-9155.** The New Mexico Snow Phone (☎ **505/984-0606**) gives statewide reports. Ski packages are available through Santa Fe Central Reservations (☎ **800/776-7669** outside New Mexico, or 505/ 983-8200 within New Mexico).

Cross-country skiers find seemingly endless miles of snow to track in the **Santa Fe National Forest** (☎ **505/988-6940**). A favorite place to start is at the Black Canyon campground, about 9 miles from downtown en route to the Santa Fe Ski Area. In the same area are the Borrego Trail (high intermediate) and the Norski Trail, 7 miles up from Black Canyon. Basic Nordic lessons and backcountry tours are offered by Bill Neuwirth's **Tracks,** 417 San Pasqual, Santa Fe, NM 87501 (☎ **505/ 982-2586**).

Other popular activities at the ski area in winter include snow-boarding, sledding, and inner-tubing. Snowboard rentals are available at the ski area.

SPAS   A common stop for skiers coming down the mountain road from the Santa Fe Ski Area is **Ten Thousand Waves,** a Japanese-style health spa about 3 miles northeast of Santa Fe on Hyde Park Road (☎ **505/988-1047** or 505/982-9304). This serene retreat, nestled in a grove of piñon, offers hot tubs, saunas, and cold plunges, plus a variety of massage and other bodywork techniques.

Bathing suits are optional in the 10-foot communal hot tub, where you can stay as long as you want for $13. Nine private hot tubs cost $18 to $25 an hour, with discounts for seniors and children. You can also arrange therapeutic massage, hot-oil massage, in-water watsu massage, herbal wraps, salt glows, and facials. New in 1996 were four treatment rooms that feature dry brush aromatherapy treatments and Ayurvedic treatments; a women's communal tub; and lodging at the Houses of the Moon, a six-room Japanese-style inn. The spa is open on Sunday, Monday, Wednesday, and Thursday from 10am to 10pm; on Tuesday from 4:30 to 10pm; and on Friday and Saturday from 10am to 11:30pm. Reservations are recommended, especially on weekends.

SWIMMING   The City of Santa Fe operates four indoor pools and one outdoor pool. The pool closest to downtown is the **Fort Marcy Complex** (☎ **505/984-6725**) on Camino Santiago off Bishop's Lodge Road. Admission is $1.25 for adults, $1 for students, and 50¢ for children 8 to 13. Call the Santa Fe Convention and Visitors Bureau for information about the other area pools.

TENNIS   Santa Fe has 44 public tennis courts and four major private facilities. The City Recreation Department (☎ **505/984-6862**) can locate all indoor, outdoor, and lighted public courts.

SPECTATOR SPORTS

HORSE RACING   The ponies run at **The Downs at Santa Fe** (☎ **505/ 471-3311**), about 11 miles south of Santa Fe off US 85, near La Cienega, from Memorial Day through September. Post time for 10-race cards is 3:30pm on Wednesday and Friday; for 12-race cards, 1:30pm on Saturday and Sunday, plus Memorial Day, the Fourth of July, and Labor Day. Admission starts at $1 and climbs depending on seating. A closed-circuit TV system shows instant replays of each race's final-stretch run and transmits out-of-state races for legal betting.

RODEO   The **Rodeo de Santa Fe,** 2801 Rodeo Rd. (☎ **505/471-4300**), is held annually the weekend following the Fourth of July.

8   Shopping

From traditional Native American crafts to Hispanic folk art to abstract contemporary works, Santa Fe is the place to shop. Galleries speckle the downtown area, and Canyon Road is well known as an artists' thoroughfare. Of course, the greatest concentration of Native American crafts is displayed beneath the portal of the Palace of the Governors. And any serious arts aficionado will try to attend one or more of the city's great arts festivals—the Spring Festival of the Arts in May, the Spanish Market in July, the Indian Market in August, and the Fall Festival of the Arts in October.

Business hours vary quite a bit between establishments, but nearly everyone is open weekdays *at least* from 10am to 5pm, with mall stores open until 9pm. Most shops are open similar hours Saturday, and many are also open Sunday afternoons during the summer. Winter hours are often more limited.

BEST BUYS

Few visitors to Santa Fe leave the city without having bought at least one item, and often several, from the Native American artisans at the Palace of the Governors. In considering purchases, keep the following pointers in mind:

Silver jewelry should have a harmony of design, clean lines, and neatness in soldering. Navajo jewelry typically features large stones, with designs shaped around the stone. Zuni jewelry usually has patterns of small or inlaid stones. Hopi jewelry rarely uses stones, instead displaying a darkened motif incised into the top layer of silver.

Turquoise of a deeper color is usually higher quality, so long as it hasn't been color treated. *Heishi* bead necklaces usually use stabilized turquoise.

Pottery is traditionally hand coiled and of natural clay, not thrown on a potter's wheel using commercial clay. It is hand polished with a stone, hand painted, and fired in an outdoor oven rather than an electric kiln. Look for an even shape; clean, accurate painting; a high polish (if it is a polished piece); and an artist's signature.

Navajo rugs are appraised according to tightness and evenness of weave, symmetry of design, and whether natural (preferred) or commercial dyes have been used.

Kachina dolls are more highly valued according to the detail of their carving: fingers, toes, muscles, rib cages, feathers, for example. Elaborate costumes are also desirable. Oil staining is preferred to the use of bright acrylic paints.

Sand paintings should display clean narrow lines, even colors, balance, an intricacy of design, and smooth craftsmanship.

Local museums, particularly the Wheelwright Museum and the Institute of American Indian Art, can give a good orientation to contemporary craftsmanship.

Contemporary artists are mainly painters, sculptors, ceramists, and fiber artists, including weavers. Peruse one of the outstanding catalogs that introduce local galleries—*The Collector's Guide to Santa Fe and Taos* by Wingspread Communications (P.O. Box 13566, Albuquerque, NM 87192); *Santa Fe and Taos Arts* by the Book of Santa Fe (535 Cordova Rd., Suite 241, Santa Fe, NM 87501); or the *Santa Fe Catalogue* by Modell Associates (P.O. Box 1007, Aspen, CO 81612). They're widely distributed at shops or can be ordered directly from the publishers.

SHOPPING A TO Z

ANTIQUES

Scarlett's Antique Shop and Gallery. 225 Canyon Rd. ☎ **505/983-7092.**

Early American antiques, fine crystal, vintage Hollywood jewelry, pre-1920 postcards, collected Western books, jewelry "confections" by international artist Helga Wagner.

William R. Talbot Fine Art. 129 W. San Francisco St. ☎ **505/982-1559.**

Antique maps, natural-history paintings and prints.

Susan Tarman Antiques and Fine Art. 923 Paseo de Peralta. ☎ **505/983-2336.**

Seventeenth- to 19th-century American, Oriental, and European furniture, porcelain, silver, and paintings.

ART

Alterman and Morris Galleries. 225 Canyon Rd. ☎ **505/983-1590.**

Nineteenth- and 20th-century American paintings and sculpture. Remington, Russell, Taos founders, Santa Fe artists, and members of the Cowboy Artists of America and National Academy of Western Art are represented here.

✪ **Joshua Baer and Company.** 116 E. Palace Ave. ☎ **505/988-8944.**

Nineteenth-century Navajo blankets, pottery, jewelry, and tribal art.

Barclay Fine Art. 424 Canyon Rd. ☎ **505/986-1400.**

This private dealership specializes in 19th- and 20th-century master paintings, drawings, and sculptures. You'll find the works of Matisse, Braque, Cassatt, Caro, Degas, Lepine, Manet, Miró, Monet, Picasso, Wyeth, and many others. Call for an appointment.

Bellas Artes. 653 Canyon Rd. ☎ **505/983-2745.**

Contemporary painting, sculpture, drawing, clay and fiber. African and pre-Columbian art as well as a sculpture garden.

Canyon Road Contemporary Art. 403 Canyon Rd. ☎ **505/983-0433.**

This gallery represents some of the finest emerging U.S. contemporary artists as well as internationally known artists. Figurative, landscape, and abstract paintings, as well as raku pottery are offered.

Dreamtime Gallery. 223¹/₂ Canyon Rd. ☎ **505/986-0344.**

If you're at all interested in Australian Aboriginal artwork, this is the place to visit. There are some very interesting Aboriginal paintings and sculptures, as well as original weavings, bark paintings, and digeridoos.

Gallery 821. 821 Canyon Rd. ☎ **505/983-2000.**

Gallery 821 represents 10 Santa Fe artists. Works are presented in a variety of different mediums and styles. Here you'll find pottery, paintings, sculpture, and etchings among other things.

Glenn Green Galleries. 50 E. San Francisco St. ☎ **505/988-4168.**

Exclusive representatives for Allan Houser, bronze and stone sculptures. Paintings, prints, photographs, and jewelry by other important artists.

Hahn Ross Gallery. 409 Canyon Rd. ☎ **505/984-8434.**

Owner Tom Ross, a children's book illustrator, specializes in representing artists who create colorful, fantasy-oriented works. Those represented here might include Rex Barron, Susan Contreras, Mary Ericksen, Peter Grieve, Kristina Hagman, Ted Larsen, Max Lehman, David Phelps, Kim Thomson, and Paul White.

Handsel Gallery. 306 Camino del Monte Sol, at Canyon Rd. ☎ **505/988-4030.**

Wonderful contemporary works that focus on images from myth, folklore, nature, and dreams.

Horwitch LewAllen Gallery. 129 W. Palace Ave. ☎ **505/988-8997.**

Contemporary art gallery exhibiting works done on canvas and paper; sculpture in stone, bronze, and glass; and ceramics, all by midcareer artists from around the United States.

The Frank Howell Gallery. 103 Washington. ☎ **505/984-1074.**

Contemporary American and American Indian art. Original works by Frank Howell. Sculpture by award-winner Tim Nicola, as well as fine art jewelry and graphics.

Chuck Jones Showroom-Animation Gallery. 135 W. Palace Ave., Suite 203. ☎ **800/290-5999** or 505/983-5999.

A comprehensive representation of animation artwork from Warner Bros. director Chuck Jones. Original production cels, lithographs, sculpture, drawings, and limited editions.

Adieb Khadoure Fine Art. 610 Canyon Rd. ☎ **505/820-2666.**

This is a working artists' studio with contemporary artists Jeff Uffelman and Hal Larsen and Santa Fe artist Phyllis Kapp. Works are shown in the gallery daily from 10am to 6pm. Beautiful rugs, furniture, and pottery from around the world are also featured.

✪ **Nedra Matteucci's Fenn Galleries.** 1075 Paseo de Peralta. ☎ **505/982-4631.**

Early Taos and Santa Fe painters; classic American impressionism, historical Western modernism, as well as contemporary Southwestern landscapes and sculpture, including monumental pieces displayed in the sculpture garden. Specialists in 19th- and 20th-century American art.

Mayans Galleries. 601 Canyon Rd. ☎ **505/983-8068.**

Twentieth-century American and Latin American paintings, photography, prints, and sculpture.

✪ **Owings-Dewey Fine Art.** 76 E. San Francisco St., upstairs. ☎ **505/982-6244.**

Nineteenth- and 20th-century American painting and sculpture. Georgia O'Keeffe, Robert Henri, Maynard Dixon, Fremont Ellis, and Andrew Dasburg are among those represented.

✪ **Gerald Peters Gallery.** 439 Camino del Monte Sol (P.O. Box 908). ☎ **505/988-8961.**

Nineteenth- and 20th-century American painting and sculpture, featuring art from the New York, Western, and Southwestern schools. Contemporary art and photography.

Photogenesis: A Gallery of Photography. 100 E. San Francisco St. ☎ **505/989-9540.**

Photography by Eileen Benjamin, Howard Bond, Edouard Boubat, Ike Fordyce, Earnest Knee, Wright Morris, David Noble, Mark Nohl, Willy Roni, Nicholas Trofimuk, Flo Vogan, and John Youngblood.

✪ **Photography: The Platinum Gallery.** 943 Canyon Rd. ☎ **505/982-2200.**

The world's first (and only) gallery to specialize in platinum prints. Works by 19th- and 20th-century masters, including Evans, Curtis, Weston, Bravo, Horst, and Gilpin. This is a wonderful gallery!

Deborah and Hudgins Fine Art Gallery. 80 E. San Francisco St. ☎ **505/988-9298.**

Exclusive representation of R. C. Gorman lithographs, bronzes, and originals. Amado Peña is also represented.

Santos of New Mexico. 2712 Paseo de Tularosa. ☎ **505/473-7941.**

Work by award-winning Santero Charles M. Carillo. Traditional New Mexican santos crafted out of cottonwood root and decorated with homemade pigments. Also, hand-adzed panels. By appointment only.

✪ **Shidoni Foundry and Gallery.** Bishop's Lodge Rd. Tesuque. ☎ **505/988-8001.**

Shidoni Foundry is one of the area's most exciting spots for sculptors and sculpture enthusiasts. At the foundry visitors may tour through the facilities to view casting processes. In addition, there is a 5,000-square-foot contemporary gallery, a bronze gallery, and a wonderful sculpture garden.

Tribal Arts. P.O. Box 4461. ☎ **505/820-2941.**

Specializing in South Pacific and African tribal arts, this gallery has recently undergone a major expansion and now includes a sculpture garden, ponds, and waterfalls. Tribal Arts is open "anytime by appointment."

Wadle Galleries. 128 W. Palace Ave. ☎ **505/983-9219.**

Fine Southwestern art, including paintings, bronzes, pottery, folk art, and traditional as well as contemporary jewelry.

BELTS
Caballo. 727 Canyon Rd. ☎ **505/984-0971.**

The craftspeople at Caballo create "one of a kind, one at a time" custom-made belts. Everything is hand-tooled, hand-carved, and hand-stamped. In addition to the belts, the buckles are something to behold in and of themselves. This shop is worth a stop.

BOOKS
Caxton Books and Maps. 216 W. San Francisco St. ☎ **505/982-6911.**

A major downtown bookstore, Caxton's collection includes a wide choice of regional works, art books, music, and maps.

Dumont Maps and Books of the West. 301 E. Palace Ave., no. 1. ☎ **505/988-1076.**

New and out-of-print works on Western history, fiction, and antique maps.

Horizons—The Discovery Store. 328 S. Guadalupe St. ☎ **505/983-1554.**

Adult and children's books, science-oriented games and toys, telescopes, binoculars, and a variety of unusual educational items.

Margolis and Moss. 129 W. San Francisco St. ☎ **505/982-1028.**

Rare books, maps, photographs, and prints.

Nicholas Potter, Bookseller. 203 E. Palace Ave. ☎ **505/983-5434.**

Rare and used hardcover books.

Palace Avenue Books. 209 E. Palace Ave. ☎ **505/986-0536.**

Books on the Southwest as well as a good collection of history and philosophy titles.

COOKING SCHOOL

✪ **Santa Fe School of Cooking.** Plaza Mercado (upper level), 116 W. San Francisco St. ☎ **505/983-4511.**

A three-hour demonstration class discusses the flavors and history of traditional New Mexican and contemporary Southwest cuisines. Prices range from $30 to $60 per class and include a meal and recipes. Specialized classes are well attended. An adjoining market offers a variety of regional foods and cookbooks, with gift baskets available.

CRAFTS

Cristof's. 106 W. San Francisco St. ☎ **505/988-9881.**

Fine contemporary Navajo weavings and jewelry.

Davis Mather Folk Art Gallery. 141 Lincoln Ave. ☎ **505/983-1660.**

New Mexican animal wood carvings, as well as folk and Hispanic arts.

Gallery 10. 225 Canyon Rd. ☎ **505/983-9707.**

Museum-quality Native American pottery, weavings, basketry, and contemporary paintings and photography.

Kania-Ferrin Gallery. 662 Canyon Rd. ☎ **505/982-8767.**

Fine Native American baskets, kachinas, jewelry, textiles, beadwork, santos, retablos, and Oceanic art and artifacts.

✪ **Nambe Mills.** 924 Paseo de Peralta, at Canyon Rd. ☎ **505/988-5528.**

An exquisite alloy is sand-cast and handcrafted to create cooking, serving, and decorating pieces. Also at Plaza Mercado, 112 W. San Francisco St. (☎ **505/988-3574**), and 216 Paseo del Pueblo Norte (Yucca Plaza), Taos (☎ **505/758-8221**).

Prairie Edge. In El Centro Mall, 102 E. Water St. ☎ **505/984-1336.**

Plains tribal art, artifacts, and jewelry.

Streets of Taos. 200 Canyon Rd. ☎ **505/983-8268.**

Navajo rugs, Pueblo jewelry, pottery, and baskets.

FASHIONS

Dewey and Sons Trading Company. 53 Old Santa Fe Trail. ☎ **505/983-5855.**

Native American trade blankets and men's and women's apparel.

Judy's Unique Apparel. 714 Canyon Rd. ☎ **505/988-5746.**

Eclectic separates made either locally or imported from around the globe. You'll find a wide variety of items here.

Origins. 135 W. San Francisco St. ☎ **505/988-2323.**

Wearable art, folk art, work of local designers, as well as imports and jewelry.

Three Sisters. At the Inn at Loretto, 211 Old Santa Fe Trail. ☎ **505/988-5045.**

Casual Southwestern clothing and fiesta ribbon shirts.

Rancho. 554 Canyon Rd. ☎ **505/986-1688.**

Authentic, comfortable, functional Western wear. This store features items by Schaefer Outfitter for both men and women, as well as by The Great American Cowboy and Wild Mustangs.

FOOD

The Chile Shop. 109 E. Water St. ☎ **505/983-6080.**

If you want to take home some chile or other New Mexican specialties, the Chile Shop is a must. You'll find everything from salsas to cornmeal and tortilla chips. The shop also stocks cookbooks and pottery items.

Cookworks Gourmet. 318 Guadalupe St. ☎ **505/988-7676.**

Gourmet food products and cooking items. Cookworks has two other shops, Cookworks Kitchen and Cookworks Tabletop, both next door.

Coyote Cafe General Store. 132 Water St. ☎ **505/982-2454.**

This store is an adjunct to one of Santa Fe's most popular restaurants. The big thing here is the enormous selection of hot sauces; however, you can also get fresh fruits and vegetables, a wide variety of Southwestern food items, T-shirts, and aprons.

Señor Murphy Candy Maker. 100 E. San Francisco St. ☎ **505/982-0461.**

This candy store is unlike any you'll find in other parts of the country because everything is made with local ingredients. The chile piñon nut brittle is a taste sensation! Señor Murphy is also located at 223 Canyon Rd. (☎ **505/983-9243**).

FURNITURE

Southwest Spanish Craftsmen. 328 S. Guadalupe St. ☎ **505/982-1767.**

Spanish Colonial and Spanish provincial furniture, doors, and home accessories.

Taos Furniture. 232 Galisteo St. ☎ **505/988-1229.**

Classic Southwestern furnishings handcrafted in solid Ponderosa pine, both contemporary and traditional pieces.

GIFTS & SOUVENIRS

El Nicho. 227 Don Gaspar Ave. ☎ **505/984-2830.**

Handcrafted Navajo and Oaxacan folk art, metal sculpture, switchplates, kachinas, jewelry, and more.

Wharton's Crafted Gifts. In the De Vargas Center Mall, N. Guadalupe St. and Paseo de Peralta. ☎ **505/983-3066.**

Native crafts including kachinas, sand paintings, jewelry, and art supplies.

JEWELRY

Mineral and Fossil Gallery of Santa Fe. 127 W. San Francisco St. ☎ **505/984-1682.**

Natural mineral jewelry, fossils, and decorative items for the home, including lamps, wall clocks, furniture, art glass, and carvings.

James Reid Ltd. 114 E. Palace Ave. ☎ **505/988-1147.**

Gold and silver jewelry and buckle sets, contemporary furniture, paintings, and sculpture.

Tresa Vorenberg Goldsmiths. 656 Canyon Rd. ☎ **505/988-7125.**

More than 30 artisans are represented in this fine jewelry store. All items are hand-crafted and custom commissions are welcomed.

MALLS & SHOPPING CENTERS

De Vargas Center Mall. N. Guadalupe St. and Paseo de Peralta. ☎ **505/982-2655.**

More than 55 merchants and restaurants are in this mall just northwest of downtown. Open Monday through Thursday from 10am to 7pm, Friday from 10am to 9pm, Saturday from 10am to 6pm, and Sunday from noon to 5pm.

Sanbusco Market Center. 500 Montezuma St. ☎ **505/989-9390.**

Unique shops and restaurants occupy this remodeled warehouse near the old Santa Fe Railroad Yard. There's a farmers market in the south parking lot. Open from 7am to noon on Tuesday and Saturday in summer.

Villa Linda Mall. 4250 Cerrillos Rd. at Rodeo Rd. ☎ **505/473-4253.**

Santa Fe's largest mall, including department stores, is near the southwestern city limits, not far from the I-25 on-ramp. Open Monday through Friday from 10am to 9pm, Saturday from 10am to 6pm, and Sunday from noon to 5pm.

MARKETS

Farmers Market. In the parking lot of Sanbusco Market Center, 500 Montezuma St. No phone.

This farmers market is held every Saturday and Tuesday from 7 to 11:30am. You'll find everything from fruits, vegetables, and flowers to cheeses, cider, and salsas.

Trader Jack's Flea Market. Hwy. 84-285 (about 8 miles north of Santa Fe). No phone.

If you're a flea market hound, you'll be happy to find Trader Jack's. More than 500 vendors here sell everything from used cowboy boots (you might find some real beauties) to clothing, jewelry, books, and furniture. The flea market is open from mid-April to late-November on Friday, Saturday, and Sunday.

POTTERY & TILES

Arius Santa Fe Art Tile. 114 Don Gaspar Ave. ☎ **505/988-1196.**

Mexican tiles are popular in this part of the country, but here you'll find hand-painted art tiles of all sorts, shapes, and varieties. Tile murals are popular custom-made items. This is a great place for tile collectors and souvenir seekers.

Canyon Road Pottery. 821 Canyon Rd. ☎ **505/983-9426.**

Handmade decorative and functional pottery. Items include stoneware, raku, earthenware, and custom dinnerware.

Santa Fe Pottery. 323 S. Guadalupe St. ☎ **505/989-3363.**

The work of more than 50 master potters from New Mexico and the Southwest is on display here. You'll find everything from mugs to lamps.

WINES

If you enjoy tasting wines of different regions, there are several wineries within driving distance of Santa Fe: **Balagna Winery/San Ysidro Vineyards,** 223 Rio Bravo Dr., Los Alamos, NM 87544 (☎ 505/672-3678); **Santa Fe Vineyards,** 20 miles north of Santa Fe on Hwy. 285 (☎ 505/753-8100); **Madison Vineyards and Winery,** Star Route 490, Ribera, NM 87560 (☎ 505/421-8020); and **Black Mesa Winery,** 1502 Hwy. 68, Valverde, NM 87582 (☎ 800/852-MESA).

The Winery. 500 Montezuma St. ☎ **505/982-WINE.**

Perhaps the best-stocked wine shop in New Mexico, The Winery also carries gourmet foods, beers, and gift baskets, and it publishes a monthly newsletter.

9 Santa Fe After Dark

Full information on all major cultural events can be obtained from the Santa Fe Convention and Visitors Bureau (☎ **800/777-CITY** or 505/984-6760) or from the City of Santa Fe Arts Commission (☎ **505/984-6707**). Current listings can be found in Friday's "Pasatiempo" edition of the *New Mexican,* Santa Fe's daily newspaper, and in the *Santa Fe Reporter,* published weekly on Wednesdays.

The **Galisteo News and Ticket Center,** 201 Galisteo St. (☎ **505/984-1316**), is the primary outlet for tickets to the opera and other major entertainment events. **Nicholas Potter, Bookseller,** 203 E. Palace Ave. (☎ **505/983-5434**), also has tickets to select events. You can order by phone from **Ticketmaster** (☎ **505/842-5387** for information, or **505/884-0999** to order). Discount tickets may be available on the nights of performances; the opera, for example, makes standing-room tickets available at a greatly reduced rate just one hour ahead of time.

A variety of free concerts, lectures, and other events are presented in the summer, cosponsored by the City of Santa Fe and the chamber of commerce under the name **Santa Fe Summerscene.** From mid-June through August, Tuesday and Thursday at noon and 6pm, events are held on the Plaza and in Fort Marcy Park and run the gamut from light opera to blues, jazz, Cajun, and bluegrass to hot salsa and New Mexican folk music. There's also a wide-ranging Noon Concert Series on Tuesday and Thursday on the Plaza. Call **800/777-2489** for more information.

The **Santa Fe Summer Concert Series,** at the Paolo Soleri Outdoor Amphitheatre on the Santa Fe Indian School campus on Cerrillos Road, has brought such name performers as Kenny Loggins, B. B. King, and the late Frank Zappa to the city. More than two dozen concerts and special events are scheduled each summer.

Note: Many companies listed here perform at locations other than their headquarters, so check the site of the performance you plan to attend.

THE PERFORMING ARTS
OPERA & CLASSICAL MUSIC

✪ **Santa Fe Opera.** P.O. Box 2408, Santa Fe, NM 87504. ☎ **505/986-5955** or 505/986-5900 for tickets. Tickets Fri–Sat $110, $80, $68, $58, $41, $26; Mon–Thurs $6 less for all seats. Rates go up for Gala Opening and Grand Finale Fiesta. Tours, first Mon in July through last Fri in Aug, Mon–Sat at 1pm; $5 for adults, free for children 7 to 15.

Even if your visit isn't timed to coincide with the opera season, you shouldn't miss seeing its open-air amphitheater. Located on a wooded hilltop 7 miles north of the city off US 84/285, the sweeping curves of this serene structure seem perfectly attuned to the contour of the surrounding terrain. At night, the lights of Los Alamos can be seen in the distance under clear skies.

Many rank the Santa Fe Opera behind only the Metropolitan Opera of New York as the finest company in the United States today. Established in 1957 by John Crosby, still the opera's artistic director, it consistently attracts famed conductors, directors, and singers.

The opera is noted for its performances of great classics, little-known works by classical European composers, and American premieres of 20th-century works.

The 9-week, 40-performance opera season runs from the first week in July through the last week in August. All performances begin at 9pm.

ORCHESTRAL & CHAMBER MUSIC

Oncydium Chamber Baroque. 210 E. Marcy St., Suite 15, Santa Fe, NM 87501. ☎ **505/988-0703.**

This new chamber ensemble presents Renaissance, classical, and baroque concerts six times during the year at various gallery spaces in Santa Fe. On Sundays in August the Oncydium Chamber Baroque performs at brunch and afternoon teas. Call for information and schedules.

Santa Fe Pro Musica. 320 Galisteo, Suite 502 (P.O. Box 2091), Santa Fe, NM 87504-2091. ☎ **505/988-4640.**

This chamber ensemble performs everything from Bach to George Crumb and William Wood (composer-in-residence at the University of New Mexico). During Holy Week the Santa Fe Pro Musica presents its annual Baroque Festival Concert. Christmas brings candlelight Christmas chamber ensemble concerts. Pro Musica's season runs from September through May.

✪ **Santa Fe Symphony and Chorus.** P.O. Box 9692, Santa Fe, NM 87504. ☎ **505/983-1414.** Tickets $15–$35 (six seating categories).

This 60-piece professional symphony orchestra has grown rapidly in stature since its founding in 1984. Matinee and evening performances of classical and popular works are presented in a subscription series at Sweeney Center from August to May. There's a preconcert lecture before each performance. During the spring there are music festivals (call for details).

CHORAL GROUPS

Desert Chorale. 219 Shelby St. (P.O. Box 2813), Santa Fe, NM 87501. ☎ **800/244-4011** or 505/988-7505. Tickets $18–$34 adults; half price for students.

This 24- to 30-member vocal ensemble, New Mexico's only professional choral group, recruits members from all over the country. It's nationally recognized for its eclectic blend of both Renaissance melodies and modern avant-garde compositions. During the summer months the chorale performs classic concerts at both the historic Santuario de Guadalupe and the St. Francis Auditorium, as well as smaller cameo concerts at more intimate settings throughout Santa Fe and Albuquerque. The chorale also performs a popular series of Christmas concerts during December. Most concerts begin at 8pm (3 or 6pm on Sunday).

Sangre de Cristo Chorale. P.O. Box 4462, Santa Fe, NM 87502. ☎ **505/662-9717.** Tickets $8–$35 depending on the season.

This 34-member ensemble has a repertoire ranging from classical, baroque, and Renaissance works to more recent folk music and spirituals. Much of it is presented a cappella. The group gives fall and spring concerts at the Santuario de Guadalupe or St. Francis Auditorium, and its Christmas dinner concerts at St. John's College (1160 Camino Cruz Blanca) are avidly attended. In October 1996 the Chorale recorded its first CD of Christmas favorites from 18 seasons of past performances.

The Santa Fe Women's Ensemble. 424 Kathryn Place, Santa Fe, NM 87501. ☎ **505/983-2137.** Tickets $15 reserved, $12 open seating.

This choral group of 12 semiprofessional singers sponsored by the Santa Fe Concert Association offers classical works sung a cappella, as well as with a variety of instrumental accompaniments during the spring and fall seasons. "A Christmas Offering" concerts as well as "Spring Offering" concerts are held in the Loretto Chapel. Tickets are sold by Nicholas Potter, Bookseller (☎ **505/983-5434;** see "Books," above), through mail order, and at the door.

Music Festivals & Concert Series

Santa Fe Chamber Music Festival. 640 Paseo de Peralta (P.O. Box 853), Santa Fe, NM 87504. ☎ **505/983-2075,** or 505/982-1890 for the box office (after June 26). Tickets $20–$32.

The festival brings an extraordinary group of international artists to Santa Fe every summer. Its six-week season of some 50 concerts runs from the second week of July through the third week of August and is held in the beautiful St. Francis Auditorium. Each festival season features chamber-music masterpieces, new music by a composer-in-residence, jazz, free youth concerts, preconcert lectures, and open rehearsals. Festival concerts are recorded for broadcast during a 13-week nationally syndicated radio series.

Performances are Monday through Friday at 8pm and on Saturday and Sunday at 6pm. Open rehearsals, youth concerts, and preconcert lectures are free to the public.

Santa Fe Concert Association. P.O. Box 4626, Santa Fe, NM 87502. ☎ **505/984-8759.** Tickets $15–$65.

Founded in 1938, the oldest musical organization in northern New Mexico, has a September-to-May season that includes more than 20 annual events. Among them are a distinguished artist series featuring renowned instrumental and vocal soloists and ensembles; a free youth concert series; a Christmas Eve special; and occasional master classes. All performances are at St. Francis Auditorium. Tickets are also sold by PROTIX (☎ 800/905-3315).

Theater Companies

✪ **Santa Fe Community Theatre.** 142 E. De Vargas St. (P.O. Box 2084), Santa Fe, NM 87504. ☎ **505/988-4262.** Tickets $10 adults, $8 students and seniors; previews require only that you "pay what you like."

Founded in the 1920s, this is the oldest existing theater group in New Mexico. Still performing in a historic adobe theater in the Barrio de Analco, it attracts thousands for its dramas, avant-garde theater, and musical comedy. Its popular one-act melodramas call upon the public to boo the sneering villain and swoon for the damsel in distress.

Dance Companies

Maria Benitez Teatro Flamenco. Behind the Radisson Hotel Santa Fe, 750 N. St. Francis Dr. ☎ 800/905-3315 or 505/982-1237. Tickets $14–$21 (subject to change).

The Benitez Company's "Estampa Flamenca" summer series is performed from early July to mid-September. True flamenco is one of the most thrilling of all dance forms, displaying the inner spirit and verve of the gypsies of Spanish Andalusia.

Major Concert & Performance Halls

Center for Contemporary Arts, 1050 Old Pecos Trail. ☎ 505/982-1338.
Paolo Soleri Amphitheatre, 1501 Cerrillos Rd. ☎ 505/989-6310.
St. Francis Auditorium at the Museum of Fine Arts, Lincoln and Palace avenues.☎ 505/827-4455.
Sweeney Convention Center, Marcy and Grant streets. ☎ 505/984-6760.

THE CLUB & MUSIC SCENE
COUNTRY, JAZZ & FOLK
✪ **El Farol.** 808 Canyon Rd. ☎ **505/983-9912.** Cover $2–$6.

The original neighborhood bar of the Canyon Road artists' quarter (its name means "The Lantern") is the place to head for local ambience. Its low ceilings and dark-brown walls are the home of Santa Fe's largest and most unusual selection of tapas (bar snacks and appetizers), from *pulpo à la Gallega* (octopus with Spanish paprika sauce) to grilled cactus with ramesco sauce. Jazz, folk, and ethnic musicians, some of national note, perform most nights.

Fiesta Lounge. In La Fonda Hotel, 110 E. San Francisco St. ☎ **505/982-5511.** No cover.

This lively lobby bar offers cocktails and live entertainment nightly.

Rodeo Nites. 2911 Cerrillos Rd. ☎ **505/473-4138.** No cover Mon–Thurs, $3 Fri–Sat, $2 Sun.

There's live country dance music nightly at this popular club.

ROCK
The Bull Ring. 150 Washington Ave. ☎ **505/983-3328.** No cover Wed and Sun, $5 Thurs–Sat.

This steakhouse is also a lively bar with dance music Wednesday through Sunday after 9pm. Bands, normally booked for a week at a time, may play rock or tunes from the 1960s and 1970s.

Chelsea Street Pub and Grill. In the Villa Linda Mall, Rodeo and Cerrillos rds. ☎ **505/473-5105.** No cover.

Burgers and beer are served here during the lunch and dinner hours, but when the shopping mall closes at 9pm the pub really starts hopping. Top bands from throughout the Southwest play dance music Monday through Saturday until 2am, Sunday until 7pm.

Edge. 125 W. Palace Ave. ☎ **505/986-1700.**

Located on the third floor of the Palace Court, Edge is Santa Fe's hottest new night club. You'll hear everything from live blues to popular dance music. Edge has a state of the art sound and light system, pool tables, a great video system, and an enormous bar. Food is served in the bar or on the balcony. Edge is open from 9pm to 2am daily.

THE BAR SCENE
Evangelo's. 200 W. San Francisco St. ☎ **505/982-9014.** No cover.

Food is not offered at Evangelo's, but the tropical decor and mahogany bar are unique to Santa Fe. More than 250 varieties of imported beer are available, and pool tables are an added attraction. Evangelo's is extremely popular with the local crowd. Open daily from noon until 1 or 2am.

Vanessie of Santa Fe. 434 W. San Francisco St. ☎ **505/982-9966.** No cover.

This is unquestionably Santa Fe's most popular piano bar. The talented Doug Montgomery and Charles Tichenor have a loyal local following. Their repertoire ranges from Bach to Billy Joel, Gershwin to Barry Manilow. They play Monday through Saturday from 8:30pm to 2am and Sunday from 8pm to midnight. There's also a great bar menu.

10 Touring the Pueblos Around Santa Fe

Within easy driving distance of Santa Fe are the "Eight Northern Pueblos." Nambe, Pojoaque, San Ildefonso, San Juan, Santa Clara, and Tesuque are all within about 30 miles. Picuris (San Lorenzo) is on the "High Road to Taos," and Taos Pueblo, of course, is just outside of the northern New Mexico town of Taos.

The southern six pueblos of this group can easily be seen in a day's round-trip from Santa Fe. Plan to focus most of your attention on San Juan and Santa Clara, including the former's arts cooperative and the latter's Puye Cliff Dwellings.

Certain **rules of etiquette** apply when visiting pueblos (see "Pueblo Etiquette: Do's and Don'ts," in chapter 6).

TESUQUE PUEBLO

Tesuque (pronounced Teh-*soo*-keh) Pueblo is located about 9 miles north of Santa Fe on US 84/285. The most visible signs that you are approaching the Pueblo are the unusual Camel Rock and a large roadside casino. Despite this concession to the late 20th century, the 400 Pueblo dwellers are faithful to traditional religion, ritual, and ceremony. Excavations confirm that there was a pueblo here as long ago as A.D. 1200; in fact, it is now on the National Register of Historic Places. A mission church and adobe houses surround the plaza, and visitors are asked to remain in that area.

Some Tesuque women are skilled potters; Ignacia Duran's black-and-white and red micaceous pottery and Teresa Tapia's miniatures and pots with animal figures are especially noteworthy. The **San Diego Feast Day** featuring buffalo, deer, flag, or Comanche dances, is November 12.

The Pueblo is open to visitors from 9am to 5pm daily. Admission is free, but permits must be obtained to use still cameras ($10), movie cameras ($50), or draw sketches ($100). The general address of the Pueblo is Rte. 5, Box 360-T, Santa Fe, NM 87501 (☎ **505/983-2667**).

Camel Rock Casino (☎ **505/984-8414**) is open 24 hours, and there is a snack bar on the premises.

In addition, Tesuque Pueblo provides an RV and campground park (☎ **505/455-2661**), which is open year-round.

POJOAQUE PUEBLO

About 6 miles farther north on US 84/285, at the junction of NM 503, is Pojoaque (Po-*hwa*-keh). Though small (population 200) and without a definable village (more modern dwellings exist now), Pojoaque is important as a center for traveler services; in fact, Pojoaque, in its Tewa form, means "water drinking place." The historical accounts of the Pojoaque people are sketchy, but we do know that in 1890 smallpox took its toll on the Pojoaque population, forcing most of the Pueblo residents to abandon their village. Since the 1930s the population has gradually increased, and in 1990 a war chief and two war captains were appointed. Today visitors won't find much to look at, but the Poeh Center, operated by the Pueblo, features a museum and crafts store. Indigenous pottery, embroidery, silverwork, and beadwork are available for sale at the Pojoaque Pueblo Tourist Center.

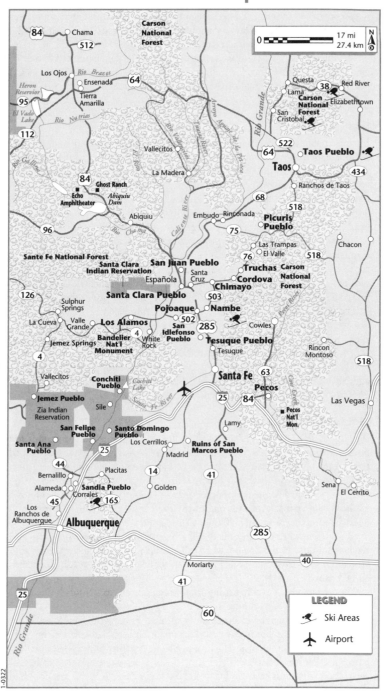

A modern community center is located near the site of the old pueblo and church. **Our Lady of Guadalupe Day,** the annual feast day celebrated on December 12, features a bow-and-arrow or buffalo dance.

The Pueblo is open to visitors during daylight hours, and admission is free. Contact the Governor's Office for information about sketching and camera fees. The general address of the pueblo is Rte. 11, Box 71, Santa Fe, NM 87501 (☎ **505/ 455-3460**).

NAMBE PUEBLO

Drive east about 3 miles from Pojoaque on NM 503, then turn right at the Bureau of Reclamation sign for Nambe Falls. Approximately 2 miles farther is Nambe (meaning "mound of earth in the corner"), a 700-year-old Tewa-speaking pueblo (population 450), with a solar-powered tribal headquarters, at the foot of the Sangre de Cristo range. Only a few of the original pueblo buildings still remain, including a large round kiva, used today in ceremonies. Pueblo artisans make woven belts, beadwork, and brown micaceous pottery.

Nambe Falls, about 4 miles beyond the Pueblo, makes a stunning three-tier drop through a cleft in a rock face, tumbling into Nambe Reservoir. A recreational site at the reservoir offers fishing, boating (nonmotor boats only), hiking, camping, and picnicking. The **Waterfall Dances** on July 4 and **the Saint Francis de Assisi Feast Day** on October 4, which has an elk dance ceremony, are observed at the sacred falls.

The Pueblo is open daily from 8am to 5pm. Admission is free; permits for still cameras cost $5; for movie cameras, $10; and for sketching, $10. The recreational site is open March and September through October from 7am to 7pm, April through May from 7am to 8pm, and June through August from 6am to 8pm. Fishing permits cost $6 per day for adults, $4 per day for children; camping is $8 per night. The address of the Pueblo is Rte. 1, Box 117, Santa Fe, NM 87501 (☎ **505/455-2036,** or 505/455-2304 for the Ranger Station).

SAN ILDEFONSO PUEBLO

If you turn left on NM 502 at Pojoaque, it's about 6 miles to the turnoff to this pueblo, nationally famous for the matte-finish black-on-black pottery developed by tribeswoman Maria Martinez in the 1920s. The pottery-making process is explained at the **San Ildefonso Pueblo Museum,** where exhibits of pueblo history, arts, and crafts are presented Monday through Friday. A couple of Westerns were filmed here in the 1940s. San Ildefonso is one of the most-visited pueblos in northern New Mexico, attracting more than 20,000 visitors a year.

San Ildefonso Feast Day (January 23) is a good time to observe the social and religious traditions of the Pueblo, when buffalo, deer, and Comanche dances are presented. Dances may be scheduled for Easter, the Harvest Festival (early September), and Christmas.

The Pueblo has a 4$\frac{1}{2}$-acre **fishing lake,** which is open April through October. Picnicking is encouraged; camping is not.

The Pueblo is open to visitors Monday through Friday from 8am to 4:30pm; call for summer weekend hours. It's closed for major holidays and tribal events. Admission is $3 for noncommercial vehicles and $10 for commercial vehicles, plus 50¢ per passenger. Permits for still cameras cost $5; for video cameras and sketching, $15 each. Fishing permits costs $8 for adults, $4 for children 6 to 12, free for children under 6. The Pueblo address is Rte. 5, Box 315A, Santa Fe, NM 87501 (☎ **505/ 455-3549**).

✪ SAN JUAN PUEBLO

If you continue north on US 84/285, you will reach the San Juan Pueblo via NM 74, a mile off NM 68, about 4 miles north of Española. The largest (population 1,950) and northernmost of the Tewa-speaking pueblos and headquarters of the Eight Northern Indian Pueblos Council, San Juan is located on the east side of the Rio Grande—opposite the 1598 site of San Gabriel, the first Spanish settlement west of the Mississippi River and the first capital of New Spain. In 1598 when the Spanish first became acquainted with the people of San Juan, they were impressed with the openness and helpfulness of the Indians; thus they decided to establish a capitol there (it was moved to Santa Fe 10 years later), making San Juan Pueblo the first to experience Spanish colonization. The Indians were generous with food, clothing, shelter, and fuel—they even helped sustain the colony when its leader Conquistador Juan de Oñate became preoccupied with his search for gold and neglected the needs of his people. Unfortunately, the Indians became somewhat like slaves. They were forced to provide the Spanish with corn, venison, cloth, and labor. They were compelled to participate in Spanish religious ceremonies and to abandon their own religious practices. Under no circumstances were Indian ceremonials allowed, and those caught participating in them were punished. In 1676 several Indians were accused of "sorcery" and jailed in Santa Fe. Later they were led to the Plaza, where they were flogged or hanged. This incident became a turning point in Indian-Spanish relations, generating an overwhelming feeling of rage in the Indian community. One of the accused, a man named Popé, a San Juan Pueblo Indian, became a leader in the Great Pueblo Revolt, which led to freedom from Spanish rule for 12 years.

The past and present cohabit here. The San Juan tribe, though Roman Catholic, still practices traditional religious rituals; thus two rectangular kivas flank the church in the main plaza, and *caciques* (pueblo priests) share influence with civil authorities. The annual **San Juan Fiesta** is June 23–24, with buffalo and Comanche dances. Another annual ceremony is the **turtle dance** on December 26.

The **Eight Northern Indian Pueblos Council** (☎ 505/852-4265) is a sort of chamber of commerce and social-service agency.

A crafts shop, **Oke Oweenge Arts and Crafts Cooperative** (☎ 505/852-2372), specializes in local wares. This is a fine place to seek out San Juan's distinctive red pottery, a lustrous ceramic incised with traditional geometric symbols. Also displayed for sale are seed, turquoise, and silver jewelry; wood and stone carvings; indigenous clothing and weavings; embroidery; and paintings. Artisans often work on the premises so that visitors can watch. The co-op is open Monday through Saturday from 9am to 4:30pm; closed San Juan Feast Day. **Sunrise Crafts,** another crafts shop, is located to the right of the coop. There you'll find one-of-a-kind handcrafted pipes, beadwork, and burned and painted gourds.

Right on the main road that goes through the pueblo is the **Tewa Indian Restaurant,** serving traditional pueblo chile stews, breads, blue-corn dishes, posole, teas, and desserts. It's open Monday through Friday from 9am to 2:30pm; closed holidays and feast days.

Fishing and picnicking are encouraged at the **San Juan Tribal Lakes,** open year-round.

Like most of the other pueblos, San Juan offers bingo. In summer, the doors open Wednesday through Sunday at 5:30pm; in winter, on Sunday afternoon at noon.

The Pueblo is open to visitors daily during daylight hours, and admission is free. Photography or sketching may be allowed with prior permission from the Governor's Office. Fishing permits costs $10 for adults, $5 for children and seniors. The general address of the Pueblo is P.O. Box 1099, San Juan Pueblo, NM 87566 (☎ **505/852-4400**).

SANTA CLARA PUEBLO

Just across the Rio Grande from Española on NM 5, Santa Clara, with a population of about 1,600, is one of the larger pueblos. For those who contact the Pueblo a week in advance (P.O. Box 580, Española, NM 87532; ☎ **505/753-7326**), driving and walking tours are offered Monday through Friday, including visits to the pueblo's historic church and artists' studios. Visitors can enter specified studios to watch artists making baskets and highly polished red-and-black pottery.

There are corn and harvest dances on **Santa Clara Feast Day** (August 12); other special days include buffalo and deer dances (early February) and children's dances (December 28).

The Pueblo is open to visitors daily during daylight. Admission is free. Permits for still cameras are $5; for video cameras, $15; and for sketching, $15. The visitor's center is open Monday through Friday from 9am to 4:30pm. Located on the Santa Clara reservation are the Puye Cliff Dwellings.

✪ **Puye Cliff Dwellings.** Santa Clara Pueblo. ☎ **505/753-7326.** Admission $5 adults, $4 children and seniors. Guided tours additional $2 charge (one week advance notice required). Open summer, daily 8am–8pm; winter, daily 9am–4:30pm.

The Santa Clara people migrated to their home on the Rio Grande in the 13th century from a former home high on the Pajarito Plateau to the west. The ruins of their previous life have been preserved at this site, an 11-mile climb west of the pueblo. It is believed that this site at the mouth of the Santa Clara Canyon (now a National Historic Landmark) was occupied from about 1250 to 1577.

High on a nearly featureless plateau, the volcanic tuff rises in a soft tan façade 200 feet high. Here the Anasazi found niches to build their houses. Visitors can descend via staircases and ladders from the 7,000-foot mesa top into the 740-room pueblo ruin, which includes a ceremonial chamber and community house. Petroglyphs are evident in many of the rocky cliff walls.

About 6 miles farther west is the **Santa Clara Canyon Recreational Area,** a sylvan summer setting for camping that is open year-round for picnicking, hiking, and fishing in ponds and Santa Clara Creek.

11 A Side Trip to Los Alamos

The atomic bomb was born in Los Alamos, a city of 12,000 spread on the craggy, fingerlike mesas of the Pajarito Plateau, between the Jemez Mountains and Rio Grande valley, 33 miles northwest of Santa Fe. Pueblo Indians lived in this rugged area for well over 1,000 years, and an exclusive boys' school operated atop the 7,300-foot plateau from 1928 to 1943. Los Alamos National Laboratory was founded in secrecy as Project Y of the Manhattan Engineer District, the hush-hush wartime program to split the atom and develop the world's first nuclear weapons.

Project director J. Robert Oppenheimer, later succeeded by Norris E. Bradbury, worked with a team of 30 to 100 scientists in research, development, and production of the weapons. Today 3,000 scientists and another 4,800 support staff work at **Los Alamos National Laboratory,** making it the largest employer in northern New Mexico. Still operated by the University of California for the federal Department of Energy (which provides more than 80% of its $600 million annual budget), its 32 technical areas occupy 43 square miles of mesa-top land.

The laboratory is known today as one of the world's foremost scientific institutions. It's still geared heavily to the defense industry—the Trident and Minuteman strategic warheads were created here, for example—but it has many other research programs, including studies in nuclear fusion and fission, energy conservation, nuclear safety, the environment, and nuclear wastes. Its international resources include a genetic sequence data bank, with wide implications for medicine and agriculture, and an Institute for Geophysics and Planetary Physics, among others.

ESSENTIALS

Los Alamos is located about 35 miles west of Santa Fe and about 65 miles southwest of Taos. From Santa Fe take US 84/285 north approximately 16 miles to the Pojoaque junction, then turn west on NM 502. Driving time is only about 50 minutes. The **Los Alamos Chamber of Commerce,** P.O. Box 640, Los Alamos, NM 87544 (☎ **505/662-8105**), has a visitor center open Monday through Friday from 8am to 5pm.

WHAT TO SEE & DO

✪ **Bradbury Science Museum.** At the Los Alamos National Laboratory, 15th St. and Central Ave. ☎ **505/667-4444.** Free admission. Tues–Fri 9am–5pm, Sat–Mon 1–5pm.

This outstanding museum is the lab's public showcase. Atomic research is emphasized in a wide variety of scientific and historical displays, including more than 35 hands-on exhibits. Visitors can peruse photographs and documents depicting the earliest days of Project Y, including a 1939 letter from Albert Einstein to Pres. Franklin D. Roosevelt suggesting research into uranium as a new and important source of energy. There are exhibits on weapons research, including an overview of the nation's nuclear arsenal; achievements in alternative-energy research, from solar and geothermal to laser and magnetic-fusion energy; biomedical research and development; computer technology; and basic research into the nature of nuclei, atoms, and molecules. Visitors can explore the museum, experiment with lasers, use computers, and view laboratory research in energy, defense, environment, and health. Educational and historical films are shown continuously.

Fuller Lodge Art Center. 2132 Central Ave. ☎ **505/662-9331.** Free admission. Mon–Sat 10am–4pm, Sun 1–4pm.

Works of northern New Mexico artists and traveling exhibitions of regional and national importance are displayed here. Four annual arts-and-crafts fairs are also held here—in May, August, October, and November.

Los Alamos Historical Museum. 2132 Central Ave. ☎ **505/662-4493.** Free admission. Summer, Mon–Sat 9:30am–4:30pm, Sun 11am–5pm; winter, Mon–Sat 10am–4pm, Sun 1–4pm.

The massive log building that once housed the dining and recreation hall for the Los Alamos Ranch School for boys is now a National Historic Landmark known as the Fuller Lodge. Its current occupants include the museum office and research archives and the Fuller Lodge Art Center (see above), which doubles as a visitor information center. The museum, located in the small log-and-stone building to the north of Fuller Lodge, depicts area history, from prehistoric cliff dwellers to the present, with exhibits ranging from Native American artifacts to school memorabilia and an excellent new permanent Manhattan Project exhibit. The museum sponsors guest speakers and operates a tax-free bookstore. Now you can even "visit" the museum on the World Wide Web at http://www.vla.com/lahistory or http://www.losalamos.com/lahistory.

WHERE TO STAY & DINE

Hilltop House Hotel. Trinity at Central, Los Alamos, NM 87544. ☎ **800/462-0936** or 505/662-2441. Fax 505/662-5913. 82 rms, 18 suites. A/C TV TEL. $88–$98 double; $98–$275 suite. Additional person $10 extra. AE, CB, MC, V.

Recently renovated, this hotel's tastefully furnished rooms include 33 efficiency units with kitchenettes. Each room has standard furnishings, satellite TV, and other modern conveniences.

The third-floor Trinity Sights Restaurant, which affords a stunning view across the Rio Grande to Santa Fe, offers a lengthy dinner menu that includes the likes of salmon grilled with Dijon mustard and apple honey, and pork chops stuffed with raisins and walnuts. Dinner main courses range from $9.95 to $17.95. A full breakfast and dinner is included in weekday rates. The restaurant is open from 6:30am to 10pm daily. The hotel also offers room service, valet laundry, secretarial service, and complimentary coffee 24 hours. Pets are accepted with a $25 deposit. Facilities include an indoor swimming pool, coin-op laundry, Avis car-rental agency, travel agent, 24-hour convenience store, adjacent gas station and liquor store, and meeting and conference facilities.

Los Alamos Inn. 2201 Trinity Dr., Los Alamos, NM 87544. ☎ **800/279-9279** or 505/662-7211. Fax 505/662-7211 (ask for fax). 116 rms, suites. A/C TV TEL. $65 double. AE, CB, DC, MC, V.

Located just a few minutes from Los Alamos National Laboratory, the inn's comfortable, spacious rooms, including some for nonsmokers and people with disabilities, have queen-size or double beds, large writing tables, remote-control satellite TV with in-room movies. Some have minibars. Ashley's restaurant is open for three meals daily. Ashley's Pub serves happy-hour hors d'oeuvres and late-night snacks. The hotel has an outdoor swimming pool, hot tub, and meeting facilities.

12 Also Worth a Look: Bandelier & Pecos National Monuments

BANDELIER NATIONAL MONUMENT

Fewer than 15 miles south of Los Alamos along NM 4, this is the nearest major prehistoric site to Santa Fe. It combines the extensive ruins of an ancient cliff-dwelling Anasazi Pueblo culture with 46 square miles of canyon-and-mesa wilderness.

Most visitors, after an orientation stop in the visitor center and museum to learn about the culture that persisted here between A.D. 1100 and 1550, follow a cottonwood-shaded, $1^1/_2$-mile trail along Frijoles Creek to the principal ruins. The pueblo site, including a great underground kiva, has been partially reconstructed. The biggest thrill for most folks, though, is climbing hardy piñon ladders to visit an alcove 140 feet above the canyon floor that was once home to prehistoric people. Tours are self-guided or led by a National Park Service ranger.

At night around a campfire, the rangers or local Native Americans talk to groups of visitors about the history, culture, and geology of the ruins, or about Indian legends. On a moonlit evening, the guided night walks reveal a different, spooky aspect of the ruins and cave houses, outlined in the two-dimensional chiaroscuro of the thin, cold light from the starry sky. In the daytime, there are nature programs for adults and children.

Elsewhere in the monument, 60 miles of maintained trails lead to more Native American ruins and ceremonial sites, waterfalls, and wildlife habitats. The separate

Tsankawi section of the monument, reached by an ancient 2-mile trail close to White Rock, contains a large unexcavated ruin on a high mesa overlooking the Rio Grande Valley.

Areas are set aside for picnicking and camping. Admission is $5 per vehicle. The national monument was named after Swiss American archeologist Adolph Bandelier, who explored here in the 1880s. It is open year-round during daylight hours, except Christmas and New Year's.

Most people are surprised to learn that the largest volcanic caldera in the world is here in northern New Mexico. **Valle Grande,** a vast meadow 16 miles in diameter and 76 square miles in area, is all that remains of a massive volcano that erupted nearly a million years ago. When the mountain spewed ashes and dust as far as Kansas and Nebraska, its underground magma chambers collapsed, forming this great valley. Lava domes that pushed up after the collapse obstruct a full view across the expanse. NM 4 skirts the caldera beginning about 15 miles west of Los Alamos.

PECOS NATIONAL MONUMENT

About 15 miles east of Santa Fe, I-25 meanders through **Glorieta Pass,** site of an important Civil War skirmish. In March 1862 volunteers from Colorado and New Mexico, along with Fort Union regulars, defeated a Confederate force marching on Santa Fe, thereby turning the tide of Southern encroachment in the West.

Take NM 50 east to **Pecos,** a distance of about 7 miles. This quaint town, well off the beaten track since the interstate was constructed, is the site of a noted Benedictine monastery. North of here 26 miles on NM 63 is the village of **Cowles,** gateway to the natural wonderland of the Pecos Wilderness. There are many camping, picnicking, and fishing locales en route.

Pecos National Monument (☎ 505/757-6032), 2 miles south of the town of Pecos off NM 63, contains the ruins of a 14th-century pueblo and 17th-century mission. The pueblo was well known to Coronado in 1540: "It is feared through the land," he wrote. With a population of about 2,000, the Native Americans farmed in irrigated fields and hunted wild game. Their pueblo had 660 rooms and many kivas. By 1620 Franciscan monks had established a church and convent. Military and natural disasters took their toll, however, and in 1838 the 20 surviving Pecos Indians abandoned their ancestral home and took up residence with relatives at the Jemez Pueblo.

The E. E. Fogelson Visitor Center tells the history of the Pecos people in a well-done, chronologically organized exhibit, complete with dioramas of pre-Hispanic lifestyles. A 1¼-mile loop trail departs from the center and leads through Pecos Pueblo and the Mission de Nuestra Señora de Los Angeles de Porciuncula, as the church was formally known. This excavated structure—170 feet long and 90 feet wide at the transept—was once the most magnificent church north of Mexico City.

Visitors to the national monument are asked to pay $2 per person, $4 per car admission, which goes to further preservation. Hours are 8am to 5pm.

13 The High Road to Taos

Unless you're in a hurry to get from Santa Fe to Taos, the "high road," also called the Mountain Road or the King's Road, is by far the most fascinating route. It transits tiny ridge-top villages where Hispanic lifestyles and traditions persist as they did a century ago.

The historic weaving center of **Chimayo** is 16 miles north of Pojoaque junction, at the junction of NM 520 and 76 via NM 503. Families like the Ortegas maintain a tradition of handwoven textiles begun by their ancestors seven generations ago, in the early 1800s, in this small village. **Ortega's Weaving Shop** and **Galeria Ortega** are fine places to take a close look at this ancient craft.

Today, however, many more people come to Chimayo to visit **El Santuario de Nuestro Señor de Esquipulas** (the Shrine of Our Lord of Esquipulas), better known simply as **El Santuario de Chimayo.** Attributed with miraculous powers of healing, this church has been the destination of countless thousands of pilgrims since its construction in 1814 to 1816. Some 30,000 people may participate in the annual Good Friday pilgrimage, many of them walking from as far away as Albuquerque.

Although only the earth in the anteroom beside the altar has healing powers ascribed to it, the entire shrine has a special serene feeling that's hard to ignore. It's quite moving to peruse the testimonies of rapid recoveries from illness or injury on the walls of the anteroom, and equally poignant to read the as yet unanswered entreaties made on behalf of loved ones.

Designated a National Historic Landmark in 1970, the church contains five beautiful *reredos,* or panes of sacred paintings, one behind the main altar and two on each side of the nave. Each year during the fourth weekend in July, the 9th-century military exploits of the Spanish saint Santiago are celebrated in a weekend fiesta, supported by the National Endowment for the Arts, including the historic play *Los Moros y Cristianos* (Moors and Christians).

Many travelers schedule their drives to have lunch at the **Restaurante Rancho de Chimayo** (☎ **505/351-4444**) on NM 76 east of the junction. The adobe home, built by Hermenegildo Jaramillo in the 1880s, has been in the food business for nearly three decades. Native New Mexican cuisine, prepared from generations-old Jaramillo family recipes, is served on terraced patios and in cozy dining rooms beneath hand-stripped vigas. Dinners run $10 to $17. The restaurant is open daily from noon to 10pm from June through August and Tuesday through Sunday from noon to 9pm the rest of the year.

The Jaramillo family also owns a bed-and-breakfast inn, **Hacienda Rancho de Chimayo,** P.O. Box 11, Chimayo, NM 87522 (☎ **505/351-2222**). Once the residence of Epifanio Jaramillo, Hermenegildo's brother, its seven guest rooms all open onto an enclosed courtyard. Each room, furnished with turn-of-the-century antiques, has a private bath and sitting area. Rates are $60 to $100. The office is open daily from 9am to 9pm.

Lovely **Santa Cruz Reservoir** has a dual purpose: The artificial lake provides water for Chimayo valley farms, but also offers a recreation site for trout fishing and camping at the edge of the Pecos Wilderness. To reach it, turn south 4 miles on NM 503, 2 miles east of Chimayo.

Just as Chimayo is famous for its weaving, the village of **Cordova,** 7 miles east on NM 76, is noted for its wood carvers. Small shops and studios along the highway display *santos* (carved saints) and various decorative items.

Anyone who saw Robert Redford's 1988 movie production *The Milagro Beanfield War* has seen **Truchas.** A former Spanish colonial outpost built at 8,000 feet atop a mesa 4 miles east of Cordova, it was chosen as the site for filming in part because traditional Hispanic culture remains pervasive. Subsistence *acequia* farming has a high profile here. The scenery is spectacular: 13,101-foot Truchas Peak dominates one side of the mesa, and the broad Rio Grande Valley the other.

Las Trampas, 6 miles east of Truchas on NM 76, is most notable for its **San Jose Church,** to some the most beautiful church built during the Spanish colonial period. It was placed on the National Register of Historic Places in 1966 through the efforts of preservationists who felt it was threatened by a highway project.

Near the regional education center of Penasco, 24 miles from Chimayo near the junction of NM 75 and 76, is the **Picuris (San Lorenzo) Pueblo** (☎ 505/587-2519). The 270 citizens of this 15,000-acre mountain pueblo, native Tiwa speakers, consider themselves a sovereign nation: Their forebears never made a treaty with any foreign country, the United States included. Thus they observe a traditional form of tribal council government. Their annual feast day at San Lorenzo Church is August 10.

Still, the people are modern enough to have fully computerized their public showcase, Picuris Tribal Enterprises. Besides the Hotel Santa Fe in the state capital, components include the **Picuris Pueblo Museum,** where weaving, beadwork, and the distinctive reddish-brown clay cooking pottery are exhibited weekdays from 8am to 4:30pm. Guided tours through the old village ruins begin from the museum; camera fees start at $5. **Hidden Valley Restaurant** serves a native Picuris menu, along with an American menu. There's also an information center, crafts shop, grocery, and other shops. Permits ($4 for adults and children) are available to fish or camp at Pu-Na and Tu-Tah lakes, regularly stocked with trout.

One mile east of Penasco on NM 75 is **Vadito,** which early this century was the center for the conservative Catholic brotherhood, the Penitentes.

Taos is 24 miles north of Penasco via NM 518. But day-trippers from Santa Fe can loop back to the capital by taking NM 75 west from Picuris Pueblo. **Dixon,** 12 miles west of Picuris, and its twin village of **Embudo,** a mile farther on NM 68 at the Rio Grande, are the homes of many artists and craftspeople who exhibit their works during an annual autumn show sponsored by the Dixon Arts Association. You can follow signs to **La Chiripada Winery** (☎ 505/579-4437), whose product is surprisingly good. The winery is open Monday through Saturday from 10am to 5pm.

Near Dixon is the **Harding Mine,** a University of New Mexico property where visitors can gather mineral specimens without going underground. If you haven't signed a liability release at the Albuquerque campus, ask at Labeo's Store in Dixon. They'll direct you to the home of a local resident who can get you started gathering almost immediately.

Two more small villages lie in the Rio Grande valley at 6-mile intervals south of Embudo on NM 68. **Velarde** is a fruit-growing center; in season, the road here is lined with stands selling fresh fruit or crimson chile *ristras* and wreaths of native plants. **Alcalde** is the location of Los Luceros, an early 17th-century home planned for refurbishment as an arts and history center. The unique Dance of the Matachines, a Moorish-influenced production brought from Spain by the conquistadors, is performed here on holidays and feast days.

The commercial center of **Española** (pop. 7,000) no longer has the railroad that was responsible for its establishment in the 1880s, but it does have perhaps New Mexico's greatest concentration of "low riders." Their owners give much loving attention to these late-model customized cars, so called because their suspension leaves them sitting exceedingly close to the ground. You can't miss seeing them cruise the main streets of town, especially on weekend nights.

Significant sights in Española include the **Bond House Museum,** a Victorian-era adobe home displaying exhibits of local history and art; and the **Santa Cruz Church,** built in 1733 and renovated in 1979, which houses many fine examples of Spanish colonial religious art. Major events include the July **Fiesta de Oñate,** commemorating the valley's founding in 1596; the **Tri-Cultural Art Festival** in October on the Northern New Mexico Community College campus; and the weeklong **Summer Solstice** celebration, staged in June by the nearby, 200-strong Ram Das Puri ashram of the Sikhs (☎ 505/753-9438).

Santa Feans sometimes take the half-hour drive to Española simply to dine at **Matilda's Cafe,** Corlett Road (☎ **505/753-3200**). Open Tuesday through Sunday from 9am to 9pm, it's noted for its New Mexican food, including vegetarian plates. There's also **El Paragua,** 603 Santa Cruz Rd. (☎ **505/753-3211**).

Full information on Española and vicinity can be obtained from the **Española Valley Chamber of Commerce,** 417 Big Rock Center, Española, NM 87532 (☎ **505/753-2831**).

If you admire the work of **Georgia O'Keeffe,** try to plan a short trip to **Abiquiu,** a tiny town in a bend of the Rio Chama, 14 miles south of Ghost Ranch and 22 miles north of Española on US 84. Once you see the surrounding terrain, it will be clear that this was the inspiration for many of her startling landscapes. Since March 1995 O'Keeffe's adobe home (where she lived and painted until her death in 1986) has been open for public tours. However, a reservation must be made in advance; the charge is $15 for a one-hour tour. As this book goes to press, tours are offered Tuesdays, Thursdays, and Fridays and are limited to six people per tour. Visitors are not permitted to take pictures. For reservations, call **505/685-4539.**

Taos   8

Taos is one of those gemlike little towns where the local regard for traditional architecture, combined with surrounding natural beauty, has drawn the eye of artists. For nearly a century painters, graphic artists, and sculptors have made Taos an art center, many of them settling here to form a sort of informal colony. It is one of the very oldest American towns: The Tiwas living in the traditional apartment complexes in Taos Pueblo nearby have been in residence for at least 1,000 years, perhaps 5,000; prehistoric ruins exist throughout the Taos Valley. The village itself was settled by the Spanish in 1617.

Taos is just 40 miles south of the Colorado border, 70 miles north of Santa Fe, and 130 miles from Albuquerque. Life here moves in and out of, and around, the Plaza, just as did life in old villages in Spain and Mexico. Although the population is only about 4,500, the summertime scene is one of crowded sidewalks, shops, and restaurants, with a never-ending traffic jam on the main road through town, for Taos has become a major tourist attraction in the Southwest. With several fine museums (including and a new one that opened in 1995) and a wide choice of accommodations and restaurants for visitors, it is well worth a visit of two to three days.

Its 6,900-foot elevation and dry climate give Taos sharp, clear air that's mild in summer and invigorating in winter, especially for skiers, who since the 1950s have flocked to the Taos area in increasing numbers to take to the slopes at five resorts. The winter season in Taos has become even busier than the summer.

Taos began as the northernmost outpost of Spain's Mexican empire. It was a hotbed of revolutionary activity throughout the late 17th century; the suppression of three rebellions helped spark the Pueblo Revolt of 1680. Through the 18th and 19th centuries Taos was an important trade center: New Mexico's annual caravan to Chihuahua, Mexico, couldn't leave until after the annual midsummer Taos Fair. French trappers began attending the fair in 1739. Plains Indians, even though they often attacked the Pueblos at other times, also attended the market festivals under a temporary annual truce. By the early 1800s Taos had become a headquarters for American "mountain men," the most famous of whom, Kit Carson, made his home in Taos from 1826 until his death in 1868.

Taos was firmly Hispanic, and stayed loyal to Mexico during the Mexican War of 1846. The city rebelled against its new U.S.

landlord in 1847, killing newly appointed Gov. Charles Bent in his Taos home. Nevertheless, it became a part of the territory of New Mexico in 1850. It fell into Confederate hands for just six weeks during the Civil War, at the end of which time Carson and two other statesmen raised the Union flag over Taos Plaza and guarded it day and night. Since then, Taos has had the honor of flying the flag 24 hours a day.

The town's international renown as an art center had its start in 1898 when two young eastern artists on a sketching tour through the Rockies had a wheel break on their horse-drawn buggy north of Taos. The pair, Ernest Blumenschein and Bert Phillips, took the wheel in for repairs, and were captivated by the dramatic light changes and their visual effect upon buildings and landscapes. They soon settled in Taos, and by 1912 the Taos Society of Artists had placed the town on the international cultural map. Today, by some estimates, more than 10% of the townspeople are painters, sculptors, writers, musicians, or otherwise earn income from an artistic pursuit.

1 Orientation

ARRIVING

BY CAR Most visitors arrive in Taos either via NM 68 or US 64. Northbound travelers exit I-25 at Santa Fe, follow US 285 as far as San Juan Pueblo, and continue on the divided highway when it becomes NM 68. Taos is 79 miles from the I-25 junction. Travelers southbound from Denver on I-25 exit 6 miles south of Raton at US 64, and follow it 95 miles to Taos. Another major route is US 64 from the west (214 miles from Farmington).

BY PLANE **Taos Airport** (☎ 505/758-4995) is about 8 miles northwest of town on US 64, en route to the Rio Grande Gorge Bridge. Call for information on local charter services. It's easiest to fly into Albuquerque International Airport, rent a car, and drive up to Taos from there. The drive will take you approximately 2 1/2 hours. If you'd rather be picked up at Albuquerque International Airport, call **Pride of Taos** (☎ 505/758-8340). They offer charter bus service to Taos town and the Taos Ski Valley daily. Faust's Transportation (☎ 800/535-1106 or 505/758-3410) offers similar service. Both services charge similar rates of $25 one way, $45 round-trip, to Albuquerque.

BY BUS The **Taos Bus Center,** Paseo del Pueblo Sur at the Chevron Station (☎ 505/758-1144), is not far from the Plaza. **Greyhound/Trailways** and **TNM&O Coaches** arrive and depart from this depot several times a day.

VISITOR INFORMATION

The **Taos County Chamber of Commerce,** P.O. Drawer I, Taos, NM 87571 (☎ 800/732-TAOS or 505/758-3873), is located at the corner of Highways 68 and 64. It's open from 8am to 5pm daily, year-round except major holidays. **Carson National Forest** also has an information center in the same building as the chamber. On the Internet you can access all sorts of information about Taos at http://www.taoswebb.com/nmusa/taos. The E-mail address is taos@taoswebb.com.

CITY LAYOUT

The Plaza is a short block west of Taos's major intersection—where US 64 (**Kit Carson Road**) from the east joins NM 68, **Paseo del Pueblo Sur** (also known

Now that you know your way around, let's move on to something simple.

1 800
CALL
ATT®

For card and collect calls.

1 800 CALL ATT is the only number you need to know when you're away from home. Dial it from any phone, anywhere* and your calls will always go through to AT&T.

AT&T

as South Pueblo Road or South Santa Fe Road). US 64 proceeds north from the intersection as **Paseo del Pueblo Norte** (North Pueblo Road). **Camino de la Placita** (Placitas Road) circles the west side of downtown, passing within a block of the other side of the Plaza. Many of the streets that join these thoroughfares are winding lanes lined by traditional adobe homes, many of them a century or more old.

MAPS

To find your way around town, pick up a copy of the Town of Taos map from the chamber of commerce.

2 Getting Around

BY CAR If you plan on renting a car during your stay in Taos, Dollar Rent-A-Car (☎ **800/369-4226** or 505/758-9501), with offices at the Taos airport, is reliable and efficient. Other car rental agencies are available out of Albuquerque. See chapter 6 for details.

Parking can be difficult during the summer rush, when the stream of tourists' cars moving north and south through town never ceases. Not everyone knows about all the free parking lots, however, especially about the municipal lot behind Taos Community Auditorium, just off Paseo del Pueblo Norte a block north of the Plaza traffic signal. Another lot just to the north of the Plaza has parking meters. Two commercial lots, one behind the Plaza and another off Kit Carson Road, charge a small fee for all-day parking.

A note for outdoor enthusiasts: Reliable paved roads lead to takeoff points for side trips up poorer forest roads to many recreation sites. Once you get off the main roads, you won't find gas stations or cafés. Four-wheel-drive vehicles are recommended on snow and much of the otherwise-unpaved terrain of the region. If you're doing some off-road adventuring, it's wise to go with a full gas tank, extra food and water, and warm clothing, just in case. At elevations of more than 10,000 feet in northern New Mexico, sudden summer snowstorms are not unknown.

BY BUS OR TAXI If you're in Taos without transportation, you're in luck, because there is now a local bus service, provided by Taos Transit (☎ **505/751-2000**). It begins at around 6:30am and ends at about 11pm. The route runs from Kachina Lodge on Paseo del Pueblo Norte and ends at the Ranchos Post Office on the south side of town. Bus fares are 50¢ one way, $1 all day, and $5 for a seven-day pass.

In addition, two private companies serve Taos. **Pride of Taos** (☎ **505/758-8340**) operates a summer trolley that runs daily from 9am to 5pm from the Sagebrush Inn to Taos Pueblo on a 45-minute schedule, for $7 ($3 for children). In winter, Pride of Taos's shuttle bus service links town hotels and Taos Ski Valley four times a day for $7 round-trip. A night bus ($10) brings skiers staying at the ski valley into town for dinner and returns them to their lodgings.

Faust's Transportation (☎ **505/758-3410**) offers town taxi service daily from 7am to 10pm, with fares of $8 anywhere within the city limits for up to two people ($2 per additional person), $35 to Albuquerque International Airport, and $25 to Taos Ski Valley from Taos town.

BY BICYCLE Rentals are available from **Gearing Up Bicycle Shop** at 129 Paseo del Pueblo Sur (☎ **505/751-0365**); **Hot Tracks Cyclery and Ski Tuning Service** at 729 Paseo del Pueblo Sur (☎ **505/751-0949**); and **Native Sons Adventures** at 715 Paseo del Pueblo Sur (☎ **800/753-7559** or 505/758-9342).

FAST FACTS: Taos

Airport   See "Orientation," above.

Business Hours   Most **businesses** are open Monday through Friday from 10am to 5pm, though some may open an hour earlier and close an hour later. Many tourist-oriented **shops** are also open on Saturday mornings, and some **art galleries** are open all day Saturday and Sunday, especially during peak tourist seasons. **Banks** are generally open Monday through Thursday from 9am to 3pm and on Friday from 6am to 6pm. Call establishments for specific hours.

Car Rentals   See "Getting Around," above.

Climate   Taos's climate is similar to that of Santa Fe. Summer days are dry and sunny, except for frequent afternoon thunderstorms; winter days are often bracing, with snowfalls common but rarely long-lived. Average summer temperatures range from 50°F to 87°F. Winter temperatures vary between 9°F and 40°F. Annual rainfall is 12 inches; annual snowfall is 35 inches in town, 300 inches at Taos Ski Valley, elevation 9,207 feet. (A foot of snow is equal to an inch of rain.)

Currency Exchange   Foreign currency can be exchanged at the Centinel Bank of Taos, 512 Paseo del Pueblo Sur (☎ **505/758-6700**).

Dentists   If you need dental work, try Dr. Walter Jakiela, 536 Paseo del Pueblo Norte (☎ **505/758-8654**); Dr. Michael Rivera (☎ **505/758-0531**); or Dr. Tom Simms, 623-B Paseo del Pueblo Sur (☎ **505/758-8303**).

Doctors   Members of the Taos Medical Group, on Weimer Road (☎ **505/758-2224**), are highly respected. Also recommended are Family Practice Associates of Taos, on Don Fernando Street (☎ **505/758-3005**), a short distance west of the Plaza.

Drugstores   There are several full-service pharmacies in Taos. Furr's Pharmacy (☎ **505/758-1203**), Smith's Pharmacy (☎ **505/758-4824** or 505/758-4823), and Wal-Mart Pharmacy (☎ **505/758-2743**) are all located on Pueblo Sur and are easily seen from the road.

Embassies/Consulates   See "Fast Facts: For the Foreign Traveler," in chapter 4.

Emergencies   Dial **911** for police, fire, and ambulance.

Eyeglasses   Taos Eyewear, in Cruz Alta Plaza (☎ **505/758-8758**), handles most needs Monday through Friday between 8:30am and 5pm. It also has emergency service.

Hospital   Holy Cross Hospital, 1397 Weimer Road, off Paseo del Canyon (☎ **505/758-8883**), has 24-hour emergency service. Serious cases are transferred to Santa Fe or Albuquerque.

Hotlines   The crisis hotline (☎ **505/758-9888**) is available for emergency counseling.

Information   See "Visitor Information," above.

Library   The Taos Public Library, on Ledoux Street (☎ **505/758-3063**), has a general collection for Taos residents, a children's library, and special collections on the Southwest and Taos art.

Liquor Laws   As in Santa Fe, bars must close by 2am Monday through Saturday and can open only between noon and midnight on Sunday. The legal drinking age is 21.

Lost Property   Check with the police (☎ **505/758-2216**).

Newspapers/Magazines   The *Taos News* (☎ **505/758-2241**) and the *Sangre de Cristo Chronicle* (☎ **505/377-2358**) are published every Thursday. *Taos Magazine* is also a good source of local information. The *Albuquerque Journal, The New Mexican* from Santa Fe, and the *Denver Post* are easily obtained at the Fernandez de Taos Bookstore on the Plaza.

Photographic Needs   Check Plaza Photo, Taos Main Plaza (☎ **505/758-3420**). Minor camera repairs can be done the same day, but major repairs must go to Santa Fe and usually require several days. Plaza Photo offers a full line of photo accessories and one-hour processing. April's 1-Hour Photos, at 613E N. Pueblo Rd. (☎ **505/758-0515**), is another good choice.

Police   In case of emergency, dial **911.** All other inquiries should be directed to Taos Police, Civic Plaza Drive (☎ **505/758-2216**). The Taos County Sheriff, with jurisdiction outside the city limits, is located in the county courthouse on Paseo del Pueblo Sur (☎ **505/758-3361**).

Post Offices   The main Taos Post Office is at 318 Paseo del Pueblo Norte, Taos, NM 87571 (☎ **505/758-2081**), a few blocks north of the Plaza traffic light. There are smaller offices in Ranchos de Taos (☎ **505/758-3944**) and at El Prado (☎ **505/758-4810**). The ZIP code for Taos is **87571**.

Radio   Local stations are KRZA-FM (88.7), the National Public Radio Station; KKIT-AM (1340) for news, sports, weather, and a daily event calendar at 6:30am; and KTAO-FM (101.7), which broadcasts an entertainment calendar daily.

Taxes   Gross receipts tax for Taos town is 6.8125% and for Taos County it's 6.3125%. There is an additional local bed tax of 4.5% in Taos town and 4% on hotel rooms in Taos County.

Television   Channel 2, the local access station, is available in most hostelries. For a few hours a day there is local programming. Cable networks carry Santa Fe and Albuquerque stations.

Useful Telephone Numbers   For information on road conditions in the Taos area, call the state police (☎ **505/758-8878**) or call **800/432-4269** (within New Mexico) for the state highway department. Taos County offices are at ☎ **505/ 758-8834.**

3 Accommodations

Taos has some 1,450 rooms in 60 hotels, motels, condominiums, and bed-and-breakfasts. Most of the hotels and motels are located on Paseo del Pueblo Sur and Norte, with a few scattered just east of the town center along Kit Carson Road. The condos and bed-and-breakfasts are generally scattered throughout Taos's back streets.

During peak seasons, visitors without reservations may have difficulty trying to find a vacant room. **Taos Central Reservations,** P.O. Box 1713, Taos, NM 87571 (☎ **800/821-2437** or 505/758-9767), might be able to help.

There are another 400 or so rooms in 15 condo/lodges at or near the Taos Ski Valley. The **Taos Valley Resort Association,** P.O. Box 85, Taos Ski Valley, NM 87525 (☎ **800/776-1111** or 505/776-2233, fax 505/776-8842), can book these as well as more than 1,300 rooms in Taos, and unadvertised condominium vacancies.

Some three dozen bed-and-breakfasts are listed with the Taos Chamber of Commerce. The **Taos Bed and Breakfast Association** (☎ **800/876-7857** or

505/758-4747), with strict guidelines for membership, will provide information and make reservations for member homes.

And **Affordable Meetings and Accommodations,** P.O. Box 1258, Taos, NM 87571 (☎ 800/290-5384 or 505/751-1292), will help you find accommodations from bed-and-breakfasts to home rentals, hotels, and cabins throughout Taos and northern New Mexico. They'll also help you arrange rental cars and reservations for outdoor activities such as white-water rafting, horseback riding, fishing/hunting trips, and ski packages.

Unlike in Santa Fe, there are two high seasons in Taos: winter (the Christmas-to-Easter ski season) and summer. Spring and fall are shoulder seasons, often with lower rates. The period between Easter and Memorial Day is notoriously slow in the tourist industry here, and many restaurants and other businesses take their annual vacations at this time. Book well ahead during ski holiday periods (especially Christmas) and during the annual arts festivals (late May to mid-June and late September to early October).

In these listings, the following categories describe peak-season prices for a double: **expensive** accommodations charge over $100 per night; **moderate,** $75 to $100; and **inexpensive,** $75 and under. A tax of 11.38% in Taos town and 9.8125% in Taos County will be added to every hotel bill.

IN THE TAOS AREA
EXPENSIVE

✪ **The Historic Taos Inn.** 125 Paseo del Pueblo Norte, Taos, NM 87571. ☎ **800/TAOS INN** or 505/758-2233. Fax 505/758-5776. 37 rms. A/C TV TEL. $85–$195, according to type of room and season. AE, DC, MC, V.

The last century of Taos history is alive and well within the walls of this atmospheric inn. The inn is made up of several separate adobe houses dating from the mid-1800s, which then surrounded a small plaza complete with communal town well. Dr. Thomas Paul Martin purchased the complex in 1895: He was Taos County's first physician, and, for many years, the only one. In 1936, a year after the doctor's death, his widow, Helen, enclosed the plaza (now the inn's magnificent two-story lobby), installed indoor plumbing (the first in Taos!), and opened the Hotel Martin. In 1981 and 1982 the inn underwent restoration; it is now listed on the state and national registers of historic places. Today, the hotel combines 20th-century elegance with 19th-century ambience. The lobby is graced with interior balconies overlooking the town well, reborn as a tiered fountain; above it rises a stained-glass cupola. Large vigas (heavy rafters) adorn the ceiling, handwoven rugs and outstanding artwork cover the walls, and Taos-style *bancos* face a sunken Pueblo-style fireplace in one corner of the room.

No two guest rooms are alike. While all are furnished in regional style, they differ in size, shape, and craft items—and thus each has a distinct personality. All rooms contain Taos-style furniture and Spanish colonial antiques built by local artisans; original Native American, Hispanic, and New Mexican art decorates the interiors. All have custom hand-loomed bedspreads and 30 rooms have fireplaces.

Dining/Entertainment: Doc Martin's, with outstanding Southwestern cuisine, is one of Taos's leading dining establishments (see "Dining," below). The Adobe Bar, popular among Taos artists and other locals, has live entertainment on select weeknights as well as a full bar menu for light lunch or dinner.

Services: Room service.

Facilities: Rooms for nonsmokers and people with disabilities, seasonal outdoor swimming pool, year-round Jacuzzi in greenhouse.

Central Taos Accommodations

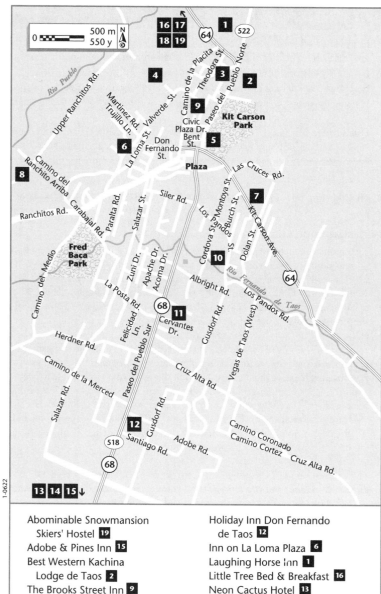

Abominable Snowmansion
  Skiers' Hostel **19**
Adobe & Pines Inn **15**
Best Western Kachina
  Lodge de Taos **2**
The Brooks Street Inn **9**
Casa de las Chimeneas **10**
Casa Europa **8**
El Monte Lodge **7**
El Pueblo Lodge **3**
The Historic Taos Inn **5**

Holiday Inn Don Fernando
  de Taos **12**
Inn on La Loma Plaza **6**
Laughing Horse Inn **1**
Little Tree Bed & Breakfast **16**
Neon Cactus Hotel **13**
Orinda B&B **4**
Quail Ridge Inn **17**
Sagebrush Inn **14**
Salsa del Salto **18**
Sun God Lodge **11**

👪 Family-Friendly Hotels

El Pueblo Lodge *(see p. 189)*   A slide, year-round swimming pool, and hot tub set on 3¹/₂ acres of land will please the kids; a barbecue, some minikitchens with microwave ovens, laundry facilities, and the rates will please their parents.

Best Western Kachina Lodge de Taos *(see p. 188)*   An outdoor swimming pool in the summer here makes a great late afternoon diversion for hot, tired, and cranky kids.

Quail Ridge Inn *(see p. 187)*   The year-round swimming pool and tennis courts will keep active kids busy during the day when it's time for a parent's siesta.

Quail Ridge Inn. Ski Valley Rd. (P.O. Box 707), Taos, NM 87571. ☎ **800/624-4448** or 505/776-2211. Fax 505/776-2949. 110 rms (60 suites). TV TEL. $60–$150 single or double; $110–$395 suite. A 3% gratuity is added to all rates. Extra person $10. Children under 18 stay free with parent. DC, MC, V.

This sports-oriented lodge bills itself as a family resort and conference center. Tennis and skiing are the recreations of note at this contemporary Pueblo-style hotel, which spreads across several acres of open sagebrush about 4 miles north of Taos and ³/₄ mile east of US 64, en route to the Ski Valley 14 miles distant.

The smallest standard rooms can sleep four on a queen-size bed and queen-size sleeper sofa. Next in size are the studios, actually semisuites with full kitchens and patios or balconies. The one-bedroom suites, the most popular accommodations, consist of a studio with a connecting standard room. A half-dozen separate *casitas* contain spacious two-bedroom suites of about 1,600 square feet each. Every room features a big fireplace, huge closets, and full shower/baths. Kitchens are fully stocked and include a stove, refrigerator, microwave oven, and dishwasher. Decor is breezy Southwestern, with light woods and various pieces of local art and artifacts.

Dining/Entertainment: Renegade Cafe (☎ **505/776-1777**), specializing in New American and Southwestern flavors with an Italian influence, is one of the more popular restaurants in the Taos area.

Services: Coin-op laundry.

Facilities: Rooms for nonsmokers, year-round heated swimming pool, hot tub and sauna. Six outdoor and two indoor tennis courts, racquetball/squash courts, summer volleyball pit. Fitness center with weights and exercise room.

MODERATE

El Monte Lodge. 317 Kit Carson Rd. (P.O. Box 22), Taos, NM 87571. ☎ **505/758-3171.** 13 rms. TV TEL. $65–$125 double. $10 extra for kitchenette units. AE, DISC, MC, V.

Century-old cottonwood trees stand in a parklike picnic area, complete with barbecue grills and children's playground, outside this friendly 1930s motel. Located four blocks east of the Plaza, it's old-fashioned but homey, built in traditional adobe style with protruding vigas, painted in a sand tone and framed by flower gardens. The rooms, many of them with fireplaces, occupy eight small buildings. The eclectic decor features considerable Pueblo art. Many rooms have fully stocked kitchenettes; there's a free guest laundry. Pets are permitted for an extra $5.

Holiday Inn Don Fernando de Taos. Paseo del Pueblo Sur (P.O. Drawer V), Taos, NM 87571. ☎ **800/759-2736** or 505/758-4444. Fax 505/758-0055. 124 rms, 26 suites. A/C TV TEL. $94–$110 double; $110–$149 suite. Christmas season rates higher. Extra person $10; children 19 and under stay free in parents' room. AE, CB, DC, DISC, JCB, MC, V.

Taos's newest major hotel (opened in 1989) is like a modern Pueblo village spread across landscaped grounds on the south side of town. Half a dozen adobe-style two-story building clusters, each named for a noted New Mexico artist, surround private courtyards. Standard rooms each feature hand-carved New Mexican wood furnishings, two double beds (or a king-size bed and sleeper sofa), and a special door-side niche for skis and boots. Each suite offers a sitting room, fireplace, and mini-refrigerator.

Breakfast, lunch, and dinner are available in **Don Fernando's Restaurant,** while **Fernando's Hideaway** lounge, built around a large adobe fireplace, presents live entertainment and features a large hors d'oeuvres buffet.

The hotel offers room service, valet laundry, courtesy van, 24-hour desk, rooms for nonsmokers and people with disabilities, outdoor swimming pool, hot tub, and tennis court.

Best Western Kachina Lodge de Taos. 413 Paseo del Pueblo Norte (P.O. Box NN), Taos, NM 87571. ☎ **800/522-4462** or 505/758-2275. Fax 505/758-9207. 118 rms, 4 suites. A/C TV TEL. $85–$125 double. Extra person $8; children under 12 stay free in parents' room. AE, DC, DISC, MC, V.

A Pueblo-style motel with bright blue trim, this long-established lodge is an art lover's dream. The art gallery, which connects the lobby with the lodge's restaurants, displays paintings and other works from the Taos Gallery. The Navajo Living Room, a comfortable space for indoor games or fireside reading, is filled with valuable antique Navajo rugs. The varied guest rooms are each appointed with custom-made Taoseño furniture. Many are furnished with a couch or love seat; all have huge bathrooms and a second sink at the vanity in an outer dressing area.

The **Hopi Dining Room** offers a family style menu. The **Kiva Coffee House** serves filling breakfasts and Mexican-style lunches. The **Zuni Lounge** is open nightly, and the **Kachina Cabaret** (see below) books big-name acts. A Taos Pueblo dance troupe performs nightly in summer.

There is a guest services desk (in summer) and the hotel van offers shuttle service. There are rooms for nonsmokers, an outdoor swimming pool, indoor hot tub, coin-op laundry, and a ski shop on the premises.

Sagebrush Inn. Paseo del Pueblo Sur (P.O. Box 557), Taos, NM 87571. ☎ **800/428-3626** or 505/758-2254. Fax 505/758-5077. 68 rms, 32 suites. A/C TV TEL. $80–$110 double; $115–$140 suite. Extra person $10. Rates include breakfast. AE, CB, DC, MC, V.

Georgia O'Keeffe, probably the most famous artist to have worked extensively in the Southwest, lived and painted for six months in the 1930s in a third-story room at this venerable hotel. Originally called the Chamisa Inn, the hotel was built in Pueblo Mission style in 1929, three miles south of the Plaza near Ranchos de Taos. In 1995, 20 new deluxe rooms with fireplaces, microwaves, and small refrigerators were added.

Most of the rooms face either an open grass courtyard or the outdoor swimming pool. Traditional viga ceilings are complemented by earth-patterned decor and standard furnishings. There are rooms for nonsmokers and people with disabilities.

The Los Vaqueros Room is open for dinner and a complimentary full breakfast is served to guests daily in the Sagebrush Dining Room. The lobby bar is one of Taos's most active nightspots for live music and dancing (see "Taos After Dark," below). Services and facilities include swimming pool, two Jacuzzis, and in-room coffee.

INEXPENSIVE

Abominable Snowmansion Skiers' Hostel. Taos Ski Valley Rd., Arroyo Seco (P.O. Box 3271), Taos, NM 87571. ☎ **505/776-8298.** Fax 505/776-2107. 60 beds. $15.50–$55 per bed, depending on size of accommodation and season. Rates include full breakfast in winter. MC, V.

Located in the small community of Arroyo Seco, about 8 miles north of Taos and 10 miles from the Taos Ski Valley, this lodging attracts many young people. It's clean and comfortable for those who like the advantages of dormitory-style accommodations. Toilets, shower rooms, and dressing rooms are segregated by sex. A two-story lodge room features a circular fireplace as well as a piano and games area. Lodging is also offered in traditional teepees and smaller bunkhouses in the campfire area. Tent camping is permitted outside. Guests can either cook their own meals or indulge in home-cooked fare.

El Pueblo Lodge. 412 Paseo del Pueblo Norte (P.O. Box 92), Taos, NM 87571. ☎ **800/ 433-9612** or 505/758-8700. Fax 505/758-7321. 60 rms, 4 suites. TV TEL. $55–$65 double; $58–$215 suite. Extra person $5–$10. Rates include continental breakfast. AE, DISC, MC, V.

The setting here is special: nicely landscaped 3¹/₂-acre grounds, complete with cottonwood and towering fir trees, gardens, barbecue pits, and lawn furniture. Throw in a year-round outdoor swimming pool and hot tub, and it's no surprise that this lodge is popular with families. All the brightly colored rooms have southwestern decor and refrigerators. There are also rooms with kitchenettes and fireplaces. Twelve new rooms were added to the property in 1996. Laundry facilities are free to guests

Laughing Horse Inn. 729 Paseo del Pueblo Norte (P.O. Box 4889), Taos, NM 87571. ☎ **800/776-0161** or 505/758-8350. 11 rms, 3 guest houses. TV. $49–$85 double; $105–$120 penthouse and guest houses.

Occupying the print shop of the 1920s "Laughing Horse Press," the inn is an unmistakable adobe structure with lilac trim. Guests can choose between sunny dorm-type loft rooms, cozy private rooms, a deluxe solar-heated penthouse, spacious private guest houses across the street, or a house on the mesa complete with views of Taos Mountain. All accommodations have cassette decks and VCRs; some have fireplaces. Bathrooms are shared in the lower portion of the inn. The penthouse has a private bedroom, enclosed sleeping loft, and a bunk set with double beds. A private bath, wood stove, big-screen TV, video and audio decks, and a small refrigerator complete the room. The inn has a common room around a kiva fireplace where a wide variety of audio- and videotapes are shelved. Breakfasts (which might be continental or full) may be eaten in the kitchen or the dining room. The refrigerator is stocked on the honor system. There's an outdoor hot tub, and mountain bikes are free for guests' use. Psychic readings are available from the innkeepers, and a massage therapist is available by appointment.

Sun God Lodge. 919 Paseo del Pueblo Sur (P.O. Box 1713), Taos, NM 87571. ☎ **800/ 821-2437** or 505/758-3162. Fax 505/758-1716. TV TEL. $75–$86 double; $101 suite; $105–$139 casita.

An adobe structure, this recently renovated motel offers 1¹/₂ acres of landscaped grounds. The rooms are done in Southwest decor; all have ceiling fans, queen- or king-sized beds (with Navajo-patterned spreads), prints and lithographs by Taos artists on the walls, and complimentary bedside coffee service. There are some new accommodations with kitchenette areas (fully supplied with dishes and utensils), coffeemakers, minirefrigerators, living rooms with kiva fireplaces (logs are supplied), remote-controlled TVs, and niches with howling coyotes or kachinas in them. There are outdoor grills and a hot-tub room.

BED-&-BREAKFASTS

✪ **Adobe and Pines Inn.** NM 68 (P.O. Box 837), Ranchos de Taos, NM 87557. ☎ **800/ 723-8267** or 505/751-0947. Fax 505/758-8423. 5 rms, 2 casitas. TV. $95–$150 double.

MC, V. Rates include breakfast. It's located directly off NM 68, just about 0.3 miles south of St. Francis Plaza. If you're driving from Santa Fe, look for the multicolored posts that mark the driveway on your right.

The inn is a 150-year-old adobe home that is one of the most beautiful and peaceful guest houses I have ever stayed in. It rests amid pine and fruit trees on sacred land (Native Americans once stopped here to pray for a good hunt on their way to the hunting grounds, and again on their way back to thank the gods for their successes). Each room has a private entrance, all have fireplaces (three even have a fireplace in the bathroom), and each is uniquely decorated. Puerta Turquese, my favorite place to stay here, is a separate guest cottage with a full kitchen. The "broken tile mosaic" floors, laid 100 years ago by a man who did only a select few in the whole town of Taos, run throughout Puerta Turquese. Two newer rooms, Puerta Violetta (the only second-story room, with a spectacular view of the Taos sky and an outdoor patio) and Puerta Rosa (with a two person soaking tub, cedar sauna, bathroom with fireplace, and a unique wrought-iron bed), are welcome competition for Puerta Turquese.

A delicious full breakfast is served in front of the fire (in winter) in the glassed-in breakfast room. Chuck and Charil Fulkerson, the owners, are very gracious hosts; they will help you plan activities to suit your interests and will even help you with dinner reservations. If I could give this place two stars I would!

The Brooks Street Inn. 119 Brooks St. (P.O. Box 4954), Taos, NM 87571. ☎ **800/758-1489** or 505/758-1489. 6 rms (all with bath). $75–$105 double; $5 less for single occupancy. AE, MC.

The Brooks Street Inn is located on a quiet, tree-lined street within walking distance from Taos Plaza. You'll recognize the rambling adobe by the circular driveway out front. Carol Frank will welcome you into her beautiful home, which is designed to make you completely at ease during your stay in Taos. The living room features a large fireplace, a comfortable sitting area, and high, beamed ceilings. Each of the guest rooms is decorated differently—the Willow Room has a willow bed, the Aspen Room features a comfortable reading banco (bench), and the Birch, Juniper, and Piñon rooms all have kiva fireplaces. Some of the rooms also have skylights, in-room coffee, and minirefrigerators.

Breakfast features a coffee bar (unique to any bed and breakfast I've ever visited), from which you may choose Taos Magic Caffe Mocha, cappuccino, espresso, or steamed almond hot chocolate, and such specialties as blue-corn pancakes and pineapple salsa; white chocolate apricot scones; and stuffed French toast topped with an apricot sauce.

✪ **Casa de las Chimeneas.** 405 Cordoba Lane at Los Pandos Road (P.O. Box 5303), Taos, NM 87571. ☎ **505/758-4777.** Fax 505/758-3976. 3 rms, 1 suite. TV TEL. $122–$130 double; $148 suite (for two). MC, V.

The "House of Chimneys" qualifies as one of Taos's luxury B&Bs. Its three rooms, each of them a work of art and with its own private entrance, look out on a beautifully landscaped private garden. The two-room suite incorporates an old library and two fireplaces. Beautiful bed linens over a sheepskin mattress pad guarantee a great night's sleep. Attention to detail is a top priority here, with plush towels, down pillows, extra firewood, books and magazines for reading, and owners eager to share tips on best restaurants, ski runs, or scenic drives. Room minirefrigerators are stocked with complimentary soft drinks, juices, and mineral water, and a full gourmet breakfast is served daily. Guests gather in the main house for complimentary afternoon hors d'oeuvres. A courtesy telephone is in the main dining room and a large hot tub is located adjacent to the garden. Smoking is not permitted. As we go to press, several improvements have been made to this B&B, and the rates may be restructured, so call ahead.

Casa Europa. 840 Upper Ranchitos Rd. (HC68, Box 3F), Taos, NM 87571. ☎ **505/758-9798.** 7 rms. $70–$135. Rates include afternoon pastries or early evening hors d'oeuvres, and a full breakfast. AE, MC, V.

This spacious 17th-century Pueblo-style adobe rests under giant cottonwood trees about 1.6 miles from Taos Plaza. It is surrounded by pastures dotted with grazing horses, and offers majestic mountain views. The elegant guest rooms have sitting areas and wood burning fireplaces. All have private baths, and two feature full-size hot tubs. The furnishings are a comfortable mix of Southwestern-style and European antiques. Smoking is not permitted.

Hacienda del Sol. 109 Mabel Dodge Lane (P.O. Box 177), Taos, NM 87571. ☎ **505/758-0287.** 9 rms. MC, V. $90–$130 double.

Not far from the Plaza on the north side of Taos, Hacienda del Sol is a lovely, quiet bed-and-breakfast in a surprising location—directly behind the Lottaburger. Like many of the homes in Taos, the 190-year-old Hacienda del Sol has a wonderful history. The home was once owned by art patron Mabel Dodge Luhan, and it was here that author Frank Waters wrote *The People of the Valley.* On the far side of the inn's well-manicured grounds is the adjoining Taos Pueblo. All of the guest rooms are constructed of adobe and furnished with handcrafted Southwestern-style furnishings, antiques, and original art (for sale), and many of them feature kiva fireplaces. Down comforters, clock radios with tape decks and a selection of cassettes, refrigerators, terry-cloth robes, and private baths (each supplied with a basket of items you might have forgotten to bring with you) are added in-room luxuries here. The casita is a separate building, housing three guest rooms that can be rented separately or as a unit. These rooms have fireplaces and great mountain views through French doors.

A full breakfast might include buttery cinnamon apples and pumpkin pancakes with walnuts and warm maple syrup; or peach bread-pudding with blueberry sauce and a selection of fresh fruit. Refreshments are also served every evening from 5pm. An outdoor hot tub offers spectacular views of Taos Mountain. Hacienda del Sol is also one of only a handful of bed-and-breakfasts that will accept children of any age.

Little Tree Bed and Breakfast. P.O. Box 960, El Prado, NM 87529. ☎ **800/334-8467** or 505/776-8467. 4 rms (all with bath). $80–$105 double. MC, V (personal checks or money orders preferred).

Little Tree is one of my favorite Taos bed-and-breakfasts, partly because it's located in a beautiful, secluded setting, and partly because it's built out of real adobe—not stucco like most of the new buildings in the area. The rooms are small but charming and very cozy. They all have adobe floors, which are warm in the winter because the heat runs through the floors, making for a much healthier environment. All rooms have queen-size beds, private baths, and access to the portal and courtyard garden. The Piñon and Juniper rooms have fireplaces and private entrances. Piñon and Aspen rooms have sunset views. The Spruce Room is Western in feeling and is decorated with beautiful quilts. In the main building, the living room has a traditional viga and latilla ceiling, and *tierra blanca* adobe, which is adobe that is naturally white. If you look closely at it you can see little pieces of mica and straw. On arrival, guests are treated to refreshments.

Neon Cactus Hotel. 1523 Paseo del Pueblo Sur (P.O. Box 5702), Taos, NM 87571. ☎ **800/299-1258** or 505/751-1258. 4 rms (all with bath). Jan, Apr–June, Sept–Dec 18, $65–$85 double, $105 quad. Rest of year $85–$125 double, $125–$145 quad. AE, DISC, MC, V.

The Neon Cactus is a delightful change of pace from some of the other hotels and bed-and-breakfasts in New Mexico. You won't find one hint of Southwestern decor anywhere in this hotel. Instead, each of the rooms here pays homage to a film star—for instance, the black-and-white Marilyn Monroe Suite is decorated with photographs that document the "many moods of Marilyn," and authentic period furnishings. The bathroom in the Marilyn Suite features a Roman-style, oversized sunken tub complete with bubble bath. The Rita Hayworth Suite is done in rich reds, has two queen-size beds, and adjoins the Casablanca Room, a small room filled with Oriental rugs, tapestries, pillows, and—the best part—a built-in Turkish-style, curtained twin bed. The other two rooms, the James Dean Room and the Billie Holiday Room, are equally well conceived. All rooms have private decks, and guests enjoy discounted rates at the adjacent Taos Spa. An extended continental breakfast is included in the rates, and there is a Jacuzzi available for guest use.

Orinda B&B. 461 Valverde St. (P.O. Box 4451), Taos, NM 87571. ☎ **800/847-1837** or 505/758-8581. 3 rms, 1 suite. $75–$85 double. $15 per additional guest. MC, V.

This B&B has the delightful advantage of being in town as well as in the country: Though only a 10-minute walk from the Plaza, it's tucked beneath huge cottonwood trees and offers views across pastureland of Taos Mountain. Thick adobe walls keep it warm in winter and cool in summer. Innkeepers Cary and George Pratt share their living room, including a TV, sound system, and kiva fireplace, with guests. Works by local artists adorn the walls of the dining room (with a wood-burning stove), where a hearty continental breakfast is served daily. Two rooms comprise the Vigil Suite, where a sitting room with a fireplace and refrigerator separates two bedrooms. The Truchas Room, with traditional Southwestern decor, has a private entrance, fireplace, and bath. Pets and smoking are not permitted.

Salsa del Salto. P.O. Box 453, El Prado, NM 87529. ☎ **505/776-2422.** 10 rms (all with bath). $85–$160 double. Extra person $10. MC, V.

Situated between Taos town and the Taos Ski Valley, Salsa del Salto is the perfect place for those seeking a secluded retreat well within short driving distance of Taos's major tourist attractions. Guest rooms are tastefully decorated in pastel shades and a Southwestern motif, and beds are covered with cozy down comforters. Each room offers views of the mountains or mesas of Taos, and the private bathrooms are modern and spacious. The focus here is on relaxation and outdoor activities. Innkeeper Mary Hockett is a native New Mexican who is extremely knowledgeable about the surrounding area and who enjoys horseback riding, skiing, biking, and tennis. Mary's French-born partner, Dadou Mayer, an accomplished chef and a former member of the French National Ski Team, serves up specialties like green chile and brie omelets served with corn muffins for breakfast. Mayer is the author of *Cuisine à Taos* and has been a supervisor of the Ski School of Taos for more than 20 years. Salsa del Salto is the only bed-and-breakfast in Taos that has a pool and hot tub as well as private tennis courts.

Inn on La Loma Plaza. 315 Ranchitos Rd. (P.O. Box 4159), Taos, NM 87571. ☎ **800/530-3040** or 505/758-1717. Fax 505/751-0155. 7 rms (all with bath). TV TEL. $95–$150 standard double; $170–$195 artist studios; $135–$300 suite. Discounts available. AE, MC, V.

Upon entering the reception area of this inn, you'll be immediately relaxed by the abundance of green plants and the slow, gurgling fountain. Local art (all for sale) is displayed in all public spaces of this comfortable, spacious adobe home (some of which was built in the 1800s).

Each room is decorated differently, though all have the same amenities, such as bathrobes, fireplaces, fresh flowers, and queen- or king-size beds. Some rooms have patios, and there are a couple of suites and artists' studios with kitchenettes. The Happy Trails Room, which is distinctly different from the rest of the rooms in the house, has wonderful pine paneling, a brass bed, and chaps and spurs hanging decoratively. A couple of the rooms have incredible views of Taos Mountain.

In the morning, a breakfast of fresh fruit, juices, fresh baked goods, and a daily special hot item is served. In the early evening, you'll find Southwestern hors d'oeuvres or homemade cookies and coffee waiting for you.

TAOS SKI VALLEY

For information on the skiing and the facilities offered at Taos Ski Valley, see "Skiing" and "Other Outdoor Activities," later in this chapter.

EXPENSIVE

Hotel Edelweiss. P.O. Box 83, Taos Ski Valley, NM 87525. ☎ **800/I-LUV-SKI** or 505/776-2301. Fax 505/776-2533. 21 rms, 3 condos. A/C TV TEL. May–Oct, hotel room $69 double; condo $125 for up to six people. Ski season, hotel room $170 double; condo $245 for up to six people. AE, MC, V.

This quiet, elegant hotel offers family style accommodations right on the ski slopes. Each of the two-bedroom/two-bathroom condominiums provides a fully equipped kitchen, living room with a fireplace, and a Jacuzzi tub in the master bathroom. There's French cuisine for breakfast and lunch, with après-ski coffees and pastries. An outdoor hot tub gazebo, indoor sauna, sundeck, and television (in the lounge) are available for guest use. There is also a masseuse on the premises.

Inn at Snakedance. P.O. Box 89, Taos Ski Valley, NM 87525. ☎ **800/322-9815** or 505/776-2277. Fax 505/776-1410. 60 rms. TV TEL. June 15–Sept 29, $75 double; Nov 27–Dec 20, $125 double; Dec 21–25, Jan 1–3, and Feb 8–Mar 29, $195 standard double, $215 fireplace double; Dec 26–31, $250 standard double, $270 fireplace double; Jan 4–Feb 7, $175 standard double, $195 fireplace double; Mar 30–Apr 5, $145 double. MC, V. Free parking at Taos Ski Valley parking lot.

Located in the heart of Taos Ski Valley, the Inn at Snakedance is the only modern hotel in the area that offers ski-in/ski-out privileges. The most attractive feature of this hotel is that it's literally 10 yards from the ski lift. The inn offers comfortable guest rooms, many of which feature wood-burning fireplaces. All of the furnishings are modern, and the windows (many of which offer mountain views) open to let in the fresh mountain air. All rooms provide cable TV, minirefrigerators, and wet bars (not stocked). Some rooms adjoin, connecting a standard hotel room with a fireplace room—perfect for families. Smoking is prohibited in the guest rooms and most public areas. Children under 6 are not welcome.

Dining/Entertainment: The **Hondo Restaurant and Bar** offers dining and entertainment daily during the ski season (schedules vary off-season), and also sponsors wine tastings and wine dinners. Grilled items, salads, and snacks are available on an outdoor deck. The slope-side bar provides great views.

Services: Shuttle service to nearby hotels, shops, and restaurants.

Facilities: Minispa (with hot tub, sauna, exercise equipment, and massage facilities), massage therapist on site, in-house ski storage and boot dryers, convenience store (with food, sundries, video rental, and alcoholic beverages).

Kandahar Condominiums. P.O. Box 72, Taos Ski Valley, NM 87525. ☎ **800/756-2226** or 505/776-2226. Fax 505/776-2481. 27 units. A/C TV TEL. May–Oct, $75–$120; ski season (four to six people per unit), $150–$350. AE, MC, V.

These condos have the highest location on the slopes—and with it, ski-in/ski-out access. Facilities include an exercise room, Jacuzzi, steam room, professional masseur, laundry, and conference/party facility. American Educational Institute seminars are held here each week during the season.

MODERATE

Amizette Inn. Taos Ski Valley Rd. (P.O. Box 756), Taos Ski Valley, NM 87525. ☎ **800/446-8267** or 505/776-2451. 12 rms. A/C TV TEL. May–Oct, $55–$110 single or double; ski season, $95–$150 single or double. AE, CB, DC, DISC, MC, V.

Open year-round, this lodge offers a hot tub and redwood sauna, tanning deck, and full-service restaurant. The spacious rooms with separate sitting areas that offer panoramic river and mountain views are perfect for a romantic getaway.

Austing Haus. Taos Ski Valley Rd. (P.O. Box 8), Taos Ski Valley, NM 87525. ☎ **800/748-2932** or 505/776-2649. Fax 505/776-8751. 53 rms. TV TEL. $49–$170 double. Rates include continental breakfast. CB, DC, DISC, MC, V.

About 1¹/₂ miles from the ski resort, the Austing Haus features a restaurant and hot tub. Guests have a choice of rooms, ranging from a standard hotel unit to luxury fireplace rooms with four-poster beds. Incidentally, this is the largest and tallest timber frame building in the United States.

Thunderbird Lodge. P.O. Box 87, Taos Ski Valley, NM 87525. ☎ **800/776-2279** or 505/776-2280. Fax 505/776-2238. 32 rms. $99–$142 double. Seven-day Ski Week Package $1,080–$1,350 per adult, depending on season and type of accommodation. Seven-day Lodge Packages are also available. Rates include three meals. AE, MC, V.

Located 150 yards from the slopes on the north ("sunny") side of the valley, the Thunderbird's extras include a superb restaurant with a large wine cellar, an excellent Saturday-evening buffet, and nightly entertainment in the bar. International jazz stars are booked annually during early January. Seven-day Ski Week Packages include seven nights, 20 meals, six days of unlimited use of all ski lifts, six daily morning ski lessons, use of all lodge facilities, a weekly wine tasting session, and two-step lessons. The lodge is equipped with saunas, Jacuzzi, and conference facilities. Twenty-four rooms in the main lodge each have a double and a single bed or a set of bunk beds. Eight rooms in the chalets are larger (including some family rooms) with king-size beds.

RV PARKS & CAMPGROUNDS

Carson National Forest. P.O. Box 558, Taos, NM 87571. ☎ **505/758-6200.**

There are nine national forest campsites within 20 miles of Taos, all open from April or May until September or October, depending on snow conditions. For information on other public sites, contact the **Bureau of Land Management,** 224 Cruz Alta Rd., Taos, NM 87571 (☎ **505/758-8851**).

Enchanted Moon Campground. No. 7 Valle Escondido Rd. (on US 64 E.), Valle Escondido, NM 87571. ☎ **505/758-3338.** 69 sites. Full RV hookup $17 per day. Closed Nov to mid-Apr.

Questa Lodge. Two blocks from NM 522 (P.O. Box 155), Questa, NM 87556. ☎ **505/586-0300.** 24 sites. Full RV hookup, $17 per day, $175 per month. Closed Nov–Apr.

Taos RV Park. Paseo del Pueblo Sur (P.O. Box 729), Ranchos de Taos, NM 87557. ☎ **800/323-6009** or 505/758-1667. Fax 505/758-1989. 29 spaces. $12 without RV hookup, $18 with RV hookup. Senior discounts are available.

Taos Valley RV Park and Campground. 120 Estes Rd. off NM 68; 7204 NDCBU, Taos, NM 87571. ☎ **800/999-7571** or 505/758-4469. Fax 505/758-4469. 92 spaces. $14.50–$15.50 without RV hookup, $18.50–$22.50 with RV hookup. MC, V. Closed Nov 1–Mar 15.

4 Dining

Restaurants in Taos are quite informal. Nowhere is a jacket and tie mandatory; in the winter you'll see diners in ski sweaters and blue jeans even at the finest restaurants. This informality doesn't extend to reservations, however; especially during the peak season, it is important to make reservations well in advance and keep them or else cancel.

EXPENSIVE

Doc Martin's. In the Historic Taos Inn, 125 Paseo del Pueblo Norte. ☎ **505/758-1977.** Reservations recommended. Main courses $15.50–$28, early diner's menu $12.95 per person; lunch $4.50–$8.50; breakfast $3.95–$7.50. AE, DC, MC, V. Daily 8am–2:30pm and 5:30–9:30pm. CONTEMPORARY SOUTHWESTERN.

Doc Martin's restaurant comprises Dr. Thomas Paul Martin's former home, office, and delivery room. In 1912, painters Bert Philips (Doc's brother-in-law) and Ernest Blumenschein hatched the concept of the Taos Society of Artists in the Martin dining room. Art still predominates here, from paintings to cuisine. The food is widely acclaimed, and the wine list has received numerous "Awards of Excellence" from *Wine Spectator* magazine.

Breakfast might include the local favorites: huevos rancheros (fried eggs on a blue-corn tortilla smothered with chile and Jack cheese) or "The Kit Carson" (eggs Benedict with a Southwestern flair). Lunch might include a Pacific ahi tuna sandwich, Caesar salad, or for the heartier appetite, the northern New Mexican casserole (layers of blue-corn tortillas, pumpkin-seed mole, calabacitas, and cheddar). For a dinner appetizer, I'd recommend the salmon gravlax (with blue corn tortilla points, red chile aioli, red chile oil, capers, cilantro, and chives) or the chile relleno. This might be followed by sesame-crusted tuna mignon (served on a noodle cake with spicy eggplant sauce, tomato jam, house pickled ginger, and bok choy) or the Southwest lacquered duck (poached, roasted, and grilled duck breast served over julienne duck-leg meat and red-chile broth with posole and mango relish).

Lambert's of Taos. 309 Paseo del Pueblo Sur. ☎ **505/758-1009.** Reservations recommended. Main courses $8–$18.50. AE, DC, MC, V. Mon–Fri 11:30am–2pm; daily 6–9pm. CONTEMPORARY AMERICAN.

Zeke Lambert, a former San Francisco restaurateur who was head chef at Doc Martin's for four years, opened this fine dining establishment in late 1989 in the historic Randall Home near Los Pandos Road. Now, in simple but elegant surroundings, he presents a new and different menu every night.

Diners might begin with homemade duck pâté with pistachios and croutons, fresh Dungeness crab cakes with Thai dipping sauce, or chile dusted deep-fried rock shrimp. Main courses always include fresh seafood, such as grilled salmon with tomato sage sauce or shrimp quesadilla (shrimp with sweet peppers and Jack cheese in a crispy tortilla with beans and salsa). Other more-or-less typical main dishes could be pepper-crusted lamb with red wine demi-glacé and garlic pasta, chicken stewed in green chile and served with black beans, or cassoulet with duck confit and lamb sausage. To accommodate different appetites, all main dishes are offered in two sizes. Desserts, like the chocolate oblivion truffle torte and sour-cream cognac cake, are outstanding. Espresso coffees, beers, and wines are served.

✪ **Stakeout Grill and Bar.** Stakeout Dr., just off NM 68. ☎ **505/758-2042.** Reservations recommended. Main courses $11.95–$25.95. AE, CB, DC, DISC, MC, V. Daily 5–10pm. CONTINENTAL.

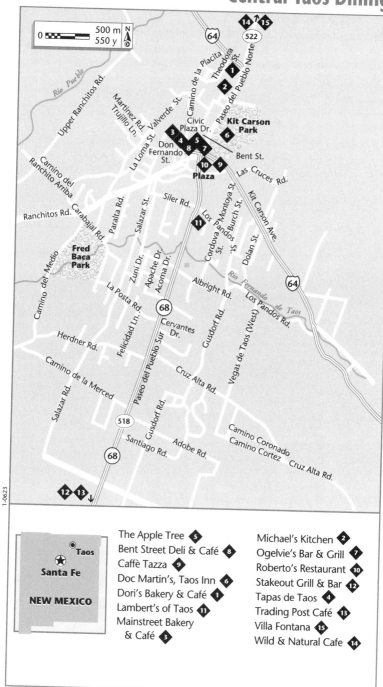

Central Taos Dining

The Apple Tree 5
Bent Street Deli & Café 8
Caffè Tazza 9
Doc Martin's, Taos Inn 6
Dori's Bakery & Café 1
Lambert's of Taos 11
Mainstreet Bakery & Café 3
Michael's Kitchen 2
Ogelvie's Bar & Grill 7
Roberto's Restaurant 10
Stakeout Grill & Bar 12
Tapas de Taos 4
Trading Post Café 13
Villa Fontana 15
Wild & Natural Cafe 14

195

👪 Family-Friendly Restaurants

El Taoseño Restaurant *(see p. 198)*   The jukebox and games room will keep the kids happy while you wait for tacos and enchiladas at low prices.

Casa de Valdez *(see p. 197)*   Parents will feel comfortable dining with children here, and the menu is simple enough to please even the pickiest of palates.

I love this restaurant. Maybe it's because you have to drive about a mile up a dirt road toward the base of the Sangre de Cristo mountains, but once you get there you'll have one of the greatest views of Taos (and the sunset). Or maybe it's because after you're inside, you're enveloped in the warmth of its rustic decor—paneled walls, creaking hardwood floors, and a crackling fireplace in the winter. The food, which focuses on steak and seafood, is marvelous. You can start with baked Brie with sliced almonds and apples, or escargots baked with walnuts, herbs, white wine, and garlic. Move on to a wonderful filet mignon, served with béarnaise sauce, or my favorite, duck Cumberland (half a duck roasted with apples and prunes and served with an orange-currant sauce); this dish is never fatty and always leaves you feeling satisfied. Among the seafood offerings are salmon, Alaskan king crab legs, scallops, and shrimp. Try to time your reservation so that you will be able to see the spectacular sunset.

✪ **Villa Fontana.** NM 522, 5 miles north of Taos. ☎ **505/758-5800.** Reservations recommended. Main courses $19–$25. AE, CB, DC, DISC, JCB, MC, V. Mon–Sat 11:30am–2pm (June–Oct only) and 6–11pm. ITALIAN.

Carlo and Siobhan Gislimberti like to talk about *peccato di gola,* "lust of the palate." The couple brought it with them to Taos when they left their home in the Italian Dolomites, near the Austrian border. They have their own herb garden, and Carlo, a master chef, is a member of the New Mexico Mycological Society—wild mushrooms are a major element in many of his kitchen preparations. Also something of an artist, Carlos displays his own work throughout the restaurant.

Meals are truly gourmet. Diners can start with *scampi alla Veneziana* (shrimp in a brandy Aurora sauce) or *pâté ricco de fegatini alla moda* (homemade chicken-liver pâté). Main courses include whole Dover sole with fresh herbs, pheasant breast with dried blueberries and demi-glacé, and grilled beef tenderloin with brandy, balsamic vinegar, and green peppercorns. Outdoor dining in the summer offers pleasant mountain and valley views.

MODERATE

The Apple Tree. 123 Bent St. ☎ **505/758-1900.** Reservations recommended. Main courses $10.95–$18.95; lunch $5.25–$9.95. CB, DC, DISC, MC, V. Mon–Fri 11:30am–3pm; light meals and snacks daily 3–5:30pm; daily 5:30–9pm; brunch Sat 11:30am–3pm, Sun 10am–3pm. INTERNATIONAL.

Eclectic music pervades the four elegant adobe rooms of this fine restaurant, a block north of the Plaza. Original paintings by Taos masters overlook the candlelit service indoors; outside, diners sit at wooden tables on a graveled courtyard beneath a spreading apple tree.

Daily specials supplement the regular international-accented menu. A very popular and excellent dish is mango chicken enchiladas. There's also a Thai red curry (either vegetarian or with shrimp), chicken moutard (boneless, skinless breast of chicken sautéed with spinach in apple cider and served with a Dijon brandy cream sauce). The Apple Tree has an award-winning wine list, and the desserts are prepared fresh daily.

✪ **Casa de Valdez.** 1401 S. Santa Fe Rd. ☎ **505/758-8777.** Reservations recommended. Main courses $8.95–$18.95. AE, DC, DISC, MC, V. Mon–Tues and Thurs–Sat 11:30am–9:30pm, Sun 3:30–9:30pm. NEW MEXICAN.

Located 2¹/₂ miles south of the Plaza, Casa de Valdez has recently been renovated. The interior is warm and welcoming and the extremely friendly staff know many of their customers by name. The menu is predictable as far as New Mexican cuisine goes, with blue-corn enchiladas, bean burritos, and tamales. The chile rellenos are exceptionally good. You can also order spareribs, barbecued chicken, steak, and shrimp. Personally, I think the sopaipillas served at the Casa de Valdez are the best around—they practically melt in your mouth.

Ogelvie's Bar and Grill. 1031 E. Plaza. ☎ **505/758-8866.** Reservations recommended. Main courses $8.50–$19.50; lunch $5.50–$9.50. AE, MC, V. Daily 11am to about 10pm. INTERNATIONAL.

This is a casual restaurant with rich wood decor. Homemade soups, burgers and other sandwiches, and huevos (eggs) de casa Ogelvie's are hits on the lunch menu. Dinner might include shrimp Hawaiian; fresh trout piñon; steaks; regional specialties like fajitas, burritos, and enchiladas; and a few pasta dishes. A lively bar with an outdoor deck overlooks the Plaza.

✪ **Trading Post Café.** 4179 Paseo del Pueblo Sur, Ranchos de Taos. ☎ **505/758-5089.** Reservations not accepted. Menu items $4–$17. AE, MC, V. Mon–Sat 11am–9:30pm. ITALIAN/ INTERNATIONAL.

Without doubt, this is Taos's hottest new restaurant. As you enter the bright, airy interior, to your right you'll see high metal stools surrounding a bar (where meals can be taken); the bar itself encloses an open exhibition kitchen. If you're dining alone or just don't feel like waiting for a table, the bar is a fun place to sit. The Trading Post's menu lists a nice variety of items without distinguishing between appetizers and main courses. This small detail speaks volumes about the restaurant. You can order whatever you want; if you feel like trying three appetizers and skipping the main course, that's fine. The tasty Caesar salad is traditional with an interesting twist: garlic chips. The menu also includes a nice variety of pastas; the angel hair pasta with chicken, wild mushrooms, and Gorgonzola cream is surprisingly light and flavorful. There's also a fresh fish of the day. Try a delicious tart for dessert.

INEXPENSIVE

Ⓢ **Bent Street Deli and Cafe.** 120 Bent St. ☎ **505/758-5787.** Reservations recommended. Main courses $10–$16; lunch $2.50–$8; breakfast $1.25–$6. MC, V. Mon–Sat 8am–9pm. DELI/ INTERNATIONAL.

This popular cafe is a short block north of the Plaza. Outside, a flower box surrounds sidewalk cafe-style seating beneath large blue-and-white umbrellas. Inside, baskets and bottles of homemade jam provide a homey, country feel. The menu features breakfast burritos and homemade granola in the morning; 18 deli sandwiches, plus a "create-your-own" column, for lunch. At dinner, the menu becomes a bit more sophisticated with dishes like beef tenderloin medallions served over fettucine with a chipotle, fontina cream, or roja shrimp (black tiger shrimp, red chile, and jicama, cilantro, and corn relish). There's heated patio dining in the winter. If you'd like to grab a picnic to go, Bent Street Deli and Cafe offers carry-out service.

Caffè Tazza. 122 Kit Carson Rd. ☎ **505/758-8706.** Reservations not accepted. All menu items under $10. No credit cards. Daily 8am–6pm (to 10pm on performance nights). CAFE.

This cozy three-room cafe is a gathering spot for local community groups, artists, performers, and poets—in fact, it's home to SOMOS, the Society of the Muse of the

Southwest. Plays, films, comedy, and musical performances are given here on weekends (and some weeknights in summer) in the cafe's main room. The walls are always hung with the works of local emerging artists who have not yet made it to the Taos gallery scene. Locals and tourists alike enjoy sitting in the cafe, taking in the scene or reading one of the assorted periodicals available while sipping a cappuccino or espresso. Of course, the food is also quite good. Soups, sandwiches, tamales, croissants, and pastries are all popular.

Dori's Cafe and Bakery. 402 Paseo del Pueblo Norte. ☎ **505/758-9222.** Menu items $3.50–$7. MC, V. Mon–Sat 7am–2:30pm; Sun 8am–1pm. AMERICAN/ITALIAN.

This delightful find, next door to the Taos Post Office, is a gathering place for the Taos literary and artistic crowd. In fact, if you read John Nichols's *Nirvana Blues,* you'll recognize the Prince Whales Cafe as Dori's. Twenty-two years ago when Dori's opened, bagels were a mainstay on the menu, but they turned out to be a hard sell in the beginning. No one in Taos had ever heard of a bagel before. Now, it's a different story. Dori's regulars come here so regularly that they keep their own personal coffee mugs hanging above the kitchen doorway. The cafe also hosts changing art exhibits and musical performances by local artists. Breakfast burritos are popular in the mornings, as are bagels, eggs, pancakes, and granola. In the afternoon, the menu offers sandwiches, soups, salads, and pizzas. Of course, pastries are homemade daily, and espresso coffees and breakfast are served all day. Beer and wine are available.

El Taoseño Restaurant. 819 S. Santa Fe Rd. ☎ **505/758-4142.** Main courses $1.25–$11.95. MC, V. Mon–Sat 6am–10pm, Sun 6:30am–3pm. NEW MEXICAN/AMERICAN.

A long-established local diner, El Taoseño features a jukebox in the corner and local art (for sale) on the walls. There are daily specials such as barbecued chicken and Mexican plates; standard fare includes everything from huevos rancheros to enchiladas and tacos. Locals flock here for the breakfast burrito. A low-fat menu is also available.

Mainstreet Bakery and Cafe. Guadalupe Plaza, Camino de la Placita. ☎ **505/758-9610.** Menu items $4.95–$12.95. No credit cards. Daily 7:30am–9pm. NATURAL FOODS.

Located about 1$^{1}/_{2}$ blocks west of the Plaza, this is one of Taos's biggest counterculture hangouts. The image is fostered by the health-conscious cuisine and the wide selection of newspapers, magazines, and other reading material advocating alternative lifestyles. Coffee and pastries are served all day. At breakfast, omelets, pancakes, French toast, and huevos rancheros are popular. The lunch menu focuses on sandwiches and pasta, but there are also several chicken dishes (like poulet Joelle, braised chicken breast with a mushroom-hazelnut cream sauce) and fish selections. In keeping with the spirit of good health promoted here, no alcoholic beverages are served, and smoking is not permitted.

☉ Michael's Kitchen. 304C Paseo del Pueblo Norte. ☎ **505/758-4178.** Breakfast $2.85–$8.45; lunch $2.65–$8.25; dinner $5.25–$10.75. MC, V. Daily 7am–8:30pm. NEW MEXICAN/AMERICAN.

A couple of blocks north of the Plaza is this eatery, a throwback to earlier days. Between its hardwood floor and viga ceiling are various knickknacks on posts, walls, and windows: a deer head here, a Tiffany lamp there, several scattered antique wood stoves. Seating is at booths and tables. Meals, too, are old-fashioned, as far as quality and quantity for price. Breakfasts, including a great variety of pancakes and egg dishes, are served all day, as are luncheon sandwiches. Dinners range from veal cordon bleu, knockwurst and sauerkraut, and plantation fried chicken to enchiladas rancheros, fish-and-chips, and New York steak. Michael's also has a full service bakery with fantastic breads. There's also a children's menu.

Roberto's Restaurant. 122 Kit Carson Rd. ☎ **505/758-2434.** Reservations recommended. Main courses around $10. MC, V. Summer, Wed–Mon noon–2:30pm and 6–9pm. Winter, most weekends. NEW MEXICAN.

Hidden within a warren of art galleries opposite the Kit Carson Museum (see below) is this local gem, which, for more than 25 years, has focused on authentic native dishes. Within this 160-year-old adobe building are three small high-ceilinged dining rooms, each with hardwood floors and a maximum of five tables; one room has a corner fireplace. Everyday dishes include tacos, enchiladas, tamales, and chile rellenos. All meals start with sopaipillas and come with homemade refried beans and chicos (dried kernels of corn). Beer and wine are served. Note that Roberto is an avid skier; thus, the restaurant's winter hours are unpredictable at best.

Tapas de Taos Cafe. 136 Bent St. ☎ **505/758-9670.** Reservations not accepted. Main courses $3.95–$12.95; tapas $3.95–$7.95. MC, V. Mon–Fri 11:30am–3pm; Mon–Sat 3–9:30pm; Sun 3–9pm. NEW MEXICAN/TAPAS.

If you're familiar with Mexican culture, you'll recognize the theme decor at Tapas de Taos Cafe; it represents the Mexican Day of the Dead (Dia de los Muertos). The rows of black skulls lining the walls of the dining room in this 300-year-old adobe may not be everyone's idea of a good time, but they certainly are unique. The tapas menu is short but excellent; it includes such items as spicy Vietnamese fried calamari, pork-and-ginger potstickers, and a shrimp-and-vermicelli fritter. Other menu offerings include chile rellenos, fajitas, enchiladas, tacos, and chimichangas. You can get a variety of coffees, including cafe macchiata, cappuccino, caffè latte, and espresso. Outdoor patio dining is available during the warmer months. There's also a kids' menu.

Wild and Natural Cafe. 812 Paseo del Pueblo Norte. ☎ **505/751-0480.** All items under $10. MC, V. Mon–Sat 7am–9pm. ORGANIC/VEGETARIAN.

When traveling it's often difficult to find a place to eat if you're a vegetarian, but in Taos the choice is easy. In fact, the Wild and Natural Cafe was voted "Natural Food Restaurant of the Year" by New Mexico Naturally in 1994. Lunches feature soups, salads, sandwiches, veggie burgers, steamed vegetables, Southwestern dishes, and low-fat daily specials. At dinner you might try the Thai green curry, East Indian curry, or lemon ginger squash. There's an espresso bar, as well as organic wine, fresh vegetable juice, local beer, fruit smoothies, and dairy-free desserts. Takeout orders are available.

5 What to See & Do

TAOS PUEBLO

No other site in Taos is as important or as famous as the ✪ **Taos Pueblo.** The community of 1,500—about 2¹⁄₂ miles north of the Plaza—forms a world of its own. The northernmost of New Mexico's 19 pueblos, it has been the home of the Tiwa tribes for more than 900 years.

Two massive, multistoried adobe apartment buildings look much the same today as they did when a regiment from Coronado's expedition first saw them in 1540. Houses are built one upon another to form porches, balconies, and roofs reached by ancient ladders. The distinctive flowing lines of shaped mud, with a straw-and-mud exterior plaster, are typical of pueblo architecture throughout the Southwest. The buildings blend in with the surrounding land since the houses are made of the earth itself. Bright-blue doors are the same shade as the sky that frames the brown buildings. Between the complexes trickles a fast-flowing creek, the Rio Pueblo de Taos. A footbridge joins the two shores. To the northeast looms Taos Mountain, its long fir-covered slopes forming a timeless backdrop to the old pueblo.

Though the Tiwa were essentially a peaceful agrarian people, they are perhaps best remembered because they spearheaded the only successful revolt by Native Americans in U.S. history. Launched by Popé (Po-*pay*) in 1680, the uprising drove the Spanish from Santa Fe until 1692 and from Taos until 1698.

Native American culture and religion have prevailed here over the centuries. Taos is one of the most conservative of all North American tribal communities, still eschewing such modern conveniences as electricity and plumbing. Arts and crafts and other tourism-related businesses support the economy, along with government services, ranching, and farming.

As you explore the pueblo and gain insights into its people's lifestyle, you can visit their studios, munch on homemade bread, look into the new **San Geronimo Chapel,** and wander past the fascinating ruins of the old church and cemetery. You're expected to ask permission from individuals before taking their photos; some will ask for a small payment, but that's for you to negotiate. Kivas and other ceremonial underground areas are taboo.

San Geronimo is the patron saint of the Taos Pueblo and his feast day (September 30) combines Catholic and pre-Hispanic traditions. **The Old Taos Trade Fair** on that day is a joyous occasion, with footraces, pole climbs, and crafts booths. Dances are performed the evening of September 29. Other annual events include a turtle dance on **New Year's Day,** deer or buffalo dances on **Three Kings Day** (January 6), and corn dances on **Santa Cruz Day** (May 3), **San Antonio Day** (June 13), **San Juan Day** (June 24), **Santiago Day** (July 23), and **Santa Ana Day** (July 24). The **Taos Pueblo Powwow,** a dance competition and parade that brings together tribes from throughout North America, is held the weekend after July 4 on reservation land off NM 522. **Christmas Eve** bonfires mark the start of the children's corn dance, the **Christmas Day** deer dance, or the three-day-long Matachines dance.

During your visit to the pueblo you will have the opportunity to purchase traditional fried and oven-baked bread as well as a variety of arts and crafts. If you want to try some traditional feast day–style meals, **Tiwa Kitchen,** near the entrance to the pueblo, is a good place to stop. Nearby Tiwa Kitchen is the **Oo-oonah Children's Art Center,** where you can see the creative works of pueblo children.

The pueblo is open to visitors daily from 8am to 5:30pm, with some exceptions. Taos Pueblo closes for one month every year in late winter or early spring—call to make sure the pueblo will be open at the time you expect to be in Taos (☎ **505/ 758-8626**). Admission is $5 per car, or $10 per van. Still camera permits cost $5; video camera permits, $10; sketching permits, $15; and painting permits, $35. No photography permitted on feast days. The mailing address of the pueblo is P.O. Box 1846, Taos Pueblo, NM 87571.

Like many of the other pueblos in New Mexico, Taos Pueblo has opened a casino featuring slot machines, blackjack, and poker. Free local transportation is available. Call **505/751-0991** for details.

OTHER TOP ATTRACTIONS

✪ **Millicent Rogers Museum.** Off NM 522, 4 miles north of Taos. ☎ **505/758-2462.** Admission $4 adults, $2 children 6–16, $3 seniors, $8 families. Daily 9am–5pm. Closed San Geronimo Day (Sept 30).

Central Taos Attractions

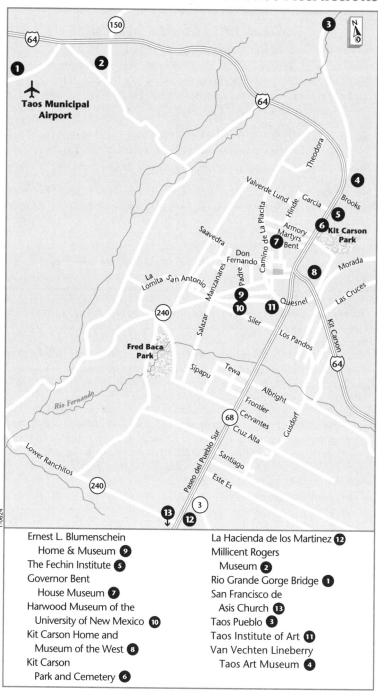

Ernest L. Blumenschein
   Home & Museum **9**
The Fechin Institute **5**
Governor Bent
   House Museum **7**
Harwood Museum of the
   University of New Mexico **10**
Kit Carson Home and
   Museum of the West **8**
Kit Carson
   Park and Cemetery **6**

La Hacienda de los Martinez **12**
Millicent Rogers
   Museum **2**
Rio Grande Gorge Bridge **1**
San Francisco de
   Asis Church **13**
Taos Pueblo **3**
Taos Institute of Art **11**
Van Vechten Lineberry
   Taos Art Museum **4**

201

Traditional Native American Bread Baking

While visiting the pueblos in New Mexico, you'll probably notice outdoor ovens (they look a bit like giant anthills), known as *hornos,* which Native Americans have used for baking bread for hundreds of years. As is true for many cultural groups, the Indians consider bread the staple of daily life. For Native Americans, making their typical bread is more than simply preparing food; it is a tradition that links them directly to their ancestors. The long process of mixing and baking also brings mothers and daughters together for what we today might call "quality time."

Usually in the evening the bread dough (made with white flour, lard, salt, yeast, and water) is made and kneaded, and the loaves are shaped. They are allowed to rise overnight. Then, in the morning, the oven is filled with wood and a fire lighted. After the fire burns down to ashes and embers, the oven is cleared and the ashes are shoveled away. Unlike modern ovens, hornos don't come equipped with thermometers, so the baker must rely on her senses to determine when the oven is the proper temperature. At that point the loaves are placed into the oven with a long-handled wooden paddle. They bake for about an hour.

If you would like to try a traditional loaf, you can buy one at the Indian Pueblo Cultural Center in Albuquerque (and elsewhere throughout the state).

Taos's most interesting collection is this museum, founded in 1953 by family members after the death of Millicent Rogers. Rogers was a wealthy Taos émigré who, beginning in 1947, compiled a magnificent array of aesthetically beautiful Native American arts and crafts. Included are Navajo and Pueblo jewelry, Navajo textiles, Pueblo pottery, Hopi and Zuni kachina dolls, paintings from the Rio Grande Pueblo people, and basketry from a wide variety of Southwestern tribes. The collection continues to grow through gifts and museum acquisitions.

Since the 1970s the scope of the museum's permanent collection has been expanded to include Hispanic religious and secular arts and crafts, from Spanish and Mexican colonial to contemporary times. Included are *santos* (religious images), furniture, weavings, *colcha* embroideries, and decorative tinwork. Agricultural implements, domestic utensils, and craftspeoples' tools dating from the 17th and 18th centuries are also displayed.

The newly remodeled museum store has some superior regional art as well as a collection of products developed exclusively for the museum (many of which were inspired by the museum's collections). Temporary exhibits, classes and workshops, lectures, and field trips are scheduled throughout the year.

Kit Carson Historic Museums. P.O Drawer P.O. CCC, Taos, NM 87571. ☎ **505/758-0505.** Admission to three museums, $8 adults, $6 seniors, $5 children 6–16, family rate $15. Two museums, $6 adults, $5 seniors, $4 children, family rate $13. One museum, $4 adults, $3 seniors, $2.50 children, family rate $6. All three museums open daily 9am–5pm (the Kit Carson Home is open daily 8am–6pm in summer).

This foundation operates three historical homes as museums, affording glimpses of early Taos lifestyles. La Hacienda de los Martinez, Kit Carson Home, and the Ernest Blumenschein Home each has unique appeal.

La Hacienda de los Martinez, Lower Ranchitos Road, Highway 240 (☎ **505/758-0505**), is one of the only Spanish colonial haciendas in the United States that is open to the public year-round. This was the home of merchant and trader Don Antonio Severino Martinez, who bought it in 1804 and lived there until his death in 1827. Located on the west bank of the Rio Pueblo de Taos about two miles south-west of the Plaza, the hacienda was built like a fortress, with thick adobe walls and no exterior windows to protect against raids by Plains tribes.

Twenty-one rooms were built around two placitas, or interior courtyards. Most of the rooms open today contain period furnishings: They include the bedrooms, servants' quarters, stables, a kitchen, and a large fiesta room. Exhibits in one newly renovated room tell the story of the Martinez family and life in Spanish Taos between 1598 and 1821, when Mexico assumed control.

Don Antonio Martinez, who for a time was *alcalde* (mayor) of Taos, owned several caravans that he used in trade on the Chihuahua Trail to Mexico. This business was carried on by his youngest son, Don Juan Pascual, who later owned the hacienda. His eldest son was Padre Antonio Jose Martinez, northern New Mexico's controversial spiritual leader from 1826 to 1867.

Kit Carson Historic Museums has developed the hacienda into a living museum with weavers, blacksmiths, and wood carvers. Demonstrations are scheduled daily, including during the Old Taos Trade Fair the last weekend in September, when the demonstrations run virtually nonstop. The Trade Fair recalls days when Natives, Spanish settlers, and mountain men met here to trade.

Kit Carson Home and Museum, East Kit Carson Road (☎ 505/758-0505), located a short block east on the Plaza intersection, is the town's only general museum of Taos history. The 12-room adobe home with walls 2 1/2 feet thick was built in 1825 and purchased in 1843 by Carson, the famous mountain man, Indian agent, and scout, as a wedding gift for his young bride, Josefa Jaramillo. It remained their home for 25 years, until both died (a month to the day apart) in 1868.

The living room, bedroom, and kitchen are furnished as they might have been when occupied by the Carsons. The Indian Room contains artifacts crafted and used by the original inhabitants of Taos Valley; the Early American Room has an array of pioneer items, including a large number of antique firearms and trappers' implements; the Carson Interpretive Room showcases memorabilia from Carson's unusual life. In the kitchen is a Spanish plaque that reads: *Nadie sabe lo que tiene la olla más que la cuchara que la menea* (Nobody better knows what the pot holds than the spoon that stirs it).

The museum bookshop, with perhaps the town's most comprehensive inventory of New Mexico historical books, is adjacent to the entry.

Ernest L. Blumenschein Home and Museum, 222 Ledoux St. (☎ 505/758-0505), 1 1/2 blocks southwest of the Plaza, recalls and re-creates the lifestyle of one of the founders (in 1915) of the Taos Society of Artists. An adobe home with garden walls and a courtyard, parts of which date to the 1790s, it was the home and studio of Blumenschein (1874–1960) and his family beginning in 1919. Period furnishings include European antiques and handmade Taos furniture in Spanish colonial style. Blumenschein was born in Pittsburgh and raised in Dayton. His arrival in Taos in 1898 came somewhat by accident. After training in New York and Paris, he and fellow painter Bert Phillips were on assignment for *Harper's* and *McClure's* magazines of New York when a wheel of their wagon broke during a mountain traverse 30 miles north of Taos. Blumenschein drew the short straw and carried the wheel by horseback to Taos for repair. He later recounted his initial reaction to the valley he entered: "No artist had ever recorded the New Mexico I was now seeing. No writer had ever written down the smell of this air or the feel of that morning sky. I was receiving . . . the first great unforgettable inspiration of my life. My destiny was being decided."

That spark later led to the foundation of Taos as an art colony. An extensive collection of work by early 20th-century Taos masters is on display in several rooms of the home. Among the modern works are paintings by Blumenschein's daughter, Helen.

Van Vechten Lineberry Taos Art Museum. 501 Paseo del Pueblo Norte (P.O. Box 1848). ☎ **505/758-2690.** Admission $5 adults, $3 students and seniors. Tues–Fri 11am–4pm, Sat–Sun 1:30–4pm.

Taos's newest museum is the Van Vechten Lineberry Taos Art Museum. It was the brainchild of Ed Lineberry, who lives in the spectacular home adjacent to the museum and conceived of it as a memorial to his late wife, Duane Van Vechten. An artist in her own right, Duane spent much time working in her studio, which now serves as the entryway to the 20,000-square-foot main gallery of the museum. The entryway features, among other things, John Dunn's roulette wheel. Lineberry traveled throughout Europe studying techniques for preservation and storage, as well as the display space, climate control, and lighting of fine museums. As a result, the Van Vechten Lineberry Taos Art Museum is state-of-the-art. The museum displays the extraordinary works of Van Vechten (by far the best works in the museum), as well as those of the original Taos artists. Each artist is represented by at least one piece. Mr. Lineberry hopes to acquire more works in the next few years. Besides the main gallery space, there are smaller areas available for traveling exhibitions and a wonderful library that will be open by appointment to researchers.

MORE ATTRACTIONS

D. H. Lawrence Ranch. San Cristobal. ☎ **505/776-2245.**

The shrine of the controversial early 20th-century author is a pilgrimage site for literary devotees. A short uphill walk from the ranch home, it is littered with various mementos—photos, coins, messages from fortune cookies—placed by visitors. The guest book is worth a long read.

Lawrence lived in Taos off and on between 1922 and 1925. The ranch was a gift to his wife, Frieda, from art patron Mabel Dodge Luhan. Lawrence repaid Luhan the favor by giving her the manuscript of *Sons and Lovers.* Lawrence died in southern France in 1930 of tuberculosis; his ashes were returned here for burial. The grave of Frieda, who died in 1956, is outside the shrine.

The shrine is the only public building at the ranch, which is operated today by the University of New Mexico as an educational and recreational retreat. To reach the site, head north from Taos 15 miles on NM 522, then another 6 miles east into the forested Sangre de Cristo range via a well-marked dirt road.

✪ **The Fechin Institute.** 227 Paseo del Pueblo Norte (P.O. Box 832), Taos, NM 87571. ☎ **505/758-1710.** Admission $3. May–Oct Wed–Sun 1–5pm, other times by appointment.

The home of Russian artist Nicolai Fechin (feh-*sheen*) from 1927 to 1933, this historic house memorializes the career of a 20th-century Renaissance man. Born in Russia in 1881, Fechin came to the United States in 1923, already acclaimed as a master of painting, drawing, sculpture, architecture, and woodwork. In Taos, he built a huge adobe home and embellished it with hand-carved doors, windows, gates, posts, fireplaces, and other features of a Russian country home. The house and adjacent studio are now used for Fechin Institute educational activities, as well as concerts, lectures, and other programs.

Governor Bent House Museum. 117 Bent St. ☎ **505/758-2376.** Admission $1 adults, 50¢ children. Daily, summer 9:30am–5pm, winter 10am–4pm.

Located a short block north of the Plaza, this was the residence of Charles Bent, the New Mexico Territory's first American governor. Bent, a former trader who established Bent's Fort in Colorado, was killed in the 1847 Indian and Hispanic rebellion. His wife and children attempted to escape by digging through an adobe wall into the house next door. The hole is still visible. Period art and artifacts are displayed.

Harwood Foundation Museum of the University of New Mexico. 238 Ledoux St. ☎ **505/758-9826.** Admission $3. Mon–Fri 10am–5pm, Sat 10am–4pm.

Some of the finest works of art ever produced in or about Taos hang on the walls of this Pueblo-style library and museum complex, a cultural and community center since 1923.

The museum shows paintings, drawings, prints, sculpture, and photographs by the artists of the Taos area from 1800 to the present. Featured are paintings from the early days of the art colony by members of the Taos Society of Artists, including Oscar Berninghaus, Ernest Blumenschein, Herbert Dunton, Victor Higgins, Bert Phillips, and Walter Ufer. In addition, there are works by Emil Bisttram, Andrew Dasburg, Leon Gaspard, Louis Ribak, Bea Mandelman, Agnes Martin, Larry Bell, and Thomas Benrimo.

Also on display are 19th-century *retablos,* religious paintings of saints that have traditionally been used for decoration and inspiration in the homes and churches of New Mexico. The permanent collection of art shows sculptures by Patrocinio Barela, one of the leading Hispanic artists of 20th-century New Mexico.

The museum also has five or six changing exhibitions each year, many of which feature the best artists currently working in Taos.

Note: The Harwood was closed at the end of 1996 for renovations. If you're traveling in early 1997, call ahead to make sure it has reopened.

Kit Carson Park and Cemetery. Paseo del Pueblo Norte.

Major community events are held in the park in summer. The cemetery, established in 1847, contains the graves of Carson and his wife, Gov. Charles Bent, the Don Antonio Martinez family, Mabel Dodge Luhan, and many other noted historical figures and artists. Plaques describe their contributions.

✪ **Rio Grande Gorge Bridge.** U.S. Hwy. 64, 10 miles west of Taos.

This impressive bridge, west of the Taos Airport, spans the Southwest's greatest river. At 650 feet above the canyon floor, it's one of America's highest bridges. If you can withstand the vertigo, it's interesting to come more than once, at different times of day, to observe how the changing light plays tricks with the colors of the cliff walls. An interesting aside is that the wedding scene in the recent movie *Natural Born Killers* was filmed here.

✪ **San Francisco de Asis Church.** Ranchos de Taos. ☎ **505/758-2754.** Donations appreciated, $2 minimum. Mon–Sat 9am–4pm, closed daily from noon to 1pm. Visitors may attend mass Sat at 5:30pm and Sun at 7am (Spanish), 9am, and 11:30am.

From NM 68, about 4 miles south of Taos, this famous church appears as a modernesque adobe sculpture with no doors or windows. It has often been photographed (by Ansel Adams, among others) and painted (for example, by Georgia O'Keeffe) from this angle. Visitors must walk through the garden on the west side of this remarkable two-story church to enter and get a full perspective of its massive walls, authentic adobe plaster, and beauty.

Displayed on the wall is an unusual painting, *The Shadow of the Cross* by Henri Ault (1896). Under ordinary light it portrays a barefoot Christ at the Sea of Galilee;

in darkness, however, the portrait becomes luminescent and the perfect shadow of a cross forms over the left shoulder of Jesus's silhouette. The artist reportedly was as shocked as everyone else to see this. The reason for the illusion remains a mystery.

The church office and gift shop are just across the driveway north of the church. A video presentation is also shown here on the half hour. Several crafts shops surround the square.

ORGANIZED TOURS

Damaso and Helen Martinez's **Pride of Taos Tours,** P.O. Box 1192, Taos, NM 87571 (☎ **505/758-8340**), offers several packages, including a Taos historical tour that lasts an hour and takes tourists to the Plaza, Martinez Hacienda, and Ranchos de Taos Church ($6 adults, $3 children 12 and under).

An excellent opportunity to explore the historic downtown area is offered by **Taos Historic Walking Tours** (☎ **505/758-4020**). Call for schedule and prices.

6 Skiing Taos

Five alpine resorts are located within an hour's drive of Taos. All offer complete facilities, including equipment rentals. Although exact opening and closing dates may vary according to snow conditions, it's usually safe to say that skiing will begin Thanksgiving weekend and continue into early April.

You can purchase ski clothing or rent ski equipment from several Taos outlets. Among them are **Cottam's Ski and Outdoor Shops,** with four locations, call **800/ 322-8267** or 505/758-2822 for the one nearest you; **Taos Ski Valley Sportswear, Ski and Boot Co.,** in Taos Ski Valley (☎ **505/776-2291**); and **Looney Tunes Ski Shop,** also in the ski valley (☎ **505/776-8839**).

AREA SKI RESORTS
TAOS SKI VALLEY

✪ **Taos Ski Valley** (Box 90), Taos Ski Valley, NM 87525 (☎ **505/776-2291.** World Wide Web: http://www.taoswebb.com/nmusa/skitaos/) is the preeminent ski resort in the southern Rocky Mountains. It was founded in 1955 by a Swiss-German immigrant, Ernie Blake. According to local legend, Blake searched for two years in a small plane for the perfect location for a ski resort equal to his native Alps. He found it at the abandoned mining site of Twining, high above Taos. Doubters predicted that Blake's enterprise would never survive, that the mountain was too steep and too remote. However, more than 40 years later, the resort is still under the command of two younger generations of Blakes and has become internationally renowned for its light, dry powder (320 inches annually), its superb ski school (one of the best in the country), and its personal, friendly manner. Even the esteemed London *Times* called the valley "without any argument the best ski resort in the world. Small, intimate and endlessly challenging, Taos simply has no equal." And, if you're sick of dealing with those yahoos on snowboards, this is the place to go—they're not permitted on the slopes of Taos Ski Valley (the only ski area in New Mexico with this restriction).

Of the 72 trails and bowls, more than half are designated for expert or advanced skiers, including the famous Al's Run, the steep, bump-laden run that greets visitors arriving at the resort's parking lot. Some say that the better skier you are, the more you will enjoy this mountain, but between the 11,819-foot summit and the 9,207-foot base, there are also ample opportunities for novice and intermediate skiers. But Taos does attract lots of expert skiers intent on challenging themselves on the mountains' steep cliffs and narrow chutes or polishing their skills in one of the ski school's Mogul Mastery workshops or week-long Ski Better programs.

The area has an uphill capacity of 15,050 skiers per hour on its five double chairs, one triple, four quads, and one surface tow. Lift tickets for all lifts, depending on the season, cost $26 to $41 adults for a full day, $25 half day; $16 to $24 for children 12 or younger for a full day, $17 half day; $18 seniors 65 to 69 for a full day; free for seniors over 70. Novice lift tickets cost $22 for adults, $16 for children. Full rental packages are $14 for adults and $7 for children. Taos Ski Valley is open daily from 9am to 4pm from Thanksgiving to the first week of April.

With its children's ski school, Taos Ski Valley has always been an excellent location for skiing families, but with the 1994 addition of an 18,000-square-foot children's center (Kinderkäfig Center), skiing with your children in Taos is an even better experience. Kinderkäfig offers every service imaginable, from equipment rental for children to baby-sitting services. Call ahead for more information.

Taos Ski Valley has 13 lodges and condominiums with nearly 700 beds. All offer ski-week packages; four of them have restaurants. There are two more restaurants on the mountain in addition to the expansive facilities of Village Center at the base. For reservations, call the **Taos Valley Resort Association** (☎ **800/776-1111** or 505/ 776-2233).

RED RIVER SKI AREA

Not far from Taos Ski Valley is Red River Ski Area, P.O. Box 900, Red River, NM 87558 (☎ **800/348-6444** for reservations, or 505/754-2223). One of the bonuses of this ski area is the fact that lodgers in Red River can walk out their doors and be on the slopes. Two other factors make this 37-year-old, family-oriented area special: First, its 57 trails are geared to the intermediate skier, though beginners and experts have their share; and second, good snow is guaranteed early and late in the year by snowmaking equipment that can work on 75% of the runs, more than any other in New Mexico. There's a 1,600-foot vertical drop here to a base elevation of 8,750 feet. Lifts include four double chairs, two triple chairs, and a surface tow, with a skier capacity of 7,920 skiers per hour. The cost of a lift ticket for all lifts is $36 for adults for a full day, $26 for a half day; $22 for children 12 and under and seniors (60 and over) for a full day, $15 for a half day. Full rental packages start at $13 for adults, $9 for children. Red River Ski Area is open daily from 9am to 4pm from Thanksgiving to March 30.

ANGEL FIRE RESORT

Also quite close to Taos is Angel Fire Resort, P.O. Drawer B, Angel Fire, NM 87710 (☎ **800/633-7463** or 505/377-6401). The 32 miles of ski runs here are heavily oriented to beginning and intermediate skiers. Still, with a vertical drop of 2,180 feet to a base elevation of 8,500 feet, advanced skiers are certain to find something they like. The area's lifts—one Poma surface tow, four doubles, and one high-speed quad—have an hourly capacity of 8,600 skiers. All-day lift tickets cost $32 for adults and $20 for children. Open from approximately Thanksgiving to April depending on the weather, daily from 8:30am to 4:30pm.

SKI RIO

Just south of the Colorado border is Ski Rio (P.O. Box 159, Costilla, NM 87524; ☎ **800/2-ASK-RIO** or 505/758-7707), a rapidly expanding ski area. Half its 83 named trails are for the intermediate skier, 30% for beginners, and 20% for experts. Also within Ski Rio are Snowboard and Snow Skate Parks, as well as 13 miles of cross-country trails. Annual snowfall here is about 260 inches, and there are three chair lifts (two triple, one double) and three tows for an uphill capacity of 5,500 per hour. At the ski base you can rent skis, snowboards, snowshoes, and snow skates, as well as find lodgings, restaurants, and a sports shop. Sleigh rides, dogsled tours, and snowmobile tours are also available. The ski school offers private and group clinics (for adults and children) in cross-country and downhill skiing, snow skating, and snowboarding. Lift tickets are $33 for adults ($22 to $27 in value season), $23 for children 7 to 12, free for children 6 and under with a paying adult. Ski Rio is open daily from 9am to 4pm from November 27 to April 6.

SIPAPU SKI AREA

The oldest ski area in the Taos region, founded in 1952, Sipapu Ski Area (P.O. Box 29, Vadito, NM 87579; ☎ **505/587-2240**) is 25 miles southeast on NM 518 in Tres Ritos canyon. It prides itself on being a small local area, especially popular with schoolchildren. Many types of overnight lodging are available, from duplexes to a bunkhouse to camping. All-day lift tickets are $28 for adults and $21 for children under 12. Open from Thanksgiving to April daily from 8am to 4pm.

CROSS-COUNTRY SKIING IN THE AREA

There are numerous popular Nordic trails in Carson National Forest. If you call or write ahead, they'll send you a booklet titled "Where to Go in the Snow," which gives cross-country skiers details about the maintained trails in Carson National Forest. One of the more popular is **Amole Canyon,** off NM 518 near the Sipapu Ski Area, where the Taos Nordic Ski Club maintains set tracks and signs along a 3-mile loop. It's closed to snowmobiles, a comfort to lovers of serenity. There are several trails open only to cross-country skiers.

Just east of Red River, with 31 miles of groomed trails in 600 acres of forest land atop Bobcat Pass, is the **Enchanted Forest Cross Country Ski Area** (☎ **505/ 754-2374**). Full-day trail passes, good from 9am to 4:30pm, are $9 for adults, much less for children. Equipment rentals and lessons can be arranged at **Miller's Crossing** ski shop on Main Street in Red River (☎ **505/754-2374**). Nordic skiers can get instruction in "skating," mountaineering, and telemarking. In addition, Enchanted Forest also sponsors various special skiing events throughout the year, including moonlight ski tours, a luminaria ski tour at Christmas, and "Just Desserts Eat and Ski," in which skiers follow a 5-kilometer tour stopping at area restaurants to sample desserts.

Taos Mountain Outfitters, 114 South Plaza (☎ **505/758-9292**), offers telemark and cross-country sales, rentals, and guide service, as do Los Rios Whitewater Ski Shop (☎ **505/776-8854**) and Southwest Nordic Center (☎ **505/758-4761**).

7 Other Outdoor Activities

Taos County's 2,200 square miles embrace a great diversity of scenic beauty, from New Mexico's highest mountain, 13,161-foot **Wheeler Peak,** to the 650-foot-deep chasm of the **Rio Grande Gorge. Carson National Forest,** which extends to the eastern city limits of Taos and cloaks a large part of the county, contains several major ski facilities as well as hundreds of miles of hiking trails through the Sangre de Cristo range. Recreation areas are mainly in the national forest, where pines and aspen provide refuge for abundant wildlife. Forty-eight areas are accessible by road, including 38 with campsites. There are also areas on the high desert mesa, carpeted by sagebrush, cactus, and frequently wildflowers. Both terrains are favored by hunters, fishermen, and horseback riders. Two beautiful areas within a short drive of Taos are the **Valle Vidal Recreation Area,** north of Red River, and the **Wild Rivers Recreation Area,** near Questa. For complete information, contact **Carson National Forest,** P.O. Box 558, Taos, NM 87571 (☎ **505/758-6200** or 505/758-6390), or the

Bureau of Land Management, 224 Cruz Alta Rd. (P.O. Box 6168), Taos, NM 87571 (☎ **505/758-8851**).

BALLOONING   As in many other towns throughout New Mexico, hot-air ballooning is a top attraction. Recreational trips are offered by Paradise Hot Air Balloon Adventure (☎ **505/751-6098**).

The **Taos Mountain Balloon Rally,** P.O. Box 3096, Taos, NM 87571 (☎ **505/758-8321**), is held each year the last full weekend of October. (See "New Mexico Calendar of Events," in chapter 3, for details.)

BIKING   Even if you're not an avid cyclist, it won't take long for you to realize that getting around Taos by bike is preferable to driving. You won't have the usual parking problems and you won't have to sit in the line of traffic as it snakes through the center of town. If you feel like exploring the surrounding area, Carson National Forest rangers recommend several biking trails in the greater Taos area, including those in Garcia Park and Rio Chiquito for beginner to intermediate mountain bikers, and a number of Gallegos and Picuris peaks for experts. Inquire at the U.S. Forest Service office next to the Chamber of Commerce for excellent materials that map out trails, tell you how to get to the trailhead, specify length, difficulty, elevation, and safety tips. You can also purchase the Taos Trails map (created jointly by the Carson National Forest, Native Sons Adventures, and Trail Illustrated). It's readily available at area bookstores and is designed to withstand water damage. Once you're out riding in Carson National Forest, you'll find trails marked in green (easy), blue (moderate), or gray (expert). **Gearing Up Bicycle Shop** (129 Paseo del Pueblo Sur; ☎ **505/751-0365**) and **Native Sons Adventures** (715 Paseo del Pueblo Sur; ☎ **505/758-9342**), offer mountain bike and equipment rentals. Rates range from $15 to $20 for a full day and $10 to $15 for a half day.

Annual touring events include Red River's **Enchanted Circle Century Bike Tour** (☎ **505/754-2366**) in mid-September.

FISHING   The fishing season in the high lakes and streams opens April 1 and continues through December, though spring and fall tend to be the best times. Naturally, the Rio Grande is a favorite fishing spot, but there is also excellent fishing in the streams around Taos. Taoseños favor the Rio Hondo, Rio Pueblo (near Tres Ritos), Rio Fernando (in Taos Canyon), Pot Creek, and Rio Chiquto. Rainbow, cutthroat, and German brown trout and kokanee (a freshwater salmon) are commonly stocked and caught. Pike and catfish have been caught in the Rio Grande as well. Jiggs, spinners, or woolly worms are recommended as lure, or worms, corn, or salmon eggs as bait, but many experienced anglers prefer fly fishing.

Licenses are required, of course; they are sold, along with tackle, at several Taos sporting-goods shops. For backcountry guides, try **Deep Creek Wilderness Outfitters and Guides,** P.O. Box 721, El Prado, NM 87529 (☎ **505/776-8423**) or **Taylor Streit Flyfishing Service,** P.O. Box 2759, Taos, NM 87571 (☎ **505/751-1312**).

FITNESS FACILITIES   The **Taos Spa and Court Club,** 111 Dona Ana Dr. (☎ **505/758-1980**), is a fully equipped fitness center that rivals any you'd find in a big city. There are treadmills, step machines, climbing machines, rowing machines, exercise bikes, NordicTrack, weight-training machines, saunas, indoor and outdoor hot tubs, a steam room, and indoor and outdoor pools. Thirty-five step aerobic classes a week, as well as stretch aerobics, aqua aerobics, and classes specifically designed for senior citizens are also offered. In addition, there are five tennis and two racquetball courts. Therapeutic massage is available daily by appointment. Children's programs include tennis and swimming camp, and babysitting programs are available in the morning and evening. The spa is open Monday through Friday from 5:30am to 9pm;

Saturday and Sunday from 7am to 8pm. Monthly, weekly, and daily memberships are available for individuals and families. For visitors there's a daily rate of $10.

The **Northside Health and Fitness Center,** at 1307 Paseo del Pueblo Norte, in Taos (☎ **505/751-1242**), is also a full-service facility, featuring top-of-the-line Cybex equipment, free weights, and cardiovascular equipment. Aerobics and Jazzercise classes are scheduled daily, and there are indoor/outdoor pools and four tennis courts, as well as children's and senior citizens' programs.

GOLF   Since the summer of 1993 the 18-hole golf course at the **Taos Country Club,** Ranchos de Taos (☎ **800/758-7375** or 505/758-7300), located just 4 miles south of the Plaza on NM 570, has been open to the public. It's a first-rate championship golf course designed for all levels of play—in fact, it's ranked as the third best course in New Mexico. It's a links-style course with open fairways and no hidden greens. In addition, there's a driving range, practice putting and chipping green, and nine-hole course and instruction by PGA professionals. Greens fees in 1996 were $27 during the week, $35 on weekends and holidays for 18 holes. Cart and club rentals are also available. It's always advisable to call ahead for tee times, but it's not unusual for people to show up unannounced and still manage to find a time to tee off.

The par-72, 18-hole course at the **Angel Fire Country Club and Golf Course** (☎ **505/377-3055**) has been endorsed by the PGA. Surrounded by stands of ponderosa pine, spruce, and aspen, at 8,500 feet, it's one of the highest regulation golf courses in the world. It also has a driving range and putting green. Carts and clubs can be rented at the course, and the club pro provides instruction.

For nine-hole play, stop at the golf course at Valle Escondido residential village just off US 64. It's a par-36 course with mountain and valley views. Greens fees are $12 for the day (children under 12 are free), clubs and pull-carts are available for rental, and the clubhouse serves refreshments.

In addition, another golf course is under construction in Red River. Call the chamber of commerce to check on its status when you're in town.

HIKING   There are hundreds of miles of hiking trails in Taos County's mountain and high-mesa country. They're especially well traveled in the summer and fall, although nights turn chilly and mountain weather may be fickle by September.

Maps (for a nominal fee) and free materials and advice on all **Carson National Forest** trails and recreation areas can be obtained from the Forest Service Building, 208 Cruz Alta Rd. (☎ **505/758-6200**), and from the office adjacent to the chamber of commerce on Paseo del Pueblo Sur. Both are open Monday through Saturday from 8am to 4:30pm. Detailed USGS topographical maps of backcountry areas can be purchased from **Taos Mountain Outfitters** on the Plaza (☎ **505/758-9292**). This is also the place to rent camping gear, if you came without your own. Tent rentals and sleeping bags are $10 each per day. Backpacks can be rented for $8 a day.

Two wilderness areas are close to Taos and offer outstanding hiking possibilities. The 19,663-acre **Wheeler Peak Wilderness** is a wonderland of alpine tundra encompassing New Mexico's highest peak (13,161 feet). One of the most popular hikes in the area is to the summit of Wheeler Peak. The trailhead can be reached from the upper portion of Taos Ski Valley parking lot. The 20,000-acre **Latir Peak Wilderness,** north of Red River, is noted for its high lake country. Both are under the jurisdiction of the Questa Ranger District, P.O. Box 110, Questa, NM 87556 (☎ **505/586-0520**).

HORSEBACK RIDING   The **Taos Indian Horse Ranch,** on Pueblo land off Ski Valley Road, just before Arroyo Seco (☎ **800/659-3210** or 505/758-3212), offers a variety of guided rides. Open from 10am to 4pm daily and by appointment, the ranch provides horses for all types of riders (English, western, bareback) and ability levels. Call ahead to reserve. Rates start at $65 to $125 for a two-hour trail ride. Horse-drawn trolley rides are also offered in summer. From late November to March, the ranch offers evening sleigh rides to a bonfire and marshmallow roast at $45 a head; for an extra $17.50, they'll throw in dinner.

Horseback riding is also offered by the **Shadow Mountain Guest Ranch,** 6 miles east of Taos on US 64 ☎ **505/758-7732**), **Rio Grande Stables** (P.O. Box 2122, El Prado; ☎ **505/776-5913**), and **Llano Bonito Ranch** (P.O. Box 99, Penasco, about 40 minutes from Taos; ☎ **505/587-2636,** fax 505/587-2636). Rates at Llano Bonito Ranch are $15 for a one-hour trail ride, $50 per person for a half-day ride ($60 if breakfast is included), and $85 per person for a full-day ride. In addition to trail rides, Llano Bonito Ranch offers three-day pack trips for $600 per person. On the three-day trip you'll spend two nights in the high country wilderness, and during the day you'll ride to an altitude of 12,500 feet. Meals are included in the pack trip.

Most riding outfitters offer lunch trips and overnight trips. Call for further details.

HUNTING   Hunters in Carson National Forest bag deer, turkey, grouse, band-tailed pigeons, and elk by special permit. On private land, where hunters must be accompanied by qualified guides, there are also black bear and mountain lions. Hunting seasons vary year to year, so it's important to inquire ahead with the **New Mexico Game and Fish Department** in Santa Fe (☎ **505/827-7882**).

Several Taos sporting-goods shops sell hunting licenses. Backcountry guides include **Agua Fria Guide Service** (☎ **505/377-3512**) in Angel Fire, **AAA Outfitters** (☎ **505/751-5474** or 505/751-1198) in Taos, and **Rio Costilla Park** (☎ **505/586-0542**) in Costilla.

ICE-SKATING   **Kit Carson Park Ice Rink** (☎ **505/758-8234**), located in Kit Carson Park, is open from Thanksgiving through February. Skate rentals are available for adults and children.

JOGGING   You can jog anywhere (except on private property) in and around Taos. I would especially recommend stopping by the Carson National Forest office in the Chamber of Commerce building to find out what trails they might recommend.

LLAMA TREKKING   **El Paseo Llama Expeditions** (☎ **800/455-2627** or 505/758-3111) uses U.S. Forest Service–maintained trails that wind through canyons and over mountain ridges. The llamas will carry your gear and food, allowing you to walk and explore, free of any heavy burdens. They're friendly, gentle animals that have a keen sense of sight and smell. Often, other animals, like elk, deer, and mountain sheep, are attracted to the scent of the llamas and will venture closer to hikers if the llamas are present. Llama expeditions are scheduled from June to early October. Day hikes cost $80 per person. Three- to five-day hikes cost $130 per person per day. **Taos Llama Adventures** (☎ **800/758-LAMA** or 505/776-1044) also offers half- or full-day, as well as overnight llama treks.

RIVER RAFTING   Half- or full-day white-water rafting trips down the Rio Grande and Rio Chama originate in Taos and can be booked through outfitters in Red River. The wild **Taos Box,** a steep-sided canyon south of the Wild Rivers Recreation Area, is especially popular. May and June, when the water is rising, is a good time to go.

One convenient rafting service is **Rio Grande Rapid Transit,** P.O. Box A, Pilar, NM 87571 (☎ **800/222-RAFT** or 505/758-9700). In addition to Taos Box ($65 per person), Rapid Transit also runs the Pilar Racecourse ($30 per person) on a daily basis. Its headquarters are at the entrance to the BLM-administered **Orilla Verde Recreation Area,** 16 miles south of Taos, where most excursions through the Taos

Box end. Several other serene but thrilling floats through the Pilar Racecourse start at this point.

Other rafting outfitters in the Taos area include **Native Sons Adventures,** 715 Paseo del Pueblo Sur (☎ **800/753-7559** or 505/758-9342) and **Far Flung Adventures** (☎ **800/359-2627** or 505/758-2628).

Safety Warning: Taos is not the place to experiment if you aren't an experienced rafter. Do yourself a favor and check with the Bureau of Land Management (☎ **505/758-8851**) to make sure that you're fully equipped to go white-water rafting without a guide. Have them check your gear to make sure that it's sturdy enough—this is serious rafting!

SPAS   Ojo Caliente Mineral Springs, Ojo Caliente, NM 87549 (☎ **800/222-9162** or 505/583-2233), is on US 285, 50 miles (a one-hour drive) southwest of Taos. This National Historic Site was considered sacred by prehistoric tribes. When Spanish explorer Cabeza de Vaca discovered and named the springs in the 16th century, he called them "the greatest treasure that I found these strange people to possess." No other hot spring in the world has Ojo Caliente's combination of iron, soda, lithium, sodium, and arsenic. The resort offers herbal wraps and massages, lodging, and meals. It's open in summer daily from 8am to 9pm; in winter (November through March) the springs are open from 9am to 5pm.

SWIMMING   The Don Fernando Pool, on Civic Plaza Drive at Camino de la Placita, opposite the new convention center, admits swimmers over age six without adult supervision.

TENNIS   Quail Ridge Inn (see above) has six outdoor and two indoor tennis courts. **Taos Spa and Tennis Club** (see "Fitness Centers," above) has five courts, and the **Northside Health and Fitness Center** (see above) in El Prado has three tennis courts. In addition there are four free public courts in Taos, two at **Kit Carson Memorial State Park,** on Paseo del Pueblo Norte, and two at **Fred Baca Memorial Park,** on Camino del Medio south of Ranchitos Road.

8 Shopping

Visitors come to Taos to buy fine art. Some 50-odd galleries are located within easy walking distance of the Plaza, and a couple of dozen more are a short drive from downtown. Most artists display in one or more of the galleries, which are generally open seven days a week, especially in high season. Some artists show their work by appointment only.

The best-known Taos artist is R. C. Gorman, a Navajo from Arizona who has made his home in Taos for over two decades. Now in his 50s, Gorman is internationally acclaimed for his bright, somewhat surrealistic depictions of Navajo women. His **Navajo Gallery,** next door to the Blumenschein House at 5 Ledoux St. (☎ **505/758-3250**), is a showcase for his widely varied work: acrylics, lithographs, silk screens, bronzes, tapestries, hand-cast ceramic vases, etched glass, and more.

A good place to begin exploring galleries is the **Stables Fine Art Gallery,** operated by the Taos Art Association at 133 Paseo del Pueblo Norte (☎ **505/758-2036**). A changing group of fine arts exhibits feature many of Taos's emerging and established artists. All types of work are exhibited, including painting (from expressionism to nonrepresentationalism), sculpture, printmaking, photography, and ceramics. Admission is free; it's open year-round Monday through Saturday from 10am to 5pm and Sunday from 1 to 5pm.

SHOPPING A TO Z
ART

Act I Gallery. 226D Paseo del Pueblo Norte. ☎ **800/666-2933** or 505/758-7831.

Watercolors, retablos, furniture, paintings, Hispanic folk art, pottery, jewelry, and sculpture.

✪ **Philip Bareiss Contemporary Exhibitions.** 15 Ski Valley Rd. ☎ **505/776-2284.**

The works of some 30 leading Taos artists, including sculptor Gray Mercer and watercolorist Patricia Sanford, are displayed here. In 1995 Philip Bareiss opened "Circles and Passageways," a sculptural installation by Gray Mercer, on the 2,500-acre Romero Range located just west of Taos. A four-wheel-drive vehicle is recommended in order to get there.

Brooks Indian Shop. 108G Cabot Plaza Mall. ☎ **505/758-9073.**

Gold and silver Native American jewelry and fine pottery.

Desurmont-Ellis Gallery. 121 North Plaza (P.O. Box 1011). ☎ **505/758-3299.**

Abstract and impressionist oils and watercolors, sculpture, ceramics, and jewelry.

✪ **El Taller de Taos Gallery and Native American Arts.** 119A Kit Carson Rd. ☎ **505/758-4887.**

Exclusive representation of Amado Peña, as well as fine art by an excellent group of Southwestern artists and Native American art and artifacts.

The Fenix Gallery. 228B Paseo del Pueblo Norte. ☎ **505/758-9120.**

The Fenix Gallery focuses on Taos artists with national and/or international collections and reputations who live and work in Taos. The work is primarily nonobjective in nature and very contemporary. Some "historic" artists are represented as well.

Franzetti Metalworks. 127B Bent St. ☎ **505/758-7872** or 505/758-8741.

Functional metal sculpture and metal art.

Gallery A. 105–107 Kit Carson Rd. ☎ **505/758-2343.**

The oldest gallery in town, Gallery A has contemporary and traditional paintings, sculpture, and graphics, including Gene Kloss oils, watercolors, and etchings.

Hirsch Fine Art. 146 Kit Carson Rd. ☎ **505/758-5460.**

Watercolors, etchings and lithographs, and drawings by early Southwest artists, including the original Taos Founders.

Lizard of Oz. 156 Vista del Valle. ☎ **505/758-0708.**

This gallery has a great collection of fine Australian art, textiles, pottery, and jewelry.

✪ **Lumina of New Mexico.** 239 Morada Rd. (P.O. Box LL). ☎ **505/758-7282.**

Located in the historic Victor Higgins home, next to the Mabel Dodge estate, Lumina is one of the loveliest galleries in New Mexico. You'll find a large variety of fine art including paintings, sculpture, and photography. This place is as much a tourist attraction as any of the museums and historic homes in town.

✪ **New Directions Gallery.** 107B North Plaza. ☎ **505/758-2771.**

Features Larry Bell's unique mixed-media "Mirage paintings" and work by acclaimed sculptor Ted Egri.

Quast Galleries—Taos. 229 and 133 E. Kit Carson Rd. ☎ **505/758-7160** or 505/758-7779.

Representational landscapes and figurative paintings and distinguished sculpture. Rotating national and international exhibits are shown here.

Second Phase Gallery. 110 Dona Luz. ☎ **505/751-0159.**

Fine antique Native American art, including Navajo rugs and blankets, Pueblo pottery, and Plains beadwork.

Shriver Gallery. 401 Paseo del Pueblo Norte. ☎ **505/758-4994.**

Traditional paintings, drawings, etchings, and bronze sculpture.

Spirit Runner Gallery. 303 Paseo del Pueblo Norte. ☎ **505/758-1132.**

Southwestern weavings, furniture, and sculpture as well as contemporary watercolors. Spirit Runner is also located at North Plaza.

The Taos Gallery. 403 Paseo del Pueblo Norte. ☎ **505/758-2475.**

Southwestern impressionism, traditional Western art, contemporary fine art, and bronze sculpture.

BOOKS

The Brodsky Bookshop. 218 Paseo del Pueblo Norte. ☎ **505/758-9468.**

Exceptional inventory of fiction, nonfiction, Southwestern and Native American studies, children's books, topographical and travel maps, cards, tapes, and CDs.

Fernandez de Taos Bookstore. 109 North Plaza. ☎ **505/758-4391.**

A substantial offering of books on Southwestern subjects, along with local and regional newspapers and a large selection of magazines.

Kit Carson Home. E. Kit Carson Rd. ☎ **505/758-4741.**

Fine collection of books about regional history.

✪ **Moby Dickens Bookshop.** 124A Bent St. ☎ **505/758-3050.**

Children's and adults' collections of Southwest, Native American, and out-of-print books. This is one of Taos's best bookstores. A renovation to add 600 square feet more of store space is currently in progress.

Taos Book Shop. 122D Kit Carson Rd. ☎ **505/758-3733.**

Founded in 1947, this is the oldest general bookstore in New Mexico. Taos Book Shop specializes in out-of-print and Southwestern titles.

CRAFTS

Clay and Fiber Gallery. 126 W. Plaza Dr. ☎ **505/758-8093.**

Clay and Fiber represents more than 150 artists from around the country; merchandise changes frequently, but you should expect to see a variety of ceramics, fiber arts, jewelry, and wearables.

Open Space Gallery. 103B E. Plaza, Taos Plaza. ☎ **505/758-1217.**

An artist-owned cooperative gallery of contemporary arts and crafts.

Southwestern Arts. In the Dunn House, Bent St. ☎ **505/758-8418.**

Historic and contemporary Navajo weavings, Pueblo pottery, and jewelry. Also photography by Dick Spas.

Southwest Moccasin and Drum. 803 Paseo del Pueblo Norte. ☎ **800/447-3630** or 505/758-9332.

Home of the All One Tribe Drum, this favorite local shop carries a large variety of drums in all sizes and styles, handmade by master Native American drum makers from Taos Pueblo. Southwest Moccasin and Drum also has the country's second-largest selection of moccasins, as well as an incredible inventory of indigenous world instruments and tapes, sculpture, weavings, rattles, fans, fetishes, bags, decor, and many handmade one-of-a-kind items. A percentage of the store's profits goes to support Native American causes.

✪ **Taos Artisans Cooperative Gallery.** 107A Bent St. ☎ **505/758-1558.**

Local handmade jewelry, wearables, clayware, glass, drums, baskets, leather work, garden sculpture, and woven Spirit Women. This is an eight-member cooperative gallery, owned and operated by local artists. You'll always find an artist in the shop.

Taos Blue. 101A Bent St. ☎ **505/758-3561.**

Fine Native American and contemporary handcrafts gallery; it specializes in clay and fiber work.

Weaving Southwest. 216 Paseo del Pueblo Norte. ☎ **505/758-0433.**

Contemporary tapestries by New Mexico artists, as well as one-of-a-kind rugs, blankets, and pillows. In May and September 1997, Weaving Southwest will hold tapestry exhibits.

FASHIONS

Blue Fish. 140 E. Kit Carson Rd. ☎ **505/758-3520.**

If you love unique articles of clothing, you'll love Blue Fish, where you'll find hand-blocked pieces of art clothing. Blue Fish also carries jewelry and gifts.

Twining Weavers and Contemporary Crafts. 135 Paseo del Pueblo Norte. ☎ **505/758-9000.**

Handwoven wool rugs and pillows by owner Sally Bachman, as well as creations by other gallery artists in fiber, basketry, and clay.

FOOD

Casa Fresen Bakery. Ski Valley Rd., Hwy. 150. ☎ **505/776-2969.**

Located on the road to the Taos Ski Valley in Arroyo Seco, this is a wonderful place to buy fresh pastries, cakes, cheeses, pâtés, specialty meats, pastas, sauces, preserves, and oils. You can enjoy a sandwich right there or select a box lunch to take along on a picnic. It's open daily from 7:30am to 6pm.

FURNITURE

Country Furnishings of Taos. 534 Paseo del Pueblo Norte. ☎ **505/758-4633.**

Here you'll find unique hand-painted folk-art furniture that has become popular all over the country. The pieces are as individual as the styles of the local folk artists who make them. There are also home accessories, unusual gifts, clothing, and jewelry.

Lo Fino. 201 Paseo del Pueblo Sur. ☎ **505/758-0298.**

Handcrafted traditional and contemporary Southwest furniture and home accessories by Northern New Mexico artisans. Lo Fino specializes in custom-built furniture.

The Taos Company. 124K John Dunn Plaza, Bent St. ☎ **800/548-1141** or 505/758-1141.

Interior design showroom, specializing in unique Southwestern antique furniture and decorative accessories.

GIFTS & SOUVENIRS

Broken Arrow Ltd. 222 N. Plaza. ☎ **505/758-4304.**

Ceramics, weaving, jewelry, baskets, paintings, and sculpture.

Charley's Corner. NW corner of Taos Plaza. ☎ **505/758-9470.**

Charley's is jam-packed full of T-shirts, pottery, jewelry, and a variety of Southwestern souvenirs.

JEWELRY

Artwares. Taos Plaza (P.O. Box 2825). ☎ **800/527-8850** or 505/758-8850.

Artwares gallery owners call their contemporary jewelry "a departure from the traditional." Indeed, each piece here is a new twist on traditional Southwest and Native American design.

Taos Gems and Minerals. 637 Paseo del Pueblo Sur. ☎ **505/758-3910.**

Now in its 30th year of business, Taos Gems and Minerals is a fine lapidary showroom. Here you can get jewelry, specimens, carvings, and antique pieces at reasonable prices.

MUSICAL INSTRUMENTS

Taos Drum Company. 5 miles south of Taos Plaza, off NM 68. ☎ **505/758-3796.**

Drum making is an age-old tradition that local artisans are continuing in Taos. The drums are made of hollowed-out logs stretched with rawhide, and they come in all different shapes, sizes, and styles. Taos Drums has the largest selection of Native American log and hand drums in the world. In addition to drums, the showroom displays Southwestern and wrought-iron furniture, cowboy art, and lamps, as well as a constantly changing selection of primitive folk art, ethnic crafts, Native American music tapes, books, and other information on drumming. To find Taos Drum Company, look for the teepees and drums off NM 68.

POTTERY & TILE

Stephen Kilborn Pottery. 136D Paseo del Pueblo Norte. ☎ **505/758-5760.**

Head up to Stephen Kilborn Pottery and you'll find some wonderful handmade pieces, both functional and decorative.

Vargas Tile Co. NM 68. ☎ **505/758-5986.**

Vargas Tile has a great little collection of hand-painted Mexican tiles at good prices. My favorite pieces are the cabinet doorknobs and the beautiful sinks.

9 Taos After Dark

Many occasional events are scheduled by the **Taos Art Association** (☎ 505/758-2052). The TAA imports local, regional, and national performers in theater, dance, and concerts—Dave Brubeck, the late Dizzy Gillespie, the American String Quartet, and the American Festival Ballet have performed here—and offers two weekly film series, including one for children. The TAA is also the best place to purchase tickets for most events.

You can get details on current events in the weekly *Taos News,* published on Thursday. The Taos County Chamber of Commerce (☎ 800/732-TAOS or 505/758-3873) publishes semiannual listings of "Taos County Events."

Major Concert Halls & All-Purpose Auditoriums

Taos Civic Plaza and Convention Center, 121 Civic Plaza Dr. ☎ **505/758-5792.** Taos's pride and joy is this new center, located just three short blocks north of the Plaza. Opened in 1990, it accommodates groups of 610 in Rio Grande Hall and another 500 in adjacent Bataan Auditorium. Major concerts and other entertainment events are scheduled here.

Taos Community Auditorium, 145 Paseo del Pueblo Norte. ☎ **505/758-4677.** The town's primary performing arts facility, this auditorium, located behind the Stables Art Gallery, seats 280 for theater. A film series is also offered on Sundays and Wednesdays (admission $4).

THE PERFORMING ARTS

Fort Burgwin Research Center. On NM 518 south of Taos. ☎ **505/758-8322.**

This historic site of the 1,000-year-old Pot Creek Pueblo, located about 10 miles south of Taos, is a summer campus of Southern Methodist University. From mid-May through mid-August, the SMU-IN-TAOS curriculum (among other studio arts, humanities, and sciences) includes courses in music and theater. There are regularly scheduled orchestral concerts, guitar and harpsichord recitals, and theater performances available to the community, without charge, throughout the summer.

✪ **Music From Angel Fire.** P.O. Box 502, Angel Fire, NM 87710. ☎ **505/377-3233** or 505/989-4772.

This acclaimed program of chamber music begins in mid-August and continues through Labor Day. Based in the small resort community of Angel Fire, about 21 miles east of US 64, it also presents concerts in Taos, Raton, and Las Vegas.

Taos School of Music. 360 State Rd., Arroyo Seco, Taos, NM 87514. ☎ **505/776-2388.**

Sponsored by the Taos Art Association, the Taos School of Music was founded in 1963. It is located at the Hotel St. Bernard in Taos Ski Valley. From mid-June to mid-August there is an intensive eight-week study and performance program for advanced students of violin, viola, cello, and piano. Students receive daily coaching by the American String Quartet and pianist Robert McDonald.

The eight-week **Chamber Music Festival**, an important adjunct of the school, offers 16 concerts and seminars for the public; performances are given by the American String Quartet, pianist Robert McDonald, guest violist Michael Tree (of the Guarneri Quartet), and the international young student artists. Performances are held at the Taos Community Auditorium and the Hotel St. Bernard.

THE CLUB & MUSIC SCENE

Adobe Bar. In the Historic Taos Inn,125 Paseo del Pueblo Norte. ☎ **505/758-2233.** No cover. Because the hours vary, be sure to call ahead.

A favorite gathering place for locals as well as visitors, the Adobe Bar is known for its live music series (Tuesday through Thursday and Sunday) devoted to the eclectic talents of Taos musicians. The schedule offers a little of everything—classical, jazz, folk, Hispanic, and acoustic. The Adobe Bar features a wide selection of international beers, wines by the glass, light New Mexican dining, desserts, and an espresso menu.

Hideaway Lounge. At the Holiday Inn, 1005 Paseo del Pueblo Sur. ☎ **505/758-4444.** No cover.

This hotel lounge, built around a large adobe fireplace, offers live entertainment and an extensive hors d'oeuvres buffet. Call for schedule.

Fireside Cantina. At Rancho Ramada, 615 Paseo del Pueblo Sur. ☎ **505/758-2900.** No cover.

Live entertainment on Friday and Saturday nights. Call for information and schedule.

Kachina Cabaret. At the Kachina Lodge, 413 Paseo del Pueblo Norte. ☎ **505/758-2275.** Cover varies according to performer, but usually $5 Fri–Sat.

Top-name country and Hispanic acts—including the Desert Rose Band, the Nitty Gritty Dirt Band, and Eddie Rabbit—have performed here. Saturday night is the big event night, starting at 9pm. The adjacent Zuni Lounge features rock bands nightly.

Sagebrush Inn. Paseo del Pueblo Sur. ☎ **505/758-2254.** No cover.

Taos's highest-energy dancing spot offers country or rock performers nightly, year-round, from 9pm.

Thunderbird Lodge. Taos Ski Valley. ☎ **505/776-2280.** Cover for Jazz Festival $10 and up.

Throughout January, the Thunderbird Jazz Festival brings leading contemporary jazz musicians to perform week-long gigs at the foot of the ski slopes. The rest of the year there's live entertainment and two-step dance lessons.

10 A Scenic Drive Around the Enchanted Circle

This 90-mile loop, a National Forest Scenic Byway, runs through the towns of Questa, Red River, Eagle Nest, and Angel Fire, incorporating portions of NM 522, NM 38, and US 64. It can be driven in two hours round-trip from Taos, but most folks take a full day, or several days, to accomplish it.

QUESTA Traveling north from Taos via NM 522, it's a 24-mile drive to Questa, whose residents are mainly employed at a molybdenum mine 5 miles east of town. En route north, the highway passes near **San Cristobal,** where a side road turns off to the D. H. Lawrence Shrine, and **Lama,** site of an isolated spiritual retreat.

If you turn west off NM 522 onto NM 378 about 3 miles north of Questa, you'll descend 11 miles on a gravel road into the gorge of the Rio Grande at the Bureau of Land Management–administered **Wild Rivers Recreation Area** (☎ **505/758-8851**). Here, where the Red River enters the gorge, is the most accessible starting point for river-rafting trips through the infamous Taos Box. Some 48 miles of the Rio Grande, south from the Colorado border, are protected under the national Wild and Scenic River Act of 1968. Information on geology and wildlife, as well as hikers' trail maps, can be obtained at the Visitors Center here. Ask for directions to the impressive petroglyphs in the gorge. River-rafting trips can be booked in Taos, Santa Fe, Red River, and other communities.

The village of **Costilla,** near the Colorado border, is 20 miles north of Questa. This is the turnoff point for four-wheel-drive jaunts into Valle Vidal, a huge U.S. Forest Service–administered reserve with 42 miles of roads.

✪ **RED RIVER** Turn east at Questa onto NM 38 for a 12-mile climb to Red River, a rough-and-ready 1890s gold-mining town that has parlayed its Wild West ambience into a pleasant resort village. Especially popular with families from Texas and Oklahoma, this community at 8,750 feet is a center for skiing and snowmobiling, fishing and hiking, off-road driving and horseback riding, mountain biking, river

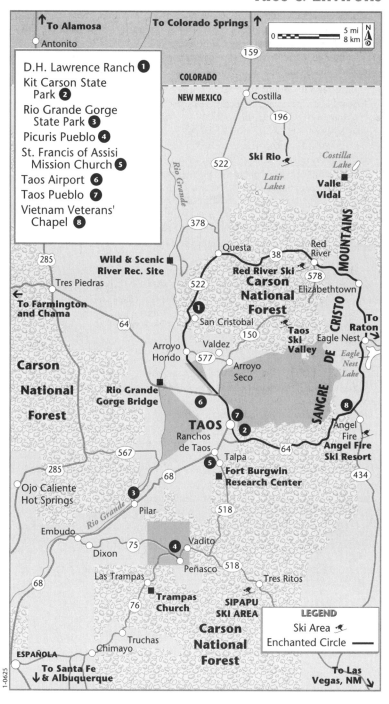

D.H. Lawrence Ranch ❶
Kit Carson State Park ❷
Rio Grande Gorge State Park ❸
Picuris Pueblo ❹
St. Francis of Assisi Mission Church ❺
Taos Airport ❻
Taos Pueblo ❼
Vietnam Veterans' Chapel ❽

To Alamosa
To Colorado Springs
Antonito

5 mi
0
8 km
N

COLORADO
NEW MEXICO

159

Costilla
196

Ski Rio

Costilla Lake

Valle Vidal

Latir Lakes

522

Rio Grande

378

285
Tres Piedras
To Farmington and Chama

64

Wild & Scenic River Rec. Site

Questa
38
Red River
578
Elizabethtown

Red River Ski
Carson National Forest

522

❶
San Cristobal

150

Taos Ski Valley

Eagle Nest

SANGRE DE CRISTO MOUNTAINS

To Raton

Arroyo Hondo
577
Valdez

Arroyo Seco

Eagle Nest Lake

Carson National Forest

Rio Grande Gorge Bridge

❻
TAOS
Ranchos de Taos

❼
❷

❽

Angel Fire
Angel Fire Ski Resort

567

64

285

❺ Talpa
Fort Burgwin Research Center

434

Ojo Caliente Hot Springs

❸
Pilar

68

518

Rio Grande

Embudo
Dixon

75

❹ Vadito

518

Peñasco

Tres Ritos

68
Las Trampas

76
Trampas Church

SIPAPU SKI AREA

Carson National Forest

Truchas
Chimayo

ESPAÑOLA

To Santa Fe & Albuquerque

To Las Vegas, NM

LEGEND
Ski Area
Enchanted Circle ——

1-0625

rafting, and other outdoor pursuits. Frontier-style celebrations, honky-tonk entertainment, and even staged shoot-outs on Main Street are held throughout the year.

The **Red River Chamber of Commerce,** P.O. Box 868, Red River, NM 87558 (☎ **800/348-6444** or 505/754-2366), lists more than 40 accommodations, including lodges and condominiums. Some are open winters or summers only.

EAGLE NEST About 16 miles east of Red River, on the other side of 9,850-foot Bobcat Pass, is the village of **Eagle Nest,** resting on the shore of Eagle Nest Lake in the Moreno Valley. There was gold mining in this area as early as 1866, starting in what is now the ghost town of Elizabethtown 5 miles north; but Eagle Nest itself (pop. 200) wasn't incorporated until 1976. The 4-square-mile lake is considered one of the top trout producers in the United States, and attracts ice fishers in winter as well as summer anglers. Sailboaters and windsurfers also use the lake, although swimming, waterskiing, and camping are not permitted. The **Laguna Vista Lodge,** P.O. Box 65, Eagle Nest, NM 87718 (☎ **800/821-2093** or 505/377-6522) is the village's best hotel/restaurant.

If you're heading to Cimarron (see Chapter 9, "Northeastern New Mexico") or Denver, proceed east on US 64 from Eagle Nest. But if you're circling back to Taos, continue southwest on US 38 and 64 to Agua Fria and Angel Fire.

Shortly before the Agua Fria junction, you'll see ✪ **DAV Vietnam Veterans Memorial.** It's a stunning structure, its curved white walls soaring high against the backdrop of the Sangre de Cristo range. Consisting of a chapel and underground visitor center, it was built by Dr. Victor Westphall in memory of his son, David, a marine lieutenant killed in Vietnam in 1968. The chapel has a changing gallery of photographs of Vietnam veterans who gave their lives in the Southeast Asian war, and a poignant inscription by young Westphall.

✪ **ANGEL FIRE** The full-service resort community of Angel Fire, 12 miles south of Eagle Nest, 21 miles east of Taos, and 2 miles south of the Agua Fria junction on NM 38, dates only from the late 1960s, but already has some 30 lodges and condominiums. Winter skiing and summer golf are the most popular activities, but there's also ample opportunity for sailing and fishing on Angel Fire Lake, tennis, racquetball, and horseback riding. The unofficial community center is the **Legends Hotel and Conference Center,** P.O. Drawer B, Angel Fire, NM 87710 (☎ **800/633-7463** or 505/377-6401), a 157-room inn and restaurant with rates starting at $65.

For more information and full accommodations listings on the Moreno Valley, contact the **Angel Fire Chamber of Commerce,** P.O. Box 547, Angel Fire, NM 87710 (☎ **800/446-8117**).

It's 21 miles back to Taos, over 9,100-foot Palo Flechado Pass, down the valley of the Rio Fernando de Taos, and through the small community of Shady Brook.

Northeastern New Mexico 9

The region north from I-40, and east of the Sangre de Cristo Mountains, is a vast prairie that, over many thousands of years, has been trodden by dinosaurs and buffalo, by early humans and Plains people, and by pioneers and settlers. Dinosaurs left footprints at Clayton Lake State Park, and Folsom Man roamed this region 12,000 years ago. Coronado passed through during his 16th-century search for Cíbola; some 300 years later, covered wagons followed the Santa Fe Trail west.

Cattle baron Lucien Maxwell controlled most of these prairies as his private empire in the latter half of the 19th century. During his era, this was truly the Wild West. The notorious town of Cimarron attracted nearly every gunslinger of the era, from Butch Cassidy to Clay Allison, Black Jack Ketchum to Jesse James; bullets still decorate the ceiling of the St. James Hotel.

Las Vegas, established long before its Nevada namesake, was the largest city in New Mexico at the turn of the 20th century, with a cosmopolitan population from all over the world. Doc Holliday, Bat Masterson, and Wyatt Earp walked its wild streets in the 1880s. A decade later, it was the headquarters of Teddy Roosevelt's Rough Riders, and early in the 20th century, it was a silent film capital (Tom Mix made movies here) and the site of a world heavyweight boxing match. Today, with a population of 15,591, it is the region's largest city, and the proud home of 900 historic properties. Raton (pop. 7,759), on I-25 in the Sangre de Cristo foothills, is the gateway to New Mexico from the north. Clayton (pop. 2,454), Tucumcari (pop. 6,706), and Santa Rosa (pop. 2,263) are all transportation hubs and ranching centers.

Two national monuments are particular points of interest. Fort Union, 24 miles north of Las Vegas, was the largest military installation in the Southwest in the 1860s and 1870s. Capulin Volcano, 33 miles east of Raton, last erupted 10,000 years ago; visitors can walk inside the crater. Kiowa National Grasslands preserves 136,000 acres of pure prairie.

Drained by the Pecos and Canadian rivers, northeastern New Mexico is otherwise notable for the number of small lakes that afford opportunities for fishing, hunting, boating, camping, and other recreational pursuits. There are 11 state parks and about a half dozen designated wildlife areas within the region. Philmont Scout Ranch, south of Cimarron, is known by Boy Scouts throughout the world.

TOURING THE REGION BY CAR

Begin exploration of this region in Las Vegas, just over an hour's drive east of Santa Fe. Start by taking the walking tour, outlined later in this chapter, through Las Vegas and visit some of the historic buildings. Next head out to Las Vegas National Wildlife Refuge where you'll be able to see more than 200 different species of birds and animals. If you're interested in pursuing some water sports, drive to Storrie Lake State Park (4 miles north via NM 518).

Stay overnight in Las Vegas, and in the morning, head north a short distance via I-25 and NM 161 to Fort Union National Monument, where you can visit the 19th-century ruins of what was once the largest military installation in the Southwest. When you've had your fill there, backtrack a bit on NM 161 up to NM 518, which begins the drive up the Mora River Valley. Turn north on NM 434, and you'll find yourself in Mora, a tiny Hispanic town founded in the early 1800s. While it's only 34 miles to the modern resort towns of Angel Fire and Eagle Nest, Mora is a place where time seems to stand still. Tall cottonwoods and ponderosa pines follow the river and surrounding ditches.

As you continue north on NM 434, in the direction of Angel Fire, you'll come to Guadalupita, a small town that once thrived on farming, ranching, and logging, but now struggles to survive. Nearby Coyote Creek State Park, a good place to stop for a breather, offers camping, picnicking, and fishing.

Next follow NM 434 north to US 64; where US 64 turns east off the Enchanted Circle, follow it to Cimarron, where you should plan to spend the night. You'll need the rest of the day to absorb this frontier village that once played host to Kit Carson, Wyatt Earp, and Jesse James, among others.

The following day, take US 64, which traces the Santa Fe Trail, northeast to Raton. Explore the town's historic district, then take US 64/87 east to Capulin Volcano National Monument. If you'd rather take a more scenic route to Capulin from Raton, follow NM 72 to Folsom, and then take NM 325 south to Capulin. It's only a 45-mile drive from Raton to Capulin, but following this route will take quite some time, so leave early. Those driving RVs should stick to the major highways, because the state highways are narrow and difficult to negotiate in larger vehicles. This, of course, is good news for motorists tired of fighting RVs for space on the road. After visiting the Capulin Volcano National Monument and at least taking the 1-mile loop hike around the crater rim and the .2-mile hike down into the crater, continue east to the ranching center of Clayton.

From Clayton, take NM 370 north a short way to Clayton Lake State Park to check out the more than 500 dinosaur footprints. When you finish there, backtrack to Clayton and then head south on NM 402 and southwest on US 54 to Tucumcari. This city and Santa Rosa, an hour west on I-40, are oases in the arid east. If you'd like to return to Las Vegas at this point, you can do so via US 84, or else you can take I-40 west to Albuquerque.

1 The Great Outdoors in Northeastern New Mexico

Northeastern New Mexico encompasses a variety of Southwest landscapes. The undulating grasslands of the eastern portion of the region eventually give way to the cliffs, canyons, and forests of the mighty Sangre de Cristo Mountains, which offer some of the best hiking and camping in the state. The area is drained by the Pecos and Canadian Rivers and is otherwise notable for the number of small streams and lakes, including Ute Lake, the second-largest in the state, that afford opportunities for fishing, including some great fly-fishing, boating, and other recreational pursuits

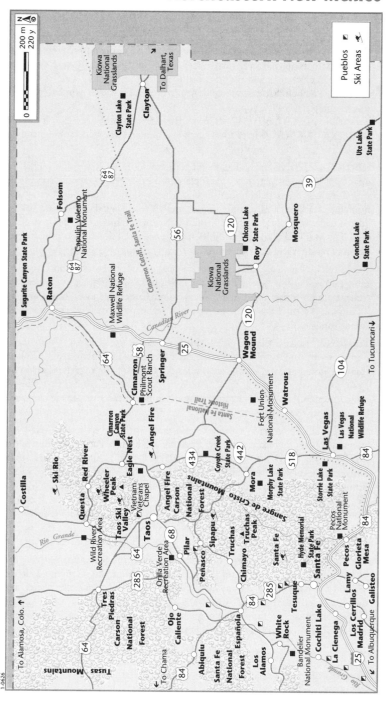

(even scuba diving) in this seemingly arid region. There are 11 state parks and about a half dozen designated wildlife areas within the region.

BIKING Favorite places to take the mountain bike in the northeastern section of New Mexico are in the areas that border Red River (particularly near Valle Vidal, discussed in chapter 8) and the areas just to the east of Santa Fe and Taos. It's best to purchase a book that describes and maps the trails for you. It's probably easiest in this region to rent your equipment in Albuquerque at **Old Town Bicycles,** 2000 Old Town Rd., NW (☎ **505/247-4926**) or **Rio Mountain Sport,** 1210 Rio Grande Blvd., NW (☎ **505/766-9970**). There are also rental shops in Santa Fe and Taos (see individual city chapters for more information).

BIRD-WATCHING The **Las Vegas National Wildlife Refuge,** just a few miles outside of Las Vegas center, is a great place for bird-watching. Species spotted year-round include prairie falcons and hawks, whereas during late fall and early winter migratory birds such as sandhill cranes, snow geese, Canada geese, and bald and golden eagles frequent the refuge. In all, more than 240 species can be sighted in the area. The **Maxwell National Wildlife Refuge,** near Raton, also boasts a rich population of resident and migratory birds, including raptors and bald eagles.

BOATING There are opportunities for boating, rafting, windsurfing, and swimming throughout this region. Two of the most popular boating areas are **Storrie Lake State Park,** 6 miles north of Las Vegas, and **Conchas Lake State Park,** near Tucumcari. Storrie Lake is especially popular among **windsurfers** who favor its consistent winds.

FISHING Isolated and primitive **Morphy Lake State Park** is a favorite destination for serious anglers. The lake is regularly stocked with rainbow trout. **Cimarron Canyon State Park** is also popular with fishers. Lake Alice in **Sugarite Canyon State Park,** just north of Raton at the Colorado border, is a good spot for fly-fishing. For more information on the best fishing opportunities in the area, see the chapters for Santa Fe and Taos (chapters 7 and 8).

GOLF Duffers can get in a few holes in or near virtually every town covered in this section. Courses I'd recommend are: **Conchas Dam State Park Golf Course** (P.O. Box 905, Conchas Dam, NM 88416; ☎ **505/868-9970**), **New Mexico Highlands University Golf Course** (Mills Ave., Las Vegas, NM 87701; ☎ **505/425-7711**); **Raton Country Club Municipal Golf Course** (83 Gardner Rd., Raton, NM 87740; ☎ **505/445-8113**); **Tucumcari Municipal Golf Course** (P.O. Box 1188, Tucumcari, NM 88401; ☎ **505/461-1849**); and **Clayton Golf Course** (P.O. Box 4, Clayton, NM 88415; ☎ **505/374-9957**).

HIKING Northeastern New Mexico abounds in great places to hike, including the trails at Capulin Volcano; however, the best places are in the mountains to the north of Las Vegas and west of Santa Fe and Taos. **Storrie Lake, Conchas Lake,** and **Villanueva** state parks all have marked hiking trails. Another great hike takes you to the top of Hermit Peak, which is only about 20 miles northwest of Las Vegas. Again, it's probably best to acquire equipment and supplies in Albuquerque before you set off. Try **REI-Albuquerque,** 1905 Mountain Rd., NW (☎ **505/247-1191**).

HOT SPRINGS In this region look for **Montezuma Hot Springs,** located on the Armand Hammer United World College of the American West Campus, near Las Vegas. See below for details.

SCUBA DIVING I know, New Mexico is landlocked—there couldn't possibly be scuba diving, could there? Exactly the question I asked when I heard scuba diving and New Mexico mentioned in the same sentence. Fact is, there is scuba diving in this dry, arid state. The best place to go is Santa Rosa, where you'll find the **Blue Hole,** an 81-foot-deep artesian spring that's a favorite of divers from around the world. The best place to rent equipment is at the **Santa Rosa Dive Center** on Blue Hole Road (☎ **505/472-3370**).

SWIMMING   Swimming is permitted at Storrie, Conchas, Ute, Morphy, and Santa Rosa lakes. See below for directions and specifics.

2 Las Vegas & Environs

Once known as the "gateway to New Mexico," this pleasant town in the foothills of the Sangre de Cristo Mountains was founded by a land grant from the Mexican government in 1835. A group of 29 Spanish colonists planted crops in the area and built a central plaza, which started out as a meeting place and a defense against Indian attack but soon became a main trading center on the Santa Fe Trail. With the advent of the Atchison, Topeka, and Santa Fe Railway in 1879, Las Vegas boomed; almost overnight the town became the most important trading center and gathering place in the state and one of the largest towns in the Rocky Mountain West, rivaling Denver, Tucson, and El Paso in size.

Town settlers who arrived by train in the late 19th century shunned the indigenous adobe architecture, favoring instead building styles more typical of the Midwest or New England. They put up scores of fancy Queen Anne– and Victorian-style houses and hotels, and the town is noted to this day for its dazzling diversity of architectural styles. Some 900 buildings in Las Vegas, both Victorian as well as earlier adobe structures, are on the National Register of Historic Buildings.

ESSENTIALS

GETTING THERE   By Car   From Santa Fe, take I-25 north (1¼ hours); from Raton, take I-25 south (1¾ hours); from Taos, follow NM 518 southeast 78 miles through Mora (2 hours); from Tucumcari, follow NM 104 west (2 hours).

By Plane   Las Vegas Municipal Airport handles private flights and charters. There is no regularly scheduled commercial service.

VISITOR INFORMATION   The **Las Vegas/San Miguel Chamber of Commerce** is at 727 Grand Ave. (P.O. Box 148), Las Vegas, NM 87701 (☎ **800/832-5947** or 505/425-8631). It's at the north end of town, between University Avenue and Bridge Street.

EXPLORING LAS VEGAS
A WALKING TOUR OF HISTORIC LAS VEGAS

(For details about the three self-guided historic-district walking tours the city has outlined, contact the chamber of commerce office listed above.)

Start next door to the chamber of commerce on Grand Avenue, at the ✪ **Rough Riders Memorial and City Museum** (727 Grand Ave.; ☎ **505/425-8726**). About 40% of Teddy Roosevelt's Spanish-American War campaigners in 1898 came from this frontier town. The museum chronicles their contribution to U.S. history and also contains artifacts relating to the history of the city. It's open Monday to Saturday 9am to 4pm, except holidays.

Most of the notable structures can be found in the Plaza–Bridge Street historic district. The 1879 **Stern and Nahm Building** has cast-iron columns and pressed and folded sheet-metal ornaments above. Decorative brickwork adorns the 1895 **Winternitz Block.** The Italianate commercial style is exemplified in the fancy arched windows of the 1884 **Anicito Baca Building,** modeled after Italian palazzos. The

E. Romero Hose and Fire Company, put up in brick in 1909, has banded piers capped by pressed-metal capitals with dentils in a strange neoclassical architecture.

The 1882 Italianate-style **Hedgcock Building** has arched window hoods like those of the Baca building, and has served both as police station and jail as well as shoe factory, saloon, and store.

The **Plaza Hotel** was the finest hotel in the New Mexico Territory back in 1881. Its three-story facade topped with a fancy broken pediment decoration was the town's pride and joy, and it has been happily restored. (See "Where to Stay," below.) The **Charles Ilfeld Building** began as a one-story adobe store in 1867, grew to two stories in 1882, and finally reached three stories with an Italianate facade in 1890. The **Louis Ilfeld Building,** nearby, shows the classic architecture coming into favor at the turn of the century in a storefront now serving as a bookstore.

The town's earlier history, going back to the first Spanish visits in the 16th century, is also seen in adobe architecture still standing alongside the ornate structures of the late 1800s. In addition, there are few places in the West with a better preserved collection of Territorial-style buildings.

OTHER ATTRACTIONS NEAR TOWN

Las Vegas has two colleges. **New Mexico Highlands University** (☎ **505/425-7511**), a four-year liberal arts school of almost 3,000 students, was established in 1893. In 1971, it hired the nation's first Hispanic college president. Located at Seventh Street and University Avenue, just west of US 85, it is especially strong in its minority education curriculum, and fields outstanding small-college athletic teams.

The **Armand Hammer United World College of the American West** (☎ **505/454-4200**), located 5 miles west of Las Vegas via NM 65, is an international school with students from more than 70 countries. It is the housed in the former **Montezuma Hotel,** a luxury resort built by the Santa Fe Railroad in 1880 and now a historic landmark. Three U.S. presidents, Germany's Kaiser Wilhelm II, and Japan's Meiji Emperor Mutsuhito stayed in the multistoried, turreted, 270-room "Montezuma Castle," as it came to be known.

Also on the campus are the **Montezuma Hot Springs.** The springs, which are open to the public, have attracted health-seekers for more than 1,000 years; there are legends that ancient Aztecs, including chief Montezuma II, journeyed here from Mexico in the early 16th century, long before the arrival of the Spanish.

EXPLORING THE AREA

Mora, a small village 31 miles north via NM 518, is the main center between Las Vegas and Taos, and the seat of sparsely populated Mora County. The 15-mile long Mora Valley is one of New Mexico's prettiest but most economically depressed regions, where large ranches have more or less pushed out small farmers.

Cleveland Roller Mill. P.O. Box 287, Cleveland, NM 87715. NM 518, about 2 miles west of Mora. ☎ **505/387-2645**. Admission $2 adults, $1 children 6–17, under 6 free. Memorial Day–Oct 31 10am–5pm and by appointment.

One vestige of a more prosperous past is this two-story adobe mill, which ground out 50 barrels of wheat flour a day, virtually every day from 1901 to 1947. It was the last flour mill to be built in New Mexico, the last to stop running, and is the only roller mill in the state to have its original milling works intact. Today, it's been converted into a museum with exhibits on regional history and culture. The Annual Millfest, on Labor Day weekend, features the mill in operation, dances, arts and crafts, music, and more.

GETTING OUTSIDE: OFF-THE-BEATEN-PATH STATE PARKS & OTHER SCENIC HIGHLIGHTS

A short drive north of the Montezuma Hot Springs takes you to a pond on the Gallinas River that provides winter skating and summer fishing.

Other nearby parklands include **Las Vegas National Wildlife Refuge** (☎ 505/425-3581), 6 miles southeast via NM 104 and NM 281, open daily from 8am to 4:30pm, boasting 220 species of birds and animals on 8,750 acres of wetland; and **Storrie Lake State Park** (☎ 505/425-7278), 4 miles north via NM 518, which offers fishing, swimming, wind-surfing, waterskiing, camping, and a visitor center with historic exhibits.

Villanueva State Park (☎ 505/421-2957), 31 miles southwest via I-25 and NM 3, offers excellent hiking, camping, and picnicking between red sandstone bluffs in the Pecos River Valley. Nearby are the Spanish colonial villages of **Villanueva** and **San Miguel del Vado;** the latter is a national historic district built around an impressive 1805 church.

Beautiful and isolated **Morphy Lake State Park** (☎ 505/387-2328) is reached via NM 518 to Mora and NM 94 south for 4 miles. Located on the edge of the Pecos Wilderness, the pretty lake is set in a basin of pine forest; it offers primitive camping, swimming, and trout fishing. Check on road conditions before going; the road to the park is rough and best suited for four-wheel-drive vehicles. Fourteen miles north via NM 434 is another out-of-the-way beauty, **Coyote Creek State Park** (☎ 505/387-2328), with campsites beside a stream dotted with beaver ponds. The fishing is good, and several well-marked hiking trails head into the mountains.

If you prefer your nature a little less primitive, head for the **Pendaries Lodge and Country Club,** P.O. Box 820, Rociada, NM 87742 (☎ 505/425-6076), located 13 miles south of Mora and 27 miles northwest of Las Vegas, on NM 105 off NM 94. This lovely foothills lodge boasts the region's finest 18-hole golf course, tennis courts, stables for horseback riding, and fishing. It also has overnight accommodations and a restaurant/lounge.

FORT UNION NATIONAL MONUMENT

Established in 1851 to defend the Santa Fe Trail against attacks from Plains Indians, Fort Union was expanded in 1861 in anticipation of a Confederate invasion, subsequently thwarted at Glorieta Pass, 20 miles southeast of Santa Fe. Its location on the Santa Fe Trail made it a welcome way station for travelers, but when the railroad replaced the trail in 1879, the fort was on its way out. It was abandoned in 1891. Today Fort Union, the largest military installation in the 19th-century Southwest, is in ruins. There's little to see but adobe walls and chimneys, but the very scope of the fort is impressive. Santa Fe Trail wagon ruts can still be seen nearby. Follow the 1.6-mile self-guided interpretive trail that wanders through the ruins and imagine yourself a weary 19th-century wagon traveler stopping for rest and supplies.

The national monument has a small visitor center and museum with exhibits and booklets on fort's history. Visitors should allow two hours to tour the ruins.

JUST THE FACTS   To reach the site from Las Vegas, drive 18 miles north on I-25 to the Watrous exit, then another 8 miles northwest on NM 161. Admission is $4 per car or $2 per person for persons aged 18 to 62. Fort Union National Monument is open Memorial Day through Labor Day from daily 8am to 6pm; during the rest of the year it is open daily from 8am to 5pm. Closed Christmas and New Year's Day.

There is a gift shop that carries a wide selection of books on New Mexico history, women's history, and frontier military books. Camping is not available at the monument, but there are facilities in nearby Las Vegas.

For more information on the monument, write to Fort Union National Monument, P.O. Box 127, Watrous, NM 87753 or call ☎ **505/425-8025.**

WHERE TO STAY IN LAS VEGAS

Most motels are on US 85 (Grand Ave.), the main north-south highway through downtown Las Vegas. (An exception is the Plaza Hotel, below.)

Inn on the Santa Fe Trail. 1133 Grand Ave., Las Vegas, NM 87701. ☎ **800/425-6791** or 505/425-6791. 42 rms (all with bath). A/C TV TEL. $44–$64 double; $65–$80 suite. Extra person $5. AE, DC, DISC, MC, V.

Built in the 1920s, the Inn on the Santa Fe Trail has been remodeled in a hacienda style with all rooms looking out onto the central courtyard and sculptured gardens, creating a quiet, intimate retreat just off the busy Grand Avenue. The small but comfortable rooms, decorated with Southwest furnishings designed and handcrafted by local artisans, have all the amenities of a major hotel, including full baths and cable TV. Every morning a complimentary "sunrise coffee buffet" is served in the fireplace room. There is a heated outdoor pool and spa. Pets are permitted at an extra charge of $5.

✪ **Plaza Hotel.** 230 Old Town Plaza, Las Vegas, NM 87701. ☎ **800/328-1882** or 505/425-3591. 37 rms, 4 suites. A/C TV TEL. $55–$65 double; $104–$110 suite. AE, DC, DISC, MC, V.

The windows of this stately old inn look out on the center of Las Vegas life, the Plaza, where in 1846 a ceremony led by Gen. Stephen Kearny marked the takeover of New Mexico by the United States. The inn was built in Italianate bracketed style in 1882, in the days when western towns, newly connected with the East by train, vied with one another in constructing fancy "railroad hotels," as they were known. Considered the finest hotel in the New Mexico Territory when it was built, it underwent a $2 million renovation exactly 100 years later. Stately walnut staircases frame the lobby and conservatory (with its piano); throughout the hotel, the architecture is true to its era.

All rooms have antique furnishings, of course, and a queen-size or two double beds. Executive rooms have desks and come equipped with modem hook ups. Numerous second- and third-floor units adjoin, and a pair of hexagonal rooms overlook the conservatory. The rooms all open onto spacious hallways with casual seating areas.

Services and facilities include limited room service, rooms accessible to people with disabilities, and meeting space.

The Landmark Grill is considered the fanciest restaurant in town. Notice the walls: The original 19th-century stenciling has been restored. The restaurant is open for breakfast, lunch, and dinner. There's often live music in the evenings at Byron T's 19th-century saloon.

CAMPING

There's plenty of camping available in and around Las Vegas. I would recommend the **KOA Las Vegas** (☎ 505/562-3423), which has 60 sites, 15 with full hookups, 26 with water and electricity. Laundry, grocery, ice, and recreational (including a pool) facilities are available. From I-25 (exit 339/US 84) go one block southeast on US 84, then 1/2 mile southwest on Frontage Road.

Also in Las Vegas is **Vegas RV Park** (☎ 505/425-5640), which offers 40 sites, 33 with full hookups, cable TV availability, and a recreation room. It's located at 504 Harris Road in Las Vegas.

If you'd rather camp at a state park, try **Storrie Lake State Park** (☎ 505/425-7278), which offers 11 sites with electricity and water, picnic tables, grills, a visitor center, and recreational facilities. Primitive camping is also available.

Camping is also allowed in the secluded **Morphy Lake State Park** as well as in **Coyote Creek State Park.** Each of these parks offers sites with picnic tables, fire rings, and pit toilets as well as primitive camping. For more information about either park, call **505/387-2328.**

WHERE TO DINE

El Alto Supper Club. Sapello St. off New Mexico Ave. ☎ **505/454-0808.** Reservations recommended. Main courses $10–$23.50. AE, MC, V. Daily 6–9pm. STEAKS/NEW MEXICAN.

Situated atop a hill overlooking the city, El Alto is a local legend: 50 years under one owner. It's known for its steaks—New York, T-bone, sirloin, filet mignon, all guaranteed $1\frac{1}{2}$ inches thick. It also has limited seafood offerings, including lobster, shrimp, trout, and frogs' legs; plus combination New Mexican meals, like enchiladas and tacos. Dinner comes with salad and tortilla chips.

Hillcrest Restaurant. 1106 Grand Ave. ☎ **505/425-7211.** Main courses $7–$13. DISC, MC, V. Daily 6am–8:30pm. AMERICAN.

Known throughout the city as a "home-style" dining establishment, the Hillcrest has everything from chicken-fried steaks to corn-fried catfish. It also has a good selection of Mexican food. The dining room is open for lunch and dinner only; the coffee shop is busy all day. The adjoining Trading Post Saloon offers full bar service. Meeting rooms are available.

The Mexican Kitchen. 717 Grand Ave. ☎ **505/454-1769.** Reservations not accepted. All items under $10. MEXICAN/AMERICAN.

Don't let the video games in the entry and Formica tables in the dining room turn you off, this is one of the best places around for enchiladas, burritos, and tacos at very reasonable prices.

3 Historic Towns on the Santa Fe Trail: Cimarron & Raton

CIMARRON

Few towns in the American West have as much lore or legend attached to them as Cimarron, 41 miles southwest of Raton via US 64. Nestled against the eastern slope of the Sangre de Cristo mountain range, the town (its name is Spanish for "wild" or "untamed") achieved its greatest fame as a "wild and woolly" outpost on the Santa Fe Trail between the 1850s and 1880s and a gathering place for area ranchers, traders, gamblers, gunslingers, and other savory characters.

ESSENTIALS

GETTING THERE   By Car   From Fort Union National Monument, head north on I-25, then head west on US 58 to Cimarron.

VISITOR INFORMATION   The **Cimarron Chamber of Commerce,** P.O. Box 604, Cimarron, NM 87714 (☎ **505/376-2417**), has complete information on the region.

EXPLORING THE WILD WEST TOWN

Frontier personalities including Kit Carson and Wyatt Earp, Buffalo Bill Cody and Annie Oakley, Bat Masterson and Doc Holliday, Butch Cassidy and Jesse James, painter Frederic Remington and novelist Zane Grey, all passed through and stayed in Cimarron—most of them at the **St. James Hotel** (see "Where to Stay & Dine," below)—at one time or another. Even if you're not planning an overnight stay here, it's a fun place to visit for an hour or two.

Land baron Lucien Maxwell founded the town in 1848 as base of operations for his 1.7-million-acre empire. In 1857, he built the **Maxwell Ranch,** which he furnished opulently with heavy draperies, gold-framed paintings, and two grand pianos. In the gaming room the tables saw high stakes, as guests bet silver Mexican pesos or pokes of yellow gold dust. Gold was struck in 1867 on Maxwell's land, near Baldy Mountain, and the rush of prospectors that followed caused him to sell out three years later.

The ranch isn't open for inspection today, but Maxwell's 1864 stone grist mill, built to supply flour to Fort Union, is. The **Old Mill Museum** houses an interesting collection of early photos and memorabilia. It's open May to October, Monday through Wednesday and Friday and Saturday from 9am to 5pm and Sunday from 1 to 5pm. Admission is $2 adults, $1 seniors and children.

Cimarron has numerous other buildings of historic note, and a walking tour map is included in the Old Mill Museum brochure.

NEARBY ATTRACTIONS

Cimarron is also the gateway to the ✪ **Philmont Scout Ranch** (☎ 505/376-2281), a 137,000-acre property donated to the Boy Scouts of America by Texas oilman Waite Phillips in 1938. Scouts from all over the world use it for backcountry camping and leadership training from June through August and for conferences the remainder of the year.

There are three museums on the ranch, all open to the public. **Villa Philmonte,** Phillips's lavish Mediterranean-style summer home, was built in 1927 and remains furnished with the family's European antiques. Located four miles south of Cimarron, it's open daily in summer for guided tours, other times by appointment. Admission is $3. The **Philmont Museum and Seton Memorial Library** commemorates the art and taxidermy of the naturalist and author who founded the Boy Scouts of America, and has exhibits on the varied history of the Cimarron area. It's open daily from June to August; closed Sunday the rest of the year. Admission is free. The **Kit Carson Museum,** 7 miles south of Philmont headquarters in Rayado, is a period hacienda furnished in 1850s style. Staff in historic costumes lead tours daily June through August. Admission is free.

GETTING OUTSIDE: CIMARRON CANYON STATE PARK

US 64 from Cimarron leads west 24 miles to Eagle Nest, passing en route to the popular, and often crowded, **Cimarron Canyon State Park** (☎ 505/377-6271), a 32,000-acre designated state wildlife area at the foot of crenellated granite formations known as the Palisades. The cliffs, which are 800 feet high in some areas, are favorites with rock climbers, while the river and the two park lakes attract anglers (for the best fishing, move away from the heavily populated campgrounds). Camping is permitted, but at least one member of every camping party must have a valid New Mexico fishing license.

Just east of Cimarron, County Road 204 offers access to the Carson National Forest's **Valle Vidal** recreation area, discussed in chapter 8.

WHERE TO STAY & DINE

✪ **St. James Hotel.** Rte. 1, Box 2, Cimarron, NM 87714. ☎ **800/748-2694** or 505/376-2664. Fax 505/376-2623. 25 rms, 2 suites. Hotel $80 single or double, $90 suite; motel $53 double. AE, DISC, MC, V.

This landmark hotel looks much the same today as it did in 1873, when it was built by Henri Lambert, previously a chef for Napoléon, Abraham Lincoln, and Gen. Ulysses S. Grant. In its early years, as a rare luxury on the Santa Fe Trail, it had a dining room, a saloon, gambling rooms, and lavish guest rooms outfitted with Victorian furniture. Today, you will find lace and cherry wood in the bedrooms, but not televisions or phones—the better to evoke the days when famous guests such as Zane Grey, who wrote *Fighting Caravans* at the hotel, were residents. Annie Oakley's bed is here, and a glass case holds a register with the signatures of Buffalo Bill Cody and the notorious Jesse James.

The St. James also was a place of some lawlessness: 26 men were said to have been killed within the two-foot-thick adobe walls, and owner Perry Champion can point out bullet holes in the pressed-tin ceiling of the dining room. The ghosts of some are believed to inhabit the hotel still.

The hotel itself has 13 rooms. There are 12 more in a recently remodeled modern annex; these lack the historic atmosphere of the hotel, but they do provide TV and telephone for those who prefer the late 20th century.

The St. James Dining Room serves the finest meals in this part of New Mexico. The menu is ambitious, featuring main courses such as shrimp Diablo, tournedos of beef, and veal marsala, most of them priced from $13 to $22. A separate coffee shop serves three meals daily. The hotel also offers an outdoor patio with bar and grill, gift shop, package store, and meeting room for 30.

RATON

Raton was founded in 1879 at the site of Willow Springs, a watering stop on the Santa Fe Trail. Mountain man "Uncle Dick" Wooton, a closet entrepreneur, had blasted a pass through the Rocky Mountains just north of the spring, and began charging toll. When the railroad bought Wooton's toll road, Raton developed as the railroad, mining, and ranching center for this part of the New Mexico Territory. Today it has a well-preserved historic district and the finest shooting facility in the United States.

East of Raton is Capulin Mountain, home to Capulin Volcano National Monument. The volcanic crater of the majestic 8,182-foot peak, inactive for 10,000 years, is open to visitors. See section 4 below for more about Capulin Volcano National Monument.

ESSENTIALS

GETTING THERE   By Car   From Santa Fe, take I-25 north; from Taos, take US 64 east.

VISITOR INFORMATION   The tourist information center is in the **Raton Chamber and Economic Development Council,** 100 Clayton Hwy. at Second Street (P.O. Box 1211), Raton, NM 87740 (☎ **800/638-6161** or 505/445-3689).

A WALKING TOUR OF HISTORIC RATON

It's best to explore the city's historic district by foot. Five blocks of Raton's original town site are listed on the National Register of Historic Places, with some 70 significant buildings.

Start at the **Raton Museum,** 216 S. First St. (☎ **505/445-8979**), where you can pick up a walking tour map. The museum, open Tuesday through Saturday from 10am to 4pm, displays a wide variety of mining, railroad, and ranching items from the early days of the town. It's housed in the **Coors Building** (1906), previously a Coors Brewing Company warehouse. Next door is the **Haven Hotel** (1913), built of ivory brick with green brick trim, and adorned with a pair of pineapples and three lion heads. At the corner of First and Cook is the **Palace Hotel** (1896), the first three-story building in Colfax County.

The **Santa Fe Depot,** First and Cook, was built in 1903 in Spanish mission revival style. It is still used by Amtrak passengers today. Next door is the **Wells Fargo Express Company,** built in 1910.

Opposite the station, heading north on First, is the **Roth Building** (1893), whose ornate metal facade boasts Corinthian pilasters and a bracketed cornice; the **Abourezk Building** (1906), with two female figureheads on the upper storefront; the **Marchiondo Building** (1882), a former dry-goods store painted bright yellow with green trim; and the **Joseph Building** (1890s), which still retains the cupids painted on its walls when it was the Gem Saloon.

Walk west one block to Second Street, and proceed south. At 131 N. Second St. is the **Shuler Theater** (☎ 505/445-5528). Built in 1915, it housed the opera company, fire station, and city offices. The interior of the theater, designed in European rococo style, has superb acoustics. The lobby is decorated with murals recalling local history. It's still in active use year-round. Open Monday to Friday from 8am to 5pm.

At the intersection of Second and Cook you'll find the **Raton Realty Building** (1928), characterized by a red tile roof and terra-cotta trimmed windows, and the **Di Lisio Building** (1918), a former bank with three Doric columns at its entrance and stained glass topping the lower windows. At Third and Cook, the neoclassical U.S. Post Office (1917) is now the **Arthur Johnson Memorial Library,** with a fine collection on Southwestern art. The south side of Cook between Second and Third is dominated by the **Swastika Hotel** (1929), now the International State Bank, a seven-story brick building decorated at the roofline with the swastika, a Native American symbol of good luck. The hotel's name was changed to the Yucca Hotel when the Nazis adopted the swastika as their symbol.

NEARBY ATTRACTIONS

The **NRA Whittington Center,** off US Highway 64 about 10 miles south of Raton, is considered the most complete nonmilitary shooting and training facility in the world. Operated by the National Rifle Association, it spans 50 square miles of rolling hills. It has 14 instructional and competitive ranges, a handful of condominium units, and hookups for campers. Classes in pistol, rifle, and shotgun shooting, firearm safety, and conservation are offered. National championship events are held annually. The center is open daily to the public for tours.

In the little town of **Springer** (pop. 1,300), 39 miles south of Raton via I-25, the **Santa Fe Trail Museum** (☎ 505/483-2341) is housed in the three-story 1881 Colfax County Courthouse. It contains pioneer artifacts and memorabilia from travelers along the Santa Fe Trail and early residents of the area, as well as a livery stable and New Mexico's only electric chair, which was used to execute seven convicted murderers between 1933 and 1956. Open Monday through Saturday from 9am to 4pm; admission is $1.50 for adults and 75¢ for children under 13. The **Colfax County Fair** takes place in Springer annually in mid-August, with a rodeo and car show.

About 30 miles east of Springer via US 56 is the **Dorsey Mansion,** a two-story log-and-stone home built in the 1880s by U.S. senator and cattleman Stephen Dorsey. With 36 rooms, hardwood floors, Italian marble fireplaces, hand-carved cherry staircase, and dining-room table that sat 60, it was quite a masterpiece! Public tours are offered by appointment (☎ 505/375-2222) Monday through Saturday from 10am to 4pm, Sunday 1 to 5pm, for an admission charge of $2 adults, $1 for children under 12.

GETTING OUTSIDE

Sugarite Canyon State Park (☎ 505/445-5607), located 10 miles northeast of Raton via NM 526, offers historic exhibits, camping, boating, and excellent fishing at three trout-stocked lakes. Lake Alice is the best place in the park for fly-fishing. Numerous hiking trails meander through the park, and a museum at the visitors' center traces the canyon's mining history.

Heading down I-25, **Maxwell National Wildlife Refuge** (☎ 505/375-2331) on the Canadian River, 24 miles from Raton, has a rich resident and migratory bird population and numerous native mammals. More than 200 species have been recorded in the refuge, which offers some of the best bird-watching in this part of the state.

South of US 56 via NM 39 is the western of the two parcels that comprise **Kiowa National Grasslands.** Travel this route to reach **Chicosa Lake State Park** (☎ 505/485-2424), on NM 120; 55 miles southeast of Springer, this park has camping, trout fishing, hiking, and historical exhibits on cattle drives along the Goodnight-Loving Trail. The 263,954-acre Kiowa National Grassland is a project to reclaim once-barren prairie land, the result of overfarming in the late 19th and early 20th centuries and the Great Plains Dustbowl of the 1930s. Today the plains are irrigated and green, and the area provides food, cover, and water for a wide variety of wildlife, such as antelope, bear, Barbary sheep, mountain lion, wild turkey, pheasant, and quail. Another portion of the grasslands is located east of here, along US 56/412, near the town of Clayton just west of the Oklahoma border.

WHERE TO STAY

Best Western Sands. 300 Clayton Hwy., Raton, NM 87740. ☎ **800/518-2581,** 800/528-1234, or 505/445-2737. 50 rms. A/C TV TEL. $53–$89 double. Extra person $3. AE, CB, DC, DISC, MC, V.

The Best Western Sands has spacious rooms, each with a king- or queen-size bed and in-room coffee. Some rooms are also outfitted with overstuffed recliners and refrigerators. Owned and operated by the same family, this motel has a more personal feeling than most chain hotels. There is a seasonal outdoor heated swimming pool as well as a hot tub, playground, gift shop and family style eatery.

Harmony Manor Hotel. 351 Clayton Rd., Raton, NM 87740. ☎ **800/922-0347** or 505/445-2763. 18 rms. A/C TV TEL. Memorial Day–Labor Day, $40–$58 single or double; rest of the year, $36–$50 single or double. AE, DC, DISC, MC, V.

The Harmony Manor Motel, located just off I-25, is a great buy. The rooms are spotlessly kept by owners Loyd and Doris Wilkins and contain all the amenities you need for a comfortable stay. Each is enormous and has king- or queen-size beds, cable TV, and direct-dial phones. Nonsmoking rooms are available. The decor is bright and airy.

Melody Lane Motel. 136 Canyon Dr., Raton, NM 87740. ☎ **800/421-5210** or 505/445-3655. 27 rms. A/C TV TEL. Mid-May to Labor Day, $41–$51 double. Labor Day to mid-May, $37–$43 double. Rates include continental breakfast. Weekly rates are available. AE, CB, DC, DISC, MC, V.

This nice property on the I-25 business loop (off Exit 454) has a wide variety of room options. Eight rooms have steam baths; many of them have king-size beds. Most have HBO cable reception and thermostat-controlled hot-water heating. Small pets are permitted.

CAMPING   There are quite a few campgrounds worth mentioning in the Raton area, including **KOA Raton,** which is located in town at 1330 S. 2nd St. (☎ **800/ 789-3488** or 505/445-3488), with 54 sites, grocery and laundry facilities, as well as picnic tables and grills.

Summerlan RV Park at 1900 S. Cedar/I-25 and US 87 (☎ **505/445-9536**), which is convenient to the interstate, has 72 sites, laundry and grocery facilities, and picnic tables.

WHERE TO DINE

The Capri Restaurant. 304 Canyon Dr. ☎ **505/445-9755.** Main courses $4.25–$10. AE, DC, DISC, MC, V. Daily 7am–9pm. ITALIAN.

Italian in the Wild West? It seems to work at this casual cafe, which draws rave reviews from locals for its homemade pastas, including stuffed manicotti, and its chicken cacciatore. It also offers a Mexican menu, steaks, and limited seafood, including a popular combination of tenderloin and brook trout.

El Matador. 1012 S. 2nd St. ☎ **505/445-9575.** Lunch and dinner $3.25–$12.25. Tues–Sun 7am–8:30pm. NEW MEXICAN.

A festive Mexican decor makes this cafe a lively spot. Tacos, enchiladas, burritos, tostadas, and other menu favorites are prepared à la carte or as part of combination plates. Steaks and other American dishes are also on the menu.

Pappas' Sweet Shop Restaurant. 1201 S. 2nd St. ☎ **505/445-9811.** Reservations suggested at dinner in summer. Lunch $5–$9; dinner $9–$30. AE, DC, DISC, MC, V. Mon–Sat 9am–2pm and 5–9pm. AMERICAN/TEX-MEX.

Don't let the name of this place fool you; it's not a bakery, as the name might suggest, but rather a fine restaurant, known for its quality beef. Prime rib, filet mignon, and steak-and-seafood combinations are popular, along with broiled breast of chicken and deep-fried shrimp. Across-the-border dishes include Tex-Mex steak, fajitas, and enchiladas. A full-service lounge adjoins the restaurant.

4 Capulin Volcano National Monument

Capulin Volcano National Monument offers visitors the rare opportunity to walk inside a volcanic crater. A 2-mile road spirals up from the visitor center over 600 feet to the crater of the 8,182-foot peak, where two self-guiding trails leave from the parking area: an energetic and spectacular 1-mile hike around the crater rim and a 100-foot descent into the crater to the ancient volcanic vent. The volcano was last active about 10,000 years ago, when it exploded and sent out the last of three lava flows; scientists still consider it potentially active. As far back as 1891 public settlement on Capulin Mountain was prohibited by Congress. In 1916 it was protected by presidential proclamation as Capulin Mountain National Monument for its scientific and geologic interest. The final name change came in 1987. One of the most interesting features of this volcano is the symmetry of the main cinder cone.

Because of the altitude, visitors are encouraged to wear light jackets in the summer and layers during the rest of the year. Be aware that the road up to the crater rim is frequently closed due to weather conditions. If you're planning on getting a quick look at the volcano, plan on spending one to three hours; a more in-depth exploration could take several days, but keep in mind that camping is not permitted at the volcano. A short nature trail behind the center introduces plant and animal life of the area and is great for kids and accessible to people with disabilities. There's also a longer hike from park headquarters up to the parking lot at the crater rim. The crater rim offers magnificent panoramic views of the surrounding landscape, the Sangre de Cristo Mountains, and, on clear days, portions of four contiguous states: Kansas, Texas, Colorado, and Oklahoma. During the summer, the volcano attracts swarms of ladybird beatles (ladybugs).

ESSENTIALS

GETTING THERE   The monument is located 30 miles east of Raton via US 64/87 and north 3 miles on NM 325.

VISITOR INFORMATION   The Visitor Center, located at the base of the northern side of the volcano, is open Memorial Day through Labor Day daily from 8am to 8pm and the rest of the year from 8:30am to 4:30pm. An audiovisual program discusses volcanism and park personnel will answer questions. Admission is $4 per car or $2 per person. For more information, contact Capulin Volcano National Monument, Capulin, NM 88414 (☎ **505/278-2201**).

CAMPING

Camping is not permitted inside the park; however, camping facilities are available in Capulin town, as well as in the neighboring towns of Raton and Clayton.

Capulin Camp (☎ **505/278-2921**) in the tiny town of Capulin has 35 sites, laundry, and picnic tables.

5 Along the Clayton Highway: Dinosaurs, Outlaws & Folsom Man

FOLSOM

Just north of Capulin Mountain, on NM 325 off the Clayton Highway (US 64/87, running 83 miles east-southeast from Raton to Clayton), is the tiny town of Folsom, the site near where cowboy George McJunkin discovered the 10,000-year-old remains of "Folsom Man." The find, excavated by the Denver Museum of Natural History in 1926, represented the first association of the artifacts of prehistoric people (spear points) with the fossil bones of extinct animals (a species of bison). Today the site, on private property, is closed to the public. But artifacts (prehistoric as well as from the 19th century) are displayed at the **Folsom Museum,** Main Street, Folsom (☎ **505/278-2122** in summer, **505/278-3616** in winter). The museum, open from 10am to 5pm daily in summer, winter by appointment, contains exhibits on prehistoric and historic Native Americans of the area, as well as Folsom's settlement by whites. Admission is $1 for adults, 50¢ for children 6 to 12.

CLAYTON

Clayton (pop. 2,454) is a ranching center just 9 miles west of the Texas and Oklahoma panhandle borders. Rich prairie grasses, typical of nearby **Kiowa National Grasslands** (☎ **505/374-9652**), led to its founding in 1887 at the site of a long-time cowboy resting spot and watering hole. In the early 19th century, the Cimarron Cutoff of the Santa Fe Trail, along which numerous bloody battles between Plains Indians and Anglo settlers and traders were waged, passed through this area. In New Mexico history, Clayton is also known as the town where Thomas "Black Jack"

Ketchum, a notorious train robber, was hanged (and inadvertently decapitated) and buried (after a doctor carefully reunited his head with his body) in 1901 after a decade of legendary heists.

Twelve miles north of town off NM 370, near the distinctive Rabbit Ears Mountains, is **Clayton Lake State Park** (☎ 505/374-8808), where tracks from eight species of dinosaurs can be clearly seen. The park has a visitor center, and offers fishing, swimming, boating, hiking, and camping. A half-mile trail on the southeast side of the lake leads across the dam to an exhibit describing the types of dinosaurs that roamed this area. From there, you can wander among the tracks along a boardwalk.

VISITOR INFORMATION   For information on other area attractions, as well as lodging and dining, contact the **Clayton-Union County Chamber of Commerce,** 1103 S. First St. (P.O. Box 476) Clayton, NM 88415 (☎ 505/374-9253).

6 The I-40 Corridor

The 216 freeway miles from Albuquerque to the Texas border cross straight, featureless prairie and very few towns. But the valleys of the Pecos River (site of Santa Rosa) and the Canadian River (location of Tucumcari) have several attractions, including natural lakes. There's not a lot to explore here, unless you're a bird-watcher or a fisher, but both towns can make a day's stopover worthwhile.

ESSENTIALS

GETTING THERE   By Car   I-40 extends from southern California to North Carolina. Travel time from Albuquerque to Tucumcari is 2 hours, 40 minutes; to Santa Rosa, 1 hour, 45 minutes.

By Plane   There's no regularly scheduled commercial service into either Tucumcari or Santa Rosa. Private planes can land at **Tucumcari Municipal Airport** (☎ 505/461-3229).

VISITOR INFORMATION   Contact the **Tucumcari–Quay County Chamber of Commerce,** 404 W. Tucumcari Blvd. (P.O. Drawer E), Tucumcari, NM 88401 (☎ 505/461-1694) or the **Santa Rosa Chamber of Commerce,** 486 Parker Ave., Santa Rosa, NM 88435 (☎ 505/472-3763).

SEEING THE SIGHTS

The **Tucumcari Historical Museum,** 416 S. Adams (☎ 505/461-4201), one block east of First Street, is open from 9am to 6pm Monday through Saturday and from 1 to 6pm Sunday in summer, and Tuesday through Saturday from 9am to 5pm and from 1 to 5pm Sunday in winter. An early sheriff's office, an authentic western schoolroom, a hospital room of the early West, a real chuck wagon, a historic windmill, and a barbed-wire collection are among the treasures.

The moonlike **Mesa Redondo,** rising 11 miles south of town via NM 209, gives visitors the sense of entering a strange unknown world. To the northwest, 34 miles distant over NM 104, is **Conchas Lake State Park** (☎ 505/868-2270), with a reservoir 25 miles long. Two modern marinas provide facilities for boating, fishing, and waterskiing. Camping and picnic areas attract visitors to the south side of the lake—there are full hookups available as well as a nine-hole golf course (☎ 505/868-2988). The northern site offers rental cabins, a trailer park with hookups, marina, store, and a restaurant.

Ute Lake State Park is 22 miles northeast on US 54, near the town of Logan. It has docking facilities, picnic tables, campsites, and rental boats. Quay County around

Tucumcari is noted for its blue-quail hunting, said to be the best anywhere in the United States.

Caprock Amphitheatre (☎ **505/461-1694**), 30 miles southeast of Tucumcari, is a natural amphitheater. Here the New Mexico Outdoor Drama Association presents an outdoor musical drama Friday and Saturday nights from mid-June to mid-August. *Billy the Kid,* first produced in 1987, is a romantic dramatization of New Mexico's Wild West days. The two-hour show starts at 8pm, following a 6:30pm barbecue on-site. Show tickets are $10 for adults, $5 for children 6 to 12. Dinner costs $6 for adults, $4 for children. The amphitheater is on NM 469, south of San Jon off I-40 (Exit 356). For advance information, write the NMODA, P.O. Box 337, San Jon, NM 88434.

Santa Rosa calls itself "the city of natural lakes." Those bodies of water include **Blue Hole,** a crystal-clear, 81-foot-deep artesian spring just east of downtown. Fed by a subterranean river that flows 3,000 gallons per minute at a constant 64°, it's a favorite of scuba divers. There's a bathhouse on site. **Park Lake,** in the middle of town, offers free swimming, picnicking, and extensive recreational facilities. **Santa Rosa Lake State Park,** P.O. Box 384, Santa Rosa (☎ **505/472-3110**), on a dammed portion of the Pecos River, has camping, hiking, excellent fishing, and a visitor information center. Ten miles south of town via NM 91, the village of **Puerto de Luna** is a 19th-century county seat with a mid-1800s courthouse and church, Nuestra Señora del Refugio.

WHERE TO STAY

In both Tucumcari and Santa Rosa, major hotels are at I-40 interchanges. Smaller "Ma and Pa" motels can be found along the main streets through town that were once segments of legendary Route 66—Tucumcari Boulevard in Tucumcari, Will Rogers Drive in Santa Rosa. All told, there are about 2,000 rooms in Tucumcari and Santa Rosa.

IN TUCUMCARI

Best Western Discovery Motor Inn. 200 E. Estrella Ave. at Exit 332, Tucumcari, NM 88401. ☎ **800/528-1234** or 505/461-4884. 107 rms. A/C TV TEL. June to mid-Sept, $54–$62 double; mid-Sept to May, $48–$60 double. AE, CB, DC, DISC, MC, V.

This spacious new motor hotel has the advantage of being off the "strip"—it's still central, but it's quieter than many others. Many rooms, all of which have king-size or two queen-size beds, look down upon the outdoor swimming pool. The hotel also has an indoor spa, guest Laundromat, game room, and gift shop. Complimentary morning coffee is an added touch. Nonsmoking and rooms for people with disabilities are available, and small pets are permitted with payment of a damage deposit.

The Headquarters House Restaurant is considered one of Tucumcari's better eating places.

Best Western Pow Wow Inn. 801 W. Tucumcari Blvd. (P.O. Box 1306), Tucumcari, NM 88401. ☎ **800/527-6996**, 800/528-1234, or 505/461-0500. Fax 505/461-0135. 90 rms, 16 suites. A/C TV TEL. $45–$55 double; $65–$90 suite. AE, CB, DC, DISC, MC, V.

A full-service downtown motor inn, the Pow Wow focuses around its beautiful outdoor swimming pool, with an artificial-turf deck. One-third of the units, including 15 ground-level suites, have kitchens (utensils not provided). Other facilities include a children's playground, a coin-op Laundromat, and a gift shop. Guests get complimentary greens fees at the local golf club. Pets are accepted, but must not be left unattended.

Route 66 Revisited: Rediscovering New Mexico's Stretch of the Mother Road

Everyone's heard of Route 66—the highway that once stretched all the way from Chicago to California was hailed as the road to freedom. In the late 1940s and '50s if you suddenly found yourself in a rut, all you had to do was hop in the car and head west on Route 66. Of course, the road existed long before it gained such widespread fascination. In fact, it was built in the late 1920s and paved in 1937, and it was the lifeblood of communities in eight different states. Nowadays the road is as elusive as the fantasies that once carried hundreds of thousands west in search of a better life. Replaced by other roads, covered up by interstates, mostly I-40, and just plain out of use, Route 66 does still exist in New Mexico, but you'll have to do a little searching and take some extra time to find it.

Motorists driving west from Texas can take a spin (make that a slow spin) on a 20-mile gravel stretch of the old highway that runs from Glenrio (Tex.) to San Jon. From San Jon to Tucumcari, drivers can get their kicks on nearly 24 continuous paved miles of vintage 66. In Tucumcari, the historic route sliced through the center of town along what is today Tucumcari Boulevard. Santa Rosa's Will Rogers Drive is that city's 4-mile claim to the Mother Road. In Albuquerque, 66 follows Central Avenue for 18 miles, from the 1936 State Fairgrounds, past original 1930s motels and the historic Nob Hill district, on west through downtown.

One of the best spots to pretend you are a 1950s road warrior crossing the desert, leaving rattlesnakes, teepees, and tumbleweeds in your wake, is along NM 124, which winds 25 miles from Mesita to Acoma in northwestern New Mexico. You can next pick up old Route 66 in Grants, along the 6-mile Santa Fe Avenue. In Gallup, a 9-mile segment of US 66 is lined with restaurants and hotels reminiscent of the city's days as a Western film capital from 1929 through 1964. Just outside Gallup, the historic route continues west to the Arizona border as NM 118.

For more information about Route 66, contact the New Mexico Route 66 Association through the Grants/Cíbola County Chamber of Commerce at **800/748-2142**. The New Mexico Department of Tourism (☎ **800/545-2040**) also publishes information about Route 66. If you want to surf the Web before you hit the road, one site to check out is http://route66.netvision.be/.

The Pow Wow Restaurant is open from 6am to 10pm. It features a daily luncheon buffet, dinners priced from $5 to $12, and a cool, low-lit lounge with live entertainment in the evenings.

CAMPING NEAR TUCUMCARI   There are four good campgrounds around Tucumcari. **KOA Tucumcari** (☎ **505/461-1841**) has 111 sites, laundry and grocery facilities, RV supplies, picnic tables, and grills. It also offers a recreation hall with video games, a heated swimming pool, basketball hoop, playground, horseshoes, and shuffleboard. To get there from I-40, get off the interstate at exit 335, and then go ¼ mile east on South Frontage Road.

Mt. Road RV Park (☎ **505/461-9628**) has 60 sites and 60 full hookups with phone availability, tenting, laundry facilities, and picnic tables. From I-40 take exit 333 to Mountain Road; the park isn't far from the US 54 bypass.

Cactus Motel and RV Park (☎ **505/461-2501**) is a bit smaller with 39 sites. Tenting is available, and there are grills. From I-40 (exit 332) go 1¼ miles north on

NM 209, then 1¹/₄ miles east on Tucumcari Boulevard. The motel and RV park are located one block east of Denny's.

Another campground is located in **Conchas Lake State Park** (☎ **505/868-2270**). It features 101 sites, 33 full hookups, lake swimming, boating, fishing, and hiking trails.

IN SANTA ROSA

Best Western Adobe Inn. E. Business Loop 40 at I-40 (P.O. Box 410), Santa Rosa, NM 88435. ☎ **800/528-1234** or 505/472-3446. 58 rms. A/C TV TEL. May–Oct $54–$56 double; Nov–Apr $44–$52 double. AE, CB, DC, DISC, MC, V.

This pleasant motel has clean, comfortable rooms with all standard furnishings, including queen-size beds in every room. There's a swimming pool and gift shop, a courtesy car, and an attached coffee shop. Small pets are allowed.

Motel 6. 3400 Will Rogers Dr., Santa Rosa, NM 88435. ☎ **505/472-3045.** 90 rms. A/C TV TEL. $32.99 double. Under 18 free with parent. AE, CB, DC, DISC, MC, V.

Rooms are basic but clean, with double beds, table and chairs, three-quarter bath, TV, and phones. The motel has an outdoor swimming pool, open seasonally. It's on the north side of I-40, opposite the town.

Super 8 Motel. 1201 Will Rogers Dr., Santa Rosa NM 88435. ☎ **505/472-5388.** Fax 505/472-5388. 88 rms (all with bath). A/C TV TEL. $40–$42 double. AE, CB, DC, MC, V.

Located near the historic Club Cafe, this Super 8 is like other Super 8s in that it's clean and has large rooms with double beds and standard furnishings. There's cable TV with pay movies, a guest laundry, and rooms for nonsmokers. Pets are not permitted.

CAMPING NEAR SANTA ROSA The **Santa Rosa KOA** (☎ **505/472-3126**) offers 94 sites, 33 full hookups, laundry and grocery facilities, fire rings, grills, a heated swimming pool, badminton, horseshoes, volleyball, and a playground for the kids. Coming from the east on I-40, take exit 277 and go 1 mile west on Business Loop; coming from the west on I-40, take exit 275 and go ¹/₄ mile east on Business Loop.

Also in the area is **Santa Rosa Lake State Park** (☎ **505/472-3110**), where visitors can camp all year. There are 75 sites as well as grills, lake swimming, boating, fishing, and hiking trails.

TWO GOOD PLACES TO EAT IN TUCUMCARI

Del's Family Restaurant. 1202 E. Tucumcari Blvd. ☎ **505/461-1740.** $3.95–$13.95. MC, V. Mon–Sat 6am–9pm. AMERICAN/MEXICAN.

The big cow atop Del's neon sign is not only a Route 66 landmark—it also points to the fine steaks inside. Sirloins, rib eyes, and other popular cuts highlight the menu. Del's also offers burgers, Mexican plates, and seafood, including an eight-ounce catfish filet. A trip through the large salad bar is a satisfying meal for many. Del's is not licensed for alcoholic beverages.

La Cita. 812 S. 1st St. ☎ **505/461-0949.** $2.95–$9.95. AE, MC, V. Mon–Sun 11am–9pm. NEW MEXICAN/AMERICAN.

A modern cafe in downtown Tucumcari since 1961, La Cita is best known for its tasty fajitas, green chile enchiladas, spicy salsa, and flat enchiladas—served with an egg on top.

10 Northwestern New Mexico

This is American Indian country, past and present. Pueblo, Navajo, and Apache share this colorful area of sandstone bluffs, treading the same ground their Anasazi ancestors did many centuries ago.

The Zuni, Acoma, and Laguna Pueblos are each located within a short distance of I-40. Acoma's "Sky City" has been continually occupied for more than nine centuries. A huge chunk of the northwest is taken up by a part of the Navajo Reservation, the largest in America; and the Jicarilla Apache Reservation stretches 65 miles south from the Colorado border. All share their arts and crafts as well as their distinctive cultures with visitors, but ask that their personal privacy and religious traditions be respected.

The past lives here, too, side by side with the present. Chaco Culture National Historical Park, with 12 major ruins and hundreds of smaller ones, represents the highest development of Anasazi civilization in the 11th century. Aztec Ruins National Monument and the nearby Salmon Ruins are similarly spectacular Pueblo preservations.

Two other national monuments in northwestern New Mexico are El Morro and El Malpais—the former a sandstone monolith known as "Inscription Rock" where travelers and explorers documented their journeys for centuries, the latter a volcanic badlands with spectacular cinder cones, ice caves, and lava tubes.

The metropolitan centers of the region are Farmington, center of the fertile San Juan valley and gateway to the Four Corners region, with about 36,500 people; Gallup, self-proclaimed "Indian capital of the world" and a mecca for silver-jewelry shoppers, with a population of about 20,000; and Grants, a former uranium-mining boomtown, with almost 8,500 residents.

Well east of Farmington, about equidistant from Santa Fe, is a fourth regional center of sorts: Chama (pop. 1,000). It's best known as the New Mexico depot for the Cumbres and Toltec Railroad—the longest and highest narrow-gauge steam railroad in the country—and as a center for hunting and fishing expeditions into New Mexico's high country.

TOURING THE REGION BY CAR

Beginning in Albuquerque, head west on I-40 via Laguna to Acoma Pueblo to tour the amazing "Sky City." Running alongside this section of I-40, though you'd barely know it today, is what was once

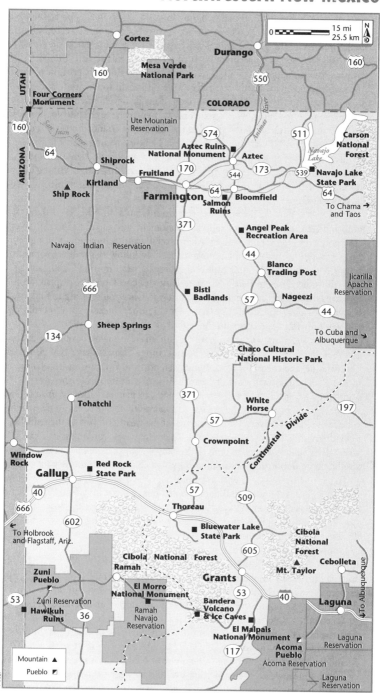

15 mi
25.5 km

N

Cortez

Durango

160

Mesa Verde National Park

160

550

UTAH

COLORADO

Four Corners Monument

Ute Mountain Reservation

574

511

San Juan River

ARIZONA

160

Carson National Forest

Navajo Lake

64

Shiprock

Aztec Ruins National Monument

170

544

Aztec

173

539

Navajo Lake State Park

Fruitland

Kirtland

▲ **Ship Rock**

Farmington

64

Bloomfield

64

Salmon Ruins

To Chama and Taos →

371

Angel Peak Recreation Area

Navajo   Indian   Reservation

44

Blanco Trading Post

Jicarilla Apache Reservation

666

■ **Bisti Badlands**

57

Nageezi

44

To Cuba and Albuquerque →

Sheep Springs

134

Chaco Cultural National Historic Park

371

White Horse

197

57

Continental   Divide

Tohatchi

Crownpoint

Window Rock

Gallup

Red Rock State Park

57

40

509

666

602

Thoreau

To Holbrook and Flagstaff, Ariz. ←

■ **Bluewater Lake State Park**

605

Cibola National Forest

▲ **Mt. Taylor**

Cebolleta

To Albuquerque →

Zuni Pueblo

Cibola   National   Forest

Ramah

Grants

53

El Morro National Monument

Bandera Volcano & Ice Caves

40

Laguna

53

Hawikuh Ruins

36

Zuni Reservation

Ramah Navajo Reservation

El Malpais National Monument

117

Laguna Reservation

Acoma Pueblo

Acoma Reservation

Mountain ▲

Pueblo ▨

Laguna Reservation

1-0627

part of historic Route 66. If you're in no real hurry to get to Acoma Pueblo, I'd recommend driving this section of Route 66. If you choose to take the road to freedom, look for today's NM 6 and follow it to Mesita where Route 66 picks up on NM 124. That will take you right through Laguna, where you might want to make a stop at Laguna Pueblo before continuing on to Acoma. During this portion of your trip through northwestern New Mexico, you'll be on Indian Reservation land, which accounts (happily, I might add) for the lack of major development in the area. After taking the tour at Acoma, which is the only way you can see the pueblo, proceed west on I-40 in the direction of Grants. Before you get to Grants, however, you should make a detour on NM 117 to see El Malpais National Monument. From there head to Grants where you'll probably want to take a room for the night. The next morning you should make a point to visit the New Mexico Museum of Mining in Grants. It's a great little museum that gives you an accurate idea of what mining life was like in New Mexico.

Later in the day, head south and west from Grants on NM 53 to Bandera Volcano and Ice Caves, El Morro National Monument, and the Zuni Pueblo. Then proceed north on NM 602 to Gallup, where you'll want to browse in trading posts for Native American jewelry and crafts and possibly follow the walking tour outlined below. If you've still got some time and energy left after touring Gallup and the area attractions, head out to Red Rock State Park and check out the displays on prehistoric Anasazi culture. It's a good little preview to what you're going to find in Chaco Canyon National Historical Park later in your journey. Next, return to Gallup where you will probably want to spend the night.

The next morning when you leave Gallup, make sure you have a full tank of gas and then head out on I-40 east to Thoreau. From Thoreau, take NM 371 north to Crownpoint, and then NM 57 east and then north to Chaco Canyon National Historical Park, the crown jewel of ancient Anasazi culture in North America. You'll want to spend at least one full day at the park, so plan accordingly. Also give yourself some time to get from the canyon to a campsite or motel. It can take a while to get out of Chaco Canyon. Please note that if the weather is bad or the roads are particularly muddy, it's best not to even try to get to the canyon unless you have a four-wheel-drive vehicle. You can camp in the canyon, but prepare accordingly—there are absolutely no opportunities to gather provisions once you enter the park.

To get to Farmington, our next stop, from Chaco Canyon, take NM 57 north to NM 44 and NM 44 north to Bloomfield and then go west on US 64. If you're camping, the towns of Bloomfield and Aztec (which leave you slightly closer to your first stop in the morning) both have campsites; otherwise, Farmington is your best bet for finding a decent motel room.

Points of interest in the Farmington/Aztec area are Aztec Ruins National Monument and the Salmon Ruins. The average visit to Aztec Ruins National Monument and Salmon Ruins combined lasts about two hours, so you'll have plenty of time to explore Navajo Lake State Park (off US 64 east), where you can take a cool dip or fish for trout, salmon, bass, or crappie before continuing on to Dulce, in the Jicarilla Apache Indian Reservation, where you'll probably want to spend the night. An alternative is to drive another half-hour down the highway to Chama, not much more than a wide spot in the road, where you can take a ride on the Cumbres and Toltec Scenic Railroad in the morning. This is one of New Mexico's premier attractions.

When you've waved the train good-bye, follow US 84 south to Santa Fe, leaving time for midway stops at the Ghost Ranch Living Museum north of Abiquiu and Georgia O'Keeffe's former home in Abiquiu. Return to Albuquerque via I-25.

1 The Great Outdoors in Northwestern New Mexico

As with the rest of New Mexico, the northwest region offers much to do in the way of outdoor recreation. If you're an outdoor enthusiast you could spend months here hiking, biking, and exploring.

BIKING **Angel Peak Recreation Area** (☎ 505/599-8900) is a good place for mountain bikers, however there are many other opportunities (and unpaved roads) available in the Grants area for avid bikers. Mountain biking is permitted throughout **Cíbola National Forest** (☎ 505/287-8833), which, in this part of the region, is located on both sides of I-40 in the Grants to Gallup area. Good trails to try are the Mount Taylor summit trail and the McGaffey Region. Additionally, bikers are also welcome at the Bureau of Land Management Conservation Area just off NM 117 near **El Malpais National Monument.** For equipment rental, try calling **Scoreboard Sporting Goods** (107 West Coal Ave. ☎ 505/722-6077) in Gallup, or **Dominic and Ray's Mountain Bikes** (☎ 505/756-2580) in Chama; or you might opt to rent something before you leave Albuquerque at either **Old Town Bicycles** (☎ 505/247-4926) or **Rio Mountainsport** (☎ 505/766-9970).

BOATING If you're towing a boat, good places to stop are **Bluewater Lake State Park** (☎ 505/876-2391), a reservoir located between Gallup and Grants, and **Navajo Lake State Park** (☎ 505/632-2278), located about 24 miles east of Aztec. Both Bluewater and Navajo Lake State Parks have boat ramps, and Navajo Lake has several marinas, picnic areas, a visitors center, and groceries for those who plan to make a day of it. **Zuni Lakes,** six bodies of water operated by the Zuni tribe, also offer opportunities for boating, although you're not allowed to use gasoline motors and you must receive a permit from tribal headquarters (☎ 505/782-5851) before setting out.

FISHING **Bluewater Lake State Park** (mentioned above for boating) is one of the best places to fish in the area. In fact, some people believe it has the highest catch rate of all New Mexico lakes. Look to catch trout here. **Ramah Lake** (no phone) was created in the late 1800s by Mormons for the purpose of irrigation, and was privately owned up until 1987 when it became available for public use. There's nothing here but the lake and the fish (bass, trout, and bluegills). Fishing is also allowed by permit at Zuni Lakes (see above). **Navajo Lake State Park** (☎ 505/632-2278) features just under 200 miles of shoreline where fishers go to catch trout, bass, catfish, and pike. Navajo Lake is one of the largest in New Mexico, and the park is very heavily trafficked, so if crowds aren't your thing, look for another fishing hole. Just four miles south of Kirtland is Morgan Lake, a quiet spot for largemouth bass and catfish. If you're in need of fishing gear while in the area, contact **Duranglers on the San Juan,** 1003 Highway 511, Navajo Dam (☎ 505/632-5952), or the nearby **Abe's Motel and Fly Shop,** 1791 Route 173, Navajo Dam (☎ 505/632-2194). In Farmington, contact **Dad's Bait, Boats, and Upholstery,** 210 E. Pinon St. (☎ 505/326-1870), or **Zia Sporting Goods,** 500 E. Main (☎ 505/327-6004).

GOLF Public golf courses in Farmington include **Pinon Hills Golf Course,** located at 2101 Sunrise Pkwy. (☎ 505/326-6066), and **Civitan Golf Course,** 2200 North Dustin (☎ 505/599-1194). If you're going to be in or near Aztec, try **Hidden Valley Country Club,** 3025 29 Rd. (☎ 505/334-3248). In Kirtland your opportunities are limited to **Riverview Golf Course,** located on County Road 6500, no. 89 (☎ 505/598-0140).

HIKING This part of the state has some great hiking trails. You'll get to see ancient archaeological ruins in places like Aztec Ruins and Chaco Canyon. In **Cíbola National Forest,** the hike to the summit of Mount Taylor is excellent. In cooler months, but not winter, try hiking around **El Malpais National Monument.** Two good hikes to try in El Malpais are the Zuni-Acoma Trail (this one is extremely taxing, so if you're not in shape, don't expect to make the 15-mile round-trip hike) and the Big Lava Tubes Trail (1 mile round-trip). For information on the above-mentioned trails, call **505/783-4774.** For quiet hiking in state parks, head to **Bluewater Lake State Park** (☎ **505/876-2391**), **Red Rock State Park** (☎ **505/722-3839**), or **Angel Peak Recreation Area** (☎ **505/599-8900**).

Sporting goods stores where you can get hiking gear include **REI-Albuquerque** at 1905 Mountain Rd. NW in Albuquerque (☎ **505/247-1191**), **Frontier Sports** at 4601 E. Main in Farmington (☎ **505/327-0800**), and **Zia Sporting Goods** at 500 E. Main, also in Farmington (☎ **505/327-6004**).

SKIING If you're tired of fighting for space on the cross-country ski trails in other parts of the state, try Mount Taylor in **Cíbola National Forest** near Grants. Contact the Ranger Station in Grants at ☎ **505/287-8833** for more information. If you need to rent ski equipment I'd recommend doing so in Albuquerque before you head north. See chapter 6 for details.

SWIMMING Good swimming is available at **Navajo Lake State Park** (☎ **505/632-2278**). Before diving in at other lakes in state parks, make sure swimming is permitted.

2 Acoma & Laguna Pueblos

Your best base for exploring Acoma and Laguna Pueblos, as well as the El Malpais and El Morro National Monuments (see section 3), is the town of Grants, 1 1/4 hours west of Albuquerque on I-40 west. Where to stay and dine in Grants, as well as details on the interesting New Mexico Museum of Mining in Grants, are discussed later in this section.

ACOMA PUEBLO

The spectacular Acoma Sky City, a walled adobe village perched high atop a sheer rock mesa 367 feet above the 6,600-foot valley floor, is said to have been inhabited at least since the 11th century—it's the longest continuously occupied community in the United States. Native legend says it has been inhabited since before the time of Christ. Both the pueblo and its mission church of San Estevan del Rey are National Historic Landmarks. When Coronado visited in 1540, he suggested that Acoma was "the greatest stronghold in the world"; those who attempt to follow the cliff-side footpath to the top (to join a guided tour), rather than take the modern road, might agree.

The Keresan-speaking Acoma (pronounced *Ack*-oo-mah) Pueblo boasts about 6,005 inhabitants, but only about 50 reside year-round on the 70-acre mesa top. Many others maintain ancestral homes and occupy them during ceremonial periods. The terraced three-story buildings face south for maximum exposure to the winter sun. Most of Sky City's permanent residents make their living off the throngs of tourists who flock here to see the magnificent church, built in 1639 and containing numerous masterpieces of Spanish colonial art, and to purchase the thin-walled white pottery, with brown-and-black designs, for which the pueblo is famous.

Many Acomas work in Grants, 15 miles west of the pueblo, or in Albuquerque; others are cattle ranchers and farm individual family gardens.

ESSENTIALS

GETTING THERE   To reach Acoma from Grants, drive east 15 miles on I-40 to McCartys, then south 13 miles on paved tribal roads to the visitor center. From Albuquerque, drive west 52 miles to the Acoma-Sky City exit, then 12 miles southwest.

VISITOR INFORMATION   For additional information before you leave home, contact the Acoma Pueblo governor's office at P.O. Box 309, Acoma, NM 87034 or call **800/747-0181** or 505/252-1139. They'll tell you everything you need to know. The office is open weekdays from 9am to 5pm.

The Pueblo is open to visitors daily from 8am to 4:30pm November through March and 8am to 7pm the rest of the year. A one-hour tour is offered every 20 minutes, and admission is $6 adults, $5 seniors, $4 children. There are additional charges for still photography sketching or painting, and video is permitted only by special permission. Acoma is not open to the visiting public during some special events; Easter weekend, July 10 to 13, and the first weekend in October.

SEEING THE HIGHLIGHTS

You absolutely cannot wander freely around Acoma Pueblo, but you can start your tour of Acoma at the visitor center at the base of the mesa. While waiting for the guided tour to begin, peruse the excellent little museum of Acoma history and crafts, or dine on Native American food in an adjoining cafe. Then board your 13-seat tour bus, which climbs through a rock garden of 50-foot sandstone monoliths and past precipitously dangling outhouses to the mesa's summit. There's no running water or electricity in this medieval-looking village; a small reservoir collects rainwater for most uses, and drinking water is transported up from below. Wood-hole ladders and mica windows are prevalent among the 300-odd adobe structures. As you tour the village there will be many opportunities to buy pottery and other pueblo treasures; however, you're going to be forced to be something of an impulse buyer if you're shopping here because the tour guide will not take you back to a spot once you've moved on. Pottery is expensive here, but you're not going to find it any cheaper anywhere else, and you'll at least be guaranteed that it's authentic if you buy it directly from the craftsperson.

DANCES & CEREMONIES

The annual San Esteban del Rey feast day is September 2, when the pueblo's patron saint is honored with a midmorning mass, a procession, an afternoon corn dance, and an arts-and-crafts fair. A Governor's Feast is held annually in February; and four days of Christmas festivals run from December 25 to 28. Cameras are not allowed on the mesa during feast days.

Other celebrations are held in low-lying pueblo villages at Easter (in Acomita), in early May (Santa Maria feast at McCartys), and August 10 (San Lorenzo Day in Acomita).

LAGUNA PUEBLO

This major Keresan-speaking pueblo consists of a central settlement and five smaller villages not far from Acoma Pueblo and just over a half hour from Grants. In fact, Lagunas are closely related to the Acomas who live just 14 miles away. Founded after the 1680 Revolt by refugees from the Rio Grande Valley, Laguna is the youngest of New Mexico's pueblos and has 6,800 residents. Today Many Lagunas are engaged in agriculture or private business, including a tribal-operated commercial center. Federal funds brought modern housing facilities and scholarship programs, one of which helped start the career of famous Laguna author Leslie Marmon Silko. The

Pueblo Pottery: A Glossary of Terms

Burnishing Potters rub a smooth stone on the surface of a pot or bowl after slip (see below) has been applied in order to create a shiny surface on the finished product.

Coiling Pieces of clay are rolled into long, snakelike pieces and then are "coiled" in order to build up the walls of a pot. After the desired size and shape have been created, the pot walls are thinned, scraped, and finally smoothed. This is the method most frequently used by Pueblo potters.

Firing Today most potters fire (bake in order to harden) their work in an electric or gas-fired kiln, but Pueblo potters fire their work in outdoor ovens using a variety of fuels, including animal dung.

Incising The cutting of designs into the surface of a pot before the firing process.

Matte The opposite of burnished, a matte finish is dull. Many Pueblo Indians, including Acoma, Picuris, and Zia, use matte finishes.

Micaceous The clay of micaceous pots contains small particles of mica, which sparkle when held up to the light. Taos and Picuris Pueblo clays contain quite a bit of mica.

Polychrome If a potter uses three or more colors on a pot, it is referred to as polychrome.

Sgraffito The scratching of a pot surface to create designs after it has been fired.

Slip Put simply, slip is very watery clay. It is applied to a piece of pottery just before firing in order to fill in air holes and create a uniform color.

employment rate here is high, and this is widely considered one of New Mexico's wealthiest pueblos.

ESSENTIALS

GETTING THERE From Grants, take I-40 east for 32 miles. The pueblo is 50 miles west of Albuquerque along I-40.

VISITOR INFORMATION For information about Laguna before you leave home, contact the tribal governor's office at P.O. Box 194, Laguna Pueblo, NM 87026, or call ☎ 505/552-6654. No admission is charged and there is no photo fee, but some restrictions apply from village to village. Visitors are welcome during daylight hours year-round.

SEEING THE HIGHLIGHTS

There are no organized tours of Laguna Pueblo, but you can wander around (respecting the fact that this is home to thousands of people) on your own at your leisure. The outlying villages of Mesita, Paguate, Paraje, Encinal, and Seama are interesting in their own rights, but the best place to visit is the old pueblo where you can see the massive stone church, San Jose de Laguna, built in 1699, and famous for its interior. It was restored in the 1930s.

DANCES & CEREMONIES

Pueblo and Navajo people from throughout the region attend St. Joseph's Feast Day (September 19) at Old Laguna Village. The fair begins in the morning with a mass and procession, followed by a harvest dance, sports events, and a carnival. New Year's Day (January 1) and Three Kings Day (January 6) are also celebrated at the pueblo with processions and dances. Each smaller village has its own feast day between July 26 and October 17; call the pueblo office for details.

AN ATTRACTION NEAR LAGUNA

Seboyeta, the oldest Hispanic community in western New Mexico, is 3¹/₂ miles north of Paguate, outside Laguna Pueblo. It still shows ruins of adobe fortress walls built in the 1830s to protect the village from Navajo attack. The Mission of Our Lady of Sorrows was built in the 1830s, as was the nearby Shrine of Los Portales, built in a cave north of town.

AN ATTRACTION IN NEARBY GRANTS

✪ **The New Mexico Museum of Mining.** 100 N. Iron St. at Santa Fe Ave. ☎ **800/ 748-2142** or 505/287-4802. Admission $2 and includes guided tour or self-guiding "sound stick." $1.50 seniors over 60; free for children 8 and under. May–Sept Mon–Sat 9am–6pm, Sun noon–6pm; Oct–Apr Mon–Sat 9am–4pm, Sun noon–4pm.

The world's only uranium-mining museum is structured over a re-creation of an actual underground mine, complete with original machinery and equipment.

Begin your tour on the first level of the museum, following a time line of dinosaur bones and ancient pueblo pottery from the prehistory of the Grants area to the industry of the late 20th century. Then an elevator, representing the "cage" of deep-rock mining, carries you into the mine shaft.

Once underground, you can touch and feel the mining tools, equipment, and cement walls. You'll start at the station, a dimly lit cavern where workers, materials, and yellow uranium ore entered and left the mine. You'll see huge ore cars and actual blasting caps. Deep in the mine, you'll duck into an open "stope," stripped of all ore and off-limits in an actual mine. Retired miners often lead tours, and their memories are worth 10 times the price of admission.

WHERE TO STAY IN NEARBY GRANTS

Grants was established in the late 19th century as a railroad town and ranching center. It didn't really come of age until 1950, when Paddy Martinez, a Navajo sheep rancher, discovered uranium near Haystack Mountain, northwest of town. Grants has boomed and declined twice since then. Mines remain active today, though in some decline. The city is the seat of expansive Cíbola County, which stretches from the Arizona border nearly to Albuquerque. For more information on the area contact the **Grants/Cíbola Country Chamber of Commerce** at 100 N. Iron Ave. (P.O. Box 297), Grants, NM 87020 (☎ **800/748-2142** or 505/287-4802). It's located in the same building as the Mining Museum.

Grants hotels are all on or near Route 66, with major properties near I-40 interchanges, and smaller or older motels nearer downtown. Lodger's tax is 5%, which is added to the gross receipts tax of 6.3125% for a total room tax of just over 11%. Parking is usually free.

Best Western Grants Inn. 1501 E. Santa Fe Ave, I-40 Exit 85 (P.O. Drawer T), Grants, NM 87020. ☎ **800/528-1234,** 800/600-5221, or 505/287-7901. Fax 505/285-5751. 125 rms. A/C FRIDGE TV TEL. $66–$97 double. AE, DC, DISC, MC, V.

Owned by Maloof Hotels, which operates six others in New Mexico, the inn offers a touch of the tropics in this semiarid land. Skylights nourish a junglelike central courtyard of lush trees and tall plants, which surround an indoor swimming pool and cafe.

Rooms are pleasant and modern. Standard units have king-size or two queen-size beds with Southwestern decor. "King suites" are set up for executive travel with a phone at a working desk, an oversize dresser, and a sleeper sofa in a sitting area. Some rooms are designated for nonsmokers and people with disabilities.

The inn's cafe offers an outdoor experience indoors beneath the skylight. Umbrellas shade the tables, while silk fuchsias and draping vines lend atmosphere. American fare is served daily for breakfast and dinner. Services and facilities include room service during restaurant hours, valet laundry, 24-hour desk, an indoor swimming pool, men's and women's saunas, hot tub, guest Laundromat, video games area, gift shop, and meeting rooms. Pets are welcome.

⑤ Sands Motel. 112 McArthur St. (P.O. Box 1437), Grants, NM 87020. ☎ **800/424-7679** or 505/287-2996. 24 rms. A/C FRIDGE TV TEL. $43 double. AE, CB, DC, DISC, MC, V.

A family style motel set back a block from Highway 66, the Sands has 24 nicely appointed rooms. Rooms have king, queen, and double beds; some have a dressing area between the bedroom and bathroom. Nonsmoking rooms are available. Fee for pets.

CAMPING   There are three excellent campgrounds with both RV and tenting facilities in Grants. **Blue Spruce RV Park** (☎ 505/287-2560) has 28 sites and 19 full hookups and is open year-round. Cable television and phone hookups are available as are laundry facilities, grills, and a recreation room. To reach to park, take I-40 to exit 81 and then go ¼ mile south on NM 53.

Cíbola Sands RV Park (☎ 505/287-4376), also open year-round, offers 54 sites, 38 full hookups, free cable TV hookup, laundry and limited grocery facilities, a recreation room, and a playground. From the junction of I-40 and NM 53 (westbound exit 81, eastbound exit 81A) go ¼ mile south on NM 53, then one block east on Frontage Road.

Lavaland RV Park (☎ **505/287-8665**) has 58 sites, 39 full hookups, and free cable and telephone hookups. Air-conditioning and heating hookups are available at an extra charge. In addition, there are cabins, laundry and limited grocery facilities, picnic tables and grills, and recreation facilities. Lavaland is open year-round. From I-40, get off at exit 85 and go 100 yards south on Access Road.

WHERE TO DINE IN NEARBY GRANTS

In general, you won't find places to eat at pueblos or national monuments, so you're best off looking for a restaurant (for dinner at least) in Grants.

✪ El Jardin Palacios. 319 W. Santa Fe Ave. ☎ **505/285-5231.** $2.50–$7.95. AE, MC, V. Mon–Fri 11am–2:30pm, Mon–Sat 5–9pm. NEW MEXICAN.

This friendly restaurant, owned and operated by the Palacio family, is located on Route 66. Plants hang in the windows, and original oils adorn the walls, giving the place a homey feeling.

The food is of high quality. Beef is shredded and sautéed for tacos, not ground and fried; the specialty is chimichangas—meat, chicken, or machaca. There is also trout, shrimp, and scampi; shrimp, beef, and chicken fajitas; and chicken enchiladas. If you have room, try the florencita, a dessert special with fruit filling. Beer and wine are served.

Grants Station Restaurant. 200 W. Santa Fe Ave. ☎ **505/287-2334.** Main courses $5–$11.95; lunch $4.25–$5.95; breakfast $2.30–$5. AE, DISC, MC, V. Daily 6am–11pm. AMERICAN.

You can't miss this place: An old red Santa Fe Railroad caboose stands outside on a length of track. The train theme extends inside with old railroad signs and other memorabilia, donated by numerous aficionados, many of them "just passing through."

This is a great place for breakfast, which is served all day. And you'll find basic American favorites: chicken-fried steak, sandwiches, salads, fried chicken, top sirloin, and filet of perch. A few Mexican dishes, like tacos, burritos, and fajitas, are also on the menu, and there's an all-you-can-eat Sunday brunch from 10am to 2pm (just $5.75). No alcohol is served.

La Ventana. 110¹/₂ Geis St., Hillcrest Center. ☎ **505/287-9393.** Reservations recommended. Main courses $3.95–$13.95; lunch $2.75–$6.75. AE, CB, DC, DISC, MC, V. Mon–Sat 11am–11pm. STEAKS.

The newly remodeled Southwestern decor displays original Navajo sand paintings and a massive metal sculpture of two horses by John F. Prazen. Prime rib and steaks are the top sellers here, and fresh seafood is served on weekends. Chicken and beef fajitas are also popular. La Ventana has a full bar.

Monte Carlo Restaurant and Lounge. 721 W. Santa Fe Ave. ☎ **505/287-9250.** Main courses $5.75–$12.95; lunch $2.50–$5.50; breakfast $1.30–$6.60. AE, DISC, MC, V. Daily 7am–10pm. NEW MEXICAN/STEAKS.

Open since 1947, this adobe restaurant is one of the few buildings in Grants that predates the uranium boom. The menu hasn't changed a lot over the years: It includes steak Marie (topped with green chile and melted cheese), chile rellenos del mar (with shrimp and crabmeat), even Navajo tacos (frybread with borracho beans, chile, and vegetables) and Mexican pizza. There's live music as well as a full bar in the Cíbola Room. Children's menu is available.

3 El Malpais & El Morro National Monuments

Northwestern New Mexico has two national monuments that are must-sees for anyone touring this region.

EL MALPAIS: EXPLORING THE BADLANDS

Designated a national monument in 1987, El Malpais (Spanish for "badlands") is considered one of the outstanding examples of volcanic landscapes in the United States. El Malpais contains 115,000 acres of cinder cones, vast lava flows, hundreds of lava tubes, ice caves, sandstone cliffs, natural bridges and arches, Anasazi ruins, ancient Native American trails, and Spanish and Anglo homesteads.

ESSENTIALS

GETTING THERE   There are two approaches to El Malpais, via NM 117 and NM 53. Route 117 exits I-40 7 miles east of Grants.

VISITOR INFORMATION   Admission to El Malpais is free (unless you're visiting the privately owned Ice Caves), and it's open to visitors year-round. The visitors center, located off route 53 between mile markers 63 and 64, is open daily from 8am to 4:30pm. Here you can pick up maps of the park, leaflets on specific trails, and other details about exploring the monument. For more information, write El Malpais National Monument, NPS, P.O. Box 939, Grants, NM 87020 or call **505/285-4641.** You can also contact the El Malpais Information center at **505/287-3407.**

SEEING THE HIGHLIGHTS

From **Sandstone Bluffs Overlook** (10 miles south of I-40 off NM 117) many craters are visible in the lava flow, which extends for miles along the eastern flank of the

Continental Divide. The most recent flows date back only 1,000 years: Native American legends tell of rivers of "fire rock." Seventeen miles south of I-40 is **La Ventana Natural Arch,** the largest accessible natural arch in New Mexico.

From NM 53, which exits I-40 just west of Grants, visitors have access to the **Zuni-Acoma Trail,** an ancient Pueblo trade route that crosses four major lava flows in a 7¹/₂-mile (one-way) hike. A printed trail guide is available. **El Calderon,** a forested area 20 miles south of I-40, is a trailhead for exploring a cinder cone, lava tubes, and a bat cave. (*Warning:* Hikers should not enter the bat cave or otherwise disturb the bats.)

The largest of all Malpais cinder cones, **Bandera Crater,** is on private property 25 miles south of I-40. The National Park Service has laid plans to absorb this commercial operation, known as **Ice Caves Resort** (☎ **505/783-4303**). Visitors pay $6 to hike up the crater or walk to the edge of an ice cave.

Perhaps the most fascinating phenomenon of El Malpais are the lava tubes, formed when the outer surface of a lava flow cooled and solidified. When the lava river drained, tunnel-like caves were left. Ice caves within some of the tubes have delicate ice-crystal ceilings, ice stalactites, and floors like ice rinks.

HIKING & CAMPING

Several hiking trails can be found throughout El Malpais, including the above-mentioned Zuni-Acoma Trail. Most are marked with rock cairns; some are dirt trails. The best times to hike this area are spring and fall, when it's not too hot. Be sure to carry plenty of water with you; do not drink surface water. You are pretty much on your own when exploring this area, so prepare accordingly. Carrying first-aid gear is always a good idea; the lava rocks can be extremely sharp and inflict nasty cuts. Hikers should wear sturdy boots, long pants, and leather gloves when exploring the lava and caves. In addition, never go into a cave alone. The Park Service advises wearing hard hats, boots, protective clothing, and gloves and carrying three sources of light when entering lava tubes. The weather can change suddenly, so be prepared; if lightning is around, move off the lava as soon as possible

Primitive camping is allowed in the park, but you must first obtain a free Back-country Permit from the visitors center.

EL MORRO NATIONAL MONUMENT

Travelers who like to look history straight in the eye are fascinated by "Inscription Rock," located 43 miles west of Grants along NM 53. Looming up out of the sand and sagebrush is a bluff 200 feet high, holding some of the most captivating messages in North America. Its sandstone face displays a written record of nearly every explorer, conquistador, missionary, army officer, surveyor, and pioneer emigrant who passed this way between 1605—when Gov. Don Juan de Onate carved the first inscription—and 1906, when it was preserved by the National Park Service. Onate's inscription, dated April 16, 1605, was perhaps the first graffiti left by any European in America, but El Morro also boasts earlier petroglyph carvings by Native Americans.

A paved walkway makes it easy to walk to the writings, and there is a stone stairway leading up to other treasures. One reads: "Year of 1716 on the 26th of August passed by here Don Feliz Martinez, Governor and Captain General of this realm to the reduction and conquest of the Moqui." Confident of success as he was, Martinez actually got nowhere with any "conquest of the Moqui," or Hopi, peoples. After a two-month battle they chased him back to Santa Fe.

Another special group to pass by this way was the U.S. Camel Corps, trekking past on their way from Texas to California in 1857. The camels worked out fine in mountains and deserts, outlasting horses and mules 10 to 1, but the Civil War ended the experiment. When Peachy Breckinridge, fresh out of the Virginia Military Academy, came by with 25 camels, he noted the fact on the stone here.

El Morro was at one time as famous as the Blarney Stone of Ireland: Everybody had to stop by and make a mark. But when the Santa Fe Railroad was laid 25 miles to the north, El Morro was no longer on the main route to California, and from the 1870s, the tradition began to die out.

Atop Inscription Rock via a short, steep trail are ruins of an Anasazi pueblo occupying an area 200 by 300 feet. Its name, Atsinna, suggests that carving one's name here is a very old custom indeed: The word, in Zuni, means "writing on rock."

ESSENTIALS

GETTING THERE   El Morro is located 43 miles west of Grants along NM 53.

VISITOR INFORMATION   Admission to El Morro is $4 per car or $2 per person. The visitors center is open in the summer from 9am to 7pm, and from 9am to 5pm in the winter. It will take you between two and four hours to visit the museum and hike a couple of trails.

Self-guided trail booklets are available at the visitors center and trails are open in the summer from 9am to 6pm, and 9am to 5pm in winter. The park is closed on December 25 and January 1.

A museum at the visitors center features exhibits on the 700 years of human activity at El Morro. A 15-minute video gives visitors a good introduction to the park. Also within the visitors center is a bookstore where you can pick up souvenirs or educational and informational books.

For more information, write El Morro National Monument, Box 43, Ramah, NM 87321, or call **505/783-4226.**

CAMPING

Though it isn't necessary to camp here in order to see most of the park, a nine-site campground at El Morro is open year-round. Fees are charged in the summer months. There are no supplies available within the park, so if you're planning on spending a night or two be sure to arrive well-equipped.

NEARBY LODGING & DINING

Two private enterprises near El Morro are worthy of note. **El Morro Lodge,** Route 2, Box 44, Ramah, NM 87321 (☎ **505/783-4612**), has cabins, and RV and tent camping.

West of El Morro, in Ramah, the **Blue Corn Restaurant,** NM 53 (☎ **505/783-4671**), serves some of the most innovative contemporary American cuisine imaginable in an isolated location like this. Daily specials, in the $10 to $12 range, include apricot-stuffed chicken breast and red snapper with cilantro cream sauce. It's open from 11am to 8:30pm, Thursday to Sunday in summer.

EXPLORING THE AREA: CÍBOLA NATIONAL FOREST

For those of you who do a lot of hiking and national forest/park exploration, you'll know that there's a big difference between a national park and a national forest. Usually national parks are 100% protected parcels of land (in some places dogs aren't even allowed), whereas national forests are federally owned pieces of land on which certain activities are permitted: logging, hunting, camping, hiking, and sometimes there are even maintained trails for motorcycles. Cíbola National Forest is actually a combination of parcels of land throughout the state that total over 1.6 million acres. Altitudes vary from 5,000 to 11,301 feet, and the forest includes the Datil, Gallinas, Bear, Manzano, Sandia, San Mateo, and Zuni Mountains.

Two major pieces of the forest flank I-40 on either side of Grants, near the pueblos and monuments described above. To the northeast of Grants, NM 547 leads some 20 miles into the San Mateo Mountains. The range's high point, and the highest point in the forest, 11,301-foot Mount Taylor, is home of the annual Mount Taylor Winter Quadrathlon in February. The route passes two campgrounds, Lobo Canyon and Coal Mine Canyon. Hiking, enjoying magnificent scenery, and elk hunting are popular in summer, cross-country skiing in winter.

To the west of Grants run the Zuni Mountains, a heavily forested range topped by 9,253-foot Mount Sedgewick. Ask at the **Grants/Cíbola County Chamber of Commerce,** 100 N Iron Ave. (☎ **800/748-2142** or 505/287-4802), or the Mount Taylor Ranger District (see address and phone below) in Grants, for the "Zuni Mountain Historic Auto Tour" brochure. This describes a 61-mile loop, including over 45 miles of unpaved road with no gas or water en route, that gives unusual insight into the region's early 20th-century logging and mining activities.

On the northern slope of the Zuni Mountains, but outside of the national forest, is **Bluewater Lake State Park** (☎ 505/876-2391). At 7,400 feet, this forested recreational site offers fishing for rainbow trout, boating (rentals available), hiking, picnicking, and camping. There is a cafe and store on the east shore, 7 miles south of I-40 Exit 63 (18 miles west of Grants). Ice fishing is popular in winter.

JUST THE FACTS   For more information about this section of Cíbola National Forest, write to Cíbola National Forest, Mount Taylor Ranger District, 1800 Lobo Canyon Rd., Grants, NM 87020, or call **505/287-8833.** For general information about different areas of the National Forest, contact Cíbola National Forest, 2113 Osuna Rd. NE, Suite A, Albuquerque, NM 87113-1001, or call **505/761-4650.**

4 Gallup: Gateway to Indian Country

There's more to Gallup than the city's seemingly endless Route 66 neon strip might at first indicate. For one thing, the city is the self-proclaimed "Gateway to Indian Country" and the site of the Intertribal Ceremonial every August. Founded on the rail line in 1881 as a coal supply town, Gallup has a frontier atmosphere that lingers among the late 19th- and early 20th-century buildings. A proliferation of Native American trading posts and pawnbrokers offers opportunities for shopping and bargaining. The city is the market center for the Navajo Reservation to the north and Zuni Pueblo to the south.

ESSENTIALS

GETTING THERE   By Car   From Albuquerque, take I-40 west (2¹/₂ hours). From Farmington, take US 64 west to Shiprock, then US 666 south (2¹/₂ hours). From Flagstaff, Arizona, take I-40 east (3 hours).

By Plane   Gallup Municipal Airport, West Highway 66 (☎ **505/722-4896**), is served several times daily by **America West Express** (☎ **800/235-9292** or 505/ 722-5404). There are regular connections to and from Farmington and Phoenix, Arizona.

VISITOR INFORMATION   The **Gallup Convention and Visitors Bureau,** 701 Montoya Blvd. (P.O. Box 600), Gallup, NM 87305 (☎ **800/242-4282** or 505/863-3841), is conveniently located in Miyamura Park, just north of the main I-40 interchange for downtown Gallup. Or contact the **Gallup-McKinley County Chamber of Commerce,** P.O. Box 1395, Gallup, NM 87305 (☎ **505/ 722-2228**).

WHAT TO SEE & DO
A WALKING TOUR OF GALLUP

Gallup has 20 buildings that are either listed on, or have been nominated to, the National Register of Historic Places. Start at the **Santa Fe Railroad Depot,** East 66 Avenue and Strong Street. Built in 1923 in modified mission style with heavy Spanish-Pueblo revival–style massing, it is earmarked to be renovated into a community transportation and cultural center. Across the highway, the **Drake Hotel** (now the Turquoise Club), built of blond brick in 1919, had the Prohibition-era reputation of being controlled by bootleggers, with wine running in the faucets in place of water. Two blocks west, the 1928 **White Cafe,** 100 W. 66 Ave., is an elaborate decorative brick structure that catered to the early auto tourist traffic. **Kitchen's Opera House,** 218 W. 66 Ave., dates from 1895; it had a second-floor stage for all kinds of functions and performances and a first-floor saloon and cafe. A block farther, the **Rex Hotel,** 300 W. 66 Ave., was constructed of locally quarried sandstone; once known for its "ladies of the night," it's now a police substation.

A block north of the police station, at 101 N. Third St., is the **C. N. Cotton Warehouse** (now Associated Grocers). Built about 1897 in the New Mexico vernacular style, with a sandstone foundation and adobe-block walls, it has a statue in front that is a city landmark: **Manuelito,** the last Navajo chief to surrender to U.S. soldiers. Mr. Cotton, a trader who admired the Navajo's bravery, commissioned the statue.

Reverse course, and head back south two blocks on Third Street. Turn east on Coal Avenue. The **Grand Hotel,** 306 W. Coal Ave., was built about 1925 as the depot for transcontinental buses on Route 66, as well as a travelers' hotel. The **Chief Theater,** 228 W. Coal Ave., was built in 1920; but in 1936 it was completely redesigned in Pueblo-deco style, with zigzag relief and geometric form, by R. E. "Griff" Griffith, brother of Hollywood producer D. W. Griffith. Almost across the street, the 1928 **El Morro Theater** is of Spanish colonial revival style with an ornate symmetry from the parapet to the corbels. Next door, the **Ruiz Optical Building** has been decorated with Native American kachinas between the second-floor windows.

South two blocks, the **McKinley County Court House,** 201 W. Hill Ave., was built in 1938 in Spanish Pueblo revival style. The bell tower and upper stories display stylized projecting vigas, while wood beams and corbels define the entry. Indian-motif reliefs, tiles, and paintings are found throughout. Back at the corner of First and Coal, the **Old Post Office** (now United Cable Television) is an eclectic mix of Mediterranean, decorative brick commercial, and Spanish Pueblo–revival styles. Large carved eagles are used as corbels, and the beams have brightly painted rope molding lines.

GETTING OUTSIDE: A NEARBY STATE PARK

Six miles east of downtown Gallup, **Red Rock State Park,** NM 566 (P.O. Box 328), Church Rock, NM 87311 (☎ 505/722-3829), with its natural amphitheater, is set against red sandstone buttes. It includes an auditorium/convention center, historical museum, post office, trading post, stables, and modern campgrounds.

The 8,000-seat arena is the site of numerous annual events, including the Intertribal Indian Ceremonial in mid-August. Red Rock Convention Center accommodates 600 for trade shows or concert performances.

The Red Rock Museum has displays on prehistoric Anasazi and modern Zuni, Hopi, and Navajo cultures, and changing art gallery exhibits. From June through September, corn, beans, and squash are grown outside in a traditional Pueblo "waffle garden." The museum is open Monday through Friday from 8:30am to 4:30pm, with extended hours in summer. Admission is $1 for adults, 50¢ for children.

SHOPPING: BEST BUYS ON JEWELRY & CRAFTS

Nowhere are the jewelry and crafts of Navajo, Zuni, and Hopi tribes less expensive than in Gallup. The most intriguing places to shop are the trading posts and pawnshops, which provide a surprising range of services for their largely Native American clientele and have little in common with the pawnshops of large American cities.

Navajoland ✪ **pawnbrokers** in essence are bankers, at least from the Navajo and Zuni viewpoint. They're like savings-and-loan institutions, but a lot less likely to fold. In fact, they're an integral part of the economic structure of the Gallup area, providing such services as the safekeeping of valuable personal goods and the payment of small collateral loans.

Security systems in Navajo hogans and Zuni pueblos are nonexistent. So Native Americans go to the trading post with their turquoise and silver jewelry, ceremonial baskets, hand-tanned hides, saddles, and guns, and "pawn" them for safekeeping. They may accept a payment far less than the value of the goods, because the smaller the amount of the loan, the easier it is to redeem the items when they are needed.

Pawnbrokers are also collateral lenders. Traditionally, Navajos visited trading posts to exchange handmade goods for cash or other products. Today, banks won't take jewelry or guns as loan collateral, but the trading post will. What's more, the trader will hold onto the items for months or even years before deeming it "dead" and putting it up for sale. Less than 5% of items ever go unredeemed.

Those shopping for jewelry should look for silver concho belts, worn with jeans and Southwestern skirts, cuff bracelets, and necklaces, from traditional squash blossoms to silver beads and *heishi,* very fine beads worn in several strands. Earrings may be only in silver, or they may be decorated with varying stones.

For men, bolo ties and belt buckles of silver and/or turquoise are popular. Silver concho hatbands go great on Stetson hats. A silver or gold handcrafted earring, sometimes decorated with turquoise, is a big seller.

Handwoven Native American rugs may be draped on couches, hung on walls, or used on floors. Also look for pottery, kachinas, and sculpture.

Most shops are open Monday through Saturday from 9am to 5pm. Some pawnbrokers in town include **Jean's All Indian Pawn Shop,** 2000 E. Hwy. 66 (☎ 505/722-4471); **T&R Pawn,** 1300 W. I-40 Frontage Rd., Rio West Mall (☎ 505/722-3473); and **Trader Billy K's,** 118 W. 66 Ave. (☎ 505/722-5151). For a look at everything from livestock to unusual souvenirs, visit **Ellis Tanner Trading Company,** Munoz Avenue between I-40 (exit 20) and Zuni Road (☎ 505/863-4434); **First American Traders of Gallup,** 2201 W. Hwy. 66 (☎ 505/722-6601); **Richardson Trading and Cash Pawn,** 222 W. 66 Ave. (☎ 505/722-4762); **Shi'ma Traders,** 216 W. Coal Ave. (☎ 505/722-5500); **Silver Dust Trading Co.,** 120 W. 66 Ave. (☎ 505/722-4848); **Tobe Turpen's Indian Trading Company,** 1710 S. Second St. (☎ 505/722-3806); and **Turney's,** 207 S. Third St. (☎ 505/863-6504).

INDIAN DANCES

Nightly Native American dance performances take place at the corner of 66 Avenue and First Street in Gallup, each evening at 7pm from Memorial Day through Labor Day. Call ☎ 505/863-1243 for more information.

WHERE TO STAY

Virtually every accommodation in Gallup is somewhere along Route 66, either near the I-40 interchanges or on the highway through downtown.

MODERATE

Best Western Gallup Inn. 3009 W. Hwy. 66, Gallup, NM 87301. ☎ **800/528-1234** or 505/722-2221. Fax 505/722-7442. 124 rms, 21 suites. A/C FRIDGE TV TEL. $64–$98 double; $68–$106 suite. AE, CB, DC, DISC, MC, V.

The trademark of this property is its huge central Atrium Courtyard that contains the hotel cafe at one end, the swimming pool at the other, and skylit trees and plants in between. Three eight-foot paintings of Native American dancers dominate the lobby.

The rooms are large and well kept, with one king-size or two queen-size beds and a big desk-dresser combination. Rooms for nonsmokers and for people with disabilities are available. The Cafe, under the roof of the Atrium Courtyard, serves breakfast and dinner daily. There is a lounge and the hotel has room service, valet laundry service, a 24-hour desk, an indoor swimming pool, hot tub, saunas, weight/exercise room, video games, guest laundry, and gift shop. Pets are allowed.

Days Inn—West. 3201 W. Hwy. 66, Gallup, NM 87301. ☎ **800/DAYS-INN** or 505/863-6889. 74 rms, 1 suite. A/C TV TEL. $45–$65 double; $80–$120 suite. AE, CB, DC, DISC, MC, V.

New in September 1990, this handsome two-story pink adobe building is built in Spanish style with a tile roof. Rooms are of average size, but they're nicely done in desert rose color schemes, with prints of regional native crafts on the walls.

Complimentary coffee, donuts, and juice are served in the lobby in the morning. The hotel offers a 24-hour desk, nonsmoking rooms and rooms accessible for people with disabilities, an indoor swimming pool, hot tub, and guest laundry. No pets.

✪ **El Rancho Hotel and Motel.** 1000 E. 66 Ave., Gallup, NM 87301. ☎ **800/543-6351** or 505/863-9311. Fax 505/722-5917. 98 rms, 2 suites. A/C TV TEL. $47–$65 double; $76 suite. AE, CB, DC, DISC, MC, V.

This historic hotel owes as much to Hollywood as to Gallup. Built in 1937 by R. E. "Griff" Griffith, brother of movie mogul D. W. Griffith, it became *the* place for film companies to set up headquarters in the Southwest. Between the 1940s and 1960s, a who's who of Hollywood stayed here. Their autographed photos line the walls of the hotel's cafe. Spencer Tracy and Katharine Hepburn stayed here during production of *The Sea of Grass;* Burt Lancaster and Lee Remick were guests when they made *The Hallelujah Trail.* Gene Autry, Lucille Ball, Jack Benny, Humphrey Bogart, James Cagney, Rhonda Flemming, Errol Flynn, Henry Fonda, John Forsythe, Paulette Goddard, Susan Hayward, William Holden, the Marx Brothers, Fred MacMurray, Robert Mitchum, Gregory Peck, Tyrone Power, Ronald Reagan, Rosalind Russell, James Stewart, Robert Taylor, Gene Tierney, John Wayne, and Mae West have all been here—the list goes on and on.

In 1986, Gallup businessman Armand Ortega, a longtime jewelry merchant, bought a run-down El Rancho and restored it to its earlier elegance. The lobby staircase rises to the mezzanine on either side of an enormous stone fireplace, while heavy ceiling beams and railings made of tree limbs give the room a hunting-lodge ambience. The hotel is on the National Register of Historic Places.

Rooms in El Rancho differ one to the next, and are named for the stars who stayed in them. There are ceiling fans, and Southwest art prints on the walls. The corridors bear small paintings of Native American life. Many rooms have balconies.

El Rancho's full-service restaurant is open from 6:30am to 10pm daily. The '49er Lounge stays lively later. Services and facilities include a 24-hour desk, courtesy car (by request), a seasonal outdoor pool, guest Laundromat, Ortega's Indian Store, and meeting space for 150.

Holiday Inn. 2915 W. Hwy. 66, Gallup, NM 87301. ☎ **800/432-2211** or 505/722-2201. Fax 505/722-9616. 212 rms. A/C TV TEL. $52–$95 single or double. AE, CB, DC, DISC, JCB, MC, V.

The spacious lobby of this hotel makes indoors feel like outdoors. A small fountain and various plants stand beneath a high ceiling, while Native American motifs and small murals are painted on some of the walls.

Rooms, many decorated with Southwest decor in tones of purple and rust, contain a king-size or two double beds, a hide-a-bed sofa or leisure chairs, a desk, and a clock radio. Some rooms accommodate nonsmokers or people with disabilities

The hotel has two restaurants and a lounge, which features live music and dancing nightly. Room service, valet laundry service, 24-hour desk, courtesy van, an indoor swimming pool, hot tub, sauna, weight equipment, guest laundry, gift shop, and meeting facilities for 800 are also available. Pets are allowed.

INEXPENSIVE

⑤ Blue Spruce Lodge. 1119 E. 66 Ave., Gallup, NM 87301. ☎ **505/863-5211.** 20 rms. A/C TV TEL. $26–$32 double. AE, CB, DC, DISC, MC, V.

This little motel is nothing fancy, but it's clean, hospitable, and a step ahead of others in friendliness. Rooms have standard furnishings; some have shower-bath combinations, others showers only. Small pets are allowed.

El Capitan Motel. 1300 E. 66 Ave., Gallup, NM 87301. ☎ **505/863-6828.** 42 rms, 5 suites. A/C TV TEL. $32–$42 double; $44–$54 suite. AE, CB, DC, DISC, MC, V.

A one-story adobe-style motel, El Capitan has recently been remodeled. Rooms are very spacious and simply but comfortably furnished with full-size beds, desk-dresser, table and chairs, and vanity/dressing area. Family suites that sleep five are a bit more eclectic in appearance than the standard guest rooms. In-room coffee is provided. Pets are accepted.

CAMPING

As in the rest of the state, there are plenty of places to pitch a tent or hook up your RV in the Gallup area. **KOA Gallup** (☎ 800/562-3915) has 145 sites, 50 full hookups (cable TV will cost extra), and cabins. There are grocery and laundry facilities. Recreation facilities include coin games, a seasonal heated swimming pool, and a playground. To reach the campground, take I-40 to the US 66/Business I-40 junction (exit 16); go 1 mile east on US 66/Business I-40.

At **Red Rock State Park** (☎ 505/722-2839) there are 200 sites—50 with no hookups and 150 with water and electricity. Group sites for tenting and RVs are available. Also accessible are a grocery store, picnic tables, and grills. Red Rock State Park, open year-round, also has a playground, horse riding trails, a sports field, and hiking trails.

WHERE TO DINE

✪ Panz Alegra. 1201 E. 66 Ave., Gallup. ☎ **505/722-7229.** Reservations recommended. Main courses $4–$12; lunch $3–$7.95. AE, CB, DC, DISC, MC, V. Mon–Sat 11am–10pm. MEXICAN, STEAK & SEAFOOD.

This brown-stone and yellow-adobe building harbors what may be Gallup's finest restaurant. Behind brick arches and planter boxes of silk flowers, diners enjoy steak-and-seafood platters, or opt for the fine New Mexican food. House specialties include carne adovada, arroz con pollo, and the Alegra steak with green chile and cheese. The restaurant has a full bar.

The Ranch Kitchen. 3001 W. Hwy. 66, Gallup. ☎ **505/722-2537.** Reservations for large parties. Main courses $5.95–$12.95; lunch $3.50–$7.95; breakfast $1.95–$5.25. AE, CB, DC, MC, V. Daily, summer 6am–10pm; winter 6am–9pm. AMERICAN/MEXICAN.

An institution since 1954, the Ranch Kitchen has the perfect location to attract tourists, wedged between Gallup's two largest accommodations at the west end of the city. It takes full advantage of that, with two gift shops flanking the entrance and a variety of colorful piñatas, kachinas, and other folk art hanging everywhere. But come for the food. It's hard to pass up the chicken and ribs, barbecued outside when weather permits. There's great chili, excellent Navajo tacos and rancho grande burritos, fine steaks, and a big soup-and-salad buffet. Children and seniors can order smaller portions from their own menus. The restaurant serves wine and beer.

5 Zuni Pueblo & the Navajo Reservation

ZUNI PUEBLO

The largest of New Mexico's occupied pueblos, Zuni was first seen by Spanish explorers in 1539. The sun reflecting off the adobe buildings created a golden glow, leading to tales of cities of gold and Coronado's search for the fabled Seven Cities of Cíbola. This encounter was the first ever by Southwestern Native Americans with Europeans.

When the Spanish first arrived, there were approximately 3,000 Zunis living in six different villages, and they had occupied the region for more than 300 years. Agriculture and trade were their primary means of support and they were strongly religious. The first and second encounters with the Spanish were tragic; in two separate misunderstandings more than 20 people were killed (mostly Zunis).

ESSENTIALS

GETTING THERE   Zuni Pueblo is located about 38 miles south of Gallup via state roads 602 and 53.

VISITOR INFORMATION   Admission is free and visitors are welcome daily from dawn to dusk. For advance information, write to the Tribal Office, P.O. Box 339, Zuni, NM 87327 or call **505/782-4481, ext. 401.** As at all Indian reservations, visitors are asked to respect tribal customs and individuals' privacy. Photography is strictly prohibited during some ceremonies, and camera permits must be obtained at other times. In addition, ceremonial dances are completely closed to outsiders

SEEING THE HIGHLIGHTS

Most of the pueblo consists of modern housing, so there isn't really that much to see; however, if you take a walk through the old pueblo you'll get a feeling for time gone by. Make a stop at the Catholic mission, dedicated to Our Lady of Guadalupe. Within you'll find a series of murals that depict events in the Zuni ceremonial calendar. In addition, there are some Native American archeological ruins on Zuni land that date from the early 1200s, but you must obtain permission from the Tribal Office well in advance of your visit in order to see them.

Today, Zuni tribal members are widely acclaimed for their jewelry, made from turquoise, shell, and jet, set in silver in intricate patterns called "needlepoint." The tribe also does fine beadwork, carving in shell and stone, and some pottery. Jewelry and other crafts are sold at the tribally owned **Pueblo of Zuni Arts and Crafts** (☎ **505/782-5531**).

If you're planning your visit for late August, call ahead and see if you're going to be around during the pueblo's annual fair and rodeo.

NAVAJO INDIAN RESERVATION

Navajos comprise the largest Native American tribe in the United States, with more than 200,000 members. Their reservation, known to them as Navajoland, spreads across 24,000 square miles of Arizona, Utah, and New Mexico. The New Mexico portion, extending in a band 45 miles wide from just north of Gallup to the Colorado border, comprises only about 15% of the total area.

Until the 1920s, the Navajo nation governed itself with a complex clan system. When oil was discovered on reservation land, the Navajos established a tribal government to handle the complexities of the 20th century. Today, the Navajo Tribal Council has 88 council delegates representing 110 regional chapters, some two dozen of which are in New Mexico. They meet at least four times a year as a full body in **Window Rock,** Arizona, capital of the Navajo nation, near the New Mexico border 24 miles northwest of Gallup.

Natural resources and tourism are the mainstays of the Navajo economy. Coal, oil, gas, and uranium earn some $45 million a year, with coal alone providing about two-thirds of that sum. Tourism provides nearly the same amount, especially on the Arizona side of the border, which contains or abuts Grand Canyon and Petrified Forest National Parks, Canyon de Chelly, Wupatki, and Navajo National Monuments, and Monument Valley Navajo Tribal Park; and in Utah, Glen Canyon National Recreation Area, Rainbow Bridge and Hovenweep National Monuments, and Four Corners Monument.

The Navajos, like their linguistic cousins the Apaches, belong to the large family of Athapaskan Indians found across Alaska and northwestern Canada and in parts of the northern California coast. They are believed to have migrated to the Southwest about the 14th century. In 1864, after nearly two decades of conflict with the U.S. Army, the entire tribe was rounded up and forced into internment at an agricultural colony near Fort Sumner, New Mexico—an event still recalled as "The Long March." Four years of near-starvation later, the experiment was declared a failure, and the now-contrite Navajos returned to their homeland.

Three to four generations later, 320 Navajo young men served in the U.S. Marine Corps as communications specialists in the Pacific during the Second World War. The code they created, 437 terms based on the extremely complex Navajo language, was never broken by the Japanese. Among those heroes still alive is artist Carl Gorman, coordinator of the Navajo Medicine Man Organization and father of internationally famed painter R. C. Gorman.

While Navajos express themselves artistically in all media, they are best known for their work in silversmithing, sand painting, basketry, and weaving. Distinctive styles of handwoven rugs from Two Grey Hills, Ganado, and Crystal are known worldwide.

ESSENTIALS

GETTING THERE   From Gallup, U.S. Route 666 goes directly through the Navajo Indian Reservation up to Shiprock and from there you can head over to Farmington (see below) on US 64. *Warning:* U.S. 666 between Gallup and Shiprock has been labeled America's "most dangerous highway" by *USA Today.* Drive carefully!

VISITOR INFORMATION   For information in advance of your trip write to P.O. Box 663, Window Rock, AZ 86515 or call **520/871-6659** or 520/871-6436.

WHAT TO SEE & DO

Attractions in Window Rock, Arizona, itself include the **Navajo Nation Council Chambers,** the **Navajo Nation Arts and Crafts Enterprise,** the **Navajo Museum** and Tribal Zoo, St. Michael's Mission Museum, and Window Rock Tribal Park, containing the natural red-rock arch after which the community is named.

In early September, the annual five-day **Navajo Nation Fair** attracts more than 100,000 people to Window Rock for a huge rodeo, parade, carnival, Miss Navajo Nation contest, arts-and-crafts shows, intertribal powwow, concerts, country dancing, and agricultural exhibits. Among smaller annual tribal fairs are the traditional October **Shiprock Navajo Fair,** 90 miles north of Gallup, and the **Eastern Navajo Fair** in Crownpoint, 55 miles northeast of Gallup.

The Crownpoint Rug Weavers Association has 12 public auctions a year, normally on Friday evenings, about five weeks apart.

LODGING & DINING

The place to stay on the reservation is the **Navajo Nation Inn,** Highway 264 (P.O. Box 1687), Window Rock, AZ 86515 (☎ **520/871-4108**). The modern guest rooms are comfortable and inexpensive, and the restaurant offers Navajo specialties. The inn has an attractive weekend package that for $160 includes two nights' lodging and a Saturday bus trip that takes in **Hubbell Trading Post National Historic Site** at Ganado, 30 miles west of Window Rock; **Canyon de Chelly National Monument,** 39 miles north of Ganado; **Navajo Community College** and its Hatathli Gallery at Tsaile, 28 miles northeast of Chinle; and the 56-mile return to Window Rock.

6 Chaco Culture National Historical Park & Aztec Ruins National Monument

These two important historical sights provide insight into the culture of the Anasazi, an advanced Indian civilization that thrived in the Four Corners region between A.D. 750 and 1300.

CHACO CULTURE NATIONAL HISTORICAL PARK

Chaco represents the high point of pre-Columbian Pueblo civilization. A must-see attraction for any visitor even vaguely interested in ancient Indians, it includes more than a dozen large Anasazi ruins occupied from the early 900s to about A.D. 1200, and hundreds of smaller sites in the wide streambed of the normally dry Chaco Wash.

ESSENTIALS

GETTING THERE The only snag to visiting Chaco is its isolation. Farmington is the nearest population center, and it's still a 75-mile, two-hour drive to these ruins. NM 44 takes you as far as the Nageezi Trading Post, but the final 26 miles are graded dirt—fine in dry weather but dangerous when it rains, and often flooded where arroyos cross it. Inquire before leaving the paved highway. (A turnoff at Blanco Trading Post, 8 miles before Nageezi, cuts 5 miles off the trip, but the road is more subject to hazardous conditions. The park can also be reached from Grants via I-40 west to NM 371, then north on NM 57 (with the final 19 miles graded dirt). There's no food, gas, or lodging nearer than Nageezi. There are two entrances, one on NM 57 and the other on San Juan County Road 7900.

VISITOR INFORMATION Admission is $4 per car or $2 per person; seniors 62 and older are admitted free. The park is open from Memorial Day to Labor Day daily from 8am to 6pm; the rest of year it is open daily from 8am to 5pm. A visitors center, with a bookstore and a museum showing films on Anasazi culture, is located in the park. Self-guiding trail brochures are obtained here, as well as permits for the overnight campground (with a water supply, tables, and fireplaces; bring your own wood or charcoal). If you want information before you leave home, write to the Park Ranger, Star Rte. 4 (P.O. Box 6500), Bloomfield, NM 87413 or call **505/786-7014.**

SEEING THE HIGHLIGHTS

Exploring the ruins and hiking are the most popular activities here. A series of pueblo ruins stand within 5 or 6 miles of each other on the broad, flat, treeless canyon floor. Plan to spend at least three or four hours here driving to and exploring the different pueblos. A one-way road from the visitors center loops up one side of the canyon and down the other. Parking lots are scattered along the road near the various pueblos; from most it's only a short walk to the ruins. Pueblo Bonito is the largest. Other ruins accessible directly from the auto road are Chetro Ketl, Pueblo del Arroyo, Kin Kletso, Casa Chiquita, Casa Rinconada, Hungo Pavi, and Una Vida. Some ruins demand half-day backcountry hikes to reach; they include Penasco Blanco, Pueblo Alto, Tsin Kletsin, and Wijiji.

Most ruins are on the north side of the canyon. **Pueblo Bonito,** constructed over three acres of land in the 11th century A.D., may have been the largest apartment house built anywhere in the world before 1887. It had four stories, 600 rooms, and 40 kivas, and may have housed as many as 1,200 people. **Chetro Ketl** had some 500 rooms, 16 kivas, and an impressive enclosed plaza. **Pueblo del Arroyo** was a four-story, D-shaped structure, with about 280 rooms and 20 kivas; **Kin Kletso** had three stories, 100 rooms, and five kivas. **Una Vida,** a short walk from the visitor center, was one of the first pueblos built and has been left only partially excavated; it had 150 rooms and five kivas. **Casa Rinconada,** on the south side of the canyon, is the largest "great kiva" in the park, and is astronomically aligned to the cardinal directions and the summer solstice. It may have been a center for the community at large, used for major spiritual observances.

The Chacoans were skilled masons, building their cities of sandstone blocks mortared with mud, with no metal tools or formal mathematical knowledge. The use of different masonry styles has helped to date the buildings.

The sweeping magnificence of this lost and ruined city, as seen from 100 feet above on the rim of the canyon, impresses visitors most—the outline of Pueblo Bonito, its many kivas forming circles within the great half circle of the community, all of it in the glowing sandstone browns and tans of the land and stone around it. Eventually there were 75 such compact towns all connected with one another in this region of New Mexico.

Aerial photos show hundreds of miles of roads connecting these towns with the Chaco pueblos, one of the longest running 42 miles straight north to Salmon Ruin and the Aztec Ruins (see below). Settlements were spaced along the road at travel intervals of one day. They were not simple trails worn into the stone by foot travel, but engineered roadways 30 feet wide with a berm of rock to contain the fill. Where the road went over flat rock, walls were built along the sides of it. It is this road network that leads some scholars to believe Chaco was the center of a unified Anasazi society.

The Chacoans' trade network, as suggested by artifacts found here, stretched from California to Texas and south into Mexico. Seashell necklaces, copper bells, and the remains of macaws or parrots were found among Chaco artifacts. Some of these items are displayed in the museum at the visitor center.

CAMPING

Gallo Campground, located within the park, is quite popular with hikers. It's located about one mile east of the visitors center; fees are $8 per night. There are 64 sites.

As I said earlier, there are no places at which to stock up on supplies once you start the arduous drive to the canyon, so if you're camping, make sure to be well supplied, especially with water, before you leave home base.

AZTEC RUINS NATIONAL MONUMENT

The ruins of a fabulous 500-room Native American pueblo, abandoned by the Anasazi seven centuries ago, make up this site, 14 miles northeast of Farmington in the town of Aztec on the Animas River. Early Anglo settlers, convinced that the ruins were of Aztec origin, misnamed the site. Despite the fact that this pueblo was built long before the Aztecs of central Mexico lived, the name persisted.

The influence of the Chaco culture is strong at Aztec, as evidenced in the preplanned architecture, the open plaza, and the fine stone masonry in the old walls. But Aztec is best known for its Great Kiva, the only completely reconstructed Anasazi great kiva in existence. About 50 feet in diameter, with a main floor sunken eight feet below the surface of the surrounding ground, this circular ceremonial room rivets the imagination. It's hard not to feel spiritually overwhelmed, and perhaps to feel the presence of people who walked here nearly 1,000 years ago.

Visiting Aztec Ruins National Monument will take you approximately one hour, even if you take the quarter-mile self-guided trail and spend some time in the visitors center, which displays some outstanding examples of Anasazi ceramics and basketry that were found in the ruins.

ESSENTIALS

GETTING THERE   Aztec Ruins is approximately $1/2$ mile north of US 550 on Ruins Road (County Road 2900) on the north edge of the city of Aztec. Ruins Road is the first street immediately west of the Animas River bridge on Highway 550 in Aztec.

VISITOR INFORMATION   Admission is $2 per person and children under 17 are admitted free. The monument is open daily in summer from 8am to 6pm and in winter until 5pm. The monument is closed on Thanksgiving, Christmas, and New Year's days. For more information, write to Park Ranger, Aztec Ruins National Monument, P.O. Box 640, Aztec, NM 87410-0640 or call **505/334-6174.**

CAMPING

Camping is not permitted at the monument. A campground nearby is **KOA Bloomfield** (☎ **505/632-8339**), which offers 83 sites, 73 full hookups, tenting, cabins, laundry and grocery facilities, picnic tables, grills, and firewood. The recreation room/area has coin games, a heated swimming pool, basketball hoop, playground, horseshoes, and volleyball. To reach the campground, take I-40 to the US 666/NM 602 junction (exit 20); go $1/2$ mile south on NM 602 and then west four blocks on Aztec Street. In addition, camping is available at **Navajo Lake State Park.**

7 Farmington: Gateway to the Four Corners Region

A river city of 36,500 residents, Farmington is the gateway to the Four Corners area. Its pride and joy is a system of five parks it's developed along the San Juan River and its tributaries, the Animas and La Plata rivers. In this desert country, it follows that Farmington is an agricultural oasis. It's also an industrial center (for coal, oil, natural gas, and hydroelectricity), and a takeoff point for explorations of the Navajo Reservation, Chaco Culture National Historical Park, and Aztec Ruins National Monument. Nearby towns of Aztec and Bloomfield offer a variety of attractions as well.

ESSENTIALS

GETTING THERE   **By Car**   From Albuquerque, take NM 44 (through Cuba) from the I-25 Bernalillo exit, then turn left (west) on US 64 at Bloomfield (45 minutes). From Gallup, take US 666 north to Shiprock, then turn right (east) on US 64 (2¼ hours). From Taos, follow US 64 all the way (4½ hours). From Durango, Colorado, take US 500 south (one hour).

By Plane   All commercial flights arrive at busy **Four Corners Regional Airport** on Navajo Drive (☎ **505/599-1395**). The principal carrier is **Mesa Airlines** (☎ **800/ MESA-AIR** or 505/326-3338), with more than a dozen daily flights connecting Farmington to Albuquerque and other major cities.

Car-rental agencies at Four Corners airport include **Avis** (☎ **800/331-212** or 505/327-9864), **Budget** (☎ **800/527-0700** or 505/327-7304), **Hertz** (☎ **800/654-3131** or 505/327-6093), and **National** (☎ **800/CAR-RENT** or 505/ 327-0215).

VISITOR INFORMATION   The **Farmington Convention and Visitors Bureau,** 203 W. Main St. (☎ **800/448-1240** or 505/326-7602), is the clearinghouse for tourist information. It shares an address with the **Farmington Chamber of Commerce** (☎ **505/325-0279**).

SEEING THE SIGHTS IN THE AREA
IN FARMINGTON
Farmington Museum. 302 N. Orchard St. ☎ **505/599-1174.** Free admission. Tues–Fri noon–5pm, Sat 10am–5pm.

This museum offers a variety of exhibits on the history of the area's diverse cultures, including a replica of a 1930s Native American trading post. Also featured are exhibits on the area's natural environment, including displays portraying this dry, barren land's days as a seacoast. There's a hands-on children's gallery and a gift shop with educational materials and unique Southwest arts and crafts.

IN NEARBY AZTEC
Aztec Museum and Pioneer Village. 125 N. Main St., Aztec. ☎ **505/334-9829.** $1 donation requested from those 13 to 61 years; free for children and seniors. Summer Mon–Sat 9am–5pm; winter Mon–Sat 10am–4pm.

The museum contains exhibits depicting local history, and the village includes an old train caboose and 13 authentically furnished buildings, both originals and replicas, from the late 1800s, including a log cabin, blacksmith shop, church, jail, school, and doctor's office. Founder's Day, held the second Saturday of September, turns the village into a living museum with demonstrations, Wild West shoot-outs, and a melodrama. In addition, the museum holds oil and gas exhibits from the 1920s, genealogy research resources of local families, and local newspapers on microfilm dating from 1899 to 1985.

IN NEARBY BLOOMFIELD
✪ **Salmon Ruin and San Juan County Archaeological Research Center.** 975 US Hwy. 64 (P.O. Box 125), Bloomfield. ☎ **505/632-2013.** Admission $2 adults, $1 children 6–15, $1.50 seniors. Daily 9am–5pm.

This massive C-shaped pueblo, overlooking the San Juan River, was built in the 11th century as a Chacoan colony. A planned community of some 150 rooms, it offers not only a great kiva in its plaza, but a remarkable, elevated ceremonial chamber or "tower kiva." Just 11 miles east of Farmington, it is one of the most recently excavated ruins in the West.

The site was actually occupied twice—first, for two generations in the 11th century, by the Chacoans; then, in the 13th century, by emigrants from the great Mesa Verde complex to the north. But they, too, soon abandoned the site.

The site today is only 30% excavated, by design. It's being saved for future generations of archeologists, who, it's assumed, will be able to apply advanced research techniques. For now, the archeological research center studies regional sites earmarked for natural-resource exploitation.

In 1990, **Heritage Park** was established on an adjoining plot of land. It comprises a series of reconstructed ancient and historic dwellings representing the area's cultures, from a paleoarchaic sand-dune site to an Anasazi pit house, from Apache wickiups and teepees to Navajo hogans, and an original pioneer homestead. Visitors are encouraged to enter the re-creations; several have arts-and-crafts exhibits or living-history demonstrations.

In the visitor center you'll find a museum displaying artifacts found at the site, a gift shop, and a scholarly research library.

Bloomfield Cultural Complex. 333 S. First St., Bloomfield. ☎ **505/632-2840.** Free admission. Mon–Fri 6am–9pm, Sat 8am–1pm.

Changing exhibits of visual arts and area cultural and historical subjects are featured here, along with hands-on programs for children. The complex also contains the community library, senior citizens' center, and a fitness center.

Bolack Trophy Museum. 3901 Bloomfield Hwy., Bloomfield. ☎ **505/325-4275.** Free admission. Mon–Sat by appointment only.

Former New Mexico governor Tom Bolack put together this collection of hundreds of mounted animal trophies from around the world.

SHOPPING

Downtown Farmington shops are generally open 10am to 6pm Monday through Saturday. Native American arts and crafts are best purchased at trading posts, either downtown on Main or Broadway streets, or west of Farmington on US 64/550 toward Shiprock. Some stores to check out are **Aztec Ruins Trading Post,** Ruins Road, Aztec (☎ 505/334-2943); **Beasley Manning's Trading Co.,** 704 Orchard Homes Dr. (☎ 505/327-5580); **Blanco Trading Post,** NM 44, 25 miles south of Bloomfield (☎ 505/632-1597); **Foutz Indian Room,** 301 W. Main St. (☎ 505/325-9413); **Hogback Trading Co.,** 3221 U.S. 64, Waterflow, 17 miles west of Farmington (☎ 505/598-5154); and **Navajo Trading Company,** 126 E. Main St. (☎ 505/325-1685).

FARMINGTON AFTER DARK: THE ANASAZI PAGEANT

The annual **Anasazi Pageant** is a summer musical about the region's multicultural heritage. Presented in the outdoor Lions Wilderness Park Amphitheater (off College Boulevard) against a sandstone backdrop, *Anasazi, the Ancient Ones* weaves a story around the early history of San Juan area settlers through original music and dance. A Southwestern-style dinner is also available. The production company also presents other musicals at the amphitheater. For information and tickets contact the Anasazi Reservation Desk at **505/327-9336** or the Farmington Convention and Visitors Bureau at **800/448-1240.**

Admission to dinner and show, $18 adults, $16 seniors, $12 children 18 and under. Pageant only, $12 adults, $10 seniors, $6 children. Tickets are sold at the Farmington Convention and Visitors Bureau and at the gate. Tuesday to Sunday, mid-June to late Aug, dinner 6:30pm, performance 8pm.

GETTING OUTSIDE: NEARBY PARKS & RECREATION AREAS

SHIPROCK PEAK

This distinctive landmark, located on the Navajo Indian Reservation southwest of Shiprock, 29 miles west of Farmington via US 64, is known to the Navajo as *Tse bidá hi*, "Rock with wings." Composed of igneous rock flanked by long upright walls of solidified lava, it rises 1,700 feet off the desert floor to an elevation of 7,178 feet. There are viewpoints off US 666, 6 to 7 miles south of the town of Shiprock. You can get closer by taking the tribal road to the community of Red Rock; but to get any nearer this sacred Navajo rock, you must have permission. Climbing is not permitted.

The town named after the rock is a gateway to the Navajo reservation and the Four Corners region. There's a tribal visitor center here.

From Shiprock you might want to make the 32-mile drive west on US 64 to Teec Nos Pos, Arizona, then north on US 160, to the **Four Corners Monument.** A marker here sits astride the only point in the United States where four states meet: New Mexico, Colorado, Utah, and Arizona. There are no facilities.

NAVAJO LAKE STATE PARK

Three recreation sites (San Juan River, Pine River, and Sims Mesa) with camping, fishing, and boating make this the most popular water-sports destination for residents of northwestern New Mexico. Trout, northern pike, largemouth bass, and catfish are caught in lake and river waters, and the surrounding hills attract hunters seeking deer and elk. A visitor center at Pine River Recreation Area has interpretive displays on natural history and on the construction and purposes of the dam.

Navajo Lake, with an area of 15,000 acres, extends from the confluence of the San Juan and Los Pinos rivers 25 miles north into Colorado. Navajo Dam, an earthen embankment, is $^3/_4$ mile long and 400 feet high. It provides Farmington-area cities, industries, and farms with their principal water supply. It's also the main storage reservoir for the Navajo Indian Irrigation Project, designed to irrigate 110,000 acres.

The park is located 40 miles east of Farmington on NM 511. For more information, call **505/632-2278.**

ANGEL PEAK RECREATION AREA

The distinctive pinnacle of 6,991-foot Angel Peak can often be spotted from Farmington. This area offers a short nature trail and a variety of unusual, colorful geological formations and canyons to explore on foot. The Bureau of Land Management has developed two campgrounds and a picnic area, all with rest rooms. There is no drinking water available. The park is located 35 miles south of Farmington on NM 44; the last 6 miles of access, after turning off highway 44, are over a graded dirt road. For more information on the park, call **505/599-8900.**

BISTI BADLANDS

A federally protected area of weird rock formations, petrified logs, and prehistoric fossils, this wilderness area is like an undiscovered planet. The wilderness offers rugged hiking among its huge turrets, buttes, spires, and pinnacles. Seventy million years ago this was a swampland that attracted many dinosaurs and primitive mammals; many fossils remain, and neither fossils nor petrified wood may be removed from the site. There are no facilities here and no motorized vehicles or bicycles are permitted. From the parking area, you must hike two miles east to reach the first rock formations. The site is administered by the Bureau of Land Management.

The wilderness is located on NM 371, 37 miles south of Farmington. For more information, call **505/599-8900.**

WHERE TO STAY
MODERATE

Holiday Inn of Farmington. 600 E. Broadway at Scott Ave., Farmington, NM 87401.
☎ **800/HOLIDAY** or 505/327-9811. Fax 505/325-2288. 150 rms, 5 suites. A/C TV TEL. $68–
$72 double; $88–$135 suite. AE, CB, DC, DISC, JCB, MC, V.

The lobby at Holiday Inn of Farmington is decorated with an Aztec motif, and
Southwestern decor predominates in the rooms. Standard units have two double beds
and normal furnishings. King rooms (with king-size beds, of course) have a sofa
sleeper, a leisure chair, and an executive desk. There are rooms for nonsmokers and
people with disabilities.

The Brass Apple Restaurant is open daily for breakfast, lunch, and dinner and offers Southwestern and continental cuisine. The Sportz Club Lounge, also open daily,
has four TV monitors, two of them big screens. The hotel provides room service during restaurant hours, valet laundry, 24-hour desk, an outdoor swimming pool, sauna,
hot tub, fitness center, and meeting space for 200. Pets are accepted; a kennel is also
available.

Best Western Inn and Suites. 700 Scott Ave., Farmington, NM 87401. ☎ **800/528-1234,**
800/600-5221, or 505/327-5221. Fax 505/327-1565. 194 rms. A/C FRIDGE TV TEL. $70–$99
double. AE, CB, DC, DISC, MC, V.

The inn is focused around a skylit central courtyard, with luxuriant trees and plants
shading a social area at one end and a swimming pool at the other.

Pleasant, modern rooms have standard furnishings and in-room coffeemakers.
Suites feature separate living and sleeping areas, microwaves, wet bar sinks, refrigerators, and two televisions. Some rooms accommodate nonsmokers or travelers with
disabilities.

The hotel's restaurant, the Riverwalk Patio and Grille, offers a wide selection of
New Mexican and Southwest Italian cuisine. Rookie's Sports Bar, which features pool
tables and televised sporting events and specials, always offers a drink special. Other
amenities include room service (during restaurant hours), valet laundry, 24-hour guest
services, heated indoor pool, Jacuzzi, saunas, complimentary in-room movies, fitness
facility, video arcade, and guest laundry. Small pets are welcome.

INEXPENSIVE

Ⓢ **Anasazi Inn.** 903 W. Main St., Farmington, NM 87401. ☎ **505/325-4564.** 66 rms,
8 suites. A/C TV TEL. $39.95 single or double; $47.95–$54.95 suite. AE, CB, DC, DISC, MC, V.

This newly renovated property, built in Pueblo style, is a real bargain. The spacious
lobby displays Navajo crafts and gift items. Pastel colors and Navajo motifs brighten
the guest rooms. There's a courtesy car and a gift shop. Nonsmoking rooms are available; small pets are permitted.

The ranch-style Coyote Restaurant, with its howling coyote motif, is open
for lunch and dinner daily. Steaks, seafood, and Mexican food are offered. The
adjoining lounge, done in a sort of "nouveau-rustique" style, sometimes features live
solo entertainment.

Enchantment Lodge. 1800 W. Aztec Blvd., Aztec, NM 87410. ☎ **800/847-2194** or 505/
334-6143. Fax 505/334-6144. 20 rms. A/C TV TEL. $44–$52 double. DISC, MC, V.

This pleasant and very reasonable small roadside motel, complete with pink neon
lights, is reminiscent of the 1950s. Popular with visiting fishermen, the motel has
been recently renovated, and has cable television, refrigerators available on request,
an outdoor heated swimming pool, and a grassy picnic area. There is also a gift shop
on the premises.

Farmington Super 8. 1601 Bloomfield Hwy. at Carlton Ave., Farmington, NM 87401. ☎ **800/800-8000** or 505/325-1813. 60 rms. A/C TV TEL. $39.50–$58.70 double. Children under 13 free with parent. AE, CB, DC, DISC, MC, V.

A handsome new property on US Highway 64, just across the Animas River from central Farmington, the Super 8 has comfortable, amply sized rooms with standard furnishings. Some rooms have water beds. A game room keeps the kids from getting bored. The motel has nonsmoking rooms, a 24-hour desk, and accepts pets (with prior arrangement).

Motel 6 Farmington. 1600 Bloomfield Hwy. at Cedar St., Farmington, NM 87401. ☎ **505/326-4501.** 134 rms. A/C TV TEL. $34.95 double. AE, DC, DISC, MC, V.

This rambling motel is located just east of downtown Farmington on US Highway 64. Rooms are clean and cozy with all the essentials but not much more. An outdoor swimming pool is open seasonally.

CAMPING

Downs RV Park (☎ **800/582-6427**) has 61 sites, 55 with full hookups and six with no hookups. Tenting, air-conditioning, and heating are allowed. Phone hookups are available. There's also a playground. The RV park is located 5 miles west of Farmington on US 64. **Mom and Pop RV Park** (☎ **800/748-2807**) has 42 sites, 32 full hookups, tenting, a recreation room/area, and a gift shop. Mom and Pop RV park is located at 901 Illionos Avenue in Farmington.

WHERE TO DINE IN FARMINGTON

❸ **Clancy's Pub.** 2703 E. 20th St. at Hutton Rd. ☎ **505/325-8176.** Main courses $3.50–$8. AE, DC, DISC, MC, V. Mon–Sat 11am–2am, Sun noon–midnight. Closed Christmas, Thanksgiving, and Easter. AMERICAN/MEXICAN.

The owners of this old adobe building call it "an Irish cantina." The atmosphere is classic pub, with a very attractive enclosed patio and rock music (sometimes live) playing almost continually. Locals love it.

The menu is heavy on sandwiches and finger food, including the Olde English burger (with cheddar cheese and bacon) and the Reuben O'Rourke (with Thousand Island dressing). There's fish-and-chips, of course, Mac McMulligan stew, and "build-your-own" baked potatoes. Enchiladas, burritos, and tacos are also served.

K. B. Dillon's. 101 W. Broadway at Orchard Ave. ☎ **505/325-0222.** Reservations recommended. Main courses $10.95–$19.95; lunch $4–$14.25. AE, MC, V. Mon–Fri 11am–2pm; Mon–Sat 5:30–10:30pm. STEAKS/SEAFOOD.

Rough wooden walls, brick arches, historic photos, and early 20th-century decor, including signs used in advertising and at railroad crossings, make this downtown restaurant seem like a page out of your grandfather's scrapbook.

The menu, by contrast, is quite modern. Selections include Fracosta (an eight-ounce top sirloin broiled and topped with sautéed sweet peppers, mushrooms, green onions, and white wine); chicken à la Dillon (a sautéed breast topped with fresh tomato, avocado, and melted provolone cheese); and fresh mountain trout amandine, Cajun, or Oscar. The restaurant has a full bar that stays open between lunch and dinner.

❸ **Something Special.** 116 N. Auburn Ave. near Main St. ☎ **505/325-8183.** Breakfast $3–$6; lunch $7; desserts $2.50. AE, DISC, MC, V. Tues–Fri 7am–2pm. GOURMET HOME COOKING.

If the aroma didn't tip you off, you might walk right past this unimposing white house, with its yellow shutters and yellow door, and not realize it's a bakery and restaurant. It's just like home, or like home ought to be. Dine indoors amid the fresh bakery smells, or outdoors beneath a vine-draped arbor.

A set lunch menu is served daily. It varies from beef Stroganoff to spinach and feta cheese croissants, from manicotti to orange-pecan chicken with avocados. Breakfasts also vary, with one criterion: Nothing is ever fried. There's always a difficult choice of nine desserts each day, from butterscotch-pecan pie to chocolate-banana torte.

8 The Jicarilla Apache Reservation

About 3,200 Apaches live on the Jicarilla Apache Indian Reservation along US Highway 64 and NM 537. Its 768,000 acres stretch from the Colorado border south 65 miles to NM 44 near Cuba, New Mexico.

The word *jicarilla* (pronounced hick-ah-*ree*-ah) means "little basket," so it's no surprise that tribal craftspeople are noted for their basket weaving and beadwork. See their work, both contemporary and museum quality, at the **Jicarilla Apache Arts and Crafts Shop and Museum,** a green building along US 64 west of downtown (☎ **505/759-3242,** ext. 274). Two isolated pueblo ruins, open to the public, are found on the reservation: **Cordova Canyon** ruins on tribal Road 13 and **Honolulu** ruin on Road 63.

This area of New Mexico offers some of the finest hunting in North America. Tribe members guide fishermen and trophy hunters, most of whom seek elk, mule deer, or bear, into the reservation's rugged wilderness backcountry. Just south of Chama on Jicarilla's northeastern flank is **Horse Lake Mesa Game Park,** P.O. Box 313, Dulce, NM 87528 (☎ **505/759-3442**), a 20,000-acre reserve surrounded by a predator-proof fence. At an altitude of around 8,500 feet, this is the home of Rocky Mountain elk, mule deer, and countless numbers of bobcat, bear, and coyote.

ESSENTIALS

VISITOR INFORMATION   Admission to Jicarilla Apache Reservation is free and visitors are welcome year-round. Fishing permits for seven reservation lakes and the Navajo River run $8 per day for adults, $6 for seniors and children under 12. Rainbow, cutthroat, and brown trout are regularly stocked. For more information on visiting the reservation, contact the Tribal Office in writing at P.O. Box 507, Dulce, NM 87528, or call **505/759-3242.**

SPECIAL EVENTS   Highlights of the Jicarilla calendar are the Little Beaver Roundup (the second or third weekend in July) and the Stone Lake Fiesta (September 14 to 15 annually).

9 Chama: Home of the Cumbres & Toltec Scenic Railroad

A village of just 1,000 people, Chama's importance exceeds its small size. It's the largest New Mexico community for two hours in any direction, the head of the fertile Rio Chama valley, and the southern terminal of the world-famous Cumbres and Toltec Scenic Railroad. Lumber and ranching, along with tourism and outdoor recreation, support the economy today. It's a hunting and fishing center in summer, a cross-country skiing and snowmobiling haven in winter. Tierra Amarilla, the Rio Arriba County seat, is 14 miles south; Dulce, governmental seat of the Jicarilla Apache Indian Reservation, is 27 miles west.

ESSENTIALS

GETTING THERE **By Car** From Santa Fe, take US 84 north (two hours). From Taos, take US 64 west (2^1/$_2$ hours). From Farmington, take US 64 east (2^1/$_4$ hours).

VISITOR INFORMATION The **Chama Welcome Center** (☎ **505/756-2235**) is at the south end of town, at the "Y" junction of US 64/84 and NM 17. The welcome center is open from 8am to 5pm daily. For complete local information, contact the **Chama Valley Chamber of Commerce,** Cumbres Mall, 499 Main St. (P.O. Box 306), Chama, NM 87520 (☎ **800/477-0149** or 505/756-2306).

ALL ABOARD THE HISTORIC C&T RAILROAD

✪ **Cumbres and Toltec Scenic Railroad.** P.O. Box 789, Chama, NM 87520. ☎ **505/756-2151.** Round-trip to Osier and return, adults $34, children 11 and under $17. Through trip to Antonito, return by van (or to Antonito by van, return by train), adults $52, children $29. Reservations highly recommended. MC, V. Memorial Day weekend to mid-Oct trains leave Chama daily at 10:30am; vans depart for Antonito at 8pm.

America's longest and highest narrow-gauge steam railroad, the historic C&T operates on a 64-mile track between Chama and Antonito, Colorado. Built in 1880 as an extension of the Denver and Rio Grande line to serve the mining camps of the San Juan Mountains, it is perhaps the finest surviving example of what once was a vast network of remote Rocky Mountain railways.

The C&T passes through forests of pine and aspen, past striking rock formations, and through the magnificent Toltec Gorge of the Rio de los Pinos. It crests at the 10,015-foot Cumbres Pass, the highest in the United States used by scheduled passenger trains.

Halfway through the route, at Osier, Colorado, the *New Mexico Express* from Chama meets the *Colorado Limited* from Antonito. They stop to exchange greetings, engines, and through passengers. Round-trip day passengers return to their starting point after enjoying a picnic or catered lunch beside the old water tank and stock pens in Osier.

A walking tour brochure, describing 23 points of interest in the Chama railroad yards, can be picked up at the 1899 depot in Chama. A registered National Historic Site, the C&T is owned by the states of Colorado and New Mexico, and operated by a concessionaire, Kyle Railways.

WHERE TO STAY

Virtually all accommodations in this area are found on NM 17 or south of the US 64/84 junction, known as the "Y."

Best Western Jicarilla Inn. U.S. Highway 64 (P.O. Box 233), Dulce, NM 87528. ☎ **800/742-1938,** 800/528-1234, or 505/759-3663. Fax 505/759-3170. 42 rms, 6 suites. A/C TV TEL $65–$85 double; $75–$95 suite. AE, CB, DC, DISC, JCB, MC, V.

Among the best motels in the area, the Jicarilla Inn is 27 miles west of Chama in Dulce, in the northeastern corner of the Jicarilla Apache Indian Reservation. Modern and well maintained, it features a skylit indoor garden down the middle of the corridor between rooms.

Guest units all have queen-size beds and attractive wood furnishings. Upstairs rooms are particularly spacious, with cathedral ceilings. Six suites have kitchenettes; kitchenware is provided on request. Some rooms accommodate nonsmokers or people with disabilities.

The inn offers a popular "Trains and Indians" package, which combines lodging and meals with a ride on the Cumbres and Toltec Scenic Railroad (see above) for rates starting at $180 double for one night, $250 for two nights.

The Hill Crest Restaurant serves New Mexican and American cuisine at breakfast, lunch, and dinner. The Timber Lake Lounge stages bingo games Thursday and Friday. The hotel also has a tourist information center, 24-hour desk, Apache Mesa Gallery and Gift Shop, and video player and tape rental shop.

Branding Iron Motel. West Main St. (P.O. Box 557), Chama, NM 87520. ☎ **800/446-2650** or 505/756-2162. 41 rms. A/C TV TEL. $65–$75 double. AE, DISC, MC, V.

This modern two-story motel, set back off the highway, has spacious, colorfully appointed motel units with all standard furnishings. Wildlife photos on the walls are reminders of the popularity of hunting in this area. The restaurant/lounge offers coffee-shop fare for breakfast, lunch, and dinner.

☉ Chama Trails Inn. 2362 Hwy. 17 (P.O. Box 975), Chama, NM 87520. ☎ **800/289-1421** or 505/756-2156. 16 rms. FRIDGE TV TEL. $43–$51 double. AE, DISC, MC, V.

An art gallery as well as a motel, this white stucco building adorned with chile *ristras* (decorative strung chiles) incorporates the work of a different artist into the decor of each room. All rooms have queen-size beds and custom-made pine furnishings. Some units have ceiling fans, gas fireplaces, and/or Mexican-tiled bathroom floors. Several rooms have been designated for nonsmokers, and a redwood sauna is available for guest use. The small but impressive art gallery here began as a hobby; now it's a major outlet for local artists' work.

✪ Elkhorn Lodge. On Hwy. 84, Chama, NM 87520. ☎ **800/532-8874** or 505/756-2105. 33 units. TV TEL. Rooms $63 double; cabins $64–$101 single or double. Extra person $6. DISC, MC, V.

Situated just outside the center of the sleepy little town of Chama, the Elk Horn Lodge is popular with both sportsmen and families. The rooms and cabins are clean and spacious and are done in dark wood paneling with beige carpeting. The furnishings include two double beds, a desk, and a table and chair. Outside the door of each room, on the motel-style porch, a folding chair is provided. There are barbecue pits available for guest use, and there is a small cafe. Small pets are welcome.

CAMPING

At an altitude of 8,100 feet, **L&L Ranch Resort** (☎ **505/588-7173**) is a lovely campground in a scenic mountain setting. There are 42 sites, 12 full hookups, and tenting is available for individuals and groups. Group RV can also be requested. Limited grocery and laundry facilities, ice, picnic tables, and firewood are provided. Recreation possibilities here include pond and stream fishing, basketball, horseshoes, hiking, volleyball, cross-country skiing, and snowmobiling. L&L is open all year. The ranch is located 10 miles east of the US 84 and US 64 junction (Tierra Amarilla Junction) on US 64.

At **Rio Chama RV Campground** (☎ **505/756-2303**) you're within easy walking distance of the Cumbres and Toltec Scenic Railroad depot. This shady campground with 60 sites along the Rio Chama is ideal for RVers and tenters who plan train rides. The campground also offers great photo opportunities of the old steam trains leaving the depot. There are hot showers, a dump station, and complete hookups available. Open mid-May through mid-October only. The campground is located 2¹/₄ miles morth of the US 84/US 64 junction on NM 17.

Twin Rivers Trailer Park (☎ 505/756-2218) has 85 sites and 50 full hookups; phone hookups are offered. Tenting is available, and there are laundry facilities, as well as ice and picnic tables. River swimming and fishing are popular activities; other sports facilities include basketball, volleyball, badminton, and horseshoes. Twin Rivers is open from April 15 to November 15 and is located 100 yards west of the junction of NM 17 and US 84/US 64 on US 84/US 64.

WHERE TO DINE

✪ **High Country Restaurant and Lounge.** Main St. (0.1 mile north of "Y"). ☎ **505/756-2384.** Main courses $4.95–$14.95; lunch $6.50–$8.50; breakfast $1.50–$6.95. AE, DISC, MC, V. Daily 7am–11pm. Closed Thanksgiving and Christmas. STEAKS/SEAFOOD.

This rustic wood-plank restaurant/saloon is like a country lodge with a big stone fireplace and an antique bar. The dinner menu features fried chicken, a variety of steaks, trout, and beer-battered shrimp. Also offered are hamburgers and Mexican food, nightly specials, and about a dozen imported beers on tap.

Ⓢ **Viva Vera's Mexican Kitchen.** Main St. (0.2 mile north of "Y"). ☎ **505/756-2557.** Main courses $6.25–$10.95; lunch $2.50–$7; breakfast $2.75–$3.95. AE, MC, V. Daily 7am–10pm. NEW MEXICAN/AMERICAN.

A small white Territorial-style roadside cafe, Vera's may be Chama's most popular hangout. Portions are generous. Try the chile stew and posole. Beer and wine are served with meals.

ON THE ROAD: WHAT TO SEE & DO ON US 84 SOUTH

Note: For a map of this area, see "Touring the Pueblos Around Santa Fe" in chapter 7.

Distinctive yellow earth provided a name for the town of **Tierra Amarilla,** 14 miles south of Chama at the junction of US 84 and 64. Throughout New Mexico, this name is synonymous with a continuing controversy over the land-grant rights of the descendants of the original Hispanic settlers. But the economy of this community of 1,000 is dyed in the wool, literally.

The organization Ganados del Valle (Livestock Growers of the Valley) is at work to save the longhaired Spanish churro sheep from extinction through breeding, to introduce other unusual wool breeds to the valley, and to perpetuate a 200-year-old tradition of shepherding, spinning, weaving, and dyeing. Many of the craftspeople work in conjunction with **Tierra Wools,** P.O. Box 118, Los Ojos, NM 87551 (☎ 505/588-7231), which has a showroom and workshop in a century-old mercantile building just north of Tierra Amarilla. One-of-a-kind blankets and men's and women's apparel are among the products displayed and sold.

Two state parks are a short drive west from Tierra Amarilla. **El Vado Lake State Park,** 14 miles on NM 112 (☎ 505/588-7247), offers boating and waterskiing, fishing, and camping in summer; cross-country skiing and ice fishing in winter. **Heron Lake State Park,** 11 miles west on NM 95 (☎ 505/588-7470), has a no-wake speed limit for motor vessels, adding to its appeal for fishing, sailing, and windsurfing. The park has an interpretive center, as well as camping and picnic sites. The scenic 5½-mile Rio Chama trail connects the two lakes.

East of Tierra Amarilla, the Rio Brazos cuts a canyon through the Tusas Mountains and around 11,403-foot Brazos Peak. Just north of Los Ojos, NM 512 heads east 7½ miles up the **Brazos Box Canyon.** High cliffs that rise straight from the valley floor give it a Yosemite-like appearance—which is even more apparent from an overlook on US 64, 18 miles east of Tierra Amarilla en route to Taos. **El Chorro,** an impressive waterfall at the mouth of the canyon, usually flows only from early May to mid-June, but this is a tremendous hiking area any time of year. There are several resort lodges in the area.

About 27 miles south of Tierra Amarilla on US 84, and 3 miles north of Ghost Ranch, is **Echo Canyon Amphitheater** (☎ **505/684-2486**), a U.S. Forest Service campground and picnic area. The natural "theater," hollowed out of sandstone by thousands of years of erosion, is a 10-minute walk from the parking area. Some 13 miles west of here, via a dirt road into the Chama River Canyon Wilderness, is the isolated **Christ-in-the-Desert Monastery** (☎ **505/843-3049**), built in 1964 by Benedictine monks. The brothers produce crafts, sold at a small gift shop, and operate a guest house.

The ✪ **Ghost Ranch Living Museum** (☎ **505/685-4312**) is a U.S. Forest Service–operated exhibit of regional plant and animal life, geology, paleontology, and ecology. Short trails lead past re-created marsh, grassland, canyon, and forest land, inhabited by 27 species of native New Mexican animals and birds, most of them brought here injured or orphaned. A miniature national forest, complete with a fire lookout tower, illustrates conservation techniques; a trail through a severely eroded arroyo affords an opportunity to study soil ecology. The new **Gateway to the Past** museum interprets the cultures of the Chama Valley. Temporary exhibits from the New Mexico Museum of Natural History are presented in an indoor display hall. It's open May through September daily from 8am to 6pm; and October through April, Tuesday through Sunday from 8am to 4:30pm. There's no admission fee, though donations are welcomed.

Celebrated artist Georgia O'Keeffe spent most of her adult life in **Abiquiu,** a tiny town in a bend of the Rio Chama 14 miles south of the Ghost Ranch, and 22 miles north of Espanola, on US 84. The inspiration for O'Keeffe's startling landscapes is clear in the surrounding terrain. Since March 1995 O'Keeffe's adobe home (where she lived and painted until her death in 1986) has been open for public tours. Reservations must be made in advance, and the charge is $15 for a one-hour tour. As this book goes to press, tours are offered Tuesdays, Thursdays, and Fridays and are limited to six people per tour. Visitors are not permitted to take pictures. For reservations, call ☎ **505/685-4539.**

Many dinosaur skeletons have been found in rocks along the base of cliffs near **Abiquiu Reservoir** (☎ **505/685-4371**), a popular boating and fishing spot formed by the Abiquiu Dam.

A good place to stay in the area is the **Abiquiu Inn,** a small country inn, restaurant, art gallery, and gift shop, ¹/₂ mile north of the village of Abiquiu (☎ **505/685-4378**). Rates are $60 to $130.

Heading south from Abiquiu, watch for **Dar al-Islam** (☎ **505/685-4515**), a spiritual center with a circular Middle Eastern mosque made of adobe; the small community of **Mendanales,** where you'll find the shop of renowned weaver Cordelia Coronado; and **Hernandez,** the village immortalized in Ansel Adams's famous 1941 photograph *Moonrise, Hernandez, New Mexico.*

11 Southwestern New Mexico

This region belongs to the Old West. Billy the Kid lived here; so did Geronimo. Rugged and infrequently visited, it was and still is a good place to hide out. But travelers who penetrate its desert, forests, and mountain ranges today will be rewarded with spectacular scenic drives in Gila National Forest, a glimpse inside a 2,000-year-old pueblo culture at Gila Cliff Dwellings National Monument, the sight of thousands of snow geese taking flight at the Bosque Del Apache Wildlife Refuge, and the chance to contemplate the vastness of space at the Very Large Array, the world's most powerful radio telescope.

The Rio Grande is southwestern New Mexico's lifeline, throughout history nourishing the Native American, Hispanic, and Anglo settlers who have built their homes beside its banks. It sketches a distinct boundary between the rugged mountains of the southwest region of the state and the desert reaching toward the southeast. The river land was especially fertile around modern Las Cruces; the settlement of La Mesilla was southern New Mexico's major center for three centuries.

West of the river, the Black Range and Mogollon Mountains rise in the area now cloaked by Gila National Forest. This was the homeland of the Mogollon Indians 1,000 years ago; Gila Cliff Dwellings National Monument preserves one of their great legacies. It was also the homeland of the fiercely independent Chiricahua Apaches in the 19th century. Considered the last North American Indians to succumb to the whites, they counted Cochise and Geronimo among their chieftains. Mining and outdoor recreation, centered in historic Silver City (pop. 11,508), are now the economic stanchions of the region. But dozens of mining towns have boomed and busted in the past 140 years, as a smattering of ghost towns throughout the region attest.

Las Cruces, at the foot of the Organ Mountains, is New Mexico's second largest city, with 71,043 people. It's a busy agricultural and education center. North up the valley are Truth or Consequences (pop. 6,285), a spa town named for the 1950s radio and TV game show, and Socorro (pop. 8,472), a historic city with Spanish roots. West, on the I-10 corridor to Arizona, are the ranching centers of Deming (pop. 13,406) and Lordsburg (pop. 3,010).

Southwestern New Mexico

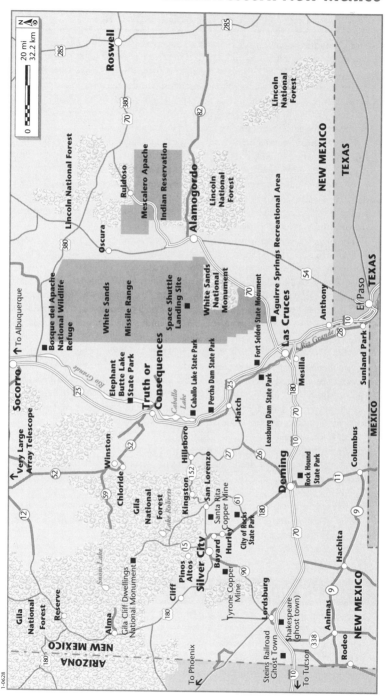

TOURING THE REGION BY CAR

From Albuquerque, follow I-25 south to Socorro, which won't take too long, so if you start early you'll have a full day of sightseeing ahead of you. You might notice Sevilleta National Wildlife Refuge during this part of the drive between La Joya and Chamizal. It's a long-term ecological research site under the direction of the National Science Foundation, open only by appointment to researchers. When you arrive in Socorro, you might want to spend an hour or so looking around, but the real points of interest are in the surrounding area.

Just south of Socorro on I-25 is Bosque del Apache National Wildlife Refuge, where you can see hundreds of species of birds, amphibians, reptiles, and mammals. If you're here in winter, you're in for a real treat. Also nearby is the Very Large Array National Radio Astronomy Observatory, which makes for an interesting visit. After seeing the sights in this area, either spend the night in Socorro or head down to Truth or Consequences, our next stop (although, in all honesty, your opportunities for food and lodging are better in Socorro).

The main attraction in Truth or Consequences is the hot springs; however, other opportunities for sightseeing await you as well. For one thing, this area is excellent for fishing and camping. From Truth or Consequences, take NM 152, which connects with US 180 for a short distance, on to Silver City. I suggest using Silver City as a base for exploring the attractions in this area: the downtown historic district and the Gila Cliff Dwellings National Monument. You'll probably want to spend a couple of nights in Silver City or at nearby campgrounds. The best way to see this area is either to leave Truth or Consequences very early and head straight over to Gila Cliff Dwellings, or to have a leisurely morning in Truth or Consequences and then explore the sights of Silver City, saving the Cliff Dwellings for the following day.

After seeing the sights in the Silver City area, it's time to head south on NM 90 to Lordsburg. It's only 40 miles to Lordsburg, so take your time getting there. You may even want to pass right by town and head over to Stein's Ghost Town first before going back to visit Shakespeare Ghost Town.

Next, drive east on I-10 to Deming, about 60 miles from Lordsburg. If rockhounding is your thing, head over to Rock Hound State Park. Plan to spend the night in Deming if you think you're going to spend the entire day poking around Lordsburg, Deming, and the surrounding areas. Otherwise, continue east to Las Cruces via I-10.

In Las Cruces you'll want to spend time at Old Mesilla Plaza, especially if you're a Wild West fanatic. There's also plenty to do in the way of sports and recreation, so plan on spending a couple of nights here.

From Las Cruces you can head north via I-25 to Albuquerque, or continue over to Alamogordo (see chapter 12) via US 70.

1 The Great Outdoors in Southwestern New Mexico

Rugged, remote, forested, and fascinating all describe southwestern New Mexico, where, lucky for you if you're looking for backcountry adventure, few tourists venture.

BIKING   A popular cycling area is located in the Socorro area at **Bosque del Apache National Wildlife Refuge** (☎ **505/835-1828**), where cyclists enjoy the 15-mile loop tour. Bikes are not allowed in the Gila Wilderness, but they are permitted in other parts of **Gila National Forest**. Contact **Gila Hike and Bike in Silver City** for rentals and guided rides in Gila National Forest (☎ **505/388-3222**).

BIRD-WATCHING **Bosque del Apache National Wildlife Refuge** (☎ 505/835-1828) is a refuge for migratory waterfowl such as snow geese and cranes. It's located 16 miles south of Socorro. **North Monticello Point,** located off Elephant Butte Lake, is a great place to see pelicans, bald eagles, and a variety of waterfowl (☎ 505/744-5421), where as **Water Canyon,** just outside of Socorro in the **Cíbola National Forest,** is home to golden eagles (☎ 505/854-2281).

BOATING In the Gila National Forest, **Lake Roberts** (☎ 505/536-2250), just north of Silver City on NM 15, and **Snow Lake** (☎ 505/533-6231), north on US 180 from Silver City and then east on NM 159, both allow boating. Lake Roberts features motor boat rentals, whereas Snow Lake only permits canoes, rowboats, and other boats without gas motors.

Elephant Butte Lake State Park (☎ 505/744-5421, which takes its name from the largest body of water in New Mexico with 200 miles of shoreline, is also popular with boating enthusiasts. Five ramps provide boating access to the lake, and there are also launching areas for smaller vessels.

FISHING **Caballo Lake State Park,** located about 16 miles south of Truth or Consequences, offers great bass, crappie, catfish, and walleye fishing in its 11,000-acre lake. For more information call **505/743-3942. Elephant Butte Lake Sate Park** (☎ 505/744-5421), also near Truth or Consequences, is another great fishing location. Look to catch bass, catfish, walleye, crappie, white bass, black bass, and stripers here. **Lake Roberts** (☎ 505/524-6090), located about 40 miles north of Silver City in the Gila National Forest, is prime trout fishing waters.

HIKING It goes without saying that there's great hiking available in the **Gila National Forest,** which has more than 1,400 miles of trails ranging in length and difficulty. Your best bet for hiking in the area is to purchase a guidebook devoted entirely to hiking the Gila Forest, but popular areas include the Crest Trail, West Fork Trail, and the Aldo Leopold Wilderness. One favorite day hike in the forest is The Catwalk, a moderately strenuous hike along a series of steel bridges and walkways suspended over Whitewater Canyon. Whenever and wherever you go hiking, be sure to carry plenty of water.

HORSEBACK RIDING If you want to go horseback riding in this area, contact **Circle S Stables** in Las Cruces, open from November to May (☎ 505/382-7708) or **Gila Wilderness Lodge** in Winston (☎ 505/722-5772).

HOT SPRINGS This is hot springs country. For locations in Truth or Consequences, call **800/831-9487** or 505/894-3536. Near City of Rocks State Park is **Faywood Hotsprings** (☎ 505/536-9663), where you can soak in outdoor pools (clothing is required and tent and RV camping are permitted). **Lightfeather Hot Spring** is a clothing optional spring near the Gila Cliff Dwellings National Monument visitors center (☎ 505/536-2250). Another clothing optional spring in the Gila National Forest is **San Francisco Hot Spring** (☎ 505/539-2481).

2 Socorro: Gateway to Bosque del Apache & the VLA

This quiet, pleasant town of 8,472 is an unusual mix of the 19th and 20th centuries. Established as a mining settlement and ranching center, its downtown area is dominated by numerous mid-1800s buildings and the 17th-century San Miguel Mission. The New Mexico Institute of Mining and Technology (New Mexico Tech) is a major research center. Socorro is also the gateway to a vast and varied two-county region that includes the Bosque del Apache National Wildlife Refuge, the Very Large Array National Radio Astronomy Observatory, and three national forests.

ESSENTIALS

GETTING THERE **By Car** From Albuquerque, take I-25 south (1¹/₄ hours). From Las Cruces, take I-25 north (2³/₄ hours).

VISITOR INFORMATION The **Socorro County Chamber of Commerce,** which is also the visitor information headquarters, is just off North California Street (Highway 85) at 103 Francisco de Avondo (P.O. Box 743), Socorro, NM 87801 (☎ 505/835-0424).

EXPLORING THE TOWN

A WALKING TOUR OF HISTORIC SOCORRO

The best introduction to Socorro is a walking tour of the historic district. Start from the parklike **Plaza,** one block west of California Street on Manzanares Street. A brochure published by the chamber of commerce points out several Territorial-style buildings from the mid-1800s, including the **J. N. Garcia Opera House,** the **Juan Nepomoceno Garcia House,** and the **Juan José Baca House.** Several impressive late 19th-century Victorian homes stand in the blocks south of the Plaza.

OTHER ATTRACTIONS IN TOWN

Old San Miguel Mission. 403 El Camino Real, NW, 2 blocks north of the Plaza. ☎ 505/835-1620. Free admission. Daily 6am–6pm.

Built during the period from 1615 to 1626 but abandoned during the Pueblo Revolt of 1680, this church was subsequently restored, and a new wing built in 1853. It boasts thick adobe walls, large carved vigas (rafters), and supporting corbel arches. English-language masses are Saturday at 5:30pm and Sunday at 10am and noon.

New Mexico Institute of Mining and Technology. College St. at Leroy St. ☎ 505/835-5011.

Founded in 1889, New Mexico Tech is a highly regarded institution of 1,700 students, whose course work focuses on science and engineering. Its internationally acclaimed research facilities include centers for petroleum recovery, explosives technology, and atmospheric research. Golfers also visit to play the 18-hole university course, considered one of the best in the state. **Macey Center** has a 600-seat auditorium for performing arts and a gallery of rotating art.

Mineral Museum. Campus Rd., New Mexico Tech campus. ☎ 505/835-5420. Free admission. Mon–Fri 8am–5pm, Sat–Sun 10am–3pm.

Run by the New Mexico Bureau of Mines and Mineral Resources, this museum has the largest geological collection in the state. Its more than 10,000 specimens include mineral samples from all over the world, fossils, mining artifacts, and photographs.

New Mexico Firefighters Training Academy. 200 Aspen Rd. in southwest Socorro, off US 60 (P.O. Box 239, Socorro, NM 87801). ☎ 800/734-6553 or 505/835-7500. Free admission. Mon–Fri 8am–5pm. Tours are available.

This school for firefighters, spread over 121 acres, is a state-of-the-art training facility with a three-story control tower, four-story drill tower, and a variety of firefighting equipment. Visitors should allow one hour.

SEEING THE SIGHTS NEARBY

SOUTH OF SOCORRO The village of **San Antonio,** the boyhood home of Conrad Hilton, is 10 miles from Socorro via I-25. During the panic of 1907, his merchant father, Augustus Hilton, converted part of his store into a rooming house. This gave Conrad his first exposure to the hospitality industry, and he went on to worldwide fame as a hotelier. Only ruins of the store/boardinghouse remain.

WEST OF SOCORRO US Highway 60, running west to Arizona, is the avenue to several points of interest. **Magdalena,** 27 miles from Socorro, is a mining and ranching town that preserves an 1880s Old West spirit. Three miles south, the ghost town of **Kelly** produced more than $40 million worth of lead, zinc, copper, silver, and gold in the late 19th and early 20th centuries.

Thirty-two miles north of Magdalena on a dead-end road is the home of the **Alamo Navajo Nation.** On special occasions, the public may be allowed to visit the band of 1,400 Navajo who live on this reservation: Inquire with the Alamo Chapter Office (☎ **505/854-2686**).

Southeast of Magdalena, atop 10,783-foot South Baldy Mountain, the **Langmuir Research Laboratory** studies thunderstorms and atmospheric electricity from June through August. There is a visitors center with exhibits. The research center can be reached by high-clearance and four-wheel-drive vehicles only; visitors should call **505/835-5423** in advance to check on road conditions.

Fifty-four miles west of Socorro via US 60 is the ✪ **Very Large Array National Radio Astronomy Observatory (VLA)** (Socorro office at 1003 Lopezville Rd. NW; ☎ **505/835-7000**), where 27 dish-shaped antennae, each 82 feet in diameter, are spread across the plains of San Agustin, forming a single gigantic radio telescope. Photographs taken are similar to the largest optical telescopes, except that radio telescopes are sensitive to low-frequency radio waves. All types of celestial objects are photographed, including the sun and its planets, stars, quasars, galaxies, and even the faint remains of the "big bang" that scientists say occurred some 10 billion years ago. The visitors center contains displays on the VLA and radio astronomy in general, and a self-guided walking tour gives visitors a closer view of the antennae, which resemble giant TV satellite dishes. Admission is free, and visitors are welcomed daily from 8:30am to sunset.

WHERE TO STAY

Most accommodations are along California Street, the main highway through town, or the adjacent I-25 frontage road. Most lodgings provide free parking.

The Eaton House. 403 Eaton Ave. (P.O. Box 536), Socorro, NM 87801. ☎ **505/835-1067.** 3 rms and 2 casitas (all with bath). A/C. $80–$130 single or double. Rates include full breakfast. No credit cards.

This charming bed-and-breakfast, constructed in 1881 by Col. E. W. Eaton, is on the New Mexico register of historic buildings. Owner Anna Appleby has decorated each room differently, from the early 19th-century Daughters' Room, with twin beds and claw-foot tub and shower, to the Colonel Eaton Room, with queen-size four-poster bed and Victorian furnishings. The Pueblo-style Chavez Casita is accessible to people with disabilities. The expertly prepared, generous breakfasts are made of only organic ingredients, and might include an apple-pie pancake with peppered bacon, blueberry French toast, or a fluffy herbed omelet with sliced ham and asparagus. Smoking and pets are not permitted; children 14 and older are welcome.

Sands Motel. 205 California St. NW, Socorro, NM 87801. ☎ **505/835-1130.** 25 rms. A/C TV TEL. $30 double. AE, CB, DC, DISC, MC, V.

Clean, comfortable lodging at very economical rates is what you'll find here; there's color cable television but few other amenities. Centrally located, the Sands is within easy walking distance of several restaurants. Pets are welcome.

Super 8 Motel. 1121 Frontage Rd. NW, Socorro, NM 87801. ☎ **800/800-8000** or 505/835-4626. Fax 505/835-3988. 63 rms, 8 suites. A/C TV TEL. $49 double; $68 suite. Rates include continental breakfast. AE, DC, DISC, MC, V.

Regular patrons of Super 8 motels return in part because the accommodations are so predictable. Each room here is clean and comfortably furnished. Complimentary continental breakfast is served in the attractive lobby. Facilities include a swimming pool, hot tub, and guest laundry.

CAMPING

Casey's Socorro RV Park (☎ 505/835-2234) offers mountain and valley views and plenty of shade. There are 100 sites and 30 full hookups. Tenting is available, as are picnic tables, grills, and ice. A playground and swimming pool are open all year. To reach Casey's, take I-25 to exit 147, then go one block west on Business I-25 and then one block south on West Frontage Road.

WHERE TO DINE

Don Juan's Cocina. 118 Manzanares Rd. ☎ **505/835-9967.** Mexican plates $3.80–$6.75. AE, DC, DISC, MC, V. Mon–Fri 10am–9pm, Sat 10am–3pm. MEXICAN.

Located in the 1885 Knights of Pythias Hall, the decor at Don Juan's is simple in the main dining room, but the festive outdoor patio has some extraordinary murals painted on its surrounding walls. If you're not particularly interested in the decor, you'll be very interested in the food: It's excellent, authentic Mexican, and inexpensive. Breakfast is served all day and might consist of the standard huevos rancheros or a breakfast burrito. Appetizers at lunch and dinner include taquitos, chile cheese fries, and sopaipillas. You can order your main course à la carte (tacos, burritos, enchiladas, and tostadas), or you might prefer to get a full Mexican plate with refried beans and rice.

✪ **Owl Bar and Cafe.** State Hwy. 1 and US Hwy. 380, San Antonio. ☎ **505/835-9946.** Main courses $2.25–$10.95. DISC, MC, V. Mon–Sat 8am–10pm. AMERICAN.

A low-lit tavern in a one-story adobe building, 7 miles south of Socorro, the Owl has earned a regionwide reputation for "the world's greatest hamburgers." It's especially proud of its green chile cheeseburger. The steak house (open 5 to 10pm Friday and Saturday only) serves T-bones, filet mignon, and catfish.

✪ **Valverde Steak House.** 203 Manzanares Ave., Socorro. ☎ **505/835-3380.** Reservations recommended. Main courses $6.75–$32.50; lunch $4.25–$6.75. AE, CB, DC, DISC, MC, V. Mon–Thurs 11am–2pm and 5–9:30pm; Fri 11am–2pm and 5–10pm, Sat 5–9:30pm, Sun noon–9pm. Closed July 4. AMERICAN.

The horseshoe-shaped Val Verde Hotel is a national historic landmark, built in 1919 in California mission style. The hotel has been converted to apartments, but the public can still enjoy the old dining room. Lunch menu items are simple but tasty: homemade soups, salads, sandwiches, plus steaks and seafood. Dinner is more elaborate. House specials include beef Stroganoff and pepper steak Capri (in Madeira sauce). Gourmet southwestern dishes are also served. The restaurant is about two blocks off California Street (Highway 85), directly east of the Plaza. A lounge provides weekend entertainment.

3 Oasis in the Desert: Bosque del Apache National Wildlife Refuge

By Ian Wilker

The barren lands to either side of I-25 south of Albuquerque seem hardly fit for rattlesnakes, much less one of the Southwest's greatest concentrations of wildlife. The plants that do find purchase in the parched washes and small canyons along the road—forbiddingly named hardies such as creosote bush, tarbush, and white thorn—serve notice that you are indeed within the northernmost finger of the great Chihuahuan Desert, which covers southern New Mexico, southwestern Texas, and runs deep into Mexico.

However, to the east of the interstate is the green-margined Rio Grande. In the midst of such a blasted landscape the river stands out as an inviting beacon to wildlife, and nowhere does it shine more brightly than at Bosque del Apache's 7,000 acres of carefully managed riparian habitat, which include marshlands, meadows, agricultural fields, arrow-weed thickets on the riverbanks, and big old-growth cottonwoods lining what were once the oxbows of the river. The refuge supports a riot of wildlife, including all the characteristic mammals and reptiles of the Southwest (mule deer, jackrabbits, and coyotes are common) and more than 300 species of birds.

The stately cottonwood, mesquite, and willow *bosque* (forest, in Spanish) lining this part of the Rio Grande used to be a familiar sight throughout the Southwest. Sadly, the last century has seen most such habitat disappear. The big trees were heavily logged, and salt cedar (tamarisk) trees, an introduced Asian species, have overpowered the native species; the spectacular birdlife—flycatchers and tanagers, among other species—that favored the old bosques has in many cases gone with them. In addition, the rivers have been dammed at many points, which has impoverished the naturally occurring wetlands that migratory waterfowl depend on: The springtime floods would spread the rivers out over floodplains, and as they waned rivers would meander through new channels each year, cutting oxbows, creating marshes, and enriching the soil.

But in the Bosque del Apache this part of the Rio Grande has enjoyed protected status since 1939, when the refuge was established. An elaborate system of canals, dikes, and water ditches was built to manage the wetlands in the absence of annual floods. In 1986 the U.S. Fish and Wildlife Service decided to make Bosque del Apache one of its flagship refuges, and in addition to refurbishing the water and implementing soil management systems began an ambitious cottonwood rehabilitation program, rooting out the salt cedars and planting thousands of cottonwoods and black willows. The refuge also began hiring local farmers to grow corn, winter wheat, and other crops to feed the wintering waterfowl and sandhill cranes.

The result has been that Bosque del Apache is a very rich, healthy environment for wildlife, particularly for wintering birds. A visit here during the peak winter season—from November through March—is one of the most consistently thrilling wildlife spectaculars you can see anywhere in the Lower 48. Bosque del Apache is, you might say, the LAX of the Central Flyway, one of four paths that migratory birds follow every year between their summer breeding grounds in the tundral north and wintering grounds in the southern United States, Mexico, even as far away as South America—and many of these birds either stop over here to recharge their batteries or settle down for the winter.

It is not enough to say that there are hundreds of species of birds on hand. The wonder is in the sheer numbers of them: In early December the refuge may harbor as many as 45,000 snow geese, 57,000 ducks of many different species, and 18,000 sandhill cranes—huge, ungainly birds that nonetheless have a special majesty in flight, pinkish in the sun at dawn or dusk. There are also plenty of raptors about—numerous red-tailed hawks and northern harriers (sometimes called marsh hawks), Cooper's hawks and kestrels, and even bald and golden eagles—as well as Bosque del Apache's many year-round avian residents: pheasants and quail, wild turkeys, and much-mythologized roadrunners (*El Paisano*, in Mexican folklore). The interest of experienced birders will be whetted by the presence of Mexican mallards, Chihuahuan ravens, burrowing owls, rare grebes, beautiful, long-billed American avocets, and especially whooping cranes (a very few remain from an experiment to imprint the migratory path of sandhills on whoopers). Everyone will be mesmerized by the huge societies of sandhills, ducks, and geese, going about their daily business of feeding, gabbling, quarreling, honking, and otherwise making an immense racket.

The refuge has a 15-mile auto tour loop, which you should drive very slowly; the south half of the loop travels past numerous water impoundments, where the majority of the ducks and geese hang out, and the north half has the meadows and farmland, where you'll see the roadrunners and other landbirds, and where the cranes and geese feed from mid-morning through the afternoon.

A few special experiences bear further explanation. Dawn is definitely the best time to be here—songbirds are far more active in the first hours of the day, and the cranes and geese will fly to the fields very early. This last is not to be missed: On my visit I was watching the geese spread across tens of acres of marsh, upwards of 30,000 birds making their characteristic hullaballoo, when as if on some mysterious cue, on the far edge of the mass, the geese began to take flight. It was as if a tsunami of wings was building toward me—it took the huge flock fully three minutes to get aloft, during which the sound of beating wings grew to a quite deafening roar. (Perhaps I should also add that when 30,000 birds fly over your head, don't be surprised when a foul rain starts to fall.)

Ducks, in their many species and numerous eccentric habits, are a lot of fun to watch. Try to pick out the different species: In addition to good old mallards, you'll also see green-winged teal, whose brown heads are cut by a marvelously iridescent bright-green stripe; shovelers, with an iridescent green head and comically long and broad bill; goldeneyes and buffleheads, whose round, puffy, elaborately plumaged heads defy description; wood ducks, perhaps the most beautiful of ducks, with intricately patterned and colored plumage; and diminutive ruddy ducks, who break up their placid paddle round the ponds with sudden dives for food—and come up so far away you'll think they simply disappeared.

Don't despair if you can't be at the Bosque del Apache during the prime winter months, for it's a special place any time of year. By April the geese and ducks have flown north, and the refuge drains the water impoundments to allow the marsh plants to regenerate; the resulting mud flats are an ideal feeding ground for the migrating shorebirds that arrive in April and May. You'll see many species of sandpipers, black-necked stilts, and yellowlegs. Summer sees numerous nesting wading birds—ibises, great-blue and green herons, and snowy egrets—along with a cormorant rookery, and plenty of songbirds: great-tailed grackles, say's phoebes, and brilliantly colored common yellowthroat, wilson's warblers, and summer tanagers. During late summer and early fall, the refuge hosts a number of migratory American white pelicans—a huge bird, with a wingspan as broad as $9^1/_2$ feet.

JUST THE FACTS   The Bosque del Apache is about a $1^1/_2$-hour drive from Albuquerque. Follow I-25 9 miles south of Socorro, then take the San Antonio exit. At the main intersection of San Antonio, turn south onto Route 1. In 3 miles you'll be on refuge lands, and another 4 miles will bring you to the excellent visitors center, which has a small museum with interpretive displays and a large shelf of field guides, natural histories, and other books of interest for visitors to New Mexico. The visitors center is open from 7am to 4pm Monday through Friday, and on weekends as well during winter. The refuge itself is open daily year-round from one hour before sunrise to one hour after sunset. For more information, write Bosque del Apache NWR, P.O. Box 1246, Socorro, NM 87801 (☎ **505/835-1828**).

4 Truth or Consequences

Originally known as Hot Springs, after the therapeutic mineral springs bubbling up near the river, the town took the name Truth or Consequences in 1950. That was the year that Ralph Edwards, producer of the popular radio and television program *Truth or Consequences,* began his weekly broadcast with these words: "I wish that some town in the United States liked and respected our show so much that it would like to change its name to Truth or Consequences." The reward to any city willing to make this change was to become the site of the 10th anniversary broadcast of the program, which would put it on the national map in a big way. The locals voted for the name change, which has survived three protest elections over the years.

Although the Truth or Consequences television program was canceled decades ago, Ralph Edwards, now in his 70s, continues to return for the annual Truth or Consequences Fiesta, the first weekend of May. Another popular annual festival is Geronimo Days, the first weekend of October.

ESSENTIALS

GETTING THERE   By Car   From Albuquerque take I-25 south (2¹/₂ hours). From Las Cruces take I-25 north (1¹/₄ hours).

By Plane   For information of private flights and charters, call Enchantment Aviation at the **Truth or Consequences Municipal Airport,** Old North Highway 85 (☎ **505/894-6199**).

VISITOR INFORMATION   The visitor information center is located at the corner of Main Street (Business Loop 25) and Foch Street in downtown Truth or Consequences. It is administered by the **Truth or Consequences/Sierra County Chamber of Commerce,** P.O. Drawer 31, Truth or Consequences, NM 87901 (☎ **800/831-9487** or 505/894-3536).

ORIENTATION   Best known as "T or C," this year-round resort town and retirement community of 6,285 is spread along the Rio Grande between Elephant Butte and Caballo reservoirs, two of the three largest bodies of water in the state. Business Loop 25 branches off from I-25 to wind through the city, splitting into Main Street (one-way west) and South Broadway (one-way east) in the downtown area. Third Avenue connects T or C with the Elephant Butte resort community, 5 miles east.

TAKING THE WATERS AT THE HISTORIC HOT SPRINGS

Truth or Consequences' "original" attraction is its hot springs. The entire downtown area is located over a table of odorless hot mineral water, 98° to 115°, that bubbles to the surface through wells or pools. The first bathhouse was built in the 1880s; most of the half dozen historic spas operating today date from the 1930s. Generally open from morning to early evening, these spas welcome visitors for soaks and massages. Baths of 20 minutes or longer start at $3 per person.

The chamber of commerce has information on all the local spas. Among them is **Sierra Grande Lodge and Health Spa,** 501 McAdoo St. (☎ **505/894-6976**) where Geronimo himself is rumored to have taken a break. **Artesian Bath House,** 312 Marr St. (☎ **505/894-2684**), has an RV park on the premises.

✪ **Geronimo Springs Museum.** 211 Main St. ☎ **505/894-6600.** Admission $2 adults, $1 students; family rates available. Mon–Sat 9am–5pm, Sun 1–4pm.

Outside the museum is Geronimo's Spring, where the great Apache shaman is said to have taken his warriors to bathe their battle wounds. Turtleback Mountain, looming over the Rio Grande east of the city, is believed to have been sacred to Native Americans.

Exhibits include prehistoric Mimbres pottery (A.D. 950–1250); the Spanish Heritage Room, featuring artifacts of the first families of Sierra County; and artists' work, including historical murals and sculptured bronzes. Exhibits in the other rooms feature army forts and mining towns; the construction of Elephant Butte Dam; local history, featuring photos and artifacts; Native American artifacts, both prehistoric and of more recent culture; the story of ranching and farming in the county; and the rise and fall of mining camps and cattle towns. An authentic miner's cabin has been moved here from the nearby mountains. The Ralph Edwards Wing contains the history and highlights of the annual fiestas, and celebrates the city's name change. The museum is geothermally heated.

GETTING OUTSIDE

Elephant Butte Lake State Park encompasses New Mexico's largest body of water, covering 36,000 acres, and has 5,000 acres of shoreline. It is one of the most popular state parks in New Mexico, attracting water-sports enthusiasts and fishers from throughout the south and central regions of the state. Fishing for black and white bass, catfish, walleye and Northern pike, and crappie goes on all year long. Trout are stocked in the Rio Grande below Elephant Butte Dam. The park has sandy beaches for tanning and swimming, and offers boating, sailing, waterskiing, windsurfing, jet-skiing, scuba diving, nature trails, and camping, at both primitive and developed sites. Bird-watchers also enjoy the park, spotting hundreds of species, including bald eagles, great blue herons, and more than 20 species of ducks during migrations in spring and fall. The lake was named for a huge rock formation that makes an island; before the inundation that created the lake, it clearly looked like an elephant! Today, it's partially submerged.

The park is 5 miles north of Truth or Consequences via I-25. For more information on the park, call **505/744-5421.**

Twenty miles south of T or C via I-25 is another recreation area, **Caballo Lake State Park** (☎ **505/743-3942**), which, like Elephant Butte, has year-round water sports, fishing, swimming, and campsites. The lofty ridge of the Caballo Mountains just to the east of the lake makes a handsome backdrop. Park facilities include a full-service marina with a shop for boaters and full hookups for recreational vehicles.

Reached from the same exit off I-25 is yet another recreation area, **Percha Dam State Park** (☎ **505/743-3942**), a lovely shaded spot under great cottonwood trees, part of the ancient bosque, or woods, the Spanish found bordering the Rio Grande when they first arrived in this area in the 1530s. The dam here diverts river water for irrigation. The park offers campsites, rest rooms and showers, hiking trails, and access to fishing.

EXPLORING THE GHOST TOWNS IN THE AREA

NORTH OF TRUTH OR CONSEQUENCES   About 40 miles from Truth or Consequences you'll find the precarious remains of Winston and Chloride, two so-called ghost towns—abandoned mining centers that nevertheless do have a few residents. **Winston,** 37 miles northwest of T or C on NM 52, was abandoned in the early 1900s when silver prices dropped and local mining became unprofitable. Some of the original structures are still standing from that era. A similar fate befell **Chloride,** 5 miles west of Winston on a side road off NM 52, where famed silver mines had such names as Nana, Wall Street, and Unknown. Chloride also figured in many battles in the turn-of-the-century war between cattle-ranching and sheep-ranching interests.

SOUTH OF TRUTH OR CONSEQUENCES   Thirty-two miles from T or C, via I-25 south to NM 152, then west, is ✪ **Hillsboro,** another ghost town fast losing its ghosts to a small invasion of artists and craftspeople, antique shops, and galleries. This town boomed after an 1877 gold strike nearby, and during its heyday produced $6 million in silver and gold. It was the county seat from 1884 to 1938. Its Labor Day weekend Apple Festival is famous throughout the state.

The **Black Range Historical Museum** (☎ **505/895-5233** or 505/895-5685) contains exhibits and artifacts from Hillsboro's mining boom. Located in the former Ocean Grove Hotel, a turn-of-the-century brothel operated by Londoner Sadie Orchard, the museum collection includes some of the madam's effects. The museum is closed Tuesdays and Wednesdays and the entire months of January and February, but open most other afternoons.

The **Enchanted Villa** bed-and-breakfast inn, P.O. Box 456, Hillsboro, NM 88042 (☎ **505/895-5686**), is a 1941 two-story adobe offering five large rooms with king-size beds and private baths. The room rate, $60 for a double, includes full hot breakfasts. Full meal service is also available.

Nine miles west of Hillsboro on NM 152, just after you've entered the Gila National Forest, is **Kingston,** born with a rich silver strike in 1880 and locally reputed to have been among the wildest mining towns in the region, with 7,000 people, 22 saloons, a notorious red-light district (conveniently located on Virtue Avenue), and an opera house. Kingston was also once the home of Albert Fall, a U.S. secretary of state who gained notoriety for his role in the Teapot Dome Scandal.

Your headquarters in Kingston should be the **Black Range Lodge,** Star Route 2, Box 119, Kingston, NM 88042 (☎ **505/895-5652**), a rustic stone lodge that dates from the 1880s, and over the years has housed miners and soldiers, as well as Pretty Sam's Casino and the Monarch Saloon. There are seven rooms—all with private baths and some with private balconies—a large game room with pool table and video games, a solar-heated hot tub, and family suites. Rates are $55 to $65 double, with multiple-night discounts; both children and pets are welcome.

Among historic buildings in Kingston are the brick assay office, **Victorio Hotel,** and the **Percha Bank,** now a museum open by appointment—ask at the lodge. The town bell in front of the Volunteer Fire Department was first used to warn residents of Native American attacks, until the Apaches' final surrender in 1886. Nearby, **Camp Shiloh** has a public outdoor swimming pool open in summer (again, ask at Black Range Lodge).

EAST OF TRUTH OR CONSEQUENCES   Had your fill of ghost towns? Then you might prefer to head east of town via NM 51 where you will find three wineries near the community of Engle producing fine wines in limited quantities. **Domaine Cheurlin** (☎ **505/894-0837**), **Duvallay Vineyards** (☎ **505/894-7122**), and **Chateau Sassenage** (☎ **505/894-7244**) all welcome visitors by appointment.

WHERE TO STAY

Best Western Hot Springs Inn. 2270 N. Date St. at I-25 Exit 79, Truth or Consequences, NM 87901. ☎ **800/528-1234** or 505/894-6665. 40 rms. A/C TV TEL. $60–$70 double. AE, CB, DC, DISC, MC, V.

This freeway-exit motel lives up to the Best Western standard with spacious, comfortable units in a pleasant setting. Rooms are tastefully appointed and have large beds, remote-control television, and a clock radio. There's an outdoor pool, open seasonally; K-Bob's steak house is adjacent.

✪ **Elephant Butte Inn.** Hwy. 195 (P.O. Box E), Elephant Butte, NM 87935. ☎ **505/744-5431.** 48 rms. A/C TV TEL. $49 double; $59 double on summer weekends and holidays. AE, CB, DC, DISC, MC, V.

Situated above the shores of Elephant Butte Reservoir, this facility caters to boaters, fishermen, and other relaxation lovers. Rooms are furnished with king- or queen-size beds. The restaurant serves American, Italian, and New Mexican meals (dinners $7 to $20) from 6am to 9pm daily, an hour later on Friday and Saturday. The Sports Bar features a lighted volleyball court, horseshoes, and live entertainment. The inn has a swimming pool, tennis courts, and room service.

Rio Grande Motel. 720 Broadway, P.O. Box 67, Williamsburg, NM 87942. ☎ **505/894-9769.** 50 rms. A/C TV TEL. $35–$48 double. DISC, MC, V.

Located in the suburb of Williamsburg near the south access to Truth or Consequences from I-25, the Rio Grande offers clean, comfortable rooms for a budget price. Some rooms have kitchenettes. There's an outdoor swimming pool, a guest Laundromat, and a restaurant next door.

River Bend Hot Springs Hostel. 100 Austin St., Truth or Consequences, NM 87901. ☎ **505/894-6183.** 16 dormitory beds, 2 apartments. Dorm beds $12 for International Youth Hostel Association members, $15 for nonmembers; apartments $38–$46.

This pleasant hostel beside the Rio Grande has the added attraction of hot mineral baths on the premises. There are kitchenette units, family units, and couples can be accommodated. There is also a campground on the property ($7.50 per person), and a small houseboat. A guest laundry is available and day tours of area attractions can be arranged.

CAMPING

Elephant Butte Lake State Park (☎ 505/744-5421) welcomes backpackers and RVs alike. There are 125 sites, picnic tables, and access points for swimming, hiking, boating and fishing. Kids love the playground.

Not far from Elephant Butte Lake is **Monticello Point RV Park** (☎ 505/894-6468), which offers 69 sites, 58 full hookups, and tenting. Laundry and grocery facilities are also on the premises as well as horseshoes and volleyball. To reach Monticello Point, take I-25 to exit 89, then go $5^{1}/_{2}$ miles east on the gravel road—follow the signs.

Lakeside RV Park and Lodging (☎ 505/744-5996), also at Elephant Butte, has 54 sites, 43 full hookups, and tenting, as well as a recreation room/area and laundry facilities. If you are headed southbound on I-25, the RV park is located 4 miles southeast of the I-25 and NM 195 junction (exit 83) on NM 195. To reach the RV park headed northbound on I-25, take I-25 to exit 79, go $^{1}/_{2}$ mile east on the paved road, then $1^{1}/_{2}$ miles north on NM 181, then $1^{1}/_{2}$ miles east on NM 171, and finally $^{1}/_{4}$ mile south on NM 195.

Camping is also available at **Caballo Lake State Park** and **Percha Dam State Park.** For information on either park, call **505/743-3942.**

WHERE TO DINE

Dam Site Restaurant. Hwy. 177, Elephant Butte. ☎ **505/894-2073.** Main courses $4.95–$12.95. AE, CB, DC, DISC, MC, V. Sat–Sun 11am–10pm, Mon–Fri 11am–9pm. AMERICAN.

It was inevitable that this lakeside restaurant and lounge would give itself the sobriquet "a dam site better." Part of the Dam Site Recreation Area, it overlooks picturesque Elephant Butte Island and bustling marina. Steaks, fish, and some Mexican dishes are the fare. Also open for breakfast Saturday and Sunday 7 to 11am, Memorial Day to Labor Day.

⑨ **La Cocina.** 280 Date St. ☎ **505/894-6499.** Main courses $3.95–$14.50. No credit cards. Mon–Thurs 11am–9pm, Fri–Sun 11am–10pm. NEW MEXICAN.

This nicely appointed traditional restaurant serves New Mexican and American meals, including excellent compuestas and chile rellenos. The walls are decorated with the work of local artists, and you'll be astonished by the size of their sopaipillas.

La Piñata. 1990 South Broadway. ☎ **505/894-9047.** Main courses $1.75–$7.85. No credit cards. Mon–Sat 7am–8pm. MEXICAN/AMERICAN.

For authentic Mexican food at low prices, La Piñata is your best bet. You'll find all the old standbys, including tostadas, chile rellenos, tamales, burritos, and stacked or rolled enchiladas, as well as hamburgers and sandwiches on the menu. The decor is a little more "flashy" than other restaurants in town, and the service is fast and friendly. You can order à la carte, or you can get a full meal complete with rice and beans. Portions are large.

✪ **Los Arcos.** 1400 Date St. (Hwy. 85). ☎ **505/894-6200.** Reservations recommended. Main courses $9–$29.95. AE, CB, DC, DISC, MC, V. Sun–Thurs 5–10:30pm, Fri–Sat 5–11pm. AMERICAN.

A spacious hacienda-style restaurant fronted by a lovely desert garden, Los Arcos is intimate and friendly in atmosphere, as if you're at an old friend's home. Its steaks are regionally famous, and its fish dishes include fresh local catches such as walleye pike and catfish. The restaurant also has a fine dessert list and cordial selection.

5 Las Cruces

Established in 1849 on El Camino Real, the "royal highway" between Santa Fe and Mexico City, Las Cruces ("the crosses") was named for the graves of travelers who had been ambushed here a generation earlier by Apaches. It became a supply center for miners prospecting the Organ Mountains and soldiers stationed at nearby Fort Selden. Today, it is New Mexico's second-largest urban area, with 66,500 people in the city and 146,600 in Doña Ana County. It is noted as an agricultural center, especially for its cotton, pecans, and chiles; as a regional transportation hub; and as the gateway to the White Sands Missile Range and other defense installations.

ESSENTIALS

GETTING THERE By Car   From Albuquerque, take I-25 south (4 hours). From El Paso, take I-10 north (^{3}/$_4$ hour). From Tucson, take I-25 east (5 hours).

By Plane Las Cruces International Airport, 8 miles west, has about a dozen arrivals and departures a day to and from Albuquerque. Contact **Mesa Airlines** (☎ **800/MESA-AIR** or 505/526-9743). **El Paso International Airport,** 47 miles south, has daily flights to Phoenix, Dallas, and Houston. The **Las Cruces Shuttle Service,** 201 E. University Ave. (☎ **800/288-1784** or 505/525-1784), provides continuing service between the El Paso airport and Las Cruces. It leaves Las Cruces 12 times daily between 4:30am and 11:45pm, with a charge of $23 ($38 round-trip). There's a $7 pickup or drop-off charge for service elsewhere than its regular stops at the Las Cruces Hilton and Holiday Inn.

VISITOR INFORMATION   The **Las Cruces Convention and Visitors Bureau** is at 311 N. Downtown Mall, Las Cruces, NM 88001 (☎ **800/FIESTAS** or 505/ 524-8521). The **Las Cruces Chamber of Commerce** can be reached by writing P.O. Drawer 519, Las Cruces, NM 88004, or calling **505/524-1968.**

WHAT TO SEE & DO IN TOWN

Las Cruces's early history is the domain of adjacent ✪ **Mesilla.** This picturesque village on Las Cruces's southwestern flank was established in the late 1500s by Mexican colonists. It became the crossroads of El Camino Real and the Butterfield Overland Stagecoach route. The Gadsden Purchase, which annexed Mesilla to the United States and fixed the current international boundaries of New Mexico and Arizona, was signed in this village in 1854.

Mesilla's most notorious resident, William Bonney, otherwise known as Billy the Kid, was sentenced to death at the county courthouse. He was sent back to Lincoln, New Mexico, to be hanged, but escaped before the sentence was carried out. Legendary hero Pat Garrett eventually tracked down and killed the Kid at Fort Sumner; later, Garrett was mysteriously murdered in an arroyo just outside Las Cruces. He is buried in the local Masonic cemetery.

Thick-walled adobe buildings, which once protected residents against Apache attacks, now house art galleries, restaurants, museums, and gift shops. Throughout Mesilla, colorful red-chile ristras decorate homes and businesses.

A Walking Tour of Historic Las Cruces

Downtown Las Cruces has numerous historical buildings, which make a walking tour very worthwhile. **Bicentennial Log Cabin,** Main Street and Lucero Avenue, Downtown Mall (☎ 505/524-1422), is a circa-1850 structure moved to Las Cruces from the Black Range Mountains, containing authentic furnishings and artifacts. This municipal museum is open April through September by appointment. The **Branigan Cultural Center,** 500 N. Water St. (☎ 505/524-1422), features traveling and local exhibits of art and local history, and presents performing arts, educational programs, and special events.

The **Old Armijo House,** Lohman Avenue at Main Street, is an 1860s home that was at one time restored with original furnishings and second-floor display rooms. Now Pioneer Savings and Loan, the building is open weekdays from 9am to 4pm, but the display rooms are no longer open to the public. **Our Lady at the Foot of the Cross Shrine,** near Water Street and Lohman Avenue, is a reproduction of Michelangelo's *Pietà,* dedicated to the Sisters of Loretto. **El Molino,** a grinding wheel from an 1853 flour mill at Water Street and Lohman Avenue, commemorates the work and hardships of early pioneers. The **Amador Hotel,** Amador Avenue and Water Street, built in 1850, once hosted Benito Juarez, Pat Garrett, and Billy the Kid; restored, it now houses county offices and is not open to the public.

Other Attractions

San Albino Church. North side of Old Mesilla Plaza. Free admission; donations appreciated. Tues–Sun 1–3pm; English-language masses Sat 6:30pm and Sun 11am, Spanish mass Sun 8am.

This is one of the oldest churches in the Mesilla valley. Constructed in 1851, the present structure was built some 55 years later (1906) on its original foundation. It was named for St. Albin, medieval English bishop of North Africa, on whose day an important irrigation ditch from the Rio Grande was completed. The church bells date to the early 1870s; the pews were made in Taos of Philippine mahogany.

Gadsden Museum. Hwy. 28 and Barker Rd. ☎ **505/526-6293.** Admission $2 adults, $1 children 6–12. Mon–Sat 9–11am, daily 1–5pm.

A famous painting of the signing of the Gadsden Purchase is a highlight of this collection, from the Albert Jennings Fountain family. The museum, three blocks east of the Old Mesilla Plaza in the 1875 Fountain family home, also houses Indian and Civil War relics and Old West artifacts. All visitors go on the museum's guided tour.

New Mexico State University. University Ave. and Locust St. ☎ **505/646-0111.**

Established in 1888, this institution of 24,000 students is especially noted for its schools of business, engineering, and agriculture. Its facilities include the Solar Energy Institute, the Water Resources Institute of New Mexico, and the New Mexico Environmental Institute.

   University Museum in Kent Hall (☎ **505/646-3739**) has exhibits of historic and prehistoric Native American culture and art; it's open Tuesday through Friday from 10am to 4pm and Sunday from 1 to 4pm, with free admission. The **University Art Gallery** (☎ **505/646-2545**) features monthly exhibits of contemporary and historical art, and a permanent collection of prints, photographs, and folk art. **Corbett Center Gallery,** in the student center (☎ **505/646-3200**), has various exhibits throughout the year; a 12-foot copper-alloy triangle outside has a notch that symbolizes the transition from youth to adulthood. **Clyde Tombaugh Observatory,** named for the discoverer of the planet Pluto (who is a current resident of Las Cruces), has a high-powered telescope open for public viewing one evening a month.

ESPECIALLY FOR KIDS

Las Cruces Museum of Natural History. Mesilla Valley Mall, Telshor Blvd. ☎ **505/522-3120.** Free admission. Mon–Thurs noon–5pm, Fri noon–9pm, Sat 10am–6pm, Sun noon–6pm.

   This small city-funded museum offers a variety of exhibits, changing quarterly, that emphasize science and natural history. The museum features live animals of the Chihuahuan Desert, hands-on science activities, and a small native plant garden. The Cenozoic Shop offers scientific toys and books about the region.

SPECTATOR SPORTS

New Mexico State University football, basketball, baseball, and other teams play intercollegiate schedules in the Big West Conference, against schools from California, Nevada, and Utah. The "Aggies" play their home games on the NMSU campus, south of University Avenue on Locust Street. Football is played in the Chili Bowl, basketball in Pan Am Center arena. For information, call the Athletic Department (☎ **505/646-1420**).

Auto Racing   Fans of motor sports will find sprint and stock car racing at **The Speedway,** at Southern New Mexico State Fairgrounds, 11 miles west of Las Cruces via I-10 (☎ **505/524-7913**), open weekends from April through November.

Horse Racing   New Mexico's longest racing season takes place 45 miles south of Las Cruces at **Sunland Park** (☎ **505/589-1131**). The ponies run Wednesday, Friday, Saturday, and Sunday, October to May.

SHOPPING

Shoppers should be aware that in Las Cruces, Monday is a notoriously quiet day. Some stores close for the day, so it's best to call ahead before traveling to a specific store.

   For **art,** visit **Lundeen Inn of the Arts,** 618 Alameda Blvd. (☎ **505/526-3326**); **Rising Sky Artworks,** 415 E. Foster (☎ **505/525-8454**), which features works in clay by local and Western artists; **Universal Community Center of the Arts,** 207 Avenida de Mesilla (☎ **505/523-0014**); and the **William Bonney Gallery,** 3 Calle Parian, just off the southeast corner of Old Mesilla Plaza (☎ **505/526-8275**).

   For **books,** try **Mesilla Book Center,** in an 1856 mercantile building on the west side of Old Mesilla Plaza (☎ **505/526-6220**).

   For native **crafts and jewelry,** check out **Silver Assets,** Calle de Santiago (☎ **505/523-8747**), 1½ blocks east of San Albino Church in Mesilla.

Got a sweet tooth? **J. Eric Chocolatier,** featuring elegant hand-dipped and molded chocolates, is on the east side of Old Mesilla Plaza (☎ **505/526-2744**).

Mesilla Valley Mall is a full-service shopping center at 700 S. Telshor Blvd., just off the I-25 interchange with Lohman Avenue (☎ **505/522-1001**), with well over 100 stores. The mall is open Monday through Saturday from 10am to 9pm, and Sunday from noon to 6pm.

There are three **wineries** in the Las Cruces area. **Blue Teal Vineyards** (☎ **505/524-0390**) has a tasting room in the historic Fountain Theater, Calle de Guadalupe, just off the southeast corner of Old Mesilla Plaza. **La Viña Winery** (☎ **505/882-7632**), south of Las Cruces off NM 28, welcomes visitors by appointment; and **Mademoiselle de Santa Fe** (☎ **505/524-0481**), has a tasting room at 3910 W. Picacho Ave., Las Cruces.

LAS CRUCES AFTER DARK

National recording artists frequently perform at NMSU's **Pan Am Center** (☎ **505/646-4413**). The NMSU Music Department (☎ **505/646-2421**) offers free jazz, classical, and pop concerts, and the **Las Cruces Symphony** (☎ **505/646-3709**) often performs here as well.

Hershel Zohn Theater (☎ **505/646-4515**), at NMSU, presents plays of the professional/student **American Southwest Theatre Company:** dramas, comedies, musicals, and original works September through May.

The **Las Cruces Community Theatre** (☎ **505/523-1200**) mounts six productions a year at its own facility on the Downtown Mall.

A popular country-music and dancing club is **Cowboys,** 2205 S. Main St. (☎ **505/525-9050**), with no cover Tuesday or Wednesday, $3 Thursday through Saturday. Free hamburgers on Thursday, free french fries on Friday. Live bands are featured Tuesday through Saturday. Cowboys is closed Sunday and Monday.

EXPLORING THE AREA

NORTH OF LAS CRUCES   The town of **Hatch,** 39 miles via I-25 or 34 miles via NM 185, calls itself the "chile capital of the world." It is the center of a 22,000-acre agricultural belt that grows and processes more chile than anywhere else in the world. The annual Hatch Chile Festival over the Labor Day weekend celebrates the harvest. For information, call the Hatch Chamber of Commerce (☎ **505/267-5050**).

✪ **Fort Selden State Monument** is located 15 miles north of Las Cruces between I-25 (exit 19) and NM 185. Founded in 1865, Fort Selden housed the famous Black Cavalry, the "Buffalo Soldiers" who protected settlers from marauding natives. It was subsequently the boyhood home of Gen. Douglas MacArthur, whose father, Arthur, was in charge of troops patrolling the U.S.-Mexican border in the 1880s. There are only eroding ruins remaining today. Displays in the visitors center tell Fort Selden's story, including photos of young Douglas and his family. The fort closed permanently in 1891. The monument is open daily from 9am to 6pm in summer, and from 7am to 5pm in winter. Admission is $2 for adults, free for children 16 and under. For more information, call **505/526-8911.**

Adjacent to the state monument, **Leasburg Dam State Park** (☎ **505/524-4068**) offers picnicking, camping, canoeing, and fishing.

SOUTH OF LAS CRUCES   **Stahmann Farms,** 10 miles south of La Mesilla on NM 28 (☎ **505/526-2453**), is one of the world's largest single producers of pecans. Several million pounds are harvested annually from orchards in the bed of an ancient lake. Tours are given by appointment. **Stahmann's Country Store** (☎ **505/526-8974**) sells pecans and pecan candy, other specialty foods, and has a small cafe. It's open weekdays from 9am to 5:30pm, weekends from 10am to 5pm.

⚙ **War Eagles Air Museum** (☎ 505/589-2000), at the Santa Teresa Airport, about 35 miles south of Las Cruces via I-10 (call for directions), has an extensive collection of historic aircraft from World War II and the Korean conflict, including a beautifully restored P-38 Lightning, P-51 Mustang, F-86 Sabre, and several Russian MIG-15s. Most of the museum's two dozen planes are in flying condition, and are kept inside a large well-lighted hangar. The museum is open Tuesday through Sunday from 10am to 4pm; admission is $4 for adults, $3 for senior citizens; children under 12 are admitted free.

EAST OF LAS CRUCES   The **Organ Mountains,** so-called because they resemble the pipes of a church organ, draw inevitable comparisons to Wyoming's Grand Tetons. Organ Peak, at 9,119 feet, is the highest point in Doña Ana County.

The **Aguirre Springs Recreation Area** (☎ 505/525-4300), off U.S. Highway 70 on the western slope of the Organ Mountains, is operated by the Bureau of Land Management. Activities include hiking, camping, picnicking, and horseback riding.

WHERE TO STAY

Best Western Mesilla Valley Inn. 901 Avenida de Mesilla at I-25, Las Cruces, NM 88005. ☎ **800/327-3314,** 800/528-1234, or 505/524-8603. Fax 505/526-8437. 166 rms. A/C TV TEL. $58–$64 double. AE, CB, DC, DISC, MC, V.

A large motel set on spacious grounds near the north-south freeway, the Mesilla Valley Inn offers rooms that are comfortably decorated in a Southwestern motif. Executive rooms are very spacious and have refrigerators, clock radios, and remote-control televisions. Some rooms have kitchenette facilities.

The hotel's restaurant serves three meals daily, and the adjacent lounge has a piano bar and sometimes books light jazz combos. The hotel has room service, valet laundry, nonsmoking rooms, rooms accessible for people with disabilities, an outdoor swimming pool, Jacuzzi, guest laundry, and meeting space for 350. There is a nominal membership fee to use a nearby health and racquet club.

Best Western Mission Inn. 1765 S. Main St., Las Cruces, NM 88005. ☎ **800/528-1234** or 505/524-8591. Fax 505/523-4740. 68 rms, 2 suites. A/C TV TEL. $58 double; $82 suite. Rates include full breakfast. AE, CB, DC, DISC, MC, V.

The grounds of this two-story motel have several trees, including a big weeping willow shading a picnic table. Rooms are spacious, with a king or two queen-size beds. Colorful flowers are stenciled on the walls, big mirrors are surrounded by Mexican tiles, and there's a tile shelf behind the beds, giving it the mission look of its name. There are rooms for nonsmokers and people with disabilities.

There is a coffee shop (open daily), a restaurant (open nightly), and a sports bar with a deejay and dancing. The inn has a 24-hour desk, same-day laundry, an outdoor swimming pool, and a playground.

⚙ **Hampton Inn.** 755 Avenida de Mesilla (I-10 exit 140), Las Cruces, NM 88005. ☎ **800/426-7866** or 505/526-8311. Fax 505/527-2015. 118 rms. A/C TV TEL. $57–$63 double. Rates include continental breakfast. AE, CB, DC, DISC, MC, V.

This handsome Hampton Inn is in a very good location for vacationers, on the southwest side of Las Cruces near the numerous shops, galleries, restaurants, and attractions of historic Old Mesilla. Rooms are comfortable and quiet, with wood-trimmed furnishings; refrigerators and microwave ovens are available.

There's a very attractive outdoor swimming pool (unheated), and the continental breakfast is among the best you'll find in town. Rooms for nonsmokers and people with disabilities are available, local phone calls and use of a local health club are free, and pets are permitted.

✪ **Las Cruces Hilton.** 705 S. Telshor Blvd., Las Cruces, NM 88001. ☎ **800/284-0616** or 505/522-4300. Fax 505/521-4707. 203 rms, 7 suites. A/C TV TEL. $77–$86 double; $104–$300 suite. Weekend packages from $75 for a family, including breakfast. AE, CB, DC, DISC, MC, V.

Las Cruces's finest hotel was built in 1986 on a hill on the east side of the city, across the street from the Mesilla Valley Mall, with an incredible view of the city and the Organ Mountains. Its pleasant tiled lobby has southwestern-style furnishings. That motif carries to the decor of the spacious rooms.

The Ventana Terrace serves casual breakfast and lunch daily, then becomes a fine gourmet dining spot serving southwestern and continental specialties in the evening.

The hotel offers rooms for persons with disabilities, limited room service, 24-hour desk, courtesy van, valet laundry, an outdoor swimming pool, whirlpool, gift shop, car rental, and an exercise facility.

BED-&-BREAKFASTS

Hilltop Hacienda. 2600 Westmoreland Rd., Las Cruces, NM 88012. ☎ **505/382-3556.** 3 rms. A/C. $65 double. Rates include full breakfast. AE, MC, V.

The bed-and-breakfast is situated on 20 acres of land, 10 minutes north of the city. A two-story, arched-adobe brick dwelling of Spanish-Moorish architectural style, it offers spectacular views of the city, Rio Grande valley, and Organ Mountains. Breakfast is served outdoors on a wide patio or indoors beside a large fireplace. No smoking is allowed. For train enthusiasts, there is a miniature, passenger-carrying, live steam train on the premises.

Lundeen's Inn of the Arts. 618 S. Alameda Blvd., Las Cruces, NM 88005. ☎ **800/553-4ART** or 505/526-3326. Fax 505/647-1334. 20 rms, 4 suites. A/C. $68 double; $78–$130 suite. Rates include breakfast. AE, CB, DC, DISC, MC, V.

Operated by Gerald Lundeen, an architect and circuit preacher, and his wife, Linda, this bed-and-breakfast establishment is also an art gallery. A late 1890s adobe built in Territorial style, it displays the works of about 30 Southwest painters, sculptors, and potters in its 14,000 square feet of floor space.

Rooms are named for noted regional artists, including Georgia O'Keeffe, Amado Peña, R. C. Gorman, Frederic Remington, Nicolai Fechin, and Gordon Snidow, and each features the flavor of that artist. Every room is different, but all have wood floors and regional touches. Two suites have kitchenettes, TVs, and telephone. Guests in the main rooms share the TV and telephone in a downstairs common area. Some rooms have fireplaces. Breakfast includes fresh fruit and eggs, pancakes, strudels, and so forth.

The inn is a popular spot for weddings and artists' workshops including classes in silversmithing, pottery, and painting. The ElderHostel program also stays here. Guests get reduced rates at a local health club, and Gerry Lundeen will take them on architectural walking tours of nearby Old Mesilla.

✪ **Mesón de Mesilla.** 1803 Avenida de Mesilla (P.O. Box 1212), Mesilla, NM 88046. ☎ **800/732-6025** or 505/525-9212. Fax 505/525-2380. 13 rms. A/C TV TEL. $58–$92 double. Rates include breakfast. CB, DC, DISC, MC, V.

This large adobe home is a landmark on Highway 28 into Mesilla, and host Chuck Walker likes to say it has the "ambience of a Wine Country inn." Surrounded by beautiful gardens and adjacent to cotton fields, it certainly has the setting.

A portico surrounds the second floor, where the homey guest rooms are located. Appointed in Southwestern motifs with clock radios, brass headboards, antiques, and ceiling fans, each room has a private bath. Phones can be used for outgoing calls only; incoming messages are taken at the switchboard. A full breakfast is served in the garden atrium of the gourmet restaurant (see "Where to Dine," below).

Facilities include an outdoor swimming pool, horseshoes, bicycles (including a tandem) free for guests' use.

CAMPING

There are quite a few campgrounds located within or near Las Cruces. All of the ones listed here include full hookups for RVs, tenting areas, and recreation areas. **Best RV Park** (☎ 505/526-6555) also offers cabins, laundry, and grocery facilities. From the junction of I-10 and US 70 (exit 135), go 1¹/₂ miles east on US 70, then ¹/₂ block south on Weinrich Road.

Other campgrounds include **Dalmont's RV Park** (☎ **505/524-2992**; if you're coming from the west, when you reach the junction of I-25 and I-10, go 2¹/₂ miles northwest on I-10 to the Main Street exit, then go two blocks west on Valley Drive; if you're coming from the east, at the junction of I-10 and Main Street, go ¹/₄ mile north on Main Street and then one block west on Valley Drive) and **Siesta RV Park** (☎ **505/523-6816;** at the junction of I-10 and NM 28, exit 140, go ¹/₂ mile south on NM 28). **Leasburg State Park** (☎ **505/524-4068**) is a smaller park that also offers tent camping, but there are no laundry or grocery facilities. Hiking and river fishing are available.

WHERE TO DINE
EXPENSIVE

✪ **Double Eagle.** 308 Calle Guadalupe, on the east side of Old Mesilla Plaza. ☎ **505/523-6700.** Reservations recommended. Main courses $12.95–$26.95; lunch $5.25–$11.50. AE, CB, DC, DISC, MC, V. Mon–Sat 11am–10pm, Sun 5–9pm. CONTINENTAL.

The recent restoration of this 150-year-old hacienda has put the imposing Territorial-style premises on the National Historic Sites register. Its 30-foot-long bar has Corinthian columns in gold leaf, and there are Gay Nineties oil paintings and 18-armed brass chandeliers hung with Baccarat crystals. A woman's ghost is said to frequent one of the several exquisite small dining rooms. Specialties of the house include quail, breast of chicken Mesilla, 16-ounce pink mountain trout, and an 18-ounce filet mignon. All portions are generous. There is a lavish salad bar, international-style desserts and coffees, and a good wine and beer list. Sandwiches and light meals are served at lunch.

Mesón de Mesilla. 1803 Avenida de Mesilla, Mesilla. ☎ **505/525-2380.** Reservations required. Main courses $17.95–$34.95; lunch $4.95–$8.95; Sun brunch $13.95. AE, CB, DC, DISC, MC, V. Wed–Fri 11am–2pm; Tues–Sat 5:30–9pm; champagne brunch Sun 11am–2pm. CONTINENTAL.

Located in an elegant bed-and-breakfast at the northeast gateway to La Mesilla (see "Where to Stay," above), this gourmet restaurant has a Spanish colonial ambience with carved wooden pillars, stained-glass windows, wrought-iron chairs, and a rich burgundy color scheme. Chef Chuck Walker's blackboard menu changes weekly, but always presents several varieties of fresh fish, chicken, beef, and Eastern veal. All meals include soup, salad, main course, vegetables, and dessert. Main courses might be sautéed quail à la meson, black sea bass, shrimp Cardinale, or chateaubriand. Lunches feature salads, sandwiches, quiches, and a buffet. There's an extensive wine and beer list.

MODERATE

Ⓢ **Peppers.** 306 Calle Guadalupe, on the east side of Old Mesilla Plaza. ☎ **505/523-4999.** Reservations for large parties only. Tapas $1.35–$4.95; lunch $4.95–$8.25; dinner $7.95–$13.95. AE, CB, DC, DISC, MC, V. Mon–Sat 11am–10pm, Sun noon–9pm. NEW MEXICAN.

This restaurant shares a building and the same ownership with the Double Eagle, but the resemblance ends there. The Eagle has age and grace; Peppers has youthful exuberance. Hispanic folk art, including traditional masks and *santos,* greets guests in the entryway. Music from the sixties and seventies plays continuously. There are cacti on the tables. A regional artist is featured in the gallery.

The cuisine is Santa Fe–style New Mexican, heavy on seafood, such as the seafood chimichanga and blue-corn catfish. Other dishes include the La Fonda strip (sirloin with black beans and a guacamole-and-chipotle sauce), shark fajitas, and shrimp enchiladas. Tapas include green-chile wontons and tortilla-wrapped shrimp with pineapple-chile salsa.

Tatsu. 930 El Paseo Rd. ☎ **505/526-7144.** Main courses $9.25–$15.95; lunch $5.95–$9.50. AE, DC, MC, V. Mon–Thurs 11am–9pm, Fri 11am–10pm, Sat noon–10pm, Sun 11am–2pm and 5–9pm. JAPANESE/NEW ORIENTAL.

Tatsu may not be classic Japanese by New York or L.A. standards, but it does well for southern New Mexico. There are no tatami rooms here, but hanging paper lanterns and other designer touches lend a feeling of authenticity. Big windows face the street in the front room. There's somewhat more traditional decor in a rear chamber, which houses a Japanese garden.

Sushi, sukiyaki, and soba plates are integral to the menu. The tempura is excellent—seafood, vegetables, and a spicy relleno pepper. "East Meets West" specials include pecan chicken katsu, ginger beef, and soft-shell crab. Imported Japanese beers, sake, and wines are served with meals. There's a children's menu as well.

INEXPENSIVE

🟢 **Henry J's Gourmet Hamburgers.** 523 E. Idaho Ave. ☎ **505/525-2211.** Sandwiches and hamburgers $2.50–$6; full meals $7.25–$11.95. AE, DISC, MC, V. Sun–Thurs 10:30am–9pm, Fri–Sat 10:30am–10pm. AMERICAN.

Much more than a huge fifties soda fountain, which it incorporates, Henry J's has seating on three levels amidst big bay windows, brass railings, framed period advertisements, and a Wurlitzer jukebox. Besides great hamburgers, Henry J's Gourmet offers beef and chicken tacos, barbecue sandwiches, and a "bottomless" soup bowl priced at just $2.50.

La Posta de Mesilla. Southeast corner of Old Mesilla Plaza. ☎ **505/524-3524.** Reservations recommended. Main courses $2.50–$12.50. AE, CB, DC, DISC, MC, V. Sun, Tues–Thurs 11am–9pm, Fri–Sat 11am–9:30pm. NEW MEXICAN/STEAKS.

La Posta occupies a historic 150-year-old adobe building, the only surviving stagecoach station of the Butterfield, Overland Mail Route from Tipton, Missouri, to San Francisco. Kit Carson, Pancho Villa, and Billy the Kid all ate here. The entrance leads through a jungle of tall plants beneath a Plexiglas roof, past a tank of piranhas and a noisy aviary of macaws, cockatiels, and Amazon parrots, to nine dining rooms with bright, festive decor.

The menu features steaks and huge Mexican dinners. Beer and wine are served.

My Brother's Place Restaurant. 336 Main St. at Amador Ave. ☎ **505/523-7681.** Main courses $4–$14. AE, CB, DC, DISC, MC, V. Mon–Thurs 11am–9pm, Fri–Sat 11am–10pm. NEW MEXICAN.

Located between the Downtown Mall and the historic Amador Hotel, the Gutierrez brothers' modern adobe hacienda boasts a central fountain, tiled planters, vigas, and arches. Mexican menu favorites include fajitas and a hot-hot green enchilada; barbecues and burgers are also popular. Lunch specials are served Monday through Friday.

Three lounges adjoin the restaurant. The Main Street Lounge has an indoor patio overlooking the street from the second story. PM's Billiards Club and the Cantina Game Room have 19 pool tables between them. Margaritas are served by the glass and the pitcher.

6 Deming & Lordsburg

New Mexico's least populated corner is this one, which includes the "boot heel" of the Gadsden Purchase that pokes 40 miles down into Mexico. These two railroad towns, an hour apart on I-10, see a lot of traffic; but whereas Deming (pop. 13,406) is thriving as a ranching center, Lordsburg (pop. 3,010) is watching its population dwindle. This is a popular area for rock hounds, aficionados of ghost towns, and history buffs: Columbus, 32 miles south of Deming, was the site of the last foreign incursion on continental American soil, by the Mexican bandit-revolutionary Pancho Villa in 1916.

ESSENTIALS

GETTING THERE By Car From Las Cruces, take I-10 west (one hour to Deming, two hours to Lordsburg). From Tucson, take I-10 east (three hours to Lordsburg, four hours to Deming).

By Plane Deming's **Grant County Airport** serves private planes only. **The Las Cruces Shuttle** (☎ **800/288-1784**) has daily runs to El Paso Airport, and Deming, Las Cruces, and Silver City.

VISITOR INFORMATION The **Deming-Luna County Chamber of Commerce** is located at 800 E. Pine St., Deming, NM 88030 (☎ **800/848-4955** or 505/546-2674) and the **Lordsburg Hidalgo County Chamber of Commerce** is located at 208 Motel Dr. (P.O. Box 699), Lordsburg, NM 88045 (☎ **505/542-9864**).

WHAT TO SEE & DO NEAR DEMING

✪ **Deming Luna Mimbres Museum.** 301 S. Silver Ave., Deming. ☎ **505/546-2382.** Admission by donation. Mon–Sat 9am–4pm, Sun 1:30–4pm.

Deming was the meeting place of the second east-west railroad to connect the Pacific and Atlantic coasts, and that heritage is recalled in this museum, run by the Luna County Historical Society. It shows some pioneer-era quilts and laces; a military room containing exhibits from the Indian Wars, Pancho Villa's raid, both world wars, and the Korean and Vietnam Wars; a room featuring the John and Mary Alice King Collection of Mimbres pottery; and a doll room with more than 800 dolls. There's a gem and mineral room; a display of ladies' fashions from the Gay Nineties to the Roaring Twenties; a variety of pioneer silver, china, and crystal; and a new Transportation Annex with a chuck wagon, a "traveling kitchen." The museum also houses a collection of 2,200 bells from all over the world, as well as about 1,800 liquor decanters.

GETTING OUTSIDE

At **Rockhound State Park,** 14 miles southeast of Deming via NM 11, visitors are encouraged to pick and take home with them as much as 15 pounds of minerals—jasper, agate, quartz crystal, flow-banded rhyolite, and other rocks. Located at the base of the Little Florida Mountains, the park is an arid, cactus-covered land with trails leading down into dry gullies and canyons. (You may have to walk a bit, as the more accessible minerals have been largely picked out.)

The campground ($7 to $11 per night), which has shelters, rest rooms, and showers, gives a distant view of mountain ranges all the way to the Mexican border. The park also has hiking trails and a playground. Admission is $3 and the park is open year-round. For more information, call **505/546-6182.**

Some 35 miles south of Deming is the tiny border town of **Columbus,** looking across at Mexico. The **Pancho Villa State Park** here marks the last foreign invasion of American soil. A temporary fort, where a tiny garrison was housed in tents, was attacked in 1916 by 600 Mexican revolutionaries, who cut through the boundary fence at Columbus. Eighteen Americans were killed, 12 wounded; an estimated 200 Mexicans died. The Mexicans immediately retreated across their border. An American punitive expedition, headed by Gen. John J. Pershing, was launched into Mexico, but got nowhere. Villa restricted his banditry to Mexico after that, until his assassination in 1923.

The state park includes ruins of the old fort and a visitors center with exhibits and a film. The park also has a strikingly beautiful desert botanical garden, worth the trip alone, plus campsites, rest rooms, showers, an RV dump station, and a playground. For more information, call **505/531-2711.**

Across the street from the state park is the old Southern Pacific Railroad Depot, which has been restored by the Columbus Historical Society and now houses the **Columbus Historical Museum** (☎ **505/531-2620**), containing railroad memorabilia and exhibits on local history. Call for hours, and write to the historical society at P.O. Box 562, Columbus, NM 88029 for additional information about the community's history.

Three miles south is Las Palomas, Chihuahua (pop. 1,500). The port of entry is open 24 hours. Numerous restaurants and tourist-oriented businesses are located in Las Palomas.

WHAT TO SEE & DO NEAR LORDSBURG

Visitors to Lordsburg can go ✪ **rockhounding** in an area rich in minerals of many kinds. Desert roses can be found near Summit, and agate is known to exist in many abandoned mines locally. Mine dumps, southwest of Hachita, contain lead, zinc, and gold. There is manganese in the Animas mountains. Volcanic glass can be picked up in Coronado National Forest, and there is panning for gold in Gold Gulch.

Rodeo, 30 miles southwest via I-10 and US 80, is the home of the **Chiricahua Gallery** (☎ **505/557-2225**), open Monday through Saturday from 10am to 4pm. Regional artists have joined in a nonprofit, cooperative venture to exhibit works and offer classes in a variety of media. Many choose to live on the high-desert slopes of the Chiricahua Range. The gallery is on Highway 80 en route to Douglas, Arizona.

Shakespeare Ghost Town. P.O. Box 253, Lordsburg, NM 88045. ☎ **505/542-9034.** Admission $3 adults, $2 children 6–12; for shoot-outs and special events $4 adults, $3 children. 10am and 2pm second and fourth weekends of every month, except the fourth weekend of December, when it is closed. Special tours by appointment.

A national historic site, Shakespeare was once the home of 3,000 miners, promoters, and dealers of various kinds. Under the name *Ralston,* it enjoyed a silver boom in 1870. This was followed by a notorious diamond fraud in 1872 in which a mine was salted with diamonds in order to raise prices on mining stock; many notables were sucked in, particularly William Ralston, founder of the Bank of California. It enjoyed a mining revival in 1879 under its new name, Shakespeare. It was a town with no church, no newspaper, and no local law. Some serious fights resulted in hangings from the roof timbers in the Stage Station.

Since 1935, it's been privately owned by the Hill family, who have kept it uncommercialized with no souvenir hype or gift shops. They offer two-hour guided tours on a limited basis, and reenactments and special events four times a year. Six original buildings and two reconstructed buildings survive in various stages of repair.

To reach Shakespeare, drive 1.3 miles south from I-10 on Main Street. Just before the town cemetery, turn right, proceed .6 mile and turn right again. Follow the dirt road .4 mile into Shakespeare.

Steins Railroad Ghost Town. Exit 3, I-10 (P.O. Box 2185, Road Forks, NM 88045). ☎ **505/542-9791.** Admission $2.50 over 12 years; under 12, free. Daily 9am–dusk.

This settlement 19 miles west of Lordsburg started as a Butterfield Stage stop, then was a railroad town of about 1,000 residents from 1880 to 1955. It was so isolated that water, hauled from Doubtful Canyon, brought $1 a barrel!

Today there remain 10 buildings, with 16 rooms filled with artifacts and furnishings from the 19th and early 20th century. There is also a petting zoo for kids and the Steins Mercantile shop. The owners have plans to build a hotel.

WHERE TO STAY
DEMING

Best Western Mimbres Valley Inn. I-10 West Frontage Rd. (P.O. Box 1159), Deming, NM 88030. ☎ **800/528-1234** or 505/546-4544. 40 rms. A/C TV TEL. $52–$60 double. AE, CB, DC, DISC, MC, V.

This motel, built in 1993, has very comfortable rooms with Southwest art, pastel-colored walls, and wood furnishings. On the west side of Deming, it is within 3 miles of a public 18-hole golf course. There's an outdoor heated pool, rooms for nonsmokers and people with disabilities, and pets are welcome.

Chilton Inn. 1709 E. Spruce St. (P.O. Box 790), Deming, NM 88031. ☎ **505/546-8813.** Fax 505/546-7095. 57 rms. A/C TV TEL. $40–$46 double. AE, CB, DC, DISC, MC, V.

Tall pillars, a brick facade, and white-shuttered windows lend an elegant appearance to this main-drag motel, which is more than adequate in many respects. Rooms are clean and comfortable, with a Southwestern decor, working desks, and vanities. The Branding Iron restaurant open daily, has American-style dinners. The property has a swimming pool, and pets are allowed.

Grand Hotel. Hwy. 70/180 east of downtown (P.O. Box 309), Deming, NM 88031. ☎ **505/546-2631.** Fax 505/546-4446. 60 rms. A/C TV TEL. $48–$52 double. AE, CB, DC, DISC, MC, V.

Looking like a redbrick Colonial Williamsburg manor, the Grand is built around a lovely central lawn and shrubbery garden with two outdoor swimming pools. The pleasant rooms have floral decor and standard furnishings, including a large bathroom and an anteroom with a dressing table and wardrobe rack. Refrigerators are available. A restaurant is open from 6am to 9pm daily and there is an adjacent lounge. A courtesy car provides service to and from the train station. Nonsmoking rooms are available.

✪ **Holiday Inn.** Off I-10 (P.O. Box 1138), Deming NM 88031. ☎ **800/HOLIDAY** or 505/546-2661. Fax 505/546-6308. 80 rms. A/C TV TEL. $58–$68 double. AE, CB, DC, DISC, MC, V.

This fully renovated motel is one of Deming's finest. The owners practically gutted the place when they bought it several years ago, and have done a wonderful job of redecorating and refurbishing the large, comfortable rooms. Many of the guest rooms look out onto the heated outdoor pool, which is open April through October; all are decorated in soft pastels and have cable TV, direct dial phones, and vanity areas separate from the bathroom. The staff is friendly and extraordinarily efficient, which is due in part to the fact that the owners live in an apartment on the premises (a rarity for hotel chains). There is a coin-operated laundry as well as valet laundry.

Fat Eddie's, the hotel's restaurant, is open for breakfast, lunch, and dinner and serves New Mexican and American cuisine. Prices are very reasonable, and there's a children's menu. Room service is available during restaurant hours. The Lazy Lizard Lounge is open for cocktails Monday through Saturday from 4pm to midnight and until 11pm on Sundays. There are rooms for nonsmokers and people with disabilities. Pets are welcome. You won't find anything to complain about at this Holiday Inn.

⑤ **Wagon Wheel Motel.** 1109 W. Pine St., Deming, NM 88030. ☎ **505/546-2681.** 19 rms. A/C TV TEL. $29–$33 double. DISC, MC, V.

You'll find clean, comfortable, and inexpensive lodging in this mom-and-pop motel, which is within walking distance of several restaurants. Built in 1958, the motel has now been completely renovated. There is a heated swimming pool open in summer, 30-channel cable television, and guest laundry. Rooms for people with disabilities and nonsmokers are available, and pets are accepted.

LORDSBURG

Best Western American Motor Inn. 944 E. Motel Dr. (Alt. I-10), Lordsburg, NM 88045. ☎ **800/528-1234** or 505/542-3591. 92 rms. A/C TV TEL. $49–$65 double. AE, CB, DC, DISC, MC, V.

Located well off I-10 on the old highway through town, the American caters to families by offering an outdoor swimming pool, a small playground with swings, and a handful of family units. Rooms have sturdy maple furnishings and scenic Southwest prints on the walls. Some king-size beds are available, along with nonsmoking rooms. The restaurant, under separate management, serves three reasonably priced meals daily, and offers a kids' menu.

Best Western Western Skies Inn. 1303 S. Main St. at I-10 (Exit 22), Lordsburg, NM 88045. ☎ **800/528-1234** or 505/542-8807. 40 rms. A/C TV TEL. $52 double. AE, CB, DC, DISC, MC, V.

A newer property at the I-10 interchange, this motel has rooms appointed in earth tones and Southwestern motifs. Each has solid maple furnishings, a large bathroom area, and dressing table/vanity. There's an outdoor pool and free coffee in the lobby beginning at 5:30am. Kranberry's family style restaurant (see "Where to Dine," below) is next door.

CAMPING IN & AROUND DEMING & LORDSBURG

City of Rocks State Park, in Deming (☎ 505/536-2800), has 54 campsites; tenting is available, and there are picnic tables, hiking trails, and a playground. **Dreamcatcher RV Park** (☎ 505/544-4004), also in Deming (take exit 85, Motel Drive, off I-10 and go one block south on Business I-10) is of similar size and offers the same amenities, with the addition of a swimming pool, grills, and laundry facilities. **Little Vineyard RV Park** (☎ 505/546-3560) near Deming (from I-10 take exit 85 and go 1 mile southwest on Business I-10 towards Deming) is a bit larger than those already mentioned, but it offers the same facilities as Dreamcatcher RV Park, with the addition of limited groceries. The campground at **Rockhound State Park** (☎ 505/546-6182) is great for rock hounds who can't get enough of their hobby. Tenting is available, and there are grills, picnic tables, and hiking trails.

If you'd rather camp near Lordsburg, try **KOA Lordsburg** (☎ 505/542-8003). It's in a desert setting, but there are shade trees and tenting is permitted. Grocery and laundry facilities are available in addition to a recreation room/area, swimming pool, playground, and horseshoes. To reach the campground, take I-10 to exit 22 and then go one block south; next go right at the Chevron station and follow the signs to the campground.

WHERE TO DINE
DEMING

Ⓢ **Cactus Cafe.** 218 W. Cedar St. off I-10 (exit 82A). ☎ **505/546-2458.** Lunch or dinner $3.90–$9.95. AE, CB, DC, DISC, MC, V. Daily 7am–9pm. AMERICAN/NEW MEXICAN.

This family restaurant has a friendly atmosphere that carries into the colorful regional decor. There's a wide choice of menu selections, including chile rellenos, shrimp fajitas, and the popular Tampiqueña steak with green chiles and onions.

K-Bob's. 316 E. Cedar St. off I-10. ☎ **505/546-8883.** Lunch or dinner $3–$17. AE, DISC, MC, V. Daily 10:30am–10pm. STEAKS.

This family style steak house offers a wide selection of steaks, chicken, and deep-fried seafood. It is home to the $2.99 chicken-fried steak, and has a large salad bar, a children's menu, and a selection of beers and wines. Soups, sandwiches, and burgers are always available.

LORDSBURG

Kranberry's Family Restaurant. 1405 S. Main St., Lordsburg, NM 88045. ☎ **505/542-9400.** Lunch and dinner main courses $2.70–$13.30. AE, CB, DC, DISC, MC, V. Daily 6am–10pm. AMERICAN/MEXICAN.

A friendly, casual family restaurant decorated with Southwest art, Kranberry's offers home-style American favorites including burgers, chicken, beef, and salads, as well as Mexican selections. Baked goods are made on the premises daily, and there's a children's menu.

7 Silver City: Gateway to the Gila Cliff Dwellings

Silver City (pop. 11,508) is an old mining town, located in the foothills of the Pinos Altos Range of the Mogollon Mountains, and gateway to the Gila Wilderness and the Gila Cliff Dwellings. Early Native Americans mined turquoise from these hills, and by 1804 Spanish settlers were digging for copper. In 1870, a group of prospectors discovered silver, and the rush was on. In 10 short months, the newly christened Silver City grew from a single cabin to more than 80 buildings. Early visitors included Billy the Kid, Judge Roy Bean, and William Randolph Hearst.

This comparatively isolated community kept pace with every modern convenience: telephones in 1883, electric lights in 1884 (only two years after New York City installed its lighting), and a water system in 1887. Typically, the town should have busted with the crash of silver prices in 1893. But unlike many Western towns, Silver City did not become a picturesque memory. Silver City capitalized on its high dry climate to become today's county seat and trade center. Copper mining and processing are still the major industry. But Silver City also can boast a famous son: astronaut Harrison (Jack) Schmitt, the first civilian geologist to visit the moon, and later a U.S. senator, was born and raised in nearby Santa Rita.

ESSENTIALS

GETTING THERE   By Car   From Albuquerque take I-25 south, 15 miles past Truth or Consequences; then west on NM 152 and US 180 (five hours). From Las Cruces take I-10 west to Deming, then north on US 180 (two hours).

By Plane   Mesa Airlines (☎ **800/MESA-AIR** or 505/388-4115) flies daily from Albuquerque to Silver City-Grant County Airport, 15 miles south of Silver City near

Hurley. Pick up a car there from **Grimes Aviation and Car Rental** (☎ 505/ 538-2142). **Silver Stage Lines** (☎ 800/522-0162) offers daily shuttle service to the El Paso and Tucson airports. **The Las Cruces Shuttle** (☎ 800/288-1784) has daily runs to El Paso Airport, and Deming, Las Cruces, and Silver City.

By Bus There's no regular commercial service into Silver City.

VISITOR INFORMATION The **Silver City-Grant County Chamber of Commerce,** at 1103 N. Hudson St., Silver City, NM 88061 (☎ 800/548-9378 or 505/ 538-3785), maintains a visitor information headquarters on NM 90, a few blocks south of US 180. The chamber produces extremely useful tourist publications.

WHAT TO SEE & DO IN TOWN

Silver City's downtown ✪ **Historic District,** the first such district to receive National Register recognition, is a must for visitors. The downtown core is marked by the extensive use of brick in construction: Brick clay was discovered in the area soon after the town's founding in 1870, and an 1880 ordinance prohibited frame construction within the town limits. Mansard-roofed Victorian houses, Queen Anne and Italianate residences, and commercial buildings show off the cast-iron architecture of the period. Some are still undergoing restoration.

An 1895 flood washed out Main Street and turned it into a gaping chasm, which was eventually bridged over; finally, the **Big Ditch,** as it's called, was made into a green park in the center of town. Facing downtown, in the 500 block of North Hudson Street, was a famous red-light district from the turn of the century until the late 1960s.

Billy the Kid lived in Silver City as a youth. You can see his cabin site a block north of the Broadway bridge, on the east side of the Big Ditch. The Kid (William Bonney) waited tables at the Star Hotel, Hudson Street and Broadway. He was jailed (at 304 N. Hudson St.) in 1875 at the age of 15, after being convicted of stealing from a Chinese laundry, but he escaped—a first for the Kid. The grave of Bonney's mother, Catherine McCarty, is in Silver City Cemetery, east of town on Memory Lane, off US 180. She died of tuberculosis about a year after the family moved here in 1873.

✪ **Silver City Museum.** 312 W. Broadway. ☎ **505/538-5921.** Free admission. Tues–Fri 9am–4:30pm, Sat–Sun 10am–4pm. Closed Mondays except Memorial Day and Labor Day.

This very well presented museum of city and regional history contains collections relating to southwest New Mexico history, mining displays, Native American pottery, and early photographs. Exhibits include a southwest New Mexico history time line; a parlor displaying Victorian decorative arts; and a chronicle of commerce in early Silver City. A local history research library is available to visitors also. The main gallery features changing exhibits.

The museum is lodged in the newly restored 1881 H. B. Ailman House, a former city hall and fire station remarkable for its cupola and Victorian mansard roof. Ailman came to Silver City penniless in 1871, made a fortune in mining, and went on to start the Meredith and Ailman Bank.

Western New Mexico University Museum. 1000 W. College, Fleming Hall, WNMU. ☎ 505/538-6386. Admission by donation. Mon–Fri 9am–4:30pm, Sat–Sun 10am–4pm.

Spread across 80 acres on the west side of Silver City, WNMU celebrated its centennial in 1993. The university boasts a 2,500-student enrollment and 24 major buildings. Among them is historic Fleming Hall, which houses this interesting museum.

The WNMU museum has the largest permanent exhibit of prehistoric Mimbres pottery in the United States. Also displayed are Casas Grandes Indian pottery, stone tools, ancient jewelry, historical photographs, and mining and military artifacts. Displays change regularly, so there is always something new to see, such as vanishing Americana, riparian fossils, Nigerian folk art, or a collection of 18th- to 20th-century timepieces. There is a gift shop here.

EXPLORING THE AREA

NORTH OF SILVER CITY   The virtual ghost town of ✪ **Pinos Altos,** straddling the Continental Divide, is 6 miles north of Silver City on NM 15. Dubbed "Tall Pines" when it was founded in the gold- and silver-rush era, Apache attacks and mine failures have taken their toll.

The adobe **Methodist-Episcopal Church** was built with William Randolph Hearst's money in 1898 and now houses the Grant County Art Guild. The **Pinos Altos Museum** displays a ³/₄-scale reproduction of the Santa Rita del Cobre Fort and Trading Post, built at Santa Rita copper mine in 1804 to protect the area from Apaches. (It was renamed Fort Webster in 1851.) It's still possible to pan for gold in Pinos Altos. The town also has the **Log Cabin Curio Shop and Museum** located in an 1866 cabin (☎ **505/388-1882**), and the Buckhorn Saloon restaurant (see "Where to Dine," below).

SOUTH OF SILVER CITY   South 12 miles on NM 90 is the **Phelps Dodge Open Pit Copper Mine** (☎ **505/538-5331**). Some 80 million tons of rock are taken out every year. An observation point is open Monday through Friday from 7am to sunset; free guided tours are offered weekdays at 9am, with a day's advance reservation.

Phelps Dodge consolidated its Tyrone holdings in 1909 and hired famous architect Bertram Goodhue to design a "Mediterranean–style" company town. **Tyrone,** later referred to as the Million Dollar Ghost Town, was constructed between 1914 and 1918. A large bank and shop building, administration office, mercantile store, and passenger depot were grouped around a central plaza. Eighty-three single and multiple-unit dwellings, accommodating 235 families, were built on the nearby hillsides; and a school, chapel, garage, restaurant, justice court, hospital, morgue, and recreation building were added. A drop in copper prices caused it to be abandoned virtually overnight.

After a pre–World War II incarnation as a luxurious dude ranch, Tyrone lay dormant for years until the late 1960s, when the town made way for the present-day open pit mine and mill. A new townsite was created 7 miles north. Most of the original homes and major buildings were removed between 1967 and 1969; today, the only remaining structures are Union Chapel, the justice court, and the pump house. The copper mine supplies copper concentrates to the modern Hidalgo Smelter near Playas, southeast of Lordsburg.

EAST OF SILVER CITY   The oldest active mine in the Southwest, and among the largest in America, is the **Chino Mines Co. Open Pit Copper Mine** at Santa Rita, 15 miles east of Silver City via US 180 and NM 152. The multicolored open pit is a mile wide and 1,000 feet deep, and can be viewed from a spectacular observation point with a small museum. Apaches once scratched the surface for metallic copper. By 1800, the Spanish, under Col. Jose Manuel Carrasco, were working "Santa Rita del Cobre." Convict labor from New Spain mined the shafts, with mule trains full of ore sent down the Janos Trail to Chihuahua, Mexico. An impressive adobe fort was built near the mine, along with smelters and numerous buildings, but Apache raids finally forced the mine's abandonment. In the late 19th century, the mine was reopened, and the town of Santa Rita was reborn. The huge open pit, started around 1910, soon consumed Santa Rita. Giant-sized machines scoop the ore from the earth and huge 175-ton ore trucks transport it to the reduction mill to the southwest of the pit.

☼ **City of Rocks State Park** (☎ **505/536-2800**), 30 miles from Silver City via US 180 and NM 61, is an area of fantastically shaped volcanic rock formations, formed in ancient times from thick blankets of ash that hardened into tuff. This soft stone, eroded by wind and rain, was shaped into monolithic blocks reminiscent of Stonehenge. For some, the park resembles a medieval village; for others, it is a collection of misshapen, albeit benign giants. Complete with a desert garden, the park offers excellent camping and picnic sites. Hot water is solar heated, while windmills pump it and make electricity; the park is thus self-sufficient.

WEST OF SILVER CITY   US 180, heading northwest from Silver City, is the gateway to Catron County and most of the Gila National Forest, including the villages of Glenwood, Reserve, and Quemado. For details on this area, see section 9, below.

WHERE TO STAY

Standard motels are strung along US 180 east of NM 90. Some of the more interesting accommodations, however, are not! Most lodgings provide free parking.

Copper Manor Motel. 710 Silver Heights Blvd. (Hwy. 180) (P.O. Box 1405), Silver City, NM 88061. ☎ **800/853-2916** or 505/538-5392. 67 rms. A/C TV TEL. $48–$54 double. AE, CB, DC, MC, V.

A standard roadside motel, the Copper Manor has the advantage of being part of a one-ownership complex that includes the Red Barn Steak House next door (see "Where to Dine," below) and the Drifter Motel and Restaurant across the street. Room decor is bold; the bathrooms quite small. Facilities include an indoor pool and whirlpool; guests can also use the Drifter's outdoor pool.

Holiday Motor Hotel. 3420 Hwy. 180 E., Silver City, NM 88061. ☎ **800/828-8291** or 505/538-3711. 80 rms. A/C TV TEL. $55–$65 double. AE, DC, DISC, MC, V.

Located about 3 miles east of downtown near the junction of US 180 and NM 15, this motel is a step above the ordinary with its landscaped grounds, attractive outdoor swimming pool, playground, all-night security guard, and guest Laundromat. Rooms are clean and comfortable, with custom-made furnishings. The restaurant serves three meals Monday through Saturday from 6am to 2pm and 5 to 8:30pm, and Sunday, from 7am to 2pm and 5 to 8:30pm, with a menu superior to the typical hotel coffee shop.

SMALLER INNS

Bear Mountain Guest Ranch. Bear Mountain Rd., Silver City, NM 88061. ☎ **800/880-2538** or 505/538-2538. 15 rms, 2 cottages. $98 double; $110–$205 suites; cottage with kitchenette (meals not included), $65–$90 for 1 to 4 persons. Rates include 3 meals daily. No credit cards. To reach the ranch, turn north off US 180 on Alabama St, 1/2 mile west of NM 90 intersection. Proceed 2.8 miles (Alabama becomes Cottage San Rd., then Bear Mountain Rd.) to turnoff; the ranch is another 0.6 miles.

Spread across 160 acres just 3 1/2 miles northwest of downtown Silver City, Myra McCormick's ranch has been a New Mexico institution since 1959. This is a nature-lover's delight—McCormick hosts birding, wild plant, and archaeological workshops throughout the year, and a "Lodge and Learn" series (for adults of all ages) is a feature every month. The ranch doesn't have horses, but visitors are urged to "bring your own." All rooms have private baths, and home-cooked meals are served in a family style setting.

The Carter House. 101 N. Cooper St., Silver City, NM 88061. ☎ **505/388-5485.** 5 rms and 20 youth-hostel bunks. $58–$69 per room, bed-and-breakfast; $14 per bed ($12 for hostel association members) in youth hostel. MC, V.

The top floor of this renovated 1906 mansion, situated next door to the Grant County Courthouse, is a classic bed-and-breakfast establishment. The lower floor is an official Hostelling International facility. It's a unique combination, but seems to work. B&B patrons feel at home with a living and dining room, library and TV room, all decorated with 19th-century prints—family heirlooms of owner Lucy Dilworth. They also can share the laundry and kitchen facilities with the hostelers in the basement.

⑤ **The Palace Hotel.** 106 W. Broadway (P.O. Box 5093), Silver City, NM 88061. ☎ **505/388-1811.** 13 rms, 7 suites. TV. $34.50–$46.50 single or double; $45–$48 suite. Rates include continental breakfast. AE, DC, DISC, MC, V.

Old-fashioned elegance and Victorian decor are earmarks of this hotel, first established 1882 and reopened in July 1990 as a historic small European-style hotel. Each of the rooms on the second floor is shaped and decorated differently. All have standard furnishings and steam heat, but bed sizes vary from king to single; some have refrigerators; two share baths; all others have bathtubs and showers. That's a sight better than in 1882! The owners provide fresh fruit, bread, juice, fruit, coffee, and tea for breakfast, which is served in the upstairs skylit garden room.

CAMPING

KOA Silver City (☎ **800/KOA-7623**) has 77 sites and 42 full hookups, and offers the same facilities and amenities you'd expect at a KOA property. The campground is 5 miles east of the NM 90/US 180 junction on US 180. **Silver City RV Park** (☎ **505/538-2239**) has 50 sites, 43 full hookups, laundry facilities, and picnic tables. Camping is also available at the Gila Cliff Dwellings, see section 8 below.

WHERE TO DINE

✪ **Buckhorn Saloon and Opera House.** 62 Main St., Pinos Altos. ☎ **505/538-9911.** Reservations strongly recommended. Main courses $12.95–$28.95. MC, V. Mon–Sat 6–10pm. CONTINENTAL/STEAKS.

Seven miles north of Silver City in Pinos Altos, the surprising Buckhorn offers elegant dining in 1860s decor. It's noted for its Western-style steaks, seafood, homemade desserts, and excellent wine list. There's live entertainment nightly; the saloon opens at 3pm during the week.

The Red Barn Steak House. 708 Silver Heights Blvd. (Hwy. 180). ☎ **505/538-5666.** Lunch $4.25–$9.50; dinner $7.50–$21.25. AE, CB, DC, DISC, MC, V. Daily 11am–10pm. AMERICAN.

This big red barn, with its white silo, is unmistakable on the south side of US 180 as it enters Silver City from the east. The interior is spacious and comfortable, with atmospheric wagon-wheel chandeliers. Steaks are the specialty, from beef teriyaki to steak Oscar. A 20-ounce T-bone is just $18.95. There's a large salad bar. At the rear of the restaurant is the Watering Hole Lounge.

8 Gila Cliff Dwellings National Monument

It takes at least 1¹/₂ to 2 hours to reach the Gila Cliff Dwellings from Silver City, but it's definitely worth the trip. First-time visitors are inevitably awed by the sight. At this stone-within-stone-on-stone relic of a long-gone civilization, reality is somehow exaggerated in the dazzling sunlight and contrasting shadow, making the dwellings look, from a distance, as two-dimensional as a stage set. The solid masonry walls are well preserved, even though they've been abandoned for seven centuries.

The cliff dwellings were discovered by Anglo settlers in the early 1870s, near where the three forks of the Gila River rise. Seven natural caves occur in the southeast-facing cliff of a side canyon; six of them contain the ruins of dwellings, which had about 42 rooms. Probably not more than 8 or 10 Mogollon families (40 to 50 people) lived in these dwellings at any one time. Tree-ring dating indicates their residence didn't last longer than 30 to 40 years at the end of the 13th century.

ESSENTIALS

GETTING THERE   From Silver City take NM 15 up 44 miles to the Gila Cliff Dwellings. Travel time from Silver City is approximately two hours. Keep in mind that there are no gas stations available between Silver City and Gila Cliff Dwellings, so plan accordingly. Once you get to the monument, you should know that vehicles are permitted on paved roads only.

VISITOR INFORMATION   Admission to the monument is free and the visitors center, where you can pick up detailed brochures on the homes in the monument, is open from 8am to 7pm from Memorial day to Labor day; from 8am to 5pm the rest of the year. The cliff dwellings are open from 9am to 7pm daily in the summer, and from 9:30am to 5pm the rest of the year. For more information about Gila Cliff Dwellings, write Box 100, Silver City, NM 88061 or call **505/536-9461.**

SEEING THE HIGHLIGHTS

Today, the dwellings allow a rare glimpse inside the homes and lives of prehistoric Native Americans. About 75% of what is seen is original, although the walls have been capped and the foundations strengthened to prevent further deterioration. It took a great deal of effort to build these homes: The stones were held in place by mortar, and all of the clay and water for the mortar had to be carried up from the stream, as the Mogollon did not have any pack animals. The vigas for the roof were cut and shaped with stone axes or fire.

The people who lived here were farmers, as shown by the remains of beans, squash, and corn in their homes. The fields were along the valley of the west fork of the Gila River and on the mesa across the canyon. No signs of irrigation have been found.

A 1-mile loop trail, rising 175 feet from the canyon floor, provides access to the dwellings.

Near the visitor center, about a mile away, the remains of an earlier (A.D. 100–400) pit house, built below ground level, and later pit houses (up to A.D. 1000), aboveground structures of adobe or wattle, have been found.

CAMPING

Camping and picnicking are encouraged in the national monument. There is a total of 20 sites on two improved campgrounds. Overnight lodging can be found in Silver City and in the nearby town of Gila Hot Springs, which also has a grocery store, horse rentals, and guided pack trips.

9 Other Adventures in Gila National Forest

Gila National Forest, which offers some of the most spectacular mountain scenery in the Southwest, comprises 3.3 million acres in four counties. Nearly one-fourth of that acreage (790,000) comprises the **Gila, Aldo Leopold,** and **Blue Range Wildernesses.** Gila National Forest also contains numerous lakes and 360 miles of mountain streams. Its highest peak is Whitewater Baldy, 10,892 feet. Big-game animals found here include mule deer, elk, antelope, black bear, mountain lion, and bighorn sheep. Anglers can head to Lake Roberts, Snow Lake, and Quemado Lake.

JUST THE FACTS For more information on the national forest, contact U.S. Forest Service, Forest Supervisor's Office, 3005 East Camino del Bosque, Silver City, NM 88061; or call **505-388-8201.** Permits are required to enter.

HIKING & OTHER ACTIVITIES

Within the forest are 1,490 miles of trails for hiking and horseback riding, and in winter, cross-country skiing and snowmobiling; outside of the wilderness areas, trail bikes and off-road vehicles are also permitted. Hiking trails in the Gila Wilderness, especially the 41-mile Middle Fork Trail, with its east end near Gila Cliff Dwellings, are among the most popular in the state, and can sometimes be crowded. If you are more interested in communing with nature than with fellow hikers, however, you will find plenty of trails to suit you, both in and out of the officially designated wilderness areas.

Most of the trails are maintained and easy to follow. Trails along river bottoms, however, have many stream crossings (so be prepared for hiking with wet feet) and may be washed out by summer flash floods. It's best to inquire about trail conditions before you set out. More than 50 trailheads provide roadside parking.

The ✪ **Catwalk National Recreation Trail** (☎ 505/539-2481), 68 miles north of Silver City on US 180, then 5 miles east of Glenwood via NM 174, is reached by foot from a parking area. It follows the route of a pipeline built in 1897 to carry water to the now-defunct town of Graham and its electric generator. About a $1/4$ mile above the parking area is the beginning of a striking 250-foot metal causeway clinging to the sides of the boulder-choked Whitewater Canyon, which in spots is 20 feet wide and 250 feet deep. Spectacular vistas are found farther up the canyon, where a suspension bridge spans the chasm. Picnic facilities are located near the parking area.

CAMPING

Eighteen campgrounds can be found in the national forest; seven with drinking water and toilets, and 11 without drinking water. Backcountry car and backpack camping are also permitted throughout the forest.

OTHER HIGHLIGHTS

The scenic ghost town of **Mogollon** is $3^{1}/_{2}$ miles north of Glenwood on US 180, then 9 miles east on NM 159, a narrow mountain road. The village bears witness to silver and gold mining booms beginning in the late 19th century, and to the disastrous effects of floods and fire in later years. Remains of its last operating mine, the Little Fanny (which ceased operation in the 1950s), are still visible, along with dozens of other old buildings, miner's shacks, and mining paraphernalia. An art gallery and museum are found along Mogollon's main street. The movie *My Name Is Nobody,* starring Henry Fonda, was shot here.

Reserve (pop. 300), Catron County seat, is noted as the place where, in 1882, Deputy Sheriff Elfego Baca made an epic stand in a 33-hour gun battle with 80 cowboys. Cochise, Geronimo, and other Apache war chiefs held forth in these mountains in the late 19th century.

12 Southeastern New Mexico

Southeastern New Mexico encompasses that part of the state east of the Rio Grande (the I-25 corridor) and south of I-40. It is a vast and surprising region that in many ways is typical of the "real" West.

Here you'll find the spectacular Carlsbad Caverns and the awesome White Sands National Monument. This is the home of the fierce Mescalero Apaches and of the world's richest horse race. Billy the Kid lived and died in southeastern New Mexico in the 19th century, and the world's first atomic bomb was exploded here in the 20th. From west to east, barren desert gives way to high, forested peaks, snow-covered in winter; to the fertile valley of the Pecos River; and to high plains beloved by ranchers along the Texas border.

The main population center in this section of the state is Roswell, a city of about 47,395. Carlsbad (pop. 26,974), 76 miles south of Roswell, and Alamogordo (pop. 29,628), 117 miles west of Roswell, are of more immediate interest to tourists. Other sizable towns are Clovis (pop. 36,091) and Hobbs (pop. 29,712), both on the Texas border, and Artesia (pop. 11,743), between Roswell and Carlsbad. Ruidoso (pop. 5,502), in the mountains between Alamogordo and Roswell, is a booming resort town.

TOURING THE REGION BY CAR

From Albuquerque, head south on I-25 to San Antonio, just beyond Socorro, then turn east on US 380 through Carrizozo. This route will take you first to the Ruidoso area, whose major attractions can be defined by a triangle formed by US 380, US 70, and NM 48. Ruidoso is the home of the world's richest horse race, and nearby Lincoln National Forest attracts outdoor enthusiasts. This is also Billy the Kid country, and the historic village of Lincoln recounts those Wild West days.

Next, drive south on US 70 to explore Alamogordo and White Sands National Monument. Spend the night in Alamogordo. I recommend camping out so you can watch the sun rise. The next day, follow US 82 east through the charming mountain village of Cloudcroft and down the valley of the Rio Penasco with its fruit orchards. At Artesia, turn south on US 285 to Carlsbad, where you can explore the town and its famous caverns.

Southeastern New Mexico

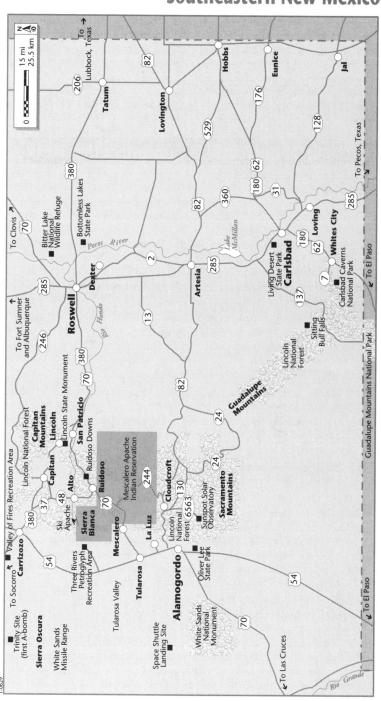

305

From Carlsbad, you can follow two routes. You can reverse course back up Highway 285 to Roswell, where you can check out the two UFO research museums or the Roswell Art Center and (via NM 20) Fort Sumner, site of Fort Sumner State Monument and Billy the Kid's grave. Or you can meander through the Llano Estacado along the Texas border, taking US 62/180 east to Hobbs, then turning north on NM 206 to Clovis. From the latter city, Fort Sumner is an hour's drive west on US 60/84. Next, head north from Fort Sumner on US 84 to I-40 at Santa Rosa; from there it's a two-hour drive west to Albuquerque.

1 The Great Outdoors in Southeastern New Mexico

BIKING Several unpaved roads in this region are favorites with mountain bikers. In the Ruisodo area, near Cloudcroft, the **Rim Trail,** a 17-mile intermediate trail that offers views of the White Sands, is considered one of the top 10 trails in the nation. To reach the trail, take NM 130 from Cloudcroft and look for the Rim Trail signs. For beginners, the Bonito Lake Road offers a scenic but easy 20-mile (round-trip) ride through the forest and around the lake. To reach the trail, take NM 48 from Ruidoso and turn off at NM 37. The road from Ski Apache Road up to Monjeau Campground as well as several other roads in the Bonito Lake area near Ruidoso are also well-traveled bike routes, as is the road up to **Carlsbad Caverns National Park** (especially in cooler months).

BIRD-WATCHING **Bitter Lake National Wildlife Refuge** (☎ 505/622-6755) is particularly good for watching migratory waterfowl, and Bluff Springs, just south of Cloudcroft, is popular with turkeys and hummingbirds (☎ **505/682-2551**). If you find turkey vultures particularly fascinating, **Rattlesnake Springs,** located south of Carlsbad (☎ **505/785-2232**), is the place to go.

BOATING Boating, waterskiing, jet skiing, and sailing are permitted at **Carlsbad Municipal Park,** which runs through town for just over a mile along the west bank of Lake Carlsbad. The lake also has 1,000 feet of beach open to swimmers. **Brantley Lake State Park** (☎ 505/457-2384), 15 miles north of Carlsbad, is popular with windsurfers who favor its consistent desert winds.

FISHING **Bonito Lake** and **Rio Ruidoso** are popular destinations for trout fishing, and **Oasis State Park** just north of Portales also offers fishing.

GOLF There are plenty of opportunities in this region. **Cree Meadows Country Club,** Country Club Drive off Sudderth Drive (☎ 505/257-5815), is an 18-hole public course. Also public are the 18-hole courses at the **Inn of the Mountain Gods,** Carrizo Canyon Road (☎ 505/257-5141); **The Links at Sierra Blanca,** 105 Sierra Blanca Dr. (☎ 505/258-5330); and the nine-hole **Carrizozo Golf Course** (☎ 505/648-2451) in Carrizozo. **Alto Lakes Golf and Country Club,** High Mesa Drive, Alto Village (☎ 505/336-4231), is an 18-hole private course.

HIKING More than 225 miles of trails weave a web through Smokey Bear Ranger District of the **Lincoln National Forest.** From Ruidoso, a favorite destination of hikers is the White Mountain Wilderness, with nine trailheads, and the Capitan Mountains Wilderness, with 11 trails. Smokey Bear Ranger District office, 901 Mechem Dr., Ruidoso, has excellent maps of each wilderness area at $4 each. Monjeau Lookout is a popular destination off Ski Run Road (NM 532). **Carlsbad Caverns National Park** (not the caves, of course), has extensive trail systems as well, and cars are not permitted. From the **Ski Apache** area there's also a 5-mile trail that leads to the top of Sierra Blanca, the area's highest mountain.

HORSEBACK RIDING   Of course, horseback riding is easily found in Ruidoso. Try the **Inn of the Mountain Gods** (☎ 505/257-5141), **Buddy's Stable** (☎ 505/258-4027) and **Cowboy Stables** (☎ 505/378-8217).

SKIING   Southern New Mexico's premier ski resort is **Ski Apache** (☎ 505/257-9001 for snow report, or 505/336-4565 for information), only 20 miles northwest of Ruidoso in the Mescalero Apache Reservation. Situated on an 11,500-foot ridge of 12,003-foot Sierra Blanca, the resort boasts a gondola, one quad chair, five triple chairs, two double chairs, a day lodge, sport shop, rental shop, ski school, first-aid center, four snack bars, and a lounge. Ski Apache has 52 trails and slopes (25% beginner, 30% intermediate, and 45% advanced), with a vertical drop of 1,900 feet and a total skier capacity of 15,300 an hour. All-day lift tickets for adults cost $34 to $37, and $21 to $23 for children (12 and under). The mountain is open Thanksgiving to Easter daily from 8:45am to 4pm. Lift-and-lodging packages can be booked through the **Inn of the Mountain Gods** (☎ 800/545-9011). **Snow Canyon** (☎ 800/333-7542 or 505/682-2333) is another small but popular ski area. In addition, it is one of only five ski resorts in the United States that offers lift-line tubing, with six 500-foot-long individual tubing chutes. There are 21 ski runs here with an uphill lift capacity of 1,900 skiers per hour. Lift tickets are $25 for adults and $16 for kids 12 and under.

2 Alamogordo

Famous for its leading role in America's space research and military technology industries, Alamogordo (pop. 29,628) first achieved worldwide fame on July 16, 1945, when the first atomic bomb was exploded at nearby Trinity Site. Today, it is home of the Space Center and International Space Hall of Fame, White Sands National Monument, and Holloman Air Force Base. Twenty miles east and twice as high, the resort village of Cloudcroft (elevation 8,650 feet) attracts vacationers to the forested heights of the Sacramento Mountains.

ESSENTIALS

GETTING THERE   By Car   From Albuquerque take I-25 south 87 miles to San Antonio; turn east on US 380, 66 miles to Carrizozo; then south on US 54 for 58 miles (four hours). From Las Cruces, take US 70 northeast (1½ hours). (This road may be closed for up to two hours during times of missile testing on White Sands Missile Range.) From El Paso, take US 54 north (1½ hours).

By Plane   Mesa Airlines (☎ 800/MESA-AIR) has connections three times daily with Albuquerque. **Avis** (☎ 505/437-3140), rents cars at the municipal airport.

VISITOR INFORMATION   The **Alamogordo Chamber of Commerce** and visitor center is at 1301 N. White Sands Blvd. Write P.O. Box 518, Alamogordo, NM 88310, or call **800/545-4021** (800/826-0294 within New Mexico) or 505/437-6120.

ORIENTATION   Alamogordo is on the eastern edge of the Tularosa Valley, at the foot of the Sacramento Mountains. US 54 (White Sands Boulevard) is the main street, extending several miles north and south. The downtown district is actually three blocks east of White Sands Boulevard, off 10th Street.

WHAT TO SEE & DO

In addition to the attractions in Alamogordo itself, also enjoyable is the small, historic village of **La Luz,** just 3 miles north of Alamogordo. It has attracted a number of resident artists and craftspeople who live, work, and display some of their products for sale. Worth seeing are the old adobe corral and the small Our Lady of Light Church.

✪ **Space Center.** Scenic Dr. and Indian Wells Rd. ☎ **800/545-4021** outside New Mexico, or 505/437-2840. Admission to Space Hall, $2.50 adults, $2 youth (6–12) and seniors (62 and older); free for children 5 and under. Theater, $4.50 adults, $3 youths and seniors. Combined visit, $6 adults, $4 youths and seniors. Triple Feature, $5 adults, $4 youths and seniors. Daily 9am–6pm summer; 9am–5pm winter.

The Space Center comes in two parts: the **International Space Hall of Fame** and the **Clyde W. Tombaugh Omnimax Theater.** Both are located on the lower slopes of the Sacramento Mountains, 2 miles east of US 54, and just above New Mexico State University's Alamogordo branch campus.

The Space Hall of Fame occupies the "Golden Cube," a five-story building with walls of golden glass. Visitors are encouraged to start on the top floor and work their way down. En route, they recall the accomplishments of the first astronauts and cosmonauts, including America's Mercury, Gemini, and Apollo programs, and the early Soviet orbital flights. Spacecraft and a lunar exploration module are exhibited. There's a space-station plan, a hands-on cutaway of crew module "Space Station 2001," and explanations of life in space aboard Skylab and Salyut. Other displays tell the history and purposes of rocketry, missiles, and satellites; provide an orientation to astronomy and exploration of other planets; and tell about New Mexico's role in space exploration history, from ancient Indians to rocketry pioneer Robert Goddard to astronauts.

On adjacent grounds is the "Sonic Wind No. 1" sled, which tested human endurance to speeds exceeding 600 m.p.h. in preparation for future space flights; the "Little Joe II" rocket, which tested Apollo launch escape systems; and other historic artifacts of space travel.

Each year, on the third Saturday of October, new members of the Space Hall of Fame are inducted in a special ceremony here.

At the Tombaugh Theater, OMNIMAX and Spitz 512 Planetarium Systems create earthly and cosmic experiences on a 2,700-square-foot dome screen. Twenty special-effects projectors can show 2,354 stars, the Milky Way, all the visible planets, the sun, and the moon, and can duplicate the night sky anywhere on earth, anytime of the year. Special programs allow visitors to take part in a laser-concert symphony of sight and sound, learn about the cosmos, and share a variety of OMNIMAX experiences.

Alameda Park Zoo. 1020 N. White Sands Blvd. ☎ **505/439-4290.** Admission $2 adults, $1 children 3–11 and seniors 62 and older. Daily 9am–5pm.

Next to the historical society museum is this seven-acre zoo, the oldest zoo in the Southwest. Established in 1898, its collection includes hundreds of mammals and birds from around the world, including a variety of American and African mammals.

Toy Train Depot. 1991 N. White Sands Blvd. ☎ **505/437-2855.** Admission $2 adults, $1.50 children; train rides $2 adults, $1.50 children. Wed–Mon noon–5pm.

A favorite of train buffs, the Toy Train Depot has more than 1,200 feet of model train track, numerous operating electric trains, and even more trains and accessories on display. Exhibits, which are appropriately housed in a genuine 1898 railroad depot, show toy trains dating from the 1800s, as well as numerous examples from the 1930s through the 1950s. There's even a reproduction of a pink electric train created by the Lionel Corporation in the 1950s as an attempt to lure more girls into the hobby. Rides through the grounds on 12-inch and 16-inch gauge trains are also offered.

SOMETHING UNUSUAL

Eagle Ranch Pistachio Groves. 7288 Hwy. 54/70. ☎ **800/432-0999** or 505/434-0035. Admission free. Gift shop and gallery daily 9am–6pm.

New Mexico's first and largest pistachio groves, Eagle Ranch offers 45-minute tours each weekday at 1:30pm, with a 10am tour added during the summer. There's also a visitors' center with an art gallery displaying the work of local artists, and a gift shop where you can buy pistachio nuts and a variety of other items.

TRINITY SITE

The world's first atomic bomb was exploded in this desert never-never land on July 16, 1945. It is strictly off-limits to civilians—except twice a year, in early April and early October. A small lava monument commemorates the explosion, which left a crater a quarter mile across, eight feet deep, and transformed the desert sand into a jade green glaze called "Trinitite" that remains today. The McDonald House, where the bomb's plutonium core was assembled 2 miles from Ground Zero, has been restored to its 1945 condition. The site is on the west slope of Sierra Oscura, 60 air miles northwest of Alamogordo. For more information, call the public affairs office of **White Sands Missile Range** (☎ **505/678-1134**).

GETTING OUTSIDE

Fifteen miles southeast of Alamogordo via US 54 and Dog Canyon Road you'll find **Oliver Lee Memorial State Park.** Nestled at the mouth of Dog Canyon, a stunning break in the steep escarpment of the Sacramento Mountains, the site has drawn human visitors for thousands of years. Springs and seeps support a variety of rare and endangered plant species, as well as a rich wildlife. Hiking trails into the foothills are well marked; the park also offers a visitor's center with excellent exhibits on local history, and picnic and camping grounds, with showers, electricity, and a dump station.

Dog Canyon was one of the last strongholds of the Mescalero Apache, and was the site of battles between Native Americans and the U.S. Cavalry in the 19th century. Around the turn of the 20th century, rancher Oliver Lee built a home near here and raised cattle; guided tours from the visitor center to his restored house give a taste of early ranch life in southern New Mexico.

The park is open daily from 7am to sunset, and admission is $3 per car. The visitor center is open daily from 9am to 4pm. Guided tours are offered Saturday and Sunday at 3pm, weather permitting. For more information, call **505/437-8284.**

EXPLORING THE AREA

✪ **Cloudcroft** is a picturesque mountain village of 705 people high in the Sacramento Mountains, surrounded by Lincoln National Forest. Though only about 20 miles east of Alamogordo via US 82, it is twice as high, overlooking the Tularosa Valley from a dizzying elevation of about 9,000 feet. It was founded in 1899 when railroad surveyors reached the mountain summit and built a lodge for Southern Pacific Railroad workers. Today, the Lodge is Cloudcroft's biggest attraction and biggest employer (see "A Great Nearby Place to Stay and Dine," below). There are also other accommodations in town, and lots of recreational opportunities and community festivals. For information, contact the **Cloudcroft Chamber of Commerce,** P.O. Box 1290, Cloudcroft, NM 88317 (☎ **505/682-2733**). It's located in a log cabin in the center of town, on the south side of US 82.

The **Sacramento Mountains Historical Museum,** US 82 east of downtown Cloudcroft (☎ **505/682-2932**), recalls the community's early days with several pioneer buildings, historic photos, and exhibits of turn-of-the-century railroad memorabilia, clothing, and other artifacts. Call for hours. Nearby, **Lincoln National Forest** (☎ 505/682-2551) maintains the unique **La Pasada Encantada Nature Trail,** a short foot path from Sleepygrass Campground, off NM 130 south of town, with signs in braille inviting walkers to touch the various plants, leaves, and trees. A new trail is a several-mile moderate hike to the historic **Mexican Canyon Railroad Trestle.** The trail head is in a U.S. Forest Service picnic area west of the junction of US 82 and NM 130, where you'll also find a short walk to an observation point offering spectacular views across White Sands Missile Range and the Tularosa Basin. This picnic area also has tables, grills, drinking water, and rest rooms.

National Solar Observatory—Sacramento Peak (☎ 505/434-7000), 18 miles south of Cloudcroft via NM 6563, a National Scenic Byway, attracts astronomers who come from around the world to study the sun and its effects on planet Earth. There are actually three observatories here, with two open to the public for self-guided tours (allow at least one hour). Free guided tours are offered Saturdays at 2pm from May through October.

Snow Canyon, 2 miles east of Cloudcroft on US 82 (☎ 800/333-7542 or 505/ 682-2333), has 21 runs and a 650-foot vertical, served by two T-bars and two rope tows. It appeals primarily to beginning and intermediate skiers, but has a few advanced pitches. When there's snow (usually December through March), it's open from 9am to 4pm daily. Snowboarding is permitted. Lift rates are $25 for adults, $16 for children.

WHERE TO STAY

All accommodations are along White Sands Boulevard, the north-south highway through town.

Days Inn Alamogordo. 907 S. White Sands Blvd., Alamogordo, NM 88310. ☎ 800/ DAYS-INN or 505/437-5090. 40 rms. A/C TV TEL. $52–$60 double. AE, CB, DC, DISC, MC, V.

Clean, comfortable rooms with standard furnishings are what you'll find at this Days Inn, which also has an outdoor unheated swimming pool and guest laundry. Rooms for nonsmokers and people with disabilities are available. Complimentary continental breakfast is offered from 6 to 10am. Pets are not accepted.

Best Western Desert Aire. 1021 S. White Sands Blvd., Alamogordo, NM 88310. ☎ 800/ 528-1234 or 505/437-2110. Fax 505/437-1898. 102 rms, 5 suites. A/C TV TEL. $58–$64 double; $56–$84 suite. Rates include continental breakfast. AE, CB, DC, DISC, MC, V.

This hotel of yellow-and-white concrete-block construction surrounds a huge central parking area. Rooms are cozy, and come with standard furnishings and minirefrigerators. Microwaves are available as well. Three-foot-deep Jacuzzis dominate a dozen "spa rooms." The hotel offers a guest recreation room, outdoor swimming pool, hot tub, and sauna.

Holiday Inn. 1401 S. White Sands Blvd., Alamogordo, NM 88310. ☎ 800/HOLIDAY or 505/ 437-7100. Fax 505/437-7100, ext. 299. 106 rms, 1 suite. A/C TV TEL. $66–$78 double; $145 suite. AE, CB, DC, DISC, JCB, MC, V.

A lovely desert garden fronts this single-story hotel, and the dining room has a carving of St. Francis. The nicely remodeled rooms have Southwestern furnishings, a king-size bed or two doubles, and a full mirror behind the vanity. Room service and many business services are offered; there's an Avis car rental on the premises, plus a hair salon, heated outdoor swimming pool, adjacent children's pool, and guest Laundromat. The hotel's restaurant serves three meals daily; prices are moderate and cuisine is American with Mexican specialties. The lounge offers daily hors d'oeuvres and four TVs that are usually tuned to sports channels.

CAMPING

Of course, you are permitted to camp (using a tent) at **White Sands National Monument,** which I'd strongly recommend, especially if you want to see the sun rise over the dunes. The park closes at dusk and if you're not camping you'll have to leave. It doesn't reopen until after dawn so there's no way you'll see the sunrise unless you camp. (Call **505/479-6124** for information.) If you'd rather stay at a full-service campground, try **KOA-Alamogordo/White Sands** (☎ **800/424-8227**). It has the usual laundry and grocery facilities as well as a recreation room/area, swimming pool, playground, shuffleboard, and planned group activities. The campground is located on 24th Street in Alamogordo, just east of the US 54/70/82 junction. If you're look-ing for something in-between, **Oliver Lee State Park** (☎ **505/437-8284**) is a good choice. There are 44 sites, 10 full hookups, picnic tables, grills, tenting availability, a playground, and hiking trails.

WHERE TO DINE

✪ **Keg's Brewery and Fine Dining.** 817 Scenic Dr. ☎ **505/437-9564.** Main courses $7.95–$19.95. DISC, MC, V. Mon–Sat 11am–10pm. Closed Christmas. STEAK/SEAFOOD.

Record albums and photos of classic cars and movie stars decorate the walls of this local favorite, located 1.3 miles south of the Space Center near 10th Street. The menu offers steak and fresh seafood, plus pasta, Mexican dishes, and deli-style sandwiches. The pub section (open until 2am) has a full bar, pool tables, a jukebox, and live rock music. Friday and Saturday nights there is a $2 cover charge. As the restaurant's name suggests, there is a microbrewery on the premises.

Mt. Carmel Restaurant and Gift Shop. 915 Texas Ave. ☎ **505/434-0722.** Main courses $8.95–$13.95; lunch $4.25–$7.50. MC, V for checks of $20 or more only. Mon–Sat 11am–3pm, Thurs–Fri 5–8pm. EUROPEAN/AMERICAN

This busy little restaurant with an attached religious/inspirational gift shop is located just south of 10th Street. A variety of specialty sandwiches plus quiche and home-made soup make up the lunch menu. There's a daily lunch special, and dinner, which features pastas, Italian specialties, and barbecue items, is offered two nights a week. Popular desserts include Mt. Carmel (caramel) pie and a brownie à la mode.

🄢 **Ramona's Restaurant.** 2913 N. White Sands Blvd. ☎ **505/437-7616.** Main courses $4.75–$9.50; lunch $2.50–$6.50; breakfast $2.50–$6.95. AE, MC, V. Daily 6am–10pm. MEXICAN/AMERICAN.

Huge arched windows face the highway from the indoor patio of this tile-roofed adobe, and a huge wallpaper mural of a Mexican city covers one wall. A favorite meal is Ramona's special: a chicken enchilada, chile relleno, and chicken burrito, with guacamole, sour cream, refried beans, rice, and salad. American dishes include chicken-fried steak and fresh mountain trout. Beer and wine are served.

Yee's Oriental Express. 1115 S. White Sands Blvd. ☎ **505/437-RICE.** Main courses $4.25–$6.95. No credit cards. Sun–Thurs 11am–9pm, Fri–Sat 11am–10pm. CHINESE FAST FOOD.

Yee's "All-U-Can Eat Buffet" ($5.95) includes 15 Chinese dishes and several Ameri-can basics such as fried chicken and corn on the cob. The regular menu includes daily specials like Szechuan beef or cashew chicken, and everyday favorites like sweet-and-sour pork, fried wontons, and butterfly shrimp. Yee's makes deliveries, or you can eat inside the bright red building, located between the Holiday Inn and the Desert Aire Motor Inn.

A GREAT NEARBY PLACE TO STAY & DINE

✪ **The Lodge at Cloudcroft.** One Corona Place (P.O. Box 497), Cloudcroft, NM 88317.
☎ **800/395-6343** in New Mexico, or 505/682-2566. Fax 505/682-2715. 59 rms, 7 suites. TV
TEL. $65–$109 single or double; $129–$199 suite. AE, DC, DISC, MC, V.

The only hotel in New Mexico listed in the "Top 100 Hotels in the United States,"
the Lodge is an antique jewel, a well-preserved survivor of another era. From the
grand fireplace in the lobby to the homey Victorian decor in the guest rooms, this
mansion exudes gentility and class. Its nine-hole golf course, one of the nation's highest, challenges golfers across rolling hills between 8,600 and 9,200 feet elevation and
is the site of numerous regional tournaments.

Rooms in the Lodge are filled with antiques, from sideboards and lamps to mirrors and steam radiators. Guests are greeted by a stuffed bear sitting on their bed with
a sampler of homemade fudge from the Lodge Mercantile. In 1991 more rooms were
added in the form of the Pavilion and the Retreat, which were built adjacent to the
Lodge. The Retreat ($269 to $299) is an entire house with four bedrooms, kitchen,
living room, and dining room. The Pavilion ($65 to $89) is a 10-room bed-and-
breakfast inn with pine paneled walls, down comforters, and fireplaces. Of course,
the guests of the recent additions also have the privilege of enjoying the amenities and
facilities of the Lodge.

Rebecca's (☎ **505/682-2566**), the hotel's restaurant, is named for the Lodge's
resident ghost, believed to have been a chambermaid in the 1930s who was killed by
her lumberjack lover. Three meals, plus a midday snack menu, are served daily. The
hotel has fax and photocopying services, a nine-hole golf course, heated outdoor
swimming pool, hot tub, sauna, massage, and a gift shop that also sells homemade
fudge.

3 White Sands National Monument

Arguably the most memorable natural area in this part of the Southwest, White Sands
National Monument preserves the best part of the world's largest gypsum dune field.
An area of 275 square miles of pure white gypsum sand reaches out over the floor
of the Tularosa Basin in wavelike dunes. Plants and animals have evolved in special
ways to adapt to the bright white environment. Some creatures here have a bleached
coloration to match the whiteness all around them, whereas some plants have evolved
means for surviving against the smothering pressures of the blowing sands.

The surrounding mountains, the Sacramentos to the east, with their forested
slopes, and the serene San Andres to the west, are composed of sandstone, limestone,
sedimentary rocks, and pockets of gypsum. Over millions of years, rains and melt-
ing snows dissolved the gypsum and carried it down into Lake Lucero. Here the hot
sun and dry winds evaporate the water, leaving the pure white gypsum to crystallize.
Then the persistent winds blow these crystals, in the form of minuscule bits of sand,
in a northeastern direction, adding them to growing dunes. As each dune grows and
moves farther from the lake, new ones form, rank after rank, in what seems an endless procession.

ESSENTIALS

GETTING THERE   The visitors center is 15 miles southwest of Alamogordo on
US 70/82, and the nearest major airport is El Paso International, which is 90 miles
away. If you'd rather, you can take a commuter flight from El Paso International to
Alamogordo–White Sands Regional Airport and drive from there. *Note:* Due to

missile testing on the adjacent White Sands Missile Range, the drive is sometimes closed for up to two hours at a time.

VISITOR INFORMATION   Admission is $4 per vehicle or $2 per person. From Memorial Day to Labor Day the visitors center is open from 8am to 7pm and Dunes Drive is open from 7am to 10pm. During the rest of the year the visitors center is open from 8am to 4:30pm and Dunes Drive is open from 7am to sunset. If you're not camping, you'll probably only want to spend a couple of hours here. Refreshments and snacks can be purchased at the visitors center, along with books, maps, posters, and other souvenirs; however, there are no dining or grocery facilities available.

If you would like more information about the monument before you leave home, write to **White Sands National Monument,** P.O. Box 1086, Holloman, AFB, NM 88330-1086, or call **505/479-6124.**

SEEING THE HIGHLIGHTS

A 16-mile Dunes Drive loops through the "heart of sands" from the visitor center. Information available at the center will tell you what to look for on your drive. Sometimes the winds blow the dunes over the road, which must then be rerouted around a dune. The dunes are in fact all moving slowly to the northeast, pushed by prevailing southwest winds, some at the rate of as much as 20 feet a year.

In the center of the monument, the road itself is made of hard-packed gypsum. (This part of the road can be especially slick after an afternoon thunderstorm, so drive cautiously!) Visitors are invited to get out of their cars at established parking areas and explore a bit; climb a dune for a better view of the endless sea of sand.

A couple of safety tips are emphasized by the Park Service: (1) tunneling in this sand can be dangerous, for it collapses easily and could suffocate a person, and (2) sand-surfing down the dune slopes, although permitted, can also be hazardous, so it should be undertaken with care, and never near an auto road. Hikers are warned about the possibility of getting lost in a sudden sandstorm should they stray from marked trails or areas.

In summer there are nature walks and evening programs in the dunes. Ranger-guided activities include orientation talks and nature walks. When driving near or in the monument, tune a radio to 1610 AM for information on what's doing.

CAMPING

Camping is permitted at White Sands, but there are no campgrounds and no facilities, so this is a backcountry adventure. You must register and get clearance from monument headquarters before you pitch a tent. If backcountry camping isn't your speed, there are other campgrounds in nearby Alamogordo and Las Cruces (see above for details).

4 Ruidoso & the Mescalero Apache Indian Reservation

Ruidoso (most New Mexicans pronounce it Ree-uh-*do*-so) is situated at 6,900 feet in the timbered Sacramento Mountains, the southernmost finger of the Rockies. It is a mountain resort town named for its site on a noisy stream and most famous for the nearby Ruidoso Downs Racetrack, where the world's richest race is run for a $2.5 million purse. Outdoor lovers, hikers, horseback riders, fishers, and hunters are drawn to the surrounding Lincoln National Forest. Southern New Mexico's most important ski resort, Ski Apache, is just out of town. The nearby Mescalero Apache Indian Reservation includes the magnificent Inn of the Mountain Gods resort hotel. Not far away, the historic village of Lincoln recalls the Wild West days of Billy the Kid.

ESSENTIALS

GETTING THERE **By Car** From Albuquerque, take I-25 south 87 miles to San Antonio; turn east on US 380, 74 miles; then south on NM 37/48 (four hours). From Alamogordo, take US 70 northeast via Tularosa (one hour). From Roswell, take US 70 west (1 1/2 hours).

By Plane Ruidoso is served by **Sierra Blanca Regional Airport** (☎ **505/336-8455**), 17 miles north, near Fort Stanton. **Mesa Airlines** (☎ **800/MESA-AIR**) has daily flights to and from Albuquerque and El Paso.

VISITOR INFORMATION The **Ruidoso Valley Chamber of Commerce** and visitor center is at 720 Sudderth Dr. For more information, contact P.O. Box 698, Ruidoso, NM 88345 (☎ **800/253-2255** or 505/257-7395). You can reach the chamber of commerce online at http://ruidoso.usa.net/.

EXPLORING RUIDOSO

Ruidoso itself, while a lovely town for wandering, shopping, and enjoying outdoor pursuits, doesn't have any sightseeing attractions *per se*—no museums, no Native American ruins, no astounding sights. The surrounding area, covered below, has plenty.

GALLERY HOPPING IN RUIDOSO

Many noted artists—among them Peter Hurd, Henriette Wyeth, and Gordon Snidow—have made their homes in Ruidoso and the surrounding Lincoln County. Dozens of other art-world hopefuls have followed them here, resulting in a proliferation of galleries in town. Among them are: **California Colors,** 201 Country Club Rd., open Tuesday to Sunday from 11am to 5pm; the **Camel House,** 714 Mechem Dr., open Wednesday to Monday from 10am to 5pm; **Crucis Art Bronze Foundry and Gallery,** 524 Sudderth Dr., open from 10am to early evening daily; **Fenton's Gallery,** 2629 Sudderth Dr., open daily from 10am to 6pm; **Grace's Art and Frame Chalet,** 2206 Sudderth Dr., open Monday to Saturday from 10am to 5pm; **Buckhorn Gallery,** Glencoe, open by appointment (☎ **505/378-4126**); **Hurd-La Rinconada,** in San Patricio, 20 miles east of Ruidoso on US 70 (see "Lincoln Loop," below), open Monday to Saturday from 10am to 5pm; **McGary Studios,** a bronze foundry at 819 Gavilan Canyon Rd.; and **Mountain Arts,** 2530 Sudderth Dr., open Monday to Saturday from 10am to 6pm and from 10am to 4pm on Sunday.

RUIDOSO DOWNS

In nearby Ruidoso Downs, 2 miles east on US 70, is the famous **Ruidoso Downs Racetrack** (☎ **505/378-4431**) with its **Museum of the Horse** (☎ **505/378-4142**), which contains a collection of more than 10,000 horse-related items, including saddles from all over the world, a Russian sleigh, a horse-drawn "fire engine," and an 1860 stagecoach. Several great American artists including Frederic Remington, Charles M. Russell, Frank Tenney Johnson, and Henry Alkins are represented here as well. The Anne C. Stradling Collection, also housed here, is composed of family memorabilia that spans six generations. There is a gift shop with some interesting books and curios. Admission is $5 for adults, $4 for seniors, and $3 for children 5 to 18 (under 5 free).

The world's richest quarter horse race, the $2.5 million All-American Futurity, is run each year on Labor Day at the racetrack. Seventy-seven other days of quarter horse and thoroughbred racing lead up to the big one, beginning the second week of May. Post time in May and June is 1pm Thursday through Sunday. Grandstand admission is free. Call for reserved seating ($2.50 up, plus boxes seating four to six persons).

MESCALERO APACHE INDIAN RESERVATION

Immediately south and west of Ruidoso, the reservation covers over 460,000 acres (719 square miles) and is home to about 2,800 members of the Mescalero, Chiricahua, and Lipan bands of Apaches. Established by order of Pres. Ulysses S. Grant in 1873, it sustains a profitable cattle-ranching industry and the Apache-run logging firm of Mescalero Forest Products.

SEEING THE HIGHLIGHTS

Even if you're not staying or dining there, don't fail to visit the **Inn of the Mountain Gods,** a luxury year-round resort owned and operated by the tribe (see "Where to Stay," below); it's the crowning achievement of Wendell Chino, president of the Mescalero Apache tribe for all but four years since 1952.

Also on the reservation, on US 70 about 17 miles southwest of Ruidoso, is the ✪ **Mescalero Cultural Center,** open from 8am to 4:30pm Monday through Friday. Photos, artifacts, clothing, craftwork, and other exhibits demonstrate the history and culture of the tribe.

St. Joseph's Church, just off US 70 in Mescalero, on a hill overlooking the reservation, is a Gothic-style structure with walls four feet thick, built between the two world wars. The interior has the symbols of Apache mountain gods along with Roman Catholic saints in paintings and carvings (see "The Lincoln Loop," below).

DANCES & CEREMONIES

Throughout the year, the center hosts powwows of colorful dancing and traditional drumming, open to the public and unrestricted as far as photography.

Restrictions do apply, however, to the annual **Coming of Age Ceremony,** held over four days in early July. A traditional rite reenacted in the tribal community of Mescalero, it includes an Apache maidens' puberty rites ceremony at dawn and a mountain spirits dance at night. Check ahead to learn what you can and can't see, and what you can and can't photograph.

For more information on the reservation before you visit, write to the Tribal Office at P.O. Box 176, Mescalero, NM 88340 or call **505/258-5445.**

LINCOLN STATE MONUMENT: WALK IN THE FOOTSTEPS OF BILLY THE KID

One of the last historic yet uncommercialized 19th-century towns remaining in the American West, this tiny community lies 37 miles northeast of Ruidoso on US 380, in the valley of the Rio Bonito. Only 70 people live here today, but it was once the seat of the largest county in the United States, and the focal point of the notorious Lincoln County War of 1878–79. The entire town is now a New Mexico State Monument and a National Historic Landmark.

The bloody Lincoln County War was fought between various ranching and merchant factions over the issue of beef contracts for nearby Fort Stanton. A sharpshooting teenager named William Bonney—soon to be known as "Billy the Kid"—took sides in this issue with "the good guys," escaping from the burning McSween House after his employer and colleague were shot and killed. Three years later, after shooting down a sheriff, he was captured in Lincoln and sentenced to be hanged. But he shot his way out of his cell in the **Old Courthouse,** now a state museum that still has a hole made by a bullet from the Kid's gun. Today's visitors can hear a talk on this famous jail escape, by request, at the Old Courthouse.

Many of the original structures from that era have been preserved and restored by State Monuments, under the aegis of the Museum of New Mexico, the Lincoln County Historical Society, or the Lincoln County Heritage Trust (☎ **505/653-4025**).

At the trust's **Historical Center,** exhibits explain the role in Lincoln's history of Apaches, Hispanics, Anglo cowboys, and the black Buffalo Soldiers, and detail the Lincoln County War. A brief slide show on Lincoln history is presented in an old-fashioned theater. Start your visit here and either join a tour, included in the admission cost, or pick up a brochure describing the trust's self-guided walking tour (50¢). Across the courtyard is the **Luna Museum Store.**

An annual folk pageant, *The Last Escape of Billy the Kid,* has been presented outdoors since 1949 as a highly romanticized version of the Lincoln County War. It's staged Friday and Saturday night and Sunday afternoon during the first full weekend in August as part of the **Old Lincoln Days** celebration. The festival also includes living-history demonstrations of traditional crafts, musical programs, and food booths throughout the village. From mid-June to mid-August, other weekend activities, including Apache dancing, historical dramas, and lectures, are scheduled.

JUST THE FACTS The monument is open May 1 through September 15 daily from 9:30am to 5:30pm, and the rest of the year from 8:30am to 4:30pm. Admission is $5 adults (includes entry to five buildings) from May through September; $4.50 adults (includes entry to three buildings) from October through April; children 16 and under are free. For more information, write P.O. Box 36, Lincoln, NM 88338, or call **505/653-4372.**

WHERE TO STAY AROUND RUIDOSO
IN TOWN

Best Western Swiss Chalet Inn. 1451 Mechem Dr. (P.O. Box 759), Ruidoso, NM 88345. ☎ **800/47-SWISS**, 800/528-1234, or 505/258-3333. Fax 505/258-5325. 81 rms, 2 suites. A/C TV TEL. $60–$78 double; $99–$139 suite. AE, CB, DC, DISC, MC, V.

This blue-and-white chalet-style motel, with Swiss flags hanging outside its entry, looks right at home in a mountain resort. The spacious rooms are very comfortable and decorated in soft colors.

In Ahna-Michelle's Restaurant, Swiss and American food, including Wiener schnitzel, wursts, Luzern Cordon Bleu, and Davos Platz (peppered beef tips), is served in an alpine atmosphere of Swiss bells and other souvenirs. The restaurant is open for breakfast and dinner (except Tuesday) daily. The inn has room service, connecting and nonsmoking rooms, an indoor swimming pool, Jacuzzi, and guest Laundromat. VCRs and videos are available at the front desk.

The Historic Carrizo Lodge and Condominiums. Carrizo Canyon Rd. (P.O. Drawer A), Ruidoso, NM 88345. ☎ **800/227-1224** or 505/257-9131. 84 rms. A/C TV TEL. $59–$89 single or double; efficiencies begin at $89. AE, CB, DC, DISC, MC, V.

Nestled among the pines beside a stream flowing east toward Ruidoso from Lake Mescalero, this lodge, on 7¹/₂ acres, is the home of the Carrizo Art School, one of America's oldest. Built in 1879 on a natural river-rock foundation, Carrizo has been designated a New Mexico cultural property and is on the National Register of Historic Places. The lodge, a rose-colored building with stucco walls, and its renovated bungalows retain their original viga (rafter) ceilings, hardwood floors, and brass fixtures. Modern luxury condominium suites all have fireplaces.

The original lodge houses the Carrizo Cafe. Facilities include a swimming pool, sauna, hot tub, video arcade, and convenience store.

Enchantment Inn. 307 US 70 (P.O. Box 4210), Ruidoso, NM 88345. ☎ **800/435-0280** or 505/378-4051. Fax 505/378-5427. 50 rms, 30 suites. A/C TV TEL. $60–$90 single or double; $70–$190 suites. AE, DC, DISC, MC, V.

Completely redecorated in the fall of 1992, this handsome and well-kept motel has Southwestern decor, with Mexican tiles and an abundance of wood and glass. Guests have use of an outdoor patio with barbecue grills, video game room, guest laundry, and indoor pool and whirlpool. The Screaming Eagle Restaurant and Lounge serves three meals daily, with most main courses priced under $10. There's also a gift shop on the premises. Rooms for nonsmokers and people with disabilities are available.

☉ Pines Motel on the River. 620 Sudderth Dr., Ruidoso, NM 88345. ☎ **800/257-4834** or 505/257-4334. 10 rms. TV TEL. $36–$75 double. AE, DISC, MC, V.

This meticulously maintained family owned-and-operated motel has six older but completely refurbished rooms, plus four new, more luxurious units overlooking the Rio Ruidoso. Rooms have color cable television and small refrigerators. Nonsmoking and connecting rooms are available. Pets are not accepted. There is no air-conditioning, but it is rarely needed at this elevation. Guests can fish for trout in the river at the back of the property, and play horseshoes in a shady area along the river.

IN UPPER CANYON

Dan Dee Cabins Resort. 310 Main Rd., Upper Canyon (P.O. Box 844), Ruidoso, NM 88345. ☎ **800/345-4848** or 505/257-2165. 12 cabins. TV. June 15 to Labor Day $82 one-bedroom cabin, $104 two-bedroom cabin; $122 three-bedroom cabin; Dec 15–Easter $76 one-bedroom, $94 two-bedroom, $116 three-bedroom; rest of year $66 one-bedroom, $84 two-bedroom, $99 three-bedroom. DISC, MC, V.

Rustic, woodsy, back-to-nature—these adjectives apply to the Dan Dee Cabins, some of which date from 1940. Built beside a stream in five acres of forest, the cabins all have sitting porches, fireplaces, kitchens with gas stoves, and their own water heaters. They're popular with honeymooners who don't want to be disturbed: The only phone is in the office. For families, there's a barbecue area and children's playground.

Shadow Mountain Lodge. 107 Main Rd., Upper Canyon (P.O. Box 1427), Ruidoso, NM 88345. ☎ **800/441-4331** or 505/257-4886. 19 rms. A/C TV TEL. Memorial Day to Labor Day and holidays $74–$89 single or double; Labor Day–Memorial Day $59–$74 single or double. Ski packages. AE, CB, DC, DISC, MC, V.

Advertising "luxury lodging for couples," this property doesn't accept pets and though children are welcome, it's not exactly the place for them. It's a place of rustic elegance, an outstanding spot for a romantic getaway. Each unit has a king-size bed, a fireplace , and a coffeemaker (with complimentary coffee and tea). Ten rooms have full kitchens; the other nine have a wet bar and microwave. A barbecue area and hot tub are available for guest use.

IN RUIDOSO DOWNS

Inn at Pine Springs. Off US 70 (P.O. Box 2100), Ruidoso Downs, NM 88346. ☎ **800/ 237-3607** or 505/378-8100. Fax 505/378-8215. 100 rms, 4 suites. A/C TV TEL. Rates include continental breakfast. Memorial Day to Labor Day $75–$88 double, $170–$189 suite; Labor Day to Memorial Day $60–$70 double, $125 suite. Children 12 and under free with parent. AE, CB, DC, DISC, MC, V.

High on a hill overlooking the racetrack, this motel is set on beautifully manicured grounds sprinkled with flowers and pine, spruce, and juniper trees. The rooms are almost too spacious; they're nicely appointed with standard furnishings and many have terrific views of the surrounding hills. A big Jacuzzi on an open-air deck is a favorite of guests.

NEARBY PLACES TO STAY
TWO HISTORIC B&BS IN LINCOLN

Casa de Patrón Bed and Breakfast. On US 380 (P.O. Box 27), Lincoln, NM 88338. ☎ **505/653-4676.** Fax 505/653-4671. 5 rms, 2 casitas. $79 double, $87–$97 casita. Rates include breakfast. MC, V.

The main building of Casa de Patrón, an adobe, was built around 1860 and housed Juan Patrón's old store (the home is on the National Register of Historic Places). In addition, Billy the Kid used part of the house as a hideout at some point during his time in the Lincoln area.

Jeremy and Cleis Jordan have created some lovely rooms in the main house and two wonderful casitas. People traveling with children are encouraged to take advantage of the casitas. The two-bedroom Casita de Paz was built with adobe bricks by the Jordans and is essentially a little house (500 square feet), whereas the cathedral ceiling in Casita Bonita gives it an even more spacious feeling. If you choose to stay in a casita, a continental-plus breakfast is delivered to your door. If you stay in the main house or the recently added Old Trail House, which holds two additional rooms, Cleis and Jeremy will prepare you a full breakfast.

Ellis Store and Co. Country Inn. US 380 (P.O. Box 15), Lincoln, NM 88338. ☎ **800/653-6460** or 505/653-4609. 7 rms (4 with bath). $69–$99 single or double. Rates include breakfast. DC, DISC, MC, V.

With part of this house dating from 1850, this is believed to be the oldest existing residence in Lincoln County. Billy the Kid spent several weeks here, although somewhat unwillingly, according to court records that show payment of $64 for two weeks' food and lodging for the Kid and a companion held under house arrest. Today, guests of innkeepers Virginia and David Vigil can come and go as they please, wandering over the inn's six quiet acres, or using the inn as a base while exploring Lincoln and nearby attractions.

Four rooms in the main house are a step back into the 1800s, with wood-burning fireplaces or stoves, antique furnishings, and handmade quilts. The separate Mill House, built of adobe and hand-hewn lumber in the 1880s, has one room with a private bath and three that share a bath. The Mill House also has a full kitchen and a large sitting room loft area available for guest use. Rooms have no televisions or telephones, but a phone is available for guest use and the Vigils are happy to take messages.

Gourmet breakfasts are cooked to order from an extensive menu, and lunches and dinners are also available by reservation. Nonguests are also welcome for meals, by reservation. Pets are not permitted inside, but kennels are available, and those with horses are invited to use the property's stables.

ADOBE GUEST HOMES

Hurd Ranch Guest Homes. P.O. Box 100, San Patricio, NM 88348. ☎ **800/658-6912** or 505/653-4331. Fax 505/653-4218. 3 casitas (all with bath). TV TEL. $100–$300 per casita (two-night minimum). AE, DISC, MC, V.

Located about 20 miles east of Ruidoso on 2,500-acre Sentinel Ranch, these attractive casitas are part of the Hurd–La Rinconada Gallery, which displays the work of well-known artists Peter and Michael Hurd, Henriette Wyeth Hurd, N. C. Wyeth, and Andrew Wyeth. The grounds also include the San Patricio Polo Fields, where matches take place from Memorial Day to Labor Day.

There are two older one-bedroom casitas, built in the early part of the century, and two new and much larger units. All have completely equipped kitchens, fireplaces, and comfortable living areas, and are decorated with antiques, primitives, and art by the Hurd-Wyeth family. The one-bedroom casitas also have private patios with barbecue grills.

A LUXURY RESORT

✪ **Inn of the Mountain Gods.** Carrizo Canyon Rd. (P.O. Box 269), Mescalero, NM 88340. ☎ **800/545-9011** or 505/257-5141. Fax 505/257-6173. 253 rms, 10 suites. A/C TV TEL. June 1 to Labor Day $120 single or double, $130 suite; Apr–May and Sept–Oct $95 single or double, $105 suite; Nov–Mar $80 single or double, $90 suite. Golf, tennis, and ski packages. AE, CB, DC, DISC, MC, V.

Southern New Mexico's most luxurious resort is this impressive property on the Mescalero Apache Reservation, 3¹/₂ miles southwest of Ruidoso. It is the successful dream of the tribal president, Wendell Chino, who wanted to help his people get into the recreation and tourism business. They picked a spectacularly beautiful location, overlooking pristine Lake Mescalero and, behind it, 12,003-foot-high Sierra Blanca.

Nine interconnected brown-shake buildings comprise the hotel and an associated convention center. Guests cross a covered wooden bridge over a cascading stream to reach the three-story lobby, dominated by a huge, cone-shaped, copper fireplace. Modern tribal art and trophies of wild animals bagged on the reservation are on display. The property includes an 18-hole golf course designed by Ted Robinson, whose work includes the famed course at the Princess in Acapulco; eight tennis courts; and horseback riding stables. In winter, buses shuttle skiers to the Ski Apache resort, also owned by the tribe.

The guest rooms are spacious and sophisticated, with high ceilings and tasteful furnishings. Lithographs on the walls depict typical 19th-century tribal scenes. There are rooms for nonsmokers and people with disabilities.

The Dan Li Ka Room (open 7am to 2:30pm and 6 to 10pm daily), a huge dining room with a view of the lake and mountain beyond, features steak, poultry, seafood, and pasta, plus reservation specialties like Southwest sautée (venison, chicken breast, and beef medallions with marsala-cilantro sauce) and broiled fresh mountain trout. Dinner main courses range from $15.25 to $32. The Apache Tee Restaurant by the golf course offers casual dining from 6:30am to 10pm. Ina Da Lounge has ample seating and a big floor for dancing and drinks. There's a piano bar off the lobby.

The hotel offers room service (7am to 10pm), valet laundry, a gift shop, and Casino Apache. Facilities include a golf course, stables, outdoor tennis courts, swimming pool, whirlpool, saunas, fishing lake stocked with rainbow trout, boating (rowboats, pedal boats, and aqua cycles can be rented), and a base for hunting trips. No pets.

A B&B IN ALTO

✪ **Sierra Mesa Lodge.** Fort Stanton Road (P.O. Box 463), Alto, NM 88312. ☎ **505/336-4515.** 5 rms. Midweek $95 double, weekend $100 double. Rates include full breakfast. DISC, MC, V.

Southern California transplants Larry and Lila Goodman operate what may be Ruidoso's friendliest and most elegant B&B for nonsmokers. Each room is faithful to its particular theme. The Country Western Room, for instance, has a huge step-up bed; the Victorian Room boasts an eagle-claw bathtub/shower. There's also the Oriental Room, the Queen Anne Room, and the French Country Room. All have private baths, period furnishings, and comforters and goose-down pillows on the brass and/or four-poster beds. The lodge has a large private spa and each afternoon offers silver tea service. The rates include afternoon tea as well as a full gourmet breakfast.

CAMPING

Lincoln National Forest has over a dozen campgrounds in the region; four of them are within the immediate area. Maps (at $2) and details can be obtained from all campground offices, including the **Smokey Bear Ranger Station,** 901 Mechem Dr., Ruidoso (☎ **505/257-4995**), open from Memorial Day to Labor Day, Saturday 7:30am to 4:30pm.

WHERE TO DINE
EXPENSIVE

✪ **Victoria's Romantic Hideaway.** 2117 Sudderth Dr. ☎ **800/959-1328** or 505/257-5440. Reservations required (one day in advance suggested). $65 per person fixed price (including tax and gratuity). AE, DISC, MC, V. Daily 6pm–close. SICILIAN.

To say one goes to Victoria's Romantic Hideaway for dinner would be a gross understatement. You go to Victoria's for a wonderful three- to four-hour dining experience, perhaps a romantic evening by soft candlelight to celebrate a special occasion. Don and Pat Baker created a unique restaurant where guests are outrageously pampered during a relaxed eight-course meal. Although the restaurant will seat up to 16, no more than five couples are usually served on any given evening, each couple in a private, elegantly decorated section of the restaurant.

One basic meal is served each night; however, dishes are customized for each particular diner. Those dining at the same table receive different meals according to the chef's choice, allowing the kitchen to show off its classic Sicilian style of cooking. Wine tasting is also part of the evening and Don serves small portions of different wines (many from Sicily) to complement the various courses. Dress is casual, except shorts are not permitted, and smoking is allowed only on an outdoor porch. Due to the abundance of Victorian antiques and the length of the evening children would be out of place here.

MODERATE

Cattle Baron Steak House. 657 Sudderth Dr. ☎ **505/257-9355.** Reservations recommended. Main courses $6.95–$20.95; lunch $3.95–$6.50. AE, DISC, MC, V. Sun–Thurs 11am–9:30pm, Fri–Sat 11am–10:30pm. STEAK/SEAFOOD.

A casually elegant restaurant with several levels of seating in a white adobe-style interior, the Cattle Baron serves up a variety of fine steaks and chicken dishes. It also boasts an extensive seafood menu, including fresh catches from the Atlantic, Pacific, and Gulf of Mexico. Prime rib is the house specialty. There's a large salad bar and a great lounge. In summer, dine in the waterfall room: Just outside the wall of windows is a lovely cascading (man-made) waterfall.

✪ **La Lorraine.** 2523 Sudderth Dr. ☎ **505/257-2954.** Reservations recommended. Main courses $12.95–$21.95; lunch $5.95–$8.95. AE, MC, V. Tues–Sat 11:30am–2pm; Mon–Thurs 5:30–9pm, Fri–Sat 5:30–9:30pm. FRENCH.

This piece of Paris is a bit hard to imagine in a New Mexico mountain town, but here it is, in an adobe building on the main street. Inside, there's French provincial decor, with lace curtains and candlelight

Le menu? Pâtés, bisques, salads, and wonderful dishes like canard (duck) à l'orange, rack of lamb, Angus rib eye, chateaubriand, and fresh salmon.

Michelena's Italian Restaurant. 2703 Sudderth Dr. ☎ **505/257-5753.** Reservations accepted. Main courses $6.95–$12.95; sandwiches $3.25–$5.50; pizzas $9.75–$15.95. DISC, MC, V. Daily 11am–9pm. Closed Mon during Apr and Nov. ITALIAN.

This pleasant Italian bistro has Chianti bottles hanging from the ceiling and traditional red-and-white checked tablecloths. All the Italian standards are offered, including chicken Alfredo, spaghetti, lasagna, ravioli, manicotti, fettuccine; or you can order a sampler plate. There are also 20 varieties of pizza, and a good selection of Italian-style sandwiches. Luncheon specials are offered Monday through Friday.

INEXPENSIVE

🟢 **Cafe Rio.** 2547 Sudderth Dr., Ruidoso. ☎ **505/257-7746.** Reservations not accepted. Main courses $4.25–$9.95. No credit cards. Daily 11am–8:30pm. Closed Dec 1–21 and for one month after Easter. INTERNATIONAL/PIZZA.

This unpretentious pizzeria-style restaurant is a lot more than it appears to be, offering a wide selection of dishes from around the world, plus a very good pizza, with everything made from scratch. There's also an extensive selection of domestic and imported beers, including seasonal beers.

Casa Blanca. 501 Mechem Dr. ☎ **505/257-2495.** Main courses $4–$12. AE, MC, V. Daily 11am–10pm. NEW MEXICAN.

This large white-stucco building, a half mile north of the Sudderth/Mechem junction toward Alto, commands a lovely valley view from its hilltop garden location. Contemporary regional art hangs on the walls inside, and a large beer garden/patio, shaded by ponderosa pines, is the location of afternoon "jams" from 2 to 6pm every summer Sunday. There's a small cantina downstairs. The menu features a wide variety of Southwestern favorites, include chimichangas and green-chile enchiladas.

Hummingbird Tearoom. 2306 Sudderth Dr., Village Plaza. ☎ **505/257-5100.** $2.55–$5.95. MC, V. Mon–Sat 11am–2:30pm (afternoon tea and desserts served until 5pm in summer). AMERICAN.

A delightful little tearoom and dessert shop, the Hummingbird also serves excellent sandwiches, salads, and homemade soups. Afternoon tea is particularly popular.

NEARBY PLACES TO DINE

✪ **Chango's.** Smokey Bear Blvd., Capitan. ☎ **505/354-4213.** Reservations strongly recommended. $12.95–$18.95. MC, V. Wed–Sat 5pm–close. INTERNATIONAL.

Jerrold Donti Flores, the owner of Chango's, left San Francisco in the late 1970s to return to the land of his birth, and after several other ventures found his calling in this small (24-seat) and highly rated restaurant in a turn-of-the-century adobe building. Flores, an accomplished avant-garde sculptor and painter, also displays his art, works by other artists, plus international primitives, in changing exhibits at the restaurant.

A choice of four to six gourmet dinners changes every other week, with selections such as fresh poached salmon with chipotle sauce, beef bourguignonne, whitefish in an asparagus-pistachio sauce, or pesto chicken. An excellent wine list includes a 26-year-old port plus Italian, Spanish, French, Australian, German, and domestic wines.

✪ **Flying J Ranch.** Hwy. 48, 1 mile north of Alto. ☎ **505/336-4330.** Reservations highly recommended. $13.50 adults; reduced children's rates. DISC, MC, V. May–Labor Day, Mon–Sat 7:30pm. CHUCK WAGON.

A treat for the whole family, this ranch is like a Western village, complete with staged gunfights and pony rides for the kids. Gates open at 6pm; a chuck-wagon dinner of beef, baked potato, beans, biscuit, applesauce cake, and coffee or lemonade is served promptly at 7:30. Then, at 8:15pm, the Flying J Wranglers present a fast-paced stage show with Western music, a world champion fiddle player, and a world champion yodeler.

Inncredible Restaurant and Saloon. Hwy. 48 North at Ski Run Rd., Alto Village. ☎ **505/ 336-4312.** Reservations recommended. Main courses $7.95–$18.95. AE, DISC, MC, V. Daily 5pm–close (bar opens 3:30pm). STEAKS/SEAFOOD.

Old West-style art hangs on the walls of this modern yet rustic restaurant, with fine etched glass and stained glass accented by large skylights. Especially known for its prime rib and Australian cold water lobster, the menu also includes steaks, such as pepper steak in brandy sauce, shrimp and crab au gratin, chicken, and pasta. There are special children's meals, and munchies are served in the bar.

✪ **Tinnie Silver Dollar Restaurant and Saloon.** Hwy. 70 E., Tinnie. ☎ **505/653-4425.** Reservations recommended. Main courses $9.95–$24.50. MC, V. Daily 11am–11pm. STEAKS/ SEAFOOD.

Housed in a Territorial-style building dating from the 1880s, this Victorian eatery is truly a relic from another era. An ornate 19th-century European music box still plays tunes on ancient metal disks. Four stained-glass windows from an old El Paso church cover the entire wall of one room. Above the fireplace in another room, Neptune is attended by mermaids in an 1880s stained-glass window from a San Francisco seafood restaurant. The restaurant has a massive oak bar, milk-glass gaslights, a bell tower, and a veranda that offers a fine view of the Rio Hondo valley.

For an appetizer, you can't miss with the layered brie, with pesto and piñon nuts. Selections include everything from rib-eye steak, grilled lamb chops, and lobster tail, to Silver Dollar prawns (basted in drawn butter), pasta Scandiffio, and enchiladas suizas.

5 A Scenic Drive Around the Lincoln Loop

An enjoyable way to see many of the sights of the area while staying in Ruidoso is on a one- or two-day 162-mile loop tour.

Heading east from Ruidoso on US 70, about 18 miles past Ruidoso Downs, is the small community of **San Patricio,** where you'll find (watch for signs) the **Hurd-La Rinconada Gallery** (☎ 505/653-4331). Late artist Peter Hurd, a Roswell native, flunked out of West Point before studying with artist N. C. Wyeth and marrying Wyeth's daughter, Henriette, and eventually returning with her to New Mexico. This gallery shows and sells works by Peter Hurd, Henriette Wyeth, their son Michael Hurd, Andrew Wyeth, and N. C. Wyeth. In addition to original works, signed reproductions are available. The gallery is open Monday through Saturday from 9am to 5pm, and Sunday from 10am to 4pm. Several rooms and guest houses are also available by the night or for longer periods (see "Nearby Places to Stay," in the Ruidoso section above).

From San Patricio, continue east on US 70 for 4 miles to the community of Hondo, at the confluence of the Rio Hondo and Rio Bonito, and turn west onto US 380. From here it's about 10 miles to **Lincoln,** a fascinating little town that is also a National Historic Landmark (see "Lincoln State Monument," above). From Lincoln, continue west on US 380 about a dozen miles to **Capitan** and **Smokey Bear Historical State Park,** 118 First St. (☎ **505/354-2748**), open daily 9am to 5pm. Smokey, the national symbol of forest fire prevention, was born near here and found as an orphaned cub by firefighters in the early 1950s. This state park (admission 50¢) has exhibits on Smokey's rescue and life at the National Zoo in Washington, D.C., as well as fire prevention from World War II to the present. Visitors can also stop at Smokey's grave, and explore a nature path that represents six vegetation zones of the area.

Heading west from Capitan about 20 miles takes you to **Carrizozo,** the Lincoln County seat since 1912. For a quick sandwich or burger, stop at **East Coast Subs,** Twelfth Street and S. US 54 (☎ 505/648-2155), before continuing west on US 380 for 4 miles to **Valley of Fires Recreation Area** (☎ 505/648-2241), where you'll find what is considered one of the youngest and best-preserved lava fields in the United States. Among the black lava formations there's a $^3/_4$-mile self-guided nature trail, and a small visitors' center and bookstore in the park campground. Admission is $4 per person or $6 per car for day use, and camping costs $7 to $12. The park is open year-round.

To continue the loop tour, return 4 miles to Carrizozo, turn south onto US 54, and go about 28 miles to the turnoff to **Three Rivers Petroglyph National Recreation Area** (☎ 505/525-4300), which is about 5 miles east on a paved road. There are some 20,000 individual rock art images here, carved by Mogollon peoples who lived in the area centuries ago. A trail about .8 mile long links many of the more interesting petroglyphs. The park also includes the partially excavated ruins of an ancient Native American village, including a multiroom adobe building, pit house, and masonry house that have been partially reconstructed. Administered by the U.S. Bureau of Land Management, the park has facilities for picnicking and camping. Day use or camping fee is $3 per vehicle. The U.S. Forest Service also has a campground in the area, about 5 miles east via a gravel road.

From the recreation area, return 5 miles to US 54 and continue south about 15 miles to **Tularosa Vineyards** (☎ 505/585-2260), which offers tours and tastings daily from noon until 5pm. Using all New Mexico grapes, the winery is especially known for its award-winning reds. Wines can be purchased by the bottle, with prices ranging from $6 to $12.

Continuing south from the winery, drive about 2 miles to Tularosa and turn east onto US 70, which you take for about 16 miles to the village of **Mescalero** on the Mescalero Indian Reservation. From US 70, turn south onto Eagle Drive to get to the imposing **St. Joseph Church,** standing over 100 feet tall to the tip of the cross, with stone walls up to four feet thick. Built between 1920 and 1939, the mission church also contains an icon of the Apache Christ, with Christ depicted as a Mescalero holy man. Local arts and crafts and religious items are for sale at the parish office. Mass is celebrated Sundays at 10:30am. From the church go south to Apache Boulevard and then east to the **Mescalero National Fish Hatchery** (☎ 505/671-4401), which has displays on the life cycle of trout and a self-guided walking tour through the tank house and raceway. The hatchery, which raises and distributes almost half a million trout annually, is open Monday through Friday from 8am to 4pm. Call for weekend hours and to arrange guided tours. Admission is free.

Returning to US 70, it's about 19 miles back to Ruidoso.

6 Roswell

Roswell (pop. 47,395) dominates a vast, sparsely populated prairie of ranch land. From its founding in 1871, it has been a center for farming, and cattle and sheep ranching. It has also become a major industrial center, with plants that produce

The Incident at Roswell

In July of 1947, something "happened" in Roswell. What was it? Debate still abounds. On July 8, 1947, a local rancher named MacBrazel found unusual debris scattered across his property. The U.S. military first released a statement saying the debris was wreckage from a spaceship crash. Four hours later, however, the military retracted the statement, claiming what fell from the sky that summer night was "only a weather balloon." Most of the community didn't believe the weather balloon story, although some did suspect that the military was somehow involved—Robert Goddard had been working on rockets in this area since the 1930s, and the Roswell Air Base was located along the city limits to the south. Eyewitnesses to the account, however, maintain the debris "was not of this world."

Theorists believe that the crash actually involved two spacecraft. One disintegrated, hence the debris across the MacBrazel ranch, and the other crash-landed, hence the four alien bodies that were also claimed to have been discovered. The current debate is not whether there was a second ship, but rather where it crashed.

There are a couple of places in Roswell where you can go to learn more about the Incident. Staffers at the **International UFO Museum and Research Center** (☎ **505/625-9495**), located in the old Plains Theater on Main Street, will be more than happy to discuss the crash and the alleged military cover-up. It's open daily from 1 to 5pm; admission is free. Or you can check out John Price's **UFO Enigma Museum** (☎ **505/347-2275**), also on Main Street (if you get to the old air base, now an industrial airport, you've gone too far, but just barely). John Price likes being next to the old air base because, he says, "it's where they took the alien bodies for autopsy." This museum is open Monday through Saturday from 9:30am to 5pm

clothing, food, airplanes, and buses. Its elevation of 3,650 feet gives it a hot climate in summer, mild in winter. The city has a very active cultural life, and a visit to its museums and nearby natural areas make it worth spending some time.

ESSENTIALS

GETTING THERE **By Car** From Albuquerque take I-40 east 59 miles to Clines Corners; turn south on US 285, 140 miles to Roswell (four hours). From Las Cruces, take US 70 east (four hours). From Carlsbad, take US 285 north (1½ hours).

By Plane **Roswell Airport,** at Roswell Industrial Air Center on South Main Street (☎ **505/347-5703**), is served commercially by **Mesa Airlines** (☎ **800/MESA-AIR** or 505/347-5501). Mesa flies to Albuquerque almost hourly throughout the day and direct to Dallas, Texas, twice daily.

VISITOR INFORMATION The **Roswell Chamber of Commerce** is at 131 W. Second St. (P.O. Box 70), Roswell, NM 88201 (☎ **505/623-5695**). The Roswell Convention and Visitors Bureau can be contacted at the same address and phone number.

SEEING THE SIGHTS

✪ **Roswell Museum and Art Center.** 100 W. 11th St., Roswell, NM 88201. ☎ **505/ 624-6744.** Free Admission. Mon–Sat 9am–5pm, Sun and holidays 1–5pm.

This highly acclaimed small museum is deservedly Roswell's number one attraction.

and Sunday from noon to 5pm; admission is $1. You can also reach Mr. Price on his website at http://members.gnn.com/ufoenigma/index.htm (a great source for information on the yearly UFO festival).

If you want to see one of the two possible crash sites, call the **Hub Corn Ranch** at **505/623-4043.** For $15, Shelia Corn will give you a great tour and fill you in on the history of the area. Presently the alleged crash site is roped off with red flags. The side of a bluff is where the alien bodies were supposedly lain. Tours are offered Monday through Saturday from 9 to 11am and from 1 to 3pm. Call ahead for reservations.

Roswell hosts a **UFO Festival** every year during the first week in July. Some of the special events include guest speakers, the Crash and Burn Expo Race, concerts, out of this world food, a laser light show, and an alien invasion at the Bottomless Lakes recreation area. For details on the event, contact festival coordinator Stan Crosby at **505/622-474.**

If you're interested in witnessing a UFO yourself, head for the **Midway Sightings Location Site,** located 9 miles southeast of Roswell on NM 2 at the Dexter/Hagerman turnoff. Becky Escamilla, a local UFO videographer, and her brother Manuel will be happy to assist you. Although not associated with the Roswell Incident, the pair claim to have caught footage of UFOs. For $10, you can participate in a program they call "This is the UFO I saw at Midway." The price includes 2 to 16 hours of filming and a dubbed tape of your UFO sighting—plus your tape will be sent off for analysis. The Escamillas are there almost every day, but weekends and the summer months are the best times to catch them; call **505/347-4228.**

By Su Hudson

Established in the 1930s through the efforts of city government, local archaeological and historical societies, and the WPA, the museum proclaims this city's role as a center for the arts and a cradle of America's space industry.

The art center contains the world's finest collection of works by Peter Hurd and his wife, Henriette Wyeth, as well as representative works by Georgia O'Keeffe, Ernest Blumenschein, Joseph Sharp, and others famed from the early 20th-century Taos and Santa Fe art colonies. There are also permanent and temporary exhibits of late 20th-century works, as well as Native American and Hispanic art. The museum has an early historical section, but its pride and joy is the Robert Goddard Collection, which presents actual engines, rocket assemblies, and specialized parts developed by Goddard in the 1930s, when he lived and worked in Roswell. Goddard's workshop has been re-created for the exhibit. A special display commemorates the Apollo XVII, which undertook the last manned lunar landing in 1972; it includes the space suit worn on the moon by New Mexican Harrison Schmitt. The Goddard Planetarium is used as a science classroom for local students and for special programs. Ask about "the Roswell Incident," an alleged UFO crash near here in 1947.

✪ **Historical Center for Southeast New Mexico.** 200 N. Lea Ave. at W. 2nd St., Roswell, NM 88201. ☎ **505/622-8333.** Admission $2. Fri–Sun 1–4pm.

The handsome mansion that houses this historical collection is as much a part of the museum as the collection itself. A three-story yellow-brick structure built between 1910 and 1912 by rancher J. P. White, its gently sweeping rooflines and large porches reflect the prairie style of architecture made popular by Frank Lloyd Wright. The White family lived here until 1972; today this home, on the National Register of Historic Places, is a monument to turn-of-the-century lifestyles.

First- and second-floor rooms, including the parlor, bedrooms, dining room, and kitchen, have been restored and furnished with early 20th-century antiques. The second floor has a gallery of changing historic exhibits, from fashions to children's toys. The third floor, once White's private library, now houses the Pecos Valley Collection and the archives of the Historical Center for Southeast New Mexico.

New Mexico Military Institute. 101 W. College Blvd. at N. Main St., Roswell, NM 88201. ☎ **505/622-6250** or 505/624-8100. Free admission. Daily (museum hours) 8am–4pm.

"West Point of the West" celebrated its centennial in 1991. Considered one of the most distinguished military schools in the United States, it is the alma mater of luminaries as disparate as football star Roger Staubach and network newsman Sam Donaldson.

On campus is the **General Douglas L. McBride Military Museum** (101 W. College Blvd.; ☎ **505/624-8220**), with a unique collection of artillery and artifacts documenting New Mexico's role in America's wars. Among the memorabilia are a machine-gun-equipped Harley Davidson used in 1916 in General Pershing's attack on Pancho Villa and items from the Bataan Death March. Tours of the campus are offered by appointment.

Spring River Park and Zoo. 1400 E. College Blvd. at Atkinson Ave., Roswell, NM 88201. ☎ **505/624-6760.** Free admisssion. Zoo, year-round, daily 10am–sunset, weather permitting. Rides and concessions, June–Labor Day daily 1–6pm; Apr–May and Sept–Oct, Sat–Sun 1–6pm.

This lovely park, covering 48 acres on either side of a stream a mile east of New Mexico Military Institute, incorporates a miniature train, antique carousel, large prairie-dog town, children's fishing pond, picnic ground, and playgrounds. There's also a children's petting zoo and Texas longhorns.

GETTING OUTSIDE IN THE AREA

Fifteen miles northeast of Roswell, on the Pecos River, is the ✪ **Bitter Lake National Wildlife Refuge,** where a great variety of waterfowl—including cormorants, herons, pelicans, sandhill cranes, and snow geese—find a winter home. The refuge, reached via US 380 and NM 265 from Roswell, comprises 24,000 acres of river bottomland, marsh, stands of salt cedar, and open range. Seven gypsum sinkhole lakes, covering an area of 700 acres, are of a peculiar beauty. If you're here between December and February, don't miss this place: The sky actually darkens with birds. Once threatened with extinction, the sandhill crane now appears, along with puddle and diving ducks every winter. Snow geese were unknown here 20 years back, but now turn up to the tune of some 40,000 every winter. All told, over 300 species of birds have been sighted. You can get information at the headquarters building at the entrance, or call **505/622-6755.**

Bottomless Lakes State Park, a chain of seven lakes surrounded by rock bluffs located 16 miles east of Roswell via NM 409 off of US 380, got its name from early cowboys, who tried to fathom the lakes' depth by plumbing them with lariats. No matter how many ropes they tied together and lowered into the limpid water, they never touched bottom. In truth, though, none of the lakes is deeper than 100 feet. The largest, Lea Lake, is so clear that skin divers frequent it. Another, aptly called Devil's Inkwell, is so shaded by surrounding bluffs that the sun rarely reaches it. Mirror, Cottonwood, Pasture, and Figure 8 lakes got their monikers with similar logic

No Name Lake, which apparently didn't have anything to distinguish it, has been renamed Lazy Lagoon.

This park is a popular recreation site for Roswell residents. There's fishing for rainbow trout, swimming and windsurfing, campsites for trailers or tents, and shelters, showers, a dump station, and a concession area with vending machines and paddleboat rentals (open 9am to 6pm Memorial Day to Labor Day). The park is open year-round from 6am to 9pm daily, and admission is $3 per vehicle. For more information, call **505/624-6058.**

Originally built to raise bass and catfish, the ✪ **Dexter National Fish Hatchery,** located 1¹/₂ miles east of Dexter on NM 190, about 16 miles southeast of Roswell via NM 2, is now a center for the study and raising of threatened and endangered fish species, such as the razorback sucker, Colorado squawfish, Chihuahuan chub, and Mexican Yaqui. Year-round, visitors can take self-guided tours among the hatchery's ponds; and from late March through October the visitors' center is open, with exhibits and an aquarium containing endangered fish. A short film is also shown. The hatchery (☎ **505/734-5910**) is open daily from 7am to 4pm, and admission is free.

WHERE TO STAY

Days Inn. 1310 N. Main St., Roswell, NM 88201. ☎ **505/623-4021.** 62 rms. A/C TV TEL. $40–$48 double. Rates include continental breakfast. AE, CB, DC, DISC, MC, V.

A colonial-style inn with a redbrick and white-wood facade, Days Inn is located on the north side of town. Guest rooms have comfortable Southwestern furnishings, king-size or two double beds, desk, and cable TV. There is a full-service restaurant and lounge on the premises, and they offer limited room service. Pets are allowed. Outdoors are a large swimming pool and hot tub.

Frontier Motel. 3010 N. Main St., Roswell, NM 88201. ☎ **800/678-1401** or 505/622-1400. Fax 505/622-1405. 38 rms and suites. A/C TV TEL. $38–$47 double; $50 suites. Rates include continental breakfast. AE, CB, DC, DISC, MC, V.

This comfortable motel just north of the center of town offers clean and attractive rooms in a variety of sizes and decors. Some of the smaller rooms have showers only, while larger rooms have shower and bath combinations. Refrigerators are available and there is an outdoor, unheated pool. Rooms for people with disabilities and nonsmokers are available, and pets are accepted.

Sally Port Inn. 2000 N. Main St., Roswell, NM 88201. ☎ **800/548-5221**, 800/528-1234, or 505/622-6430. Fax 505/623-7631. 124 rms. A/C TV TEL. $64–$68 double. Summer weekend specials. AE, CB, DC, DISC, MC, V.

A Best Western property, this two-story white-brick building adjacent to New Mexico Military Institute boasts a huge atrium courtyard. A cafe and swimming pool are at opposite ends of this skylit area.

Guest rooms, all of which have interior access, have double and queen-size beds, two sinks (one at the vanity), brass fixtures, and a working table. Executive king units have a refrigerator as well as a king-size bed. Some rooms are designated for nonsmokers and people with disabilities.

The atrium cafe serves three meals daily, and there's also a separate bar. The inn has room service, courtesy van, valet laundry, swimming pool, whirlpool, sauna, weight room, coin-op laundry, hair salon, and gift shop.

CAMPING

Trailer Village Campgrounds (☎ **505/623-6040**) in Roswell is your best bet, they have 53 sites and 53 full hookups. Cable TV and phone hookups are available, and air-conditioning and heating are provided at an extra charge. Tenting is available and so are group tent sites. Laundry and limited grocery facilities are also available. The campgrounds are located 1¹/₃ miles east of the US 285 and US 70/380 junction on US 380.

WHERE TO DINE

El Toro Bravo. 102 S. Main St. at 1st St. ☎ **505/622-9280.** Main courses $5.75–$10.95; lunch $3.95–$6.95. AE, MC, V. Mon–Fri 11am–2:30pm, Sat 11am–5pm; Mon–Sat 5–9pm. NEW MEXICAN.

Mexican souvenirs adorn the walls of this dimly lit restaurant, which occupies two large rooms. Plants hang from the high ceiling. The menu has a wide selection of regional dishes, including stuffed sopaipillas, chalupas, chile colorado, and carne asada. There's a $4.95 luncheon buffet Monday through Friday.

Keuken Dutch Restaurant. 12th and N. Main Sts. ☎ **505/624-2040.** Main courses $4.99–$10.99; lunch $2.70–$6; breakfast $3–$6.50. AE, CB, DC, DISC, MC, V. Daily 5am–11pm. DUTCH/AMERICAN.

This restaurant is straight from New Holland. Blue-and-white delft pottery and Dutch dolls brighten the decor of this family restaurant, while servers in traditional outfits, wearing bonnets and aprons, provide attentive service. Standard American dishes share the menu with Dutch specialties like eggs hollandaise and fruit koeken (pancakes) for breakfast, a Dutch burger with Gouda cheese for lunch, and Metworst sausage with warm red cabbage and German potato salad for dinner. There's free coffee for early risers (5 to 6am).

✪ **Mario's.** 200 E. 2nd St. ☎ **505/623-1740.** Main courses $4.95–$13.95; lunch $3.70–$4.95. AE, MC, V. Mon–Thurs 11am–9pm, Fri–Sat 11am–10pm. AMERICAN.

The works of regional artists such as Peter Hurd and R. C. Gorman hang on the walls, while stained-glass lamps/ceiling fans are suspended above the booths and tables. Dinners include prime rib and New York strip steak, country chicken, and blackened or Southern (cornmeal-fried) catfish. "Heart Smart" (low-fat, low-cholesterol) items are indicated on the menu. All dinners include the expansive salad bar and a miniloaf of bread. An adjoining lounge has complimentary hors d'oeuvres and a big-screen TV. In fine weather you can dine on the patio.

⬢ **Nuthin' Fancy Cafe.** 2103 N. Main St. ☎ **505/623-4098.** Main courses $3.75–$10.25; breakfast $1–$5.75. DISC, MC, V. Daily 6am–9pm. AMERICAN.

This large comfortable room with Western decor seems just right for a restaurant with the motto "Home cooking without the mess." The menu is basic American diner, prepared better than most. There are also a few Mexican dishes, such as huevos rancheros and breakfast burritos, which join the standard eggs, pancakes, and waffles on the breakfast menu. Lunch and dinner selections include sandwiches, burgers, chicken-fried steak, meat loaf, and grilled chicken and fish.

7 Also Worth a Look: Fort Sumner & Environs

This little town of 1,300 people, located 84 miles north of Roswell via US 285 and NM 20, is important in New Mexico history for two big reasons: It's the site of Fort Sumner State Monument and the burial place of the notorious Billy the Kid.

Fort Sumner State Monument (☎ 505/355-2573) recalls a tragic U.S. Army experiment (1864–68) to create a self-sustaining agricultural colony for captive Navajos. That native tribe still recalls it as the "Long March," the saddest chapter in their noble history. Today, a visitor center (open daily from 9am to 5pm) tells the story of the fort, and the **Old Fort Sumner Museum** (☎ 505/355-2942) displays artifacts, pictures, and documents. It's located 7 miles southeast of the modern town, via US 60/84 and NM 272.

Behind the museum is the **Grave of Billy the Kid,** a six-foot tombstone engraved to "William H. Bonney, alias 'Billy the Kid,' died July 16, 1881," and to two previously slain comrades with whom he was buried. Those curious about the notorious young outlaw, just 21 when Sheriff Pat Garrett shot him in Fort Sumner, can learn more at the **Billy the Kid Museum** (☎ **505/355-2380**), 2 miles east of downtown Fort Sumner on US 60/84. It contains more than 60,000 relics of the Old West, including some recalling the life of young Bonney himself.

The **Old Fort Days** celebration, the second week of June, is Fort Sumner's big annual event. It includes the World's Richest Tombstone Race (inspired by the actual theft of Billy's tombstone, since recovered), two nights of rodeo, a country music show, barbecue, and parade.

Sumner Lake State Park (☎ **505/355-2541**), 16 miles northwest of Fort Sumner via US 84 and NM 203, is a 1,000-acre property with a campground and cabin sites. Boating, fishing, swimming, and waterskiing are popular recreations.

For more information on the town, write or phone the **De Baca County Chamber of Commerce,** P.O. Box 28, Fort Sumner, NM 88119 (☎ **505/355-7705**). To learn more about Billy the Kid and Pat Garrett, write **Billy the Kid Outlaw Gang,** P.O. Box 1881, Taiban, NM 88134 (☎ **505/355-9935**).

CLOVIS/PORTALES

Clovis, 110 miles northeast of Roswell via US 70, is a major market center on the Texas border. Founded in 1906 as a railway town, it is now the focus of an active ranching and farming region, with about 36,091 population. **Cannon Air Force Base,** a part of the Tactical Air Command, is just northwest of the city. The **Lyceum Theatre,** 411 Main St. (☎ **505/763-6085**), is a magnificent restoration of a former vaudeville theater; it's now the city's center for performing arts. The **H. A. "Pappy" Thornton Homestead and Museum** in Ned Houk Park (no phone) displays antique farming equipment in a prairie farmhouse. A major rodeo on the national circuit is held the first weekend in June. "Clovis Man," who hunted mammoths in this region about 10,000 B.C., was first discovered at a site near the city.

South of Clovis 19 miles is **Portales,** a town of 12,280 people that is the home of the main campus of **Eastern New Mexico University.** On campus are the **Roosevelt County Historical Museum** (☎ **505/562-2592**) of regional ranching history and the **Natural History Museum** (☎ **505/562-2174**), with wildlife exhibits, including a bee colony. There are anthropology and paleontology exhibits at the **Blackwater Draw Museum** (☎ **505/562-2202**), 7 miles northeast of Portales on U.S. Highway 70 toward Clovis.

For lodging in the Clovis/Portales area, try the **Best Western LaViata Inn,** 1516 Mabry Dr. (U.S. Highway 60/70/84), Clovis, NM 88101 (☎ **800/528-1234** or 505/762-3808), or the **Holiday Inn,** 2700 Mabry Dr., Clovis, NM 88101 (☎ **800/HOLIDAY** or 505/762-4491). Clovis is the flagship of the **K-Bob's Steakhouse** chain, when you're hungry. The restaurant is at 1600 Mabry Dr. (☎ **505/763-4443**).

8 Carlsbad & Environs

Carlsbad is a city of 26,500 on the Pecos River. Founded in the late 1800s, its area was controlled by Apaches and Comanches until just a little over a century ago. Besides a good tourist business from Carlsbad Caverns, the town thrives on farming, with irrigated crops of cotton, hay, and pecans. Pecans grow so well in Carlsbad that it is said the nuts from just two trees in your yard will pay your property taxes. The area is the largest producer of potash in the United States. The town was named for the spa in Bohemia of the same name.

The caverns (see section 9, below) are the big attraction, having drawn more than 33 million visitors since opening in 1923. A satellite community, Whites City, was created 20 miles south of Carlsbad at the park entrance junction. The family of Jack White Jr. owns all of its motels, restaurants, gift shops, and other attractions.

ESSENTIALS

GETTING THERE   By car   From Albuquerque take I-40 east 59 miles to Clines Corners; turn south on US 285, 216 miles to Carlsbad via Roswell (six hours). From El Paso, take US 62/180 east (three hours).

By Plane   Cavern City Air Terminal (☎ 505/885-5236) is 4 miles south of the city via National Parks Highway (US 62/180). **Mesa Airlines** (☎ 800/MESA-AIR or 505/885-0245) provides commercial service with four flights to and from Albuquerque and two flights to and from Dallas, Texas. You can rent a car at the airport from Hertz (☎ 800/654-3131 or 505/887-1500).

VISITOR INFORMATION   The **Carlsbad Chamber of Commerce** and the **Carlsbad Convention and Visitors Bureau,** both at 302 S. Canal St. (Highway 285) at Green Street (Highway 62/180), P.O. Box 910 Dept. B, Carlsbad, NM 88221-0910 (☎ 800/221-1224 or 505/887-6516), are open from 8am to 5pm Monday to Friday.

SEEING THE SIGHTS

Carlsbad's pride and joy is its river, with a 3½-mile **Riverwalk** along both banks of the pretty Pecos River, beginning near the north end of Riverside Drive. Annual **Christmas on the Pecos** pontoon boat rides take place each evening from Thanksgiving to New Year's Eve (except Christmas Eve), past a fascinating display of Christmas lights on riverside homes and businesses. Advance reservations are required, available from the chamber of commerce. Cost is $6 per person; lap tickets are available free for children under three.

The **Carlsbad Museum and Art Center,** 418 W. Fox St., one block west of Canal Street (☎ 505/887-0276), contains Apache relics, pioneer artifacts such as guns and saddles, and an impressive art collection. The museum is open Monday through Saturday from 10am to 6pm; admission is free, although donations are welcome.

GETTING OUTSIDE

Recreational facilities in the Carlsbad area include some two dozen parks, several golf courses, numerous tennis courts and swimming pools, a municipal beach, and a shooting and archery range. Contact the **City of Carlsbad Recreation Department** (☎ 505/887-1191).

✪ **Living Desert Zoo and Gardens State Park.** 1504 Miehls Dr. (P.O. Box 100), Carlsbad, NM 88221-0100. ☎ **505/887-5516.** Admission $3, children 6 and under free. Group rates are available. Memorial Day weekend–Labor Day 8am–6:30pm; rest of year 9am–3:30pm. Closed Christmas. Take Miehls Dr. off US 285 west of town and proceed just over a mile.

Situated within 1,200 acres of authentic Chihuahuan Desert, this park contains more than 50 species of desert mammals, birds, and reptiles, and almost 500 varieties of plants. Paved walkways lead through a variety of habitats past native plants, and into a greenhouse that shelters unusual cacti and exotic succulents from around the world.

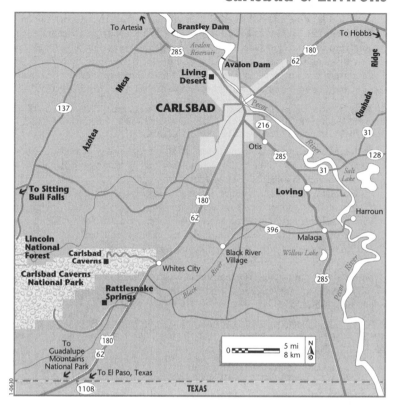

Rehabilitation programs provide the park's animals, who have been sick or injured and could no longer survive in the wild. You'll see golden eagles and great horned owls among the birds of prey in the aviary, and large animals such as deer, antelope, elk, and bison in large outdoor pastures. An arroyo exhibit houses javelina, and you'll also see bears, bobcats, and cougars. A prairie dog town is a children's favorite, and a visitors' center houses additional exhibits and a gift shop.

The view from the park, high atop the Ocotillo Hills on the northwest side of Carlsbad, is superb.

WHERE TO STAY

Most properties are along the highway south toward Carlsbad Caverns.

Best Western Cavern Inn. 17 Carlsbad Cavern Hwy. at N.M. Hwy. 7 (P.O. Box 128), White's City, NM 88268. ☎ **800/CAVERNS** or 505/785-2291. Fax 505/785-2283. 63 rms. A/C TV TEL. May 15–Sept 15 $59–$75 single or double; Sept 16–May 14 $49–$65 single or double. AE, CB, DC, DISC, MC, V.

This motel and the overflow properties flanking it—the 44-room Guadalupe Inn and the 25-unit adobe Walnut Canyon Inn—suffice as places to rest one's head before or after a visit to Carlsbad Caverns. Guest registration is in the arcade with the western facade on the south side of the highway; the motel is on the north side. Rooms are very spacious, with a Southwestern decor.

Most folks dine and drink across the highway at the Velvet Garter Saloon and Restaurant (see "Where to Dine," below). The White's City arcade contains a post office, grocery store, gift shop, Million Dollar Museum of various antiques and paraphernalia, and Granny's Opera House, a theater for weekend melodramas. Between the Cavern Inn and its neighbor properties, there are two swimming pools, two hot tubs, and a court for tennis, volleyball, and basketball. Pets are not allowed.

☉ Best Western Motel Stevens. 1829 S. Canal St., Carlsbad, NM 88220. ☎ **800/ 730-2851,** 800/528-1234, or 505/887-2851. Fax 505/887-6338. 202 rms, 15 suites. A/C TV TEL. $70–$80 double; $70 and up suite. AE, CB, DC, DISC, MC, V.

Well-landscaped gardens surround this handsome property, composed of several buildings spread across the spacious grounds. The very attractive lobby and restaurant are located in a central brick building with a tile roof.

Rooms are good sized, with Southwestern decor, and most have two queen beds. All have remodeled bathrooms with large mirrors and spacious vanities. Some units, with peaked ceilings to make them feel even larger, have backdoor patios. A microwave/refrigerator combo is available and suites have kitchenettes.

There are rooms for people with disabilities and nonsmokers. Pets are allowed.

The Flume (see "Where to Dine," below), open daily from 6am to 10pm, is a beautiful fine-dining establishment specializing in American cuisine. The motel has room service, courtesy car, guest laundry, 24-hour desk, swimming and wading pools, and playground.

Continental Inn. 3820 National Parks Hwy., Carlsbad, NM 88220. ☎ **505/887-0341.** Fax 505/885-0508. 60 rms and suites. A/C TV TEL. $39.95–$44.95 double; suites from $49.95. AE, CB, DC, DISC, MC, V.

This economical motel has all the necessities for travelers on a budget. Rooms have coffeemakers; most have queen-size beds, there are a few kings, and one room has a water bed. Suites are equipped with refrigerators, and the Honeymoon Suite has a heart-shaped tub below a mirrored ceiling, and a shower for two. There's an outdoor heated swimming pool, nonsmoking rooms, and rooms for people with disabilities. A 24-hour restaurant is nearby.

✪ Holiday Inn. 601 S. Canal St. (P.O. Box 128), Carlsbad, NM 88220. ☎ **800/742-9586,** 800/HOLIDAY, or 505/885-8500. Fax 505/887-5999. 100 rms. A/C TV TEL. $86–$96 double. AE, CB, DC, DISC, JCB, MC, V.

A handsome New Mexico Territorial-style building houses this first-rate full-service hotel in downtown Carlsbad. Rooms have Southwestern decor, and there's a beautiful outdoor heated swimming pool, sauna, and whirlpool, plus an exercise room and playground. Guests have self-service laundry facilities. Rooms for nonsmokers and people with disabilities are available (some with roll-in showers).

The hotel has two restaurants: Ventanas offers fine dining, serving steaks, prime rib, seafood, veal, and pastas; the Phenix Bar and Grill has sandwiches, burgers, soups, salads, and prime rib.

Stagecoach Inn. 1819 S. Canal St., Carlsbad, NM 88220. ☎ **505/887-1148.** 55 rms. A/C TV TEL. $45–$59 double. AE, DISC, MC, V.

A large, tree-shaded playground area with a picnic table set back from the highway is the earmark of this motel, which also features an adult pool and children's wading pool. Pets are permitted. Rooms have ample space, and are simply but comfortably furnished. Facilities include a coin-op guest laundry.

The adjacent restaurant specializes in Mexican food, burgers, and barbecue and is open daily.

CAMPING

Brantley Lake State Park (☎ 505/457-2384) in Carlsbad has RV hookups as well as tent camp sites. Picnic tables, grills, and recreational facilities are available. Boating and lake fishing are popular here. **Carlsbad Campground** (☎ **505/885-6333**) is a large, full-service campground with a swimming pool and playground. In Artesia, try **Bill's RV Park** (☎ **505/746-6184**), a more moderately sized campground located on Hermosa Drive just south of the junction of US 82 and US 285. Laundry facilities are available.

WHERE TO DINE

✪ **The Flume.** At Best Western Motel Stevens, 1829 S. Canal St. ☎ **505/887-2851.** Reservations recommended for dinner. Main courses $7.50–$15.95; lunch $3.25–$7.95. AE, CB, DC, DISC, MC, V. Mon–Sat 6am–10pm, Sun 6am–9pm. AMERICAN.

This elegant restaurant has a Southwestern feel, with rich wood and upholstery, lovely chandeliers, wall sconces, and candlelight. The menu includes lots of steaks, a New Orleans shrimp plate, and a special teriyaki chicken breast. Lighter dinners, called "Young and Young-at-Heart" meals, are available.

Lucy's. 701 S. Canal St. ☎ **505/887-7714.** Reservations recommended on weekends. Main courses $3.75–$11.95. AE, CB, DC, DISC, MC, V. Mon–Sat 11am–10pm. MEXICAN.

Since 1974, Lucy and Justo Yanez's friendly, casual downtown restaurant has made diners—visitors and locals alike—feel right at home. It's dedicated to the words of a Mexican proverb printed on the menu: *El hambre es un fuego, y la comida es fresca* (Hunger is a burning, and eating is a coolness). The food is superb, with Lucy's personal adaptations of old favorites: steak ranchero, caldillo de Miguel (beef stew), Tucson chimichanga, and shrimp fajitas. Finish with a dessert of buñelos, sprinkled with cinnamon sugar. Children's plates are available; diners can choose how hot they like their red or green chiles.

Sirloin Stockade. 710 S. Canal St. ☎ **505/887-7211.** Main courses $5.99–$12.99. MC, V. Daily 11am–10pm. STEAKS.

Part of a statewide eight-restaurant chain of family steak houses, the Sirloin Stockade serves a variety of steaks, chicken, and shrimp platters. There are several buffet food bars offering soups, salads, hot dishes, and desserts; and children's and senior citizens' menus are available.

Velvet Garter Saloon and Restaurant. 26 Carlsbad Cavern Hwy., White's City. ☎ **505/785-2291.** Reservations recommended in summer. Main courses $6.95–$12.95. AE, CB, DC, MC, V. Daily 4–9pm. AMERICAN.

This comfortable coffee shop near the Carlsbad Caverns Highway junction boasts two beautiful stained-glass windows portraying the caverns and the Guadalupe Mountains. The menu includes steaks, chicken, and fish. Nearby Fat Jack's caters to fast-food diets with three meals daily; the saloon is unmistakable, with the longhorns mounted over the door.

EXPLORING THE ENVIRONS
A SIDE TRIP TO TEXAS: GUADALUPE MOUNTAINS NATIONAL PARK

Some 250 million years ago, the Guadalupe Mountains were an immense reef poking up through a tropical ocean. Marine organisms fossilized this 400-mile-long Capitan Reef as limestone; later, as the sea evaporated, a blanket of sediments and mineral salts buried the reef. Then just 10 to 12 million years ago, a mountain-building uplift exposed a part of the fossil reef. This has given modern scientists a unique opportunity to explore Earth's geologic history and outdoor lovers a playground for wilderness experience.

The steep southern end of the range makes up the park, while the northern part lies within Lincoln National Forest and Carlsbad Caverns National Park. Deer, elk, mountain lion, and bear are found in the forests, which contrast strikingly with the desert around them. In these isolated basins and protected valleys is a proliferation of vegetation rare elsewhere in the Southwest.

JUST THE FACTS   To reach the park, take US 62/180 55 miles southwest of Carlsbad. Admission to the park is free, and the visitor center is open from June to August from 8am to 6pm; September to May from 8am to 4:30pm. For more information, write to Park Ranger, Box 400, Salt Flat, TX 78947 or call **915/828-3251.**

SEEING THE HIGHLIGHTS   The Visitors Center offers a variety of exhibits and slide programs telling the story of the Guadalupe Mountains, as well as ranger-guided walks and lectures. Information, maps, and backcountry permits can also be obtained at McKittrick Canyon Visitor Center (10 miles northeast via US 62/180 and a side road) and Dog Canyon Ranger Station (reached through Carlsbad via NM 137 and County Road 414, about 70 miles).

McKittrick Canyon, protected by its high sheer walls, with a green swatch of trees growing along the banks of its spring-fed stream, is a beautiful location. It is a great spot for bird-watching and viewing other wildlife, and an especially lovely sight during fall foliage time, late October to mid-November. Most of the national park's 86,416 acres are reached only by 80 miles of foot or horse trail through desert, canyon, and high forest. Backcountry hikers require water and permits; camping must be in designated areas.

CAMPING   Pine Springs and Dog Canyon both have developed camping areas, with rest rooms and water, but no hookups or showers. Fires, including charcoal, are not permitted. Fees at Pine Springs and Dog Canyon Campgrounds are $8 per night.

ARTESIA

The principal attraction of this quiet town of 11,743 people, 36 miles north of Carlsbad on US 285, is the **Artesia Historical Museum and Art Center,** housed in a Victorian home at 505 W. Richardson Ave., Artesia (☎ **505/748-2390**). Open Tuesday to Saturday from 10am to noon and from 1 to 5pm, it exhibits Native American and pioneer artifacts, traveling exhibits, and art shows.

Visitors looking for a stopover in Artesia might consider the **Best Western Pecos Inn,** 2209 W. Main St. (Highway 82), Artesia, NM 88211 (☎ **505/748-3324**). Further information can be obtained from the **Artesia Chamber of Commerce,** P.O. Box 99, Artesia, NM 88211 (☎ **505/746-2744**).

HOBBS

Located 69 miles east of Carlsbad on US 62/180, on the edge of the Llano Estacado tableland, Hobbs (pop. 29,712) is at the center of New Mexico's richest oil field. Many oil companies have their headquarters here.

Points of interest include the **Lea County Cowboy Hall of Fame and Western Heritage Center** at New Mexico Junior College, on the Lovington Highway (☎ **505/392-1275**). It honors the area's ranchers, both men and women, and rodeo performers and is open from 10am to 5pm Monday through Friday, and from 1 to 5pm Saturday (closed college holidays). The **Confederate Air Force Museum** (☎ **505/397-3203**) at Lea County Airport, on US 62/180, displays World War II aircraft, and the **Soaring Society of America** (☎ **505/392-1177**) has its national headquarters at the Hobbs Industrial Air Park, north of town on NM 18. Native American artifacts and pioneer mementos are displayed by appointment at the **Linam Ranch Museum** (☎ 505/393-4784), located west of town on US 62/180.

Twenty-two miles northwest of Hobbs via NM 18, at the junction of U.S. Highway 82, is the town of **Lovington** (pop. 9,500), another ranching and oil center. The **Lea County Historical Museum,** 103 S. Love St. (☎ 505/396-5311), presents memorabilia of the region's unique history in a World War I-era hotel.

If you plan to stay in Hobbs, try the **Ramada Inn,** 501 N. Marland St. (☎ 505/397-3251). You can get a good square meal at the **Cattle Baron Steak and Seafood Restaurant,** 1930 N. Grimes St. (☎ 505/393-2800). **Harry McAdams State Park,** 4 miles north of Hobbs on NM 18 (☎ 505/392-5845), has campsites and a visitor center. For more information, contact the **Hobbs Chamber of Commerce,** 400 N. Marland St. (☎ 800/658-6291 or 505/397-3202).

9 Carlsbad Caverns National Park

One of the largest and most spectacular cave systems in the world, Carlsbad Caverns comprise some 80 known caves that snake through the porous limestone reef of the Guadalupe Mountains. Fantastic and grotesque formations fascinate visitors, who find every shape imaginable (and unimaginable) naturally sculpted in the underground world—from frozen waterfalls to strands of pearls, from soda straws to miniature castles, from draperies to ice-cream cones.

Although Native Americans had known of the caverns for centuries, they were not discovered by whites until about a century ago, when settlers were attracted by sunset flights of bats from the cave. Jim White, a guano miner, began to explore the main cave in the early 1900s and to share its wonders with tourists. By 1923, the caverns had become a national monument, upgraded to national park in 1930.

ESSENTIALS

GETTING THERE Visitors arrive via US 62/180 from either Carlsbad, New Mexico (see below), which is 23 miles to the northeast, or El Paso, Texas (150 miles west). The scenic entrance road to the park is 7 miles long and originates at the park gate at White's City.

Arriving by Bus From White's City, south of Carlsbad, van service to Carlsbad Caverns National Park is provided by **Sun Country Tours/White's City Services** (☎ 505/785-2291).

VISITOR INFORMATION General admission to the park is $5 for adults, $3 for children 6 to 15, and children under 6 are free. Admission is good for three days and includes entry to the two self-guided walking tours. Guided tours range in price from $4 to $12 depending on the type of tour, and reservations are required. The visitor center and park are open daily from Memorial Day to mid-August from 8am to 7pm; the rest of the year they're open from 8am to 5:30pm. For more information about the park, write to Carlsbad Caverns National Park, 3225 National Parks Hwy., Carlsbad, NM 88220, or call **505/785-2232** (ask for ext. 429 if you're calling about guided tours) or 505/785-2107 (for recorded information).

TOURING THE CAVES

Two caves, Carlsbad Cavern and Slaughter Canyon (formerly New) Cave, are open to the public. The National Park Service has provided facilities, including elevators, to make it easy for everyone to visit the cavern, and a kennel for pets is available. Visitors in wheelchairs are common.

Carlsbad Caverns National Park

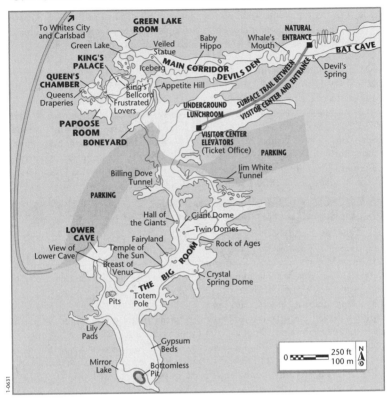

In addition the tours described below, visitors should inquire at the visitor center information desk about other ranger-guided tours, including climbing and crawling "wild" cave tours. Spelunkers who seek access to the park's undeveloped caves require special permission from the park superintendent.

CARLSBAD CAVERN TOURS

Visitors to the park may tour the caverns in one of three ways, depending on their time, interest, and level of ability. The first, and least difficult, option is to take the elevator from the visitor center down 750 feet to the start of the self-guided tour of the Big Room. More difficult and time-consuming is the 1-mile self-guided tour along the Natural Entrance route, which follows the traditional explorer's route, entering the cavern through the large historic natural entrance. The paved walkway through the natural entrance winds into the depths of the cavern and leads through a series of underground rooms; this tour takes about an hour. Parts of it are steep. At its lowest point, the trail reaches 750 feet below the surface, ending finally at an underground rest area.

Both visitors who take the elevator and those who take the Natural Entrance route begin the self-guided tour of the spectacular Big Room near the rest area. The floor of this room covers 14 acres; the tour, over a relatively level path, is 1 1/4 miles in length and takes about an hour.

The third option is the 1 1/2-hour ranger-guided Kings Palace tour, which also departs from the underground rest area. This tour descends 830 feet beneath the surface of the desert to the deepest portion of the cavern open to the public. Reservations are required and an additional fee is charged.

TOUR TIPS   Everyone is advised to wear flat shoes with rubber soles and heels because of the slippery paths. A light sweater or jacket feels good in the constant temperature of 56°, especially when it's 100° outside in the sun. The cavern is well lit, but you might want to bring along a flashlight as well. Rangers are stationed in the cave to answer questions.

SLAUGHTER CANYON CAVE TOUR

Slaughter Canyon Cave was discovered in 1937 and was mined for bat guano commercially until the 1950s. It consists of a corridor 1,140 feet long with many side passageways. The lowest point is 250 feet below the surface, and the passage traversed by the ranger-guided tours is 1^3/$_4$ miles long, but more strenuous than hiking through the main cavern; there is also a strenuous 500-foot rise hike from the parking lot to the cave mouth. The tour lasts about 2^1/$_2$ hours. No more than 25 people may take part in a tour, and then by reservation only. Everyone needs a flashlight, hiking boots or shoes, and a container of drinking water. Slaughter Canyon Cave is reached via US 180, south 5 miles from White's City, to a marked turnoff that leads 11 miles into a parking lot.

BAT FLIGHTS

Every sunset from early spring through October, a crowd gathers at the natural entrance of the cave to watch a quarter of a million bats take flight for a night of insect feasting. (The bats, and some of the people, winter in Mexico.) All day long the Mexican free-tailed bats, approximately one million of them, sleep in the cavern; at night they all strike out on an insect hunt. A ranger program is offered about 7pm (verify the time at the visitor center) at the outdoor Bat Flight Amphitheater. On the second Thursday in August (usually), the park sponsors a **Bat Flight Breakfast** from 5 to 7am, during which visitors watch the bats return to the cavern.

OTHER PARK ACTIVITIES

Aside from the caves, the national park offers a 10-mile one-way scenic loop drive through the Chihuahuan Desert to view Rattlesnake and Upper Walnut Canyons. Picnickers can head for Rattlesnake Springs Picnic Area, on County Road 418 near Slaughter Canyon Cave, a water source for hundreds of years for the Native Americans of the area. Backcountry hikers must register at the visitor center before going out on any of the trails in the 46,766 acres of the park.

Index

FROMMER'S COMPLETE TRAVEL GUIDES

(Comprehensive guides to destinations around the world, with selections in all price ranges—from deluxe to budget)

Acapulco/Ixtapa/Zihuatenjo
Alaska
Amsterdam
Arizona
Atlanta
Australia
Austria
Bahamas
Bangkok
Barcelona, Madrid & Seville
Belgium, Holland & Luxembourg
Berlin
Bermuda
Boston
Budapest & the Best of Hungary
California
Canada
Cancún, Cozumel & the Yucatán
Caribbean
Caribbean Cruises & Ports of Call
Caribbean Ports of Call
Carolinas & Georgia
Chicago
Colorado
Costa Rica
Denver, Boulder & Colorado Springs
Dublin
England

Florida
France
Germany
Greece
Hawaii
Hong Kong
Honolulu/Waikiki/Oahu
Ireland
Italy
Jamaica & Barbados
Japan
Las Vegas
London
Los Angeles
Maryland & Delaware
Maui
Mexico
Mexico City
Miami & the Keys
Montana & Wyoming
Montréal & Québec City
Munich & the Bavarian Alps
Nashville & Memphis
Nepal
New England
New Mexico
New Orleans
New York City
Northern New England
Nova Scotia, New Brunswick & Prince Edward Island

Paris
Philadelphia & the Amish Country
Portugal
Prague & the Best of the Czech Republic
Puerto Rico
Puerto Vallarta, Manzanillo & Guadalajara
Rome
San Antonio & Austin
San Diego
San Francisco
Santa Fe, Taos & Albuquerque
Scandinavia
Scotland
Seattle & Portland
South Pacific
Spain
Switzerland
Thailand
Tokyo
Toronto
U.S.A.
Utah
Vancouver & Victoria
Vienna
Virgin Islands
Virginia
Walt Disney World & Orlando
Washington, D.C.
Washington & Oregon

FROMMER'S FRUGAL TRAVELER'S GUIDES

(The grown-up guides to budget travel, offering dream vacations at down-to-earth prices)

Australia from $45 a Day
Berlin from $50 a Day
California from $60 a Day
Caribbean from $60 a Day
Costa Rica & Belize from $35 a Day
Eastern Europe from $30 a Day

England from $50 a Day
Europe from $50 a Day
Florida from $50 a Day
Greece from $45 a Day
Hawaii from $60 a Day
India from $40 a Day
Ireland from $45 a Day
Italy from $50 a Day

Israel from $45 a Day
London from $60 a Day
Mexico from $35 a Day
New York from $70 a Day
New Zealand from $45 a Day
Paris from $60 a Day
Washington, D.C. from $50 a Day

FROMMER'S PORTABLE GUIDES

(Pocket-size guides for travelers who want everything in a nutshell)

Charleston & Savannah   Las Vegas   Washington, D.C.   New Orleans   San Francisco

FROMMER'S FAMILY GUIDES

(The complete guides for successful family vacations)

California with Kids   New England with Kids   San Francisco with Kids
Los Angeles with Kids   New York City with Kids   Washington, D.C. with Kids

FROMMER'S AMERICA ON WHEELS

*(Everything you need for a successful road trip, including full-color
road maps and ratings for every hotel)*

California & Nevada	Midwest & the Great	Northwest & the	Southwest
Florida	Lake States	Great Plains States	Texas & the South-
Mid-Atlantic	New York & the New	Southeast	Central States
	England States		

FROMMER'S WALKING TOURS

(Memorable neighborhood strolls through the world's great cities)

Berlin	Montréal & Québec City	Spain's Favorite Cities
Chicago	New York	Tokyo
England's Favorite Cities	Paris	Venice
London	San Francisco	Washington, D.C.

SPECIAL-INTEREST TITLES

Arthur Frommer's Branson!
Arthur Frommer's New World of Travel
The Civil War Trust's Official Guide to the
   Civil War Discovery Trail
Frommer's America's 100 Best-Loved State
   Parks
Frommer's Caribbean Hideaways
Frommer's Complete Hostel Vacation Guide to
   England, Scotland & Wales
Frommer's Food Lover's Companion to France
Frommer's Food Lover's Companion to Italy
Frommer's Great European Driving Tours

Frommer's National Park Guide
Outside Magazine's Adventure Guide to New
   England
Outside Magazine's Adventure Guide to
   Northern California
Places Rated Almanac
Retirement Places Rated
USA Sports Traveler's and TV Viewer's
   Golf Tournament Guide
USA Sports Minor League Baseball Book
USA Today Golf Atlas
Wonderful Weekends from NYC

FROMMER'S IRREVERENT GUIDES

(Wickedly honest guides for sophisticated travelers)

Amsterdam	Manhattan	Paris	U.S. Virgin Islands
Chicago	Miami	San Francisco	Walt Disney World
London	New Orleans	Santa Fe	Washington, D.C.

UNOFFICIAL GUIDES

(Get the unbiased truth from these candid, value-conscious guides)

Atlanta	Euro Disneyland	Mini-Mickey
Branson, Missouri	The Great Smoky & Blue	Skiing in the West
Chicago	Ridge Mountains	Walt Disney World
Cruises	Las Vegas	Walt Disney World Companion
Disneyland	Miami & the Keys	Washington, D.C.

BAEDEKER
(With four-color photographs and a free pull-out map)

Amsterdam	Florence	London	Scotland
Athens	Florida	Mexico	Singapore
Austria	Germany	New York	South Africa
Bali	Great Britain	Paris	Spain
Belgium	Greece	Portugal	Switzerland
Budapest	Greek Islands	Prague	Thailand
California	Hawaii	Provence	Tokyo
Canada	Hong Kong	Rome	Turkish Coast
Caribbean	Ireland	San Francisco	Tuscany
China	Israel	St. Petersburg	Venice
Copenhagen	Italy	Scandinavia	Vienna
Crete	Lisbon		

FROMMER'S BY NIGHT GUIDES
(The series for those who know that life begins after dark)

Amsterdam	London	Miami	Paris
Chicago	Los Angeles	New Orleans	San Francisco
Las Vegas	Manhattan		

FROMMER'S BEST BEACH VACATIONS
(The top places to sun, stroll, shop, stay, play, party, and swim, with ratings for each beach)

California	Hawaii	New England
Carolinas & Georgia	Mid-Atlantic (from New	
Florida	York to Washington, D.C.)	

FROMMER'S BED & BREAKFAST GUIDES
(Selective guides with four-color photos and full descriptions of the best inns in each region)

California	Great American Cities	New England	The Rockies
Caribbean	Hawaii	Pacific Northwest	Southwest

FROMMER'S DRIVING TOURS
(Four-color photos and detailed maps outlining spectacular scenic driving routes)

Australia	France	Italy	Spain
Austria	Germany	Scandinavia	Switzerland
Britain	Ireland	Scotland	U.S.A.
Florida			

FROMMER'S BORN TO SHOP
(The ultimate guides for travelers who love to shop)

France	Hong Kong		Mexico
Great Britain	London		New York

TRAVEL & LEISURE GUIDES
(Sophisticated pocket-size guides for discriminating travelers)

Amsterdam	Hong Kong	New York	San Francisco
Boston	London	Paris	Washington, D.C.